COOK'S

ILLUSTRATED

~ 2016 ~

$35.00

Published by
America's Test Kitchen
17 Station Street
Brookline, MA 02445

ISBN: 978-1-940352-73-2
ISSN: 1933-639X

To get home delivery of *Cook's Illustrated* magazine, call 800-526-8442 inside the U.S., or 515-247-7571 if calling from outside the U.S., or subscribe online at www.CooksIllustrated.com.

In addition to *Cook's Illustrated* Annual Hardbound Editions available from each year of publication (1993–2016), America's Test Kitchen offers the following cookbooks and DVD sets:

THE COOK'S ILLUSTRATED COOKBOOK SERIES

The Cook's Illustrated Meat Book
The Cook's Illustrated Cookbook
The Cook's Illustrated Baking Book
The Science of Good Cooking
The America's Test Kitchen Menu Cookbook
Soups, Stews & Chilis
The Best Skillet Recipes
The Best Slow & Easy Recipes
The Best Chicken Recipes
The Best International Recipe
The Best Make-Ahead Recipe
The Best 30-Minute Recipe
The Cook's Illustrated Guide to Grilling and Barbecue
Best American Side Dishes
The Best Cover & Bake Recipes
The New Best Recipe
Steaks, Chops, Roasts, and Ribs
Baking Illustrated
Perfect Vegetables
Italian Classics
The Best American Classics
The Best One-Dish Suppers

THE AMERICA'S TEST KITCHEN SERIES COMPANION COOKBOOKS

America's Test Kitchen: The TV Companion Cookbook (2010–2017 Editions)
The Complete America's Test Kitchen TV Show Cookbook (2010–2016 Editions)
America's Test Kitchen: The TV Companion Cookbook (2009)
Behind the Scenes with America's Test Kitchen (2008)
Test Kitchen Favorites (2007)
Cooking at Home with America's Test Kitchen (2006)
America's Test Kitchen Live! (2005)
Inside America's Test Kitchen (2004)
Here in America's Test Kitchen (2003)
The America's Test Kitchen Cookbook (2002)

THE AMERICA'S TEST KITCHEN SERIES DVD SETS
(featuring each season's episodes from our hit public television series)
The *America's Test Kitchen* 4-DVD Set (2002–2016 Seasons)
The *America's Test Kitchen* 2-DVD Set (2001 Season)

AMERICA'S TEST KITCHEN ANNUALS

The Best of America's Test Kitchen (2007–2017 Editions)
Cooking for Two (2009–2013 Editions)
Light & Healthy (2010–2012 Editions)

THE AMERICA'S TEST KITCHEN LIBRARY SERIES

The How Can It Be Gluten-Free Cookbook
The How Can It Be Gluten-Free Cookbook: Volume 2
The America's Test Kitchen Complete Vegetarian Cookbook
The Best Mexican Recipes
The Make-Ahead Cook
The America's Test Kitchen Do-It-Yourself Cookbook
Slow Cooker Revolution
Slow Cooker Revolution 2: The Easy Prep Edition
Healthy Slow Cooker Revolution
Comfort Food Makeovers
From Our Grandmothers' Kitchens

ADDITIONAL BOOKS FROM AMERICA'S TEST KITCHEN

Naturally Sweet
Foolproof Preserving
Cook it in Cast Iron
Master of the Grill
100 Recipes: The Absolute Best Way to Make the True Essentials
Cook's Country Eats Local
Kitchen Hacks: How Clever Cooks Get Things Done
The America's Test Kitchen New Family Cookbook
The Complete Cooking for Two Cookbook
The America's Test Kitchen Quick Family Cookbook
The America's Test Kitchen Healthy Family Cookbook
The America's Test Kitchen Family Cookbook
The America's Test Kitchen Family Baking Book
The America's Test Kitchen Cooking School Cookbook
Pressure Cooker Perfection
The Complete Cook's Country TV Show Cookbook
Cook's Country Annual Hardbound (2005–2016)

Visit our online bookstore at www.CooksIllustrated.com to order any of our cookbooks and DVDs listed above. You can also order subscriptions, gift subscriptions, and any of our cookbooks and DVDs by calling 800-611-0759 inside the U.S., or at 515-246-6911 if calling from outside the U.S.

BC = Back Cover

COOK'S ILLUSTRATED INDEX 2016

COOK'S ILLUSTRATED INDEX 2016

COOK'S
ILLUSTRATED

Perfect Baked Potato
Yes, You Need Our Recipe

Easiest Beef Stew
One-Step Approach

Shrimp Scampi
Amping Up the Shrimp Flavor

Roast Chicken and Winter Vegetables

Fluffy Dinner Rolls
New Japanese Technique

Testing Full-Size Food Processors

Top Kitchen Tools
21 You Have to Have

Stovetop Cauliflower
Pear Upside-Down Cake
Penne Arrabbiata
Tasting Beef Broths

CooksIllustrated.com
$6.95 U.S. & $7.95 CANADA

7 25274 62805 6

02>

CONTENTS

January & February 2016

BACK COVER ILLUSTRATED BY JOHN BURGOYNE

Swiss Cheeses

The most common Swiss cheese is the deli staple EMMENTALER, which is strewn with holes and tastes nutty yet sweet. Lush, creamy RACLETTE is traditionally melted on its wheel and scraped onto cooked potatoes, pearl onions, and cornichons. TOMME DE VERBIER oozes like Brie when ripe but is a tad saltier and more complex. Musty and sharp TÊTE DE MOINE recalls a monk's head because the stout cylinder is exposed at the top. GRUYÈRE ALPAGE is aged for at least a year and boasts nutty tang—like a cross between good sharp cheddar and Parmesan. Dry and deeply nutty PLAN DE L'OUGE is a Gruyère relative with a distinct crystalline structure. The pleasant funk and sherry-like sweetness of STERNENBERGER develop as the cheese is washed and aged for at least six months. Creamy VACHERIN FRIBOURGEOIS, which packs assertive bite and a tingly finish, adds smoothness and punch to fondue.

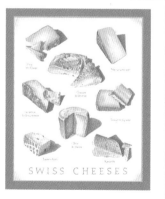

SWISS CHEESES

COOK'S
ILLUSTRATED

Founder and Editor	Christopher Kimball
Chief Creative Officer	Jack Bishop
Editorial Director, Magazines	John Willoughby
Executive Editor	Amanda Agee
Test Kitchen Director	Erin McMurrer
Deputy Editor	Rebecca Hays
Executive Managing Editor, Magazines	Todd Meier
Executive Food Editor	Keith Dresser
Executive Tastings & Testings Editor	Lisa McManus
Senior Editors	Hannah Crowley
	Andrea Geary
	Andrew Janjigian
	Dan Souza
Senior Editors, Features	Elizabeth Bomze
	Louise Emerick
Copy Editors	Jillian Campbell
	Krista Magnuson
Associate Editors	Lan Lam
	Chris O'Connor
Test Cooks	Daniel Cellucci
	Steve Dunn
	Annie Petito
Assistant Editors	Miye Bromberg
	Lauren Savoie
	Kate Shannon
Assistant Test Cooks	Allison Berkey
	Matthew Fairman
Executive Assistant	Christine Gordon
Assistant Test Kitchen Director	Leah Rovner
Test Kitchen Manager	Alexxa Grattan
Senior Test Kitchen Assistant	Meridith Lippard
Kitchen Assistants	Blanca Castanza
	Maria Elena Delgado
	Ena Gudiel
Executive Producer	Melissa Baldino
Co-Executive Producer	Stephanie Stender
Associate Producer	Kaitlin Hammond
Production Assistant	Madeline Heising
Contributing Editor	Dawn Yanagihara
Science Editor	Guy Crosby, PhD
Creative Consultant	Amy Klee
Managing Editor, Web	Christine Liu
Social Media Manager	Jill Fisher
Senior Editor, Web	Roger Metcalf
Assistant Editor, Web	Terrence Doyle
Senior Video Editor	Nick Dakoulas
Product Manager, Cooking School	Anne Bartholomew
Senior Editor, Cooking School	Mari Levine
Design Director, Print	Greg Galvan
Photography Director	Julie Cote
Art Director	Susan Levin
Associate Art Director	Lindsey Chandler
Art Director, Marketing	Jennifer Cox
Deputy Art Director, Marketing	Melanie Gryboski
Associate Art Director, Marketing	Janet Taylor
Designer, Marketing	Stephanie Cook
Staff Photographer	Daniel J. van Ackere
Associate Art Director, Photography	Steve Klise
VP, Print & Direct Marketing	David Mack
Circulation Director	Doug Wicinski
Circulation & Fulfillment Manager	Carrie Fethe
Partnership Marketing Manager	Pamela Putprush
Marketing Assistant	Andrea Hampel
Chief Operating Officer	Rob Ristagno
VP, Digital Products	Fran Middleton
Production Director	Guy Rochford
Imaging Manager	Lauren Robbins
Production & Imaging Specialists	Heather Dube
	Sean MacDonald
	Dennis Noble
	Jessica Voas
Director, Business Systems	Alice Carpenter
Project Manager	Britt Dresser
Director of Engineering	Welling LaGrone
Senior Controller	Theresa Peterson
Customer Loyalty & Support Manager	Amy Bootier
Customer Loyalty & Support Reps	Caroline Augliere
	Rebecca Kowalski
	Andrew Straaberg Finfrock
VP, New Business Development	Michael Burton
Director, Marketing & Sales	Deborah Fagone
Client Services Manager	Kate Zebrowski
Sponsorship Sales Associate	Morgan Mannino
Director, Retail Book Program	Beth Ineson
Retail Sales Manager	Derek Meehan
Human Resources Director	Adele Shapiro
Publicity	Deborah Broide
Associate Director, Publicity	Susan Hershberg
Cover Illustration	Robert Papp

PRINTED IN THE USA

THIS OLD HOUSE

Our house in Vermont was built in 1827. It's still upstanding with four-pane vertical windows, white clapboards, a steep roof, marble mounting blocks in front for horses, and a narrow porch around three sides. It has a large mudroom, claw-footed bathtubs instead of showers, and a small railroad kitchen. The attic contains a brick cistern, originally fed by gutters, with the water drawn down to the rest of the house by gravity.

It sits next to Sherman's Country Store, a local institution stocked with Labatts and Papps, cold cuts, and a wheel of Vermont cheddar (the cat sleeps on the scale). A coffee booth sits next to the front window and there are stuffed animals, including woodchuck, wild boar, and a jackalope for the tourists.

Our house has one other feature. It's haunted.

Mysterious lights appear in top-floor windows. Visitors who are sensitive to otherworldly vibrations have refused to venture to the third floor. The basement is a classic of the genre with a dirt-floor root cellar reminiscent of *The Blair Witch Project*. And, more practically speaking, there is the usual collection of errant mice and the occasional bat that has to be shooed out the front door with a fishing net.

Ten years ago, a neighbor was downstairs cleaning and heard someone walking around upstairs. She didn't think much of it until heavy, deliberate footfalls started down the main staircase. She paused in her work, looked up, and saw an old-fashioned preacher without a face.

Besides offering a spiritual home to prior residents, our house has two distinctly different sides.

The half with the kitchen and dining room is three stories, with two square bedrooms on the second floor and two smaller rooms on the third, separated by a stepped brick chimney. The staircase's treads are cherry, as is the foyer; the windows almost reach almost to the floor; and there is a faux marble fireplace in the dining room. The other side has a rough-built staircase with narrow painted treads, plain moldings, and a small hobbit-size door connecting the two sides on the second floor. One side is rather grand, and the other looks like it was built for farmhands.

Stories about the provenance of the house include its use as a girls' school and how one owner sold homemade candy out of the basement (there is a small take-out window built into one of the basement partitions), but nobody remembers why it is two houses joined together. Even the original stone foundation tells no tales—the house was clearly built at one time; nothing has been added on.

It's also a bit of a hodgepodge. An outside porch door once led only into a bathroom. Seven doors lead off the dining room. Old plumbing gives one a clue that the kitchen was once in the mudroom. Each side of the house had only one bathroom.

I recently went to see a chiropractor trained in kinesiology. One extends an arm, and the practitioner measures your resistance to a substance (a mineral, for example) by lightly pushing down on that arm. Don't ask me how or if this works. Although

Christopher Kimball

I was told that my energy field was lacking (that's a new-age putdown if I have ever heard one), I left the office skeptical but intrigued, willing to give the unseen a chance.

I claim no special knowledge of or belief in spirits, hauntings, vibrations, planetary forces, or chakras—all the things that may in fact control the universe or just go bump in the night. I do know that I live in a house that is alive. How many times have family and friends sat in close quarters after dinner, in a room full of radiators and pipes, doorways and windows, and felt shrouded in happiness, floating on a buoyant sea of ancient evenings? Our house is always good company.

These days, I observe the reflections in the faces around the table and see the expected—a common cause, shared passions, and hard times as well as years transformed into history much like this house; old doorways blocked, intentions obscured. Yet there is new life, a bright coat of paint and a renovated kitchen, renewed inspiration and a fresh start. The past is the foundation for the future.

It's late and I'm finishing up the dishes. I hear a creak on the stairs and a dull clang from the basement. It could be a ghost or just the house trying to speak up, to say that it's happy that both new life and old walk across its well-worn floorboards. It's a reminder that old houses have lives of their own. They live and breathe, inviting us in from the storm when we most need shelter.

FOR INQUIRIES, ORDERS, OR MORE INFORMATION

CooksIllustrated.com
At CooksIllustrated.com, you can order books and subscriptions, sign up for our free e-newsletter, or renew your magazine subscription. Join the website and gain access to 23 years of *Cook's Illustrated* recipes, equipment tests, and ingredient tastings, as well as companion videos for every recipe in this issue.

COOKBOOKS
We sell more than 50 cookbooks by the editors of *Cook's Illustrated*, including *The Cook's Illustrated Cookbook* and *The Science of Good Cooking*. To order, visit our bookstore at CooksIllustrated.com/bookstore.

COOK'S ILLUSTRATED MAGAZINE
Cook's Illustrated magazine (ISSN 1068-2821), number 138, is published bimonthly by Boston Common Press Limited Partnership, 17 Station St., Brookline, MA 02445. Copyright 2015 Boston Common Press Limited Partnership. Periodicals postage paid at Boston, MA, and additional mailing offices, USPS #012487. Publications Mail Agreement No. 40020778. Return undeliverable Canadian addresses to P.O. Box 875, Station A, Windsor, ON N9A 6P2. POSTMASTER: Send address changes to *Cook's Illustrated*, P.O. Box 6018, Harlan, IA 51593-1518. For subscription and gift subscription orders, subscription inquiries, or change of address notices, visit AmericasTestKitchen.com/support, call 800-526-8442 in the U.S. or 515-248-7684 from outside the U.S., or write to us at *Cook's Illustrated*, P.O. Box 6018, Harlan, IA 51593-1518.

FOR LIST RENTAL INFORMATION Contact Specialists Marketing Services, Inc., 777 Terrace Ave., 4th Floor, Hasbrouck Heights, NJ 07604; phone: 201-865-5800.

EDITORIAL OFFICE 17 Station St., Brookline, MA 02445; 617-232-1000; fax: 617-232-1572. For subscription inquiries, visit AmericasTestKitchen.com/support or call 800-526-8442.

QUICK TIPS

⇒ COMPILED BY ANNIE PETITO ⇐

No-Mess Nut Chopper

Whenever Chris Wilson of Laurel, Miss., chops nuts, they scatter all over the counter. To contain them, he loads the nuts into the bowl of a manual citrus juicer, squeezes to break them up, shakes to redistribute the contents, and repeats the method until all the nuts are evenly chopped.

Corralling Eggs on the Counter

Louise Oates, of Grass Valley, Calif., keeps eggs from rolling off the counter by "corralling" them with the joined plastic rings that hold together two large bottles of juice.

Grating over Parchment Paper

When grating chocolate or hard cheese, Bonnie Stern of Monroe, Conn., works directly over a sheet of parchment paper, which is nonstick and easily catches all the shavings. When finished, she rolls up the sides of the parchment to pour the shavings directly into a bowl.

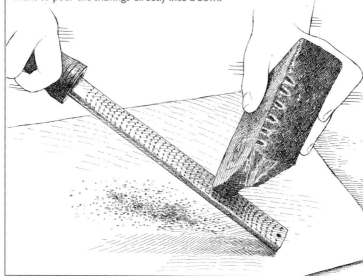

Storing Pastes in the Fridge

Mary Addison-Lamb of Springville, Tenn., finds that pastes sold in tubes (such as tomato) can sometimes leak in the fridge or become sticky at the opening, dirtying neighboring ingredients. By storing the tubes facing down in tall glass jars, she keeps the contents contained.

Fruit Cushion

When shopping for delicate pieces of fruit, Brian Solomon of Narberth, Pa., puts the fruit in a plastic bag and blows air into it before tying a knot to seal the opening. The air creates a protective cushion that allows him to put the fruit in his shopping cart or in a bag for the trip home without fear of bruising.

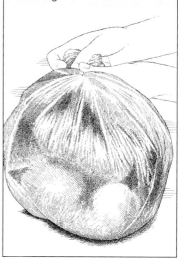

Crack That Cork

Whenever Lisa Ashley Tichenor of Sarasota, Fla., tries to open a bottle of champagne and finds that the cork is stuck, she uses an old-fashioned nutcracker to remove it. She first places a towel over the cork and then uses a slight twisting motion, as one would do with a wrench, to safely remove it.

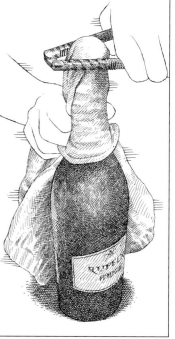

SEND US YOUR TIPS We will provide a complimentary one-year subscription for each tip we print. Send your tip, name, address, and daytime telephone number to Quick Tips, *Cook's Illustrated*, P.O. Box 470589, Brookline, MA 02447, or to QuickTips@AmericasTestKitchen.com.

Stray Pepper Catcher

Michael Grady of Warwick, R.I., discovered a novel way to catch the stray pepper flecks that fall from the bottom of his pepper mill and get left behind on the shelf: He stores the mill on top of an upside-down jar lid, which makes it easy to discard the flecks in between uses.

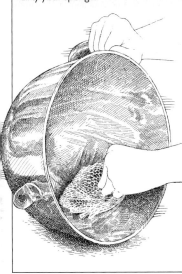

Moving the Mixer

It was hard for Fran Curtis of Eugene, Ore., to move her heavy stand mixer out of the corner when she wanted to use it—until she put the mixer on top of a cotton place mat. Now she is able to easily slide the mixer across the counter when needed.

Peeling Away Foil from a Wine Bottle

Jim Holladay of Gordonsville, Va., has found that the easiest way to remove the tight foil cover from the top of a wine bottle is with a vegetable peeler. Starting at the bottom of the foil, he peels away a thin strip, which loosens the rest for easy removal.

Securing Pot Lids

Needing to transport a large pot of hot soup to a potluck, Pat Short of West Lafayette, Ind., came up with the following trick to keep the lid tightly shut. Using large rubber bands (like those wrapped around bunches of broccoli or leeks), she looped two bands around the lid's handle on opposite sides and then stretched the bands over the outer handles on the sides of the pot.

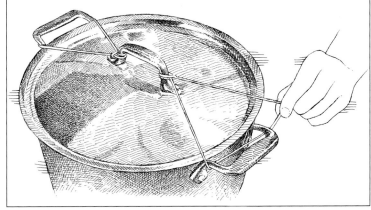

Disposable Scouring Pads

Rose Goldberg of Fullerton, Calif., saves the plastic mesh bags that onions come in and turns them into disposable abrasive scouring pads. She cuts the bags into 3-inch sections and uses the strips to scrub away stuck-on residue (such as from cheese or dough) from bowls. The bits stick to the plastic mesh, which can then be discarded—no need to dirty your sponge.

Trussing a Chicken Without Twine

Helas Wolf of New York, N.Y., discovered that you don't need kitchen twine to truss a chicken. Instead, she uses the pocket of extra fat near the opening of the bird, cutting two slits in the pocket and then crossing the legs and pulling the ankles through the slits.

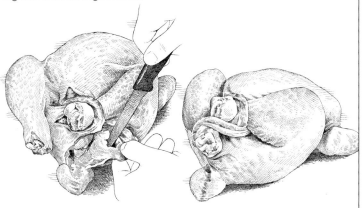

1. Cut slit in fat pocket on 1 side of cavity and thread leg opposite it into and through flap.

2. Cut second slit in fat pocket on other side of cavity and thread second leg into and through slit.

Stringing Up Citrus Zest

When steeping citrus peels in soups or stews, Michael Drury of Boulder, Colo., discovered an easy method for removing them without wrapping them in cheesecloth or fishing around in the pot: He pokes a hole in each strip, threads it with twine, and ties it to the handle of the pot.

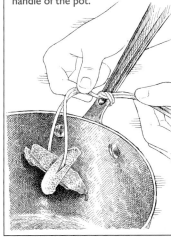

Best Roast Chicken and Vegetables

The secret to a perfect marriage of roast chicken and root vegetables is to keep them apart until the wedding day.

≥ BY ANDREW JANJIGIAN ≤

The idea of roasting a whole chicken with an abundance of root vegetables—think potatoes, carrots, parsnips—has a lot of appeal. Not only do you get a twofer of entrée and side dish from a single pan, but the result promises to turn everyday ingredients into something greater: a delicious, bronzed centerpiece and a side of vegetables that are beautifully caramelized and infused with deep, savory chicken flavor.

That said, I've always found it challenging to roast both components in the same pan without compromising the results. Surrounding the chicken with vegetables slows down the cooking of the thighs, the part of the bird you actually want to cook more quickly (it's the delicate breast meat that needs to cook slowly). This arrangement also prevents the skin on the lower portion of the bird from browning. Meanwhile, the crowded vegetables steam in their juices rather than brown, and because a whole chicken sheds quite a bit of fat, the vegetables also wind up greasy.

While there are ways around these issues, I wondered if it would be easier to achieve presentation-worthy chicken and perfectly roasted vegetables by cooking the two components separately. I'd just have to find another way to infuse the vegetables with rich chicken flavor.

Skillet Solution

It was essential to use the drippings from the chicken to flavor the vegetables, so I needed to find a way to produce evenly cooked dark and white meat and nicely browned skin and a good amount of drippings. I settled on a 12-inch skillet. Its low sides let air circulate around the skin for even browning, and its narrow diameter ensured that the drippings would pool and brown rather than burn as they would in a wide roasting pan. I also decided to preheat the skillet so that the thighs, which were in contact with the pan, would get a jump start, helping them finish cooking at the same time as the white meat.

▶ **See the Twofer Process**
Video available free for 4 months at CooksIllustrated.com/feb16

While the chicken rests, we blast the vegetables in a 500-degree oven to develop flavorful browning.

When the chicken had finished roasting, I set it aside on a carving board to rest and admired the thick, dark golden deposit of flavorful proteins, or fond, on the bottom of the skillet—just the stuff the vegetables were waiting for. I poured a little bit of water into the skillet to loosen the fond and give me more liquid to work with. I could simply toss the vegetables (potatoes for now) with this rich liquid before roasting them, which would certainly imbue them with chicken-y flavor, but the extra moisture might also hinder browning. A better idea: I poured the liquid into a fat separator to create two types of flavor bases—fat and concentrated juices. I tossed the potatoes with a few tablespoons of the fat, which would help them brown and crisp, and then placed them on a baking sheet in a hot oven.

Once they were tender and nicely browned, I tossed them with the concentrated juices and returned them to the oven for a few minutes. The result? In a word, spectacular. The potatoes were coated with a deeply savory glaze that tasted of pure chicken.

But it took about 40 minutes to cook the vegetables;

I wanted a faster method. First, however, there were a few minor improvements to the chicken to attend to. One: The meat was a bit dry—it required some pretreatment. Because I was after a streamlined recipe, I opted to brine rather than salt, since salting can take significantly longer. I also added sugar to my brine. It wouldn't really make the meat taste sweet so much as boost its underlying flavor. Plus, it would help the coated vegetables caramelize even more for better flavor. Two: The skin was nicely browned but unevenly crisp because some pockets of fat didn't fully render. Pricking the fat deposits before cooking solved this problem, and also helped the brine season the meat more quickly. I also rubbed the skin with olive oil before cooking to keep it from turning leathery and to enhance browning.

Uncovering the Best Approach

Now back to the vegetables. My new plan was to cook the vegetables most of the way through in the oven on a rack below the chicken and then finish them while the chicken rested. The problem with this approach was that the vegetables' exteriors dried out before their interiors had turned tender, leaving them shriveled and tough. Parboiling them before finishing them in the oven had potential but seemed fussy—and I knew of a better way. In the past we've roasted root vegetables by arranging the pieces in a single layer on a baking sheet and then covering the sheet with foil to trap moisture so that they can steam and cook through evenly. We then remove the foil to let moisture evaporate and return the vegetables to a very hot oven to brown.

After a few tests, I had my method: Cook the vegetables on a baking sheet, covered, beneath the chicken for 30 minutes. Then remove the foil and let them sit while the chicken finished up (another 20 minutes, give or take). In this time, the excess moisture evaporated from residual heat. Once the chicken was finished, I set it aside, deglazed the pan and separated the fat as before, and tossed the potatoes with a few tablespoons of the fat before returning them to the oven to brown. Once they were nicely browned, I poured the chicken-y liquid from the pan over the potatoes and cooked them until the liquid had reduced to a glazy coating. I found that they browned most evenly and quickly with the oven turned up to

500 degrees. A few more tests confirmed that the technique worked on a wide variety of root vegetables, including potatoes, carrots, parsnips, turnips, beets, celery root, and even shallots and leeks, provided they were each cut into sizes that let them cook through at a similar rate. With a perfectly cooked, beautifully browned chicken and plenty of richly flavorful root vegetables, this was a recipe that finally delivered on the promise of this old-fashioned classic.

BEST ROAST CHICKEN WITH ROOT VEGETABLES
SERVES 4 TO 6

Cooking the chicken in a preheated skillet will ensure that the breast and thigh meat finish cooking at the same time. See "Mixing Up the Medley" for instructions on how to substitute other vegetables for the parsnips and/or carrots. This recipe requires brining the chicken for 1 hour before cooking. If using a kosher chicken, do not brine in step 1, but season with ½ teaspoon salt in step 3.

1	(3½- to 4-pound) whole chicken, giblets discarded
	Salt and pepper
½	cup sugar
1½	pounds Yukon Gold potatoes, peeled and cut into 2-inch pieces
12	ounces carrots, peeled, halved crosswise, thick halves halved lengthwise
12	ounces parsnips, peeled, halved crosswise, thick halves halved lengthwise
4	teaspoons extra-virgin olive oil
¼	cup water
1	teaspoon minced fresh thyme
1	tablespoon chopped fresh parsley

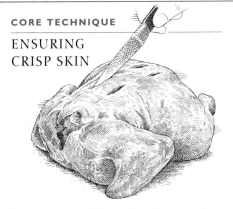

CORE TECHNIQUE

ENSURING CRISP SKIN

Because pockets of fat can thwart the goal of golden-brown, crisp chicken skin, we take a few steps to help the fat render properly. First, we cut slits along the back to allow fat to escape. Next, we use our fingers to loosen the skin covering the breast and thighs so that rendering fat can trickle out. Finally, we use a skewer to poke holes in the fat deposits on top of the breast and thighs to provide channels for fat to escape.

Separation, Without Anxiety

Half the allure of a roast chicken and vegetable dinner is having vegetables that are infused with rich, savory chicken flavor. So if it isn't ideal to cook the vegetables in the same pan with the chicken, how do you get chicken-y vegetables? Here's what we do.

SEPARATE
Create two flavor bases by separating the chicken fat from the juices.

TOSS WITH FAT
Coat the parcooked vegetables with some of the fat to help them brown.

TOSS WITH JUICES
Add the juices near the end of cooking so they reduce to a savory glaze.

If You Don't Have a Fat Separator . . .

➤ **PAPER CUP/FREEZER**
1) Pour pan drippings into paper cup. Freeze until fat has begun to solidify on top, about 10 minutes.
2) Over small bowl, poke hole in bottom of cup with skewer. Let drippings run out through hole.

➤ **COOKING SPOON**
Let liquid settle for about 10 minutes. Use wide, shallow spoon to skim fat from surface.

➤ **BULB BASTER**
Let liquid settle for about 10 minutes. Plunge baster into liquid beneath fat and draw into baster, then deposit in another container.

1. With chicken breast side down, use tip of sharp knife to make four 1-inch incisions along back. Using your fingers, gently loosen skin covering breast and thighs. Use metal skewer to poke 15 to 20 holes in fat deposits on top of breast halves and thighs. Dissolve ½ cup salt and sugar in 2 quarts cold water in large container. Submerge chicken in brine, cover, and refrigerate for 1 hour.

2. Adjust oven racks to upper-middle and lower-middle positions and heat oven to 450 degrees. Place 12-inch ovensafe skillet on upper rack and heat for 15 minutes. Spray rimmed baking sheet with vegetable oil spray. Arrange potatoes, carrots, and parsnips with cut surfaces down in single layer on baking sheet and cover sheet tightly with aluminum foil.

3. Remove chicken from brine and pat dry with paper towels. Combine 1 tablespoon oil and ½ teaspoon pepper in small bowl. Rub entire surface of chicken with oil-pepper mixture. Tie legs together with twine and tuck wingtips behind back.

4. Carefully remove skillet from oven (handle will be hot). Add remaining 1 teaspoon oil to skillet and swirl to coat. Place chicken, breast side up, in skillet. Return skillet to upper rack and place sheet of vegetables on lower rack. Cook for 30 minutes.

5. Remove vegetables from oven, remove foil, and set aside. Rotate skillet and continue to cook chicken until breasts register 160 degrees and thighs register 175 degrees, 15 to 25 minutes longer.

6. Transfer chicken to carving board and let rest, uncovered, for 20 minutes. Increase oven temperature to 500 degrees. Add water to skillet. Using whisk, stir until brown bits have dissolved. Strain sauce through fine-mesh strainer into fat separator, pressing on solids to remove any remaining liquid. Let liquid settle for 5 minutes. Pour off liquid from fat separator and reserve. Reserve 3 tablespoons fat, discarding remaining fat.

7. Drizzle vegetables with reserved fat. Sprinkle vegetables with thyme, 1 teaspoon salt, and ½ teaspoon pepper and toss to coat. Place sheet on upper rack and roast for 5 minutes. Remove sheet from oven. Using thin, sharp metal spatula, turn vegetables. Continue to roast until browned at edges, 8 to 10 minutes longer.

8. Pour reserved liquid over vegetables. Continue to roast until liquid is thick and syrupy and vegetables are tender, 3 to 5 minutes. Toss vegetables to coat, then transfer to serving platter and sprinkle with parsley. Carve chicken and transfer to platter with vegetables. Serve.

Mixing Up the Medley

We recommend sticking with 1½ pounds of potatoes for half the vegetable mixture, but to switch things up, you can substitute 1½ pounds of the following vegetables for the carrots and parsnips.

Turnips	Peel and cut into 1-inch pieces.
Beets/Celery Root	Peel and cut into ½-inch pieces.
Shallots	Peel and halve lengthwise, leaving root end attached. Place on sheet cut side down.
Leeks	Using white and light green parts only, halve pieces lengthwise, leaving root end attached. Place on sheet cut side down.

Easiest-Ever Beef Stew

This meaty, clean-tasting Portuguese version of beef stew, called *alcatra*, requires mere minutes of hands-on work.

⇒ BY LAN LAM ⇐

A few times a year, I labor over a great beef stew. Based on a classic French approach to braising, the recipe I follow calls for batch-searing pieces of beef chuck—a step that splatters grease on my stovetop but generates valuable savory browning. From there, I sauté vegetables, aromatics, and flavor boosters like minced anchovies and tomato paste in the rendered fat, followed by a little flour to thicken the cooking liquid; deglaze the pot with wine and scrape up the flavorful browned bits of fond on the bottom of the pot; add broth, water, and a chunk of salt pork for even more meaty flavor; and then braise the stew in the oven for a few hours, just enough time to turn the tough pieces of chuck roast fork-tender.

All those steps and ingredients yield a meaty, complex, and satisfying stew but one that I make infrequently. However, my assumption about making beef stew changed when a colleague brought in his mother-in-law's Portuguese version, which called for just a handful of ingredients and was supposedly dead-simple to make. Best of all, the dish, called *alcatra*, from the Azorean island of Terceira, tasted fabulous without requiring any browning of the meat or aromatics. All you do is pack chunks of beef into a pot (traditionally a clay pot called an *alguidar*) with onions, wine, bacon or chorizo, garlic, and spices; cover it and put it in the oven; and forget about it until it's done.

You wouldn't think that the result would taste nearly as good as a stew made the French way, but it does. The pork, onions, and spices (often peppercorns, allspice, and bay leaves) add surprising depth to what is, essentially, boiled beef and yield a brothy cooking liquid that's flavorful but clean-tasting. Crusty bread or boiled potatoes are often served alongside to sop up the flavorful juices. Needless to say, I could see myself making a dish this easy all winter long.

▶ **Alcatra Comes to Life**
Video available free for 4 months at CooksIllustrated.com/feb16

In *alcatra*, there is no flour or thickener to mute the taste of the intensely flavored jus, which we soak up with crusty bread or potatoes.

Cut Out for Braising

My recipe research revealed that, despite its narrow regional provenance, alcatra can vary quite a bit—from the cut of beef to the type of wine and particular seasonings. Tackling the beef first, I prepared batches of a basic recipe with three different cuts of meat: rump (the name "alcatra" comes from *alcatre*, the Portuguese word for rump), shank, and chuck, which is our usual choice for braising. After cutting the meat into roughly 2½-inch pieces and seasoning them with salt, I packed the pieces of each cut into three Dutch ovens (my alguidar substitute). I then added a couple of sliced onions; a cheesecloth bundle of peeled and smashed garlic cloves, black peppercorns, allspice berries, and bay leaves; 8 ounces of chopped bacon; and just a few cups of white wine (chosen over red for its cleaner taste), so as not to dilute the flavor of the meat, to each pot.

Not a Flower Pot

The traditional Portuguese vessel for *alcatra* is an unglazed clay pot called an *alguidar*. We used a Dutch oven instead.

Next, I covered the pots, slid them into 325-degree ovens, and cooked each batch until the meat was very tender. Tasters agreed that the seasonings in each batch were more or less on target: savory and faintly sweet from the onions, garlic, and warm spices, with bright, clean acidity from the wine. They weren't wild about the bacon's heavy smoke flavor, but I'd revisit that after I settled on the beef.

As for the meat, the rump tasted comparatively dull and even a bit liver-y, which we've found can happen when this cut cooks for a prolonged period of time. It was the first to go. Meanwhile, the shank and chuck were superbeefy and cooked up beautifully tender, but the shank offered two distinct advantages that made it particularly good for braising. First, whereas chuck is a relatively fatty cut that made the cooking liquid a bit greasy (it required skimming before serving), shank is quite lean, so its broth wasn't the least bit fatty. Second, shank is loaded with collagen, the major protein in connective tissue that breaks down during cooking into gelatin; the gelatin coats the muscle fibers, rendering the lean meat supple and silky and the cooking liquid full-bodied and glossy. (For more information about beef shank, see "Shank: The Ultimate Cut for Braising.")

The Missing Link

Back to the pork: While bacon's assertive smokiness can be a great addition to stews, I liked the idea of a cleaner-tasting stew and hoped that chorizo would offer savory support with subtler smoke.

Markets in the United States usually carry two main varieties of chorizo, Mexican and Spanish. I picked Spanish because it's seasoned with smoked paprika and tastes faintly sweet and fruity (not unlike some varieties of dried chiles). When I sliced ½ pound into 1-inch chunks and added it to a fresh batch of my stew along with the onions, its sweet-smoky flavor matched up perfectly with the other warm spices. The downside was that it dried out considerably during the lengthy braise, so I tried delaying its

Shank: The Ultimate Cut for Braising

Shank (also called shin), a cut from the upper portion of a steer's legs, is an excellent cut for braising for a number of reasons. First, it's at least as beefy-tasting as more popular stew cuts like chuck or short ribs—but unlike those cuts, shank is quite lean, so the cooking liquid requires little, if any, skimming. Second, it's loaded with collagen, the major protein in connective tissue that liquefies into gelatin during cooking, giving the meat and the cooking liquid a silky richness. Third, it's a bargain cut, cheaper than both chuck and short ribs.

Shank is typically sold in two forms: boneless long-cut and crosscut, which can be sold with or without the bone. We prefer long-cut because it contains more collagen, but crosscut can be used; remove the bones before cooking (they're great for roasting—see page 30) and reduce the cooking time by about half an hour.

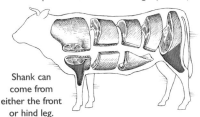

Shank can come from either the front or hind leg.

LONG-CUT

Both long-cut and crosscut shank work in our stew, but we prefer the former, which is sold boneless and contains more collagen.

CROSSCUT

---

addition until the last 20 minutes of cooking. The results were better but inconsistent; some pieces were fully submerged and overcooked quickly, while others sat on the surface and stayed nicely moist.

I finally got the texture right when I took advantage of Spanish chorizo's other notable trait: Unlike the Mexican variety, it's sold cured and/or fully cooked and thus doesn't need prolonged cooking. Going forward, I simply sliced it into ¼-inch-thick coins (they would warm through quickly); added them to the pot after braising the beef, making sure they were fully submerged by flipping the pieces of beef on top of the sausage; and let the stew sit covered off the heat for about 20 minutes.

Keep It Simple

My version of alcatra was solid and dead simple, but I had an idea for amping up its savory flavor just a bit more: packing the sliced onions at the bottom of the pot where they would be completely submerged in the liquid. The reason—though it sounds counterintuitive—is that cooking cut onions causes them to form a meaty-tasting compound called 3-mercapto-2 methylpentan-1-ol, or MMP for short. The payoff was evident in this latest batch of stew, which tasted even more flavorful. I also made a point of submerging the spice packet in the liquid to ensure that those flavors were thoroughly infused.

For due diligence, I ran a final series of tests in which I added supporting flavors I'd seen in published recipes: tomato paste (too sweet), butter (unnecessarily rich), and carrots (too vegetal). The only change I made was to add a little ground cinnamon, which underscored the warmth of the black pepper and allspice.

This stew was complex and bright-tasting—as satisfying as any beef stew I'd ever had. Even better, it was truly one of the easiest meals I'd ever made.

Don't Cook Cooked Sausage

Because Spanish chorizo is a fully cooked sausage, it doesn't require prolonged cooking. For this recipe, we simply slice it into thin coins and add them to the pot off the heat so that the pieces warm through but don't dry out.

PORTUGUESE-STYLE BEEF STEW (ALCATRA)
SERVES 6

Beef shank is sold both long-cut and crosscut (with and without bones). We prefer long-cut since it has more collagen. You can substitute 4 pounds of bone-in crosscut shank if that's all you can find. Remove the bones before cooking and save them for another use (see page 30 for how to roast marrowbones). Crosscut shank cooks more quickly, so check the stew for doneness in step 2 after 3 hours. A 3½- to 4-pound chuck roast, trimmed of fat and cut into 2½-inch pieces, can be substituted for the shank. Serve this dish with crusty bread or boiled potatoes.

- 3 pounds boneless long-cut beef shanks
  Salt and pepper
- 5 garlic cloves, peeled and smashed
- 5 allspice berries
- 4 bay leaves
- 1½ teaspoons peppercorns
- 2 large onions, halved and sliced
- 2¼ cups dry white wine
- ¼ teaspoon ground cinnamon
- 8 ounces Spanish-style chorizo sausage, cut into ¼-inch-thick rounds

1. Adjust oven rack to middle position and heat oven to 325 degrees. Trim away any fat or large pieces of connective tissue from exterior of shanks (silverskin can be left on meat). Cut each shank crosswise into 2½-inch pieces. Sprinkle meat with 1 teaspoon salt.

2. Cut 8-inch square of triple-thickness cheesecloth. Place garlic, allspice berries, bay leaves, and peppercorns in center of cheesecloth and tie into bundle with kitchen twine. Arrange onions and spice bundle in Dutch oven in even layer. Add wine and cinnamon. Arrange shank pieces in single layer on top of onions. Cover and cook until beef is tender, about 3½ hours.

3. Remove pot from oven and add chorizo. Using tongs, flip each piece of beef over, making sure that chorizo is submerged. Cover and let stand until chorizo is warmed through, about 20 minutes. Discard spice bundle. Season with salt and pepper to taste. Serve.

Few Ingredients, Little Work

Unlike a classic French beef stew, which requires many steps and ingredients to build robust savory flavor, Portuguese *alcatra* is built with just a few carefully chosen ingredients and minutes of hands-on work—but the result is no less satisfying.

WHITE WINE
Braising the beef in a few cups of white wine—which provides more complexity than commercial broth or water does—ensures that the meaty flavor isn't diluted.

MEATY-TASTING ONIONS
Cooking cut onions in liquid causes them to form a meaty-tasting compound called MMP that balances the acidity of the wine with savory flavor.

SMOKY SAUSAGE
Subtly smoky and sweet Spanish chorizo adds richness and depth.

SPICE BLEND
A faintly warm and sweet combination of bay leaves, allspice berries, black peppercorns, and a little cinnamon complements the meaty flavors of the beef and sausage.

Perfecting Shrimp Scampi

Making a passable version of this restaurant standard is easy enough, but for truly first-rate results, we took stock of every detail.

> BY ANDREW JANJIGIAN <

Shrimp scampi is rarely awful—it's unusual for things to go terribly wrong when garlic, wine, and butter are involved—but restaurant versions always make me wish I'd ordered differently. I have never been presented with the ultimate scampi, the one that I can almost taste when I peruse the menu: perfectly cooked, briny beauties in a garlicky, buttery (but not greasy) white wine sauce.

When I last made my way through a mediocre rendition, I decided it was time to realize this ideal scampi vision at home. Since shrimp are susceptible to overcooking, which can make them dry and tough, I gave my shrimp (1½ pounds, enough to serve four) a short dunk in a saltwater solution to season them and help preserve moisture. I then heated extra-virgin olive oil in a skillet, sautéed a few cloves of minced garlic and a dash of red pepper flakes, and added the shrimp. Once the shrimp turned opaque, I splashed in some dry white wine and followed it with a chunk of butter, a big squeeze of lemon juice, and a sprinkle of parsley.

My guests and I didn't go hungry that night, but the scampi was far from perfect. One problem was that the sauce separated into a butter-and-oil slick floating on top of the wine—not ideal in the looks department or for dunking bread into. (While some serve shrimp scampi over a pile of spaghetti, I think it's best with a crusty loaf.) Then there were the shrimp: Some were a little overdone, while others were still translucent. Finally, the overall dish was shy on both seafood and garlic flavors. For results that I'd be truly satisfied with, some adjustments were in order.

Shrimp Tales

Back in the test kitchen, I thought about ways to improve the shrimp. Flavorful crustaceans are often thought of as sweet, so would adding sugar to the brine be beneficial? Sure enough, my colleagues agreed that when used judiciously (2 tablespoons of

▶ **See How It's Done**
Video available free for 4 months
at CooksIllustrated.com/feb16

One detail perfected: Since lots of minced garlic can give the sauce a grainy quality, we use thinly sliced cloves instead.

sugar along with 3 tablespoons of salt in 1 quart of water), the sugar subtly boosted the natural flavor of the shrimp. I also found that using untreated shrimp, with no added salt or preservatives, produced the best results (see "The Right Shrimp").

Another detail to consider was the cooking method. The inconsistent doneness of my first batch had come from crowding the skillet, so I needed to sauté the shrimp in batches. Or did I? What if, instead of sautéing the shrimp and then adding the wine, I gently poached the shrimp in the wine? As it turned out, this approach cooked all of the shrimp just right and in unison, as long as the skillet was covered with a lid to trap steam.

Now that I had flavorful, properly cooked shrimp, it was time to tackle the sauce. I had three items on my to-do list. First: Seriously bump up the flavor. (I'd found that the 5 minutes or so that it took to cook the shrimp wasn't long enough to impart much of a seafood taste to the dish.) Second: Add extra garlic for a more robust punch. Third: Fix the separated consistency.

Waste Not, Want Not

A few ladles of stock made from trimmings, bones, or other ingredient scraps can be a great way to infuse flavor into a sauce. Here I could make a stock from the shrimp shells, so I started buying shell-on shrimp instead of the prepeeled type (to save time, I started using the jumbo size so I'd have fewer to peel). To coax out every bit of savoriness, I first browned the shells in a little olive oil and then simmered them in the wine for 30 minutes with a few sprigs of thyme for a little more complexity. But the stock didn't taste all that shrimpy. My incorrect assumption was that simmering the shells for a longer period of time would extract more flavor from them. A timing test conducted by a fellow test cook debunked that myth, finding that you get more flavor out of shrimp shells if you simmer them for only 5 minutes (see "When Less Time Means More Flavor"). This was an easy change I was happy to make.

Next, I doubled the amount of garlic. It worked to boost the garlic flavor but not without a cost: All of those minced pieces gave the sauce a gritty quality. To prevent this, I switched from mincing the cloves to slicing them into thin rounds. But since sliced garlic is milder in flavor than minced (garlic's bite is created in the act of damaging its cells; the finer it's cut, the stronger its flavor will be) the switch required that I double the number of cloves, to eight.

All that remained was to bind the fats and wine together into a cohesive sauce. In other words, I needed a stabilizer. I considered my choices: Flour, gelatin, and even pectin would work, but cornstarch seemed like the best option since it would require virtually no cooking to get the job done. I could hydrate the cornstarch in some of the wine, but I decided that it would be more convenient to use the lemon juice I was adding to the sauce for brightness. A mere teaspoon of cornstarch worked like a charm. I stirred the mixture into the sauce before adding the butter, which easily whisked into the rest of the sauce and stayed there, giving it a creamy, silky texture. In fact, it was so rich and creamy that I was able to scale back the amount of butter to 4 tablespoons without anyone finding it too lean. And there it was: the scampi I'd been looking for all along.

When Less Time Means More Flavor

It's easy to view shrimp shells simply as an impediment to the sweet, briny flesh within, but the shells actually contain lots of flavorful compounds that can be extracted into a stock. We've always assumed that, as with beef bones, the longer shrimp stock simmered, the more intense its flavor would be. But was that really true? To find out, we designed a test to determine the optimal simmering time. –Dan Souza

EXPERIMENT

We simmered batches of shrimp shells in water, covered, for 5, 10, 15, and 30 minutes and then strained out the shells. We asked tasters to evaluate the flavor of each sample.

RESULTS

Tasters almost unanimously chose the 5- and 10-minute simmered samples as "more potent," "shrimpier," and "more aromatic" than the 15- and 30-minute simmered samples.

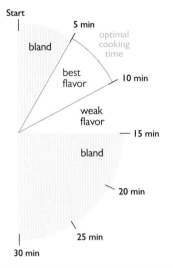

Start
5 min
optimal cooking time
bland
best flavor
10 min
weak flavor
15 min
bland
20 min
25 min
30 min

EXPLANATION

While some of the savory compounds found in shrimp shells are stable (i.e., they stay in the stock, rather than release into the atmosphere), the compounds that we associate with shrimp flavor are highly volatile. The longer a stock is simmered, the more of these molecules will release into the air, and the blander the stock will be.

TAKEAWAY

For the most flavorful shrimp stock, simmer shells for just 5 minutes.

Mini Prep Bowl Sets

Many cooks use mini prep bowls to help them complete their *mise en place*, the preparation and arrangement of ingredients for tidier, better-organized cooking.

We gathered seven of the most widely available sets (priced from $5.49 to $22.06) to assess how easy they were to fill and empty and how well they contained different volumes of food. We also evaluated them for durability and ease of cleanup. With the exception of the silicone bowls, which were small, floppy, and retained food odors, most of the sets worked pretty well.

Glass mini prep bowls dominate the market, and for good reason. They're oven-, microwave-, and dishwasher-safe; they tend to be fairly sturdy; and they're easy to clean, retaining no off-odors or food stains. Our favorite set from Anchor Hocking includes six nested glass bowls of different sizes. Made of heavy glass, the relatively wide, shallow bowls were easy to fill, empty, and clean. Plus, a slight lip around the rim made them comfortable to grip. For complete testing results, go to CooksIllustrated.com/feb16. –Miye Bromberg

RECOMMENDED
ANCHOR HOCKING
6-Piece Nesting Prep Bowl Set

MODEL: 92025L11

PRICE: $11.00

COMMENTS: Our winning set performed ably on almost every test. Its microwaveable bowls were easy to fill, empty, and clean.

SHRIMP SCAMPI
SERVES 4

Extra-large shrimp (21 to 25 per pound) can be substituted for jumbo shrimp. If you use them, reduce the cooking time in step 3 by 1 to 2 minutes. We prefer untreated shrimp, but if your shrimp are treated with sodium or preservatives like sodium tripolyphosphate (see "The Right Shrimp"), skip the brining in step 1 and add ¼ teaspoon of salt to the sauce in step 4. Serve with crusty bread. For our free recipe for Shrimp Scampi for Two, go to CooksIllustrated.com/feb16.

- 3 tablespoons salt
- 2 tablespoons sugar
- 1½ pounds shell-on jumbo shrimp (16 to 20 per pound), peeled, deveined, and tails removed, shells reserved
- 2 tablespoons extra-virgin olive oil
- 1 cup dry white wine
- 4 sprigs fresh thyme
- 3 tablespoons lemon juice, plus lemon wedges for serving
- 1 teaspoon cornstarch
- 8 garlic cloves, sliced thin
- ½ teaspoon red pepper flakes
- ¼ teaspoon pepper
- 4 tablespoons unsalted butter, cut into ½-inch pieces
- 1 tablespoon chopped fresh parsley

1. Dissolve salt and sugar in 1 quart cold water in large container. Submerge shrimp in brine, cover, and refrigerate for 15 minutes. Remove shrimp from brine and pat dry with paper towels.

2. Heat 1 tablespoon oil in 12-inch skillet over high heat until shimmering. Add shrimp shells and cook, stirring frequently, until they begin to turn spotty brown and skillet starts to brown, 2 to 4 minutes. Remove skillet from heat and carefully add wine and thyme sprigs. When bubbling subsides, return skillet to medium heat and simmer gently, stirring occasionally, for 5 minutes. Strain mixture through colander set over large bowl. Discard shells and reserve liquid (you should have about ⅔ cup). Wipe out skillet with paper towels.

3. Combine lemon juice and cornstarch in small bowl. Heat remaining 1 tablespoon oil, garlic, pepper flakes, and pepper in now-empty skillet over medium-low heat, stirring occasionally, until garlic is fragrant and just beginning to brown at edges, 3 to 5 minutes. Add reserved wine mixture, increase heat to high, and bring to simmer. Reduce heat to medium, add shrimp, cover, and cook, stirring occasionally, until shrimp are just opaque, 5 to 7 minutes. Remove skillet from heat and, using slotted spoon, transfer shrimp to bowl.

4. Return skillet to medium heat, add lemon juice–cornstarch mixture, and cook until slightly thickened, 1 minute. Remove from heat and whisk in butter and parsley until combined. Return shrimp and any accumulated juices to skillet and toss to combine. Serve, passing lemon wedges separately.

The Right Shrimp

Many manufacturers add salt or sodium tripolyphosphate to shrimp to prevent darkening or water loss, but we found that these treatments made the shellfish watery and bland; the latter also produced a chemical taste. When buying frozen shrimp, look for a brand with "shrimp" as the only ingredient listed on the bag. Some supermarkets, such as Whole Foods, sell only untreated shrimp.

CORE TECHNIQUE

HOW TO PEEL AND DEVEIN SHRIMP

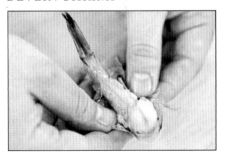

Many supermarkets carry easy-peel shrimp. The shells have been split open along the back for easy removal and the shrimp have already been deveined. If you can't find them, here is how to do the job yourself.

1. Peel shell away from flesh, starting at swimming legs, and then gently pull meat from tail.

2. Make ¼-inch-long incision along back of shrimp, then use tip of paring knife to remove vein.

Tuscan-Style Roast Pork

Arista means "the best." This dish promises a superlative pork loin flavored with garlic, rosemary, and deep browning. Too bad few versions live up to their name.

≥ BY ANNIE PETITO ≤

Boneless pork loin is a popular cut for good reason. It's widely available and affordable, and its uniform shape lends itself to even cooking and easy serving. But it has its flaws, too. Pork loin is lean and mild, and it's prone to overcooking. That's why I recently became intrigued by a classic Tuscan roast pork dish, *arista*, which derives its name from the Greek word *aristos*, meaning "the best." It promises to transform the loin into a flavorful roast with a deeply browned crust and plenty of rosemary and garlic in every bite. Though it can be made with a bone-in or boneless roast, I was drawn to the simplicity of using a boneless loin and the opportunity to turn this everyday cut into something more special.

Despite the simple concept, no two recipes I found were alike. Oven temperatures varied (anywhere from 325 to 475 degrees) as did roasting times (45 minutes to 4 hours) and ways to incorporate the garlic and rosemary (from simply rubbing the seasonings over the exterior to making a tunnel through the middle of the roast in which to deposit them). Regardless of the approach—and I tried them all—the outcome was the same: not good. The meat was usually underseasoned, dry, and tough. And it didn't stop there. The "crusts" were closer to beige than brown, and the rosemary and garlic flavors came across as either fleeting or aggressively harsh.

Something had obviously been lost in translation, and I was determined to find an approach that would deliver a version of arista that lived up to its name.

Pampering Pork Loin

American pork contains little marbling, and pork loin is one of the leanest cuts of pork, so avoiding overcooking can be a challenge. And it's only compounded by attempts to deeply brown the exterior, which typically leads to overcooking the meat just below the surface. But we've dealt with this issue

▶ Annie Shows You How
Video available free for 4 months at CooksIllustrated.com/feb16

After cooking the pork, we caramelize a halved lemon and use the juice to make a quick vinaigrette-style sauce for a bright, slightly sweet finish.

before in the test kitchen; our solution is to reverse-sear. Cooking the meat through very gently in a low-temperature oven ensures that it cooks evenly from edge to center, and browning it in a hot skillet on the stovetop gets the job done so quickly that it avoids overcooking much of the meat beneath the surface. The long time in the oven also helps dry the exterior, encouraging a nicely browned, crisp crust. It's a technique we've used with flank steak, rack of lamb, and strip steaks, so I felt confident that it would work here, too.

I cooked the loin through in a 275-degree oven, pulling it out when it was just below the medium mark (135 degrees), knowing that carryover cooking would continue to raise the temperature to 145 to 150 degrees, my target for doneness. Then I browned the roast over high heat in a few tablespoons of oil. To guard against overcooking, I browned just three

For Better Taste, Cook the Paste

Most recipes call for applying raw garlic and rosemary to the pork before roasting, but this results in harsh flavors. By pre-cooking our paste, we expose the garlic and rosemary to high temperatures and ensure that their flavors are mellowed.

sides (no one would see the unbrowned fourth side). Now I had a pork loin roast with a perfectly cooked interior, but I was surprised to find that the browning was patchy. Also, the meat was still bland and could stand to be a bit juicier.

The solution to the latter two problems was pretreating the meat. Salting the roast before cooking would draw the seasoning into the meat and help it retain moisture during cooking by changing the protein structure. And unlike brining, salting wouldn't add excess liquid that might impede browning.

In the past we found that simply salting the exterior of a pork loin doesn't season deeply enough. Instead, we double-butterfly the roast. Making two cuts into the meat allows you to essentially unroll the loin, exposing lots of surface area (see "How to Double-Butterfly a Pork Loin"). I rubbed each side with 1½ teaspoons of kosher salt and then rolled it back up and tied it with twine. After refrigerating it for an hour, I roasted it as before. Tasters confirmed: The meat was now well seasoned and far juicier.

Ensuring Even Flavor

Next up: how to incorporate the garlic and rosemary. Recipes I'd tried called for applying the garlic and rosemary in such a way that the flavor was either superficial (on the exterior only) or not evenly dispersed. But no matter the method, the flavor was spotty; I wanted garlic and rosemary in every bite. Given how well the double-butterflying method allowed me to season the meat with salt, it seemed like the obvious way to also distribute the garlic and rosemary. Rubbing a mixture made with a hefty amount of chopped garlic, rosemary, and a bit of red pepper flakes and lemon zest for some brightness into one side of the salted butterflied pork before rolling it up definitely distributed the flavors well, but tasters noted that the garlic and rosemary tasted raw and harsh. They were basically steaming inside the pork. Simmering the mixture in some oil before spreading it over the meat helped mellow its flavor, and because I wanted a clean garlic flavor, I used plenty of oil and opted for a nonstick skillet to cook the minced garlic until soft while avoiding browning. Then I simply strained off the oil. And because the pork loin tasted a bit lean, I decided to add some meaty reinforcement to the mixture. Minced in the food processor, pancetta's concentrated pork flavor and richness did the trick.

Creating a Crust

It was time to circle back to the issue of uneven browning. I realized that the problem was that the pork wasn't making even contact with the oil. I'd been using a 12-inch skillet with a couple of tablespoons of oil. This setup works fine when browning cuts of meat that fill up most of the pan, but here the skinny, cylindrical roast covered only the center of the skillet, leaving the oil to pool around the edges. Downsizing to a 10-inch skillet created a more snug setup, with an even layer of oil across the surface of the pan. This was also a good chance to use the oil I'd strained off from the rosemary and garlic.

After browning, I let the meat rest for 20 minutes, tented with foil to keep it warm, before serving it to my tasters. The meat was juicy and flavorful, and the crust certainly looked the part, but it had turned soggy. It had been steaming under the foil. The fix was quick: I simply changed the order of things. After removing the roast from the oven, I let it rest, and *then* I patted away any excess moisture, browned it on the stove, and served it immediately.

Traditionally arista is served with just juices from the pan, but I decided that it wouldn't be much more work to put together a more polished sauce. I made a quick vinaigrette-style sauce with the remainder of the infused olive oil strained from the herb mixture and the juice from the lemon I had zested earlier. This tasted a little too acidic, so I tried halving the lemon and, before browning the pork, cooking it cut side down in the skillet over high heat until it softened and browned. I squeezed this caramelized juice into the oil. Bright, slightly sweet, and perfumed with garlic and rosemary, this quick sauce was the perfect finishing touch for the pork.

TUSCAN-STYLE ROAST PORK WITH GARLIC AND ROSEMARY (ARISTA)
SERVES 4 TO 6

We strongly prefer natural pork in this recipe, but if enhanced pork (injected with a salt solution) is used, reduce the salt to 2 teaspoons (1 teaspoon per side) in step 3. After applying the seasonings, the pork needs to rest, refrigerated, for 1 hour before cooking.

- 1   lemon
- ⅓   cup extra-virgin olive oil
- 8   garlic cloves, minced
- ¼   teaspoon red pepper flakes
- 1   tablespoon chopped fresh rosemary
- 2   ounces pancetta, cut into ½-inch pieces
- 1   (2½-pound) boneless center-cut pork loin roast, trimmed
     Kosher salt

1. Finely grate 1 teaspoon zest from lemon. Cut lemon in half and reserve. Combine lemon zest, oil, garlic, and pepper flakes in 10-inch nonstick skillet. Cook over medium-low heat, stirring frequently, until garlic is sizzling, about 3 minutes. Add rosemary and cook, 30 seconds. Strain mixture through fine-mesh strainer set over bowl, pushing on garlic-rosemary mixture to extract oil. Set oil aside and let garlic-rosemary mixture cool. Using paper towels, wipe out skillet.

2. Process pancetta in food processor until smooth paste forms, 20 to 30 seconds, scraping down sides of bowl as needed. Add garlic-rosemary mixture and continue to process until mixture is homogeneous, 20 to 30 seconds longer, scraping down sides of bowl as needed.

3. Position roast fat side up. Insert knife one-third of way up from bottom of roast along 1 long side and cut horizontally, stopping ½ inch before edge. Open up flap. Keeping knife parallel to cutting board, cut through thicker portion of roast about ½ inch from bottom of roast, keeping knife level with first cut and stopping about ½ inch before edge. Open up this flap. If uneven, cover with plastic wrap and use meat

pounder to even out. Sprinkle 1 tablespoon kosher salt over both sides of roast (½ tablespoon per side) and rub into meat to adhere. Spread inside of roast evenly with pancetta-garlic paste, leaving about ¼-inch border on all sides. Starting from short side, roll roast (keeping fat on outside) and tie with twine at 1-inch intervals. Set wire rack in rimmed baking sheet and spray with vegetable oil spray. Set roast fat side up on prepared rack and refrigerate for 1 hour.

4. Adjust oven rack to middle position and heat oven to 275 degrees. Transfer roast to oven and cook until meat registers 135 degrees, 1½ to 2 hours. Remove roast from oven, tent with aluminum foil, and let rest for 20 minutes.

5. Heat 1 teaspoon reserved oil in now-empty skillet over high heat until just smoking. Add reserved lemon halves, cut side down, and cook until softened and cut surfaces are browned, 3 to 4 minutes. Transfer lemon halves to small plate.

6. Pat roast dry with paper towels. Heat 2 tablespoons reserved oil in now-empty skillet over high heat until just smoking. Brown roast on fat side and sides (do not brown bottom of roast), 4 to 6 minutes. Transfer roast to carving board and remove twine.

7. Once lemon halves are cool enough to handle, squeeze into fine-mesh strainer set over bowl. Press on solids to extract all pulp; discard solids. Whisk 2 tablespoons strained lemon juice into bowl with remaining reserved oil. Slice roast into ¼-inch-thick slices and serve, passing vinaigrette separately.

TECHNIQUE | HOW TO DOUBLE-BUTTERFLY A PORK LOIN

Opening up the pork loin with two parallel cuts exposes more of the meat's surface area to salt and the garlic-rosemary paste, for a better-seasoned, more flavorful roast.

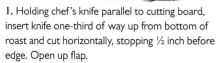

1. Holding chef's knife parallel to cutting board, insert knife one-third of way up from bottom of roast and cut horizontally, stopping ½ inch before edge. Open up flap.

2. Make another horizontal cut into thicker portion of roast about ½ inch from bottom, stopping about ½ inch before edge. Open up this flap, smoothing out rectangle of meat.

Perfecting Penne Arrabbiata

What's the trick to making this classic Italian sauce spicy but balanced? More chiles.

⇒ BY STEVE DUNN ⇐

Arrabbiata means "angry" in Italian, and one bite of this peasant-style pasta sauce will confirm that it was aptly named. The simplest versions blend tomatoes, garlic, olive oil, and, of course, red pepper flakes to create the dish's signature fiery kick. While I appreciate the simplicity, this bare-bones template produces a thin, one-dimensional sauce that's dominated by mouth-searing heat. Recipes that look beyond this short ingredient list—to additions like onion, fresh hot chiles, tomato paste, fresh herbs, and grated cheese—seemed much more promising. After all, heat is much more enticing when it's one element of a more complex dish and not the sole attraction. Crafting a better version of this classic would require enhancing its body and boosting its complexity and depth of flavor while being careful to maintain the vibrancy and peppery kick that are its hallmarks.

I began with the tomatoes: fresh or canned? And, if the latter, which type? Diced fresh tomatoes were a popular choice among the recipes I found, but given that this spicy dish is a great cold-weather meal, I eliminated fresh tomatoes from the running. Diced canned tomatoes (which are treated with calcium chloride) didn't break down enough to thicken the sauce properly, while crushed tomatoes, though they lent better body, came across as too cooked. In the end, whole canned tomatoes, which are the least processed of the canned tomato options, had the brightest flavor. A few pulses in the food processor broke them down just enough.

Next, I focused on ingredients that would enhance the savory depth and complexity of my arrabbiata. Dried oregano, though ubiquitous in Italian cooking, made the sauce taste like it came from a jar, so it was out. Fresh parsley and basil

▶ **Watch: We Make Pasta Angry**
Video available free for 4 months at CooksIllustrated.com/feb16

didn't add enough to warrant their purchase, and the texture and sweetness of onion distracted from the sauce's signature pepperiness. However, freshly grated Pecorino Romano did make the cut; stirring ¼ cup of the cheese into the sauce improved both its body and flavor. Another winning addition was tomato paste, which, like the cheese, is rich in glutamates—a couple of tablespoons gave the sauce savory, umami notes. Anchovies were a less obvious candidate because, while often found in Italian cooking, they are rarely seen in arrabbiata. Still, we use them often in the test kitchen as an umami booster, and my tasters welcomed a few minced fillets.

With the body and flavor of the sauce now much improved, it was time to focus on the heat component. I wanted more complexity than the one-dimensional heat that comes from using red pepper flakes alone, but I didn't want to make the sauce overwhelmingly spicy. In addition to 1 teaspoon of red pepper flakes, I tried arbol chiles, the closest available substitute for the rehydrated dried Italian red chiles called for by some recipes I found. But while the arbols were mild enough, they added an out-of-place smoky, earthy flavor. I had better luck with sweet paprika. Made from dried sweet red-pepper pods, it offered pepper flavor without upping the heat quotient.

What the dish still lacked was fresh bite, so I tried adding jalapeños, which appeared in a restaurant version of the dish that I'd tested early on; unfortunately, they added too much of a green-grassy taste and too much heat, even when seeded first. Fresh red cherry peppers, which appeared occasionally as an ingredient during my recipe research, seemed promising, but I couldn't find them. As a substitute, I gave pickled cherry peppers a try and had surprisingly good results. The sauce was too spicy, but the vinegar from the peppers' pickling brine was a turning point. My tasters loved the balance and brightness the acidity lent to the sauce.

The better option was *pepperoncini*. Also known as Tuscan peppers, these pickled peppers are much milder than cherry peppers but still delivered the acidity I was looking for. Vinegar is often added as

a finishing touch to recipes, bringing all the flavors together while retaining its brightness, but when I added the pepperoncini late in the cooking time, their flavor and vinegar-y punch were too dominant. Adding them at the beginning of the cooking process allowed their flavor to meld perfectly with the sauce. With that, the final piece of my arrabbiata puzzle clicked into place.

I finally had what I was looking for: a quick pasta sauce with sting that remained true to its "angry" roots but had a richness and complexity that offered more to love than just heat.

Pick Three Peppers

With their fiery kick, red pepper flakes made a good start for our version of *arrabbiata*, but we wanted more than one-dimensional pepper flavor. Paprika imparts sweet, fruity flavor, while pickled pepperoncini lend a mild kick along with a vinegary bite that brightens up the whole sauce.

PEPPERONCINI, PAPRIKA, AND RED PEPPER FLAKES

PENNE ARRABBIATA
SERVES 6

This recipe will work with other short tubular pastas like ziti or rigatoni. For our free recipe for Penne Arrabbiata for Two, go to CooksIllustrated.com/feb16.

- 1 (28-ounce) can whole peeled tomatoes
- ¼ cup extra-virgin olive oil
- ¼ cup stemmed, patted dry, and minced pepperoncini
- 2 tablespoons tomato paste
- 1 garlic clove, minced
- 1 teaspoon red pepper flakes
- 4 anchovy fillets, rinsed, patted dry, and minced to paste
- ½ teaspoon paprika
  Salt and pepper
- ¼ cup grated Pecorino Romano, plus extra for serving
- 1 pound penne

1. Pulse tomatoes and their juice in food processor until finely chopped, about 10 pulses.

2. Heat oil, pepperoncini, tomato paste, garlic, pepper flakes, anchovies, paprika, ½ teaspoon salt, and ½ teaspoon pepper in medium saucepan over medium-low heat, stirring occasionally, until deep red in color, 7 to 8 minutes.

3. Add tomatoes and Pecorino and bring to simmer. Cook, stirring occasionally, until thickened, about 20 minutes.

4. Bring 4 quarts water to boil in large pot. Add pasta and 1 tablespoon salt and cook, stirring often, until al dente. Reserve ½ cup cooking water, then drain pasta and return it to pot. Add sauce and toss to combine, adjusting consistency with reserved cooking water as needed. Season with salt and pepper to taste. Serve, passing extra Pecorino separately.

Skillet-Roasted Cauliflower

For tender, richly caramelized florets, we threw out the culinary rule book.

⇒ BY STEVE DUNN ⇐

Roasting cauliflower is a good way to caramelize its sugars and transform this mild vegetable into something sweet and nutty-tasting. But between preheating the oven and the actual roasting time, the process can take 45 minutes to 1 hour. Could a stovetop method deliver the same results in a time frame more suitable for a busy weeknight?

Following a standard sautéing method, I heated olive oil in a skillet until it started to shimmer and then added a head of cauliflower divided into florets. Cauliflower's dense texture means it can take a while to cook through, so it was no surprise when the craggy exteriors browned before the interiors had a chance to soften. I made another batch, this time pouring a little water into the pan and covering it. The trapped steam cooked the florets through, but now they looked—and tasted—anemic.

It was time to consider straying from the fundamentals. Since a hot pan browned the florets too quickly, how about starting with a cold one? I put a skillet with the cauliflower and oil on the stove, turned on the heat, and let it cook, covered, over medium-high heat for 5 minutes. I then removed the lid and let it continue to cook for another 12 minutes, stirring now and again. It was an unusual approach, but it delivered: Now I had tender florets with some deep-brown, caramelized spots. Even better, it all happened in less than 20 minutes.

Why did it work? The gentle cold start encouraged the cauliflower to release its moisture so that the florets steamed without any additional liquid. This meant there was no dilution of flavor. That said, my florets still needed more browning. Because of their irregular, rounded shape, very few of their surfaces actually rested on the bottom of the pan. To fix that, I sliced the entire head of cauliflower into ¾-inch-thick planks and then cut around the core to divide each cross section into florets.

Finally, inspired by a classic gremolata, I found that a combination of sautéed garlic and lemon zest, with fresh chopped parsley added at the finish, perked up the cauliflower without overwhelming it. With a sprinkle of toasted fresh bread crumbs for crunch, my newfangled skillet-roasted cauliflower was complete.

▶ **Steve Makes the Planks**
Video available free for 4 months
at CooksIllustrated.com/feb16

Cutting the cauliflower into thick crosswise planks and then florets provides lots of flat surfaces for browning.

SKILLET-ROASTED CAULIFLOWER
WITH GARLIC AND LEMON
SERVES 4 TO 6

For the first 5 minutes of cooking, the cauliflower steams in its own released moisture, so it is important not to lift the lid from the skillet during this time. For our free recipes for Skillet-Roasted Cauliflower with Curry, Raisins, and Almonds and for-two versions of the master recipe and all variations, go to CooksIllustrated.com/feb16.

- 1 head cauliflower (2 pounds)
- 1 slice hearty white sandwich bread, torn into 1-inch pieces
- 5 tablespoons extra-virgin olive oil
- Salt and pepper
- 1 garlic clove, minced
- 1 teaspoon grated lemon zest, plus lemon wedges for serving
- ¼ cup chopped fresh parsley

1. Trim outer leaves of cauliflower and cut stem flush with bottom of head. Turn head so stem is facing down and cut head into ¾-inch-thick slices. Cut around core to remove florets; discard core. Cut large florets into 1½-inch pieces. Transfer florets to bowl, including any small pieces that may have been created during trimming, and set aside.

2. Pulse bread in food processor to coarse crumbs, about 10 pulses. Heat bread crumbs, 1 tablespoon oil, pinch salt, and pinch pepper in 12-inch nonstick skillet over medium heat, stirring frequently, until bread crumbs are golden brown, 3 to 5 minutes. Transfer crumbs to bowl and wipe out skillet.

3. Combine 2 tablespoons oil and cauliflower florets in now-empty skillet and sprinkle with 1 teaspoon salt and ½ teaspoon pepper. Cover skillet and cook over medium-high heat until florets start to brown and edges just start to become translucent (do not lift lid), about 5 minutes.

4. Remove lid and continue to cook, stirring every 2 minutes, until florets turn golden brown in many spots, about 12 minutes.

5. Push cauliflower to edges of skillet. Add remaining 2 tablespoons oil, garlic, and lemon zest to center and cook, stirring with rubber spatula, until fragrant, about 30 seconds. Stir garlic mixture into cauliflower and continue to cook, stirring occasionally, until cauliflower is tender but still firm, about 3 minutes longer.

6. Remove skillet from heat and stir in parsley. Transfer cauliflower to serving platter and sprinkle with bread crumbs. Serve, passing lemon wedges separately.

SKILLET-ROASTED CAULIFLOWER
WITH CAPERS AND PINE NUTS

Omit bread and reduce oil to ¼ cup. Reduce salt in step 3 to ¾ teaspoon. Substitute 2 tablespoons capers, rinsed and minced, for garlic. Substitute 2 tablespoons minced fresh chives for parsley and stir in ¼ cup toasted pine nuts with chives in step 6.

SKILLET-ROASTED CAULIFLOWER
WITH CUMIN AND PISTACHIOS

Omit bread and reduce oil to ¼ cup. Heat 1 teaspoon cumin seeds and 1 teaspoon coriander seeds in 12-inch nonstick skillet over medium heat, stirring frequently, until lightly toasted and fragrant, 2 to 3 minutes. Transfer to spice grinder or mortar and pestle and coarsely grind. Wipe out skillet. Substitute ground cumin-coriander mixture, ½ teaspoon paprika, and pinch cayenne pepper for garlic; lime zest for lemon zest; and 3 tablespoons chopped fresh mint for parsley. Sprinkle with ¼ cup pistachios, toasted and chopped, before serving with lime wedges.

The Perfect Baked Potato

We wanted a uniformly fluffy interior encased in thin, crisp skin—
and we baked nearly 200 pounds of potatoes to get it.

⇒ BY LAN LAM ⇐

Baking a potato is about as basic as cooking gets—so basic, in fact, that it doesn't even seem to require a recipe. Simply stick a russet in a moderately hot oven directly on the rack, and after about an hour, give it a squeeze. If it's still firm, bake it longer; if it gives to pressure, it's done.

The beauty of that method is its simplicity, but how often does it produce a truly great baked potato? In my experience, almost never. Whether the center is dense and gummy or the skin is soggy, shriveled, or chewy, the best I can do is slather on as much butter or sour cream as possible to cover up the flaws.

I want more from a baked potato than a dense or desiccated log of starch, and I was determined to examine every variable to nail down ideal results. That meant a fluffy interior encased in thin, crisp skin.

Degrees of Doneness

Russets are the classic choice for baked potatoes because they're a dry, floury variety, meaning they contain a relatively high amount (20 to 22 percent) of starch. (So-called in-between varieties like Yukon Golds, or waxy types like Red Bliss, contain 16 to 18 percent and about 16 percent starch, respectively.) The more starch a potato contains, the more water from inside the potato can be absorbed during baking. As the starch granules swell with water within the spud's cell walls, they eventually force the cells to separate into clumps that result in the texture we perceive as dry and fluffy.

But when exactly does a potato reach that dry and fluffy stage—the point at which it is done? Taking a closer look at the bake-until-it's-squeezable approach would at least give me a baseline temperature to work from, so I pricked an 8-ounce russet a few times with a fork and placed it in a 400-degree oven. Once the exterior had softened, I cut slits to open up the potato and stuck an instant-read thermometer in several places. The outer ½ inch or so, which was soft

It's crucial to cut the potatoes open immediately after baking to allow steam to escape; otherwise, even a perfectly baked potato will be gummy.

▶ Look: It's Perfect
Video available free for 4 months
at CooksIllustrated.com/feb16

enough to squeeze but not quite fluffy, registered 195 degrees, while the dense core, which was clearly underdone, was 175 degrees. From there, I baked off several more potatoes, placing probes at exterior points in each and removing them from the oven at different temperatures. At 200 degrees the outer edge was light and fluffy, while the core was just tender, but at 205 degrees the whites of the potatoes were at their best: fluffy from edge to center. A few more tests revealed that the method was somewhat forgiving; I could bake the potatoes as high as 212 degrees and still achieve perfectly light and fluffy results. The only hitch, I discovered, was that it was crucial to cut the potatoes open immediately after baking to let steam escape; if they sat for even 10 minutes, they retained more water than potatoes that were opened immediately and turned dense and gummy even after cooking to 205 degrees.

Must You Prick?

Everyone knows that you have to prick potatoes before baking them so steam doesn't build up inside and cause them to explode. Well, we baked 40 potatoes without doing this, and not one exploded. But since it takes so little effort, here's one time we'll err on the side of caution. It could be the 41st one that explodes.

Working from the Inside Out

Now that I knew exactly when the potato was cooked through, I wanted to see how fast I could get it there. Microwaving the potatoes would surely speed up the cooking, I assumed. But further tests proved that this was actually the worst approach. Whether I used the microwave alone or in tandem with the oven, the potatoes always cooked unevenly and were often gummy and dense. Why? Because microwaves heat potatoes very unevenly, rendering some portions fully cooked while others are still rock-hard.

Back to the oven. The potatoes took between 60 and 80 minutes to cook through at 400 degrees, so I hoped that cranking the heat up to 500 would hasten things. Unfortunately, this caused the outer portion of the potato to overbrown and almost char in spots, leading to a slightly burned flavor. Going forward, I turned the oven temperature down notch by notch and eventually found 450 degrees for 45 minutes or so to be the sweet spot—the interior was soft and light, the skin nicely browned. Now I just had to see about crisping it up.

Skin Care

Since frying potatoes in oil crisps and browns their exteriors, I hoped that coating the russets' skin with oil might do the same as they baked. But as it turned out, painting the spuds with vegetable oil (1 tablespoon coated four potatoes nicely) and then baking them yielded disappointingly soft and chewy skins. The problem was that the oil created a barrier on the skin's exterior that prevented moisture from escaping, so the skins weren't able to dry out and crisp.

The better method was to apply the oil once the potatoes were cooked, by which point the skins had dehydrated considerably. Returning them to the oven for 10 more minutes rendered them deep brown and crisp (the extra time increases the interior temperature of the potatoes by just 2 or 3 degrees).

I was very pleased with my method, which really wasn't much more work than baking a potato without a recipe. But one variable lingered: seasoning.

We're Not Kidding About the Thermometer!

It might sound fussy to take the temperature of a baked potato to see if the center has reached 205 degrees, but it's the only way to guarantee that you're getting a uniformly fluffy interior. The usual approach to checking for doneness, squeezing the potato, doesn't work because while the outer edge might feel soft, the center is likely dense and firm. This cross section shows how different the texture (and temperature) can be from the surface to the center.

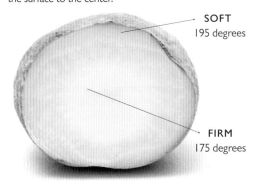

SOFT
195 degrees

FIRM
175 degrees

Sure, I'd sprinkle salt and pepper on the potato at the table, but what I really wanted was even seasoning all over. My first attempt, brining the potatoes for 1 hour before baking, delivered skins with fantastic flavor, but did I really have to add that much more time to the method? Instead, I tried simply wetting the raw potatoes and sprinkling them with salt—and when that failed (the salt crystals didn't stick), I simply dunked the potatoes in salty water. The flavor was just as full and even as that of the brined potatoes, but this step added mere seconds to my recipe. The last tweak I made, baking the potatoes on a rack set in a rimmed baking sheet, prevented drips of salt and water from staining the bottom of my oven and allowed the hot air to circulate evenly around the potatoes during baking.

Crisp and thoroughly seasoned on the outside and light and fluffy within, my baked potatoes were perfect as-is, though nobody disagreed that a pat of butter or sour cream was in order. And for the times when I wanted a real showstopper of a side dish (or even a main course with a salad), I put together a few simple toppings that could be made while the potatoes baked. Topped with a creamy egg salad–like mixture or herbed goat cheese, these spuds were an unqualified hit at the dinner table.

Why You Shouldn't Microwave

A microwave might seem like a fast way to "bake" a potato, but we found two reasons why it's actually the worst approach. First, microwaves heat foods very unevenly, so some parts of the potato might rapidly reach 205 degrees while others get to only 180 degrees. Second, rapidly heating a potato causes pressure to build and cell walls to burst, releasing starch molecules that glue together the broken cell walls.

Finding the Best—and Quickest—Way to Bake a Potato

We found that if a baked potato reached between 205 and 212 degrees, the interior was uniformly fluffy—just the way we like it. The question was how quickly we could achieve that texture and if we could crisp the skin, too.

HOW FAST CAN WE COOK IT?

METHOD: Microwave for 6 minutes
RESULT: Uneven cooking; gummy, stodgy interior; shriveled skin.

METHOD: Pressure-cook for 40 minutes
RESULT: Fluffy inside, soggy skin, not much time savings.

METHOD: Bake at 500 degrees for 40 minutes
RESULT: Overbrowns and slightly chars exterior, leading to burned flavor.

SOLUTION: Bake at 450 degrees for 45 to 60 minutes
The sweet spot for evenly cooked potatoes.

BEST WAY TO CRISP THE SKIN?

METHOD: Deep-fry fully baked potato
RESULT: Skin crisps nicely, but too much work.

METHOD: Butter skin
RESULT: Water in butter keeps skin from crisping.

METHOD: Oil skin before baking
RESULT: Oil keeps moisture in skin from evaporating; cooks up soggy.

SOLUTION: Oil skin when almost done
Skin dehydrates during baking, then crisps in oil.

BEST BAKED POTATOES
SERVES 4

Open up the potatoes immediately after removal from the oven in step 3 so steam can escape. Top them as desired, or with one of our toppings. For our free recipes for Best Baked Potatoes for Two and Smoked Trout Topping, go to CooksIllustrated.com/feb16.

  Salt and pepper
4 (7- to 9-ounce) russet potatoes, unpeeled, each lightly pricked with fork in 6 places
1 tablespoon vegetable oil

1. Adjust oven rack to middle position and heat oven to 450 degrees. Dissolve 2 tablespoons salt in ½ cup water in large bowl. Place potatoes in bowl and toss so exteriors of potatoes are evenly moistened. Transfer potatoes to wire rack set in rimmed baking sheet and bake until center of largest potato registers 205 degrees, 45 minutes to 1 hour.

2. Remove potatoes from oven and brush tops and sides with oil. Return potatoes to oven and continue to bake for 10 minutes.

3. Remove potatoes from oven and, using paring knife, make 2 slits, forming X, in each potato. Using clean dish towel, hold ends and squeeze slightly to push flesh up and out. Season with salt and pepper to taste. Serve immediately.

CREAMY EGG TOPPING
MAKES 1 CUP

3 hard-cooked large eggs, chopped
4 tablespoons sour cream
1½ tablespoons minced cornichons
1 tablespoon minced fresh parsley
1 tablespoon Dijon mustard
1 tablespoon capers, rinsed and minced
1 tablespoon minced shallot
  Salt and pepper

Stir together eggs, sour cream, cornichons, parsley, mustard, capers, and shallot. Season with salt and pepper to taste.

HERBED GOAT CHEESE TOPPING
MAKES ¾ CUP

4 ounces goat cheese, softened
2 tablespoons extra-virgin olive oil
2 tablespoons minced fresh parsley
1 tablespoon minced shallot
½ teaspoon grated lemon zest
  Salt and pepper

Mash goat cheese with fork. Stir in oil, parsley, shallot, and lemon zest. Season with salt and pepper to taste.

Essential Tools (and Ingenious Gadgets)

Decades of testing have taught us what every well-equipped kitchen should have. Here are our favorite tools—plus a handful of other useful gadgets. BY SARAH SEITZ

THE MUST-HAVES

These models are the best of the best in their respective categories.

Bench Scraper

Dexter-Russell 6" Dough Cutter/Scraper—Sani-Safe Series ($7.01)
➤ Its sharp beveled edge cuts, scrapes, and scoops with ease.

Can Opener

Fissler Magic Smooth-Edge Can Opener ($29.00)
➤ It tidily removes lids; plus, its long handle offers great leverage.

Coarse Grater

Rösle Coarse Grater ($35.95)
➤ This flat paddle with grippy feet can grate over any surface or bowl.

Colander

RSVP International Endurance Precision Pierced 5 Qt. Colander ($25.99)
➤ Tiny, all-over perforations drain water quickly but don't allow food to slip through.

Dry Measuring Cups

Amco Housewares Professional Performance 4-Piece Measuring Cup Set ($14.95)
➤ Long, clearly marked handles make the "dip and sweep" method easy.

Garlic Press

Kuhn Rikon Stainless Steel Epicurean Garlic Press ($39.95)
➤ Conical holes produce a fine, uniform mince for even flavor. Easy to squeeze and clean.

Instant-Read Thermometer

ThermoWorks Splash-Proof Super-Fast Thermapen ($96.00)
➤ So fast and easy to use, you'll wonder how you ever lived without it.

Kitchen Shears

Kershaw Taskmaster Shears/Shun Multi-Purpose Shears ($49.95)
➤ These shears are sharp enough to butcher chicken yet nimble enough to trim pie dough.

Ladle

Rösle Hook Ladle with Pouring Rim ($34.00)
➤ The Rösle's angled handle offers control when reaching into any pot.

Liquid Measuring Cup

Pyrex 2-Cup Measuring Cup ($5.99)
➤ It's everything you need: sturdy tempered glass etched with clear, fade-resistant markings.

Mandoline/V-Slicer

Swissmar Börner Original V-Slicer Plus Mandoline ($29.99)
➤ It can slice faster and more precisely than a skilled chef with a knife.

Measuring Spoons

Cuisipro Stainless Steel Measuring Spoon Set ($11.95)
➤ The oval bowls of these spoons fit in small jars and are flush with the handles for level measuring.

Metal Spatula

Wüsthof Gourmet Slotted Turner/Fish Spatula ($34.95)
➤ The best tool for sliding under fish—not to mention cookies, pancakes, and roasted vegetables.

Pepper Mill

Cole & Mason Derwent Gourmet Precision Pepper Mill ($40.00)
➤ The grind size selection is simple, it loads easily, and its transparent body shows the fill level.

Rasp Grater

Microplane Classic Zester Grater ($12.35)
➤ With minimal effort, it grates wisps of cheese or citrus zest and makes paste of garlic or ginger.

Salad Spinner

OXO Good Grips Salad Spinner ($29.99)
➤ The OXO dries greens more thoroughly than any other model.

Silicone Spatula

Rubbermaid Professional 13½-Inch High-Heat Scraper ($18.99)
➤ Its firm-but-flexible edge scrapes as well as it stirs.

Timer

American Innovative Chef's Quad Timer ($29.95)
➤ This perfectly accurate timer is sleek and solidly built. You set the time with a dial, not buttons.

Tongs

OXO Good Grips 12-Inch Locking Tongs ($12.09)
➤ The shallow pincers grip heavy roasts as easily as they do slender asparagus spears.

Vegetable Peeler

Kuhn Rikon Original Swiss Peeler ($3.50)
➤ This lightweight, cheap peeler skins anything from dense butternut squash to knobby ginger.

Whisk

OXO Good Grips 11" Balloon Whisk ($9.99)
➤ This lightweight model features a long handle that won't slip into bowls or pots.

CLEVER USES FOR CORE TOOLS

Some of our favorite tools have hidden talents.

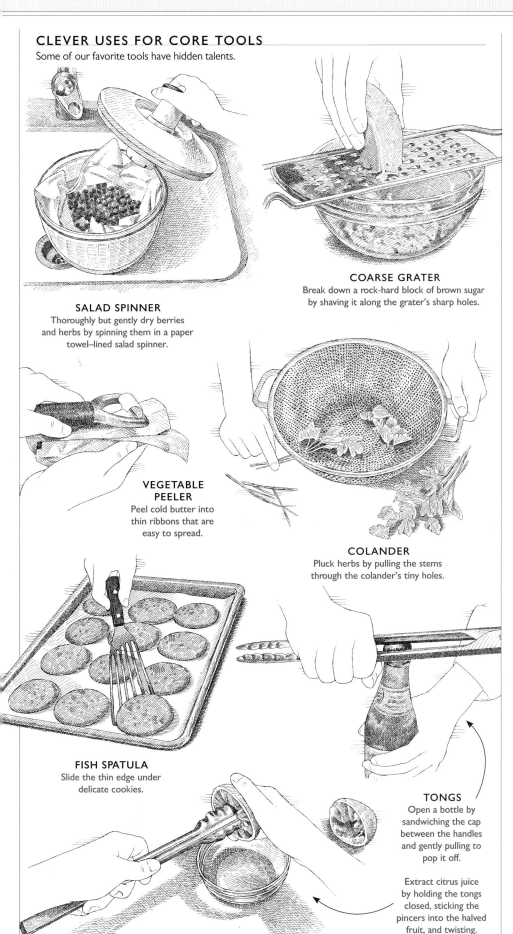

SALAD SPINNER
Thoroughly but gently dry berries and herbs by spinning them in a paper towel–lined salad spinner.

COARSE GRATER
Break down a rock-hard block of brown sugar by shaving it along the grater's sharp holes.

VEGETABLE PEELER
Peel cold butter into thin ribbons that are easy to spread.

COLANDER
Pluck herbs by pulling the stems through the colander's tiny holes.

FISH SPATULA
Slide the thin edge under delicate cookies.

TONGS
Open a bottle by sandwiching the cap between the handles and gently pulling to pop it off.

Extract citrus juice by holding the tongs closed, sticking the pincers into the halved fruit, and twisting.

GADGETS WORTH BUYING

We've tested hundreds of quirky gadgets over the years, but only a handful have stood out as useful.

Adjustable Measuring Cup: KitchenArt Adjust-A-Cup Professional Series, 2-Cup
Price: $12.95

Why It's Worth Owning: This clear plastic barrel with measurement markings and a plunger insert makes it easy to measure—and extract—semisolid or sticky ingredients like mayonnaise, honey, or peanut butter. Simply draw back the plunger to the desired marking, fill the cup, and then push forward to eject the ingredient—no fussy scraping necessary.

Boil-Over Prevention: Kuhn Rikon Spill Stopper
Price: $24.95

Why It's Worth Owning: This bowl-shaped flexible silicone lid (which doubles as a splatter guard) has six central flaps that open just enough to let milk foam flow over its surface, where it is contained by curved edges. It's dishwasher-safe, but it cleans up almost as easily by hand.

Bowl Anchor: Staybowlizer
Price: $19.95

Why It's Worth Owning: This two-sided silicone gadget solves the problem of mixing bowls that spin or rock on the counter, leaving our hands free to whisk oil into vinaigrette, beat eggs, or mix cookie dough.

Jar Opener: Amco Swing-A-Way Jar Opener
Price: $5.99

Why It's Worth Owning: By using a combination of traction and pressure, this model releases the vacuum on jars of all sizes and loosens tight threads on plastic lids. It also works well on previously opened jars.

Wine Aerator: Nuance Wine Finer
Price: $19.95

Why It's Worth Owning: This long, tube-like aerator improved wine's flavor and aroma without the usual wait for the wine to breathe. It slides into the neck of the bottle, leaving only a pouring spout for neat, hands-free aerating.

Pear-Walnut Upside-Down Cake

The underrated pear makes for a more refined version of this simple cake—if you know just how to treat it.

≥ BY ANNIE PETITO ≤

Pears are sometimes referred to as the queen of fruit, but you'd never know it from a baking standpoint. Their popularity in desserts has always been a distant second to apples, perhaps because there's a lack of good information about them. Pear recipes tend to offer few guidelines, often not naming a variety and suggesting that the pieces be "firm but ripe"—a description that I've never been entirely clear on.

With pear season well under way, I figured it was a great time to explore pear upside-down cake, which requires a fair amount of fruit and would be a perfect way to showcase pears' subtle floral flavor and graceful shape. To make the best version, I would have to learn more about determining pear ripeness and how different varieties function when baked.

Pear Picking

My first move was to consult pear experts from Oregon State University and the Pear Bureau Northwest about the best way to check for ripeness. They explained that the best method is to "check the neck," which means pressing lightly on the fruit near the stem end, where the fruit should give to gentle pressure (for more information, see "Understanding Pears"). Armed with that advice, I shopped for the four most readily available varieties (Bosc, Anjou, Bartlett, and Comice), gathering several pounds of each.

I'd seen a few recipes for pear upside-down cakes where the fruit was cut into thick chunks, but for the polished presentation I had in mind, I peeled, halved, and sliced them into long wedges. Then I fanned the pears (three per cake) around the bottom of 9-inch round pans over a simple upside-down cake topping of butter, brown sugar, and a touch of salt that I had briefly simmered in a saucepan. I poured a basic yellow cake batter evenly over the fruit and slid the pans into 350-degree

▶ **Step-by-Step Video**
Video available free for 4 months at CooksIllustrated.com/feb16

One advantage of making an upside-down cake with pears: There's no need to precook the fruit to remove excess moisture or soften the texture.

ovens to bake for about 40 minutes. When they were done, I carefully turned them out onto cooling racks, attempting to make sure that none of the gooey topping was left behind.

One thing was immediately clear: Bosc pears stood out not just for their elongated necks, which looked particularly graceful, but also because they boasted a unique combination of sweetness and a nicely dense texture. Further research confirmed my findings: Unlike other varieties, the flavor of Bosc pears is sweeter and more pronounced even before their flesh has fully softened, which meant that there was a wider window in which they'd be good for baking.

But when I went to cut a slice, the cake was wet and there were streaks down the sides where liquid had obviously seeped in. I figured that the pears had shed a lot of moisture during baking, as other fruits do, so I ran a series of tests to remove or soak up the excess liquid: microwaving and draining the pears, tossing them in cornstarch, and coating them in panko bread crumbs. But none of the fixes worked.

Would adding a couple of teaspoons of cornstarch to the topping absorb and trap any moisture that leaked out? Sure enough, the next cake was moist but not damp and looked tidier, with no streaks down the sides.

I also used these tests to make two subtle refinements to my method. First, I realized that I didn't need to cook the topping separately; I could simply pour melted butter into the cake pan and sprinkle a mixture of brown sugar, cornstarch, and salt over the top. Second, I came up with a reliable technique for unmolding the cake cleanly every time: lining the bottom of the pan with parchment paper and letting the baked cake rest in the pan for 15 minutes, which I found was the sweet spot for ensuring that the fruit didn't stick to the pan and that the bottom of the cake wasn't so warm that it steamed and turned gummy (for more information, see "Unmolding Upside-Down Cakes").

Going Nuts

I'd made good progress: The pears looked and tasted great, and the cake was easy. But the components weren't good matches because all three elements—the cake, topping, and pears—were sweet. For better contrast, I needed a less-sweet cake with more character.

At first I tried simply tweaking the yellow cake by adding cornmeal. But instead of the pleasantly coarse crumb I was hoping for, its texture was gritty. I had better luck when I switched to an almond cake from the test kitchen archives, which offered more distinct flavor and—because the cake gets its structure from whipping egg whites and sugar in a food processor rather than from an abundance of flour—a light but sturdy texture and more open crumb.

The only drawback to the almonds was their understated taste, so I tried walnuts in their place. This was a great move: The walnuts' earthy, faintly astringent flavor (from the tannins in their skins) offset the fruit's sweetness just enough and lent the cake an attractively speckled appearance.

My pear-walnut upside-down cake was a refreshing change from the usual apple or pineapple—and, dare I say, more sophisticated, too. With a dollop of not-too-sweet crème fraîche alongside, it could even make an ultrasimple yet elegant holiday dessert.

PEAR-WALNUT UPSIDE-DOWN CAKE
SERVES 8 TO 10

We strongly recommend baking this cake in a light-colored cake pan with sides that are at least 2 inches tall. If using a dark-colored pan, start checking for doneness at 1 hour, and note that the cake may dome in the center and the topping may become too sticky. Serve with crème fraîche, lightly sweetened whipped cream, or our Yogurt Whipped Topping (page 29).

Topping
4	tablespoons unsalted butter, melted
½	cup packed (3½ ounces) dark brown sugar
2	teaspoons cornstarch
⅛	teaspoon salt
3	ripe but firm Bosc pears (8 ounces each)

Cake
1	cup walnuts, toasted
½	cup (2½ ounces) all-purpose flour
½	teaspoon salt
¼	teaspoon baking powder
⅛	teaspoon baking soda
3	large eggs
1	cup (7 ounces) sugar
4	tablespoons unsalted butter, melted
¼	cup vegetable oil

1. FOR THE TOPPING: Adjust oven rack to middle position and heat oven to 300 degrees. Grease 9-inch round cake pan and line bottom with parchment paper. Pour melted butter over bottom of pan and swirl to evenly coat. Combine sugar, cornstarch, and salt in small bowl and sprinkle evenly over melted butter.

2. Peel, halve, and core pears. Set aside 1 pear half and reserve for other use. Cut remaining 5 pear halves into 4 wedges each. Arrange pears in circular pattern around cake pan with tapered ends pointing inward. Arrange two smallest pear wedges in center.

3. FOR THE CAKE: Pulse walnuts, flour, salt, baking powder, and baking soda in food processor until walnuts are finely ground, 8 to 10 pulses. Transfer walnut mixture to bowl.

4. Process eggs and sugar in now-empty processor until very pale yellow, about 2 minutes. With processor running, add melted butter and oil in steady stream until incorporated. Add walnut mixture and pulse to combine, 4 to 5 pulses. Pour batter evenly over pears (some pear may show through; cake will bake up over fruit).

5. Bake until center of cake is set and bounces back when gently pressed and toothpick inserted in center comes out clean, 1 hour 10 minutes to 1¼ hours, rotating pan after 40 minutes. Let cake cool in pan on wire rack for 15 minutes. Carefully run paring knife or offset spatula around sides of pan. Invert cake onto wire rack set in rimmed baking sheet; discard parchment. Let cake cool for about 2 hours. Transfer to serving platter, cut into wedges, and serve.

CORE TECHNIQUE | UNMOLDING
UPSIDE-DOWN CAKES

If an upside-down cake is turned out of the pan too quickly, the bottom of the cake steams and turns gummy; if the cake cools completely in the pan, the fruit will stick. Our approach is to line the pan with parchment paper, which ensures that the fruit releases cleanly; let the cake rest in the pan for just 15 minutes before turning it out onto a rack.

Understanding Pears

While you can find a variety of pears in most supermarkets, the flavor and texture differences among them are relatively subtle. (Bosc is an exception; see below for more information.) The most important factors to consider when selecting pears are whether you're buying them for eating or for cooking and when you plan to use them.

SHOPPING

➤ For Cooking
Since heat causes the pectin in pears—the source of their structure—to break down and soften, it's important to cook with pears that are firm but not rock-hard. When you press the neck, it should give only slightly and feel a bit softer than a russet potato—the meaning of "firm but ripe."

➤ For Eating
Pears for eating should yield slightly more when pressed at the neck, like a ripe avocado. Avoid pears that are soft at the base, which are overripe.

➤ Why Check the Neck?
Pears ripen from the inside out, so checking at the neck—the fruit's narrowest point—will be the earliest indication that the pear has started to ripen. Waiting for the thicker base of the pear to soften before using will result in overripe fruit.

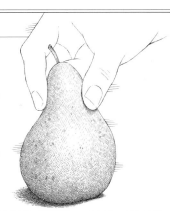

STORAGE
If pears are not fully ripe when you buy them, keep them at a cool room temperature and allow them to ripen slowly. In a pinch, you can speed up the ripening process a bit by storing the pears in a paper bag, but avoid plastic bags, which will greatly accelerate ripening and can cause them to degrade. Once the pears are fully ripe, move them to the refrigerator, where they'll keep for up to 5 days. Whether they're stored on the counter or in the fridge, avoid proximity to strong-smelling foods, as pears readily absorb odors.

Bosc: The Cooking Pear
When we compared Bosc pears with other common varieties in our upside-down cake recipe, the other pears tasted bland and washed-out, but the Bosc pears were sweet and complex. As it turns out, Bosc pears develop sweetness and flavor earlier in the ripening process than most other varieties, so even when shy of fully ripened, they'll still have plenty of their characteristic musky, floral sweetness. They also have a more naturally firm texture, which helps keep them from turning mushy when cooked. One aesthetic benefit: Their elongated necks make Boscs a more elegant choice for poaching or fanning over a cake or tart than rounder, squatter varieties.

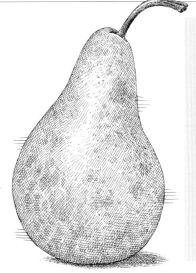

SCIENCE
Pears Ripen Best Off the Tree
Pears that have ripened off the tree have a better texture than those that spent longer than needed on the tree. Ripening on the branch causes them to develop deposits of lignin and cellulose called "stone cells" that make the flesh gritty. To avoid this, pears are picked when immature and placed in chilled storage for anywhere from days to months. The cold storage "conditions" the fruit, allowing precursors to ethylene to form, which in turn help the pears ripen fully at room temperature with a texture that's smooth and juicy throughout.

The Fluffiest Dinner Rolls

We thought the classic light, tender American dinner roll couldn't get any better.
Then we tried a cutting-edge Asian baking technique.

⇒ BY ANDREA GEARY ⇐

I used to think that the Old Testament adage "There is nothing new under the sun" could be applied to bread baking. Most "new" bread recipes are actually just modern twists on established recipes or resurrections of bygone techniques. So I was intrigued when I read about *tangzhong*, an oddball bread-making technique that originated in Japan and was popularized by pastry chef Yvonne Chen in the early 2000s.

Instead of simply combining the dry and wet ingredients and kneading as you would to make a conventional loaf, you begin by cooking a portion of the flour and liquid to form a pudding-like paste that you then let cool and mix into the dough. Fans of the method claimed not only that it produced bread with a particularly moist, airy, feathery crumb but also that the loaf remained fresh and soft longer than conventional bread.

Curious, I made a popular published Japanese milk bread recipe (a soft, rich sandwich loaf with a snow-white crumb that's a staple in Asian bakeries) that employs the tangzhong method and was immediately won over: The dough was soft and silky, and its pillowy crumb was made up of delicate, almost croissant-like sheets. Eating it gave me the kind of satisfaction I get from a really good dinner roll—except that this bread was even fluffier and, as promised, maintained its impressively moist, plush crumb over the next couple of days.

So, what if I applied this Japanese technique to my usual pull-apart dinner roll recipe? If it worked, it could potentially yield the best dinner rolls I'd ever made and give them a perk that most rolls don't have: make-ahead potential.

Well-Hydrated

In the recipes I found that employ the tangzhong method, the paste is about 5 parts liquid to 1 part flour and makes up 15 to 20 percent of the total dough weight. My standard dinner roll recipe yields 25 ounces of dough, so to make about 5 ounces of paste, I whisked together ½ cup of water and 3 tablespoons of bread flour in a saucepan. As I stirred the mixture over medium heat, its consistency went from heavy cream to thick pudding. I set the paste aside to cool while

Besides boasting a particularly moist and feathery crumb, these rolls can be made a day in advance and still taste great.

I added the remaining ingredients to the stand mixer bowl: 2 cups of bread flour, instant yeast, a little sugar and salt, 4 tablespoons of softened butter, an egg, and ¼ cup milk. Then I added the cooled paste and started mixing. But after 3 minutes, I knew something was wrong: The dough, which is usually slightly sticky and workable was dry and tight.

I knew this wasn't typical for a tangzhong dough, because the Japanese milk loaf dough I'd made had

What Makes These Rolls Unique?

An Asian bread-making technique called *tangzhong* produces exceptionally moist rolls by incorporating a good amount of water. Ten minutes of kneading creates the structure needed to support the extra liquid, and a special shaping method delivers delicate, sheet-like layers.

MORE WATER

MORE STRUCTURE

LAYERED SHAPING

been soft and smooth. It wasn't until I compared the hydrations of the two doughs that I discovered the discrepancy: My standard dough had a hydration of 60 percent (meaning there were 6 parts liquid to every 10 parts flour), while the hydration of the Japanese milk bread was 80 percent, which I later learned was typical for a dough using the tangzhong method. Ordinarily, that much liquid would make a dough slack, sticky, and hard to shape, but not so with my milk bread.

I made another batch of rolls with a hot-water paste, but this time I added extra milk (½ cup total) to the dough to bring the hydration to 80 percent. Sure enough, the dough was soft and silky, not sticky, and held its shape nicely after kneading.

So why wasn't it a sticky mess? In a standard dough, where you mix cold water and flour, most of the water is not absorbed, so the stickiness you feel is so-called free water. But as I learned making Mandarin pancakes for Mu Shu Pork (March/April 2015), flour can absorb twice as much hot water as cold water. Heating the water for the paste allows it to be fully absorbed by the flour; in essence, a portion of what would be free water in a standard dough gets locked away. Thus, when the flour paste is mixed with the rest of the ingredients, the dough is smooth, not sticky.

From there, I knocked the air out of the doubled dough to eliminate large air bubbles and encourage a fine crumb, portioned it into 12 pieces, rolled each into a taut ball, and arranged the rolls in a greased cake pan to rise. Baked at 375 degrees until they were deep golden brown, these rolls were moist and flavorful—but they were a bit squat and the crumb was coarse.

Building Strength

A close look at some tangzhong recipes revealed my mistake: I had added more moisture to my dough without building any additional structure to support the greater expansion of steam produced by the extra water. So I made a few changes. First, I added an autolyse—a brief resting period between mixing and kneading the dough that alters the gluten-forming proteins so they can link up more effectively. Withholding sugar and salt until after the autolyse makes this little power nap even more effective, since those ingredients would otherwise slow the alteration of the proteins. Second, I waited until the second half of the kneading period—when the gluten was well established—to add the butter, since fat makes the gluten strands slippery and unable to "grab" each other to form a network. I also streamlined my method by microwaving the flour paste; roughly 60 seconds on high did the trick. And rather than wait for the hot paste to cool (so it wouldn't kill the yeast on contact), I added it to cold milk and whisked them together until the mixture was merely warm.

With those changes, my rolls were lighter and boasted a finer crumb, so I was definitely on the right track. But those gossamer-thin layers were still missing, and I wondered if altering my shaping method might help.

When dough is kneaded, the flour proteins link up in a fairly random way. Rounding each portion of dough into a tight ball, as you typically would when shaping dinner rolls, organizes the proteins on the exterior into a kind of membrane (bakers call this a "gluten cloak") but does not affect the proteins on the interior, which remain random. The Japanese milk bread's shaping method was elaborate, and now I suspected that it was the key to the bread's delicate vertical layers. To shape that loaf, I had divided the dough into four pieces, rolled each one into a rectangle, and folded each rectangle into thirds like a business letter; then I flattened each piece of dough out again and rolled it up again like a jelly roll before nestling it into the loaf pan with the others.

Because I was shaping 12 dinner rolls instead of four larger dough pieces, I tried a simplified version, flattening each piece into a long, narrow rectangle before rolling it up and placing it in the pan. When

Rolling the dough into balls, as most recipes instruct, causes the gluten to organize randomly and the crumb to be sponge-like. Stretching and rolling the dough into tight spirals organizes the gluten into sheets, and the rolls develop delicate, distinct layers.

FORM Gently stretch and press dough into 8 by 2-inch strip.

ROLL Starting at 1 end, roll strip into snug cylinder.

ARRANGE Place cylinders seam side down in prepared pan.

the rolls had doubled, they looked especially smooth and plump, thanks to the strong gluten development. I baked them to a deep golden brown, removed them from the pan, and brushed them with ½ tablespoon of melted butter.

When I pulled one roll from the round, it separated from the others cleanly, and I delightedly peeled away layer after delicate layer. The combined effect of the added liquid in the flour paste, the well-developed gluten, and the unusual shaping had given me the ideal dinner roll: moist, tender, and particularly fluffy. The most convincing part of all: The rolls were great the next day when I refreshed them in the oven, a real bonus when making them for a holiday dinner.

FLUFFY DINNER ROLLS
MAKES 12 ROLLS

We strongly recommend weighing the flour for the dough. The slight tackiness of the dough aids in flattening and stretching it in step 5, so do not dust your counter with flour. This recipe requires letting the dough rest for at least 2 hours before baking. The rolls can be made a day ahead. To refresh them before serving, wrap them in aluminum foil and heat them in a 350-degree oven for 15 minutes.

Flour Paste
- ½ cup water
- 3 tablespoons bread flour

Dough
- ½ cup cold milk
- 1 large egg
- 2 cups (11 ounces) bread flour
- 1½ teaspoons instant or rapid-rise yeast
- 2 tablespoons sugar
- 1 teaspoon salt
- 4 tablespoons unsalted butter, softened, plus ½ tablespoon, melted

1. FOR THE FLOUR PASTE: Whisk water and flour together in small bowl until no lumps remain. Microwave, whisking every 20 seconds, until mixture thickens to stiff, smooth, pudding-like consistency that forms mound when dropped from end of whisk into bowl, 40 to 80 seconds.

2. FOR THE DOUGH: In bowl of stand mixer, whisk flour paste and milk together until smooth. Add egg and whisk until incorporated. Add flour and yeast. Fit stand mixer with dough hook and mix on low speed until all flour is moistened, 1 to 2 minutes. Let stand for 15 minutes.

3. Add sugar and salt and mix on medium-low speed for 5 minutes. With mixer running, add softened butter, 1 tablespoon at a time. Continue to mix on medium-low speed 5 minutes longer, scraping down dough hook and sides of bowl occasionally (dough will stick to bottom of bowl).

4. Transfer dough to very lightly floured counter. Knead briefly to form ball and transfer, seam side down, to lightly greased bowl; lightly coat surface of dough with vegetable oil spray and cover with plastic wrap. Let rise until doubled in volume, about 1 hour.

5. Grease 9-inch round cake pan and set aside. Transfer dough to counter. Press dough gently but firmly to expel all air. Pat and stretch dough to form 8 by 9-inch rectangle with short side facing you. Cut dough lengthwise into 4 equal strips and cut each strip crosswise into 3 equal pieces. Working with 1 piece at a time, stretch and press dough gently to form 8 by 2-inch strip. Starting on short side, roll dough to form snug cylinder and arrange shaped rolls seam side down in prepared pan, placing 10 rolls around edge of pan, pointing inward, and remaining 2 rolls in center. Cover with plastic and let rise until doubled, 45 minutes to 1 hour.

6. When rolls are nearly doubled, adjust oven rack to lowest position and heat oven to 375 degrees. Bake rolls until deep golden brown, 25 to 30 minutes. Let rolls cool in pan on wire rack for 3 minutes; invert rolls onto rack, then reinvert. Brush tops and sides of rolls with melted butter. Let rolls cool for at least 20 minutes before serving.

▶ **Tangzhong in Action**
Video available free for 4 months at CooksIllustrated.com/feb16

Red Lentil Soup

Pantry staples and a familiar kitchen tool are the keys to a smooth, flavorful soup.

> BY ANDREA GEARY

If you'd like to cook more beans but are unsure of where to begin, red lentils are the ideal gateway legumes. For one thing, they're quick to prepare. Unlike green and brown lentils, the red ones have had their skins removed; as a result, they split in two during processing, which leaves them so tiny that they cook in less than 20 minutes, with no presoaking or brining required. But the best thing about cooking red lentils is that you get to sidestep the biggest challenge of bean cookery: getting the interiors of the beans to soften before the skins rupture. With no skins to contain them, red lentils disintegrate when you cook them. No amount of vigilance or technique can prevent it. In countries like Egypt and Morocco, cooks embrace this inevitability by turning their red lentils into soup. They add them to sautéed aromatics, stir in some warm spices, and then simmer it all in broth or water. Less than half an hour later, they have a satisfying soup.

To develop my own recipe, I started simply. I sautéed onions in a bit of butter until they were soft, and then I stirred in some minced garlic and ground cumin, coriander, and black pepper and cooked them briefly in the warm mixture. When the spices were fragrant, I added a cup of lentils, and because many recipes called for some form of tomato, I added one can of diced. For my cooking liquid, I began with the easiest option: water.

After 15 minutes of simmering, the lentils were fully softened and about half had disintegrated, but the consistency of the soup was thinner than I had anticipated. The tomato added a nice acidity, but it made the soup seem even more watery. To thicken the soup, I added 50 percent more lentils in the next round. I ditched the diced tomatoes for a tablespoon of tomato paste, and to give the soup a bit more backbone, I replaced some of the water with chicken broth. I also added more of the warm spices found in North African versions of the soup: cinnamon, ginger, and just a pinch of cayenne.

A swirl of paprika-mint butter adds richness.

This batch was more substantial, but the lentils had settled to the bottom; the top was somewhat watery. And the overall flavor was still a bit flat. But before I perfected the flavor, I evened out the consistency. A quick whir in the blender or food processor would do the trick, but it seemed like overkill for such a simple soup. Instead I tried boiling it vigorously after the lentils had softened, thinking that the turbulence would break up the lentils and help thicken things up. It did, but it also scorched on the bottom of the saucepan, so the soup tasted burnt.

I knew that constant stirring while boiling would prevent scorching, but then it occurred to me: Maybe I could skip the boiling if I just changed stirring implements. When the next batch of lentils had softened, I swapped my wooden spoon for a whisk. Thirty seconds of whisking did the trick: Now I had a coarse puree that was homogeneous from top to bottom.

Following the lead of North African cooks, I added 2 tablespoons of lemon juice to the pureed soup. The effect was like adjusting the focus on a manual camera: All the flavors were instantly more vibrant and defined. Now the soup needed just a touch of richness. I melted 2 tablespoons of butter and then stirred in some dried mint and paprika. I ladled out some soup, drizzled some spiced butter on top, and sprinkled it with fresh cilantro.

Whisk Away

Red lentils, which have had their skins removed, cook in just 15 minutes. Even better, they soften so completely that they can be whisked into a puree, no blender needed.

⏵ **Watch the Soup Happen**
Video available free for 4 months
at CooksIllustrated.com/feb16

RED LENTIL SOUP
WITH NORTH AFRICAN SPICES
SERVES 4 TO 6

Pair this soup with a salad and bread for lunch or a light supper.

4	tablespoons unsalted butter
1	large onion, chopped fine
	Salt and pepper
¾	teaspoon ground coriander
½	teaspoon ground cumin
¼	teaspoon ground ginger
⅛	teaspoon ground cinnamon
	Pinch cayenne
1	tablespoon tomato paste
1	garlic clove, minced
4	cups chicken broth
2	cups water
10½	ounces (1½ cups) red lentils, picked over and rinsed
2	tablespoons lemon juice, plus extra for seasoning
1½	teaspoons dried mint, crumbled
1	teaspoon paprika
¼	cup chopped fresh cilantro

1. Melt 2 tablespoons butter in large saucepan over medium heat. Add onion and 1 teaspoon salt and cook, stirring occasionally, until softened but not browned, about 5 minutes. Add coriander, cumin, ginger, cinnamon, cayenne, and ¼ teaspoon pepper and cook until fragrant, about 2 minutes. Stir in tomato paste and garlic and cook for 1 minute. Stir in broth, water, and lentils and bring to simmer. Simmer vigorously, stirring occasionally, until lentils are soft and about half are broken down, about 15 minutes.

2. Whisk soup vigorously until it is coarsely pureed, about 30 seconds. Stir in lemon juice and season with salt and extra lemon juice to taste. Cover and keep warm. (Soup can be refrigerated for up to 3 days. Thin soup with water, if desired, when reheating.)

3. Melt remaining 2 tablespoons butter in small skillet. Remove from heat and stir in mint and paprika. Ladle soup into individual bowls, drizzle each portion with 1 teaspoon spiced butter, sprinkle with cilantro, and serve.

Testing Food Processors

How much do you need to spend to get a machine that makes light work of chopping, slicing, shredding, and mixing?

⇒ BY LISA McMANUS ⇐

Here in the test kitchen, we demand a food processor that can handle lots of chopping, slicing, and shredding while delivering professional-quality results, and we think home cooks deserve the same. It had better be able to not only puree a dip and whip up creamy mayonnaise but also cut fat into a pie crust in seconds, grind beef into hamburger, and knead heavy pizza dough. And of course we want our food processor to be simple to use and quick to clean.

We bought eight full-size food processors, priced from $59.99 to $299.99, with capacities of 11 to 14 cups, a size we deemed big enough to handle most recipes. (We also tested two professional-style food processors with suggested retail prices of more than $400.00; see "Overpriced, Underperforming" on page 25.) We put each model through 21 tests, measuring their performance on a range of tasks, all while comparing construction and user-friendliness. We considered everything from the feel of the pulse button and the weight and shape of the workbowl to the capacity of the feed tube and how often we'd have to handle sharp, pokey blades. In terms of blades, some models were equipped with just the basics—a chopping blade and a shredding/slicing disk—while others arrived with sizable boxes of extra attachments. We assessed which of these were actually useful and which were just window dressing.

On the Chopping Block

While food processors are designed to do a variety of jobs, we most often call upon them for chopping. So we ran several chopping tests and weighted those results heaviest in our final ratings: prepping *mirepoix* (a combination of diced carrot, celery, and onion used as a foundation for many sauces, soups, and stews), grinding whole almonds, mincing fresh parsley, and grinding chunks of beef and cold butter into fresh hamburger meat. We wanted to achieve uniform pieces of food at whatever size we desired, but the reality was often a disappointment. For example, while we were aiming for ¼-inch pieces of crisply cut mirepoix, in some cases we ended up with a crushed mixture strewn with bigger chunks. One of the biggest factors in chopping performance was the length of time the machine ran once we'd pushed the pulse button—short, powerful, jerky pulsing is essential to

The Slice Is Right

A well-designed food processor should be as proficient at slicing and shredding as it is at chopping and mixing.

WINNER: CLEAN CUT
Our favorite model consistently made even, smooth cuts.

OTHERS: A REAL SMASHUP
Some machines either pulverized food or left behind unprocessed pieces.

help toss ingredients around the bowl and into the cutting action. The best models had pulses that ran for only as long as we were pushing the button (a fraction of a second in our top models), giving us excellent control; the worst kept running for nearly 2 seconds, processing the food too much and often letting bigger pieces ride the spinning blades without getting chopped. The other important factor for even chopping was the distance of the blades from the bottom and sides of the workbowl, which ranged from 3 millimeters to more than 10 millimeters. Smaller gaps were critical to making sure that chunks of food didn't escape the blades.

Any Way You Slice It

Slicing and shredding with a food processor can be a huge timesaver, especially when you're prepping large quantities. A good machine takes seconds to produce piles of carrot shreds for a salad, mounds of shredded cheese for a pizza, or pounds of potato slices for gratin. We shredded soft cheddar cheese and crunchy carrots, and we sliced delicate tomatoes and firm potatoes, considering not just the quality of the processed food but also how much was wasted, whether trapped in the machine or pretrimmed so the food would fit inside feed tubes. The best models left almost nothing behind. The worst left jagged chunks stuck atop the cutting disk or made us trim up to a third of the food off to make it fit.

Blade quality mattered, too: Dull blades bruised and hacked up the food, splattering the workbowl with juices. The top machines had sharp, efficient blades that made clean, dry cuts—you could barely tell the tomato or potato had been through the processor until you fanned out the slices like a deck of cards.

A few models had special slicing features, but not all were successful. A slice-thickness adjustment lever on the front of the KitchenAid model lacks numerical markings, so we had to use trial and error to attain slices with a specific thickness. We preferred adjustments like the one on the Breville, which lets you simply dial up a precise setting by millimeters.

Mixing It Up

Efficient mixing is a key feature, whether you're making a quick pie crust, kneading a sticky dough, or emulsifying mayonnaise. We tried all three tasks with each machine, and we assessed the speed and thoroughness of the mixing action by processing yogurt with drops of yellow and blue food coloring, timing how long it took for the yogurt to turn green. The worst ran for over a minute while still leaving distinct streaks of color. Better models created a smooth, even green hue in 25 seconds or less.

When it came to pushing the machines' upper limits, double batches of pizza dough were a real challenge for a few models. The KitchenAid model shut itself down repeatedly. A light flashed on the Breville, indicating distress, and the Cuisinart Elemental model left clumps of flour. The manual of the Hamilton Beach processor said it was not meant for dough; when we gave it a try anyway, it made a lot of noise (as it did throughout testing) and jumped around the counter, but the dough actually emerged in good shape. (We wouldn't recommend processing dough in this model routinely since it could burn out the motor over time.) Another, by Black + Decker, advised us not to process more than 3½ cups of dough but did fine with 4 cups. (Again, we wouldn't recommend going over the upper limit often since it risks damaging the motor.) The top performers, including our front-runner, yielded silky, bouncy dough with little apparent strain.

Mayonnaise was another failure point for several machines. Our recipe yields about 1 cup, so whenever a mini bowl was included with the food processor, we used it for this small job. Still, half the models

⏵ **See the Tests**
Video available free for 4 months at CooksIllustrated.com/feb16

TESTING FOOD PROCESSORS

HIGHLY RECOMMENDED

CUISINART Custom 14 Food Processor

MODEL: DFP14-BCN
PRICE: $161.99
MINI BOWL: None

CHOPPING ★★★
SLICING ★★★
SHREDDING ★★★
MIXING ★★★
PUREEING ★★★
EASE OF USE ★★★
LEAKING? NO

COMMENTS: With a powerful, quiet motor; responsive pulsing action; sharp blades; and a simple, pared-down-to-basics design, our old favorite aced every test, surprising us time and again by outshining pricier, more feature-filled competitors. It was one of the few models that didn't leak at its maximum stated liquid capacity. It's also easy to clean and store, because it comes with just a chopping blade and two disks for shredding and slicing. Additional blade options are available à la carte.

RECOMMENDED

THE BREVILLE Sous Chef 12-Cup Food Processor

MODEL: BFP660SIL
PRICE: $299.99
MINI BOWL: None

CHOPPING ★★★
SLICING ★★★
SHREDDING ★★★
MIXING ★★
PUREEING ★★★
EASE OF USE ★★½
LEAKING? NO

COMMENTS: Quiet and quick at most tasks, with a well-designed workbowl that slides smoothly into place and pours neatly, this model excelled at chopping, slicing, and shredding, but its motor clearly struggled when mixing a double batch of pizza dough. And with blades spinning out of reach in the big bowl, mayonnaise never emulsified and dyed yogurt never turned uniformly green. Turning the shaft on the slicing blade offered eight thickness settings clearly marked in millimeters, a nice design touch.

BLACK + DECKER Performance Food Processor

MODEL: FP6010B
PRICE: $149.99
MINI BOWL: 4 cups

CHOPPING ★★½
SLICING ★★★
SHREDDING ★★★
MIXING ★★★
PUREEING ★★
EASE OF USE ★½
LEAKING? NO

COMMENTS: This model performed surprisingly well in many areas, despite a cheap, flimsy feel to its construction. The tall, skinny accessory box shattered after taking a tumble. Suction-cup feet on its lightweight base failed to stabilize the machine when it was working, and its motor was loud. The pulse button continued running a bit long, and chopping was a bit uneven. That said, its slicing and shredding were impressive, and its dicing attachment worked very well.

RECOMMENDED WITH RESERVATIONS

CUISINART Elite Collection 2.0 12-Cup Food Processor

MODEL: FP-12DC
PRICE: $249.00
MINI BOWL: 4 cups

CHOPPING ★★½
SLICING ★★
SHREDDING ★★★
MIXING ★★
PUREEING ★★½
EASE OF USE ★★½
LEAKING? YES

COMMENTS: We liked this machine's responsive pulse button and simple control panel; shredding was exemplary, and chopping was more than acceptable. But the innovative snap-on lid didn't always latch; we often found it running ajar. The motor struggled when mixing heavy pizza dough, and flour flew up into the lid and fell out messily after making pie crust. Nooks and crannies in the workbowl lid slowed cleanup.

RECOMMENDED WITH RESERVATIONS CONTINUED

CUISINART Elemental 11 Food Processor

MODEL: FP-11GM
PRICE: $149.00
MINI BOWL: None

CHOPPING ★★½
SLICING ★★★
SHREDDING ★★
MIXING ★★½
PUREEING ★★½
EASE OF USE ★½
LEAKING? NO

COMMENTS: With a lid that usually went on a bit stiffly and off-kilter, this machine was some work to open and close, and its lightweight base and parts felt less solidly constructed than its Cuisinart siblings; a piece of the handle became loosened by the end of testing. The motor was very loud. Too-long, too-weak pulses made the chopping action less efficient, as did narrower blades that left gaps around the edges for food to slip through. Pizza dough was a struggle, leaving us to finish kneading the still-lumpy dough by hand.

NOT RECOMMENDED

HAMILTON BEACH Stack & Snap Food Processor

MODEL: 70725
PRICE: $59.99
MINI BOWL: None

CHOPPING ★★
SLICING ★★★
SHREDDING ★½
MIXING ★½
PUREEING ★★
EASE OF USE ★★
LEAKING? YES

COMMENTS: This model's claim to fame is that the jar and lid snap on with no twisting, but the plastic flaps that snap down the lid felt like they might snap off. More critically, gaps between blades and bowl allowed food to sit on the bottom and avoid the chopping overhead. It failed to make mayonnaise, and it leaked when filled with liquid to capacity. Lightweight, inexpensive construction meant the machine wobbled on its suction-cup feet. Though we made pizza dough in this model, the manual instructs not to use it for dough.

OSTER Designed for Life 14-Cup Food Processor with 5-Cup Mini Chopper

MODEL: FPSTFP5273-DFL
PRICE: $69.00
MINI BOWL: 5 cups

CHOPPING ★★
SLICING ★
SHREDDING ★★½
MIXING ★★
PUREEING ★★½
EASE OF USE ★½
LEAKING? NO

COMMENTS: While this is one of the lowest-priced products in the lineup, it also felt lightweight and flimsy, and running it required earplugs (think jackhammer crossed with dentist drill: Ree! REE!). It wobbled on its suction-cup feet, pumped a stream of air at us as it ran, and blew flour and bits of food all over the interior of the workbowl like confetti. Gaps between blade and bowl allowed some pieces to pass under the blades unchopped, while mayonnaise failed to emulsify.

KITCHENAID 11-Cup Food Processor with ExactSlice System

MODEL: KFP1133
PRICE: $199.95
MINI BOWL: 3 cups

CHOPPING ★★
SLICING ★★★
SHREDDING ★½
MIXING ★★½
PUREEING ★★
EASE OF USE ½
LEAKING? YES

COMMENTS: With a remarkably stiff pulse button that was painful to push and somewhat unresponsive, comparatively weak chopping action, a draggy gasket that made the lid difficult to twist on or off, and abundant crannies that trapped food and moisture and made cleaning complicated, this machine made us work too hard. While its actual slicing was crisp and neat, the thickness-adjusting lever on the front is unmarked, so choosing a specific thickness involves trial, error, and wasted food.

Performance Criteria

We tested eight food processors with capacities of 11 to 14 cups, rating them on their ability to chop, slice, shred, mince, emulsify, puree, and mix pie crust and pizza dough, as well as perform other common tasks that call for a food processor. We also rated them on ease of use and cleanup. We purchased all models online. They appear in order of preference.

CHOPPING

Testers chopped onion, carrot, and celery into *mirepoix*; ground whole almonds; minced fresh parsley; and ground beef chunks and butter into hamburger. This category was weighted most highly in our ratings.

SLICING

We sliced ripe plum tomatoes and russet potatoes, giving highest marks to models that cut crisply and neatly, rendering little to no juice, which would indicate that food was sliced, not crushed.

SHREDDING

We shredded carrots and cheddar cheese, rating models highest if pieces were crisp and uniform with little to no unprocessed, trapped food.

MIXING

We mixed pie dough and a double batch of heavy pizza dough, made mayonnaise (in small workbowls where available), and conducted a timed test using drops of blue and yellow food coloring in yogurt to show how efficiently machines made a uniformly green mixture.

PUREEING

We processed large cans of whole tomatoes in each machine until smooth; high-rated models made velvety puree.

EASE OF USE

We rated each machine throughout testing on its handling, intuitiveness of assembly and controls, shape of workbowl and lid, weight and stability, quality of construction, noise, and other factors relating to its design and ergonomics, including the convenience of any included accessory boxes or other extra features.

LEAKING

We filled each machine to its "maximum liquid fill" line and compared actual to stated capacity; we then ran machines on high for 1 minute, checking for leaks.

Anatomy of a Great Food Processor

For a machine that can handle everything from slicing tomatoes and mincing herbs to kneading heavy pizza dough, it takes more than just a sharp blade and a strong motor.

❶ WELL-DESIGNED FEED TUBE
Big enough to minimize pretrimming and waste but narrow enough to hold food upright.

❷ MINIMAL GAPS BETWEEN BLADE AND BOWL
The space between the end of the blade and the side of the bowl as well as the space between the base of the blade and the bottom of the bowl should be small. This ensures more efficient, thorough mixing and food that is evenly chopped.

❸ SMALL SPACE BETWEEN DISKS AND FEED TUBE
Ensures that all the food gets shredded or sliced.

❹ WEIGHTY, COMPACT BASE
Space-saving and keeps machine anchored during heavy mixing.

❺ RESPONSIVE PULSE BUTTON
Enables quick stop-start so ingredients are tossed around the bowl and into the cutting action.

---

that lacked mini bowls (including our winner) were able to emulsify the mayonnaise. Once again, the failures seem to be caused by excessive space between the blades and the bottom of the bowl, which caused the blades to spin uselessly over unmixed oil and egg.

To test how well the machines processed chunky food into a smooth puree, we blended 28-ounce cans of whole tomatoes. While most handled this task acceptably well, it made us wonder how much liquid the workbowls could handle without leaking. We filled each with water to its maximum volume and ran them all on high. A few erupted in overflowing waves, while a few more sent forth a steady trickle. Our favorite never spilled a drop, despite lacking a rubber gasket in the lid. These gaskets, designed to seal the workbowl from leaks, weren't always effective. Instead, they mostly made lids hard to slide on or off.

Wash 'n' Go

Cleanup was the final factor. Complicated nooks and crannies inside the lid and on the pusher and feed tubes of the KitchenAid 11-cup model trapped food and were a chore to clean and dry. The same could be said for multipart shafts that held blades inside workbowls on other models. Our favorite machines had smooth, simple surfaces that were a snap to clean and dry, so they were ready for the next job. Our favorite models' workbowls are all dishwasher-safe (blades should be hand-washed to keep them sharp).

In the end, nothing beat our old favorite, the Cuisinart Custom 14 Food Processor ($161.99). It may not be the cheapest food processor available, but

it proves its worth in its sturdiness and performance, and it outshone fancier models costing up to three times as much. It comes with just three basic blades, for chopping, slicing, and shredding. After all of our testing, we decided that these are all you really need for most jobs (though it's worth noting that Cuisinart offers a variety of additional blades on its website), and fewer blades equals less stuff to store. With a plain, heavy base; just two simple, lever-style bars to operate; a responsive pulsing action that makes chopping efficient; sharp blades set close to the base and bottom of the workbowl that don't miss a thing; and a pared-down design that is easy to clean, handle, and store, our old winner takes the top prize again.

Overpriced, Underperforming

We tested two high-end professional-style food processors to see if they offered any features that made them worth nearly two to three times the price of an ordinary food processor. Although they are decent machines overall, we found that they couldn't outperform cheaper models. Our lower-cost winner, from Cuisinart, not only performs better but is a quarter of the cost. For our complete testing of high-end processors, go to CooksIllustrated.com/highendprocessors.

DON'T BOTHER High-end processors, like the one we tested from KitchenAid, are not worth the money.

NOTE: We recently noticed that after 18 months of heavy use in the test kitchen and constant exposure to our powerful commercial dishwasher, most of the S-shaped chopping blades from our winning Cuisinart Custom 14 food processors either showed hairline cracks or had small pieces of metal broken off. Cuisinart is in the process of updating blades for this model. In the meantime, if you own this food processor, we recommend checking the S-blade every time you use it; this would also be a good practice with the chopping blade of any food processor. Go to CooksIllustrated.com/apr16 for the most up-to-date information on the Cuisinart Custom 14, including what to do about replacing a damaged blade.

The Truth About Beef Broth

Commercial beef broths contain almost no beef. So what exactly are these products adding to your recipes?

⇒ BY KATE SHANNON ⇐

It's hard to beat the convenience of store-bought broth. Truth be told, we turn to it often when making soups, stews, and gravies. Our winning commercial chicken broth is a pretty good stand-in for the real thing, but we've had less luck finding a decent beef broth. Part of the reason is that we expect more of beef broth. We typically rely on chicken broth to bolster the savory backbone of a recipe. But when we turn to beef broth, we want it to literally beef up the flavor of a dish.

A slew of new products have hit the beef broth market since our last tasting, and not just the mainly liquid contenders we've seen in the past. Hopeful that a better, truly beefy broth had come along, we rounded up 10 options from top-selling brands—including liquids as well as pastes, powders, and cubes that must be reconstituted with hot water—that contained at least 450 milligrams of sodium per serving (in previous broth tastings, we've found that products with less sodium taste underseasoned). We sampled these broths simply warmed, simmered in a beef and vegetable stew, and reduced in gravy.

Unfortunately, we were once again largely unimpressed with all the products we tasted. None delivered anything close to true beef flavor. At best, the broths contributed a savory taste, while the worst were either bland, overwhelmingly salty, or plagued by "bitter," "charred," or "burnt" off-notes. In the end, we had just one product to recommend. Though lacking in actual beefy taste, it delivered "fuller" flavor than any of the other products.

Where's the Beef?

There's an obvious explanation for the absence of beefy flavor in commercial broth products: They lack beef. To meet U.S. Department of Agriculture standards, liquid products labeled "beef stock" or "beef broth" (the government doesn't distinguish between the two) need only contain 135 parts moisture to 1 part protein (which may be derived from meat or bones). The regulations that guide the pastes,

We made gravy and stew with each broth, as well as sampled them plain.

powders, and cubes in our lineup are similarly paltry or don't exist at all. A look at the nutrition labels confirms how little meat goes into them: Five of the 10 products have 1 gram or less of protein per cup, including our new winner. Meanwhile, our homemade beef broth, made with 6 pounds of meat and 2 pounds of bones per 2 quarts of water, has more than 4 grams of protein per cup.

Ultimately, however, the amount of protein in a broth had little to do with its ranking. In fact, though the liquid broths had more protein than products requiring reconstitution, in general they performed less well, exhibiting blandness or off-notes.

We learned one reason for their lackluster flavor: Most liquid broths (as well as some products requiring reconstitution) start with the same source—weak generic stock supplied by a handful of specialty stock producers. Stephanie Lynch, vice president of technology and sales at International Dehydrated Foods, one of the companies that create these stock bases, told us that they simmer water and bones—not actual meat—in large pressurized vats to create a broth base with deliberately mild flavor that can provide a blank slate for a variety of uses. The broth is dehydrated for cheaper shipping and sold to broth manufacturers, who can build on it with other flavors.

Flavor Makers

The problem is, in lieu of adding actual meat to their products, broth manufacturers mainly use chemistry to amp up flavor. According to Michael Noble, corporate chef at Ariake USA (a large commercial stock producer based in Virginia), it's common for major broth manufacturers to hire flavor chemists to help them choose from a vast assortment of highly concentrated flavorings that can contribute a range of very specific tastes to a product. When such flavorings are distilled or extracted from natural sources, they appear as "natural flavorings" or "natural flavor" on an ingredient list; synthetically produced flavorings must be identified as "artificial." These flavorings can help make a product taste distinct from others and yield consistent results from batch to batch. But their use can also backfire. In the products we tasted from Swanson and Imagine, for example, tasters picked up on "charred" and "burnt" notes. Though neither company would elaborate on the source of the flavors in their products, it seems likely that the off-notes we noticed came from concentrated "natural flavorings" intended to mimic the flavor of cooked beef.

The broth with the highest protein content by far at 7 grams per cup—College Inn—failed for an entirely different reason. Tasters detected bitter, metallic notes that almost certainly came from the inclusion of potassium chloride, the main ingredient in many salt substitutes. (With 750 grams of sodium per serving, it already had one of the highest sodium levels in the lineup.)

No matter what the form—liquid or dehydrated—what really benefited these products was the presence of yeast extract, a substance that's loaded with glutamates and nucleotides. Glutamates are savory on their own, and nucleotides work in synergy with them to amplify their flavor. Together these compounds can boost a broth's savory, meaty-tasting flavors twentyfold. All 10 broths include yeast extract, but our winner (and the second-place broth) also contains hydrolyzed soy protein, another powerful source of flavor potentiators that might have given it an edge over the others. Our new winner, Better Than Bouillon Beef Base, trumped our previous favorite from Rachael Ray, which simply wasn't beefy enough to compete with our winner's ultrasavory punch.

We're still hopeful that someday broth manufacturers will put more actual beef in their products. In the meantime, our winner is an economical choice that stores easily, costs just 16 cents per cup, and does a good job of boosting savory depth in soups and stews.

➤ Taking It Up a Notch

For broths with genuinely beefy flavor, try making our recipe for Rich Beef Broth (CooksIllustrated.com/richbeefbroth) or our recipe for Quick Beef Broth (CooksIllustrated.com/feb16), which adds real beef to our winning commercial broth.

TASTING BEEF BROTH

We tasted 10 top-selling national supermarket beef broths plain (served warm), reduced in gravy, and in beef stew. Results of the plain, gravy, and soup tastings were averaged, and products appear below in order of preference. Nutritional data for a 1-cup serving of broth is taken from product labels.

RECOMMENDED

BETTER THAN BOUILLON Beef Base

PRICE: $6.99 for 8 oz ($0.02 per reconstituted fl oz)

STYLE: Paste (1 tsp per cup of water, makes 38 cups)

SODIUM: 680 mg FAT: 0 g PROTEIN: 1 g

INGREDIENTS: Roasted beef with concentrated beef stock, salt, hydrolyzed soy protein, sugar, corn syrup solids, flavoring, yeast extract, dried whey (milk), potato flour, caramel color, corn oil, xanthan gum

COMMENTS: Though lacking in actual beefy taste, a goodly amount of salt and multiple powerful flavor enhancers delivered "fuller flavor than other samples." The paste is economical, stores easily, and dissolves quickly in hot water.

RECOMMENDED WITH RESERVATIONS

WYLER'S Reduced Sodium Beef Flavor Cubes

PRICE: $2.00 for 2 oz ($0.02 per reconstituted fl oz)

STYLE: Bouillon cubes (1 cube per cup of water, makes 15 cups)

SODIUM: 540 mg per cup FAT: 0 g PROTEIN: 0 g

INGREDIENTS: Beef bouillon type flavor (sugar, hydrolyzed soybean/corn protein, hydrolyzed soybean protein, hydrolyzed corn gluten, monosodium glutamate, natural flavoring, hydrolyzed wheat gluten, autolyzed yeast extract, beef, salt, maltodextrin [corn], beef extract, caramel color, onion powder, garlic powder, spice and herb), salt, sugar, corn syrup solids, potassium chloride, water, monosodium glutamate, onion powder, cornstarch, beef fat (beef fat, bha, bht, citric acid), contains less than 2% of: garlic powder, caramel color, disodium inosinate and guanylate, red 40. Contains soy, wheat

COMMENTS: With little actual beef and four different forms of hydrolyzed vegetable protein, monosodium glutamate, and yeast extract, these bouillon cubes delivered savory flavor that was more "mushroomy" than beefy.

KITCHEN ACCOMPLICE Reduced Sodium Beef Style Broth Concentrate

PRICE: $4.99 for 12 oz ($0.02 per reconstituted fl oz)

STYLE: Liquid concentrate (2 tsp per cup of water, makes 28 cups)

SODIUM: 480 mg FAT: 0 g PROTEIN: <1 g

INGREDIENTS: Beef stock, maltodextrin, sea salt, yeast extract, natural flavors, tapioca starch, salt, vegetable stock (carrot, celery and onion stocks), beef fat, xanthan gum, leek juice concentrate, spices

COMMENTS: Although soup and gravy tasted "meaty," the flavors were generically "savory" instead of distinctly beefy.

RACHAEL RAY Stock-in-a-Box All-Natural Beef-Flavored Stock (made by Colavita)

PRICE: $3.49 for 32 oz ($0.11 per fl oz)

STYLE: Liquid

SODIUM: 480 mg FAT: 0 g PROTEIN: 3 g

INGREDIENTS: Concentrated beef stock (contains: beef stock, sea salt, yeast extract), vegetable stock (carrot, celery, onion, leek, natural flavor)

COMMENTS: This broth didn't have the off-flavors that we found in other products. But compared to more heavily seasoned broths, our top-rated liquid broth didn't just lack real beef flavor—it also tasted "watery" and "flat."

SWANSON Cooking Stock, Beef

PRICE: $2.99 for 32 oz ($0.09 per fl oz)

STYLE: Liquid

SODIUM: 500 mg FAT: 0 g PROTEIN: 3 g

INGREDIENTS: Beef stock, yeast extract, salt, natural flavoring, honey, onion juice concentrate, tomato paste, beef fat, carrots, cabbage, beef extract, onions, celery, celery leaves, parsley

COMMENTS: Yeast extract gave this stock a boost of savory flavor, but tasters found the soup and gravy "bitter" and "charred."

RECOMMENDED WITH RESERVATIONS CONTINUED

IMAGINE Organic Beef Flavored Cooking Stock

PRICE: $5.29 for 32 oz ($0.17 per fl oz)

STYLE: Liquid

SODIUM: 670 mg FAT: 0 g PROTEIN: 2 g

INGREDIENTS: Filtered water, organic beef stock (organic beef stock, sea salt, flavoring), sea salt, organic caramel color, natural flavors (includes yeast extract), organic evaporated cane syrup

COMMENTS: While some tasters found this broth "roasty," many also picked up on "burnt," "slightly bitter" flavors reminiscent of "charred onions."

NOT RECOMMENDED

COLLEGE INN Bold Stock Tender Beef Flavor

PRICE: $2.99 for 17.6 oz ($0.17 per fl oz)

STYLE: Liquid

SODIUM: 750 mg FAT: 0 g PROTEIN: 7 g

INGREDIENTS: Beef stock, contains less than 2% of the following: yeast extract, salt, celery, sugar, carrot puree, onion juice, dextrose, potassium chloride, caramel color, beef fat, corn syrup solids, soy lecithin, xanthan gum, di- and mono-sodium phosphate, tomato paste, potato flour, gum arabic. Contains: soy

COMMENTS: Despite its high protein count, this broth was marred by "weird," "tinny" flavors that were also "bitter" and "metallic." This is most likely due to the inclusion of potassium chloride, which is known to add such off-flavors.

KNORR Homestyle Beef Stock

PRICE: $3.99 for 4.66 oz ($0.04 per reconstituted fl oz)

STYLE: Paste (1 tub per 3½ cups of water, makes 14 cups)

SODIUM: 710 mg FAT: 0.5 g PROTEIN: 0 g

INGREDIENTS: Water, salt, palm oil, maltodextrin (corn), autolyzed yeast extract, sugar, carrots, beef extract, spinach, leeks, xanthan gum, disodium guanylate, disodium inosinate, citric acid, garlic powder, onion powder, locust bean gum, soy sauce powder (soybeans, wheat, salt), lactic acid, beef fat, caramel color, natural flavor, spice, beta carotene (for color)

COMMENTS: Six ingredients—including salt—precede the mention of beef, so it's no wonder that this Jell-O–like concentrate had one of the highest perceived salt levels in gravy. We also had a practical complaint: Each tub of concentrate (one package contains four tubs) yields 3½ cups of broth, an amount that doesn't match up with most recipes.

PACIFIC Organic Beef Broth

PRICE: $3.99 for 32 oz ($0.12 per fl oz)

STYLE: Liquid

SODIUM: 570 mg FAT: 0 g PROTEIN: 3 g

INGREDIENTS: Water, beef stock (water, beef), sea salt, cane sugar, onion powder, yeast extract, garlic powder, caramel color, black pepper

COMMENTS: Tasters were turned off by this broth's "murky" green-yellow color and its unappealingly vegetal flavor.

ORRINGTON FARMS Beef Broth Base & Seasoning

PRICE: $2.79 for 12 oz ($0.01 per reconstituted fl oz)

STYLE: Powder (2 tsp per cup of water, makes 56 cups)

SODIUM: 950 mg FAT: 1 g PROTEIN: 0 g

INGREDIENTS: Salt (includes sea salt), maltodextrin (made from corn), dextrose (made from corn), soybean oil, caramel color, yeast extract, beef (dehydrated cooked beef, beef extract), beef stock, dehydrated onion, natural flavor, dehydrated garlic, disodium inosinate & disodium guanylate (flavor enhancer), lactic acid, white pepper, black pepper, spice extract

COMMENTS: Tasters were unequivocal: This powdery concentrate made stew and gravy "taste more of salt than anything else." It's no surprise, given that each serving contains a whopping 950 milligrams.

⇒ BY STEVE DUNN, ANDREA GEARY & LAN LAM ⇐

Tasting Harissa

Harissa is a North African chili paste that's used as a condiment and as an ingredient. It's potent, so just a dollop adds a jolt of bright, spicy flavor to everything from soups and stews to sautéed vegetables and fried eggs. Harissa is always made with some combination of hot and/or mild chiles, garlic, and oil and often includes aromatic spices like cumin, coriander, and caraway. To find the best packaged version, we scooped up four nationally available products, priced $0.45 to $2.00 per ounce, and sampled them plain and stirred into a North African vegetable soup.

The consistencies of the products varied considerably: Straight from the container, they ranged from loose and spreadable to coarsely chopped, with visible pieces of garlic and chile seeds. Although we generally found a cohesive mix more appealing for a condiment, all of the harissas were deemed to have an acceptable texture, and all incorporated easily into the hot soup.

As for flavor, our panel demanded a fair amount of heat and gave top marks to a product that reminded them of familiar chili-garlic sauces like Thai Sriracha sauce. But in addition to heat, harissa offers complexity. Our winner tasted of garlic and sweet bell pepper, our runner-up boasted sweet sun-dried tomato flavor, and the other two products tasted either markedly salty or citrusy, drawing comparisons to preserved lemons. Although some tasters loved the vibrancy of these last two, others on our panel couldn't get past their intensity.

We recommend two products. Our top scorer, Mina Harissa, Spicy, packs a fiery, garlicky punch that is perfect for heat-seekers. Those who shy away from heat will enjoy our runner-up, the sweeter, milder Les Moulins Mahjoub Traditional Harissa Spread. For complete tasting results, go to CooksIllustrated.com/feb16. –Kate Shannon

RECOMMENDED

MINA Harissa, Spicy

PRICE: $5.99 for 10-oz jar ($0.59 per oz)

INGREDIENTS: Red bell pepper, red chili pepper, garlic, extra virgin olive oil, vinegar, salt

COMMENTS: This harissa combines coarsely chopped chiles and garlic in a loose, spreadable sauce. Heat-seekers on our panel loved "the gradual burn that comes in strong for the finish."

LES MOULINS MAHJOUB Traditional Harissa Spread

PRICE: $12.99 for 6.5-oz jar ($2.00 per oz)

INGREDIENTS: Sundried piments, extra virgin olive oil, garlic, sundried tomatoes, salt, coriander, caraway seeds

COMMENTS: Gentle heat pairs up with the "earthy sweetness" of sun-dried tomatoes in this product. It's our recommendation for people who want harissa's signature flavors but with less-bracing heat.

RECOMMENDED WITH RESERVATIONS

PIQUANT Harissa

PRICE: $2.49 for 5-oz can ($0.50 per oz)

INGREDIENTS: Hot peppers, sweet peppers, carrots, water, vegetable oil, salt, caraway, coriander, garlic, citric acid

COMMENTS: Many people liked its "vibrancy" and "floral" flavor, contributed by the citric acid, but others described it as "off-putting" and "funky."

Bloomed Chocolate: Is It Ruined?

Improper storage of chocolate can cause a superficial white film, called a bloom, to develop. There are two types: Cocoa butter bloom occurs when the chocolate softens so much that the cocoa butter crystals melt and molecules of fat migrate to the surface where they form new crystals. Sugar bloom happens when water condenses on the chocolate and dissolves some of its sugar. When that water evaporates, a fine layer of sugar crystals is left behind.

When we compared batches of dark chocolate truffles and chocolate chunk cookies made with bloomed chocolate with samples made with properly stored chocolate, tasters found no differences. But when we dipped cookies in melted bloomed chocolate, we found that the chocolate took longer to set up and the bloom reappeared. That's because chocolate maintains its characteristic snap and sheen only when its fat molecules are properly aligned. The bottom line: Bloomed chocolate is fine for baking—just don't use it for dipping. –L.L.

NOT FINE FOR DIPPING
The white film on melted bloomed chocolate is still there.

FINE FOR BAKING
In baking recipes, the bloom on chocolate isn't noticeable.

Whole-Grain Panade

Recipes for meatloaf, meatballs, and hamburgers often incorporate a paste of bread and dairy. This mixture, a panade, helps keep the meat moist and also prevents it from tightening up into a dense mass during cooking. Though most panades are made with white sandwich bread since it imparts little flavor, we wondered if a whole-grain bread would make an acceptable substitute.

To find out, we swapped in 100 percent whole-wheat bread and 12-grain bread in batches of meatballs and compared them with a control made with white bread. Tasters detected a faint, yet not unpleasant, wheaty flavor in the whole-wheat meatballs. Twelve-grain meatballs also tasted fine, though the occasional seed detracted slightly from their overall tenderness. Even with these distractions, both types of bread make a respectable alternative to white bread. –L.L.

Chickpea Meringues

When we heard that the liquid from a can of chickpeas could be substituted for egg whites to make meringue—a win for people with egg allergies—we had to try it. We subbed 4 ounces of chickpea liquid for the four large egg whites called for in our Classic Meringue Cookies (March/April 2008). We whipped the chickpea liquid for 5 minutes, slowly added the sugar, and then continued to whip for a whopping 5 minutes more. (We omitted the salt since the chickpea liquid was already salty.)

To our surprise, the liquid produced a more-than-decent facsimile. Just like regular meringues, these were snow white with crisp piping lines. In terms of taste and texture, they were more coarse, with a sweeter, more starchy taste and a hint of salt.

So why does it work? Our science editor conjectures that when whipped, the dissolved carbohydrates and proteins in canned chickpea liquid behave like egg whites, forming a network that coats the air bubbles to make a stable foam. If you have an egg allergy, think twice before discarding chickpea liquid—you could whip up a quick batch of cookies instead. –A.G.

WEIRD BUT GOOD
Swapping in chickpea canning liquid for egg whites is surprisingly successful.

A Tip for Cooking Grass-Fed Beef

We've often heard that grass-fed beef cooks faster than grain-fed beef because it's leaner. To put this claim to the test, we cooked seven grain-fed prime strip steaks alongside seven grass-fed strip steaks (grass-fed beef is not graded). Though the grass-fed steaks rose in temperature a bit more quickly than grain-fed in all but one of the tests, the difference between the quickest and the slowest steak was 4 minutes or less, and all of the samples cooked within our given time range. The takeaway? Check grass-fed beef's temperature at the beginning of a recommended time range. –A.G.

The Best Way to Rehydrate Sun-Dried Tomatoes

When buying sun-dried tomatoes, we typically purchase the oil-packed kind, since the dry-packed variety have tougher skins and a chewier texture. But dry-packed sun-dried tomatoes do have their advantages: They can cost just one-third of the price of oil-packed, and they don't have herbs or seasonings that may not suit your recipe. Some sources suggest that you can approximate oil-packed tomatoes by soaking the dry-packed variety in olive oil overnight, but we found that the tomatoes were still too tough.

Rehydrating is best, but with what liquid? We tried using plain water or wine, but the former left the tomatoes waterlogged and diluted their flavor, and the latter overpowered the tomatoes' natural acidity. We had better luck with broth (vegetable or chicken, depending on your recipe), which infuses them with a complementary savory flavor and an appealing saltiness. Alternately, you could soak them in salt water. Here's our preferred method (which you can scale as needed):

Place ½ cup tomatoes in heatproof bowl, cover with 1 cup broth or ½ teaspoon salt dissolved in 1 cup warm water, then cover with plate and microwave for 2 minutes. Let sit until skin side of tomato can be pierced easily with fork, 5 to 10 minutes. Drain and blot well with paper towels. Leftovers can be topped with oil and refrigerated in airtight container for up to 2 weeks. –S.D.

REHYDRATE In heatproof bowl, cover sun-dried tomatoes with liquid and microwave, covered, for 2 minutes.

DRAIN AND BLOT Let tomatoes sit in liquid until skins can be easily pierced with fork, then drain and blot dry.

A Lighter Whipped Topping

For sweet desserts like our Pear-Walnut Upside-Down Cake (page 19), a tangy whipped topping made with heavy cream and sour cream can make an even better accompaniment than plain whipped cream. We wondered if we could create a topping that was not only tangy but lighter as well by using yogurt. Indeed, a ratio of ½ cup Greek yogurt to ¾ cup heavy cream delivered a likable combination of creaminess and tang. We found that Greek yogurt was essential, as the regular variety produced a looser, less stable topping. Even better, we found that not only did the full-fat kind work but 2 percent and nonfat Greek yogurt also produced great results, with the nonfat tasting the tangiest.

To make 1½ cups of Yogurt Whipped Topping: Using stand mixer fitted with whisk, whip ¾ cup chilled heavy cream and ½ cup chilled plain Greek yogurt on medium speed until combined, about 10 seconds. Increase speed to high and beat to soft peaks, about 1 minute more. For stiff peaks, beat 30 seconds to 1 minute longer. Add sugar, if desired. –S.D.

DIY RECIPE Sauerkraut

A classic pairing with bratwurst and in Reuben sandwiches, sauerkraut packs a tangy, sour punch. And yet it's nothing more than shredded cabbage and salt that have been tossed, packed, and left to ferment. We discovered that the correct amount of salt was key. Too little salt and the kraut quickly spoiled; too much and the fermentation slowed to a halt. We found the temperature at which the cabbage ferments was also critical. At higher temperatures, the cabbage fermented more quickly, resulting in a sauerkraut that tasted sharp and pungent. –Anne Wolf

SAUERKRAUT
MAKES ABOUT 6 CUPS

To help the cabbage stay submerged, we place a bag of brine on top to weigh it down. We use brine (rather than water) because if the bag breaks it won't ruin the careful balance of salinity inside the jar. For a balanced flavor, we prefer fermenting at a cool room temperature of 65 degrees (consider locations such as a basement, den, or cabinet in an air-conditioned room). We don't recommend fermenting above 70 degrees as the flavor suffers, and above 75 degrees food safety becomes a concern. You will need cheesecloth for this recipe.

- 1   head green cabbage (2½ pounds), quartered, cored, and shredded
- 2   tablespoons pickling and canning salt
- 1½   teaspoons juniper berries
- 2   cups water

1. Cut out parchment paper round to match diameter of ½-gallon glass or ceramic container. Toss cabbage with 4 teaspoons salt in large bowl. Using your hands, forcefully knead salt into cabbage until it has softened and begins to release moisture, about 3 minutes. Stir in juniper berries.

2. Tightly pack cabbage mixture and any accumulated liquid in jar, pressing down firmly with your fist to eliminate air pockets as you pack. Press parchment round flush against surface of cabbage.

3. Dissolve remaining 2 teaspoons salt in water and transfer to 1-quart zipper-lock bag; squeeze out air and seal bag well. Place bag of brine on top of parchment and gently press down. Cover jar with triple layer of cheesecloth and secure with rubber band.

4. Place jar in cool location (50 to 70 degrees; do not expose cabbage to temperatures above 70 degrees) away from direct sunlight and let ferment for 6 days; check jar daily, skimming residue and mold from surface and pressing to keep cabbage submerged. After 6 days, taste sauerkraut daily until it has reached desired flavor (this may take up to 7 days longer; sauerkraut should be pale and translucent with a tart and floral flavor).

5. When sauerkraut has reached desired flavor, remove cheesecloth, bag of brine, and parchment and skim off any residue or mold. Serve. (Sauerkraut and accumulated juices can be transferred to clean jar, covered, and refrigerated for up to 2 months; once refrigerated, flavor of sauerkraut will continue to mature.)

TOSS AND KNEAD WELL
Toss cabbage with salt, then knead forcefully.

PACK FIRMLY
Use your fist to tightly pack cabbage and remove any air pockets.

KITCHEN NOTES

≫ BY MIYE BROMBERG, STEVE DUNN, ANDREA GEARY, ANDREW JANJIGIAN, LAN LAM & ANNIE PETITO ≪

WHAT IS IT?

While this instrument might look like something from a woodworker's bench or even an antique doctor's bag, it is in fact a champagne tap. Taps such as this were first patented in France in 1828. Back then, champagne was often prescribed as a medicinal, and the tap allowed just a small "dose" to be dispensed by penetrating the cork of a bottle so some champagne could be poured out without having to remove the cork.

To use, the tap is screwed into the cork until the tip of the spike has penetrated the cork and is visible inside the bottle. Pulling up on the handle withdraws the spike, allowing the liquid to flow out through the hollow worm. The tap is then closed off with a side valve. To pour, you invert the bottle over a glass and turn the valve to open it. We found that the tap worked well as intended, but in terms of keeping champagne fresh, it was no match for our modern-day equivalent. After two days the champagne preserved with the tap had gone flat, while a week later the bottle preserved with our favorite champagne saver, the Cilio Champagne Bottle Sealer ($7.50), was still going strong. –S.D.

CHAMPAGNE TAP
Though it preserved a bottle of bubbly's effervescence reasonably well, it was no match for our favorite champagne preserver.

Rest, Sear, and Serve

When developing our recipe for Tuscan-Style Roast Pork with Garlic and Rosemary (Arista) (page 11), we found that most recipes call for letting the roast rest under foil after it's been cooked through and browned and then serving it. This allows time for the internal juices to redistribute and for carryover cooking to bring the roast up to the final serving temperature. But covering a well-browned roast with foil will trap steam and cause the crust to soften. By letting it rest after cooking and then searing it and serving it immediately, we guarantee a perfectly crisp crust at the table. –A.P.

Body Builder for Pan Sauces

We often add gelatin to stews and braises to give them a silky, rich texture that you'd otherwise get only if you started with a homemade broth (the bones and meat used to make broth contain lots of collagen, which breaks down to form gelatin). When developing our recipe for Better Chicken Marsala (November/December 2015), we realized that adding gelatin to the sauce enhanced its texture in just the same way, giving it a great silky texture. Another test confirmed that the trick worked equally well for enhancing our All-Purpose Gravy (November/December 2003). In fact, just about any preparation that calls for canned broth will likely benefit from the addition of gelatin. We found that 2 teaspoons of gelatin per cup of broth thickens sauces and braises appropriately, while 1 teaspoon per cup is best for dishes with a larger amount of broth, such as soups. Here's how to incorporate it:

If the broth or sauce is being boiled and then strained (as it is for our gravy), simply add powdered unflavored gelatin along with the broth; if not, bloom the gelatin in a few tablespoons of cold water for 30 seconds to prevent clumping before adding it to the recipe. –A.J.

SAVE THOSE MARROWBONES

If you can find only bone-in crosscut beef shank for our Portuguese-Style Beef Stew (Alcatra) (page 7), you'll need to remove the bones before you begin—but don't throw them out. When roasted, the marrow inside the bones softens and becomes richly flavored. Simply scoop it out and spread it on toasted bread for a decadent appetizer or side dish. Before roasting the marrowbones, we soak them in a brine and refrigerate them for up to two days. In addition to seasoning, brining dissolves proteins in the marrow that would otherwise turn an unattractive dark gray color during cooking.

To roast the marrowbones: Dissolve ¼ cup salt in 2 quarts water, add bones to brine, and refrigerate until marrow turns creamy in color, 1 to 2 days. Arrange bones cut side down on foil-lined baking sheet and roast on middle rack in 350-degree oven until skewer inserted in marrow slides in and out with ease, 20 to 25 minutes. –L.L.

SOAK Brining the bones for one to two days in a saltwater solution seasons the marrow and prevents it from turning an unappealing gray when roasted.

ROAST Just 20 to 25 minutes on the middle rack in a 350-degree oven will soften the marrow so it's easy to scoop out and spread on toast.

Foolproof Rice Without a Rice Cooker

Rice cookers make the task convenient and foolproof, but what if you don't own this single-task appliance? Is there another way to guarantee perfect results every time? Knowing that electric rice cookers automatically switch from "cook" to "keep warm" mode when a sudden rise in temperature indicates that all the water has been absorbed, we devised a method using a probe thermometer, aluminum foil, and a saucepan. We inserted the probe until it touched the bottom of the pot (since this was the simplest, most foolproof location). We set the target temperature for 214 degrees, 2 degrees above boiling, to allow for any inaccuracies and the slightly higher temperature of the bottom of the pot. We found that the temperature stayed below 214 degrees until all of the water in the pot had been absorbed by the rice, at which point the temperature rose to 214 degrees and beyond, meaning the rice was done.

MAKESHIFT RICE COOKER
A probe thermometer and aluminum foil help produce perfect rice in a saucepan.

Here's how you do it: Combine 2 cups rinsed white rice and 3 cups water in saucepan and bring to boil. Reduce heat to simmer, then cover pot tightly with aluminum foil. Insert probe, poking through foil, until tip is touching bottom of pot and set target temperature to 214 degrees. When alarm sounds, remove foil and probe, place dish towel folded in half over top, and cover with saucepan lid. Let rice stand for 10 to 15 minutes. Fluff with fork and serve. –A.G.

For Identical Loaves and Layers, Use a Scale

It's easy and efficient to mix up a double or triple batch of quick bread in a big bowl, but it's important to distribute the batter evenly among the pans, or a smaller loaf may overbake while the others are still cooking through. To be absolutely sure that all your loaves are the intended size, use your scale.

First, determine the weight of the batter by weighing it in an empty bowl set on a scale tared to zero. Divide that weight by the number of pans you intend to fill. Place each prepared pan on the scale, tare the scale to zero, and add the appropriate amount of batter. This technique is also handy for ensuring that the cakes in a layer cake will be exactly the same. –A.G.

WEIGHING IN
The most accurate way to divide a big batch of batter into individual pans is to weigh it.

Tips for Making Better Waffles

Preheating a waffle iron is key to producing crispy, evenly browned waffles. After making hundreds of waffles for our waffle iron testing (page 32), we learned that it's not as simple as waiting for a preheat indicator to signal that the iron is ready. Here's what we recommend:

➤ Preheat for longer than recommended. We found that preheat indicators signaled that the irons were ready after about 4 minutes, but that's not nearly long enough. That's because preheat indicators rely on a simple sensor that tells you when only one particular area of the iron plate has reached the desired temperature—not when the cooking surface is uniformly hot. For a cooking surface that is heated evenly from edge to edge, we recommend preheating the waffle iron (no matter the brand) for at least 10 minutes (or up to 20 minutes if you have the time) before using.

➤ Reheat between batches. In our tests, most waffle irons took between 1 and 2 minutes to rebound to their properly preheated temperatures after a waffle was removed. By giving your empty waffle iron time to heat up again, you lessen the chances of anemic, soft waffles. –M.B.

Freezing Thin-Crust Pizza Dough

Our Thin-Crust Pizza dough (January/February 2011) relies on refrigeration to slow down the fermentation for better flavor and texture, but this technique has the added benefit of convenience—you can make the dough on one day, place it in the fridge, and then it's ready to bake anywhere from one to three days later. We recently confirmed that it also works well if you want to freeze the dough for later use, something typical room-temperature doughs aren't well suited to.

Freezing pizza dough involves putting the yeast into suspended animation. The problem with doing this with room-temperature doughs is that as they thaw, the yeast awakens from its slumber and the dough can easily overproof if you don't bake it at just the right moment. But with refrigerated doughs, the process is slowed down enough that the flexibility remains intact.

Here's the method: Place prepared dough in refrigerator and allow to proof for 24 hours. Divide and shape dough into balls, then place on baking sheet or plate lined with parchment paper. Cover loosely with plastic wrap and freeze until firm, about 3 hours or up to overnight. Wrap frozen dough balls individually in plastic and store in zipper-lock bags in freezer for up to 2 weeks. To thaw, unwrap ball, place in lightly oiled bowl, cover with plastic, and let sit in refrigerator for 12 to 24 hours before making pizza. –A.J.

SCIENCE **Shimmer and Smoke**

When sautéing or pan-frying, we often call for heating oil until just smoking. What happens if you add your food to the pan too soon, before it's actually smoking? We ran an experiment to demonstrate.

EXPERIMENT

We cooked two sirloin strip steaks in identical 12-inch skillets. For one steak, we heated 1 tablespoon of vegetable oil until shimmering, which took about 2 minutes. In the other pan, we heated 1 tablespoon of oil until it reached the smoke point, which took 6 minutes. We cooked both steaks until well browned on both sides.

RESULTS

The steaks cooked in the oil heated to the smoke point browned quickly and evenly, in about 6 minutes, with a minimal overcooked gray band beneath the surface. Those cooked in the shimmering oil took 10 minutes to brown, and the meat just beneath the surface overcooked, leaving a larger gray band.

EXPLANATION

Shimmering oil only reaches about 275 degrees, rather than the 400 degrees of vegetable oil at its smoke point. Making sure the oil is sufficiently hot helps keep the pan from cooling down too much once the food has been added and guarantees quick, even, and thorough browning. If the oil is below the smoke point when the food is added, browning will take too long and the food will overcook.

TAKEAWAY

For food that is properly browned with minimal overcooking beneath the surface, make sure to heat the oil until just smoking. It's easy to think you've seen a wisp of smoke and rush to add the food to the pan. But oil that has actually hit the smoke point is unmistakable—you'll see multiple wisps rising from the pan. And don't worry too much about overheating the oil; as long as you have your food at the ready, there is little risk since the oil will cool quickly once you add the food. (If you have overheated it, you will know because the oil will turn dark. In these cases, throw out the oil and start over.) –A.J.

SHIMMERING OIL, GRAY BAND
Browning takes 10 minutes, so the meat overcooks beneath the surface.

SMOKING OIL, NO GRAY BAND
Browning happens in just 6 minutes, so the meat remains rosy from edge to center.

▶ **SCIENCE OF COOKING:**
Wild versus Farmed Salmon
The type of salmon you buy can make all the difference. Free for 4 months at CooksIllustrated.com/feb16

EQUIPMENT CORNER

⇒ BY MIYE BROMBERG, LAUREN SAVOIE & KATE SHANNON ⇐

HIGHLY RECOMMENDED
CHEF'N
FreshForce Citrus Juicer
Model: 102-159-017
Price: $23.04

HIGHLY RECOMMENDED
THERMOWORKS
TimeStick
Model: TX-4200-GR
Price: $25.00

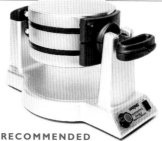

RECOMMENDED
WARING PRO
Double Belgian Waffle Maker
Model: WMK600
Price: $89.99

HIGHLY RECOMMENDED
CHICAGO METALLIC
Set of 4 Mini Loaf Pans
Model: 59400
Price: $11.99

UPDATE Manual Citrus Juicers

After replacing our favorite manual citrus juicer every few months because of worn enamel, we decided that it was time to revisit the category. We tried 12 models (priced from $5.99 to $23.04) in three styles: countertop reamers, handheld reamers, and presses. Handheld reamers performed the worst, spraying juice and letting seeds drop into the bowl. Worse, they collected on average 30 percent less juice than the top-performing model. Tabletop reamers fared somewhat better, but their built-in collection bowls and seed grates meant more to disassemble and clean. In general, the press-style models extracted the most juice with the least effort and also quickly trapped seeds. Though some smaller models had trouble with larger lemons, our favorite, the Chef'n FreshForce Citrus Juicer ($23.04), could handle up to medium (baseball-size) oranges. It extracted far and away the most juice of any model in the lineup, and its slat-like openings let juice drain without splattering or overflowing. Plus, it showed no signs of wear, even after squeezing more than 200 pieces of fruit. –L.S.

UPDATE Wearable Timers

Timers that hang from the neck or clip to clothing allow you to move freely about the house while tracking the progress of a recipe. Our longtime favorite from Polder ($13.45) is compact and reliable, but the small crevices around its buttons trap food. To explore other options, we rounded up five new wearable models (priced from $15.99 to $35.00). In the main, we preferred models with clock, stopwatch (count up), and timer (count down) options and the ability to quickly toggle from one mode to another. Testers strongly preferred timers with numbered buttons that allowed for efficient, direct time entry. One model's click-through hour, minute, and second buttons took nearly three times as long to set, and because it was unidirectional, we had to clear the display and start over if we overshot our desired setting.

When it came to wearability, clip-on styles refused to stay put. Models that hung from lanyards slipped easily overhead, and their slim silhouettes fit inside shirt pockets. The ThermoWorks TimeStick ($25.00) jumped ahead of our old favorite, thanks to a smooth, water-resistant exterior that eliminates food-trapping crevices and keeps the timer safe from wet hands and spills. –K.S.

TESTING Belgian Waffle Irons

Belgian waffle makers produce waffles that are taller and have deeper pockets than conventional waffles. To ferret out the best machine, we tested 13 models priced under $100.00. We considered rotary-style models, in which the machine either turns on a hinge or spins 180 degrees on a stand, as well as stationary machines. The irons needed to consistently produce tall, evenly browned waffles with crisp shells and moist crumbs without requiring trial and error, and they had to be easy to use, clean, and store.

Many of the irons heated unevenly or ran too hot or too cool. The best machines maintained an average interior temperature between 400 and 435 degrees. We awarded bonus points to machines with a good drip tray and audible and/or visual alerts that told us when our waffles were ready. Our winning iron, the Waring Pro Double Belgian Waffle Maker ($89.99), made picture-perfect waffles, two at a time, in less than 5 minutes. And while it lacked a removable drip tray, it had a good, loud alert. –M.B.

TESTING Mini Loaf Pans

Mini loaf pans make it a snap to churn out petite breads and cakes for homemade holiday gifts. Since most recipes designed for a 9 by 5-inch pan will produce three mini loaves, we homed in on five roughly 5½ by 3-inch models (priced from $8.75 to $28.95) that come in sets of three or more, as well as one tray-style option with four wells. We baked pound cake and quick breads in each, looking for tall, nicely domed, evenly browned loaves with precise edges.

The material and weight of the pans were key. One set made of light-colored, light-weight aluminum produced loaves with flat, browned tops and pale, spongy sides. The other pans, made of heavier, darker metal, performed better. All of the pans released baked goods cleanly, and the individual pans offered more control than the tray-style model. The Chicago Metallic Set of 4 Mini Loaf Pans ($11.99) won top marks for producing loaves with tall, even doming and the prettiest golden-brown coloring. –K.S.

For complete testing results, go to CooksIllustrated.com/feb16.

U.S. POSTAL SERVICE STATEMENT OF OWNERSHIP, MANAGEMENT AND CIRCULATION

1. Publication Title: Cook's Illustrated; 2. Publication No. 1068-2821; 3. Filing Date: 9/22/15; 4. Issue Frequency: Jan/Feb, Mar/Apr, May/Jun, Jul/Aug, Sep/Oct, Nov/Dec; 5. No. of Issues Published Annually: 6; 6. Annual Subscription Price: $41.70; 7. Complete Mailing Address of Known Office of Publication: 17 Station Street, Brookline, MA 02445; 8. Complete Mailing Address of Headquarters or General Business Office of Publisher: 17 Station Street, Brookline, MA 02445; 9. Full Names and Complete Mailing Addresses of Publisher, Editor, and Managing Editor: Publisher: Christopher Kimball, 17 Station Street, Brookline, MA 02445; Editor: Jack Bishop, 17 Station Street, Brookline, MA 02445; Managing Editor: Rebecca Hays, 17 Station Street, Brookline, MA 02445; 10. Owner: Boston Common Press Limited Partnership, Christopher Kimball, 17 Station Street, Brookline, MA 02445; 11. Known Bondholders, Mortgagees, and Other Securities: None; 12. Tax Status: Has Not Changed During Preceding 12 Months; 13. Publication Title: Cook's Illustrated; 14. Issue Date for Circulation Data Below: September/October 2015; 15a. Total Number of Copies: 1,056,883 (Sep/Oct 2015: 899,452); b. Paid Circulation: (1) Mailed Outside-County Paid Subscriptions Stated on PS Form 3541: 881,144 (Sep/Oct 2015: 889,300); (2) Mailed In-County Paid Subscriptions Stated on PS Form 3541: 0 (Sep/Oct 2015: 0); (3) Paid Distribution Outside the Mail Including Sales Through Dealers and Carriers, Street Vendors, Counter Sales, and Other Paid Distribution Outside the USPS: 41,545 (Sep/Oct 2015: 0); (4) Paid Distribution by Other Classes of Mail Through the USPS: 0 (Sep/Oct 2015: 0); c. Total Paid Distribution: 922,689 (Sep/Oct 2015: 889,390); d. Free or Nominal Rate Distribution: (1) Free or Nominal Rate Outside-County Copies Included on PS Form 3541: 4,123 (Sep/Oct 2015: 3,605); (2) Free or Nominal Rate In-County Copies Included on Form PS 3541: 0 (Sep/Oct 2015: 0); (3) Free or Nominal Rate Copies Mailed at Other Classes Through the USPS: 0 (Sep/Oct 2015: 0); (4) Free or Nominal Rate Distribution Outside the Mail: 500 (Sep/Oct 2015: 500); e. Total Free or Nominal Rate Distribution: 4,623 (Sep/Oct 2015: 4,105); f. Total Distribution: 927,312 (Sep/Oct 2015: 893,495); g. Copies Not Distributed: 129,572 (Sep/Oct 2015: 5,957); h. Total: 1,056,884 (Sep/Oct 2015: 899,452); i. Percent Paid: 99.50% (Sep/Oct 2015: 99.54%).

INDEX
January & February 2016

FOLLOW US ON SOCIAL MEDIA
facebook.com/CooksIllustrated
twitter.com/TestKitchen
pinterest.com/TestKitchen
google.com/+AmericasTestKitchen
instagram.com/TestKitchen
youtube.com/AmericasTestKitchen

BONUS ONLINE CONTENT
*More recipes, reviews, and videos are available
at* CooksIllustrated.com/feb16.

RECIPES

EXPANDED REVIEWS

▶ RECIPE VIDEOS
Want to see how to make any of the
recipes in this issue? There's a video for that.

▶ MORE VIDEOS
Science of Cooking: Wild versus
    Farmed Salmon
Testing Food Processors

Fluffy Dinner Rolls, 21

Shrimp Scampi, 9

Portuguese-Style Beef Stew (Alcatra), 7

Skillet-Roasted Cauliflower, 13

Best Roast Chicken with Root Vegetables, 5

Pear-Walnut Upside-Down Cake, 19

Red Lentil Soup, 22

Tuscan-Style Roast Pork (Arista), 11

America's Test Kitchen
COOKING SCHOOL

Visit our online cooking school today, where we offer
180+ online lessons covering a range of recipes and
cooking methods. Whether you're a novice just starting
out or are already an advanced cook looking for new
techniques, our cooking school is designed to give you
confidence in the kitchen and make you a better cook.

Start a 14-Day Free Trial at
OnlineCookingSchool.com

Cook's Illustrated on iPad

Enjoy *Cook's* wherever you are
whenever you want.

Did you know that *Cook's Illustrated* is available on
iPad? Go to **CooksIllustrated.com/iPad** to download
the app through iTunes. You'll be able to start a
free trial of the digital edition, which includes bonus
features like recipe videos, full-color photos, and
step-by-step slide shows of each recipe.

Go to CooksIllustrated.com/iPad to download our app through iTunes.

Penne Arrabbiata, 12

Best Baked Potatoes, 15

PHOTOGRAPHY: CARL TREMBLAY; STYLING: MARIE PIRAINO

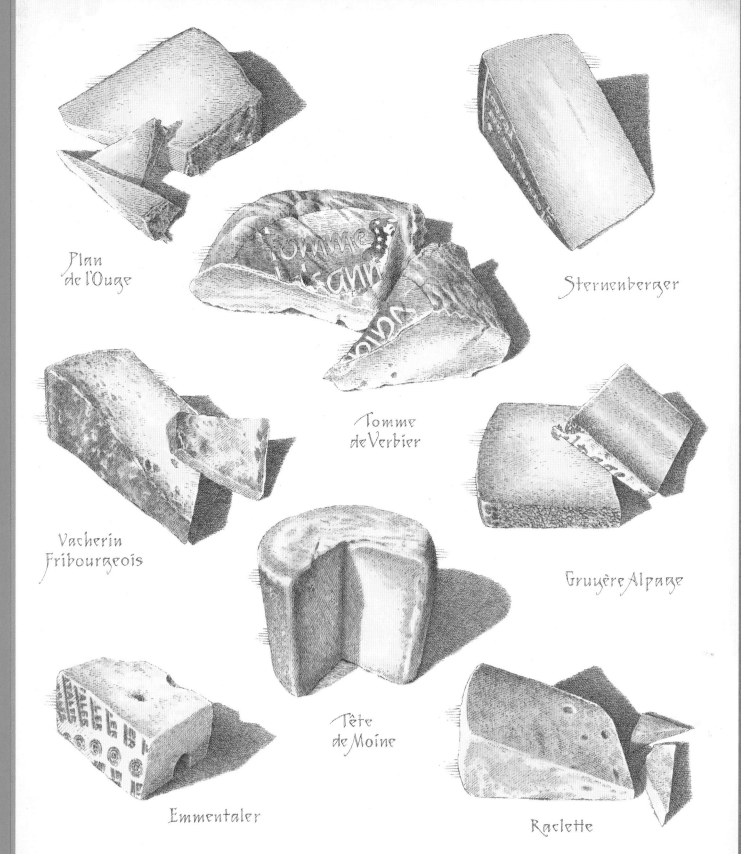

Plan
de l'Ouge

Sternenberger

Tomme
de Verbier

Vacherin
Fribourgeois

Gruyère Alpage

Tête
de Moine

Emmentaler

Raclette

SWISS CHEESES

NUMBER 139

MARCH & APRIL 2016

COOK'S
ILLUSTRATED

How to Cook Bone-In Chicken Breasts
Hint: Treat Them Like Steaks

Stir-Fried Beef
Classic Technique Simplified

Best Chicken Broth
Three Options for Homemade

A New Approach to Making Vinaigrette

Hard-Cooked Eggs
New Easy-Peel Method

Pantry Pasta Sauces
Dinner in 15 Minutes

Persian-Style Rice
Plump Grains plus Crispy Crust

Perfect Roasted Asparagus
Taste Test: Greek Yogurt
Homemade Corned Beef

CooksIllustrated.com
$6.95 U.S. & $7.95 CANADA

7 25274 62805 6   04>

COOK'S ILLUSTRATED

MARCH & APRIL 2016

ASIAN DUMPLINGS

BACK COVER ILLUSTRATED BY JOHN BURGOYNE

Asian Dumplings

To eat a Shanghainese soup dumpling (XIAO LONG BAO), bite open the thin-skinned sac and slurp out the unctuous pork broth. Wrinkly, thin-skinned Hong Kong–Style WONTONS are often served in broth with noodles. Boiled wontons (SHUI JIAO) hold ground pork or shrimp and leeks or cabbage. A Cantonese dim sum spread features several dumplings; among them: open-faced SHU MAI stuffed with pork and shrimp; shell-shaped, translucent HAR GOW loaded with steamed shrimp; and WU GOK—wispy fried taro dumplings filled with pork. TIBETAN MOMOS house a meaty center—often beef, lamb, or yak. The hallmark of Japanese potstickers (GYOZA) is their crisp base. Thai chive cakes (KANOM GUI CHAI) are crisp, chewy, and loaded with garlicky Chinese chives. The peppery pork-and-shrimp filling of Vietnamese BÁNH BỘT LỌC stands out against the clear, gelatinous cover.

America's Test Kitchen is a real 2,500-square-foot kitchen located just outside Boston. It is the home of more than 60 test cooks, editors, and cookware specialists. Our mission is to test recipes until we understand exactly how and why they work and eventually arrive at the very best version. We also test kitchen equipment and supermarket ingredients in search of products that offer the best value and performance. You can watch us work by tuning in to *America's Test Kitchen* (AmericasTestKitchen.com) and *Cooks Country from America's Test Kitchen* (CooksCountry.com) on public television, and listen to us on our weekly radio program on PRX. You can also follow us on Facebook, Twitter, Pinterest, and Instagram.

SMALL MIRACLES

Cooking with science may sound intimidating. But at *Cook's Illustrated* it doesn't refer to cooking *sous vide* or creating foams and powders. Instead, it means taking advantage of the scientific principles inherent in traditional, everyday cooking. Very often, this means unlocking the hidden powers of the most familiar ingredients in your pantry.

It all started with salt.

In the very first year of this magazine, we discovered that soaking your Thanksgiving turkey in a salt brine not only seasoned it more deeply but also caused the bird to retain more moisture as it cooked, so it ended up more tender. It was a revelatory discovery. (Though, amusingly, we boast in that article about testing 30 turkeys to make this discovery; these days, 30 turkeys would just be the beginning of our testing.)

For 22 years since then, we've been exploring the simple magic of familiar ingredients. It continues in the issue you're holding now. Our goal for the Beef Stir-Fry with Bell Peppers and Black Pepper Sauce recipe on page 7, for example, was to mimic the ultratender texture of stir-fried beef you find in high-end Chinese restaurants. We ran through test after test trying to duplicate it, but in the end we discovered that the secret was just a bit of good old baking soda. Simply put, a quick bath with a little baking soda makes the meat more alkaline (as opposed to acidic). This in turn causes certain enzymes in the meat, called calpains, to become more active and cut the meat's muscle fibers. As the meat's fibers break down, its texture softens. And since the meat's looser consistency retains water better, it's less likely to

contract and expel moisture when heated.

On page 19, you'll find yet another ordinary ingredient (though this one may be farther toward the back of your pantry) that has hidden culinary virtues. Molasses, it turns out, contains large compounds called malanoidins that, among other things, cause the oil-and-water emulsion of a vinaigrette to last not just for hours but for days.

We don't deny the appeal of complex cooking, nor are we immune to the joys of technology. We use food processors, microwaves, stand mixers, and all the modern machines with pleasure and with appreciation of the way they can make culinary tasks faster and easier.

But very often, the key to a great, foolproof recipe is in a familiar box or jar in your pantry. Come along with us as we continue to explore the everyday magic that is cooking with science.

The Editors of *Cook's Illustrated*

FOR INQUIRIES, ORDERS, OR MORE INFORMATION

COOK'S ILLUSTRATED MAGAZINE

Cook's Illustrated magazine (ISSN 1068-2821), number 139, is published bimonthly by Boston Common Press Limited Partnership, 17 Station St., Brookline, MA 02445. Copyright 2016 Boston Common Press Limited Partnership. Periodicals postage paid at Boston, MA, and additional mailing offices, USPS #012487. Publications Mail Agreement No. 40020778. Return undeliverable Canadian addresses to P.O. Box 875, Station A, Windsor, ON N9A 6P2. POSTMASTER: Send address changes to *Cook's Illustrated*, P.O. Box 6018, Harlan, IA 51593-1518. For subscription and gift subscription orders, subscription inquiries, or change of address notices, visit AmericasTestKitchen.com/support, call 800-526-8442 in the U.S. or 515-248-7684 from outside the U.S., or write to us at *Cook's Illustrated*, P.O. Box 6018, Harlan, IA 51593-1518.

CooksIllustrated.com

At the all new CooksIllustrated.com, you can order books and subscriptions, sign up for our free e-newsletter, or renew your magazine subscription. Join the website and gain access to 23 years of *Cook's Illustrated* recipes, equipment tests, and ingredient tastings, as well as companion videos for every recipe in this issue.

COOKBOOKS

We sell more than 50 cookbooks by the editors of *Cook's Illustrated*, including *The Cook's Illustrated Cookbook* and *Paleo Perfected*. To order, visit our bookstore at CooksIllustrated.com/bookstore.

EDITORIAL OFFICE 17 Station St., Brookline, MA 02445; 617-232-1000; fax: 617-232-1572. For subscription inquiries, visit AmericasTestKitchen.com/support or call 800-526-8442.

Cleaner Cheese Crumbling

Rebekah Mahoney of Grafton, Mass., recently discovered a less messy way to crumble soft cheeses such as blue or goat before adding them to salads: She places the refrigerator-cold cheese in a zipper-lock bag and crumbles it directly in the bag before turning it out onto her dish.

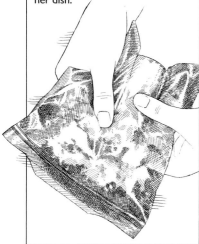

Saving Pasta Scraps

Mimicking the bags of mixed pasta scraps commonly sold in Italy, Pauline Fanuele of Nesconset, N.Y., saves strands and pieces of short store-bought pastas to use in soups and stews.

QUICK TIPS

⇒ COMPILED BY ANNIE PETITO ⇐

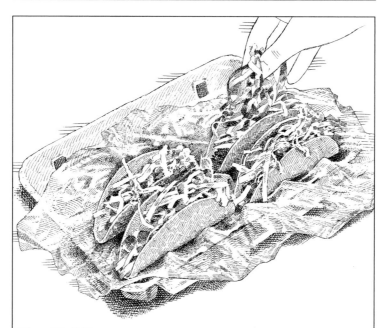

Taco Shell Prop

Roger Cummings of Olympia, Wash., garnishes four hard-shell tacos at a time by steadying them in an empty, plastic wrap–lined egg carton. Plus, any garnishes that drop onto the plastic are easily discarded afterward.

Getting a Grip on Radish Prep

Laura Candler of Sewanee, Tenn., finds it difficult to grasp small, round radishes while cutting them, so instead of trimming off the root tail before cutting, she leaves it attached and uses it as a grip.

Cake Stand Organizer

When she's not using her cake stand for displaying desserts, Stephanie Kohn of Jacksonville, Fla., discovered that it can do double duty as an organizer for core ingredients like salt, pepper, and olive oil, or even for soap dispensers and sponges. The stand's elevation keeps countertop clutter to a minimum.

Measuring-Spoon Chain

Sara Joyce of Westford, Mass., was frustrated that she kept losing the chain to her measuring spoons, which left them loose and difficult to find in the drawer. She found that a cable key ring, which is durable and washable, makes a great long-lasting substitute.

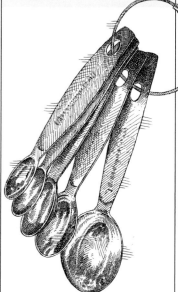

SEND US YOUR TIPS We will provide a complimentary one-year subscription for each tip we print. Send your tip, name, address, and daytime telephone number to Quick Tips, *Cook's Illustrated*, P.O. Box 470589, Brookline, MA 02447, or to QuickTips@AmericasTestKitchen.com.

Easy Label Removal

To make it easy to remove homemade masking tape labels from food storage containers, Sakura Amend of Brooklyn, N.Y., folds the end of the masking tape onto itself to make an easy-to-pull tab before adhering it to her container.

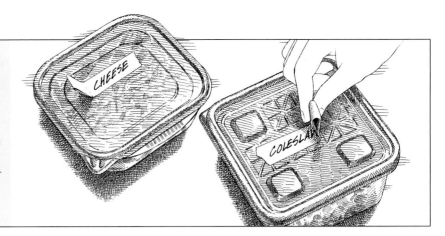

Noodle Knife Block

Brad Mumsford of St. Louis, Mo., has a surprising use for uncooked spaghetti: a homemade knife block. He packs a tall container with the dried strands and then slides the knives in point side down to store them.

Shoeshining the Counter

When baking, Adrian Bartoli of San Francisco, Calif., has found that flour and crumbs inevitably fall on his kitchen counter, where they become lodged in corners and crevices. For easy cleanup, he keeps a spare (unused) shoeshine brush on hand; the soft, sturdy bristles dig into tight spaces and easily sweep up the debris.

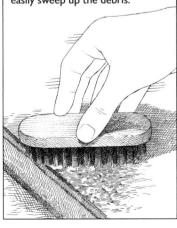

Compound Butter for Company

When serving flavored butters to dinner guests, Jenell Moore of Elon, N.C., lines a ramekin or cookie cutter (sitting on a plate) with plastic wrap and then fills the vessel with butter, making sure to push it into the corners. Once chilled, the shaped butter is easy to remove from the cutter with no messy cleanup.

Securing a Dip Bowl on a Platter

To keep a dip bowl from sliding around on a platter, Janet Tarrant of Prescott, Ariz., folds a piece of plastic wrap into a small square and places it on the platter before placing the bowl on top, pressing on the bowl to secure it. The plastic is virtually invisible, and the bowl of dip stays securely anchored to the platter.

Slot Machine for Herb Prep

When plucking large amounts of parsley or cilantro, Leslie Croyle of Bay Village, Ohio, threads the stems through the holes of a perforated spoon and pulls the herbs through. The leaves gather in the bowl of the spoon, and the stems can be discarded.

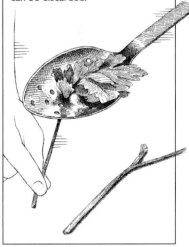

Good to the Last Squeeze

To get every last bit from tubes of tomato or anchovy paste, Sue Ringgold of Jacksonville, Fla., found that using her toothpaste winder works just as well as it does on toothpaste. When the tube is empty, she removes the winder and slips it onto a new tube.

How to Cook Bone-In Chicken Breasts

Skin and bones lend chicken breasts exactly what the boneless, skinless variety lacks: flavor and moisture. But how do you cook them? Like steak.

≈ BY ANDREA GEARY ≈

Choosing boneless, skinless chicken breasts over less expensive bone-in breasts is like paying extra for a car that has had its air bags removed. You're spending more for less protection. Boneless, skinless breasts are entirely exposed to the heat during cooking, and the bare meat turns leathery as it dries out. But bone-in chicken breasts, with skin on one side and bone on the other, have protection built right in. What's more, the crispy, nicely browned skin of roasted chicken adds flavor and textural contrast.

Bone-in breasts have only one problem that I can see: People view the bone and skin as a complication rather than an asset. In fact, in my research I couldn't find a single recipe for how to actually cook them well. I resolved to devise an easy method that would deliver juicy, well-seasoned meat and crispy brown skin.

I started with the simplest approach. I placed four bone-in breasts on a rimmed baking sheet, sprinkled them with salt, and roasted them in a 425-degree oven. In 25 minutes, they had reached the target temperature of 160 degrees, and the skin was crackly and brown. But the meat was quite dry, especially at the narrow end of each breast, and the seasoning had not penetrated beyond the surface. Lowering the oven temperature to 375 helped: The narrow ends of the breasts weren't as dry, and the chicken was slightly juicier. The skin was still flabby and pale, but I'd deal with that later.

Since the more moderate oven had produced juicier meat, how about dropping the temperature more drastically? I decided to try the reverse-sear technique, a method we often use with steaks. We cook the meat in a low oven until it reaches the desired temperature and then sear it in a skillet on the stovetop. The interior stays incredibly juicy, while the oven-dried exterior browns quickly, with little mess and minimal chance of overcooking the meat just beneath the surface.

For juicy meat and well-browned skin, we take a hint from our method for cooking steak: Start in a moderate oven and finish quickly in a hot skillet.

After poking holes in the skin to help the fat render, I baked the next batch of chicken in a 250-degree oven. When it reached 160 degrees, I placed the pieces skin side down in a hot skillet. After 3 minutes, the skin was brown and supercrispy. The meat was terrifically moist, too. I noted just two problems: There was zero seasoning once you got past that beautiful skin. And that stint in the oven? It was 1 hour and 45 minutes long.

Three Strikes and You're Out

A cooking time approaching 2 hours was not an option, so I ran through several tests to find the temperature that would produce juicy chicken in a reasonable amount of time. The sweet spot was 325 degrees for about 40 minutes.

The meat was juicy and the skin was crispy, but the chicken still tasted bland. I had hoped to forgo pretreatments like salting and brining because I didn't want to add time to the recipe. My technique was working so well that I could get away with skipping the salt for its moisture-retaining effect, but I realized that I did need it for seasoning. Before putting the next batch in the oven, I carefully peeled back the skin on each breast and sprinkled 1½ teaspoons of kosher salt over all four before smoothing the skin back into place. After 40 minutes in the oven and a quick sear on the stovetop, this was the juiciest and most flavorful batch yet.

As for the searing, I found that there was often a small amount of collected moisture hiding underneath the skin, which caused the chicken to splatter alarmingly when I placed it in a smoking-hot skillet. Rather than try to remove the moisture (and possibly mar the skin in the process), I kept the heat low until the chicken was safely transferred and then turned it up. By the time the pan was hot enough to splatter, the hidden water had evaporated.

Except for the salting at the beginning and the quick sear at the end, my method was pretty much hands-off. That left me with time to make a sauce, which I could put together, start to finish, while the chicken was in the oven. Because chicken breast meat

---

Why buy bone-in chicken breasts? First, the crisped skin adds flavor and nice textural contrast. Second, bone-in breasts are far less expensive than boneless. Lastly, unlike boneless, skinless breasts, which have no barrier against drying, bone-in breasts have built-in protection (skin and bone), making them more foolproof to cook.

▶ **Keep Abreast of the Method**
A step-by-step video is available at CooksIllustrated.com/apr16

PRONE TO DRYING OUT
Boneless, skinless breasts are entirely exposed to the heat.

EASIER TO KEEP MOIST
The skin and bone provide protection.

is quite lean, I would base the sauce on a rich ingredient: mayonnaise. Jalapeño and lime added zing while cilantro lent some freshness. With that, I had a sauce that was as uncomplicated to prepare as the chicken.

ROASTED BONE-IN CHICKEN BREASTS
SERVES 4

Be sure to remove excess fatty skin from the thick ends of the breasts when trimming. You may serve these chicken breasts on their own or prepare a sauce (recipe follows) while the chicken roasts. For our free recipes for Roasted Bone-In Chicken Breasts for Two, Tahini and Honey Sauce, and Spicy Butter Sauce, go to CooksIllustrated.com/apr16.

   4   (10- to 12-ounce) bone-in chicken breasts, trimmed
1 ½ teaspoons kosher salt
   1   tablespoon vegetable oil

1. Adjust oven rack to lower-middle position and heat oven to 325 degrees. Line rimmed baking sheet with aluminum foil. Working with 1 breast at a time, use your fingers to carefully separate chicken skin from meat. Peel skin back, leaving it attached at top and bottom of breast and at ribs. Sprinkle salt evenly over all chicken, then lay skin back in place. Using metal skewer or tip of paring knife, poke 6 to 8 holes in fat deposits in skin. Arrange breasts skin side up on prepared sheet. Roast until chicken registers 160 degrees, 35 to 45 minutes.

2. Heat 12-inch skillet over low heat for 5 minutes. Add oil and swirl to coat surface. Add chicken, skin side down, and increase heat to medium-high. Cook chicken without moving it until skin is well browned and crispy, 3 to 5 minutes. Using tongs, flip chicken and prop against side of skillet so thick side of breast is facing down; continue to cook until browned, 1 to 2 minutes longer. Transfer to platter and let rest for 5 minutes before serving.

JALAPEÑO AND CILANTRO SAUCE
MAKES 1 CUP

For a spicier sauce, reserve and add some of the chile seeds to the blender.

   1   cup fresh cilantro leaves and stems, trimmed and chopped coarse
   3   jalapeño chiles, stemmed, seeded, and minced
 ½ cup mayonnaise
   1   tablespoon lime juice
   2   garlic cloves, minced
 ½ teaspoon kosher salt
   2   tablespoons extra-virgin olive oil

Process cilantro, jalapeños, mayonnaise, lime juice, garlic, and salt in blender for 1 minute. Scrape down sides of blender jar and continue to process until smooth, about 1 minute longer. With blender running, slowly add oil until incorporated. Transfer to bowl.

TESTING Robot Vacuums

With the push of a button, robotic vacuums do the cleaning for you; many can even be programmed to work when you're out of the house. When active, they scoot around the floor vacuuming, and most automatically return to their charging base when they're done cleaning (or when their power runs low).

Some robot vacuums cost nearly a thousand dollars, and we wondered if we could find one we liked for a whole lot less. We rounded up seven robots, priced from $119.99 to $499.99, and set them to work, first picking up a messy combination of flour, salt, wet coffee grounds, chopped vegetables, and garlic peels from a hard floor and then cleaning up sprinkles spilled in a carpeted office. We quantified cleaning ability by weighing all the debris before scattering it on the floor; when the robots were done cleaning, we weighed the contents of their collection bins, calculated the percentage of debris picked up, and then averaged the two scores. We also sent each robot home with a different editor for a week of home use.

None of the robots worked flawlessly, and they're not a replacement for your regular vacuum. Every model eventually got hung up on an obstacle, usually around power cords or in cramped spaces. Most also missed corners or sections along walls, and they weren't strong enough to handle large amounts of debris. That said, our testers loved the better-performing models for maintenance cleaning.

What made some robots work better than others? While we didn't find much difference in the vacuums' suction power, we did find a huge difference in coverage. To track how the robots navigated through a cleaning cycle, we took a series of long-exposure photos as they cleaned. We discovered three distinct movement patterns: random lines, concentric circles, and methodical grids. Robots that moved in random lines had uneven coverage and cleaned poorly. Those that worked in circles had better coverage but took much longer to clean a room; these robots also had trouble steering out of tight corners. The clear winners were the two robots that traveled in methodical grids. These robots, made by Neato Botvac (our winner) and Moneual Rydis (our Best Buy), employed advanced mapping technologies to "see" the room and plot their course for efficiency—they provided thorough coverage and did it in about a third of the time of the other models. Visit CooksIllustrated.com/apr16 for the complete testing results. –Lauren Savoie

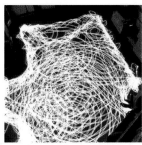

GRID: BEST

CIRCLES: DECENT

RANDOM LINES: POOR

Restaurant-Style Stir-Fried Beef

The ultrasupple texture of beef stir-fried in Chinese restaurants normally requires a messy coating and a dip in hot oil. We looked for an easier way.

> BY STEVE DUNN

Years ago, the test kitchen nailed down our approach to stir-frying beef: Choose flank steak for its big, beefy flavor and relatively reasonable price; soak the meat briefly in a soy sauce–based marinade; and cook it in batches in a large nonstick skillet. Follow those guidelines, and you're well on your way to a satisfying dish. And yet there is one quality that method doesn't deliver: a texture typical of Chinese restaurant stir-fries, in which the meat is almost meltingly tender, with a luxurious, silky softness. I am a big fan of this texture and wanted to find a way to add it to our beef stir-fries.

Seeking Softness

The supple meat served at Chinese restaurants is achieved via a traditional technique called velveting. It involves marinating the meat in egg whites, cornstarch, water or rice wine, and salt for 15 to 30 minutes, during which time the mixture forms a gossamer-thin coating on the meat and the alkaline egg whites tenderize the meat by changing its pH. The meat is then blanched in simmering water or oil to set the coating, which will protect the meat against the

We tie this stir-fry together with a spicy-sweet-salty sauce made from soy and oyster sauces, brown sugar, and 2 teaspoons of ground black pepper.

blazing heat of the wok. The coating turns plush and silky as it cooks, delivering its namesake texture.

I decided to give velveting a try using oil blanching, which the Chinese call *jau yau*, or "passing through oil." Keeping in mind that slicing meat against the grain shortens the muscle fibers and makes them easier to chew, I prepped the steak by dividing it into strips and then cutting those strips against the grain into thin, bite-size pieces.

Next, I submerged the steak pieces in a thin paste of egg whites, cornstarch, rice wine, and soy sauce (my replacement for the usual salt). After a brief soak, I blanched the pieces in a pot of hot oil, drained them, and transferred them to a skillet to be quickly stir-fried. Sure enough, the resulting meat seemed ridiculously tender, just like that which

▶ See the Tenderness Happen
A step-by-step video is available at CooksIllustrated.com/apr16

I'd enjoyed in Chinese restaurants. That said, the process was messy and fussy—no wonder velveting is typically practiced only in professional kitchens. In a home kitchen, an extra blanching step just makes things too complicated.

Transferring the beef straight from the egg white–cornstarch mixture into the skillet without first blanching to set the coating seemed like a good shortcut to try. Alas, this resulted in an outer layer

more akin to scrambled eggs than to the plush coating I was after. Clearly blanching was nonnegotiable when egg whites were involved. Well then, how about getting rid of the egg whites? Happily, a simple marinade of cornstarch, rice wine, and soy sauce resulted in beef that, while not as silky or tender as traditionally velveted meat, came close.

To finish the job, I applied a tenderizing trick that has practically become standard practice in the test kitchen and works by the same principle as egg whites. Soaking meat in a solution of baking soda and water raises the pH on the meat's surface, making it more difficult for the proteins to bond, which keeps the fibers tender and moist. In the past, we've historically called for baking soda soaks at concentrations that required rinsing the meat prior to cooking, lest the meat taste soapy or metallic. But after some experimentation, I found that a lower ratio of baking soda (just ¼ teaspoon to 1 tablespoon of water) still made a noticeable difference in the meat's tenderness and made rinsing unnecessary.

Because the small amount of baking soda was performing the same role as the egg white, I was able to achieve my goal—extremely supple and tender beef—without adding any extra work to the process.

Now that the beef was sliced, pretreated, and marinated, it was time to stir-fry. Batch-cooking the meat was a must to ensure proper browning by not overcrowding the pan. What's more, we have found that arranging the meat in an even layer and allowing it to cook undisturbed for a full minute—forget about keeping the pieces in constant motion—guarantees

---

TECHNIQUE | CUTTING FLANK STEAK FOR STIR-FRY

Cut steak with grain into 2- to 2½-inch strips, then cut each strip crosswise against grain into ¼-inch-thick slices.

deep browning. With flavorful, ultratender, well-browned meat at the ready, it was time to turn the bare-bones beef into a full-fledged stir-fry.

A Peppery Punch

I've long been a fan of steak au poivre, the iconic French union of beef and black pepper, so I wondered if there was a Chinese dish that also celebrated this pairing. Indeed, black pepper beef (*hei hu jiao niu liu*)—a Cantonese standard of beef, green bell peppers, and yellow onions bathed in a black pepper sauce—seemed to fit the bill perfectly.

For the vegetables, which took their turn in the pan right after the meat was removed, I deviated from the original. I traded onion for scallions, swapped some of the green pepper for red, and mixed in fresh ginger and garlic. To tie it all together, I whipped up a salty-sweet-spicy sauce with soy and oyster sauces, a little brown sugar, and 2 full teaspoons of coarsely ground black pepper. When combined with my extra-tender beef, these ingredients delivered the best beef stir-fry I'd ever had, in or out of a restaurant.

BEEF STIR-FRY WITH BELL PEPPERS AND BLACK PEPPER SAUCE
SERVES 4

Prepare the vegetables and aromatics while the beef is marinating. Serve with steamed white rice. For our recipe for Beef Stir-Fry with Bell Peppers and Black Pepper Sauce for Two, go to CooksIllustrated.com/apr16.

1	tablespoon plus ¼ cup water
¼	teaspoon baking soda
1	pound flank steak, trimmed, cut into 2- to 2½-inch strips with grain, each strip cut crosswise against grain into ¼-inch-thick slices
3	tablespoons soy sauce
3	tablespoons dry sherry or Chinese rice wine
3	teaspoons cornstarch
2½	teaspoons packed light brown sugar
1	tablespoon oyster sauce
2	teaspoons rice vinegar
1½	teaspoons toasted sesame oil
2	teaspoons coarsely ground pepper
3	tablespoons plus 1 teaspoon vegetable oil
1	red bell pepper, stemmed, seeded, and cut into ¼-inch-wide strips
1	green bell pepper, stemmed, seeded, and cut into ¼-inch-wide strips
6	scallions, white parts sliced thin on bias, green parts cut into 2-inch pieces
3	garlic cloves, minced
1	tablespoon grated fresh ginger

1. Combine 1 tablespoon water and baking soda in medium bowl. Add beef and toss to coat. Let sit at room temperature for 5 minutes.

2. Whisk 1 tablespoon soy sauce, 1 tablespoon sherry, 1½ teaspoons cornstarch, and ½ teaspoon

sugar together in small bowl. Add soy sauce mixture to beef, stir to coat, and let sit at room temperature for 15 to 30 minutes.

3. Whisk remaining ¼ cup water, remaining 2 tablespoons soy sauce, remaining 2 tablespoons sherry, remaining 1½ teaspoons cornstarch, remaining 2 teaspoons sugar, oyster sauce, vinegar, sesame oil, and pepper together in second bowl.

4. Heat 2 teaspoons vegetable oil in 12-inch nonstick skillet over high heat until just smoking. Add half of beef in single layer. Cook without stirring for 1 minute. Continue to cook, stirring occasionally, until spotty brown on both sides, about 1 minute longer. Transfer to bowl. Repeat with remaining beef and 2 teaspoons vegetable oil.

5. Return skillet to high heat, add 2 teaspoons vegetable oil, and heat until beginning to smoke. Add bell peppers and scallion greens and cook, stirring occasionally, until vegetables are spotty brown and crisp-tender, about 4 minutes. Transfer vegetables to bowl with beef.

6. Return now-empty skillet to medium-high heat and add remaining 4 teaspoons vegetable oil, scallion whites, garlic, and ginger. Cook, stirring frequently, until lightly browned, about 2 minutes. Return beef and vegetables to skillet and stir to combine.

7. Whisk sauce to recombine. Add to skillet and cook, stirring constantly, until sauce has thickened, about 30 seconds. Serve immediately.

SCIENCE Just ¼ Teaspoon = Meat That's 20% More Tender

Just like egg whites, baking soda raises the pH on the surface of the meat, making it more difficult for the proteins to bond and therefore keeping the meat tender and moist. To demonstrate the effect of treating meat with baking soda, we soaked one batch of flank steak in a baking soda mixture and left a second batch untreated. We cooked both samples *sous vide* to 160 degrees and then used a texture analyzer to see how much force was required to "bite" into slices. The results: Meat treated with baking soda was about 20 percent more tender than untreated meat. –S.D.

Stir-Fry Fundamentals

No matter what you're stir-frying, follow these guidelines to ensure success.

➤ Be ready for quick cooking: Prep ingredients in advance.

➤ For even browning, use a nonstick skillet, not a wok.

➤ Limit stirring so meat and vegetables can develop color.

➤ Sear in batches so meat doesn't steam.

➤ Add aromatics last to preserve flavor and avoid scorching.

Velvety Beef, Without Velveting

The ultratender texture of the stir-fried beef served in Chinese restaurants comes from a classic technique known as velveting, which involves coating the meat and blanching it in a pot of oil before stir-frying even takes place. We looked for a more streamlined way to protect and tenderize the meat.

TRADITIONAL VELVETING: Marinate in cornstarch and egg white; blanch in oil to set coating
➤ Results: Good but messy and time-consuming

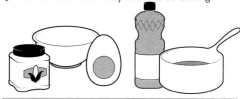

TEST 1: Keep cornstarch and egg white; skip blanching in oil
➤ Results: Curdled mess

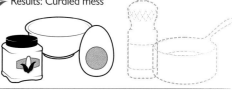

TEST 2: Keep cornstarch; omit egg white
➤ Results: Silky but not tender enough

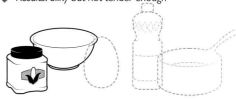

TEST 3: Keep cornstarch; add baking soda
➤ Results: Extra-supple meat and less fuss

BEST METHOD

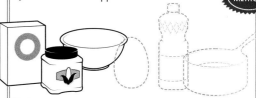

Introducing Fougasse

If you're a fan of a crisp crust, then this rustically elegant Provençal bread is for you.
(Don't worry: It's easier than it looks.)

⇉ BY ANDREW JANJIGIAN ⇇

If ever there was a bread made for crust-lovers, it has to be *fougasse*. Revered by professional bakers, this loaf is still relatively unknown to everyday cooks, at least outside its home territory of Provence. It is related by name and pedigree to focaccia, which comes from just over the border in Italy. But unlike its Italian cousin, fougasse gets an elegant twist: After being stretched and flattened, the dough is given a series of cuts, usually in fanciful geometric patterns, to create multiple openings in the finished flatbread.

As pretty as the sculpted breads are, the openings are not just aesthetic: They dramatically increase the crust-to-crumb ratio so that nearly every bite includes an equal share of crisp crust and tender, airy interior. The cuts also help the bread bake very quickly.

And while tearing off a chunk of fougasse and dipping it in extra-virgin olive oil is a terrific way to go, the relatively flat shape makes a good canvas for bold additions. Some, like chopped olives, anchovies, or lardons (bacon), are mixed into the dough, while others, such as cheese or herbs, are sprinkled on top prior to baking.

The decorative slashes do more than add charm; they increase the crust-to-crumb ratio so there's plenty of crunch to complement the airy interior.

Finding Fougasse

Most bakeries don't make a separate dough for fougasse. Instead, they simply repurpose extra dough from some other product, such as baguettes, ciabatta, or sourdough. The only requirement is that the dough be fairly wet to ensure an open crumb and a crisp, light crust. (For more information on how hydration affects bread, see "Dough Hydration" on page 30.)

So when I set out to create a fougasse recipe of my own, it made sense to mix up the test kitchen's baguette dough. (Shaping baguettes can be intimidating, but the dough itself is quite simple to prepare.) This dough had the appropriate wet texture, and it turned out a flavorful loaf—thanks to some whole-wheat flour and a slow overnight fermentation.

▶ See How to Shape It
A step-by-step video is available at CooksIllustrated.com/apr16

It was also convenient since it proofed in the fridge overnight, allowing for some flexibility as to when it could be shaped and baked.

Here's how that dough comes together: First, sift whole-wheat flour to remove the larger pieces of sharp-edged bran, which would otherwise interfere with gluten formation and compromise the dough's structure. In a stand mixer, combine the sifted whole-wheat flour with all-purpose flour, yeast, salt, and water. Knead the mixture to form a cohesive dough, and then transfer it to a bowl and give it a series of gentle folds every 30 minutes for 2 hours, by which time the consistency will be smooth and the gluten well developed. (Folding the dough to develop gluten slowly, rather than mixing it fully right from the start, helps develop a light, airy, and irregular crumb.)

Fougasse Timeline

DAY BEFORE BAKING:
- Mix dough; let rest for **30 minutes.**
- Fold dough and let rise for **30 minutes**; repeat, folding 3 more times for **2 hours** total.
- Refrigerate for **16 to 48 hours.**

DAY OF BAKING:
- Create 2 rough triangles; let rest for **30 minutes to 1 hour.**
- Roll and cut first loaf; let rest for **30 to 45 minutes.**
- **20 minutes** after shaping first loaf, roll and cut second loaf.

I made a batch of this dough and put it in the fridge to rise slowly overnight. The following morning, I considered possible shapes. Some bakers make sand dollar–shaped fougasse; others fashion a ladder-like pattern. But the most typical form is a leaf shape with a long central "vein" cut surrounded by shorter angled ones.

I opted to start with the leaf shape, so I patted half the dough into a rough 8-inch-long leaf. I cut slits in the dough to create a vein pattern and carefully transferred it to a sheet of parchment paper to proof, opening up the cuts to accentuate the form. Thirty minutes later, the dough was puffy and ready to bake, so I placed it on a baking stone that I'd preheated on the upper rack of a 500-degree oven. The hot stone helped the bread spring up quickly, ensuring good stature. After 20 minutes, the fougasse was crisp and brown and, following a brief cooling period, ready to sample.

The baguette formula made for a very good start indeed. The fougasse boasted an airy, open crumb; its crust was substantial; and the flavor was—as expected—wonderful. But it wasn't entirely perfect. For starters, parts of the crust were a little too tough, especially where it was overly browned or even verging on burnt. Plus, the browning was spotty. Most important, my fougasse was not so much leaf-shaped as it was amoeboid: uneven in thickness and anything but symmetrical. Clearly, my shaping and cutting technique left something to be desired. But that would come with practice; first I needed to perfect the baking method.

Evening out the browning of the crust was relatively easy: I simply dropped the baking stone to the lower-middle rack and reduced the oven temperature to 450 degrees, both of which slowed things down enough to even out the browning and prevent the loaves from getting too dark before they were fully baked.

To make the crust less hard, I first tried adding olive oil to the dough, as I'd seen in some recipes.

MAKING LEAF-SHAPED FOUGASSE

Before being shaped and cut, the dough pieces are rolled into rough triangles and then left to rest.

I. Roll dough into triangular shape with 8-inch base and 10-inch sides, about ½ inch thick.

2. Make 6-inch-long cut in center, leaving 1½-inch border. Make three 2- to 3-inch diagonal cuts on each side, leaving 1-inch border.

3. Gently stretch dough to widen cuts and emphasize leaf shape; loaf should measure about 10 by 12 inches.

Why Add Whole Wheat?

Blending a small amount of whole-wheat flour into our fougasse dough gives the bread complexity and depth, thanks to the nutty-tasting bran. This outer layer of the grain is stripped away from the grain in refined flour. The only trick: Since the large pieces of bran have sharp edges that can cut gluten strands and inhibit rise, we sift the whole-wheat flour first.

Sure enough, this was effective at eliminating any overly crunchy spots—so much so that there was no trace of crispness left. Brushing the bread with oil before it went into the oven worked much better, producing a delicate, almost fried crispness.

Shape, Stretch, and Cut

With that, I moved on to the shaping and cutting technique. There were three main areas to finesse: evening out the thickness of the dough, improving the symmetry of the overall shape, and achieving nicely formed, distinct openings.

The uneven dough thickness was fixed by switching from stretching the dough by hand to using a rolling pin. Normally I'd eschew the use of a pin when shaping dough, especially one that is meant to be airy, since it would be apt to press out too much gas. However, used gently, a rolling pin proved to be the ideal tool for ensuring a level result.

As for the overall shape of the loaf, this was best addressed early on in the process. Trying to coax a ball of dough into a leaf shape is difficult since gluten causes the dough to tighten up and spring back under your hands. A better approach was to preshape the refrigerated dough into a rough triangle, let it rest for 30 minutes to 1 hour to allow the gluten to relax, and then roll it into the finished shape.

As for the cutting itself, bakers typically use a metal bench scraper, pressing it straight through the

Alternative Shapes

For instructions on creating these shapes, go to CooksIllustrated.com/ fougasseshapes.

SAND DOLLAR   **LADDER**

dough to the counter. (A regular knife tends to drag through the dough, causing it to tear.) My 6-inch bench scraper did a fine job when the openings needed to be at least as long as the tool, but anything shorter required another implement. I found that a pizza wheel worked nicely for cuts of any length.

And there I had it: a fougasse that was delicious, beautiful, and best of all, fairly simple to make. In fact, I would recommend it as a starting point for any baker wanting to experiment with artisanal loaves.

FOUGASSE
MAKES 2 LOAVES

If you can't find King Arthur all-purpose flour, you can substitute bread flour. For the best results, weigh your ingredients. You'll also need to plan ahead: The dough needs to rise in the refrigerator for at least 16 hours. For our free recipes for Fougasse with Asiago and Black Pepper, Fougasse with Bacon and Gruyère, and Olive Fougasse, go to CooksIllustrated.com/apr16.

  ¼   cup (1⅓ ounces) whole-wheat flour
  3   cups (15 ounces) King Arthur all-purpose flour
      Salt
  1   teaspoon instant or rapid-rise yeast
1½   cups (12 ounces) water
      Cornmeal or semolina flour
  ¼   cup extra-virgin olive oil
  1   tablespoon chopped fresh rosemary
  2   teaspoons coarse sea salt

1. Sift whole-wheat flour through fine-mesh strainer into bowl of stand mixer; discard bran remaining in strainer. Add all-purpose flour, 1½ teaspoons salt, and yeast to mixer bowl. Fit stand mixer with dough hook, add water, and knead on low speed until cohesive dough forms and no dry flour remains, 5 to 7 minutes. Transfer dough to lightly oiled large bowl, cover with plastic wrap, and let rest at room temperature for 30 minutes.

2. Holding edge of dough with your fingertips, fold dough over itself by gently lifting and folding edge of dough toward center. Turn bowl 45 degrees;

fold again. Turn bowl and fold dough 6 more times (total of 8 folds). Cover with plastic and let rise for 30 minutes. Repeat folding and rising every 30 minutes, 3 more times. After fourth set of folds, cover bowl tightly with plastic and refrigerate for at least 16 hours or up to 48 hours.

3. Transfer dough to lightly floured counter, stretch gently into 8-inch round (do not deflate), and divide in half. Working with one piece of dough at a time, gently stretch and fold over 3 sides of dough to create rough triangle with 5-inch sides. Transfer to lightly floured rimmed baking sheet, seam side down, and repeat with remaining piece of dough. Cover dough loosely with plastic lightly coated with vegetable oil spray and let rest at room temperature until dough is relaxed and no longer cool to the touch, 30 minutes to 1 hour.

4. Place baking stone on lower-middle rack of oven and heat oven to 450 degrees. Line two overturned rimmed baking sheets with parchment paper and dust liberally with cornmeal. Transfer one piece of dough to lightly floured counter and, using rolling pin, gently roll into triangular shape with 8-inch base and 10-inch sides, about ½ inch thick. Transfer dough to parchment with base facing short side of pan.

5. Using pizza cutter, make 6-inch-long cut down center of triangle, through dough to sheet, leaving about 1½ inches at either end. Make three 2- to 3-inch diagonal cuts through dough on each side of center cut, leaving 1-inch border on each end of cuts, to create leaf-vein pattern (cuts should not connect to one another or to edges of dough).

6. Gently stretch dough toward sides of pan to widen cuts and emphasize leaf shape; overall size of loaf should measure about 10 by 12 inches. Cover loosely with plastic lightly coated with oil spray and let rest at room temperature until nearly doubled in size, 30 to 45 minutes. Twenty minutes after shaping first loaf, repeat rolling, cutting, and shaping with second piece of dough. (Staggering shaping of loaves will allow them to be baked in succession.)

7. Brush top and sides of first loaf with 2 tablespoons oil. Sprinkle loaf evenly with 1½ teaspoons rosemary and 1 teaspoon coarse salt. Using pizza peel, transfer loaf, on parchment, to baking stone and bake until golden brown, 18 to 22 minutes, rotating parchment halfway through baking. Transfer to wire rack and let cool for at least 15 minutes before serving. Repeat topping and baking with second loaf.

Introducing Persian Rice

Iran's national dish takes rice to a whole new level, with perfectly plump, separate grains and a crispy, buttery, nutty-tasting crust.

⋝ BY ANNIE PETITO ⋜

To Americans, rice is an everyday side dish made with minimal fuss. But in Iran, a rice pilaf known as *chelow* (pronounced CHEH-lo) is one of the most important dishes in the cuisine—and actually defines a cook's reputation in the kitchen. What makes the dish so good is contrast: a marriage of unusually light and fluffy grains with a golden-brown, crispy crust that's so buttery that you can't help but go back for more. It's a showpiece pilaf.

The trade-off has always been the effort involved, as most shortcut recipes yield gummy, overcooked rice and pale, flavorless crusts. The best versions I've made call for rinsing the rice before soaking it for 24 hours, parboiling it, packing some of the rice down in hot oil to make a crust, and mounding the rest on top. The whole thing is then steamed for over an hour before being turned out onto a platter.

My goal was a middle-ground approach, where I'd streamline the best versions without sacrificing the pilaf's defining qualities.

Treat It Right

Traditional recipes call for Persian rice, which isn't readily available in the United States, so nutty and aromatic long-grain basmati rice is the usual substitute (for information on shopping for basmati rice, see "Seeking Out Authentic Basmati" on page 29). As for the cooking vessel, since the size of the pot's base determines the size of the crust and I wanted plenty to go around, I grabbed a large, wide Dutch oven.

I started by focusing on the pilaf portion of the rice—specifically, the rinsing and soaking steps. Starch granules are the primary component of rice; as the granules absorb water during cooking, they swell and can eventually burst, releasing gummy starch molecules that glue the grains together. Rinsing was a must to remove excess surface starch that would otherwise swell and burst. Soaking, meanwhile, helps hydrate the grains before cooking. But was it necessary?

▶ Watch Every Step
A step-by-step video is available at CooksIllustrated.com/apr16

Adding yogurt to the rice that forms the crust on the bottom of the pot enriches the crust's flavor and helps make it easier to remove.

A quick test comparing rice that was rinsed and then soaked for 24 hours with rice that was only rinsed confirmed that both rinsing and soaking yielded fluffier pilaf with more separate grains. After a few more tests and some analysis, I determined that a 15-minute bath in hot tap water provided almost as much hydration as a 24-hour soak—the grains' presoak weight increased by 25 percent and 29 percent, respectively. Taste tests confirmed that there was little difference; a 15-minute hot soak and a 24-hour room-temperature soak produced grains that were equally fluffy and individual. I also discovered that adding salt to the water seasoned the grains for better flavor.

Besides the two-step prep process, the recipes from my research called for a two-stage cooking process: The rice is first parboiled in plenty of water and then drained and steamed in a well-oiled pot. Eliminating the parboiling step wasn't an option, since the rice is steamed in too little water for the grains to cook fully and evenly. But accurately timing the parboiling step proved critical. I found that I needed to start timing from the moment I added the rice to the water.

Thanks to the jump start that soaking had given the rice, it needed only 3 to 5 minutes in the pot to reach al dente. I also found that transferring the rice to a strainer and rinsing it under cool water before moving on to the steaming step helped avoid overcooking.

The second cooking stage is really a hybrid of steaming and frying. Recipes call for adding fat (I opted for oil) to the empty pot, packing in a layer of rice for the crust, and then adding the rest of the rice and drizzling it with water. After an initial blast of high heat to jump-start the crust formation, I reduced the heat and let the rice steam. In Iran, a special cloth "shower cap" is wrapped around the lid to pull excess moisture from the rice as it steams. The test kitchen does a similar thing with rice pilaf—we place a dish towel under the lid after cooking to absorb moisture—so I knew that a step like this would be worth it. Some recipes note that the longer the rice is steamed, the drier and fluffier the grains will be, but I found that 30 minutes did the trick—longer stints made a nominal difference. The pilaf portion of the rice was the fluffiest I'd ever made, so now I could move on to the crust, or *tahdig* (pronounced ta-DEEG), which needed some work.

Ta-da, Tahdig

I wanted a tahdig that was deep golden brown, with a crunchy—but not tough—texture and a rich, nutty-buttery, toasted flavor. But my results tasted somewhat lean and bland, the grains cooked a bit unevenly, and I also had some problems getting it out of the pot. I knew how to fix the uneven cooking problem. When packing the rice into the pot, the grains inevitably started cooking as soon as they hit the hot oil. So I moved the operation off the heat. I stirred the oil and rice together in a bowl, packed the mixture into the pot off heat, and only then moved it onto the stove.

Some recipes called for mixing beaten egg or plain yogurt into the rice before spreading it into the pot to both enrich the flavor and bind the grains to help the crust come out more easily. The egg's flavor was a bit too distinct, but Greek yogurt added richness without identifying itself. What's more, the proteins in the yogurt helped facilitate browning for improved flavor.

But the crust was still not exactly easy to get out of the pot. Brushing a tablespoon of oil on the sides and bottom of the pot was helpful in this regard but

Special Occasion Rice

There are four main styles of rice preparation in Iran, and *chelow* (top right) is often reserved for special occasions to impress guests with its beautiful crust and perfectly separate grains. The crust is sometimes presented intact to be broken up at the table. Here, it is served alongside salads, lavash bread, and cherries.

still not perfect. In the end, tradition had the answer: Set the pot on a dampened dish towel or dip it into cool water after the rice finishes cooking. The rapid cooling causes the rice grains to contract, helping the crust release more easily. It seemed easier to let the pot sit on a damp towel, so I went with that approach. Just 5 minutes was all it took to get the rice to slip easily out of the Dutch oven with the help of a spatula.

Once the rice is cooked, some cooks flip the whole dish onto a platter. While this can look impressive, it's tricky to pull off. I found it much easier to scoop the rice onto a platter, use a thin metal spatula to break the crust into shards as I removed it from the pot, and then arrange the crispy pieces around the pilaf.

For my last tweak to the process, I considered how I'd been putting the parboiled rice back in the pot. After packing down the rice for the crust, traditional recipes call for mounding the remainder in a pyramid shape on top. Was this really necessary? As it turned out, yes. When I simply poured the rice into the pot and spread it out evenly, steam couldn't escape from the bottom of the pot as easily, and the crust cooked up chewy instead of crispy.

Final Flavors

Both the pilaf portion and the crust looked impressive, and the flavor was close but needed a few tweaks. Some recipes call for pouring oil over the rice for enrichment, but I followed the lead of recipes that opted to use butter, poking holes into the mounded rice and inserting bits of butter into them. This added the flavor and richness the rice needed. (The water in the butter contributed a little extra steaming power, too.) For more complexity, I looked to the spice rack. Many recipes call for saffron, but I was satisfied with simple (and more affordable) whole cumin seeds, which added a distinct earthiness. Finally, some chopped parsley lent fresh, bright flavor and color.

The light, fluffy rice and golden, buttery shards of crust were a huge hit, immediately winning over those who weren't familiar with the dish. When I'm serving rice and want to impress, this is the recipe I'll turn to.

PERSIAN-STYLE RICE WITH GOLDEN CRUST (CHELOW)
SERVES 6

We prefer the nutty flavor and texture of basmati rice, but Texmati or another long-grain rice will work. For the best results, use a Dutch oven with a bottom diameter between 8½ and 10 inches. It is important not to overcook the rice during the parboiling step, as it will continue to cook during steaming. Begin checking the rice at the lower end of the given time range. Do not skip placing the pot on a damp towel in step 7—doing so will help free the crust from the pot. Serve this pilaf alongside stews or kebabs.

- 2 cups basmati rice
- Salt
- 1 tablespoon plus ¼ cup vegetable oil
- ¼ cup plain Greek yogurt
- 1½ teaspoons cumin seeds
- 2 tablespoons unsalted butter, cut into 8 cubes
- ¼ cup minced fresh parsley

1. Place rice in fine-mesh strainer and rinse under cold running water until water runs clear. Place rinsed rice and 1 tablespoon salt in medium bowl and cover with 4 cups hot tap water. Stir gently to dissolve salt; let stand for 15 minutes. Drain rice in fine-mesh strainer.

2. Meanwhile, bring 8 cups water to boil in Dutch oven over high heat. Add rice and 2 tablespoons salt. Boil briskly, stirring frequently, until rice is mostly tender with slight bite in center and grains are floating toward top of pot, 3 to 5 minutes (begin timing from when rice is added to pot).

3. Drain rice in large fine-mesh strainer and rinse with cold water to stop cooking, about 30 seconds. Rinse and dry pot well to remove any residual starch. Brush bottom and 1 inch up sides of pot with 1 tablespoon oil.

4. Whisk remaining ¼ cup oil, yogurt, 1 teaspoon cumin seeds, and ¼ teaspoon salt together in medium bowl. Add 2 cups parcooked rice and stir until combined. Spread yogurt-rice mixture evenly over bottom of prepared pot, packing it down well.

5. Stir remaining ½ teaspoon cumin seeds into remaining rice. Mound rice in center of pot on top of yogurt-rice base (it should look like small hill). Poke 8 equally spaced holes through rice mound but not into yogurt-rice base. Place 1 butter cube in each hole. Drizzle ⅓ cup water over rice mound.

6. Wrap pot lid with clean dish towel and cover pot tightly, making sure towel is secure on top of lid and away from heat. Cook over medium-high heat until rice on bottom is crackling and steam is coming from sides of pot, about 10 minutes, rotating pot halfway through for even cooking.

7. Reduce heat to medium-low and continue to cook until rice is tender and fluffy and crust is golden brown around edges, 30 to 35 minutes longer. Remove covered pot from heat and place on damp dish towel set in rimmed baking sheet; let stand for 5 minutes.

8. Stir 2 tablespoons parsley into rice, making sure not to disturb crust on bottom of pot, and season with salt to taste. Gently spoon rice onto serving platter.

9. Using thin metal spatula, loosen edges of crust from pot, then break crust into large pieces. Transfer pieces to serving platter, arranging evenly around rice. Sprinkle with remaining 2 tablespoons parsley and serve.

A Blueprint for the Best Rice You'll Ever Eat

This is no ordinary side dish. The combination of fluffy rice pilaf and the crispy, browned crust can't help but make *chelow* a star attraction. After the rice has been rinsed, soaked, and parboiled, it is steamed in a Dutch oven. The unusual setup is key to producing rice with two very distinct textures in a single pot.

GREASED POT
Helps with crust removal

POCKETS OF BUTTER
Add flavor and more steam during cooking for even fluffier rice

PACKED RICE LAYER
Creates evenly browned, crispy crust

TOWEL-WRAPPED LID
Absorbs excess moisture for fluffy, not gummy, rice

MOUNDED RICE
Allows steam to escape so rice crust beneath cooks up crispy, not soggy

DAMP TOWEL
Makes grains contract to help *tahdig* release from pot

Easy-Peel Hard-Cooked Eggs

You no longer need to fear the drudgery of peeling hard-cooked eggs— with the right cooking method, the shells practically fly off.

⇒ BY ANDREA GEARY ⇐

The test kitchen has a sure-fire method for producing perfect hard-cooked eggs: Put the eggs in a saucepan, cover them with an inch of cold water, bring the water to a boil, cover the pot, let the eggs sit off the heat in the cooling water for 10 minutes, and then transfer them to an ice bath for 5 minutes before peeling. You'll get tender whites and uniformly opaque (but not chalky) yolks every time.

But eggs cooked this way can be difficult to peel—a problem that has more to do with the membrane that lines the shell than with the shell itself. When that membrane cements itself to the egg, it must be painstakingly peeled away and often takes pieces of the white with it, leaving an unappealingly pitted exterior—an unacceptable result when you need flawless eggs for deviled eggs or garnishing a salad.

The Impact of Age

"Fresh eggs are harder to peel than older eggs." This piece of conventional wisdom seemed like the natural place to start my testing. Could the key to success really be as simple as choosing the proper eggs to cook?

Here's the science behind the claim: The white in a fresh egg is slightly alkaline. As the egg ages, the white becomes more alkaline as the dissolved carbon dioxide (a weak acid) it contains dissipates—and the more alkaline the white, the easier it is to peel when cooked. Why? Because the higher alkalinity causes the egg white proteins to bond to each other, not to the membrane directly under the shell. That's the theory, anyway.

To test it, I used our foolproof method to cook 18 fresh and 18 month-old eggs, peeling them all right after they'd cooled. As expected, many of the fresh eggs were difficult to peel, and a few were downright impossible. But the older eggs weren't a guarantee for easy peeling either—some were actually quite difficult—so I moved on.

> ▶ **See How Easily They Peel**
> A step-by-step video is available
> at CooksIllustrated.com/apr16

The key to easy peeling isn't about the age of the eggs. It's about the starting temperature of the water.

Environmental Influences

Having exhausted my options in terms of ingredients (there was only one), I moved on to the cooking method. Our foolproof approach makes it impossible to overcook the eggs, but if another method would make peeling easier, I was willing to branch out.

I compared five methods—our foolproof method, boiling in already-boiling water, steaming in a pressure cooker, steaming over boiling water, and baking—cooking 10 eggs each way and peeling them all right after cooling them in a 5-minute ice bath.

I graded each method from A to F: If most of the eggs cooked a certain way peeled easily, the method got an A. If the shell clung stubbornly to most of the eggs, forcing me to tear the whites, it received a lesser grade.

The foolproof and baking methods produced eggs that were challenging to peel; they each scored a C (but unlike the nicely cooked foolproof eggs, the baked ones sported green rings around their yolks). The pressure-cooked eggs were nicely cooked, and the method earned a B. But the steaming and

boiling methods each earned an A. Their shells slipped off to reveal perfectly smooth whites. What made them (and the pressure-cooked eggs) succeed?

Peeling Away the Answer

The only real common denominator of the boiled and steamed eggs was that both went directly into a hot environment, whereas eggs cooked by our foolproof method started out cold and warmed up slowly as the water came up to a boil. The baked eggs also qualified as using a cold start because the oven's air is a slow and inefficient conductor of energy.

Our science editor explained what was happening: Plunging raw eggs into boiling water (or hot steam) rapidly denatures the outermost proteins of the white, which reduces their ability to bond with the membrane. Plus, those rapidly denaturing proteins shrink as they start to bond together, and that causes the white to pull away from the membrane. Thus, these eggs are easy to peel. (The pressure-cooked eggs are a unique case: Though they start out in cold water, the water gets hot very rapidly and can reach as high as 250 degrees, which likely causes additional shrinkage of the proteins, making the eggs easy to peel.) Conversely, proteins that rise in temperature slowly, as in the eggs started in cold water or baked in the oven, have more time to bond to the membrane before they bond with each other, so the membrane is difficult to remove.

SCIENCE **Blame the Membrane**
Most cooks assume that when an egg is difficult to peel, it's because the shell is sticking to the egg white. But it's the membrane between the shell and the white that's really the problem. When an egg is very fresh or when it's cooked slowly, the proteins in the white bond to the membrane instead of to one another, and the membrane becomes cemented to the white and impossible to peel away. The solution: Plunging the eggs directly into hot steam, which causes the egg white proteins to denature and shrink, reducing their ability to bond with the membrane.

A Report Card on Peelability

We compared five methods, cooking 10 eggs per method and peeling them all after letting them cool for 5 minutes in an ice bath. We then assigned a grade to each method based on the condition of the peeled eggs. Our takeaway: The steaming and boiling methods each earned an A, as nine of the 10 peeled eggs cooked each way were flawlessly smooth.

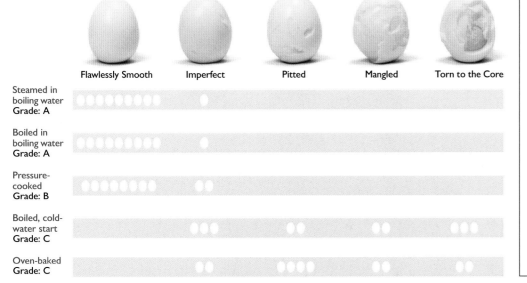

	Flawlessly Smooth	Imperfect	Pitted	Mangled	Torn to the Core
Steamed in boiling water Grade: A	●●●●●●●●●	●			
Boiled in boiling water Grade: A	●●●●●●●●●	●			
Pressure-cooked Grade: B	●●●●●●●●	●●			
Boiled, cold-water start Grade: C		●●●	●●	●●	●●●
Oven-baked Grade: C		●●	●●●●	●●	●●

Peel Six Eggs in 41 Seconds!

Combined with our hot-start cooking method, this novel approach to peeling is so efficient that the shells slip right off. Instead of preparing the ice bath in a bowl, use a plastic container with a tight-fitting lid. Once the eggs are chilled, pour off half the water and, holding the lid in place, shake the container vigorously using a vertical motion (the eggs will hit the top of the container) until the shells are cracked all over, about 40 shakes. Peel, rinse, and use as desired.

Full Steam Ahead

As for which hot-start method it would be—steaming or boiling—I had an idea. When I developed a recipe for Soft-Cooked Eggs (January/February 2013), I determined that steaming was a superior method to boiling because adding eggs to a pot of boiling water lowers the temperature of the water, making it hard to nail down a precise cooking time that will give you dependable results every time. Eggs that steam in a steamer basket, on the other hand, don't touch the water, which means they don't lower the water temperature, so the same cooking time produces consistently perfect results. Plus, steaming is faster because there's less water to bring to a boil.

To prove the point, I compared the two methods: I filled one saucepan with water, brought the water to a boil, carefully lowered six eggs into the water, covered the pot, and then turned down the heat slightly so the eggs wouldn't jostle and break. In another saucepan, I brought 1 inch of water to a boil and then placed a steamer basket loaded with six eggs into it before covering the pot. After 13 minutes (which a few tests showed was ideal), I transferred all the eggs to an ice bath and chilled them for 15 minutes.

Sure enough, I preferred the texture of the steamed eggs. Their yolks were uniformly cooked but not chalky, while the yolks of the boiled eggs were just a tiny bit translucent at the center, just a bit undercooked—likely due to a temporary dip in temperature when the cold eggs went in.

I had one last challenge: Would my steaming method make even notoriously difficult fresh eggs easy to peel? Indeed it did. I was able to peel six eggs in just over 2 minutes. (When I used a novel method of enclosing eggs in a plastic container with water and shaking them vigorously, I cut that time to mere seconds. See "Peel Six Eggs in 41 Seconds!")

I was so pleased that I decided to showcase the eggs' beautifully smooth exteriors by making deviled eggs. The test kitchen already has a recipe for the classic version, so I created a few new approaches: curry, bacon-chive, and chipotle pepper with pickled radishes. Thanks to my new cooking method, throwing these together couldn't have been easier.

EASY-PEEL HARD-COOKED EGGS
MAKES 6 EGGS

Be sure to use large eggs that have no cracks and are cold from the refrigerator. If you don't have a steamer basket, use a spoon or tongs to gently place the eggs in the water. It does not matter if the eggs are above the water or partially submerged. You can use this method for fewer than six eggs without altering the timing. You can also double this recipe as long as you use a pot and steamer basket large enough to hold the eggs in a single layer. There's no need to peel the eggs right away. They can be stored in their shells and peeled when needed.

6   large eggs

1. Bring 1 inch water to rolling boil in medium saucepan over high heat. Place eggs in steamer basket. Transfer basket to saucepan. Cover, reduce heat to medium-low, and cook eggs for 13 minutes.

2. When eggs are almost finished cooking, combine 2 cups ice cubes and 2 cups cold water in medium bowl. Using tongs or spoon, transfer eggs to ice bath; let sit for 15 minutes. Peel before using.

CURRY DEVILED EGGS
MAKES 12 EGGS

To slice eggs, lay each egg on its side and sweep the blade cleanly down the center. Wipe the knife after each egg. You may use either regular or reduced-fat mayonnaise in this recipe. If preferred, use a pastry bag fitted with a large plain or star tip to fill the egg halves. For our free recipes for Bacon and Chive Deviled Eggs and Chipotle Deviled Eggs with Pickled Radishes, go to CooksIllustrated.com/apr16.

1   recipe Easy-Peel Hard-Cooked Eggs
3   tablespoons mayonnaise
1   tablespoon minced fresh parsley, plus 12 small whole parsley leaves for garnishing
1½   teaspoons lemon juice
1   teaspoon Dijon mustard
1   teaspoon curry powder
        Pinch cayenne pepper

1. Slice each egg in half lengthwise with paring knife. Transfer yolks to bowl; arrange whites on serving platter. Mash yolks with fork until no large lumps remain. Add mayonnaise and use rubber spatula to smear mixture against side of bowl until thick, smooth paste forms, 1 to 2 minutes. Add minced parsley, lemon juice, mustard, curry powder, and cayenne and mix until fully incorporated.

2. Transfer yolk mixture to small, heavy-duty plastic bag. Press mixture into 1 corner and twist top of bag. Using scissors, snip ½ inch off filled corner. Squeezing bag, distribute yolk mixture evenly among egg white halves. Garnish each egg half with parsley leaf and serve.

Homemade Corned Beef

Once you find the right curing method, corning beef requires no work, just time. And the results are superb.

⇒ BY LAN LAM ⇐

You can make a decent corned beef dinner by buying a corned beef brisket, simmering it in a big pot of water for a few hours, and adding carrots, potatoes, and cabbage at the end of cooking so they soak up some of the seasoned liquid. But you can make a superb corned beef if you skip the commercially made stuff and "corn" the meat yourself. (The Old English term refers to the "corns," or kernels of salt, used to cure the meat for preservation.) When this curing process is done properly, the meat isn't just generically salty (or overly salty, as commercial versions often are). It's seasoned but balanced, with complex flavor thanks to the presence of aromatics and spices. And although the process takes several days, it's almost entirely hands-off.

I'd never corned beef but had always wanted to try. In addition to having an easy one-dish meal for serving a crowd, I could use the leftover corned beef in sandwiches and hash. The trick would be figuring out just the right curing formula and length of time to produce tender, well-seasoned meat.

In Search of a Cure

I knew I'd be using a flat-cut brisket, the most common cut for corned beef. As for the curing method, I had two options: wet or dry. Wet curing works much like brining: You submerge the meat in a solution of table and curing, or "pink," salt (more on that later) and water along with seasonings. Over time, the salt penetrates the meat, seasoning it and altering its proteins so that they retain moisture. Dry curing works more like salting: The meat gets rubbed with the salt mixture and seasonings, wrapped in plastic wrap, and weighed down with a heavy plate or pot. As the meat sits, the salt draws water out of it, creating a superconcentrated brine. To expose all of the meat to the brine, the meat is flipped daily. Whichever approach you use, the cured brisket gets simmered in water to break down its abundant

Simmering the vegetables in the meaty cooking liquid seasons them nicely.

collagen, the connective tissue that converts to gelatin during cooking and coats the meat fibers so that they appear more tender and juicy.

I tried both methods, wet-curing one 5-pound flat-cut brisket for seven days and dry-curing another for 10, the average length of time for each method that I found in recipes, to see how the flavor of the cured meats would differ. (For now, I left out the pink salt and seasonings.) I placed each in a Dutch oven with water and simmered them for 5 hours, which was a bit fussy since I had to adjust the stove dial to ensure

gentle heat. The briskets tasted virtually the same, so I moved ahead with the wet cure, which was considerably faster and easier, with no need for daily flipping.

(Not Just) Pretty in Pink

Now for the pink salt. This specialty product (which is dyed pink to distinguish it from conventional salt) is a mixture of sodium chloride (table salt) and sodium nitrite. Only a small amount, combined with conventional table salt, is needed for curing. Nitrites prevent the oxidation of fats, which would otherwise lead to off-flavors and certain types of bacterial growth, especially *Clostridium botulinum*. Hence, their preservative effect. They're also responsible for the attractive pink color of cured meats.

Since I wasn't relying on the pink salt for preservation, I wanted to confirm that it improved the flavor of the brisket, not just its color. I cured one with pink salt and one without and then offered both up to blindfolded tasters. The results were close, but the majority of tasters preferred the flavor of the pink salt batch. Plus, once the blindfolds came off, every single taster preferred the rosy-hued meat. With that, I knew pink salt was a must. (For more information, see "Can You Taste the Pink?")

Finally, the seasonings: garlic cloves, allspice berries, bay leaves, coriander seeds, and brown sugar—the flavors of which truly put the meat a notch above commercial corned beef.

As for how long to cure the meat, I'd been following recipes from my research that called for seven days, but others called for as few as four—and both seemed rather arbitrary. I wanted a more precise

Calculating a Cure to the Core

By removing and simmering a core sample of the brisket each day, we learned that the pink color—the indication that the meat was cured—moved inward ¼ inch per day on all sides. Thus, a brisket that was 2½ to 3 inches thick required six days to thoroughly cure.

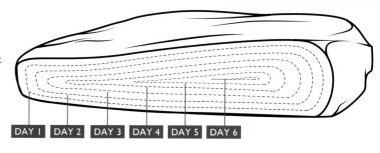

DAY 1 DAY 2 DAY 3 DAY 4 DAY 5 DAY 6

method to determine when the meat was thoroughly cured, and I realized that the pink salt could help.

I started another batch and removed a sample of the core from the brisket each day, simmering them (the meat's color only changes when it's cooked) and looking for the point at which the center of the meat turned distinctly pink. The pink crept inward about ¼ inch per day. For the 2½- to 3-inch briskets I was using, that meant a six-day cure was the answer.

Slow and Steady

I wanted to try simmering the brisket in the oven, a method we often use when braising meat because the heat is more gentle and even. Waiting for the water to come to a boil in the oven would greatly prolong the cooking time, so I added the meat (rinsed first to remove the loose spices) and brought the water to a simmer on the stove before moving the pot to a 275-degree oven.

Three hours later, the brisket was fork-tender, at which point I transferred it to a platter to rest, ladling over some of the cooking liquid to keep it moist. Then I moved the pot back to the stove and cooked the vegetables in the meaty liquid: carrots and red potatoes (added first so they cooked through) as well as cabbage wedges. As they simmered, I sliced the brisket thinly against the grain, which ensures that each bite is tender.

Texturally, the meat and vegetables were spot-on, but both components tasted a tad washed-out, so I added a cheesecloth bundle of more garlic and curing spices to the cooking liquid (the cheesecloth meant I didn't have to pluck out any stray spices). This added subtle but clear depth to the dish, which was as impressive-looking as it had been easy to prepare—and so very worth making from scratch.

HOME-CORNED BEEF WITH VEGETABLES
SERVES 8 TO 10

Pink curing salt #1, which can be purchased online or in stores specializing in meat curing, is a mixture of table salt and nitrites; it is also called Prague Powder #1, Insta Cure #1, or DQ Curing Salt #1. In addition to the pink salt, we use table salt here. If using Diamond Crystal kosher salt, increase the salt to 1½ cups; if using Morton kosher salt, increase to 1⅛ cups. This recipe requires six days to corn the beef, and you will need cheesecloth. Look for a uniformly thick brisket to ensure that the beef cures evenly. The brisket will look gray after curing but will turn pink once cooked. For tips on purchasing brisket, see page 28.

Corned Beef
- 1 (4½- to 5-pound) beef brisket, flat cut
- ¾ cup salt
- ½ cup packed brown sugar
- 2 teaspoons pink curing salt #1
- 6 garlic cloves, peeled
- 6 bay leaves
- 5 allspice berries
- 2 tablespoons peppercorns
- 1 tablespoon coriander seeds

Vegetables
- 6 carrots, peeled, halved crosswise, thick ends halved lengthwise
- 1½ pounds small red potatoes, unpeeled
- 1 head green cabbage (2 pounds), uncored, cut into 8 wedges

1. FOR THE CORNED BEEF: Trim fat on surface of brisket to ⅛ inch. Dissolve salt, sugar, and curing salt in 4 quarts water in large container. Add brisket, 3 garlic cloves, 4 bay leaves, allspice berries, 1 tablespoon peppercorns, and coriander seeds to brine. Weigh brisket down with plate, cover, and refrigerate for 6 days.

2. Adjust oven rack to middle position and heat oven to 275 degrees. Remove brisket from brine, rinse, and pat dry with paper towels. Cut 8-inch square triple thickness of cheesecloth. Place remaining 3 garlic cloves, remaining 2 bay leaves, and remaining 1 tablespoon peppercorns in center of cheesecloth and tie into bundle with kitchen twine. Place brisket, spice bundle, and 2 quarts water in Dutch oven. (Brisket may not lie flat but will shrink slightly as it cooks.)

3. Bring to simmer over high heat, cover, and transfer to oven. Cook until fork inserted into

thickest part of brisket slides in and out with ease, 2½ to 3 hours.

4. Remove pot from oven and turn off oven. Transfer brisket to large ovensafe platter, ladle 1 cup of cooking liquid over meat, cover, and return to oven to keep warm.

5. FOR THE VEGETABLES: Add carrots and potatoes to pot and bring to simmer over high heat. Reduce heat to medium-low, cover, and simmer until vegetables begin to soften, 7 to 10 minutes.

6. Add cabbage to pot, increase heat to high, and return to simmer. Reduce heat to low, cover, and simmer until all vegetables are tender, 12 to 15 minutes.

7. While vegetables cook, transfer beef to cutting board and slice ¼ inch thick against grain. Return beef to platter. Using slotted spoon, transfer vegetables to platter with beef. Moisten with additional broth and serve.

Homemade Chicken Broth Three Ways

Homemade broth brings everything to a higher level. With these simple recipes and tips, you may never go back to the commercial stuff. BY ELIZABETH BOMZE

BUILDING BLOCKS OF GOOD BROTH

Great chicken broth is like culinary liquid gold: a backbone of savory cooking that can transform even the simplest soup, sauce, rice, or pasta into something flavorful and satisfying. To work in a variety of applications, the broth should taste rich yet balanced and neutral—not assertive, vegetal, sour, or sweet. And unlike watery commercial broths, good homemade versions should boast gelatin-rich body. The first trick to a good broth is choosing the right ingredients.

What Parts Go in the Pot?

Historically, thrifty cooks made chicken broth with leftover carcasses or older hens that were too tough for eating. Today, most homemade versions use anything from a whole bird to scraps like backs and wings. To see which parts make the best broth, we compared four batches of broth made with 4 pounds of all wings, all backs, all legs, and a combination of backs and wings, choosing these parts because they contain relatively high levels of collagen. We deliberately left out breasts because they offer little collagen. We also opted to omit whole birds—they contain a high proportion of breast meat—and thighs, which offer similar traits to legs but cost more.

All four broths were flavorful and full-bodied, but the batch made with the combination of backs and wings offered the richest flavor and the most viscous consistency. The backs are full of collagen that breaks down into gelatin during cooking; they also contain a little muscle and fat. Wings boast a large amount of skin and multiple joints, both of which are abundant sources of collagen as well as flavorful meat, making them a better choice than legs, which contain fewer joints. Chicken backs are often available at supermarket butcher counters during colder months. You can also freeze backs if you butcher a whole chicken at home.

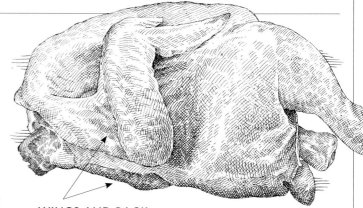

WINGS AND BACK:
Good sources of collagen and meat (and some fat)

Body Builder for Quicker Broths
Because our Quick and Cheater Chicken Broths don't call for a long simmering time (the latter isn't made with gelatin-rich bones or skin), they lack the body of our Classic Chicken Broth. But there's a quick fix: unflavored gelatin. Adding 1 teaspoon per cup of liquid gives these broths surprisingly good body.

For Clearer Broth, Simmer; Don't Boil

Boiling will cause soluble proteins and rendered fat from the meat to emulsify into the cooking liquid, turning it greasy and cloudy. By simmering, you minimize the amount of fat that gets emulsified, so the broth is clearer, and the sediment simply settles to the bottom of the pot, where it can be avoided.

KEEP IT SIMPLE
For the best flavor, we add only onion and bay leaves.

Minimize Other Flavors
Because we want our broths to taste as chicken-y as possible, we skip the traditional *mirepoix*—the mixture of chopped onions, carrots, and celery used as a base for soups and stews—as well as other popular additions like garlic and thyme. Instead, we use only chopped onion and bay leaves, which add just enough dimension and flavor to the broth without making it taste too vegetal.

SIMMERING	BOILING
Fine bubbles constantly breaking at the surface; wisps of steam	Large bubbles constantly breaking at the surface; heavy steam

TWO HANDY TOOLS

A good pot is critical for making broth—we use our favorite, the Le Creuset 7¼-Quart Round French Oven ($349.99)—and these two tools make the process easier and more efficient.

LAMSONSHARP 7-Inch Meat Cleaver ($48.00)
➤ This reasonably priced model offers a comfortable handle and a sharp blade.

CIA Masters Collection Fine-Mesh Strainer ($27.49)
➤ This model sits securely on most bowls, thanks to a wide bowl rest.

CLASSIC CHICKEN BROTH
MAKES ABOUT 8 CUPS

This classic approach to making chicken broth calls for gently simmering a mix of chicken backs and wings in water for several hours but requires almost no hands-on work. The long, slow simmer helps the bones and meat release both deep flavor and gelatin.

➤ Why Make This Broth
Rich flavor and body with very little hands-on work
　　Prep time: about 5 minutes
　　Cook time: about 5 hours

If you have a large pot (at least 12 quarts), you can easily double this recipe to make 1 gallon.

　4　pounds chicken backs and wings
3½　quarts water
　1　onion, chopped
　2　bay leaves
　2　teaspoons salt

1. Heat chicken and water in large stockpot or Dutch oven over medium-high heat until boiling, skimming off any scum that comes to the surface. Reduce heat to low and simmer gently for 3 hours.
2. Add onion, bay leaves, and salt and continue to simmer for another 2 hours.
3. Strain broth through fine-mesh strainer into large pot or container, pressing on solids to extract as much liquid as possible. Let broth settle for about 5 minutes, then skim off fat.

An Alternate Fat-Removal Method
If you do not plan to use the broth right away, you can refrigerate it and let the fat solidify. Use a wide, shallow spoon to skim the solidified fat from the surface and deposit it into another container to save for another use.

Save the Fat
Flavorful chicken fat makes a great substitute for butter or oil in a number of savory applications, such as sautéing aromatics, roasting root vegetables, and frying eggs. Store it in an airtight container in the refrigerator for up to one month or in the freezer for up to six months, adding more fat as desired.

QUICK CHICKEN BROTH
MAKES ABOUT 8 CUPS

When time is limited, this method ekes out remarkably rich flavor in a little over an hour. We chop the chicken into small pieces (more surface area means faster flavor extraction) and then brown and sweat them to draw out their flavorful juices before adding the cooking liquid.

➤ Why Make This Broth
Great flavor for the time it takes
　　Prep time: about 20 minutes
　　Cook time: about 60 minutes

A meat cleaver makes quick work of chopping the chicken into small pieces, but a hefty, sharp chef's knife will also work.

　1　tablespoon vegetable oil
　1　onion, chopped
　4　pounds chicken backs and wings, cut into 2-inch pieces
　2　quarts water
　8　teaspoons unflavored gelatin
　2　bay leaves
　2　teaspoons salt

1. Heat oil in large stockpot or Dutch oven over medium-high heat until shimmering. Add onion and cook until lightly browned and softened slightly, 2 to 3 minutes; transfer to large bowl.
2. Add half of chicken pieces and cook on both sides until lightly browned, 4 to 5 minutes. Transfer cooked chicken to bowl with onion. Repeat with remaining chicken pieces. Return onion and chicken pieces to pot, reduce heat to low, cover, and cook until chicken releases its juices, about 20 minutes.
3. Increase heat to high and add water, gelatin, bay leaves, and salt. Bring to simmer, then cover and barely simmer until broth is rich and flavorful, about 20 minutes, skimming off any scum that comes to surface.
4. Strain broth through fine-mesh strainer into large pot or container, pressing on solids to extract as much liquid as possible. Let broth settle for about 5 minutes, then skim off fat.

Best Way to Cool Broth
For safety reasons, the U.S. Food and Drug Administration (FDA) recommends cooling liquids to 70 degrees within 2 hours after cooking and 41 degrees within 4 hours after that.
　We found that the best way to cool down the hot liquid—without raising the temperature of the refrigerator and risking the spoilage of other food—is to first let the liquid cool to 85 degrees on the counter, which takes about an hour. At that point, it's safe to transfer to the fridge, and the total time it takes to cool to 41 degrees is 4 hours and 30 minutes—well within the FDA's recommended range.

CHEATER CHICKEN BROTH
MAKES ABOUT 8 CUPS

To quickly improve the flavor of commercial broth, we skip the bones and start by browning ground chicken, which has lots of surface area and thus gives up its flavor fast. Simmering the sautéed ground meat in the broth for just 30 minutes gives the broth a significant chicken-y boost.

➤ Why Make This Broth
An upgrade to commercial broth that's fast and easy
　　Prep time: about 5 minutes
　　Cook time: about 40 minutes

Since commercial chicken broth contains almost no fat, leave a little on the broth's surface when skimming to enhance its flavor. Both dark and white meat ground chicken will work in this recipe. Our favorite chicken broth is Swanson Chicken Stock.

　1　tablespoon vegetable oil
　1　pound ground chicken
　1　onion, chopped
　1　quart water
　1　quart chicken broth
　8　teaspoons unflavored gelatin
　2　bay leaves
　2　teaspoons salt

1. Heat oil in large saucepan over medium-high heat until shimmering. Add chicken and onion and cook, stirring frequently, until chicken is no longer pink, 5 to 10 minutes.
2. Add water, broth, gelatin, bay leaves, and salt and bring to simmer. Reduce heat to medium-low, cover, and cook for 30 minutes. Strain broth through fine-mesh strainer into large pot or container, pressing on solids to extract as much liquid as possible. Let broth settle for about 5 minutes, then skim off fat.

Freezing Broth in Portions
Portioning broth before freezing it makes it easy to defrost only as much as you need (from a few tablespoons for a sauce to a few cups for soup). Broth portions can be frozen for up to three months.

Ice cube trays or nonstick muffin tins
➤ Pour the broth into the tray or muffin cups. Once the portions are frozen, transfer them to a zipper-lock bag and freeze until needed.

Zipper-lock bags
➤ Pour the cooled broth into a zipper-lock bag placed in a 4-cup measuring cup (the cup holds the bag open so you can use both hands to pour). Seal the bag (double up for extra protection) and lay it flat to freeze.

Make-Ahead Vinaigrette

What if you could make a vinaigrette that would stay emulsified and taste great for a week?

≥ BY ANDREW JANJIGIAN ≤

I make a lot of salads, so I like to mix up a large batch of vinaigrette to last for several days. But no matter how carefully I whisk the oil into the other ingredients, it doesn't stay emulsified for long. Even our Foolproof Vinaigrette (September/October 2009) only holds together for a few hours—fine for dinner one night but not the next. One option is to rewhisk the dressing in a bowl, but it never truly comes back together.

But recently I stumbled on a potential solution in an unusual ingredient. Finding myself short on wine and sherry vinegars, I supplemented with some of the thick, syrupy aged balsamic vinegar that I would ordinarily drizzle on steak, good cheese, or berries. This vinaigrette had a thick, viscous consistency. Not only that—and this was key—but it had remarkable staying power. The mixture remained fully emulsified the next day and for several days after that. It wasn't until the week was nearly over that a thin layer of vinegar sat at the bottom of the jar—and even then, a quick shake was all it took to restore a tight emulsion. This was a dressing I wanted to investigate further.

The Three Ms

I wanted to create a basic recipe for long-lasting vinaigrette, a template in which I could switch up the acid, using any type of wine vinegar or even lemon juice. That meant I had to figure out what property of the aged balsamic gave the vinegar its remarkable hold on the emulsion. Once I had discovered that, I'd see if I could replicate the effect with other ingredients.

I thought the balsamic's high concentration of sugar might be the answer, since it's known to lend viscosity to dressings. I prepared two batches of Foolproof Vinaigrette, combining (for now) white wine vinegar, Dijon mustard (valuable for its tangy flavor and emulsifying properties), a touch of mayonnaise (another emulsifier), salt, and pepper, plus a few teaspoons of honey and maple syrup; then I whisked

> ▶ **Watch It Emulsify**
> Video available free for 4 months
> at CooksIllustrated.com/apr16

Our superstable vinaigrette keeps well in the fridge for days.

3 tablespoons of extra-virgin olive oil into each. Both sweeteners thickened up the dressing, but neither one produced a dressing that held for more than an hour or so.

It wasn't until I asked our science editor that we hit upon the key component: melanoidins. These compounds, abundant in aged balsamic vinegar, are formed when sugars and proteins are heated and undergo the Maillard reaction, the chemical reaction that generates deep browning and flavor. Because the molecules of these compounds are extremely large, they increase the viscosity of emulsions so much that it becomes difficult for the oil droplets to move around and coalesce into larger droplets and eventually separate from the water; thus, the dressing is very slow to separate. (Melanoidins also happen to be responsible for the aged vinegar's inky color.)

Knowing that, I did a search for other ingredients that contain similar concentrations of melanoidins, and sure enough, I found one sitting in my pantry: molasses. The trick would be to add enough of the gooey sugar syrup to stabilize the dressing but not so much that its flavor was pronounced, so I made more batches of the vinaigrette until I hit upon the ideal

combination: ¾ cup of extra-virgin olive oil, ¼ cup of vinegar (our standard ratio of oil to vinegar for a balanced vinaigrette), 1 tablespoon each of mustard and mayonnaise, and 1 tablespoon of light molasses (the dark, smoky blackstrap variety would taste too strong and bitter). The emulsion held for a week, and the dressing tasted even better than with the balsamic because the molasses's flavor wasn't as recognizable and left only a bit of background sweetness.

There were just two more questions to answer: If the melanoidins created such a strong emulsion, did I need the emulsifying powers of the mustard and mayonnaise? And was it necessary to slowly whisk in the olive oil, or could I simply shake the jar to mix the components?

I made three more batches of dressing, omitting the mustard in one, the mayo in a second, and both in a third. In each case the dressings lacked cohesion—particularly the mustard-free batch. The emulsion completely separated after just a few hours. Eventually, I learned that mustard and melanoidins work differently. While the mustard helps the emulsion form, the melanoidins prevent it from separating. It's basically the difference between emulsifiers and stabilizers (for more information, see "Secrets to a Dressing with Staying Power").

As for shaking the dressing as a method of forming the emulsion, it worked beautifully as long as I stirred together the vinegar, mustard, mayonnaise, molasses, and salt with a fork and then added the oil ¼ cup at a time and shook vigorously. Over the coming days, a very thin layer of vinegar did eventually settle out onto the bottom of the jar, but it was easily reincorporated with a quick shake before serving.

Two Oils Are Better Than One

The only hitch to including the mayonnaise was that the dressing needed to be refrigerated, and doing so caused the oil to solidify and the emulsion to break completely once it came to room temperature. But I had an idea.

I knew that extra-virgin olive oil solidifies when its molecules form a lattice and crystallize, and I knew I could prevent crystallization by cutting it with another type of oil. Vegetable oil would be the easiest and most neutral addition, so I tried ratios ranging from 10:1 to 2:1 of olive oil to vegetable oil and eventually found that the 2:1 ratio kept the dressing smooth and pourable directly from the refrigerator while still allowing the distinct flavor of the olive oil to come through.

My recipe was not only ideal for making ahead, but without the whisking, it was easier than any other vinaigrette I'd ever made. Plus, I could substitute other oils (like hazelnut or walnut) for the olive oil, use any number of wine vinegars or lemon juice, or even throw in aromatics like garlic and shallots. The template complemented just about any salad green I tried, from plain leafy lettuces to the heartier combinations I created using cooked chicken with spinach, watercress, and arugula. Making vinaigrette had just become a weekly rather than a daily affair.

MAKE-AHEAD VINAIGRETTE
MAKES ABOUT 1 CUP

Regular or light mayonnaise can be used in this recipe. Do not use blackstrap molasses. You can substitute toasted hazelnut or walnut oil for the extra-virgin olive oil. For our free recipe for Arugula Salad with Cherry Tomatoes, Chickpeas, Hard-Cooked Eggs, and Pecorino, go to CooksIllustrated.com/apr16.

- 1 tablespoon mayonnaise
- 1 tablespoon molasses
- 1 tablespoon Dijon mustard
- ½ teaspoon salt
- ¼ cup wine vinegar
- ½ cup extra-virgin olive oil
- ¼ cup vegetable oil

1. Combine mayonnaise, molasses, mustard, and salt in 2-cup jar with tight-fitting lid. Stir with fork until mixture is milky in appearance and no lumps of mayonnaise or molasses remain. Add vinegar, seal jar, and shake until smooth, about 10 seconds.

2. Add ¼ cup olive oil, seal jar, and shake vigorously until thoroughly combined, about 10 seconds. Repeat, adding remaining ¼ cup olive oil and vegetable oil in 2 additions, shaking vigorously until thoroughly combined after each addition. (After third addition, vinaigrette should be glossy and lightly thickened, with no pools of oil on its surface.) Refrigerate for up to 1 week. Shake briefly before using.

MAKE-AHEAD
SHERRY-SHALLOT VINAIGRETTE

Substitute sherry vinegar for wine vinegar. Add 2 teaspoons finely minced shallot and 2 teaspoons minced fresh thyme to jar with mayonnaise, mustard, and molasses.

MAKE-AHEAD LEMON-GARLIC-CHIVE
VINAIGRETTE

Substitute lemon juice for wine vinegar. Add 2 teaspoons grated lemon zest, 2 teaspoons minced fresh chives, and 1 finely minced garlic clove to jar with mayonnaise, mustard, and molasses.

SPINACH SALAD WITH CHICKEN, RADISHES, AND GRAPEFRUIT
SERVES 4 TO 6 AS A MAIN DISH

Crumble the feta when it's cold so it won't smear.

- 1 red grapefruit
- 10 ounces (10 cups) baby spinach
- 6 radishes, trimmed and sliced thin
- ¼ cup Make-Ahead Vinaigrette
   Kosher salt and pepper
- 2 cups shredded cooked chicken
- 2 ounces feta cheese, crumbled (½ cup)
- ½ cup roasted pepitas, chopped coarse

1. Cut away peel and pith from grapefruit. Holding fruit over bowl, use paring knife to slice between membranes to release segments. Set aside segments.

2. Toss spinach and radishes with 3 tablespoons vinaigrette in large bowl. Season with salt and pepper to taste and transfer to serving platter. Add chicken to now-empty bowl along with remaining 1 tablespoon vinaigrette and toss to combine. Arrange chicken over spinach, followed by grapefruit segments. Sprinkle with feta and pepitas and serve.

WATERCRESS SALAD WITH CHICKEN, FENNEL, AND PICKLED SHALLOTS
SERVES 4 TO 6 AS A MAIN DISH

Use a vegetable peeler to shave the gouda.

- ⅓ cup red wine vinegar
- 2 tablespoons sugar
   Kosher salt and pepper
- 2 shallots, sliced thin
- 10 ounces (10 cups) watercress, torn into bite-size pieces
- 1 fennel bulb, fronds minced, stalks discarded, bulb halved, cored, and sliced thin
- ¼ cup Make-Ahead Vinaigrette
- 2 cups shredded cooked chicken
- 2 ounces aged gouda cheese, shaved
- ½ cup dry-roasted peanuts, chopped coarse

1. Bring vinegar, sugar, and pinch salt to simmer in small saucepan over medium-high heat, stirring occasionally, until sugar dissolves. Remove pan from heat, add shallots, and stir to combine. Cover and let cool completely, about 30 minutes. Drain and discard liquid.

2. Toss watercress and fennel fronds and bulb with 3 tablespoons vinaigrette in large bowl. Season with salt and pepper to taste and transfer to serving platter. Add chicken to now-empty bowl along with remaining 1 tablespoon vinaigrette and toss to combine. Arrange chicken over watercress mixture, followed by pickled shallots. Sprinkle with gouda and peanuts and serve.

Point of Separation

Our Make-Ahead Vinaigrette stays emulsified for much longer than a traditional vinaigrette or plain oil and vinegar.

OIL AND VINEGAR
No emulsifiers or stabilizers

OUR FOOLPROOF VINAIGRETTE
Contains emulsifiers: mustard and mayonnaise

NEW MAKE-AHEAD VINAIGRETTE
Contains emulsifiers and stabilizers:
mustard, mayonnaise, and molasses

SCIENCE Secrets to a Dressing with Staying Power

Our Make-Ahead Vinaigrette relies on mustard and mayonnaise (emulsifiers) to help the oil and vinegar combine into a unified sauce. Mustard contains a polysaccharide, and the egg yolks in mayonnaise contain lecithin; both of these agents attract oil and are compatible with water, so they hold the two disparate components together. Molasses (a stabilizer) contains large compounds called melanoidins that increase the viscosity of the emulsion and make it difficult for the oil droplets to coalesce and separate from the water.

EMULSIFIERS
Mustard and mayonnaise

STABILIZER
Molasses

Pantry Pasta Sauces

For a quick weeknight pasta sauce, we balance garlic's sweet and fiery sides and then add a few pantry staples—all in the time it takes to boil spaghetti.

≥ BY LAN LAM ≤

I like to maintain a revolving door–style kitchen pantry, rotating items in and out depending on my mood. It's how I pull off memorable dinners even when the fridge is nearly empty. While many ingredients come and go, there are three constants I make sure never to be without: spaghetti, garlic, and extra-virgin olive oil. Italians turn this trio into a quick pasta called *aglio e olio*, an ultrasimple recipe that coaxes loads of flavor from the garlic. But there are also many variations in which the garlic is augmented by a few additional ingredients. To make my weeknight sauces even better, I set out to perfect the garlic, pasta, and olive oil components as a base to which I could add other ingredients I had on hand.

As a first step, I needed to figure out how to infuse the oil with as much garlic flavor as possible. My second step would be to determine the best way to coat the spaghetti with the oil. I quickly discovered that it wasn't going to be as easy as I thought.

Many recipes call for sliced garlic, but I found that thinner slices turned dark brown (going from toasty-sweet to harshly acrid) by the time thicker slices became straw-colored. With a solution in mind, I put a pot of spaghetti on to boil and then pushed a few garlic cloves through a press to create identical bits. I cooked the minced garlic in ¼ cup of oil—enough to ensure that the bits were totally submerged—over low heat. After 10 minutes, the garlic was uniformly golden brown and the pasta was al dente. I set aside 1 cup of pasta cooking water, drained the spaghetti, and returned it to the pot. In went the garlic oil along with the starchy cooking liquid, which would help form a clingy sauce. For zing, I added ½ teaspoon of raw minced garlic at the last minute.

A few forkfuls revealed great flavor—and an oily consistency. I couldn't decrease the amount of oil because that would cause the garlic to toast unevenly. Doubling the starchy cooking liquid eliminated greasiness, but the spaghetti became bloated as it soaked up the excess water. That said, the extra starch did a great job of helping create a cohesive sauce. My solution: Boil the pasta in 2 quarts of water instead of 4, effectively doubling the amount of starch in the cooking water. This way I could stick with adding just

▶ **Look: Near-Instant Dinner**
A step-by-step video is available at CooksIllustrated.com/apr16

A mix of cooked and raw garlic punches up the flavor.

1 cup of cooking water, ensuring that the dish was neither greasy nor soggy.

Finally, I fiddled with supplementary ingredients. Incorporating toasted pine nuts, lemon juice and zest, Parmesan, and slivers of fresh basil made for a vibrant dish. Then, following the same template, I created a few more variations, all with the same amount of oomph.

GARLICKY SPAGHETTI WITH LEMON AND PINE NUTS
SERVES 4

A garlic press makes quick work of uniformly mincing the garlic. For our for-two versions of these recipes, go to Cooks Illustrated.com/apr16.

- 2 tablespoons plus ½ teaspoon minced garlic
- ¼ cup extra-virgin olive oil
- ¼ teaspoon red pepper flakes
- 1 pound spaghetti
  Salt and pepper
- 2 teaspoons grated lemon zest plus 2 tablespoons juice
- 1 cup chopped fresh basil
- 1 ounce Parmesan, grated (½ cup), plus extra for serving
- ½ cup pine nuts, toasted

1. Combine 2 tablespoons garlic and oil in 8-inch nonstick skillet. Cook over low heat, stirring occasionally, until garlic is pale golden brown, 9 to 12 minutes. Off heat, stir in pepper flakes; set aside.

2. Bring 2 quarts water to boil in large pot. Add pasta and 2 teaspoons salt and cook, stirring frequently, until al dente. Reserve 1 cup cooking water, then drain pasta and return it to pot. Add remaining ½ teaspoon garlic, lemon zest and juice, reserved garlic-oil mixture, and reserved cooking water to pasta in pot. Stir until pasta is well coated with oil and no water remains in bottom of pot. Add basil, Parmesan, and pine nuts and toss to combine. Season with salt and pepper to taste. Serve, passing extra Parmesan separately.

GARLICKY SPAGHETTI WITH ARTICHOKES AND HAZELNUTS

Omit lemon zest and reduce lemon juice to 1 tablespoon. Stir in 1½ teaspoons fennel seeds, coarsely ground, with pepper flakes in step 1. Stir 1 (14-ounce) can artichoke hearts, chopped, into pasta with lemon juice. Omit basil and substitute ½ cup hazelnuts, toasted, skinned, and chopped, for pine nuts.

GARLICKY SPAGHETTI WITH CAPERS AND CURRANTS

Omit lemon zest and reduce lemon juice to 1 tablespoon. Stir 3 tablespoons capers, rinsed and minced; 3 tablespoons currants, minced; and 2 anchovy fillets, rinsed, patted dry, and minced, into pasta with lemon juice. Omit basil and pine nuts.

GARLICKY SPAGHETTI WITH CLAMS

Omit lemon zest and reduce lemon juice to 2 teaspoons. Stir 2 (6½-ounce) cans whole clams, drained and chopped, and 4 anchovy fillets, rinsed, patted dry, and minced, into pasta with lemon juice. Increase Parmesan to ¾ cup, substitute 2 tablespoons chopped fresh parsley for basil, and omit pine nuts.

GARLICKY SPAGHETTI WITH GREEN OLIVES AND ALMONDS

Omit lemon zest and reduce lemon juice to 1 tablespoon. Stir 1 cup green olives, chopped fine, into pasta with lemon juice. Substitute Pecorino Romano for Parmesan and toasted sliced almonds for pine nuts.

Perfecting Roasted Asparagus

A blazing-hot oven is only part of the formula for deeply browned, crisp-tender spears.

⇒ BY STEVE DUNN ⇐

I like to roast asparagus because the method allows me to cook enough to feed my large clan and requires very little hands-on attention. My usual approach couldn't be simpler: Toss the spears with some oil, salt, and pepper; spread them on a baking sheet; and pop them into a 400-degree oven until they are deeply browned—the hallmark of any good roasted vegetable.

But while the outcome has been good enough, I have always had a nagging sense that it could be much better if I concentrated on figuring out the ideal recipe (and made it foolproof while I was at it).

I was already aware of one downside to roasting: Unlike heartier vegetables such as cauliflower or potatoes, which can withstand longer roasting times to develop good color, slender asparagus spears often overcook by the time they brown, giving up their fresh flavor and tender snap and trading their grass-green color for a duller shade of army fatigue.

To nail the ideal—spears that are both crisp-tender and well-browned—I had to start with the right size asparagus. I was pretty sure that thicker specimens (at least ½ inch in diameter) would hold up better to the heat than the pencil-thin kind. Roasting a bunch of each size according to my usual method provided confirmation, as the skinnier spears practically wilted by the time they were sufficiently roasted. They were also comparatively chewy, thanks to their higher ratio of fibrous skin to tender flesh.

With thicker spears, the question was how to remove their woody stems: Should I trim them with a knife or snap them off at the spears' so-called natural break point? I tested both methods on multiple asparagus bunches and realized that using a knife was the way to go because it produced less waste. Then, to remove the remaining tough outer skin, I grabbed a vegetable peeler and stripped the stalks down to their creamy white flesh—a step that added a few minutes to the prep but maximized the stalks' tenderness as well as their visual appeal (see "Peeling Asparagus—Is It Worth the Fuss?" on page 28).

Back to the cooking method. Recipes that I found called for a wide range of oven temperatures (from 350 to 500 degrees) and cooking times, but since I already knew that the spears were taking too long to brown at 400 degrees for 12 minutes, I set my sights on a hotter oven. Sure enough, when I tested different roasting temperatures at various time increments, the batch I blasted at 500 degrees for no more than 10 minutes was the best: bright with a tender snap.

But unfortunately the degree of browning was only fair. The leap I wanted to make for color development was essentially the difference between a moderate

For deep but fresh flavor, brown just one side.

sauté and a hard sear—and once I thought about it that way, the problem became obvious. I was starting the asparagus on a cold baking sheet. The better plan would be to preheat the sheet in the oven on the bottom rack (closest to the element) so that the spears would essentially sear upon contact. This change made all the difference; the next round of testing offered up spears with flavorful but spotty browning.

I knew I was on the right track, but when I retested this method, I made one useful mistake. Midway through the roasting time, I shook the baking sheet to ensure that the spears browned evenly on all sides. The resulting spears were indeed evenly browned, but not deeply browned. For the next test, I resisted the urge to shake the sheet, leaving the spears to cook undisturbed, and the results were the best yet: vibrant green on one side with a deep, flavorful sear on the other. Tasters didn't seem to mind that the spears weren't evenly browned.

As good as this asparagus was, I wanted to develop some quick seasonings to give the dish more variety. Fresh garnishes would enhance the stalks' vibrancy, so I whipped up a gremolata, the Italian minced-herb condiment usually made with lemon zest, garlic, and parsley. But instead of the classic profile, I took a broader approach and came up with variations that traded the lemon zest for orange or lime zest and some of the parsley for mint, tarragon, or cilantro.

ROASTED ASPARAGUS
SERVES 4 TO 6

This recipe works best with thick asparagus spears that are between ½ and ¾ inch in diameter. The asparagus can be served as is or sprinkled with the gremolata topping (recipe follows) right before serving. For information on peeling asparagus, see page 28. For our recipes for Tarragon-Lemon Gremolata and Cilantro-Lime Gremolata, go to CooksIllustrated.com/apr16.

- 2 pounds thick asparagus
- 2 tablespoons plus 2 teaspoons extra-virgin olive oil
- ½ teaspoon salt
- ¼ teaspoon pepper

1. Adjust oven rack to lowest position, place rimmed baking sheet on rack, and heat oven to 500 degrees.

2. Trim bottom inch of asparagus spears and discard. Peel bottom halves of spears until white flesh is exposed. Place asparagus in large baking pan and toss with 2 tablespoons oil, salt, and pepper.

3. Transfer asparagus to preheated sheet and spread into even layer. Roast, without moving asparagus, until undersides of spears are browned, tops are vibrant green, and tip of paring knife inserted at base of largest spear meets little resistance, 8 to 10 minutes. Transfer asparagus to serving platter, drizzle with remaining 2 teaspoons oil, and serve immediately.

MINT-ORANGE GREMOLATA
MAKES ABOUT ¼ CUP

To avoid harsh garlic flavor, don't mince the garlic until you're ready to mix the gremolata.

- 2 tablespoons minced fresh mint
- 2 tablespoons minced fresh parsley
- 2 teaspoons grated orange zest
- 1 garlic clove, minced
  Pinch cayenne pepper

Combine all ingredients in bowl.

▶ **Steve Shows You How**
A step-by-step video is available
at CooksIllustrated.com/apr16

Introducing Lemon Posset

This classic English specialty transforms cream, sugar, and lemon into a lush pudding with clear citrus flavor. It's the easiest dessert you've never made.

⇒ BY ANNIE PETITO ⇐

It may sound like a small mammal, but posset is actually an old-time English dessert that most Americans have never encountered. Until fairly recently, even most English cooks would likely have associated the name with a tart, creamy drink dating back to the Middle Ages.

But today's posset, which has been taken up by English celebrity chefs and cookbook writers and is starting to appear on American restaurant menus, is something altogether different: a chilled dessert with the marvelously plush texture of a mousse or pudding that comes together almost by magic from nothing more than sugar, cream, and citrus juice. There are no temperamental egg yolks or add-ins like gelatin, flour, or cornstarch needed to help the mixture thicken and set—or to interfere with the clean, bright taste of citrus.

Eager to bring this supremely simple dessert into the test kitchen, I gave a few recipes a whirl, choosing to focus on classic lemon versions (lime, orange, grapefruit, and combinations thereof are also common). The technique rarely varied: Heat cream with sugar until the sugar dissolves, add lemon juice, and chill as you wait for the mixture to gel to a velvety texture. As for the results, every single one appealed to my weakness for creamy, buttery-smooth desserts. But that didn't mean there wasn't room for improvement. Some possets were a bit too thin and almost runny, while others turned out firm but overly sweet, lacking enough citrusy tang to cut the cream's richness. And I wondered if I could make the lemon flavor a bit more complex. With a little finessing, I was sure I could transform these three ingredients into a silky, creamy dessert (think crème brûlée) with enough bright-tart flavor to balance the richness of the cream.

▶ Look: Culinary Magic
A step-by-step video is available at CooksIllustrated.com/apr16

Considering the Posset-bilities

My first step was to understand the magic behind how the dessert works. Here's how it goes: When acid is added to milk (or when milk turns sour

This rich, creamy pudding sets best in individual servings.

over time), the change in pH causes the milk's casein proteins to lose the negative charge that ordinarily keeps them separate. Instead, they bond together in clusters, and the milk becomes grainy, or curdled. When acid is added to cream—which is a more viscous liquid than milk thanks to its smaller amount of water and greater amount of fat (at least 36 percent fat as opposed to whole milk's 3.25 percent)—the effect is different. The fat in cream outweighs the casein proteins 10 to 1 (in milk they are about equal) and so interferes with the proteins' ability to form tight curds. As a result, a smooth, creamy consistency develops instead of a grainy one. Heating the cream for posset also has an effect: It causes the whey proteins in the dairy to unwind and attach themselves to the casein molecules and so helps stabilize the gelled liquid.

With that in mind, I realized that the key to perfect posset would simply be determining the optimal ratio of ingredients to achieve the ideal texture as well as flavor. I decided to nail down sweetness first. I simmered 2-cup batches of heavy cream with different amounts of sugar (from ¼ cup up to ⅔ cup) for 5 minutes, stirred 4 tablespoons of lemon juice into each batch, and then portioned and chilled the mixtures until they were set. Tasting the samples, it was clear that the sugar's role in the dessert was more critical than I initially realized: The less sugar in the mix, the thinner and looser the dessert was. That's because dissolved sugar binds water molecules, increasing viscosity, and therefore gives the gel structure as well as a velvety mouthfeel. (Think of how thick a sugar syrup is compared with plain water.) I decided to move forward using ⅔ cup of sugar, which produced a nicely set consistency. However, I would need to compensate for the sweetness since this amount of sugar made the posset somewhat cloying.

That meant adding more lemon juice. After some fiddling, I found that 6 tablespoons of freshly squeezed juice provided a sharp, tangy—but not harsh—flavor. But that amount of juice also produced a slightly looser set than I liked. I had thought that more lemon juice might create a firmer texture. But by adding more juice, I was also adding more water—enough, it seemed, to hamper the acid's ability to fully gel the cream.

I had a thought: Cream also contains water, so what if I reduced the cream to remove some of its water? That might get the overall liquid in the mix closer to

A Concoction Fit for Royalty

A mention of posset even made it into one of Shakespeare's plays: Lady Macbeth drugged King Duncan's guards with poisoned posset that she probably served up in a vessel like this one. Since old-fashioned versions of the concoction contained a foamy or semisolid layer floating above the sweet liquid, the spout allowed the liquid part to be drunk before the thick layer was eaten with a spoon.

POSSET POT
Since posset was traditionally a drink favored by aristocrats, it warranted its own elegant serving vessel.

A REAL DRIP
Extra lemon juice made the posset too liquidy.

ALL SET
Boiling the cream delivered the right set consistency.

Too Loose? Crank Up the Heat

Bumping up the amount of lemon juice in our posset got the flavor where we wanted it, but it also made the pudding too loose. Our solution? Boil the cream. This not only caused water to evaporate but also broke up the fat droplets in the cream. Cream is an emulsion of fat and water, and more droplets of fat made it even harder for the water molecules to move about, resulting in a thicker, more viscous mixture.

TECHNIQUE | FOR FOOLPROOF REDUCTION, USE A RULER

When reducing a liquid to a specific volume, such as in our Lemon Posset with Berries recipe, you can monitor progress by pouring it into a measuring cup at regular intervals, but here's another way: Fill a measuring cup with water to the desired volume. Pour the liquid into the saucepan you plan to use, mark the water level on a ruler or chopstick, and then reduce your liquid to that line.

what it had been with 2 cups of cream and 4 tablespoons of lemon juice, which in turn might let me use a full 6 tablespoons of lemon juice and still have the firm set I wanted. For my next batch, instead of simmering the cream and sugar, I turned up the heat and boiled it hard for a few minutes. I stirred in 6 tablespoons of lemon juice and put the mixture in the refrigerator. When I checked it a few hours later, it was not only firm but also had the most dense, luxuriously creamy texture of any posset I'd made yet. Was there something else going on besides the removal of water?

A Drastic Reduction

As it turns out, yes. Our science editor explained that by boiling, I was also concentrating the proteins and fats in the cream, which would lead to a firmer set. Additionally, the vigorous action of boiling the cream instead of simmering it breaks up the fat into more numerous, smaller droplets. This has a twofold effect: There are more of the droplets to get in the way of the casein proteins forming tight curds, which leads to an even creamier texture. At the same time, the increase in the number of fat droplets leads to a thicker consistency. This is because cream is an emulsion of fat and water, and the more fat droplets present to break up the water, the more viscous the mixture (think of a well-emulsified vinaigrette).

To ensure consistent results, I elected to boil the cream and sugar not for a certain period of time but to a particular volume. With some experimentation, I found that reducing the cream and sugar to 2 cups (about a 30 percent reduction) before adding the lemon juice produced dense, ultraplush results.

Finishing Touches

I had the texture of my posset exactly right, but its flavor needed to be a little brighter and more complex. The obvious thing to do was to incorporate some of the zest, which contains oils that are more resistant to breaking down under heat than the juice and would impart a more well-rounded lemon flavor than the juice alone. I added a full tablespoon of finely grated zest to the cream-sugar mixture before boiling it. Then, after I poured in the lemon juice, I let the mixture steep off heat for 20 minutes before straining out the zest as well as any skin that formed, ensuring that there would be no skin on the final dessert. (For

more information on the skin, see "A Tidy Way to Avoid Skin on Custards" on page 30.) The result was a livelier flavor and just the right amount of lemony punch to cut through the sweetness and richness of the cream.

Pleased with my results, I portioned the posset into ramekins (portioning was key; spooning the set dessert from one large serving bowl caused the texture to suffer). One-third cup servings seemed like plenty, since the dessert is so rich. After 3 hours in the fridge, the possets were cold, fully set, and ready to be garnished with a handful of fresh mixed berries. This British classic was so easy and elegant that I knew it would become a staple in my repertoire.

LEMON POSSET WITH BERRIES
SERVES 6

This dessert requires portioning into individual servings. Reducing the cream mixture to exactly 2 cups creates the best consistency. Transfer the liquid to a 2-cup heatproof liquid measuring cup once or twice during boiling to monitor the amount. Do not leave the cream unattended, as it can boil over easily.

- 2 cups heavy cream
- ⅔ cup (4⅔ ounces) granulated sugar
- 1 tablespoon grated lemon zest plus 6 tablespoons juice (2 lemons)
- 1½ cups blueberries or raspberries

1. Combine cream, sugar, and lemon zest in medium saucepan and bring to boil over medium heat. Continue to boil, stirring frequently to dissolve sugar. If mixture begins to boil over, briefly remove from heat. Cook until mixture is reduced to 2 cups, 8 to 12 minutes.

2. Remove saucepan from heat and stir in lemon juice. Let sit until mixture is cooled slightly and skin forms on top, about 20 minutes. Strain through fine-mesh strainer into bowl; discard zest. Divide mixture evenly among 6 individual ramekins or serving glasses.

3. Refrigerate, uncovered, until set, at least 3 hours. Once chilled, possets can be wrapped in plastic wrap and refrigerated for up to 2 days. Unwrap and let sit at room temperature for 10 minutes before serving. Garnish with berries and serve.

Three-Ingredient Magic
Lemon juice, cream, and sugar practically make themselves into posset. Here's how it works.

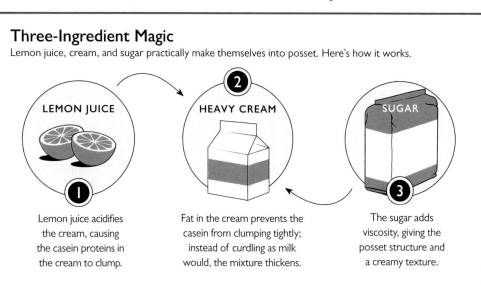

LEMON JUICE ① Lemon juice acidifies the cream, causing the casein proteins in the cream to clump.

HEAVY CREAM ② Fat in the cream prevents the casein from clumping tightly; instead of curdling as milk would, the mixture thickens.

SUGAR ③ The sugar adds viscosity, giving the posset structure and a creamy texture.

Why You Should Buy a Saucier

An ordinary saucepan has its uses, but once you experience the ease of stirring in a saucier, you'll wonder how you ever did without one.

> BY KATE SHANNON <

Mention the word "saucier" in the test kitchen, and you're in for an earful. The loyalists among us rave that these vessels, which are essentially rounded saucepans with wider mouths, flared walls, and rolled lips, can do everything a conventional saucepan can do—and that their distinct design features make some cooking tasks even easier. These include preparations like oatmeal, risotto, and polenta, where the food is prone to getting lodged in corners and burning, as well as custards and sauces that require frequent stirring. And as their name and wide-mouth design imply, they're built for reducing sauces. ("Saucier" is also the name given to French cooks who prepare sauces, stocks, and soups.) And though models vary in shape and size, sauciers offer depth and capacity, as well as easy access to their interiors and corner-free surfaces that are easy to clean.

But while a saucepan is standard in any kitchen, sauciers have mainly been the domain of restaurant chefs. We thought it was time this changed. We gathered eight models with capacities ranging from 3 to 3½ quarts—the most common large size—and compared them with our favorite 4-quart saucepan from All-Clad. Six of these pans were fully clad, meaning they were made of alternating layers of steel and aluminum, which takes advantage of the best qualities of each metal. We also tested a "disk bottom" model (only the base is fully clad, and the sides are a single layer of stainless steel) and a hefty model made of enameled cast iron. In them, we prepared risotto, gravy, and pastry cream, noting their cooking performance as well as how comfortable they were to maneuver. We also tested their reduction speed by boiling a measured amount of water in each model for 10 and 20 minutes and weighing the results. Finally, since their curvy sides are known for being easier to clean than L-shaped saucepans, we washed each model by hand.

Surface Tensions

The good news: Every model delivered creamy risotto, satiny gravy, and smooth pastry cream, and it was a pleasure to whisk and stir in most of them. Our

▶ **Should You Buy a Saucier?**
A video that answers that question is at CooksIllustrated.com/apr16

A rounded bottom makes whisking a snap; flared sides aid evaporation.

utensils glided against their curvy walls—a noticeable difference from the stiffer, bumpier movements they made in the saucepan. The Paderno was the exception; its L-shaped corners meant that it behaved more like a saucepan, trapping custard and rice.

The diameter of the base separated top performers from lesser models, affecting how frequently we had to stir the contents to ensure that food cooked evenly. When softening aromatics for risotto and gravy, testers using sauciers that measured less than about 5¾ inches across the bottom had to stir continuously, lest the vegetables pile atop one another and steam. The same diligence was also required if the base was too broad, since the too-thin layer of vegetables was prone to scorching. Pans with bottom surfaces measuring between 5¾ and 7 inches were best.

As for reduction rates, water evaporated faster in all of the sauciers than it did in the All-Clad saucepan; the fastest, by Le Creuset, evaporated about 13 percent more water than the saucepan did after 20 minutes. That's proof that these flared pans are more efficient for sauce-making, though the disparity isn't so great that a recipe designed for a saucepan will fail in a saucier. When using a saucier, expect that the food might be done on the earlier end of the cooking time range.

How's It Handle?

The more distinct discrepancy among these pans was their overall design: the size and shape of their handles, how much they weighed, and how comfortable they were to maneuver. All testers struggled with stumpy, skinny, or sharp-edged handles that slipped from or dug into our palms, and we docked points from models with handles that became too hot and forced us to use potholders. The best models sported relatively long (about 8 inches), wide (2½ to 3 inches around) handles that were easy to grasp, stayed relatively cool, and offered enough leverage to lift the saucier with one hand.

The cast-iron Tramontina literally sank into last place. Clocking in at nearly 6 pounds, it outweighed every other pot by at least 2 pounds and was a bear to maneuver. Other, less-heavy models felt just as solid, and none chipped or scratched when we sharply rapped them with a metal utensil.

But there were also a few lighter-weight models that were cumbersome to handle, thanks to the awkward angle at which the handle extended from the bowl. For example: The handle on the lighter-weight Mauviel pot jutted so sharply that testers struggled to move it. Likewise, the handle on the hefty Demeyere curved steeply upward and offered little leverage. According to Jack Dennerlein, professor of ergonomics and safety at Northeastern and Harvard Universities, the key consideration is "the line of your hand and forearm compared to the line of the pan," which affects how much leverage you have.

Finally, there was cleanup—which might be the most convincing reason to invest in a saucier. In the best models, the absence of sharp corners meant not only that there was nowhere our utensils couldn't reach and no crevices in which rice grains or drops of custard could get stuck, but that it was easy and natural to swipe a sponge along the curved walls and wipe out every speck of food.

Our favorite, the Le Creuset 3½ Quart Stainless Steel Saucier Pan ($250.00) has it all: Its wide bowl with walls that slope gently down to a 5¾-inch cooking surface encouraged broad, efficient strokes with a whisk, rubber spatula, or sponge. The long, wide, comfortable handle gave us great control, and its relatively straight extension from the pot made it easy to maneuver. It's pricey and won't replace our favorite All-Clad saucepan—the latter's 4-quart capacity is a must for any kitchen—but give this pan a spot on your pot rack and you'll be reaching for it almost every day.

TESTING SAUCIERS

We tested eight sauciers with capacities ranging from 3 to 3½ quarts (the largest common size). In them, we prepared risotto, gravy, and pastry cream, noting their cooking performance as well as how comfortably they handled and how easy they were to clean by hand. Products were purchased online and appear below in order of preference.

PERFORMANCE

We stirred Parmesan risotto, sautéed aromatic vegetables and reduced broth to make gravy, and whisked pastry cream. To test reduction speed, we filled each model with 1,840 grams (about 8 cups) of 75-degree water, timed how long each took to boil over high heat on the same burner, boiled the water for 10 minutes, weighed the results, and repeated the weighing again after 10 more minutes of boiling. Sauciers received high marks if they produced good-quality results in the three recipe tests and offered a relatively broad cooking surface and a rounded shape that made it easy to stir and whisk.

EASE OF USE

We evaluated the length, circumference, and angle of the handles, as well as the weight of the pans (without lids)—all of which contributed to the pans' ease of use.

CLEANUP

We washed the sauciers by hand throughout testing, noting how easy they were to scrub with a sponge and whether or not they showed any visible scrub marks, scratches, or discoloration.

RECOMMENDED

LE CREUSET 3½ Quart Stainless Steel Saucier Pan
MODEL: SSP6100-24P PRICE: $250.00
CAPACITY: 3.5 quarts WEIGHT: 2 lb 12 oz
COOKING SURFACE DIAMETER: 5¾ in
HANDLE LENGTH: 8¼ in

CRITERIA	
PERFORMANCE	★★★
EASE OF USE	★★½
CLEANUP	★★½

TESTERS' COMMENTS
With gently sloping sides and a generous opening, this pan made whisking and stirring a pleasure. It was also the most efficient at the evaporation test. Its lightweight frame and straight-angled handle make it very easy to lift. One criticism: The handle became hot over time, forcing us to use a potholder.

ZWILLING J.A. HENCKELS Aurora 3.5 qt Stainless Steel Saucier
MODEL: 66080-240 PRICE: $219.99
CAPACITY: 3.5 quarts WEIGHT: 3 lb 13 oz
COOKING SURFACE DIAMETER: 7 in
HANDLE LENGTH: 9¼ in

CRITERIA	
PERFORMANCE	★★★
EASE OF USE	★★½
CLEANUP	★★½

TESTERS' COMMENTS
Our runner-up is heftier than our winner, with walls that slope just slightly less gently toward the cooking surface. Still, it cooks food beautifully, and its wide, easy-to-grip handle extends at a comfortable angle from the pan.

RECOMMENDED WITH RESERVATIONS

ALL-CLAD Stainless Steel 3-Quart Saucier with Lid
MODEL: 4213 PRICE: $189.95
CAPACITY: 3 quarts WEIGHT: 2 lb 10¾ oz
COOKING SURFACE DIAMETER: 5¼ in
HANDLE LENGTH: 8½ in

CRITERIA	
PERFORMANCE	★★½
EASE OF USE	★★
CLEANUP	★★½

TESTERS' COMMENTS
This lightweight pan is easy to maneuver around the stovetop, though its cooking surface is on the small side and its walls are more sharply sloped than our top pots; that might explain why it was the slowest model to reduce water. Some testers complained that the handle's edges were sharp, but most found it easy to grip without slippage.

DEMEYERE Atlantis 3.5 qt Stainless Steel Saucier
MODEL: 55924-41524 PRICE: $319.99
CAPACITY: 3.5 quarts WEIGHT: 3 lb 11 oz
COOKING SURFACE DIAMETER: 6½ in
HANDLE LENGTH: 9¼ in

CRITERIA	
PERFORMANCE	★★★
EASE OF USE	★½
CLEANUP	★★

TESTERS' COMMENTS
The walls of this pricey saucier come close to forming saucepan-like corners. As a result, testers had to hold their utensils at a sharper angle to stir, but the food it produced was flawless. Lifting its heavier frame was made more difficult by its steeply angled handle, which felt awkward and uncomfortable.

CALPHALON Tri-Ply Stainless Steel 3-qt Covered Chef's Pan
MODEL: 1767724 PRICE: $93.49
CAPACITY: 3 quarts WEIGHT: 2 lb 6 oz
COOKING SURFACE DIAMETER: 5 in
HANDLE LENGTH: 7½ in

CRITERIA	
PERFORMANCE	★★
EASE OF USE	★½
CLEANUP	★★★

TESTERS' COMMENTS
The walls of this saucier slope smoothly down to the cooking surface without a hint of a corner, and testers loved the way spatulas glided around the interior, but its cooking surface is relatively skimpy. Short and slim, the handle rested uncomfortably against our palms, and cooks with large hands struggled to get a firm grip. Without rivets, cleanup was a breeze.

NOT RECOMMENDED

MAUVIEL M'cook Stainless Steel Curved Splayed Saute Pan, Cast Stainless Steel Handle, 3 qt
MODEL: 5212.24 (pan), 5218.24 (lid)
PRICE: $225.00 ($170.00 for pan, $55.00 for lid)
CAPACITY: 3 quarts WEIGHT: 2 lb 14⅜ oz
COOKING SURFACE DIAMETER: 6½ in
HANDLE LENGTH: 9¼ in

CRITERIA	
PERFORMANCE	★★★
EASE OF USE	★
CLEANUP	★★

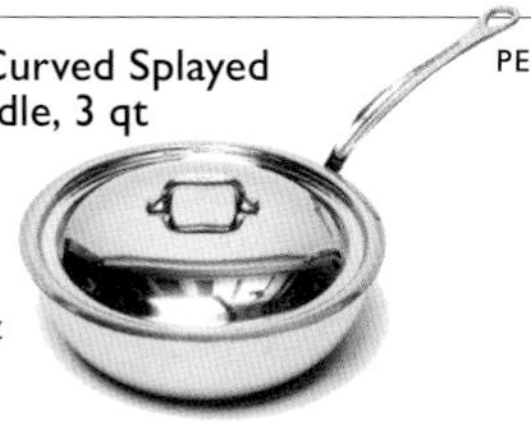

TESTERS' COMMENTS
We have no complaints about the size or shape of the pan itself (despite its name, it is a saucier). Unfortunately, we can't say the same for the skinny handle, which bends upward at a sharp angle that provides poor leverage and makes the pot awkward to move, lift, and turn.

PADERNO World Cuisine Grand Gourmet Stainless Steel Saucier, 3½ Quart
MODEL: 11113-24 (pan), 11161-24 (lid)
PRICE: $156.19 ($123.81 for pan, $32.38 for lid)
CAPACITY: 3.5 quarts WEIGHT: 3 lb 8⅜ oz
COOKING SURFACE DIAMETER: 7½ in
HANDLE LENGTH: 9¾ in

CRITERIA	
PERFORMANCE	★★
EASE OF USE	★
CLEANUP	★

TESTERS' COMMENTS
Although the manufacturer confirmed that it considers this pot a saucier, the vessel's L-shaped walls make it behave more like a shallow saucepan; namely, its sharp corners trapped food, so cleanup was a chore. Testers struggled to keep the thin layer of vegetables from scorching on the extra-broad cooking surface, and the sharp-edged handle sacrifices several inches to a hook that's too flat to hang securely.

TRAMONTINA 3 Qt. Covered Saucier
MODEL: 80131/061DS PRICE: $69.95
CAPACITY: 3 quarts WEIGHT: 5 lb 15⅝ oz
COOKING SURFACE DIAMETER: 4¾ in
HANDLE LENGTH: 6 in

CRITERIA	
PERFORMANCE	★½
EASE OF USE	½
CLEANUP	★★

TESTERS' COMMENTS
We had to lug this cast-iron heavyweight around the stovetop, and its stumpy, scorching-hot handle was no help. The small, cramped cooking surface forced us to stir vegetables frequently to ensure that they didn't steam. The abrasive side of a sponge scratched the enameled surface.

Tasting Whole-Milk Greek Yogurt

Nonfat products used to dominate this market, but now whole-milk versions are taking over. Does more fat equal better yogurt?

> BY LISA McMANUS <

Greek yogurt has taken the American supermarket by storm, growing from just 1 percent of the yogurt market in 2007 to nearly 50 percent today. High in protein and indulgently thick and creamy, it's a satisfying snack and also acts as a key ingredient in savory dips and sauces or as a substitute for sour cream or cream cheese in baking. We last tasted Greek yogurt in 2010 and thought it was time for a fresh look.

At the time of our last tasting, most Greek yogurts were available only in nonfat versions. Today, the whole-milk variety is on the verge of taking over. Because we generally prefer to work with whole-milk dairy in the test kitchen, we decided to focus on it for this tasting (we also held a separate tasting of nonfat Greek yogurt; see "What About Nonfat?"). We stuck with "plain" flavor, not only because it is commonly used as an ingredient but also because it would give any flavor or textural flaws no place to hide. Interestingly, none of the "Greek" yogurts we tasted—we selected seven nationally available products—are made in Greece. Our former favorite, Olympus Yogurt, the only Greek import in our last tasting, is no longer sold in the United States.

We held two blind tastings, with the yogurt first unadorned and then used in *tzatziki*, a Greek sauce

Looks Good and Tastes Good

Our winning yogurt, Fage, has a creamy texture, but it is also so thick that we could stand a spoon in it. Fage produces that texture the traditional way: by straining off the liquid whey. Other manufacturers took shortcuts to achieve the thick texture associated with Greek yogurt, adding a thickener instead of straining. In these cases, the ingredient list will also include whey protein concentrate, milk protein concentrate, or pectin. These additives may make the yogurt look thick, but chalky texture will give them away.

OUR FAVORITE
Fage yogurt is thick, and naturally so.

featuring yogurt, shredded cucumber, garlic, and dill. The textures of the yogurts ranged from thick enough to hold a spoon upright to as thin and runny as regular (non-Greek) yogurt. Some were weighty and dense, others as airy as whipped cream. When it came to flavor, the amount of yogurty tang varied greatly. Two products lost points for off-flavors; one reminded tasters of goat cheese, and the other tasted like "cooked milk." A handful more were practically flavorless. A select few—our favorites—offered clean, milky-sweet flavor with mild but definite tang, and they were nicely thick, which proved to be very important to our tasters. How could plain yogurt vary so much?

Thick or Thin

Yogurt is made by adding live, active bacterial cultures to warm milk. As the bacteria digest lactose, milk's naturally occurring sugar, they produce lactic acid, which lowers its pH, coagulates the proteins into a gel, and creates yogurt's characteristic tang. To make Greek yogurt, the fermented milk is strained for several hours through cheesecloth to drain off most of the clear liquid called whey. Because so much liquid is strained out, traditional Greek yogurt starts with three or four times the amount of milk as is necessary to make regular yogurt. (It's because of this straining that Greek yogurt costs more and is so much higher in protein than regular yogurt.)

That's the basic traditional process, but modern manufacturers have a bag of tricks that allow for customization: choice of bacterial cultures, type of milk (such as from grain- or grass-fed cows) and its fat level, fermenting time and temperature, and the way in which the yogurt reaches its final thick consistency.

Since texture was paramount to our tasters, we started our investigation there. Most manufacturers today use a costly machine called a yogurt separator, which relies on centrifugal force to wring out the whey. But some opt to add a thickening agent—pectin, milk protein concentrate, or whey protein concentrate—instead to avoid the need for investment in costly separators or waste-processing systems for the strained whey. With this method, manufacturers also avoid losing all that volume to whey that's poured down the drain.

What About Nonfat?

In a separate tasting of nonfat Greek yogurts, we found that thick texture was key. Our favorite was Fage Total 0%. As one taster raved, "It's impossible that this is nonfat." For the full tasting results, go to CooksIllustrated.com/apr16.

SURPRISINGLY RICH

Unlike pectin, protein concentrates will increase the yogurt's protein content to be closer to that of a strained yogurt, but that didn't matter to our tasters, who clearly preferred the creamy thickness of strained brands. Both Cabot's yogurt, thickened with protein concentrates, and the pectin-thickened yogurt from The Greek Gods lost points for being "grainy" or "chalky," with "a slight grittiness," while tasters also noticed that Cabot had a slight "funky," "cheesy" "off-flavor." Mirjana Curic-Bawden, principal scientist at Chr. Hansen, a leading international supplier of food cultures that supplies approximately 40 percent of the yogurt cultures used in the United States, said milk protein concentrate can not only give yogurt a powdery, chalky mouthfeel but also readily absorbs odors. If the milk protein concentrate is stored near fragrant substances (such as cheese), those aromas will be transferred to the yogurt.

Still, not all strained brands were well liked. Tasters found that Maple Hill, our bottom-ranked brand, "slumped like soft meringue," while Chobani was likewise too "loose" and "wet," characteristics Curic-Bawden said can result from "mechanical shear" during processing. If the yogurt is pumped through the processing lines with too much pressure, it will damage the structure by breaking the bonds that create thickness in the yogurt.

A Matter of Taste

The choice of bacterial cultures is equally important to creating the desired texture as it is to creating the desired acidity (or mildness) and flavor, so we wondered if looking at the cultures listed on the label might help inform our preferences. According to Curic-Bawden, while manufacturers might tout using five or even more live and active cultures, you actually need only one pair, *Lactobacillus bulgaricus* and *Streptococcus thermophilus*, to make yogurt. Unless yogurt contains a documented probiotic strain (which is then clearly labeled with alphanumeric strain identity), any other cultures beyond these two are basically window dressing. However, there are endless variations (or strains) of *L. bulgaricus* and *S. thermophilus* that will produce radically divergent results. Some are faster to acidify, some affect texture more, and others produce more tangy flavor. But the exact strains are proprietary and a closely guarded secret, so beyond recognizing brands that are trying to woo consumers with those extra "bonus" cultures, we realized we couldn't draw conclusions by looking at cultures on the label.

Secondary to a thick, dense texture, our tasters made it clear that some—but not too much—tang is essential. When we measured the yogurts' titratable acidity at an independent laboratory (a higher number means more acidity), the results ranged from 1.05 percent in our blandest yogurt to 1.47 percent in a yogurt with an "assertive" tanginess. Our top choice was right in the middle with 1.26 percent.

As the main ingredient, the type of milk also has an impact on flavor, mostly when unusual choices are made. One disadvantage of our bottom-ranked yogurt was its hint of "barnyard funk" from its use of grass-fed cows' milk, which has a stronger taste than milk from grain-fed cows. This was a dividing point for our panel, and even many of those who loved it concluded it was just too atypical for "plain" Greek yogurt.

Focus on Fat

Finally, we compared fat levels in the yogurts. We were astonished that the range was anywhere from 9 grams to 22 grams per cup—far beyond the 8 to 9 grams in a cup of whole milk. Yogurt makers can adjust the fat level either at the outset when the milk is cultured or by making yogurt with skim milk and adding varying amounts of cream at the end of the process. But interestingly, fat levels didn't matter to our tasters as much as the *perceived* richness of the yogurt—which circled us back to texture. For example, the two leanest yogurts in our lineup each had 9 grams of fat. One scored near the top of our rankings and the other near the bottom. One of them, Dannon Oikos, made up for its leanness with an extra-thick consistency that left an impression that it was "thick, rich, silky." By contrast, Chobani was thin and loose, so those same 9 grams of fat came across as "too lean" and "disappointingly virtuous." Our favorite, Fage Total, contained 11 grams of fat per cup—only half the fat of our highest-fat yogurt—but, bolstered by the thickest, most spoon-standing density in the lineup, it satisfied our tasters.

In the end, Fage Total ($8.49 for 35.3 oz) won top marks across the board. It struck just the right balance of thick and creamy and was mildly tangy, with a fresh, rich dairy flavor that tasted great plain and provided a welcome balance to the pungent tzatziki sauce. One minor note: Yogurt can continue to exude whey even in an unopened container; typically you must stir that whey back in. Fage adds a round of absorbent parchment on top of each tub of yogurt, a nice touch that meant we could skip that step. It's our new favorite whole-milk Greek yogurt.

WHOLE-MILK GREEK YOGURT

We tasted seven nationally available supermarket plain-flavor whole-milk Greek yogurts in two blind tastings, plain and in *tzatziki* sauce. Scores were averaged, and products appear below in order of preference. Nutritional information was taken from labels. Titratable acidity was measured by an independent laboratory.

RECOMMENDED

FAGE Total Classic Greek Yogurt
PRICE: $8.49 for 35.3 oz ($0.24 per oz)
INGREDIENTS: Grade A Pasteurized Milk and Cream, Live active yogurt cultures (*L. bulgaricus, S. thermophilus, L. acidophilus, Bifidus, L. casei*)
FAT: 11 g per cup   PROTEIN: 20 g per cup
TITRATABLE ACIDITY: 1.26%

With a "faintly sweet," "super-rich, fresh dairy taste," "like cream" or "butter," and "not terribly tangy, just enough to know it's yogurt," this "dense" and "decadent" yogurt was the thickest of the lineup. High protein and no added stabilizers or thickeners listed on the label indicate that this is traditionally strained yogurt. It held its own against the garlic's sharpness in tzatziki sauce.

DANNON OIKOS
Traditional Plain Greek 4% Yogurt
PRICE: $5.39 for 32 oz ($0.17 per oz)
INGREDIENTS: Cultured Grade A milk
FAT: 9 g per cup   PROTEIN: 20 g per cup
TITRATABLE ACIDITY: 1.47%

With a "yogurt taste that is more assertive" than our winner's, this yogurt was "tangier than I generally like, but the richness balances it." Its "whipped texture" offered "less body than I'd expect," but it had "great, fresh dairy taste." It won the top spot in our tzatziki tasting. (Note: "Cultured milk" in this yogurt's ingredient list does not indicate a different processing method.)

WALLABY ORGANIC Whole Milk Greek Yogurt Plain
PRICE: $7.79 for 32 oz ($0.24 per oz)
INGREDIENTS: Organic cultured pasteurized milk and cream. Live and active yogurt cultures (*L. acidophilus. L. bulgaricus, S. thermophilus, Bifidus, L. paracasei*)
FAT: 10 g per cup   PROTEIN: 19 g per cup
TITRATABLE ACIDITY: 1.29%

With a "supersmooth," "creamy," even "velvety" texture, this yogurt won fans, especially among those who don't like sour flavor in their yogurt. Tasters said it had a "very mild taste," though for some it "borders on bland." In tzatziki sauce, it was "good all around, but not very tangy" and "a little loose."

RECOMMENDED WITH RESERVATIONS

THE GREEK GODS Greek Yogurt Traditional Plain
PRICE: $4.29 for 24 oz ($0.18 per oz)
INGREDIENTS: Cultured Pasteurized Grade A Milk, Cream, Pectin, Live and active yogurt cultures (*S. thermophilus, B. lactis, L. acidophilus, L. casei, L. rhamnosus, Lactobacillus lactis, L. bulgaricus*)
FAT: 14 g per cup   PROTEIN: 9 g per cup
TITRATABLE ACIDITY: 1.05%

This "stiff," "bland" yet watery yogurt adds pectin to simulate traditional yogurt's thick, strained consistency, which explains why it has one of the lowest levels of protein per serving in our lineup. The flavor was "pretty neutral" in tzatziki. It was also sweet, not from added sugar but as a result of not straining (lactose, milk's natural sugar, is normally removed when yogurt is strained).

CABOT Greek Plain Greek-Style Yogurt
PRICE: $3.99 for 32 oz ($0.12 per oz)
INGREDIENTS: Pasteurized milk, cream, whey protein concentrate, milk protein concentrate, live active yogurt cultures (*L. acidophilus, Bifidus, L. bulgaricus, and S. thermophilus*), Vitamins A, C, D, E
FAT: 22 g per cup   PROTEIN: 16 g per cup
TITRATABLE ACIDITY: 1.22%

This very "pillowy," extremely high-fat yogurt adds whey protein concentrate and milk protein concentrate to boost protein content and artificially thicken the yogurt. Tasters complained of a "chalky" aftertaste and a "savory, cooked" flavor. In tzatziki sauce, tasters said, it was "missing tang."

CHOBANI Greek Yogurt Whole Milk Plain
PRICE: $6.59 for 32 oz ($0.21 per oz)
INGREDIENTS: Yogurt (cultured pasteurized nonfat milk, cream). Contains live and active cultures (*S. thermophilus, L. bulgaricus, L. acidophilus, Bifidus, and L. casei*)
FAT: 9 g per cup   PROTEIN: 20 g per cup
TITRATABLE ACIDITY: 1.37%

With one of the tangiest tastes and one of the thinnest textures, Chobani slid toward the bottom of the pack. "Almost like regular yogurt," complained one taster. While a few enjoyed its "sour cream"–like tang, others just called it "very sour." In tzatziki it was "watery—both in texture and flavor." One taster summed it up: "For full-fat Greek yogurt, this seems disappointingly virtuous."

NOT RECOMMENDED

MAPLE HILL CREAMERY
100% Grass-Fed Organic Whole Milk Greek Yogurt
PRICE: $2.29 for 5.3 oz ($0.43 per oz)
INGREDIENTS: Pasteurized Whole Milk, live active cultures (*L. delbrueckii* subsp. *bulgaricus, S. thermophilus*)
FAT: 9 g per cup   PROTEIN: 18 g per cup
TITRATABLE ACIDITY: 1.25%

This yogurt, made with milk from grass-fed cows, has a strong, savory flavor that stood out as very different. While a few tasters loved it, most found the "barnyard funk" too challenging. It was also much looser than our preferred Greek yogurt.

Tasting Prepared Pesto

Great pesto is all about the quality of its few ingredients: basil, extra-virgin olive oil, cheese (traditionally Parmesan), garlic, and pine nuts. This simplicity gave us high hopes for prepared pesto purchased from the supermarket. We found seven options (six shelf-stable, one refrigerated), priced from $2.99 to $11.49 per container, and tasted them plain and tossed with pasta.

To our chagrin, most of the pestos were bad—which wasn't surprising when we found ingredients like potato flakes, spinach, cashews, and white balsamic vinegar listed on their labels. Several products suffered from musty, bitter, and sour off-flavors. Why? Nuts and oil go rancid quickly when exposed to light or air, and basil's flavor starts to fade once it is chopped. Any of these ingredients can also go bad before packaging. As a result, many manufacturers rely on preservatives like lactic and acetic acids. Although they're added to ensure freshness, they can impart noticeable sourness.

The best product was the only refrigerated pesto and one of just two products without preservatives. The other, our runner-up (but only recommended with reservations), was a cheese-free, shelf-stable pesto sold in a glass jar. Both products use primarily olive oil, which is slower to oxidize and go rancid than vegetable oils. Our favorite, Buitoni Pesto with Basil, is made with both Parmesan and Romano. For complete tasting results, go to CooksIllustrated.com/apr16. –Kate Shannon

RECOMMENDED	RECOMMENDED WITH RESERVATIONS
BUITONI Pesto with Basil	**SEGGIANO** Fresh Basil Pesto Genovese
PRICE: $6.29 for 7-oz tub ($0.90 per oz)	PRICE: $11.49 for 7-oz jar ($1.64 per oz)
PACKAGING: Refrigerated plastic tub	PACKAGING: Shelf-stable glass jar
COMMENTS: Tasters liked its "creamy flavor and texture" and the richness that comes with two kinds of cheese. We just wish the basil's flavor was a bit stronger. 	COMMENTS: With more cashews than basil or pine nuts, this pesto was pleasantly chunky, but some tasters bemoaned the lack of cheesy flavor. Shelf-stable without acidic preservatives, it avoided sour flavors.

Fresh Curry Leaves

Deep green and glossy, fresh curry leaves have a faint lemony aroma and a complex flavor—our tasters noted hints of cumin, menthol, popcorn, and grass. While sometimes used in curries, curry leaves are unrelated to and only rarely found in curry powder—and they are definitely not a curry powder substitute. Since heating in fat helps draw out their mostly oil-soluble flavor compounds, curry leaves are typically fried lightly in oil or butter before other ingredients are added. We tasted them in a red lentil dish (*masoor dal*) and in a potato samosa filling and found that their unique flavor was a welcome contribution. However, we needed to use eight to 10 leaves rather than the three or four some recipes recommend. The leaves are typically left whole for cooking and are tender enough to eat, though they can be removed before serving. Freeze fresh leaves in a zipper-lock bag for up to a month to preserve their flavor. You can find them at Indian markets, and they're increasingly available at grocery stores. –A.J.

Peeling Asparagus—Is It Worth the Fuss?

When developing our recipe for Roasted Asparagus (page 21), we considered different ways to prep the spears. We finally settled on trimming 1 inch off the base of each spear and then peeling the lower half of each stalk to remove its woody exterior. These spears certainly looked prettier than those we trimmed using our old method—snapping each stalk at its natural breaking point—but we realized there's another reason to trim and peel the spears: There's less waste.

To find out exactly how much less, we divided bunches of standard and jumbo spears (we knew it wouldn't be worth peeling pencil-thin spears) in half and snapped one group of spears and trimmed and peeled the other. We weighed the spears before and after. What did we find? Spears that were snapped lost an average of half their weight, while trimming and peeling resulted in a loss of less than 30 percent. The thicker the spear, the more pronounced the difference when snapped.

Bottom line? You'll throw away more asparagus if you snap off the ends, and the spears won't look as long and elegant. For many reasons, we think trimming and peeling is worth the effort. –S.D.

SNAPPED
Snapping at the natural breaking point means losing half the weight of almost every spear.

PEELED
Trimming 1 inch and then peeling the woody exterior results in a heftier spear.

Tips for Buying Brisket

When buying brisket for recipes like our Home-Corned Beef with Vegetables (page 15) or Barbecued Beef Brisket (July/August 2007), be aware that butchers typically sell two types: flat cut and point cut. These two pieces together make up a full brisket, a large slab of muscle from the cow's chest. The knobby point cut overlaps the rectangular flat cut. The point cut has more marbling, while the flat cut is lean but topped with a thick fat cap. Because the flat cut is easy to find, cheap, and fairly uniform in shape, it's the cut we generally prefer. Make sure to trim the fat cap according to the instructions in whatever recipe you are using. In the case of our corned beef recipe, for example, leaving too much fat in place will impede the curing process, while too little will result in overcooking. A small fat cap provides the best flavor. –L.L.

| **POINT CUT**
Knobby shape with more marbling | **FLAT CUT**
Fairly uniform with a thick fat cap; our preferred cut |

Jerusalem Artichokes: Another Tasty Tuber

Jerusalem artichokes are neither from Jerusalem nor are they artichokes. These knobby-looking North American natives (*Helianthus tuberosus*) are a species of the sunflower genus. When cooked briefly until just tender, they have a creamy texture and taste like a cross between potatoes and artichokes. Our tasters preferred them cooked longer until they were softer, with the consistency of a baked sweet potato. The longer cooking time also made them sweeter, with a deeper artichoke-like flavor. We recommend peeling Jerusalem artichokes before cooking them to remove their fibrous skin. When shopping for them, look for those that are the least knobby. They will be the easiest to peel.

How to cook them: Peel and cut 1 pound Jerusalem artichokes into 2- to 3-inch pieces. Cook in large saucepan over medium-high heat with 1 tablespoon of butter until browned. Season with salt and pepper, then add sprig of thyme and enough water to cover artichokes halfway. Cover saucepan tightly and simmer until artichokes are softened, about 25 minutes. Remove lid and cook until sauce reduces to glazy consistency. Discard thyme sprig and serve. –L.L.

Seeking Out Authentic Basmati

Supermarket shelves teem with a multitude of boxes, bags, and burlap sacks labeled "basmati." Does it matter which you choose? In a word, yes. True basmati can only come from India or Pakistan. The real deal must meet standards for grain dimension, amylose content, and grain elongation during cooking, as well as for aroma. In addition, unlike American basmati, authentic basmati is aged for a minimum of a year (and often much longer) before packaging. Aging dehydrates the rice, which translates into cooked grains that expand greatly in length—more so than any other long-grain rice. While our recipe for Persian-Style Rice with Golden Crust (Chelow) (page 11) will work with standard long-grain or Texmati rice, these options will lack the aromatic quality and more delicate, lengthy grains of Indian- or Pakistani-grown basmati. Our favorite is Tilda Pure Basmati Rice. When buying other brands, look for rice grown in India or Pakistan; some packages will also note that the rice has been aged, another good indicator that it is authentic basmati. –A.P.

DIY RECIPE Whole-Grain Mustard

Homemade mustard is easy to prepare and packs a lot more punch than the store-bought stuff. For our recipe, we start with a 1:1 ratio of milder yellow mustard seeds to more pungent, spicier brown seeds. A little brown sugar tempers the mustard seeds' bite while cider vinegar (rather than straightforward white vinegar) adds complexity. We soak the seeds before processing them in a food processor with the other ingredients. This step not only softens the seeds but also ensures that they break down evenly when processed. Reserving ½ cup of the soaked seeds and stirring them back into the pureed mustard gives it an appealingly grainy consistency. If sampled right after mixing, the mustard might taste a little bitter. We found it best to let the mustard "ripen" on the counter for a few days to allow bitter compounds to dissipate and spicy ones to develop. Refrigeration will halt these enzymatic reactions, so chill it once it reaches your desired heat level. –Amanda Rumore

WHOLE-GRAIN MUSTARD
MAKES 2 CUPS

Don't be tempted to hurry the soaking time by using hot water, as heat activates an enzyme that will kill the mustard's flavor.

¾	cup cider vinegar
½	cup water
⅓	cup yellow mustard seeds
⅓	cup brown mustard seeds
2	tablespoons packed light brown sugar
1¼	teaspoons salt

MAKING IT WHOLE GRAIN
Stirring in some whole mustard seeds delivers the right texture.

1. Combine vinegar, water, yellow mustard seeds, and brown mustard seeds in medium bowl. Cover with plastic wrap and let stand at room temperature for at least 8 hours or up to 24 hours.

2. Measure out ½ cup vinegar–mustard seed mixture and set aside. Combine remaining vinegar–mustard seed mixture, sugar, and salt in food processor and process until coarsely ground and thickened, 1 to 2 minutes, scraping down bowl as needed; return to medium bowl. Stir in reserved vinegar–mustard seed mixture.

3. Using funnel and spoon, portion mustard into two 1-cup jars. Cover and let mustard stand at room temperature until it has reached desired spiciness, 1 to 2 days. (Mustard will become spicier as it rests at room temperature, so refrigerate it once it has reached desired spice level. Once refrigerated, its flavor will continue to mature, but it will not become more spicy. Mustard can be refrigerated for up to 6 months.)

SQUEAKY CLEAN LEEKS

The typical way to clean a leek—trim the leaf ends and the roots, cut the leek in half lengthwise, and wash grit and sediment from the halves under cold running water—doesn't always do the job. The greatest concentration of dirt is usually found at the leek's base, where the layers are tightly packed. Unless the leeks are going to be served halved (as in braised leeks), we prefer this method. We recommend using three times as much water as there are leeks for the rinsing step. –A.G.

1. Lay trimmed, halved leeks cut side down on cutting board and cut to desired size.

2. Transfer leeks to bowl of cold water and rub together until layers separate. Set aside for 1 minute to allow grit to settle to bottom of bowl.

3. Lift leeks from water and transfer to colander to drain. (Do not pour leeks from bowl into colander, or you'll pour dirt over them again.)

KITCHEN NOTES

⇒ BY STEVE DUNN, ANDREA GEARY, ANDREW JANJIGIAN, LAN LAM & ANNIE PETITO ⇐

WHAT IS IT?

Though it resembles a tortilla press, this is a turn-of-the-century cast-iron waffle maker designed to be used over a gas flame or on top of a wood- or coal-burning stove. We found that its wooden handles and ball hinge facili-

tate easy flipping during cooking as intended, but the problem was in the cooking surface. As with all cast-iron cookware, proper seasoning is critical to create a nonstick surface, and it's especially important in this case since the peaks and valleys give waffle batter lots of places to stick. Even after we seasoned the iron multiple times and brushed it with plenty of oil just before adding the batter, waffles made in the Griswold, though they baked up properly, refused to release.

GRISWOLD STOVETOP WAFFLE IRON
Though the waffles appeared to cook up nicely in this antique iron, the fact that it wouldn't release them made it a bust.

If we want to make waffles, we'll stick with our winning modern-day waffle iron, the Waring Pro Double Belgian Waffle Maker ($89.99), whose nonstick coating produced—and released—perfect waffles every time. –S.D.

BAKING CLASS Dough Hydration

The amount of water a bread dough contains greatly affects a bread's texture. Simply put, dough hydration is the weight of the water in a dough relative to the total weight of flour it contains, expressed as a percentage. For example, a 75-percent-hydration dough has 75 grams of water for every 100 grams of flour. Hydration affects bread texture because of the way water and gluten—the protein responsible for providing most of the structure in bread—interact with one another.

Gluten is a network of stretchy flour proteins capable of containing the carbon dioxide produced by yeast while the bread proofs. The more water surrounding the gluten, the more pliable it is, and—up to a point—the more it can expand around the gas bubbles as they grow larger. However, with too much water in the dough, the gluten network weakens, and the structure collapses.

To demonstrate how hydration can affect a dough, we made three versions of our Fougasse (page 9) at varying hydration levels. When we used 10 ounces of water (60 percent hydration), the relatively low amount of water resulted in a stiff dough that was unable to expand properly, producing a compact fougasse with a dense crumb. At the opposite extreme, when we used 14 ounces of water (90 percent hydration), some of the gluten trapping air bubbles in the soupy dough collapsed, resulting in irregular, large gaps in the fougasse. When we used 12 ounces of water (the amount we call for in the recipe)—a hydration of 75 percent—the fougasse rose up nicely, with a good mixture of large and small holes, the ideal structure for this rustic loaf. –A.J.

60% HYDRATION   **90% HYDRATION**   **75% HYDRATION**

Avoid Old Eggs When Hard-Cooking

Conventional wisdom holds that when making hard-cooked eggs, you should choose older eggs (such as those that have been sitting around in your fridge for a few weeks) rather than fresh ones. Why? Because they are supposedly easier to peel. Happily, our new method for hard-cooked eggs (page 13) makes any egg, whether just laid or weeks old, easy to peel. On top of that, we've learned that you are actually better off using fresh eggs over older ones for three specific reasons.

Flat End

Because the air sac inside an egg becomes larger as the egg ages (that's why older eggs float), it can make the broad end of an older egg awkwardly flat. Fresh eggs, with their smaller air sacs, are more likely to have a smooth ovoid shape when peeled, which looks more appealing in applications such as deviled eggs.

Off-Center Yolk

Fresher eggs are more likely (though not guaranteed) to have centered yolks, again leading to more attractive deviled eggs.

More Likely to Form a Green Ring

A freshly laid egg has a slightly alkaline white. As the egg ages, the white becomes increasingly alkaline. The more alkaline the white, the more quickly sulfur in the white reacts with iron on the yolk's surface when the egg is heated, forming the ferrous sulfide that creates that green ring in cooked eggs. While this green ring can be a symptom of overcooking, we confirmed that it is more likely to happen with older eggs. Fresh eggs could be cooked for a full 15 minutes (2 minutes past our cooking time) without forming a green ring, but the yolks of month-old eggs started turning green even within our recommended cooking times.

The Takeaway?

When hard-cooking eggs, ignore conventional wisdom and go with the freshest eggs you can find. If in doubt, try looking at the "best if used by" date. –A.G.

A Tidy Way to Avoid Skin on Custards

A thin, dry "skin" forms on the surface of puddings because as the mixture is heated, two things happen: Water evaporates, and proteins and sugar become more concentrated. Together, this results in a dry barrier on the liquid's surface. You can prevent the skin from forming during cooking by stirring, but what about afterward? The most common method is to press parchment paper onto the surface, which prevents evaporation. But this approach can be messy and fussy, particularly when dealing with individual portions in cups or ramekins.

When developing our recipe for Lemon Posset with Berries (page 23), we came up with a simpler way: We let the mixture sit until a skin had formed, passed it through a fine-mesh strainer, and then portioned the pudding and refrigerated it until serving time. The strainer broke up the clumped proteins and sugar, returning the posset to a smooth consistency throughout. We found that this technique will work equally well on other puddings and custards like our Creamy Chocolate Pudding (September/October 2011). After cooking, simply let the pudding or custard cool until a skin forms, about 20 minutes, and then pour it through a fine-mesh strainer into a large bowl. Portion it, and then refrigerate the portions, uncovered, until cool. Cover the cooled portions with plastic wrap (no need to press it onto the surface of the pudding) until serving time. –A.P.

To keep the recipe for our Roasted Bone-In Chicken Breasts (page 5) simple, we decided to forgo brining and salting. But since we wanted well-seasoned chicken, we knew we had to put salt under the skin, not just on top. In the past we've advised working your fingers between the skin and flesh to loosen the skin and then going back underneath to apply the salt. But doing so can be messy and awkward, and getting the salt evenly distributed over the meat can be a challenge. Here's our new approach. –A.G.

Using your fingers, carefully separate chicken skin from meat. Peel skin back, leaving it attached at top and bottom of breast and at ribs. Repeat with remaining breasts. Sprinkle measured amount of salt evenly over all chicken, then lay skin back in place.

Season Your Salad, Not Just the Dressing

Even though all salad dressing and vinaigrette recipes, including our Make-Ahead Vinaigrette on page 19, contain a measured amount of salt, most professional cooks like to season the salad itself as well. It's a good idea for two reasons: First, it allows you to adjust the seasoning as needed; we generally dress salad greens and then toss in add-ins (radishes, carrots, etc.), so you can season based on how little or much you add. Second, it creates appealing distinct bites of salt throughout. For that reason, we prefer kosher and flaked salts, such as Maldon. Add-ins like fruits and nuts particularly benefit from the contrast of salty bites. So the next time you are serving a salad, add salt just after dressing it to get the seasoning just right. –A.J.

Lighten Up (Your Cake Pans)

Dark-colored pans absorb heat more efficiently than light-colored pans, so the sides and bottoms of items baked in dark pans will cook and brown more quickly than the same items cooked in light pans. This is an asset when baking cinnamon rolls and deep-dish pizza, where a brown crust is desired, but it can be a problem with other recipes. Because the batter near the edges in a dark pan will reach its maximum temperature sooner than the batter near the edges in a light pan, a cake baked in a dark pan will have sides that are overly brown and set early, leading to stunted height, while the center continues to rise. This results in a domed shape, which is particularly problematic for a layer cake.

So what do you do if you own dark pans? Wrap the pans in aluminum foil. We found that a cake baked in a dark pan wrapped in foil looked identical to a cake baked in a light-colored pan: level, with tender, lightly browned sides and bottom. Make sure to wrap the exterior of the pans with foil as snugly as you can. At the top of the pan, fold the edge of the foil back onto itself; do not fold the foil over onto the interior. The shiny side can be in or out; we found it made no noticeable difference. –A.G.

MAKE A FOIL WRAPPER
Cakes baked in foil-wrapped dark pans come out as perfect as those baked in light pans.

EXPERIMENT Roasting Temp and Resting Time

Whether it is a pork tenderloin or a large beef roast, we always let meat rest after roasting. One of the reasons we do this is that resting allows the meat fibers—which contract when hot—to relax and reabsorb juices they've squeezed out. If cut too soon, the roast will release these juices onto your cutting board. In the past, we've gone by the rule of thumb that the larger the piece of meat, the longer it needs to rest. We wondered recently whether the oven temperature used to cook the meat also affects the resting time, so we ran an experiment.

EXPERIMENT

We roasted six 1-pound pork loins; three at 250 degrees and three at 450 degrees, cooking them all to an internal temperature of 140 degrees. We then let pairs from each set rest for different amounts of time before slicing. We sliced the first set immediately, the second set after a 10-minute rest, and the third after a 20-minute rest. We then measured the amount of juices lost as a percentage of total weight for each pork loin.

RESULTS

Both of the roasts that were carved immediately lost a significant (and unacceptable) amount of their weight in juices (6.5 percent from the low-oven roast and 8.6 percent from the hot-oven roast). At the other end of the spectrum, the two roasts that sat for 20 minutes before slicing lost roughly equal amounts of juice (about 4 percent). The most notable difference was between the roasts that had rested for 10 minutes: The hot-oven roast lost almost twice as much juice when sliced after 10 minutes (7.9 percent) as the low-oven roast (which lost 4.3 percent).

LOW HEAT, SHORTER REST
After roasting at 250 degrees and resting for 10 minutes, this roast lost just 4 percent of its juices.

HIGH HEAT, SHORTER REST
After roasting at 450 degrees and resting for 10 minutes, this roast lost 7.9 percent of its juices.

EXPLANATION

While all of the roasts were cooked to the same internal temperature, the roasts cooked in the 450-degree ovens were significantly hotter around their perimeters than at their centers compared with the roasts cooked in the 250-degree ovens. Therefore, the muscle fibers around the perimeter in these roasts were much more contracted and needed more time to relax and reabsorb juices.

TAKEAWAY

When roasting low and slow, meat needs a shorter rest than does a high-temperature roast. The muscle fibers do not tighten as much, so juices lost are minimized, and there's nominal benefit to extra waiting time—your roast will simply cool off more. –L.L.

SCIENCE OF COOKING:
The Key to Perfectly Cooked Salmon
It turns out that a thermometer is just as crucial when grilling salmon as it is when grilling steak. A video explaining why is available for 4 months at CooksIllustrated.com/apr16.

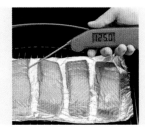

EQUIPMENT CORNER

⇒ BY MIYE BROMBERG, LISA McMANUS & KATE SHANNON ⇐

    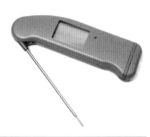

RECOMMENDED	**HIGHLY RECOMMENDED**	**RECOMMENDED**	**NOT RECOMMENDED**	**HIGHLY RECOMMENDED**
LODGE 12-inch Tempered Glass Cover	BONAVITA 8-Cup Coffee Maker with Thermal Carafe	OXO Good Grips Salad Dressing Shaker	NORPRO Spice Grinder	THERMOWORKS Thermapen Mk4
MODEL: GC12	MODEL: BV1900TS	MODEL: 1188500	MODEL: 775	MODEL: 234-XX7
PRICE: $25.81	PRICE: $189.99	PRICE: $14.99	PRICE: $8.48	PRICE: $99.00

TESTING Lids for Cast-Iron Skillets

Our favorite traditional cast iron manufacturer, Lodge, now makes dedicated lids that fit its 12-inch traditional skillet, the winner of our most recent cast-iron skillet testing. One lid is made of tempered glass and costs about $26; the other is made of cast iron and costs about $33. We put both through their paces by covering frying eggs, caramelizing onions, and bubbling tomato sauce, washing each by hand (and oiling the cast-iron lid per Lodge's recommendation) after every use. The verdict? You don't need a lid made of cast iron to cover a cast-iron skillet—it's simply too heavy to be practical—plus, it needs the special care and maintenance required of cast iron. The tempered glass lid is cheaper, works well, and is much easier to use, clean, and store. –M.B.

UPDATE Bonavita Coffee Maker

Our highly recommended Best Buy coffee maker, the Bonavita 8-Cup Coffee Maker with Thermal Carafe, has been redesigned. In addition to a $40 price hike to $189.99, the biggest changes were to the coffee brew basket (formerly cone-shaped, it is now flat-bottomed), additional holes in the hot water "showerhead," and the thermal carafe (which is now double-lined with stainless steel instead of glass).

We measured the brew time and temperature, brewed multiple pots of coffee and cleaned up to assess user-friendliness, and then held a blind tasting comparing identical coffee brewed in the old and new models. The Specialty Coffee Association of America certified that this new model also meets its coffee-brewing standards for optimal flavor. We found that the changes still met our standards as well and produced coffee our tasters enjoyed. In sum: A very good coffee maker is now even better. We also preferred the new version's more durable and better-insulated carafe.

However, just like the older model, the updated model lacks a brew-through lid, so you must replace the brew basket with the lid to keep coffee hot. And there's nowhere on the machine to store the lid during brewing or to put the basket when the carafe lid is on. Those complaints aside, we like the improvements to this machine, and it remains our Best Buy. –L.M.

TESTING Salad Dressing Shakers

Salad dressing shakers promise to emulsify, dispense, and store vinaigrette more easily than a lidded jar. But out of the seven we purchased (all under $16), there is only one, the OXO Good Grips Salad Dressing Shaker, that we can recommend. The models that failed had many problems: Some were too small or awkwardly large, lacked pour spouts, had leaky seals, and/or were hard to clean. By contrast, our winner has a wide mouth, a tight seal, and a spout that pours beautifully. –M.B.

TESTING Manual Spice Grinders

As with pepper, the flavor and aroma of dried spices are more potent when you grind them fresh. But our favorite electric grinder, the Krups Fast-Touch Coffee Mill (we keep one dedicated to spice grinding), can feel oversized for grinding just a teaspoon or two. Are manual spice grinders—hand-cranked cousins of pepper mills—the answer to quick, small-batch ground spices?

To find out, we tested six models (priced from $8.48 to $24.22) by grinding measured amounts of cumin seeds at the finest and coarsest settings and then grinding a teaspoon of dried rosemary needles into a fine powder in each model. The majority of the models looked and worked a lot like pepper mills: You load a clear glass jar with spices, screw on a stainless-steel or plastic grinder housing, and hold it steady while you twist the jar. The majority of grinders had a small knob on the grinding mechanism that adjusted the space between the two grinding elements and thus the size of the grind.

Sadly, we can't recommend any of the models we tried. The worst offender was the Norpro Spice Grinder. It had a tiny spice reservoir, and it wasn't adjustable. At best, we could achieve only a single, fairly coarse grind, and we often found whole cumin seeds mixed in with the crushed. We'll stick with our favorite electric grinder for spices. –K.S.

UPDATE Thermapen

ThermoWorks recently released an updated version of our favorite instant-read thermometer, the Splash-Proof Super-Fast Thermapen. The new model, called the Thermapen Mk4, has a number of additional features: New sensors allow the display to automatically rotate, wake up, turn off, and light up in darker conditions. The Mk4 is more water-resistant, and ThermoWorks claims that a switch from lithium batteries to a single AAA alkaline battery doubles usage time from 1,500 hours to 3,000. The Mk4 costs $99; ThermoWorks plans to keep selling the older model, now called the Classic Super-Fast Thermapen, for $79.

To see if the improvements were worth having, we bought four Mk4s and tested them extensively in our kitchen against the Classic. We found little difference between the two models in terms of accuracy or speed; both read precise temperatures in 2 to 3 seconds. (One of the Mk4s failed to turn on consistently, so we ordered five additional units to make sure that the problem wasn't systemic. We'll continue to monitor their performance, but so far, all the other units have worked great.) Which Thermapen should you get? In the end, the new features give the Mk4 a slight edge, but if you don't care about the Mk4's new features, the classic model is still a top performer and is also cheaper. –M.B.

For complete testing results, go to CooksIllustrated.com/apr16.

INDEX
March & April 2016

BONUS ONLINE CONTENT
More recipes, reviews, and videos are available at CooksIllustrated.com/apr16

▶ RECIPE VIDEOS
Want to see how to make any of the recipes in this issue? There's a video for that.

▶ MORE VIDEOS
Recipes, reviews, and videos available free for 4 months at CooksIllustrated.com/apr16

Roasted Bone-In Chicken Breasts, 5

Roasted Asparagus, 21

Fougasse, 9

Home-Corned Beef with Vegetables, 15

Beef Stir-Fry with Black Pepper Sauce, 7

Make-Ahead Vinaigrette, 19

Lemon Posset with Berries, 23

Persian-Style Rice with Golden Crust, 11

Garlicky Spaghetti with Lemon and Pine Nuts, 20

Curry Deviled Eggs, 13

PHOTOGRAPHY: CARL TREMBLAY; STYLING: MARIE PIRAINO

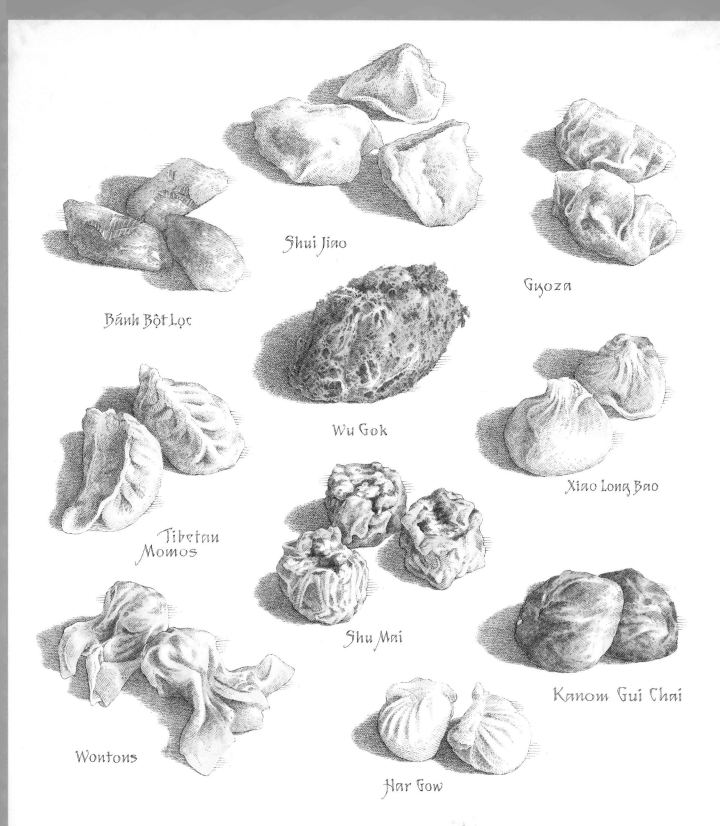

Shui Jiao

Gyoza

Bánh Bột Lọc

Wu Gok

Xiao Long Bao

Tibetan Momos

Shu Mai

Kanom Gui Chai

Wontons

Har Gow

ASIAN DUMPLINGS

NUMBER 140

MAY & JUNE 2016

COOK'S
ILLUSTRATED

Best Strawberry
Shortcake

Pan-Seared Salmon
Crisp Crust, Moist Flesh

Lemon Chicken
Tender Chicken in Silky Sauce

Grill-Roasted
Beef Tenderloin
How to Get Real Grill Flavor

Spanish-Style
Fried Potatoes

Rating Gas Grills
It's Not About the BTUs

Easy Italian Soufflé
Less Fuss, Just As Elegant

Dinner Rice Bowl
How to Cook Sugar Snap Peas
Best Sticky Buns

CooksIllustrated.com
$6.95 U.S. & $7.95 CANADA

COOK'S ILLUSTRATED

MAY & JUNE 2016

PAGE 20

DOUGHNUTS

BACK COVER ILLUSTRATED BY JOHN BURGOYNE

Doughnuts

CINNAMON-SUGAR CAKE doughnuts get their lift from baking powder; a spiced sugar coating adds delicate crunch. With a custard filling and a smear of chocolate icing, BOSTON CREAM doughnuts are a nod to the cake of the same name. CRULLERS are made by piping egg-enriched dough into an elongated twist; the ring-shaped variety are called FRENCH CRULLERS. A generous portion of sweet berry jelly fills the center of raised JELLY doughnuts. DOUGHNUT HOLES are the bite-size treats made from the dough taken from the center of ringed doughnuts. CHOCOLATE GLAZED doughnuts feature cocoa- and/or chocolate-enriched cake dunked in a confectioners' sugar glaze. The featherlight dough used to make HONEY GLAZED doughnuts yields a soft, delicate result. BEIGNETS were established by the French in New Orleans and are often enjoyed with café au lait. A thin track of cinnamon swirls through glazed COFFEE ROLLS.

AMERICA'S TEST KITCHEN
RECIPES THAT WORK®

America's Test Kitchen is a real 2,500-square-foot kitchen located just outside Boston. It is the home of more than 60 test cooks, editors, and cookware specialists. Our mission is to test recipes until we understand exactly how and why they work and eventually arrive at the very best version. We also test kitchen equipment and supermarket ingredients in search of products that offer the best value and performance. You can watch us work by tuning in to *America's Test Kitchen* (AmericasTestKitchen.com) and *Cooks Country from America's Test Kitchen* (CooksCountry.com) on public television, and listen to us on our weekly radio program on PRX. You can also follow us on Facebook, Twitter, Pinterest, and Instagram.

EDITORIAL STAFF

Chief Executive Officer David Nussbaum
Chief Creative Officer Jack Bishop
Editorial Director John Willoughby
Executive Editor Amanda Agee
Deputy Editor Rebecca Hays
Executive Managing Editor Todd Meier
Executive Food Editor Keith Dresser
Senior Editors Andrea Geary, Andrew Janjigian, Dan Souza
Senior Editors, Features Elizabeth Bomze, Louise Emerick
Associate Editors Lan Lam, Chris O'Connor
Test Cooks Daniel Cellucci, Steve Dunn, Annie Petito
Assistant Test Cooks Allison Berkey, Matthew Fairman
Copy Editors Jillian Campbell, Krista Magnuson
Science Editor Guy Crosby, PhD

Executive Tastings & Testings Editor Lisa McManus
Managing Editor, Tastings & Testings Scott Kathan
Senior Editor Hannah Crowley
Assistant Editors Miye Bromberg, Lauren Savoie,
    Kate Shannon

Test Kitchen Director Erin McMurrer
Assistant Test Kitchen Director Leah Rovner
Test Kitchen Manager Alexxa Grattan
Senior Test Kitchen Assistants Meridith Lippard,
    Taylor Pond
Kitchen Assistants Gladis Campos, Blanca Castanza,
    Maria Elena Delgado, Heather Ecker, Ena Gudiel

Design Director, Print Greg Galvan
Photography Director Julie Cote
Art Director Susan Levin
Associate Art Director Lindsey Chandler
Deputy Art Director, Marketing Melanie Gryboski
Associate Art Director, Marketing Janet Taylor
Designer, Marketing Stephanie Cook
Staff Photographer Daniel J. van Ackere
Associate Art Director, Photography Steve Klise
Assistant Photography Producer Mary Ball
Styling Catrine Kelty, Marie Piraino

Design Director, Digital John Torres
Managing Editor, Web Christine Liu
Social Media Manager Jill Fisher
Senior Editor, Web Roger Metcalf
Assistant Editor, Web Terrence Doyle
Senior Video Editor Nick Dakoulas
Test Kitchen Photojournalist Kevin White

BUSINESS STAFF

VP, Print & Direct Marketing David Mack
Circulation Director Doug Wicinski
Circulation & Fulfillment Manager Carrie Fethe
Marketing Assistant Andrea Hampel
Production Director Guy Rochford
Imaging Manager Lauren Robbins
Production & Imaging Specialists Heather Dube,
    Sean MacDonald, Dennis Noble, Jessica Voas

Chief Digital Officer Fran Middleton
Chief Financial Officer Jackie McCauley Ford
Senior Controller Theresa Peterson
Director, Business Systems Alice Carpenter
Project Manager Mehgan Conciatori

VP, New Business Development Michael Burton
Partnership Marketing Manager Pamela Putprush
Client Services Manager Kate Zebrowski
Sponsorship Sales Associate Morgan Mannino
VP, Strategic Analytics Deborah Fagone
Customer Loyalty & Support Manager Amy Bootier
Senior Customer Loyalty & Support Specialist
    Andrew Straaberg Finfrock
Customer Loyalty & Support Specialists Caroline Augliere,
    Rebecca Kowalski, Ramesh Pillay
Senior VP, Human Resources & Organizational
    Development Colleen Zelina
Human Resources Director Adele Shapiro
Director, Retail Book Program Beth Ineson
Retail Sales Manager Derek Meehan
Associate Director, Publicity Susan Hershberg

Cover Illustration (Plums) Robert Papp

YOU'RE THE BOSS

Confession time: We don't really run this magazine. You do.

Okay, maybe that's a bit of hyperbole. But not very much. Because before we do anything, we ask you if we should do it. Then we solicit your input along the way. And then, when we're finished, we ask you how we did.

Here's how it works. When we're considering what recipes to develop, we survey a random panel of you readers, asking, for each dish, whether it's something you really want. If 80 percent of you say yes, we start testing incessantly to come up with the best possible version. When we think we've got it, we ask those of you who have volunteered to do so to actually make the recipe in your own kitchens and give us feedback. If fewer than 80 percent of you say you're so happy with our recipe that you'll add it to your regular repertoire, we go back to the drawing board (or, more accurately, the kitchen counter) to address your concerns. Then we send it out to you again. No matter how much work we've done, if we can't get at least 80 percent of you to love a recipe, we ditch it. (Ask our test cooks about the famous chocolate fudge recipe that, despite two months of testing, sits in the dustbin of our culinary history.) Finally, a postpublication survey lets us know how much you liked not only the recipes but also the stories and even the art in the issue.

It's all about giving you not what we think you should have, but what you really want.

One interesting thing about this is that what you want changes over time. In this issue, for example, you'll find plenty of what you might call "American classics," from Refined Strawberry Shortcake to easy

Skillet-Roasted Chicken in Lemon Sauce, smoky Grill-Roasted Beef Tenderloin, and a new (and better) version of Sticky Buns. These types of recipes will always be a major part of our magazine.

But there are also recipes here that would never have appeared in our pages 10 years ago. There's Patatas Bravas, a classic Spanish potato tapa; Korean Rice Bowl, which features the newly popular Asian condiment *gochujang*; and Parmesan Farrotto, based on a grain that has only recently come to the attention of American cooks. Oh, and when you read about the sticky buns, you'll find that the secret to their amazing texture is a cutting-edge Japanese technique known as *tangzhong*.

It seems that our world—or, really, your world—is getting larger. We hope you like what we're adding to it. We'll soon find out.

The Editors of *Cook's Illustrated*

FOR INQUIRIES, ORDERS, OR MORE INFORMATION

COOK'S ILLUSTRATED MAGAZINE

Cook's Illustrated magazine (ISSN 1068-2821), number 140, is published bimonthly by Boston Common Press Limited Partnership, 17 Station St., Brookline, MA 02445. Copyright 2016 Boston Common Press Limited Partnership. Periodicals postage paid at Boston, MA, and additional mailing offices, USPS #012487. Publications Mail Agreement No. 40020778. Return undeliverable Canadian addresses to P.O. Box 875, Station A, Windsor, ON N9A 6P2. POSTMASTER: Send address changes to *Cook's Illustrated*, P.O. Box 6018, Harlan, IA 51593-1518. For subscription and gift subscription orders, subscription inquiries, or change of address notices, visit AmericasTestKitchen.com/support, call 800-526-8442 in the U.S. or 515-248-7684 from outside the U.S., or write to us at *Cook's Illustrated*, P.O. Box 6018, Harlan, IA 51593-1518.

CooksIllustrated.com

At the all-new CooksIllustrated.com, you can order books and subscriptions, sign up for our free e-newsletter, or renew your magazine subscription. Join the website and gain access to 23 years of *Cook's Illustrated* recipes, equipment tests, and ingredient tastings, as well as companion videos for every recipe in this issue.

COOKBOOKS

We sell more than 50 cookbooks by the editors of *Cook's Illustrated*, including *The Cook's Illustrated Cookbook* and *Paleo Perfected*. To order, visit our bookstore at CooksIllustrated.com/bookstore.

EDITORIAL OFFICE 17 Station St., Brookline, MA 02445; 617-232-1000; fax: 617-232-1572. For subscription inquiries, visit AmericasTestKitchen.com/support or call 800-526-8442.

QUICK TIPS

≈ COMPILED BY ANNIE PETITO ≈

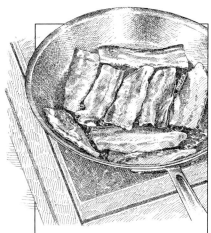

More (and Better) Bacon in the Pan

To ensure that bacon cooks evenly in the pan, Rob Hughes of Soquel, Calif., cuts the slices in half crosswise before cooking. The shorter strips (which happen to be the perfect size for sandwiches) lay completely flat against the surface; plus, he's able to fit two extra half-slices in the pan without overcrowding.

A Steadier Pour from Syrup

Because it's easy to pour out too much maple syrup over pancakes or waffles, Mara Morgan of Boise, Idaho, controls the pour and creates a steady stream by affixing a spare liquid pourer (the kind she uses for cruets of oil and vinegar) to the top of the syrup bottle. The pourer does get sticky, so she removes and washes it between uses.

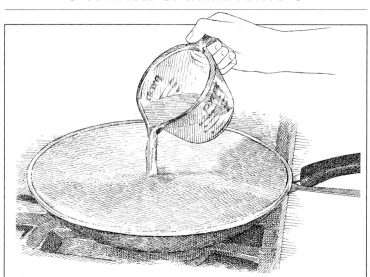

Splatter-Free Deglazing

Pouring liquid into a hot skillet to deglaze it can cause messy splatters. To keep his stovetop cleaner, Skip Redman of San Diego, Calif., covers the pan with a splatter screen and pours the liquid directly through the mesh into the pan. Once the splatter and sizzle subside, he removes the screen to stir and incorporate the browned bits of fond.

No More Sticky Jar Lids

After struggling to open sticky honey, syrup, and jam jars, Katherine James of Atlanta, Ga., now sprays the rim of the jar with nonstick spray before twisting the lid back on. A couple of tricks: Hold the jar at an angle with the opening facing away from you so you don't spray directly into the food, and pulse gently on the nozzle to avoid spraying too much.

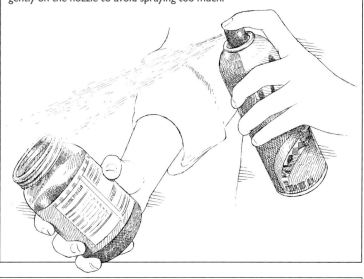

Faster Food Wrapping

To avoid repeatedly cutting plastic wrap to individually seal up multiple portions of foods like muffins or raw burger patties, Jennifer Siegel of Westfield, N.J., uses this more efficient method.

1. Tear off a very long piece of plastic wrap. Place individual portions evenly along the bottom half of the wrap.

2. Fold the top half of the plastic wrap down over the portions, and press down between them and on the ends to seal.

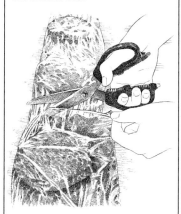

3. Cut between the portions to create individual packets, folding the edges under to close. (Wrapped foods can be placed in a zipper-lock bag or stored individually.)

SEND US YOUR TIPS We will provide a complimentary one-year subscription for each tip we print. Send your tip, name, address, and daytime telephone number to Quick Tips, *Cook's Illustrated*, P.O. Box 470589, Brookline, MA 02447, or to QuickTips@AmericasTestKitchen.com.

A Grate Way to Transfer Food

To quickly transport cheese or vegetables that he's shredded on his box grater, Tim Granger of Dayton, Ohio, wedges a bench scraper that is wide enough to cover the opening underneath the grater as he works. Then, he holds the two tools tightly together to contain the food as he transfers it to the mixing bowl.

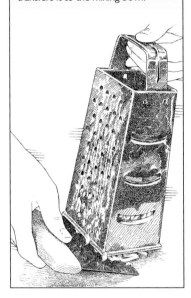

Easy-to-Recognize Hard-Cooked Eggs

When Megan Homan of Rockwood, Mich., makes a few hard-cooked eggs for the coming week, she marks their spaces on the cardboard carton with the letter H so she doesn't confuse them with the uncooked eggs.

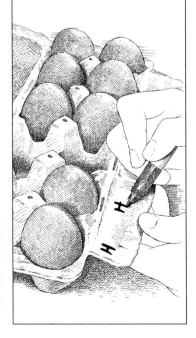

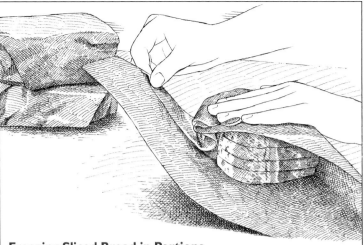

Freezing Sliced Bread in Portions

To easily remove and thaw slices of bread for sandwiches from loaves stored in the freezer, Isabel Aybar of Houston, Texas, divides the whole loaf into groups of two or four slices. She then wraps each portion in parchment or plastic wrap before putting them all back in the original bag to freeze.

Butter Wrapper Doubles as Dough Presser

When pressed into a baking pan for bar cookies, dough often sticks to the utensil. To avoid this, instead of using a spoon or spatula, Bridget Sciales of New York, N.Y., uses the wrapper from the stick of butter called for in the recipe, which is slick enough to press against the dough without any worry of sticking.

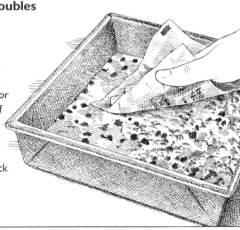

Bookmarking Recipes

When Nora Thompson of Bandon, Ore., finds a recipe she wants to try in a cooking magazine, she bookmarks the page with a sticky note on which she writes the ingredients she'll need to buy. When she's ready to shop, all she has to do is grab the note as her shopping list.

Containing Marinating Meat

Miriam Miltenberger of St. David, Ariz., found that an empty plastic salad greens container (one with no holes in the bottom) works well for marinating smaller cuts or chunks of meat. The plastic top snaps tightly to keep the meat contained; the container is flat, so it stacks easily in the fridge; and the container can be rinsed and recycled after use.

Frugal Fruit Infusion

Rather than throwing strawberry tops in the trash, Alexis Patrissi of Ardsley, N.Y., saves them for flavoring water. Steeping the tops from 1 pound of strawberries in 4 cups of water for 1 hour yields a lightly sweet, fruity beverage, and because the strawberries have already been washed, there is no extra prep. (Spent citrus halves also work well.)

Rao's Lemon Chicken, Our Way

Getting a reservation at this New York institution is nearly impossible, so we decided to re-create its beloved lemony chicken dish at home.

⋟ BY ANNIE PETITO ⋞

Even if you've never landed a table at Rao's, New York City's legendary Italian restaurant, you may have heard of its famous roast lemon chicken. The dish is a take on *pollo al limone* in which two small chickens are cut in half and cooked under the restaurant's powerful broiler (called a salamander). The deeply bronzed birds are then cut into pieces and bathed in a simple, pungent sauce of lemon juice (a full cup per bird), olive oil, red wine vinegar, garlic, and dried oregano before being briefly broiled again and served with crusty bread for dipping.

With its simple, bold preparation, the dish is undeniably appealing, and the restaurant's recipe (published in its cookbook and on the Internet) is hugely popular. But it's not perfect. When I tried to replicate it, I hit a number of snags. First: The small, quick-cooking birds used at Rao's are not available in most supermarkets, and home broilers are not nearly as powerful or even-heating as restaurant broilers. As a result, the skin on the larger supermarket birds (which has more fat than the skin on the younger birds used at Rao's) browned unevenly and was flabby since it didn't fully render. Then there was the sauce. Pouring it over the chicken made the skin soggy, and marrying the two components at the last minute made the flavor transfer between them superficial. Plus, the sauce was thin—fine as a bread dipper but not viscous enough to cling to the meat—and downright puckery.

The good news was that all of these flaws seemed fixable, so I set my sights on making a more accessible version of the Rao's classic and refining its flavors.

Problematic Elements

My first task: picking the right chicken. As an easy alternative to the small birds, I decided to use bone-in chicken parts; 3 pounds of mixed white and dark meat would roughly approximate the yield of two small chickens and would serve four. The Rao's recipe

▶ **Watch It Come Together**
A step-by-step video is available at CooksIllustrated.com/june16

To keep the skin crisp, we pour the lemon gravy around—rather than over—the chicken before serving.

doesn't call for brining or salting the chicken, but we've found that both methods season the meat and help keep it moist. To make this a weeknight-friendly dish, I chose brining, which can be done in 30 minutes (salting bone-in chicken pieces takes at least 6 hours to have an impact). I dried the brined meat's exterior well so as not to inhibit browning.

As for the cooking method, a comparison of conventional home broilers to salamanders explained why the former was yielding such uneven results. Most salamanders comprise multiple closely aligned parallel elements that disperse heat evenly over the surface of the food. With home broilers, the design of the heating element can vary considerably: Some models have a single bar running down the middle of the oven, others a serpentine coil—and neither projects widespread, even heat. Plus, the heat output and the distance you can put between the element and the food vary; I needed to lower the oven rack 10 inches from the element in our test kitchen ovens to ensure that the chicken pieces cooked through before burning, but not every home oven offers that option.

The more foolproof approach would be to sear the chicken on the stovetop and then finish cooking it in the oven in the sauce. Doing so meant I could incorporate the flavorful fond left in the pan after searing the chicken pieces into the sauce, and I could also maximize the flavor transfer between the chicken pieces and the sauce.

After patting the chicken parts dry, I browned them in a 12-inch ovensafe skillet, transferred them to a plate, and briefly sautéed minced garlic and shallot in the rendered chicken fat. To balance the acidity, I reduced the amount of lemon juice to ¼ cup and skipped the vinegar (we couldn't taste it with all the citrus). To this mixture I added 1 cup of chicken broth—which was just enough liquid to submerge the bottom halves of the chicken pieces while leaving the skin exposed. In essence, I'd be braising the meat—but uncovered so that the exposed skin could crisp in the oven's heat.

In less than 15 minutes, the skin was crisp and the white meat was cooked through; the downside was that I had to remove the breasts from the pan before the legs and thighs, which took longer to cook, were done. As for the sauce, cooking the lemon juice had weakened the fruit's flavor, and the consistency was still too thin.

New York's Toughest Table

Unless you're a New York City A-lister, you probably haven't dined at Rao's. The tiny East Harlem institution, famous for its Italian American classics and quirky policies, is like a club for longtime regulars and celebrities, including Al Pacino, Woody Allen, and Robert DeNiro.

Better Results with a Backward Method

Most recipes for roasted chicken with a sauce call for cooking the chicken and then making the sauce. But here we quickly brown the chicken and then braise the meat in the sauce, which not only melds the flavors of the meat and sauce but also eliminates the need to tent the chicken and compromise its crackly skin while making the sauce.

BROWN THE CHICKEN TO BUILD FLAVOR
After searing the chicken to develop the flavorful brown bits called fond (and crisp the skin), we sauté minced shallot and garlic in butter.

ADD THE AROMATICS, FLOUR, AND LIQUID
We use a generous amount of flour to thicken the braising liquid (lemon juice and chicken broth)—no need to reduce it once the meat is done.

WHISK IN THE HERBS AND REMAINING FOND
Just before serving, we whisk the sauce to incorporate the herb mixture and any fond that has built up around the skillet during braising.

Through Thick and Thin

The easiest way to synchronize the doneness of the white and dark meats in the oven was to extend the cooking time of the dark meat on the stovetop, browning it on both sides rather than just the skin side so that it went into the oven at a higher temperature than the white meat. Problem solved.

Since I was cooking the lemon juice, I knew that adding more of it to the sauce would only increase the acidity, not the flavor. Added at the end of cooking, it made the sauce sour. But the aromatic compounds in lemon zest are more stable and retain more fruity lemony flavor when heated. After trying various amounts of zest, I settled on introducing 1 tablespoon right before I added the chicken for the bright, citrusy boost I was after. (For more information, see "The Chemistry of Cooked Lemon Flavor.")

As for thickening the sauce, I first tried the most conventional tactic—removing the cooked chicken from the liquid and tenting it with foil to keep it warm, whisking some cornstarch into the sauce, and

briefly simmering it. It worked, but at the expense of the chicken's skin, which steamed under the foil and lost its crispiness. But what if I thickened the sauce at the beginning instead by adding flour, which is more heat-stable than cornstarch, to the aromatics? The tricky part was that as the chicken cooked, it shed juices that thinned the sauce, so it took a few tests before I determined that 4 teaspoons of flour made for full-bodied, lemony gravy. I also swapped in butter for the chicken fat because I found that the rendered fat varied from batch to batch. Two tablespoons of butter gave me a perfectly rich sauce. After transferring the chicken to a serving platter, I gave the mixture a whisk to smooth it out and scrape the flavorful fond from the sides of the pan back into the sauce.

A combination of chopped oregano, parsley, and more lemon zest—stirred into the sauce and sprinkled over top—added fruity brightness that complemented the crisp skin; moist, flavorful meat; and silky, lemony sauce. This wasn't exactly Rao's chicken, but in the spirit of New York, I could say I did it my way.

SCIENCE The Chemistry of Cooked Lemon Flavor

Virtually all of the lemon flavor we perceive is due to volatile aroma compounds that enter our noses as we chew and swallow food—a phenomenon called retronasal smell. In fact, the only flavors we actually perceive from our tastebuds are sour and bitter compounds. Both lemon juice and zest contain volatile aroma compounds (limonene in juice; neral, geranial, and linalool in zest), but because the compounds in each behave very differently when exposed to heat, we use a combination of juice and zest in our lemon sauce to achieve a balance of fruitiness and acidity.

JUICE KEEPS ITS ACIDITY
The aroma compounds in lemon juice, which are suspended in water, are highly volatile and readily evaporate when heated. But its acidic compounds are unaffected by heat, so juice added during cooking will contribute bright tanginess but little fruity flavor.

most fruity aroma compounds evaporate
acidity is unaffected
COOKED JUICE

ZEST KEEPS ITS FRUITINESS
The aroma compounds in zest are less volatile than those in juice when exposed to heat because they are trapped in oil glands within the peel's cell walls. Zest added during cooking will thus lend noticeable lemony taste to food; we add more at the end of cooking for a final hit of fruity flavor.

few fruity aroma compounds evaporate
fruity flavor stays largely intact
COOKED ZEST

We serve our version of Rao's chicken with crusty bread, but it can also be served with rice, potatoes, or egg noodles. To ensure crisp skin, dry the chicken well after brining and pour the sauce around, not on, the chicken right before serving.

- ½ cup salt
- 3 pounds bone-in chicken pieces (2 split breasts cut in half crosswise, 2 drumsticks, and 2 thighs), trimmed
- 1 teaspoon vegetable oil
- 2 tablespoons unsalted butter
- 1 large shallot, minced
- 1 garlic clove, minced
- 4 teaspoons all-purpose flour
- 1 cup chicken broth
- 4 teaspoons grated lemon zest plus ¼ cup juice (2 lemons)
- 1 tablespoon fresh parsley leaves
- 1 teaspoon fresh oregano leaves

1. Dissolve salt in 2 quarts cold water in large container. Submerge chicken in brine, cover, and refrigerate for 30 minutes to 1 hour. Remove chicken from brine and pat dry with paper towels.

2. Adjust oven rack to lower-middle position and heat oven to 475 degrees. Heat oil in ovensafe 12-inch skillet over medium-high heat until just smoking. Place chicken skin side down in skillet and cook until skin is well browned and crisp, 8 to 10 minutes. Transfer breasts to large plate. Flip thighs and legs and continue to cook until browned on second side, 3 to 5 minutes longer. Transfer thighs and legs to plate with breasts.

3. Pour off and discard fat in skillet. Return skillet to medium heat; add butter, shallot, and garlic and cook until fragrant, 30 seconds. Sprinkle flour evenly over shallot-garlic mixture and cook, stirring constantly, until flour is lightly browned, about 1 minute. Slowly stir in broth and lemon juice, scraping up any browned bits, and bring to simmer. Cook until sauce is slightly reduced and thickened, 2 to 3 minutes. Stir in 1 tablespoon zest and remove skillet from heat. Return chicken, skin side up (skin should be above surface of liquid), and any accumulated juices to skillet and transfer to oven. Cook, uncovered, until breasts register 160 degrees and thighs and legs register 175 degrees, 10 to 12 minutes.

4. While chicken cooks, chop parsley, oregano, and remaining 1 teaspoon zest together until finely minced and well combined. Remove skillet from oven and let chicken stand for 5 minutes.

5. Transfer chicken to serving platter. Whisk sauce, incorporating any browned bits from sides of pan, until smooth and homogeneous, about 30 seconds. Whisk half of herb-zest mixture into sauce and sprinkle remaining half over chicken. Pour some sauce around chicken. Serve, passing remaining sauce separately.

Great Grill-Roasted Beef Tenderloin

To deliver great grill flavor to beef tenderloin, we had to upend the most commonly held notion about the source of that flavor.

⋛ BY LAN LAM ⋜

Grilled to a perfect medium-rare, a rosy-pink, ultratender beef tenderloin is a great centerpiece for summer entertaining. The only trouble is, this cut's flavor is fairly mild. To amp things up, many recipes call for smoking the tenderloin over wood chips, wrapping it with cured meats like pancetta or bacon, or rubbing it with an abundance of spices. The result? The meat's delicate flavor is overwhelmed. I wanted a grilled beef tenderloin that tasted beefy—not smoky or porky or spicy—with just enough flavor from the grill to complement and amplify the roast's natural flavor. And of course, I wanted the roast to be perfectly cooked.

Inner Perfection

I settled on a ready-to-go center-cut tenderloin (also known as Châteaubriand) rather than a larger whole tenderloin. The center-cut option comes cleaned of fat and silverskin by the butcher and makes enough to serve a small group. All I had to do was tie the roast at 1½-inch intervals to keep it uniform in shape, ensuring even cooking and an attractive presentation.

No, that bacon isn't an accompaniment to the meat. It's there to drip fat onto the coals—in this case not a problem but a solution.

After seasoning my roast with salt and pepper and giving it a thin coating of oil to encourage browning, I fired up the grill. I decided I'd start my testing on a gas grill since it would be more challenging to produce grill flavor; once I'd perfected the cooking method, I would translate the recipe for a charcoal grill.

Many recipes call for grilling tenderloin over medium heat, but this necessitates constantly turning the roast to ensure even cooking, and inevitably some of the meat just beneath the surface overcooks. I knew I'd rely on indirect, low-and-slow heat to cook my roast through since it would be the most gentle and even. The higher the heat the meat is exposed to, the more its proteins contract, and thus squeeze out juices, so by keeping the roast away from

▶ See the Proper Setup
A step-by-step video is available at CooksIllustrated.com/june16

intense direct heat, I would also be minimizing the juices lost. After the grill was preheated, I turned off all but the primary burner and placed the roast on the cooler side of the grill. With a little experimentation, I found that keeping the grill at 300 degrees and placing the tenderloin about 7 inches from the primary burner yielded a roast with an interior that was rosy and juicy from edge to edge.

Dripping with Flavor

With the inside of the roast looking good, I turned my focus to improving its flavor and exterior appearance—it needed some browning, and it didn't taste grilled. The two attributes are related. Part of grill flavor is attributed to browning—both the deep color the roast develops where it comes in contact with the bars of the grill's cooking grate and the overall browning the exterior develops through indirect heat. That much is pretty well known. Less widely known is the fact that grill flavor also comes from the meat's drippings hitting the heat diffusers on a gas grill (also known as

flavorizer bars) or the hot coals on a charcoal grill. These drippings break down into new flavorful compounds and then vaporize, waft up, and condense when they hit the food, sticking to it and adding that grill flavor.

The drippings are generally a combination of fat and juices, but a conversation with our science editor informed me that the fats have a much bigger role in creating grilled flavor. Problem: Châteaubriand is a very lean cut, so I didn't have much to work with. But I had an outside-the-box thought: What if I put something else on the grill alongside the tenderloin that could provide the fat that translates into great grill flavor? Whatever I chose, though, would have to be cheap and readily available. I came up with a short list of options: bacon and salt pork. I made two tenderloins, using a different potential grill "flavorizer" for each. In both cases, I put the flavorizer directly over the lit burner to maximize the rendered fat it exuded.

Bacon won out. It was easier to work with, and it boosted the grilled flavor of my roast without producing a hard-to-control fire as the salt pork did. That is, as long as I didn't lay the strips out flat on the grill. The key was shaping a few strips of bacon into a compact block by stacking three slices and then threading them accordion-style onto a metal skewer. Positioned over the heat diffusers, the bacon heated through slowly, rendering its fat at a measured pace.

Over the hour-long (give or take) cooking time, the bacon definitely boosted the grill flavor of the tenderloin, but my tasters agreed that it still wasn't as good as they thought it could be. My roast looked burnished, but it wasn't really browned. I needed

Oil Meat for Looks and Flavor

Rubbing the meat with oil before grilling helps prevent sticking, of course, and also helps develop flavor and color. When heated, the oil's unsaturated fatty acids quickly break down and join with meat proteins to form compounds that accelerate browning and add flavor. (These compounds form as part of the Maillard reaction as well as a separate reaction.) So for the prettiest, most flavorful meat that doesn't stick, oil it.

the savory flavors that occur when meat browns via a process called the Maillard reaction for the best, most rounded grill flavor.

Browning Basics

I headed back outside to try again. This time, I cooked the tenderloin quickly over high heat until it was lightly browned, keeping in mind that too much time spent over direct heat would lead to overcooking. I then moved it to the cooler part of the grill to cook through. The results were promising—the roast tasted grilled—but I wanted even more flavor.

More time on the heat wasn't an option; I needed a way to speed up the browning. I knew from test kitchen experience that the Maillard reaction occurs more readily as pH increases. And the easiest way to raise the pH in this situation would be to apply some baking soda. I made a paste by combining baking soda with the salt, pepper, and oil I was already rubbing on the tenderloin's exterior and carefully applied this mixture. This time, the tenderloin browned more readily, and the difference in flavor between this roast and my previous attempts was obvious. Each bite of juicy, pink meat offered up all the flavor that grilled meat should have.

Translating this recipe for a charcoal grill was fairly simple. I used just 4 quarts of charcoal (enough to fill a large chimney starter two-thirds full) and spread the coals evenly over half the grill. Instead of centering the bacon skewer over the coals, where the fire is hottest, I kept it near the center of the grill where the heat is gentler so that it wouldn't render too quickly.

While the roast cooked, I put together a couple of no-cook sauces to serve with the tenderloin. Both chimichurri and a chermoula worked well, lending fresh, bright flavor with plenty of herbs. They were the ideal summery match for my savory, meaty grilled tenderloin.

GRILL-ROASTED BEEF TENDERLOIN
SERVES 4 TO 6

Center-cut beef tenderloin roasts are sometimes sold as Châteaubriand. You will need one metal skewer for this recipe. The bacon will render slowly during cooking, creating a steady stream of smoke that flavors the beef. Serve the roast as is or with our Chermoula Sauce (recipe follows). For our Argentinian Chimichurri Sauce recipe, go to CooksIllustrated.com/june16.

- 2¼ teaspoons Kosher salt
- 1 teaspoon pepper
- 2 teaspoons vegetable oil
- 1 teaspoon baking soda
- 1 (3-pound) center-cut beef tenderloin roast, trimmed and tied at 1½-inch intervals
- 3 slices bacon

1. Combine salt, pepper, oil, and baking soda in small bowl. Rub mixture evenly over roast and let stand while preparing grill.

2. Stack bacon slices. Keeping slices stacked, thread metal skewer through bacon 6 or 7 times to create accordion shape. Push stack together to compact into about 2-inch length.

3A. FOR A CHARCOAL GRILL: Open bottom vent halfway. Light large chimney starter two-thirds filled with charcoal briquettes (4 quarts). When top coals are partially covered with ash, pour evenly over half of grill. Set cooking grate in place, cover, and open lid vent halfway. Heat grill until hot, about 5 minutes.

3B. FOR A GAS GRILL: Turn all burners to high, cover, and heat grill until hot, about 15 minutes. Turn primary burner to medium and turn off other burner(s). (Adjust primary burner as necessary to maintain grill temperature of 300 degrees.)

4. Clean and oil cooking grate. Place roast on hotter side of grill and cook until lightly browned on all sides, about 12 minutes. Slide roast to cooler side of grill, arranging so roast is about 7 inches from heat source. Place skewered bacon on hotter side of grill. (For charcoal, place near center of grill, above edge of coals. For gas, place above heat diffuser of primary burner. Bacon should be 4 to 6 inches from roast and drippings should fall on coals or heat diffuser and produce steady stream of smoke and minimal flare-ups. If flare-ups are large or frequent, slide bacon skewer 1 inch toward roast.)

5. Cover and cook until beef registers 125 degrees, 50 minutes to 1¼ hours. Transfer roast to carving board, tent with aluminum foil, and let rest for 20 minutes. Discard twine and slice roast ½ inch thick. Serve.

CHERMOULA SAUCE
MAKES ABOUT 1 CUP

To keep the sauce from becoming bitter, whisk in the olive oil by hand.

- ¾ cup fresh cilantro leaves
- 4 garlic cloves, minced
- 1 teaspoon ground cumin
- 1 teaspoon paprika
- ¼ teaspoon cayenne pepper
- ¼ teaspoon salt
- 3 tablespoons lemon juice
- ½ cup extra-virgin olive oil

Pulse cilantro, garlic, cumin, paprika, cayenne, and salt in food processor until coarsely chopped, about 10 pulses. Add lemon juice and pulse briefly to combine. Transfer mixture to medium bowl and slowly whisk in oil until incorporated and mixture is emulsified. Cover with plastic wrap and let stand at room temperature for at least 1 hour. (Sauce can be refrigerated for up to 2 days; bring to room temperature and rewhisk before serving.)

When Fat Sizzles, Grill Flavor Builds

A common assumption about grill flavor is that it comes from burning coals. While the compounds rising up from burning charcoal may deliver some flavor, far more significant is the flavor imparted when fatty drippings hit the coals (or the heat diffusers of a gas grill). As these drippings sizzle and pop, new complex compounds are created that waft up and get deposited back on the food. These compounds (along with the browning and char the food develops on its exterior) are responsible for characteristic grill flavor.

So what does this mean for beef tenderloin? Since this lean cut doesn't have much to offer in the way of fatty drippings, we needed to find a different source. The answer: bacon.

1 The skewered bacon is placed at the edge of the coals, where some (but not all) of its drippings will hit the coals, minimizing the chance of flare-ups.

2 The fat in the drippings breaks down into new complex compounds.

3 These flavor compounds vaporize and waft up.

4 The compounds condense on the tenderloin (which cooks over indirect heat on the cooler side of the grill), adding characteristic grill flavor.

Spanish Fried Potatoes

Crispy potatoes served with a smoky, spicy sauce—*patatas bravas*—are hugely popular in tapas bars. To make them at home, we had to rethink deep frying.

≽ BY ANNIE PETITO ≼

Patatas bravas are a quintessential tapas offering, the perfect bite to nibble between sips of sherry. These chunks of crispy fried potatoes are served with a smoky, spicy tomato sauce (*bravas* means "fierce") and sometimes a thick, garlicky mayonnaise, or *alioli*, to balance the heat. In Spain, patatas bravas are served at virtually every tapas bar but rarely, if ever, made at home.

That being the case—and because I've always wanted to be able to serve these at home with drinks or even alongside a simple roast—I was glad to find that recipes for the dish abound. But when I tried a handful in the test kitchen, the results were disappointing. The potatoes didn't have the supercrispy, well-browned exteriors and fluffy interiors of those I've enjoyed in tapas bars, and the bravas sauces lacked complexity. Finally, most of the recipes were very involved, but I wanted the workload to be reasonable.

The Road to Supercrispy

Though some recipes called for waxy potatoes, I went straight to floury russets, whose tightly packed, starch-filled cells swell up and separate from one another during cooking, resulting in just the dry, fluffy interiors I was after. I began by trying the twice-frying method called for by many recipes. It involves parcooking the potatoes in relatively cool oil (about 250 degrees) and then giving them a second, brief fry in hotter oil to crisp and brown. During the initial fry, some of the starch molecules (mostly amylose) on the exterior of the potato loosen and are hydrated by moisture in the potato. This starchy gel settles on the outside of the potato, creating a thin shell that crisps up during the second fry.

Indeed, double-frying delivered good, nicely crispy results. However, it was time-consuming and required multiple batches.

▶ Watch Patatas Happen
A step-by-step video is available at CooksIllustrated.com/june16

If you prepare the sauce and parcook the potatoes in advance, all you need to do at tapas time is fry the potatoes.

In a test kitchen recipe for home fries, we call for parcooking the potatoes in water instead of oil. In that recipe, we add baking soda to the boiling water to help create a starchy coating. Here's how it works: Alkaline baking soda triggers a chain reaction that causes the pectin on the exteriors of the potatoes to break down and release a substantial layer of amylose from the potato cells that, when fried, develops into a thick crust. We also toss the drained, parcooked spuds with kosher salt to rough up the layer of potato cells and create lots of nooks and crannies. The extra surface area means there are more pathways by which moisture can escape and oil can enter the potatoes during frying—a process that leads to a thick, porous, ultracrispy coating.

To give this method a try here, I added ½ teaspoon of baking soda to 2 quarts of water, brought the water to a boil, and added the potato pieces. Once the water returned to a boil, I set a timer for 1 minute—just long enough for the pectin in the exterior potato cells to break down—and then drained the spuds, put them back into the empty pot, and

let them dry out for about 1 minute over low heat. Next, I added 1½ teaspoons of kosher salt, vigorously stirring until the exteriors were coated in a thick paste. I spread the pieces on a baking sheet while I heated 10 cups of vegetable oil (most recipes call for about this much) in a large Dutch oven. Once the oil hit 350 degrees, a standard temperature for deep frying, into the hot fat went the potatoes. I fried them in three 6- to 7-minute batches until they were deep golden brown, draining each batch and sliding them onto a baking sheet and into a 200-degree oven to keep warm as they finished cooking.

As soon as I crunched into my first bite, I knew that things had gone according to plan. The potatoes were encased in shells that were even thicker and crunchier than the ones I'd produced with the double-fry method. Plus, they stayed that way, even when dunked in sauce (a placeholder recipe, for now). I still had tweaking to do, though. First, some of the potato chunks, which hadn't been in the hot oil for very long, were undercooked at the very center. Second, I had been hunched over the stove for what felt like an age, shuttling batches in and out of the oil and transferring them to the low oven to keep warm. Could I streamline the process?

Not-So-Deep Frying

One place to trim back was the amount of oil: I wondered if 10 cups, which took a long time to heat up, was overkill. Sure enough, the potato pieces only needed to be just submerged—not swimming—in oil. Three cups of oil was enough to just cover the pieces (any less would require flipping to ensure allover browning).

I had cut the amount of oil by more than two-thirds; could I also reduce the amount of hands-on time? The simplest solution would be to fry all of the potatoes in one shot. This would increase the overall cooking time, but maybe that wasn't all bad since the potatoes were emerging a bit underdone anyway. Since the oil temperature would surely drop when I added so many spuds, I heated the oil to 375 degrees instead of 350. It fell to about 300 degrees when I added the potatoes and crept up to 350 during frying.

For Supercrispy Potatoes, Put a Shell on Them

Patatas bravas are commonly made by frying the potatoes twice. The first fry creates an exterior "shell" of gelatinized starch that turns crispy during the second fry. Double frying works well, but it's time-consuming, so we looked for an alternate method. We found that boiling the spuds in baking soda–laced water and then tossing them with kosher salt before frying produced a crust that was even more substantial than that of the double-fried potatoes. Here's how it works: Baking soda causes the pectin on the exterior of the potatoes to break down, releasing a gloppy, starchy paste that fries up crispy. Kosher salt roughs up the surfaces of the potatoes, creating many nooks and crannies through which steam can escape. As the steam escapes, it leaves behind small holes, and the hot oil fills those holes, helping to create a substantial, brittle crust. –Annie Petito and Dan Souza

TRADITIONAL WAY
Double-fried potatoes boast a nice crispy shell, but the process is messy and time-consuming.

FRIED ONCE
Frying the potatoes without any pretreatment isn't ideal. They emerge from the oil pale and lacking a crispy coating.

PARBOILED AND FRIED
Parboiling the potatoes prior to frying helps cook them through but doesn't create a crispy shell.

OUR WAY
For crispy potatoes with less fuss, we parboil them with baking soda, rough them up with kosher salt, and then fry them once.

Happily, the process worked beautifully and was mostly hands-free: I only nudged the potato pieces occasionally with a wire skimmer (a slotted spoon would also work) while they were frying to separate any that were sticking together and to encourage even browning. About 20 minutes later, I pulled out a single batch of supercrispy, browned potatoes. Deep frying had never been so easy.

Getting Saucy

With the potatoes perfected, I moved on to the smoky, spicy tomato sauce. I sautéed sweet smoked paprika with minced garlic, salt, and a healthy dose of cayenne, cooking the mixture until it sent up wafts of heady fragrance. For the tomato element, I turned to tomato paste thinned with water, which provided bright, sweet flavor and a smooth consistency. Finally, after simmering the sauce briefly, I stirred in a couple of teaspoons of tangy sherry vinegar. The result was vibrant, tomatoey, and full of spice and smoke.

I was tempted to whip up an alioli (the Spanish take on aïoli) as well, but in an effort to save time, I decided to experiment with a hybrid sauce. While not entirely traditional, adding just ¼ cup of store-bought mayonnaise to the bravas mixture created a twofer sauce featuring the best of both worlds: The mayo added creaminess and helped the sauce cling to the potatoes, but the sauce still boasted plenty of brightness and heat to cut through the richness of the potatoes.

To re-create a tapas experience, I spread some sauce on a platter and piled the potatoes on top, passing the remaining sauce for dipping. When I noticed the pace at which my colleagues consumed this batch of potatoes, I smiled—and started to prep a second batch.

PATATAS BRAVAS
SERVES 4 TO 6

While this dish is traditionally served as part of a tapas spread, it can also be served as a side dish with grilled or roasted meat. Bittersweet or hot smoked paprika can be used in place of sweet, if desired. If you make this substitution, be sure to taste the sauce before deciding how much cayenne to add, if any. A rasp-style grater makes quick work of turning the garlic into a paste. For information about our favorite smoked paprika, see "Tasting Smoked Paprika" on page 28.

Sauce
- 1 tablespoon vegetable oil
- 2 teaspoons garlic, minced to paste
- 1 teaspoon sweet smoked paprika
- ½ teaspoon kosher salt
- ½–¾ teaspoon cayenne pepper
- ¼ cup tomato paste
- ½ cup water
- 2 teaspoons sherry vinegar
- ¼ cup mayonnaise

Potatoes
- 2¼ pounds russet potatoes, peeled and cut into 1-inch pieces
- ½ teaspoon baking soda
  Kosher salt
- 3 cups vegetable oil

1. FOR THE SAUCE: Heat oil in small saucepan over medium-low heat until shimmering. Add garlic, paprika, salt, and cayenne and cook until fragrant, about 30 seconds. Add tomato paste and cook for 30 seconds. Whisk in water and bring to boil over high heat. Reduce heat to medium-low and simmer until slightly thickened, 4 to 5 minutes. Transfer sauce to bowl, stir in vinegar, and let cool completely. Once cool, whisk in mayonnaise. (Sauce can be refrigerated for up to 24 hours. Bring to room temperature before serving.)

2. FOR THE POTATOES: Bring 8 cups water to boil in large saucepan over high heat. Add potatoes and baking soda. Return to boil and cook for 1 minute. Drain potatoes.

3. Return potatoes to saucepan and place over low heat. Cook, shaking saucepan occasionally, until any surface moisture has evaporated, 30 seconds to 1 minute. Remove from heat. Add 1½ teaspoons salt and stir with rubber spatula until potatoes are coated with thick, starchy paste, about 30 seconds. Transfer potatoes to rimmed baking sheet in single layer to cool. (Potatoes can stand at room temperature for up to 2 hours.)

4. Heat oil in large Dutch oven over high heat to 375 degrees. Add all potatoes (they should just be submerged in oil) and cook, stirring occasionally with wire skimmer or slotted spoon, until deep golden brown and crispy, 20 to 25 minutes.

5. Transfer potatoes to paper towel–lined wire rack set in rimmed baking sheet. Season with salt to taste. Spoon ½ cup sauce onto bottom of large platter or 1½ tablespoons sauce onto individual plates. Arrange potatoes over sauce and serve immediately, passing remaining sauce separately.

TWO SAUCES IN ONE

In tapas bars, *patatas bravas* are often served with two condiments: a smoky, spicy, tomatoey bravas sauce as well as a garlicky mayonnaise, or *alioli*. We took a shortcut and threw together a tomato paste–based bravas sauce, using sweet smoked paprika and cayenne pepper to provide the signature smoke and heat and then mixing in ¼ cup of store-bought mayonnaise. The result? A smoky, spicy, tomatoey, and creamy hybrid sauce—in short order.

The Best Pan-Seared Salmon

For a crisp crust and a juicy interior, the key is doing less, not more.

⇒ BY ANDREW JANJIGIAN ⇐

Pan-searing salmon sounds so straightforward that I've never given much thought to the technique. Normally, I'd add a little oil to a nonstick skillet, get it good and hot, sprinkle a few skinless fillets on both sides with salt and pepper, slide them into the pan, and cook them on both sides until the fish was cooked through and nicely browned on the exterior but still pink on the inside.

But when I gave this approach a more critical look, I could see that it had two flaws. While the fish had a nice rosy interior at its thickest point, it was a bit overcooked and dry at the thinner end. (Pieces cut from the center of the fillet are our preference for their more uniform thickness, but even these taper on one end.) Secondly, the exteriors of the fillets were more tough than crisp. I wanted to take advantage of the intense heat of the skillet to produce a golden-brown, ultracrisp crust on salmon fillets while keeping their interiors moist.

The solution to the dryness problem was relatively easy: salt. We salt and brine meat all the time, and both techniques apply just as well to fish. Beyond seasoning the flesh, the salt also helps keep it moist. Salting would keep the exterior of the fish drier than brining and thus would seem like the better choice since my goal was crisp, browned crust. But, this being a quick weeknight dinner, I didn't want to wait 2 hours for the salt to do its job. Brining took about 15 minutes, and as long as I patted the fillets dry with paper towels before cooking, I found that the treatment didn't significantly inhibit browning.

As for that browning, I decided to focus on getting a really nice sear on only the flesh side since it would be facing up when the fillet was plated. Plus, attempting to brown both sides would just lead to overcooking. Cooking the fish through with the flesh side down the entire time produced a wonderfully crisp crust, but it also left me with an unworkable dilemma: Either the face-up (skinned) side was nearly sushi-raw, or the rest of the fillet overcooked while I waited for the face-up side to cook through. Covering the pan with a lid toward the end helped cook the fish through more evenly, but this trapped moisture, softening the crust.

There was one piece left to tinker with: the heat level. What if I added the fish to a cold pan and

▶ See How to Do It
A step-by-step video is available at CooksIllustrated.com/june16

then turned on the heat? This would allow the fish to cook through gently as the pan slowly came up to temperature. I'd then flip the fillets over after the skillet was good and hot so they could form a crust and finish cooking through.

I quickly discovered a problem starting with a not-so-hot skillet: No matter how gently I cooked the first side, it tended to dry out and turn tough on the very exterior. When I was skinning the salmon for my next test, I came up with the solution: Leave the skin on. It could serve to protect that first side as it cooked, and I could simply remove it after flipping the fish. Removing the skin at this stage was also a whole lot easier than removing it from the uncooked flesh.

Sure enough, this worked perfectly. Even better, the skin shed enough fat as it cooked that I was able to cook the fish without needing to add a single drop of oil to the pan.

This salmon was excellent with just a squirt of lemon, but a mango-mint salsa and a cilantro-mint chutney were both easy to make, and their bright flavors balanced the salmon's richness.

PAN-SEARED SALMON
SERVES 4

To ensure uniform cooking, buy a 1½- to 2-pound center-cut salmon fillet and cut it into four pieces. Using skin-on salmon is important here, as we rely on the fat underneath the skin as the cooking medium (as opposed to adding extra oil). If using wild salmon, cook it until it registers 120 degrees. If you don't want to serve the fish with the skin, we recommend peeling it off the fish after it is cooked. Serve with lemon wedges or Mango-Mint Salsa (recipe follows). For our recipes for Cilantro-Mint Chutney and Pan-Seared Salmon for Two, go to CooksIllustrated.com/june16.

> Kosher salt and pepper
> 4 (6- to 8-ounce) skin-on salmon fillets
> Lemon wedges

1. Dissolve ½ cup salt in 2 quarts water in large container. Submerge salmon in brine and let stand at room temperature for 15 minutes. Remove salmon from brine and pat dry with paper towels.

2. Sprinkle bottom of 12-inch nonstick skillet evenly with ½ teaspoon salt and ½ teaspoon pepper. Place fillets, skin side down, in skillet and sprinkle tops of fillets with ¼ teaspoon salt and ¼ teaspoon pepper. Heat skillet over medium-high heat and cook fillets without moving them until fat begins to

The skin insulates the fish during cooking and releases its fat—no oil is necessary.

render, skin begins to brown, and bottom ¼ inch of fillets turns opaque, 6 to 8 minutes.

3. Using tongs, flip fillets and continue to cook without moving them until centers are still translucent when checked with tip of paring knife and register 125 degrees, 6 to 8 minutes longer. Transfer fillets skin side down to serving platter and let rest for 5 minutes before serving with lemon wedges.

MANGO-MINT SALSA
MAKES ABOUT 1 CUP

Adjust the salsa's heat level by reserving and adding the jalapeño seeds, if desired.

> 1 mango, peeled, pitted, and cut into ¼-inch pieces
> 1 shallot, minced
> 3 tablespoons lime juice (2 limes)
> 2 tablespoons chopped fresh mint
> 1 jalapeño chile, stemmed, seeded, and minced
> 1 tablespoon extra-virgin olive oil
> 1 garlic clove, minced
> ½ teaspoon salt

Combine all ingredients in bowl.

Easy Italian Soufflé

A custardy *sformato* has the plush elegance of a soufflé with a fraction of the fuss.

⇒ BY SARAH MULLINS ⇐

A towering cheese soufflé is my favorite brunch offering, but some may consider whipping egg whites and assembling a water bath too much work for a Sunday morning. An ideal alternate dish combines the richness and elegance of a cheese soufflé with less work.

Enter *sformato*, an elegant Italian baked egg custard with a plush but light texture. It's surprisingly easy to make: Most recipes I found were based on a béchamel (a mixture of butter cooked with flour and milk) and then thickened with eggs and flavored with sharp cheese like Parmesan or Pecorino Romano. Some included vegetables that were processed into the batter, which was ladled into a baking dish (or ramekins for individual *sformati*) and baked in a moderate oven for about 30 minutes. A restaurant version I'd had was turned out of a ramekin (the dish's name comes from the Italian verb *sformare*, meaning "to unmold") and garnished with minced fresh herbs.

My attempts at a recipe resulted in loose, soggy, or curdled custards—hardly company-worthy. So I got to work on rich, dense, but silky sformati with pronounced cheese flavor and elegant form.

Like any custard, the texture of my sformati would largely depend on the ratio of dairy to eggs, as the proteins in eggs provide structure. When heated, these proteins link up and form a network that traps water: The more dilute the egg proteins, the looser the resulting custard. Several soupy custards contained just two eggs in relation to several cups of béchamel, so upping the number of eggs was a given.

My béchamel was basic: a roughly 1:1 ratio of butter and flour (plus minced garlic for aromatic depth) cooked until a paste formed, into which I whisked a few cups of milk. I seasoned it with salty, rich Pecorino Romano, plus black and cayenne peppers for a touch of heat. To that base, I added a range of eggs (from four to eight), ladled the custard into six ramekins, and baked them (set on a wire rack in a rimmed baking sheet for stability and airflow under the ramekins) in a 325-degree oven. Cooked to about 175 degrees, the sformati were nicely set and silky; letting them rest for about 20 minutes allowed them to set up further and ensured that they turned out of the ramekins cleanly.

I wasn't surprised that more eggs delivered richer, nicely firm results—but even with eight eggs, the custards weren't quite as creamy as I'd hoped. An extra yolk made them more decadent but also overly eggy. Instead, I built extra richness into the béchamel by swapping half the milk for half-and-half.

With my a silky base set, I varied the flavors by processing roasted red peppers into one version and thawed frozen spinach into another. To dress up the sformati, I enhanced a classic Italian gremolata with butter-toasted panko crumbs and extra Pecorino.

Rich, silky, and elegant, my take on sformato was textbook brunch fare—with a minimum of fuss.

LEMON-HERB SFORMATI
SERVES 6

The *sformati* will soufflé in the oven but will settle back to their original size while cooling. To take the temperature of the sformati, touch the probe tip to the bottom of the ramekin and pull it up about 1 inch. Fresh thyme can be used in place of fresh tarragon, if desired. The sformati can be served warm or at room temperature. For our free recipes for Roasted Red Pepper Sformati and Spinach Sformati, go to CooksIllustrated.com/june16.

Sformati

- 8 large eggs
- 1 teaspoon salt
- 6 tablespoons unsalted butter
- 1 garlic clove, minced
- ¼ cup plus 2 tablespoons (1¾ ounces) all-purpose flour
- 1½ cups whole milk
- 1½ cups half-and-half
- 1½ ounces Pecorino Romano cheese, grated (¾ cup)
- ¼ teaspoon pepper
- Pinch cayenne pepper
- 2 tablespoons chopped fresh chives
- 2 teaspoons chopped fresh tarragon
- ½ teaspoon grated lemon zest

Gremolata

- 1 tablespoon unsalted butter
- 1 garlic clove, minced
- ¼ cup panko bread crumbs
- ¼ cup grated Pecorino Romano cheese
- ¼ cup chopped fresh chives
- 1 teaspoon finely grated lemon zest
- Salt and pepper

1. FOR THE SFORMATI: Adjust oven rack to upper-middle position and heat oven to 325 degrees. Grease six 6-ounce ramekins and place on wire rack set in rimmed baking sheet. Whisk eggs and salt together in bowl until homogeneous and set aside.

2. Melt butter in medium saucepan over medium heat. Add garlic and cook until fragrant, about 30 seconds. Stir in flour and cook for 1 minute. Slowly whisk in milk and half-and-half until smooth. Increase heat to high and bring to simmer, 2 to 4 minutes. Continue to cook, stirring constantly, 1 minute longer. Remove pan from heat and whisk in Pecorino, pepper, and cayenne until smooth. Let béchamel cool for 5 minutes.

3. Whisk chives, tarragon, lemon zest, and reserved eggs into béchamel until smooth. Divide mixture evenly among ramekins (filling should be ¼ inch from top of each ramekin). Bake until centers register 175 to 180 degrees, 30 to 35 minutes.

4. FOR THE GREMOLATA: While sformati are baking, melt butter in 8-inch skillet over medium-low heat. Add garlic and cook until fragrant, about 30 seconds. Add panko and cook, stirring frequently, until golden brown, 1 to 2 minutes. Let mixture cool for 2 minutes, then stir in Pecorino, chives, and lemon zest. Season with salt and pepper to taste.

5. Remove sformati from oven and let cool for 20 minutes. Invert sformati onto individual plates. Sprinkle evenly with gremolata and serve.

Let the sformati cool for 20 minutes before unmolding.

⊙ **See the Proper Texture**
A step-by-step video is available at CooksIllustrated.com/june16

Korean Rice Bowl

This comforting combination of rice, vegetables, eggs, spicy sauce, and a crisp crust is a restaurant favorite. We wanted an efficient way to make it at home.

⇒ BY ANDREA GEARY ⇐

At its most basic, a rice bowl is not so much a recipe as it is a practical style of eating popular across Asia: Top warm rice with an array of seasoned vegetables, a fried egg, maybe a small amount of meat, and a piquant sauce, and stir it up for a complete meal that's true comfort food: nourishing, flavorful, texturally interesting, and healthy.

To me, the ultimate interpretation of a rice bowl is Korean *dolsot* bibimbap, where the rice takes on a brown, crisp crust that makes the dish very satisfying. *Bibim* means "mixed," *bap* means "rice," and a dolsot is the heavy single-serving stone bowl in which the bibimbap is traditionally assembled. The vessel is heated and then coated with sesame oil so the soft rice sizzles when it's piled in. While the garnishes are arranged on top, the heat retained in the stone crisps the bottom layer of rice, which gets combined with the softer rice and other components when the dish is mixed together.

I don't own a set of the stone bowls, so I usually go to a Korean restaurant for bibimbap. But since many of the ingredients are staples, I wanted to try simulating stone-bowl bibimbap at home. And why stop at the traditional single-serving size? The assembled dish is so impressive that I knew I'd want to show off for guests and make a family-style dish that would serve at least four.

Bibimbap Basics

First I'd make the rice and the sauce, which could sit while I prepared the garnishes. Korean cooks use soft, slightly resilient short-grain white rice for bibimbap because its clingy surface helps it form a more cohesive crust than smooth long-grain rice would. I rinsed the grains in several changes of cool water to wash away excess starch that makes the rice too sticky. I then simmered equal parts rice and water, plus a bit of salt, in a covered saucepan while I turned my attention to the sauce.

▷ **See the Bowl Come Together**
A step-by-step video is available at CooksIllustrated.com/june16

To ensure that all the components are done at the same time, fry the eggs while the rice sizzles and forms a crust.

The primary component would be *gochujang*, a thick Korean chile paste that's sweet, savory, and spicy. The rest of the sauce, which I based on a Korean recipe, was toasted sesame oil and a bit of sugar along with enough water to make the mixture just runny enough for drizzling.

Part of what makes bibimbap so impressive to serve—the tidy piles of colorful and texturally varied garnishes—is also what makes it a bit of a marathon to prepare. One shortcut would be to cut back on the number of garnishes, starting with the meat. Authentic but hard-to-find dried ferns and daikon radishes were next to go, and I slimmed the rest of the list to a mix of chopped spinach, shredded carrots, and sliced shiitake mushrooms. I sautéed them sequentially in a skillet for even cooking, seasoning each batch with soy sauce, sugar, garlic, and scallions before returning them to individual bowls.

Easy to Make— and Make Ahead

Don't let the lengthy recipe intimidate you. The pickles, chile sauce, and vegetables can all be prepared ahead, so all that's left to do on the day of is cook the rice and eggs. Plus, leftover pickles and chile sauce make great condiments for other applications like sandwiches, burgers, noodles, and eggs.

To build a substantial crust of rice, I'd need something that, like a dolsot, held heat for a long time. It occurred to me that my cast-iron skillet behaves the same way. I set it over high heat, added vegetable oil and a little sesame oil for a flavor boost, carefully added the rice, and patted it into an even layer. I let the rice cook for 2 minutes to get the crust going and then arranged the garnishes on top before frying the eggs in a separate skillet I had warmed. I placed the finished eggs in the center of the vegetables, drizzled on the sauce, removed the pan from the heat, and stopped briefly to admire the lovely sight. Later I would be glad I had paused, because things were about to get ugly.

All Mixed Up

Stirring transforms the orderly bibimbap into a jumble of colors and textures. It's an impressive sight, but it was especially dramatic this time because my skillet was too shallow to contain everything; rice, vegetables, eggs, and sauce went everywhere. Plus, the crust had broken into very small pieces that quickly lost their crunch in the soft rice.

The first change was obvious: Switch to a deeper Dutch oven to better accommodate the mixing step. I'd still have to cook the three vegetables separately, but since they were all seasoned similarly, I made a mixture of soy sauce, sugar, scallions, and garlic (and a little bit of water to help things cook) that I could add in measured amounts to each batch. Both stainless-steel and cast-iron Dutch ovens worked, but the heftier enameled cast-iron pot yielded a more substantial crust, so I went with that.

Finally, I was tempted to try a controversial step: not rinsing the rice. I made two batches—one with rinsed rice and one with unrinsed—and, frankly, the shortcut was worth it. There's so much going on in this dish that my tasters didn't notice much of a difference.

To make sure everyone got substantial pieces of crust, I mixed the bibimbap in two stages, first combining the vegetables, eggs, and soft rice and then digging deep and scraping up the crust in big pieces that stayed crunchy.

I was delighted with my family-style bibimbap, but it was missing a crisp, pungent element. In a Korean household or restaurant, a dish of the spicy fermented cabbage known as kimchi would fill that role—and if you can get it (kimchi is available in many supermarkets and Asian markets), it's a great addition. As a stand-in, I quickly pickled a mixture of bean sprouts and sliced cucumbers. It made for a bright, fresh accompaniment that could also be prepared ahead of time—and it completed my version of this hearty, savory one-pot meal.

KOREAN RICE BOWL (DOLSOT BIBIMBAP)
SERVES 6

For a quick dinner, prepare the pickles, chile sauce, and vegetables a day ahead (warm the vegetables to room temperature in the microwave before adding them to the rice). You can also substitute store-bought kimchi for the pickles to save time. The Korean chile paste *gochujang* is sold in Asian markets and some supermarkets. If you can't find it, an equal amount of Sriracha can be substituted. But because Sriracha is more watery than gochujang, omit the water from the chile sauce and stir just 1 tablespoon of sauce into the rice in step 9. For a true bibimbap experience, bring the pot to the table before stirring the vegetables into the rice in step 9.

Pickles
1	cup cider vinegar
2	tablespoons sugar
1½	teaspoons salt
1	cucumber, peeled, quartered lengthwise, seeded, and sliced thin on bias
4	ounces (2 cups) bean sprouts

Chile Sauce
¼	cup gochujang
3	tablespoons water
2	tablespoons toasted sesame oil
1	teaspoon sugar

Rice
2½	cups short-grain white rice
2½	cups water
¾	teaspoon salt

Vegetables
½	cup water
3	scallions, minced
3	tablespoons soy sauce
3	garlic cloves, minced
1	tablespoon sugar
1	tablespoon vegetable oil
3	carrots, peeled and shredded (2 cups)
8	ounces shiitake mushrooms, stemmed, caps sliced thin
1	(10-ounce) bag curly-leaf spinach, stemmed and chopped coarse

Bibimbap
2	tablespoons plus 2 teaspoons vegetable oil
1	tablespoon toasted sesame oil
4	large eggs

1. FOR THE PICKLES: Whisk vinegar, sugar, and salt together in medium bowl. Add cucumber and bean sprouts and toss to combine. Gently press on vegetables to submerge. Cover and refrigerate for at least 30 minutes or up to 24 hours.

2. FOR THE CHILE SAUCE: Whisk gochujang, water, oil, and sugar together in small bowl. Cover and set aside.

3. FOR THE RICE: Bring rice, water, and salt to boil in medium saucepan over high heat. Cover, reduce heat to low, and cook for 7 minutes. Remove rice from heat and let sit, covered, until tender, about 15 minutes.

4. FOR THE VEGETABLES: While rice cooks, stir together water, scallions, soy sauce, garlic, and sugar. Heat 1 teaspoon oil in Dutch oven over high heat until shimmering. Add carrots and stir until coated. Add ⅓ cup scallion mixture and cook, stirring frequently, until carrots are slightly softened and moisture has evaporated, 1 to 2 minutes. Using slotted spoon, transfer carrots to small bowl.

5. Heat 1 teaspoon oil in now-empty pot until shimmering. Add mushrooms and stir until coated with oil. Add ⅓ cup scallion mixture and cook, stirring frequently, until mushrooms are tender and moisture has evaporated, 3 to 4 minutes. Using slotted spoon, transfer mushrooms to second small bowl.

6. Heat remaining 1 teaspoon oil in now-empty pot until shimmering. Add spinach and remaining ⅓ cup scallion mixture and stir to coat spinach. Cook, stirring frequently, until spinach is completely wilted but still bright green, 1 to 2 minutes. Using slotted spoon, transfer spinach to third small bowl. Discard any remaining liquid and wipe out pot with paper towel.

7. FOR THE BIBIMBAP: Heat 2 tablespoons vegetable oil and sesame oil in now-empty pot over high heat until shimmering. Carefully add cooked rice and gently press into even layer. Cook, without stirring, until rice begins to form crust on bottom of pot, about 2 minutes. Using slotted spoon, transfer carrots, spinach, and mushrooms to pot and arrange in piles that cover surface of rice. Reduce heat to low.

8. While crust forms, heat remaining 2 teaspoons vegetable oil in 10-inch nonstick skillet over low heat for 5 minutes. Crack eggs into small bowl. Pour eggs into skillet; cover and cook (about 2 minutes for runny yolks, 2½ minutes for soft but set yolks, and 3 minutes for firmly set yolks). Slide eggs onto vegetables in pot.

9. Drizzle 2 tablespoons chile sauce over eggs. Without disturbing crust, use wooden spoon to stir rice, vegetables, and eggs until combined. Just before serving, scrape large pieces of crust from bottom of pot and stir into rice. Serve in individual bowls, passing pickles and extra chile sauce separately.

What Makes It Dolsot Bibimbap?

Dolsot bibimbap is distinguished by a variety of flavors, colors, and textures, including a crunchy rice crust. In our version of this Korean classic, we cut back on the number of ingredients but still feature five essential elements.

➤ **SAVORY, GARLICKY VEGETABLES**
In our version, carrots, shiitake mushrooms, and spinach—sautéed separately in a sweet soy-garlic mixture and arranged over the rice—add color and freshness.

➤ **CRUNCHY RICE CRUST**
When placed in the hot, well-oiled vessel, the steamed rice forms a crisp, nicely browned crust.

➤ **FRIED EGG**
In Korean restaurants, bibimbap may be topped with a fried egg or a raw egg yolk that cooks as it's stirred into the hot rice. We opt for fried eggs.

➤ **CRISPY, TANGY PICKLES**
Traditionally, the spicy fermented cabbage called kimchi adds a crisp, pungent element to bibimbap. Instead, we add pickled cucumber and bean sprouts for a tangy crunch that brightens our dish's rich and spicy flavors.

➤ **BOLD SPICY-SWEET SAUCE**
Gochujang, a thick, spicy Korean chile paste, forms the base for this sauce. (For more information, see "Our Asian Pantry" on page 16.) We thin it with toasted sesame oil, sugar, and water to yield a spicy-salty-sweet condiment that's just the right consistency for drizzling.

A Bowl That Holds the Heat

Traditionally, *dolsot* bibimbap is served in individual stone bowls that retain heat and crisp the bottom layer of rice. Instead, we make a family-size portion in a heavy Dutch oven.

Dressing Up Strawberry Shortcake

Loads of fresh berries were a given. But for a refined version of this classic dessert, the key was engineering a cake that could take the juice—and hold on to the berries.

≥ BY LAN LAM ≤

Plenty of juicy, sweet berries and whipped cream are a must for strawberry shortcake, but what about the shortcake itself? Some opt for biscuits, but I've always been drawn to the style featuring light, fluffy cake, since it seems better suited to soaking up the berry juice. For my ideal version, a flavorful cake that wouldn't fall apart when soaked with the juice was a must, and I liked the idea of a whole cake since it would offer a more elegant presentation. As for the strawberries, I wanted to pack in as many as possible.

Cake Walk

What kind of cake would be best? Recipes were split between butter and sponge cakes. Butter cakes practically dissolved when soaked with juice. Sponge cakes, which rely on whipped eggs or egg whites for leavening and structure, held up much better. (For more detail, see page 30.) I settled on a type of sponge called genoise, which has a rich flavor from whole eggs and melted butter.

But genoise isn't without problems. Recipes call for whipping the eggs and sugar until the mixture has more than tripled in volume and then gently folding in the dry ingredients (just cake flour and salt) followed by the melted butter and any flavorings. But since the batter contains no chemical leaveners, if the eggs aren't fully aerated or if the batter is deflated during folding, the cake turns out dense, flat, and rubbery.

First I considered how the eggs were whipped. Most recipes call for whisking the eggs and sugar over a pan of simmering water until the sugar is dissolved and then whipping this mixture in a stand mixer until it reaches the ribbon stage, so called because it forms a ribbon that holds its shape when dribbled down into the bowl from the whisk, indicating that it's stable.

Some recipes skip heating the mixture, but I found that in these cases the whipped eggs deflated very quickly. Why? When eggs are whipped, their

▶ **Watch: It's the Berries**
A step-by-step video is available at CooksIllustrated.com/june16

By removing the center from one cake layer and stacking the resulting ring on top of an uncut layer, we create a barrier that holds the berries in place.

proteins unwind, link up, and trap both the air introduced by whipping and the water in the eggs. The water provides support to the network, or foam, but over time the water seeps out, weakening the foam, and air escapes. Heating the sugar and water as opposed to just stirring them together ensures that all of the sugar dissolves, which makes for a more viscous mixture. And the more viscous a liquid, the slower the water it contains escapes. This leads to a more stable foam.

So the heating step was key. I put my sugar and eggs in the bowl of the stand mixer and placed the bowl over a saucepan of simmering water. I found that heating the mixture to 115 to 120 degrees before whipping it fully dissolved the sugar and delivered the sturdiest egg foam.

One key to maximizing airiness is minimizing the number of strokes used to fold in the dry ingredients. Sifting them over the foam and folding them into it

Slices, Not Chunks

Sliced strawberries pack more tightly than quartered berries, and their greater surface area means they also release more juices when they're combined with sugar and left to sit (a process known as maceration).

in batches, which many recipes call for, was a must, ensuring that there were no clumps of flour that needed aggressive mixing. Transferring the egg foam from the narrow mixer bowl to a wide, shallow bowl made the folding process even more efficient since fewer strokes were required.

Last to go into the batter were the butter, vanilla extract, and lemon zest. Just folding them in didn't work well, however. Because the mixture was more dense than the egg foam, it took a lot of strokes to incorporate it. To address this, I whisked ¾ cup of the egg foam into the melted butter mixture and then folded this lightened mixture into the batter. The resulting cake was perfectly airy with a uniform crumb—and, best of all, I got these same results cake after cake.

Now I just needed to figure out how to corral the berries, which would tumble off if I simply arranged them on top. One approach I read about cut a well in the cake. To simplify this idea, I divided the batter between two 9-inch cake pans. I'd cut the center from one of the baked layers and set the ring on top of the uncut layer. The ring would act like a retaining wall, securely holding the strawberries in place.

It's the Berries

As for the strawberries, I hulled 2 pounds and, instead of quartering them as some recipes call for, I sliced them thin. Slices would lay flatter, not only allowing me to pack in more berries but also giving the filling a neater appearance. Slices were also more helpful for the macerating step (see "Slices, Not Chunks").

I assembled my cake, placing the cake ring on the uncut layer, scooping the berries into the well, and topping it off with lightly sweetened whipped cream, which also included a little crème fraîche for tang. This cake looked the part, but when I sliced into it, I saw that the juice wasn't evenly distributed, and the berries slipped and slid as I sliced.

I tried again. To make the berry filling more cohesive, I strained the juice from the macerated berries, thickened a small portion with cornstarch, and then combined this gelled mixture with the berries.

I brushed the remaining juice evenly over the cake before adding the berries and tangy whipped cream.

This cake looked elegant and sliced easily, and each bite delivered that perfect combination of fresh strawberries, light-as-air cake, and tangy whipped cream. I knew even the staunchest biscuit-style shortcake fans wouldn't be able to resist it.

REFINED STRAWBERRY SHORTCAKE
SERVES 8

For the best texture, mix the cake batter quickly but gently, and have your equipment ready and ingredients measured before beginning. Cool the melted butter only slightly, to between 95 and 110 degrees. This recipe was written for light-colored cake pans; if your pans are dark, reduce the baking time in step 7 to 10 to 13 minutes. For ideas about how to use the leftover cake, go to CooksIllustrated.com/june16.

Strawberries
- 2 pounds strawberries, hulled and sliced vertically ¼ inch thick (6 cups)
- ¼ cup (1¾ ounces) granulated sugar
- 2 teaspoons lemon juice
- Pinch salt
- ½ teaspoon cornstarch

Cake
- 4 tablespoons unsalted butter, melted and cooled slightly
- 1 teaspoon vanilla extract
- ½ teaspoon grated lemon zest
- 1¼ cups (5 ounces) cake flour
- ¼ teaspoon salt
- 5 large eggs
- ¾ cup (5¼ ounces) granulated sugar

Whipped Cream
- 1 cup heavy cream
- ⅓ cup crème fraîche
- 3 tablespoons confectioners' sugar, plus extra for dusting

1. FOR THE STRAWBERRIES: Toss strawberries with sugar, lemon juice, and salt in large bowl. Set aside for at least 1½ hours or up to 3 hours.

2. FOR THE CAKE: Adjust oven rack to middle position and heat oven to 350 degrees. Spray two 9-inch round cake pans with baking spray with flour. Line with parchment paper and spray parchment with baking spray with flour. Combine melted butter, vanilla, and lemon zest in medium bowl. Whisk flour and salt together in second bowl.

3. Combine eggs and sugar in bowl of stand mixer; place bowl over medium saucepan filled with 2 inches simmering water, making sure that water does not touch bottom of bowl. Whisking constantly, heat until sugar is dissolved and mixture registers 115 to 120 degrees, about 3 minutes.

4. Transfer bowl to stand mixer fitted with whisk. Beat on high speed until eggs are pale yellow and have tripled in volume, about 5 minutes. (Egg foam will form ribbon that sits on top of mixture for 5 seconds when dribbled from whisk.) Measure out ¾ cup egg foam, whisk into butter mixture until well combined, and set aside.

5. Transfer remaining egg foam to large, wide bowl and sift one-third of flour mixture over egg foam in even layer. Using rubber spatula, gently fold batter 6 to 8 times until small streaks of flour remain. Repeat folding 6 to 8 times with half of remaining flour mixture. Sift remaining flour mixture over batter and gently fold 10 to 12 times until flour is completely incorporated.

6. Pour butter mixture over batter in even layer. Gently fold until just incorporated, taking care not to deflate batter. Divide batter evenly between prepared pans.

7. Bake until centers of cakes are set and bounce back when gently pressed and toothpick inserted in center comes out clean, 13 to 16 minutes. Remove cakes from pans, discarding parchment, and let cool completely on wire rack, about 2 hours.

8. Drain berries in fine-mesh strainer over bowl. Measure out 2 tablespoons juice into small bowl (reserve remaining juice in bowl) and stir in cornstarch

Sponge cake is the ideal type of cake for this recipe since it soaks up berry juice like, well, a sponge.

until well combined. Microwave, stirring every 10 seconds, until mixture is very thick and translucent, 30 to 45 seconds. Set aside.

9. Place 1 cake layer right side up on platter. Place second layer upside down on cutting board. Using paring knife, cut circle from center of cake on board, leaving 1-inch-wide ring of cake. (Reserve circle for another use.) Place upside-down cake ring on top of layer on platter. Using pastry brush, brush all of unthickened strawberry juice onto bottom cake layer and inner sides of cake ring. Gently combine berries and reserved thickened juice in now-empty bowl. Spoon berry mixture into cake ring, forming even layer.

10. FOR THE WHIPPED CREAM: Using stand mixer fitted with whisk, whip cream and crème fraîche on low speed until foamy, about 1 minute. Add sugar, increase speed to medium-high, and whip until soft peaks form, about 2 minutes. Dollop 2 tablespoons whipped cream onto center of cake. Transfer remaining whipped cream to serving bowl. Dust cake ring with confectioners' sugar. Cut and serve, passing extra whipped cream separately.

KEEPING THE AIR IN AIRY CAKE

For our Refined Strawberry Shortcake, we use a style of sponge cake known as a genoise. Like any sponge, a genoise should have an airy, springy texture—but if the whipped eggs intended to give it this texture aren't fully aerated or deflate during folding, the cake turns out dense, flat, and rubbery. Here's how we made it foolproof.

HEAT EGGS WITH SUGAR
Fully dissolving the sugar in the eggs makes the mixture more viscous and better able to hold in air when whipped.

WHIP TO RIBBON STAGE
A ribbon of foam that holds for 5 seconds when dribbled from the whisk indicates a stable structure that will hold air.

FOLD IN FLOUR IN WIDE BOWL
Sifting the flour over a broad area means fewer strokes are needed to mix it in—minimizing the risk of deflating the foam.

LIGHTEN UP MELTED BUTTER
Whisking some egg foam into the butter mixture lightens the mixture and makes it easier to incorporate into the batter.

Our Asian Pantry

While the universe of Asian ingredients is vast, we turn to these staple ingredients to bring authentic flavor to Asian recipes. And in some cases, the right product can be critical.

BY ELIZABETH BOMZE

Chili-Garlic Sauce

➤ A puree of chiles, garlic, vinegar, and salt, this complex, spicy sauce adds brightness and heat to countless stir-fries, sauces, and glazes. The popular Huy Fong, or "Rooster" brand, is available in many supermarkets.

Can't find it? Substitute Sriracha: Sriracha sauce, which contains similar ingredients, makes a spicier, less acidic stand-in. For 1 tablespoon of chili-garlic sauce, use 2 teaspoons of Sriracha.

Chinese Egg Noodles

➤ There are countless varieties of egg noodles, both dried and fresh. Wavy fresh ones (sometimes labeled "lo mein noodles") offer just the right springy chew for stir-fries. Many supermarkets stock them alongside tofu. Avoid vacuum-packed "Chinese-style" fresh noodles, which can be gummy.

Can't find them? Use dried linguine: Though not authentic, we've found that linguine offers a similar firm chew.

Chinese Rice Wine (Shaoxing)

➤ Like Japanese mirin, Shaoxing is made from fermented rice, but its flavor is deeper, more aromatic, and not as sweet. It's a staple in stir-fries, sauces, and glazes.

Can't find it? Use dry sherry: For cooking, Taylor Dry Sherry ($5.99 for 750 milliliters) will do just fine.

Coconut Milk

➤ The sweet, rich liquid strained from shredded raw coconut meat that's been steeped in water, coconut milk is used extensively in Thai and Vietnamese cooking.

Good to know: We found that products with relatively low amounts of sugar (less than 1 gram per ⅓ cup) boasted more coconutty flavor; those with at least twice as much sugar tasted saccharine.

What about light coconut milk? This style is far less creamy, and we found that it can ruin the texture of desserts. But it's acceptable in soups and curries.

Our favorite: Chaokoh Coconut Milk ($1.79 for 13.5 ounces)

Didn't use the whole can? Stored in an airtight container, coconut milk will last up to a week in the fridge and a month in the freezer. The milk will break when defrosted; to re-emulsify it, blend it with an immersion blender for about 30 seconds.

Dried Rice Noodles

➤ Made from ground rice and water, rice noodles are cut into myriad shapes and thicknesses, but when cooked, all should taste like fresh rice with a tender but pleasantly resilient bite.

Good to know: Unlike other dried noodles, which must be boiled to soften them, dried rice noodles are usually just soaked in hot water until tender before being added to stir-fries or salads.

Our favorite: A Taste of Thai Straight Cut Rice Noodles ($6.59 for 16 ounces)

Fish Sauce

➤ This liquid product of fermented anchovies, which is used as both an ingredient and a condiment, boasts a rich and savory saltiness that adds depth to countless Thai and Vietnamese dishes. It's strong stuff with an intense aroma.

Good to know: We use this sauce not just in Asian dishes but also to season marinades. Used judiciously, it adds savoriness, not fishy flavor.

Our favorite: Red Boat 40°N Fish Sauce ($7.99 for 8.45 ounces)

Our vegan alternative: Simmer 3 cups water, ¼ ounce dried sliced shiitake mushrooms, 3 tablespoons salt, and 2 tablespoons soy sauce over medium heat until reduced by half. Strain, cool, and refrigerate for up to 3 weeks. Makes 1½ cups.

Gochujang

➤ This moderately spicy, salty, savory paste made from chiles, glutinous rice, fermented soybeans, and salt makes a powerful base for Korean sauces and marinades (such as the chile sauce for our Korean Rice Bowl, page 13).

Good to know: This paste is our new favorite flavor booster. Stir it into soup, barbecue sauce, ketchup, mayonnaise, or butter, or thin it with water to a drizzling consistency and use it as a condiment for eggs, vegetables, rice, noodles, or dumplings.

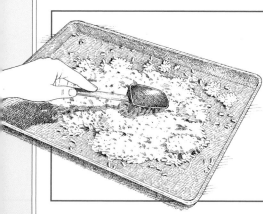

Making Fried Rice Without Leftovers

Chilled, hardened leftover rice is crucial in fried rice since fresh rice turns mushy. But we don't always have leftovers on hand. Here's our work-around: Heat 2 tablespoons vegetable oil in large saucepan over medium heat until shimmering. Add 2 cups jasmine or long-grain white rice; stir to coat. Add 2⅔ cups water and bring to boil. Reduce heat to low, cover, and simmer until liquid is absorbed, about 18 minutes. Off heat, remove lid and place dish towel over saucepan. Let stand, covered, until rice is just tender, about 8 minutes. Spread cooked rice onto rimmed baking sheet. Let cool for 10 minutes, then refrigerate for 20 minutes. Makes 6 cups.

Hoisin Sauce

➤ A thick, reddish-brown mixture of soybeans, sugar, vinegar, garlic, and chiles, hoisin sauce is used in many classic Chinese dishes, including barbecued pork, Peking duck, and *mu shu* pork.

Good to know: Hoisin should pack a punch, but some products taste flat. The best sauces balance sweet, salty, pungent, and spicy elements so that no one flavor dominates.

Our favorite: Kikkoman Hoisin Sauce ($2.89 for 9.3 ounces)

Jasmine Rice

➤ This rice variety's delicate floral, buttery scent, prized in Southeast Asian cuisines, isn't a byproduct of jasmine plants. It's the result of a flavor compound common to all rice varieties, which occurs in high levels in aromatic rices such as jasmine and basmati.

Good to know: Look for packages stamped with a green seal from Thailand's Department of Foreign Trade, an indication that at least 92 percent of the rice is the purest form called Hom Mali ("good smelling").

Our favorite: Dynasty Jasmine Rice ($4.59 for 2 pounds)

Mirin

➤ This Japanese rice wine adds sweetness and acidity to sauces and glazes like teriyaki. Hard-to-find traditional mirin contains no added ingredients; supermarket brands usually contain sweeteners and salt.

Our favorite: Mitoku Organic Mikawa Mirin Sweet Rice Seasoning ($8.83 for 10 fluid ounces, plus shipping)

Our best buy: Eden Mirin Rice Cooking Wine ($7.16 for 10.5 fluid ounces)

Can't find it? Use this: For 1 tablespoon of mirin, use an equal amount of white wine plus 1 teaspoon of sugar.

Oyster Sauce

➤ Made from a reduction of boiled oysters, this condiment adds salty-sweetness (not fishiness) and body to stir-fries.

Good to know: Though it may look like hoisin sauce, oyster sauce lacks hoisin's fruity, spicy, pungent profile. Oyster sauce should taste deeply savory with a hint of sweetness. Lesser brands can taste like little more than gloppy soy sauce.

Our favorite: Lee Kum Kee Premium Oyster Flavored Sauce ($4.69 for 9 ounces)

Try These Classics

With a well-stocked Asian pantry, you can make many of our best Asian recipes. Find these at CooksIllustrated.com/june16.

➤ **GRILLED BEEF SATAY**
Key flavors: coconut milk, fish sauce, and lemon grass

➤ **THAI-STYLE CHICKEN WITH BASIL**
Key flavors: fish sauce and oyster sauce

➤ **SICHUAN STIR-FRIED GREEN BEANS**
Key flavors: soy sauce, toasted sesame oil, and white peppercorns

➤ **PORK STIR-FRY WITH NOODLES (LO MEIN)**
Key flavors: chili-garlic sauce, Chinese rice wine, hoisin sauce, oyster sauce soy sauce, and toasted sesame oil

➤ **STIR-FRIED SICHUAN-STYLE SHRIMP WITH ZUCCHINI, RED BELL PEPPER, AND PEANUTS**
Key flavors: chili-garlic sauce, Chinese rice wine, Sichuan peppercorns, and toasted sesame oil

---

Rice Vinegar

➤ Not to be confused with rice wine, rice vinegar (sometimes incorrectly called rice wine vinegar) has malty sweetness and mild acidity. It's primarily used to season sushi rice and stir-fries and makes a less-sharp alternative to other vinegars in dressings.

Good to know: It's sold seasoned or unseasoned. The latter contains no added salt or sugar, so it can be used in a variety of dressings and sauces. Use the seasoned kind for applications like quick pickles where you want both acidity and sweetness.

Sichuan Peppercorns

➤ Not actually peppercorns but dried fruit rinds from a Chinese citrus tree, these contribute a unique tingling sensation and a piney, citrusy aroma. We bloom them in oil or grind them and sprinkle them over Chinese dishes like *ma pao* tofu and salt and pepper shrimp.

Good to know: Since Sichuan peppercorns don't actually contribute any heat, they shouldn't be subbed in for black or red pepper.

Our favorite: Dean & DeLuca Szechuan Peppercorns ($6.25 for 1 ounce)

Soy Sauce

➤ Made from soybeans fermented in a brine with roasted wheat, this savory condiment is used globally in Asian cuisines to season and add depth.

Good to know: Different types serve different purposes: We use a more robust-tasting brand in cooked applications and reserve pricier long-aged soy sauce for dipping.

Our favorite for cooking: Lee Kum Kee Tabletop Premium Soy Sauce ($1.99 for 5.1 ounces)

Our favorite for dipping: Ohsawa Nama Shoyu Organic Unpasteurized Soy Sauce ($6.49 for 10 ounces)

What about tamari? A byproduct of miso production, tamari has a similarly salty-savory flavor to soy sauce; the two can be used interchangeably. Many tamaris are also gluten-free.

Toasted Sesame Oil

➤ While plain sesame oil has very little color, smell, or flavor, toasted (or roasted) sesame oil boasts deeper color and much stronger, richer flavor. We've found that a little goes a long way in dressings, dipping sauces, and stir-fries in Chinese, Korean, and Japanese recipes.

Good to know: Due to its potent flavor and relatively low smoke point, it shouldn't be used as a primary cooking oil. But try adding a few drops to neutral vegetable or peanut oil when stir-frying to give food a mildly nutty flavor boost.

To keep flavor fresh: Store it in the refrigerator.

White Peppercorns

➤ These are simply skinned black peppercorns, which taste less spicy and more floral than black pepper since skinning removes much of the spicy compound piperine. They're a common seasoning in Chinese and Thai dishes; we also use them in non-Asian applications like spaetzle, mayonnaise, and spice rubs.

What about subbing in black? Only substitute black pepper if the amount called for is less than 1 teaspoon—otherwise, the pepper may mask other flavors.

Staple Fresh Flavors

In addition to everyday aromatics and herbs like garlic, shallots, scallions, and cilantro, lemon grass and ginger are also worth keeping on hand.

Lemon Grass

➤ Native to India and tropical Asia, this grassy herb imparts citrusy, floral flavors to South Asian soups, curries, and stir-fries. Look for stalks that are green, firm, and fragrant.

Strip to the core: Remove the dry outer layers to expose the tender inner stalk before mincing.

Sub dried for fresh? Dried lemon grass works in soups and curry paste but not in stir-fries, where there isn't enough liquid to rehydrate the pieces.

Ginger

➤ A rhizome grown largely in Jamaica, China, and India, ginger is bright and floral but also packs heat thanks to its pungent gingerol, a relative of the spicy compounds in chiles.

Old is OK: Ginger dries out and loses pungency as it ages. So if your ginger is older, use more of it than a recipe calls for and add it toward the end of cooking (heat also dulls its pungency).

Scrape; don't peel: Scraping off the knotty skin with a spoon is easier than peeling with a knife or vegetable peeler.

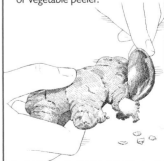

Introducing Farro Risotto

This Italian grain's flavorful bran layer makes it a challenge to coax into creamy *farrotto*.

≥ BY STEVE DUNN ≤

Risotto has been a staple in American restaurants and home kitchens for years, but *farrotto* has only recently gained a footing stateside. As the name suggests, it's a twist on the classic Italian rice-based dish, made with farro, an ancient form of wheat that's been grown in Italy for centuries and that boasts a nutty flavor and a tender chew. Using this whole grain instead of rice yields a more robust dish that still cooks relatively quickly and functions well as a blank slate for any type of flavor addition—from cheese and herbs to meats and vegetables.

There's just one pitfall to farrotto: bran. Arborio or *carnaroli* rices have been stripped of their bran layer and thus readily give up their amylopectin, the starch molecule that makes risotto creamy. Farro retains most of its bran (how much depends on whether it's been "pearled," or had its bran at least partially rubbed away), which gives it bite and earthy flavor but also traps the starch inside the grain. Hence, most farrottos lack risotto's velvety body and cohesion. I wanted both: the distinct flavor and chew of farro with the creamy consistency of risotto.

My instinct was to first try pearled farro; since it has less bran, it might cook up creamier. I had a leg up on a basic cooking method, which I'd borrow from our Almost Hands-Free Risotto (May/June 2010). The trick in that recipe is to add most of the liquid up front, rather than in several stages, which helps the grains cook evenly so that you need to stir only a couple of times rather than constantly. We also use a lidded Dutch oven, which helps trap and distribute the heat evenly so every grain is tender.

To start, I softened onion and garlic in butter, added the farro to toast in the fat, and finally added the liquid. But the pearled farro not only lacked the robust flavor of whole farro but also resulted in farrotto that was too thin. I would have to stick with whole farro.

My breakthrough came from an outlier farrotto recipe, which called for "cracking" the farro before cooking by soaking the grains overnight to soften them and then blitzing them in a food processor. This gave the starch an escape route and yielded a silkier dish. The only drawback was that lengthy soak.

I tried skipping the soak, and I also tried a hot soak to see if I could soften the grains quickly. In both cases the hard grains just danced around the processor bowl without breaking. Switching to a blender created a vortex that drew the unsoaked grains into the blade. Six pulses cracked about half of them so

that there was plenty of starch but still enough chew.

Seasoned with Parmesan, herbs, and lemon juice, my farrotto was hearty and flavorful—and more satisfying than any risotto I've eaten. I also created variations with spring vegetables and mushrooms, both of which can stand as one-pot meals.

PARMESAN FARROTTO
SERVES 6

We prefer the flavor and texture of whole farro. Do not use quick-cooking or pearled farro. The consistency of *farrotto* is a matter of personal taste; if you prefer a looser texture, add more of the hot broth mixture in step 6. For our recipe for Mushroom Farrotto, go to CooksIllustrated.com/june16.

- 1½ cups whole farro
- 3 cups chicken broth
- 3 cups water
- 4 tablespoons unsalted butter
- ½ onion, chopped fine
- 1 garlic clove, minced
- 2 teaspoons minced fresh thyme
- Salt and pepper
- 2 ounces Parmesan, grated (1 cup)
- 2 tablespoons minced fresh parsley
- 2 teaspoons lemon juice

1. Pulse farro in blender until about half of grains are broken into smaller pieces, about 6 pulses.

2. Bring broth and water to boil in medium saucepan over high heat. Reduce heat to medium-low to maintain gentle simmer.

3. Melt 2 tablespoons butter in large Dutch oven over medium-low heat. Add onion and cook, stirring frequently, until softened, 3 to 4 minutes. Add garlic and stir until fragrant, about 30 seconds. Add farro and cook, stirring frequently, until grains are lightly toasted, about 3 minutes.

4. Stir 5 cups hot broth mixture into farro mixture, reduce heat to low, cover, and cook until almost all liquid has been absorbed and farro is just al dente, about 25 minutes, stirring twice during cooking.

5. Add thyme, 1 teaspoon salt, and ¾ teaspoon pepper and continue to cook, stirring constantly, until farro becomes creamy, about 5 minutes.

6. Remove pot from heat. Stir in Parmesan, parsley, lemon juice, and remaining 2 tablespoons butter. Season with salt and pepper to taste. Adjust

Break 'em Up

A few quick pulses in a blender crack the farro grains, allowing some of their starches to escape and thicken the cooking liquid into a creamy, cohesive sauce.

Asparagus, peas, and pancetta round out this version.

consistency with remaining hot broth mixture as needed. Serve immediately.

FARROTTO WITH PANCETTA, ASPARAGUS, AND PEAS

Add 4 ounces asparagus, trimmed and cut on bias into 1-inch lengths, to broth-water mixture in step 2 and cook until crisp-tender, 2 to 3 minutes. Using slotted spoon, transfer asparagus to bowl and set aside. Reduce heat as directed. Cook 4 ounces pancetta, cut into ¼-inch pieces, in large Dutch oven over medium heat until lightly browned and fat has rendered, about 5 minutes. Proceed with step 3, reducing butter to 1 tablespoon and adding butter and onion to pot with pancetta. Substitute 1 cup thawed frozen peas and 2 teaspoons minced fresh tarragon for thyme and reduce salt to ¾ teaspoon and pepper to ½ teaspoon in step 5. In step 6, add 1 teaspoon grated lemon zest and reserved asparagus with remaining 2 tablespoons butter, reduce Parmesan to ¾ cup and lemon juice to 1 teaspoon, and substitute 1 tablespoon minced fresh chives for parsley.

▶ **Watch: Blender Technique**
A step-by-step video is available at CooksIllustrated.com/june16

Sautéed Sugar Snap Peas

What's the secret to tender pods that retain their namesake snap? Steam.

≥ BY SANDRA WU ≤

If I'm going to cook fresh peas, I usually go for the sugar snap variety. These pods are a cross between snow peas and shelling peas and, in my opinion, offer the best traits of both: the former's easy preparation (just pull away the tough strings along the pod's seam—no shelling required) and the latter's fresh pop, sweetness, and delicate crunch.

I like to sauté sugar snap peas because the method allows me to flavor them with a little garlic in the pan. But unlike when sautéing other vegetables such as cauliflower or mushrooms, my goal isn't to brown the snap peas, because doing so muddies their fresh sweetness. The other difficulty of cooking them—and part of what makes my goal challenging—is that snap peas are a two-part vegetable, and it's tricky to get the peas within to cook through before the exterior pod browns. What I needed was a way to sauté them so that they turned crisp-tender inside and out but retained their fresh, clean flavor.

A Simple Trick for Tasty Pods

Halving the snap pea pods on the bias creates handy pockets that capture the seasonings.

Since high heat inevitably imparts color, I started testing over a moderate flame, adding a couple of teaspoons of vegetable oil to a large nonstick skillet, setting the dial to medium, adding 12 ounces of snap peas, and stirring them to ensure even cooking. But it was a failed attempt; while the pods didn't brown, they turned limp, dull, and greasy by the time the peas had cooked through.

I needed the peas inside to cook faster—and it occurred to me that introducing water might do the trick, since it transfers heat more efficiently than air. Blanching and shocking the snap peas—that is, dropping them into boiling water for about a minute and then plunging them into ice water to stop their cooking—before sautéing them was too much trouble for a side dish. Instead, I tried a hybrid steam-then-sauté method, in which I heated the oil over a moderate flame, added the snap peas with a small amount of water, briefly covered the pan to trap the steam, and then removed the lid and allowed the water to evaporate.

That gave me exactly what I wanted: both pods and peas that were evenly crisp-tender. Now they just needed some seasonings. First, I added a little minced garlic to the pan after the snap peas had steamed. Then, instead of covering them with heavy or assertive sauces, I dressed the snap peas up with variations inspired by *dukka*, a light, crunchy Egyptian condiment that's a blend of chopped nuts, seeds, and spices. I paired pine nuts and fennel seeds with lemon zest and red pepper flakes for a vaguely Italian profile; almonds, coriander seeds, and orange zest for a Moroccan version; and sesame seeds, lemon, ginger, and scallions for a Japanese one.

These flavorful blends were a cinch to prepare, but there was just one small issue: the small bits slid off the pods. The easy fix was halving the snap peas on the bias before cooking, which created pockets that captured the seasonings. The vegetable's tender snap paired with the distinct flavors and delicate crunch of the dukka mixtures was a combination I'd be making all season long.

SUGAR SNAP PEAS WITH PINE NUTS, FENNEL, AND LEMON ZEST
SERVES 4

Do not substitute ground fennel for the fennel seeds in this recipe.

- 3   tablespoons pine nuts
- 1   teaspoon fennel seeds
- ½   teaspoon grated lemon zest
- ½   teaspoon kosher salt
- ⅛   teaspoon red pepper flakes
- 2   teaspoons vegetable oil
- 12 ounces sugar snap peas, strings removed, halved crosswise on bias
- 2   tablespoons water
- 1   garlic clove, minced
- 3   tablespoons chopped fresh basil

1. Toast pine nuts in 12-inch skillet over medium heat, stirring frequently, until just starting to brown, about 3 minutes. Add fennel seeds and continue to toast, stirring constantly, until pine nuts are lightly browned and fennel is fragrant, about 1 minute longer. Transfer pine nut mixture to cutting board. Sprinkle lemon zest, salt, and pepper flakes over pine nut mixture. Chop mixture until finely minced and well combined. Transfer to bowl and set aside.

2. Heat oil in now-empty skillet over medium heat until shimmering. Add snap peas and water, immediately cover, and cook for 2 minutes. Uncover, add garlic, and continue to cook, stirring frequently, until moisture has evaporated and snap peas are crisp-tender, about 2 minutes longer. Remove skillet from heat; stir in three-quarters of pine nut mixture and

Nuts, seeds, and spices flavor this snappy side dish.

basil. Transfer snap peas to serving platter, sprinkle with remaining pine nut mixture, and serve.

SUGAR SNAP PEAS WITH ALMONDS, CORIANDER, AND ORANGE ZEST

Slivered almonds can be used in place of sliced almonds. Do not use ground coriander in this recipe.

Substitute sliced almonds for pine nuts, coriander seeds for fennel seeds, ¼ teaspoon orange zest for lemon zest, and cilantro for basil. Omit red pepper flakes.

SUGAR SNAP PEAS WITH SESAME, GINGER, AND LEMON ZEST

Black or white sesame seeds can be used in this recipe.

Substitute 2 tablespoons sesame seeds for pine nuts, ½ teaspoon grated fresh ginger for garlic, and 1 thinly sliced scallion for basil. Omit fennel seeds and red pepper flakes.

▶ Watch: It's a Snap
A step-by-step video is available at CooksIllustrated.com/june16

Perfect Sticky Buns

Sticky buns look inviting, but most are dry and overly sweet, with a topping that threatens your dental work. We wanted a version that fulfilled its promise.

⇒ BY ANDREA GEARY ⇐

I once made sticky buns at home, and I enjoyed every step of the baking process, from rolling the spiced sugar filling up in the firm, smooth dough to nestling the tidy spirals in the nutty caramel topping to flipping the baked buns onto a platter and watching the glaze drip down the sides. But when it came to the final step—actually eating a bun—I felt betrayed.

Even when slightly warm, the bread part was drier and tougher than I had anticipated, and the topping was so firm that I feared for my fillings. A few hours later, the buns were downright hard from top to bottom, but it didn't really matter. They were so overwhelmingly sweet that finishing one had been a feat, and I couldn't muster enough enthusiasm to repeat the experience.

When I was finally ready to attempt sticky buns again, I set some firm goals: This time around the bread would be moist, soft, and fluffy, and the topping would be substantial enough to sit atop the buns without sinking in but not so hard that it stuck in my teeth. And, of course, I'd keep the overall sweetness in check so that I could eat an entire bun.

A Hard Case

Most sticky bun recipes follow a common procedure: First, you make a yeast dough, and while it rises you mix up a filling and a topping. The filling is often just sugar and a bit of spice but may also include ingredients such as softened butter, dried fruit, and chopped nuts. The topping usually involves cooking butter and sugar and maybe honey or maple syrup together in a saucepan, pouring the mixture into a baking pan, and scattering the surface with nuts. You flatten the risen dough into a rectangle, sprinkle the filling over it, and roll it up like a jelly roll. Cut the dough cylinder into pieces, place them in the pan, let them rise, and then bake, flip, and enjoy (in theory).

I chose simple formulas to act as placeholders for the filling and topping so I could concentrate

▶ **Andrea Shows You How**
A step-by-step video is available at CooksIllustrated.com/june16

Using three sweeteners—brown and granulated sugars plus corn syrup—was key to a topping that was perfectly sweet and just sticky enough.

on creating a dough that would bake up soft and light. I started with a couple of basic yeast doughs made with flour, milk, sugar, butter, and eggs, as well as some that included ingredients like rolled oats and instant mashed potatoes for their purported moisture-retaining qualities.

In dough form, each of these was pleasantly smooth and springy, a joy to work with. Unfortunately, all of the recipes—even those with oats and mashed potatoes—yielded buns that were drier and harder than my ideal. I was quickly learning that, while firm, smooth doughs are the least sticky and as such the easiest to shape, they inevitably yield tight, tough bread.

Fair enough. I was willing to struggle with a slack, sticky dough if it gave me the light, moist results I was after, so I mixed together a buttery, eggy brioche dough. As expected, its softness made it difficult to roll into a cylinder, and when I sliced it into pieces, they stuck to the knife, which left them mangled. But that's not what discouraged me. When baked, the rich, sugar-filled brioche topped with buttery, nutty

caramel was just too much of a good thing. I couldn't finish a full portion.

It seemed that the three qualities I wanted most in a dough—easy to work with, not too rich, light and fluffy when baked—were incompatible. And then I realized that I had tackled a similar problem a few months earlier.

Lighten Up

While developing a recipe for dinner rolls, I had learned about an interesting Asian bread-baking technique called *tangzhong*, in which a portion of the flour and liquid in a recipe is cooked together until it forms a pudding-like gel, which is then added to the bread dough. This allows you to add more liquid to the dough, yet the added water doesn't make the dough sticky or difficult to work with because that precooked gel traps it. The extra water converts to steam during baking, which made my rolls fluffy and light. And with a fraction of the eggs and butter found in a rich brioche and just a few tablespoons of sugar, they aren't too decadent.

Easy to work with? Light and moist without too much richness? Obviously the sticky bun–tangzhong marriage was meant to be.

Given that sticky buns are a bit of work and something that you tend to make for an occasion, I wanted to make enough to fill a 13 by 9-inch pan, so I increased my dinner roll recipe by one-third. I cooked a small amount of flour and water together in the microwave until it had formed a smooth paste and then whisked the mixture with milk to cool it down to ensure that it wouldn't kill the yeast. I stirred in eggs, flour, and instant yeast and let the mixture rest for 15 minutes before adding some salt and a modest amount of sugar. I then let the mixer knead the dough for 5 minutes. Next, I added some softened butter and mixed for 5 minutes more before setting the dough aside to rise while I made the filling and topping.

Why wait to add the salt and sugar? They are hygroscopic, which means they attract water and would have diverted moisture away from the flour, delaying the formation of gluten. Pausing before adding salt and sugar allows the gluten-forming proteins to fully hydrate so that they can link up and create structure, giving the buns height and lightness when baked. And because my sticky buns would

The Ideal Sticky Bun

Most sticky buns are dense and dry, with a filling that's fussy to work with and a topping so sticky that chewing it makes your jaw ache. Plus, the whole package is usually so rich that you can't finish an entire bun. Here's how we made a better bun.

FILLING THAT STAYS INSIDE
Moist brown sugar doesn't scatter like granulated when the dough is rolled.

SOFT, FLUFFY BREAD
Adding extra water to our dough creates more steam, which results in more lift and a lighter bun.

STICKY BUT NOT HARD TOPPING
Corn syrup and water help keep the topping soft.

NOT TOO SWEET OR TOO RICH
Keeping the eggs and sugar in the dough to a minimum means you can eat a whole bun.

have a heavy topping to support, a sound structure would be crucial.

I turned the risen dough out onto the counter and patted and stretched it to form a rectangle, a technique I found easier and more effective than rolling this soft dough with a pin. I sprinkled on the filling, rolled the dough into a tight cylinder, and sliced it into portions using a length of dental floss, which kept the pieces neat and round. I transferred the pieces to the pan, let them rise, and then baked them.

When I retrieved the buns from the oven, I found that almost every one had blossomed into a tall cone shape (see "Go Easy"), which was kind of charming but not ideal. Problematic geometry aside, these moist, fluffy buns were a success. After a few more tests, I realized that their fluffiness was what had caused their odd shape: The dough expanded so much when it baked that it had nowhere to go but up. Simply keeping the cylinder a little looser produced tall but level buns.

Topped Off

With the dough sorted out, it was time to examine the filling and topping. My placeholder filling was just ¾ cup of sugar and 1 teaspoon of cinnamon. It tasted okay, but the dry, loose mixture had a maddening tendency to roll and shift over the surface of the dough when I formed the cylinder, which left some pieces with less filling than others—and a lot of sugar on my counter.

Some bakers encourage the filling to stick by brushing the dough with melted butter (a little rich) or water (drippy and a bit messy) or by mixing butter into the filling and smearing it over the dough (both rich and messy and also a pain). Instead I simply used dark brown sugar instead of white. Its moistness helped it stick to the tacky dough, so I could roll it up easily.

The topping required a little more trial and error. My placeholder was a mixture of brown sugar, butter, honey, and cream that was cooked in a saucepan, poured into the baking pan, and covered evenly with

a layer of chopped pecans (some might opt to leave the nuts out, but I preferred them for the visual and textural appeal they lent). It baked up a bit too firm, and I wasn't crazy about the assertive flavor of the honey or the overall sweetness.

The first thing to go was the saucepan. I simply melted the butter in a bowl in the microwave and then stirred the other ingredients into it. If it wasn't going to be honey, I decided a liquid sugar of some form was a must. Because these liquid sweeteners contain water, they produce a softer texture than I'd get with just granulated or brown sugar; plus, the sugar in these liquid ingredients is fully dissolved, which helps avoid grainy results. Substituting dark corn syrup for the honey was the answer. It gave me a topping that was a little less sweet and also a little less distinctive, so it didn't overpower the cinnamon in the filling or the pleasant yeastiness of the bread. I went with a mixture of dark brown and granulated sugars to give the topping just the right rich color.

But that cream bothered me. I was using just 2

Go Easy

Because these sticky buns bake up so soft and fluffy, it's important to roll the dough loosely when forming the cylinder in step 7.

BAD BUNS
If rolled too tightly, the buns will expand upward.

tablespoons, so it was hardly worth buying a carton, but eliminating it made the topping even firmer. And then it occurred to me: Cream is mostly water and fat, and my buttery topping was hardly lacking in the fat department. As odd as it seemed, substituting water for the cream did the trick and, in fact, was an improvement. By decreasing the fat and increasing the liquid with this swap, I created a topping that was substantial, gooey, and sticky—yet not too firm.

Though I'd typically make these buns to give to a crowd, they're now so fluffy and light that the prospect of keeping more than one for myself is pretty tempting.

STICKY BUNS
MAKES 12 BUNS

These buns take about 4 hours to make from start to finish. For dough that is easy to work with and produces light, fluffy buns, we strongly recommend that you measure the flour for the dough by weight. The slight tackiness of the dough aids in flattening and stretching it in step 6, so resist the urge to use a lot of dusting flour. Rolling the dough cylinder tightly in step 7 will result in misshapen rolls; keep the cylinder a bit slack. Bake these buns in a metal, not glass or ceramic, baking pan. We like dark corn syrup and pecans here, but light corn syrup may be used, and the nuts may be omitted, if desired.

Flour Paste
- ⅔ cup water
- ¼ cup (1⅓ ounces) bread flour

Dough
- ⅔ cup milk
- 1 large egg plus 1 large yolk
- 2¾ cups (15⅛ ounces) bread flour
- 2 teaspoons instant or rapid-rise yeast
- 3 tablespoons granulated sugar
- 1½ teaspoons salt
- 6 tablespoons unsalted butter, softened

Topping
- 6 tablespoons unsalted butter, melted
- ½ cup packed (3½ ounces) dark brown sugar
- ¼ cup (1¾ ounces) granulated sugar
- ¼ cup dark corn syrup
- ¼ teaspoon salt
- 2 tablespoons water
- 1 cup pecans, toasted and chopped (optional)

Filling
- ¾ cup packed (5¼ ounces) dark brown sugar
- 1 teaspoon ground cinnamon

1. FOR THE FLOUR PASTE: Whisk water and flour together in small bowl until no lumps remain. Microwave, whisking every 25 seconds, until mixture thickens to stiff, smooth, pudding-like consistency that forms mound when dropped from end of whisk into bowl, 50 to 75 seconds.

The Road to Moist Sticky Buns

Our ideal was a light, moist bun that wasn't too rich or sweet, so we could eat the whole thing without regret. Here's how we got there.

TEST 1
BASIC YEASTED DOUGH
Why We Tried It:
Most are not too sticky, which makes them easy to work with.
Result: Buns were dense and dry.

TEST 2 REPLACE SOME FLOUR WITH ROLLED OATS
Why We Tried It:
We hoped the oats would help retain moisture and soften the buns.
Result: No improvement.

TEST 3
ADD MASHED POTATOES
Why We Tried It:
Instant mashed potatoes also have moisture-retaining properties for the promise of a softer bun.
Result: No improvement.

TEST 4
ADD EGGS AND BUTTER
Why We Tried It:
Eggs and butter add fat; eggs also add water.
Result: Buns were tender but too rich; dough was overly sticky.

BEST METHOD

TEST 5 ADD A COOKED FLOUR-AND-WATER PASTE
Why We Tried It:
Also known as *tangzhong*, this technique allowed us to add more water without making the dough too wet.
Result: Buns were light and moist; dough was simple to roll and cut.

2. FOR THE DOUGH: In bowl of stand mixer, whisk flour paste and milk together until smooth. Add egg and yolk and whisk until incorporated. Add flour and yeast. Fit stand mixer with dough hook and mix on low speed until all flour is moistened, 1 to 2 minutes. Let stand for 15 minutes. Add sugar and salt and mix on medium-low speed for 5 minutes. Stop mixer and add butter. Continue to mix on medium-low speed for 5 minutes longer, scraping down dough hook and sides of bowl halfway through (dough will stick to bottom of bowl).

3. Transfer dough to lightly floured counter. Knead briefly to form ball and transfer seam side down to lightly greased bowl; lightly coat surface of dough with vegetable oil spray and cover bowl with plastic wrap. Let dough rise until just doubled in volume, 40 minutes to 1 hour.

4. FOR THE TOPPING: While dough rises, grease 13 by 9-inch metal baking pan. Whisk melted butter, brown sugar, granulated sugar, corn syrup, and salt together in medium bowl until smooth. Add water and whisk until incorporated. Pour mixture into prepared pan and tilt pan to cover bottom. Sprinkle evenly with pecans, if using.

5. FOR THE FILLING: Combine sugar and cinnamon in small bowl and mix until thoroughly combined; set aside.

6. Turn out dough onto lightly floured counter. Press dough gently but firmly to expel air. Working from center toward edge, pat and stretch dough to form 18 by 15-inch rectangle with long edge nearest you. Sprinkle filling over dough, leaving 1-inch border along top edge; smooth filling into even layer with your hand, then gently press mixture into dough to adhere.

7. Beginning with long edge nearest you, roll dough into cylinder, taking care not to roll too tightly. Pinch seam to seal and roll cylinder seam side down. Mark gently with knife to create 12 equal portions. To slice, hold strand of dental floss taut and slide underneath cylinder, stopping at first mark. Cross ends of floss over each other and pull. Slice cylinder into 12 portions and transfer, cut sides down, to prepared baking pan. Cover tightly with plastic wrap and let rise until buns are puffy and touching one another, 40 minutes to 1 hour. (Buns may be refrigerated immediately after shaping for up to 14 hours. To bake, remove baking pan from refrigerator and let sit until buns are puffy and touching one another, 1 to 1½ hours.) Meanwhile, adjust oven racks to lowest and lower-middle positions. Place rimmed baking sheet on lower rack to catch any drips and heat oven to 375 degrees.

8. Bake buns on upper rack until golden brown, about 20 minutes. Tent with aluminum foil and bake until center of dough registers at least 200 degrees, 10 to 15 minutes longer. Let buns cool in pan on wire rack for 5 minutes. Place rimmed baking sheet over buns and carefully invert. Remove pan and let buns cool for 5 minutes. Using spoon, scoop any glaze on baking sheet onto buns. Let cool for at least 10 minutes longer before serving.

Use the Correct Pan

If a recipe specifies a particular pan—metal or glass—don't be tempted to swap one for the other. Each material conducts heat at a different rate, and baking for more or less time to account for that difference won't give you identical results. Case in point: Our Sticky Buns recipe calls for a metal baking pan. When we tried baking the buns in a glass baking dish, which conducts heat more slowly than a metal pan, we had to extend the baking time by 10 minutes to ensure that the buns in the center of the dish were done. But since glass retains heat longer than metal, the buns on the edges of the dish turned dry and hard. For best results, stick with the pan the recipe calls for.

THESE BUNS PALE IN COMPARISON
Our buns baked in glass instead of metal were pale and undercooked in the center.

The Best Gas Grill Under $500

It doesn't matter how powerful a grill is. If it can't distribute and hold the heat where you want it, your food will suffer.

≥ BY LISA McMANUS ≤

It's easy to drop several hundred dollars on a gas grill and not get what you need. We've cooked on models that never got hot enough; models that were too small to cook more than a couple of burgers at once; models that rusted, wobbled, and warped; and models that couldn't handle anything beyond the simplest jobs—never mind roasting a holiday turkey or smoking tender ribs. The bottom line: For the best results, you need a well-designed, responsive, durable grill.

The winner from our previous gas grill testing was discontinued, so we went shopping for some new models to test, priced at $500 or less. We focused on six major brands, asking them to help us choose their best contender. The grills in our lineup were outfitted with three to five burners, as well as two wing-like side tables. All but one grill were equipped with side burners set into one of the wings. All were fitted with warming racks, narrow wire shelves suspended across the back of the grill, and all featured built-in lid thermometers. You can buy a gas grill fully assembled or opt to put it together yourself. After trying both, we would strongly encourage you to order your grill assembled. Some stores do it for free.

We fired up the grills to cook (and smoke) a variety of foods, from burger patties to thick strip steaks to 5-pound pork butts. We checked that a 12-pound turkey fit under each lid with room to spare. We used slices of white bread to map each grill's heating pattern, and we checked the accuracy of the grills' lid thermometers with a calibrated thermocouple.

Along the way, we observed design elements of each grill that made cooking easier or more complicated. Scrubbing down grills after cooking and emptying grease trays showed which were simplest to maintain. And rolling them in and out of our grill garage over bumpy pavement revealed grills that fought us and rattled to pieces—literally—while others glided steadily and remained sturdily intact.

The Heat Is On

Most people choose a gas grill because it's convenient: Turn a knob and you can start cooking in minutes. But whether that grill performs as it should is another matter. For simple grilling, the most important requirement is strong heat that spreads evenly across the grates. To determine which grills met the mark, we preheated each grill on high for 15 minutes (our standard method) and mapped the heat by covering the entire grill surface with white sandwich bread. Top grills gave us evenly browned toast. The worst made

an uneven patchwork of black, brown, and white toast. Others dried out the bread, leaving it white with black stripes. Wrecked toast is no big deal, but when we grilled a quartet of pricey, thick New York strip steaks, the same thing happened. Spreading 4-inch burger patties across the hot grills, we saw those heat patterns a third time.

So what made the difference in how well food cooked? While manufacturers may try to dazzle customers with their burners' high BTUs (British Thermal Units, a measure of heat output per hour), in our tests this number turned out to be less relevant than the grill's construction and heat distribution. All gas grills share a similar construction: At the bottom, perforated metal tubes (the burners) produce a row of flames when the gas is ignited. Above them are metal heat diffusers shaped like inverted Vs. As we used the grills, we realized that these tent-like bars are very important. First, they shield burners to keep fallen food from clogging holes. Second, when dripping fat hits them, the fat turns into smoke that makes food taste grilled (they are sometimes called "flavorizer bars" for this reason). Third, and perhaps most important, they help spread heat horizontally across the grill. The flames' heat wants to rise straight up, and without these tent-like bars to deflect it there would be distinct hot spots directly over each burner and cooler zones everywhere else.

All of the grills we tested had bars right over each burner, but our top-performing grills had further design tweaks to help spread out the rising heat for more even distribution and much-improved cooking results. One achieved this with extra bars between the burners, while the other featured a full layer of perforated stainless-steel plates beneath the grates, which, like the tent-like bars, diffused heat.

While powerful, even heat is critical in a good grill, so are a few other factors. First up: capacity. Sometimes you want to feed a hungry crowd. When we packed our grills with hamburger patties, the

results were surprising. While the grills in our lineup featured different numbers of burners, more burners didn't always correspond to more cooking space. The "smallest" grill—the only one with just three burners—held 19 burgers, while one of the four-burner models fit just 15 burgers. As it turned out, the four-burner grill was only 2 inches wider than the three-burner model (they were the same depth), a negligible advantage that was negated by the fact that the four-burner grill's wide warming rack blocked access to the back of its cooking grates. Other grills shared this design flaw.

Grate material also mattered: Our two highest-ranking grills had cast-iron grates, while most of the lower-ranked ones used stainless steel. Cast iron did a better job of transferring heat for crisp, flavorful grill marks. Finally, the angle of the open lid also mattered. Curved, low-angled lids directed smoke right into our faces, even when fully open. Our favorite grills had lids that opened wide to let smoke flow straight up.

Slow Down

Direct cooking is important, but a good gas grill must also excel at cooking with indirect heat for roasting large cuts of meat or smoking them low and slow. To do this, after preheating the grill, you leave one burner on, turn off the rest, and set the meat over the unlit burners. For our test, we put wood chip packets over each lit burner and set pork butts (each cut into three pieces) over pans of water on the cooler side of each grill, maintaining a temperature of 300 degrees by watching the grills' lid thermometers. All of the roasts should have reached an internal temperature of 200 degrees in 4 hours, yet even after a whopping 7½ hours,

What's Under the Grate?

If you look beneath the cooking grate on a gas grill, you'll notice tent-shaped metal bars covering each of the burners. These flame tamers, or heat diffusers, deflect heat, making them critical to how evenly a grill heats—without them there would be distinct hot spots and cool zones. They also help flavor the food (one manufacturer appropriately calls them "flavorizer bars") since drippings from the food hit the bars, vaporize, and then waft up and adhere to the food.

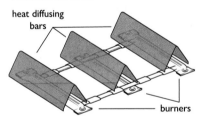

heat diffusing bars

burners

EVENING OUT THE HEAT
Metal tents spread the heat rising up from each burner, minimizing hot and cool zones.

● Lisa Explains It All
A video of our testing is available at CooksIllustrated.com/june16

What Makes Our Winner Great? It's Not the BTUs.

With one of the lowest BTU numbers of any of the models we tested, our winning grill, the Weber Spirit E-310, produced better results (richly browned, evenly cooked food) than grills with up to 72 percent more firepower. The real measure of a great grill? How well it retains heat (and smoke) and spreads it across the grates.

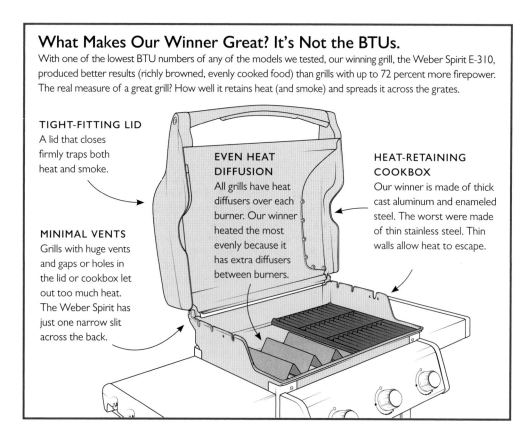

TIGHT-FITTING LID
A lid that closes firmly traps both heat and smoke.

MINIMAL VENTS
Grills with huge vents and gaps or holes in the lid or cookbox let out too much heat. The Weber Spirit has just one narrow slit across the back.

EVEN HEAT DIFFUSION
All grills have heat diffusers over each burner. Our winner heated the most evenly because it has extra diffusers between burners.

HEAT-RETAINING COOKBOX
Our winner is made of thick cast aluminum and enameled steel. The worst were made of thin stainless steel. Thin walls allow heat to escape.

some roasts still weren't done. Others yielded tender meat but no smoke flavor. Only one grill rendered the meat both tender and smoky.

We realized that the problem causing this almost-uniformly poor performance lies in the grills' construction and is, in fact, endemic to gas grills.

For indirect grill-roasting or barbecuing on charcoal, you push all of the coals to one side of the grill, put the meat on the other side, and then adjust the vents to customize heat level and airflow, putting the lid vent over the meat on the cooler side to draw heat and smoke over it. But all of this control is out of your hands with gas grills. The clamshell-shaped "cookbox" on a gas grill has nonadjustable vents, and all of those vents are in one place: across the back of the box. That means hot air and smoke flow in one direction when the lid is closed: straight out the back of the grill. This didn't cause a problem with our previous winning grill (nor with several other models from our last testing). Its burners ran from side to side, so we could send the smoke and heat over the meat by turning on the burner in the front of the grill, putting the wood chips on this burner, and putting the meat directly behind. Heat and smoke traveled front to back, over the meat, on the way to the vents. But the burners in all of the grills for our current testing run from front to back. We're not sure why manufacturers have all gone this route, but it means that the lit burner with the chip packet is always to the side of the meat, and so heat and smoke travel straight back to the vent—bypassing the meat.

Because of this, the integrity of the cookbox—specifically the box material and the number and position of the vents—became essential to success. Even though we had confirmed that the lid ther-

mometers were all accurate and we had been adjusting the heat as needed to maintain a temperature of 300 degrees, we realized that the thermometer was only monitoring the air behind it and not the entire cooking surface. Lower-performing grills had row after row of vents that perforated the back of their cookboxes (some even lacked full back panels). The boxes themselves were thin, with lids that closed loosely over the grates. This translated to an inability to retain heat. When we tried a second time, placing meat much closer to the lit burner, the recipe timing and meat tenderness improved, but smoke flavor was still absent from most.

By contrast, our top grill—the only one that gave us smoky, tender meat—has a cookbox with its bottom and sides made of thick cast aluminum and a heavy, double-layered steel lid. The lid seals tightly, and the box has just one narrow vent across the back. Meat cooked properly in a timely manner every time because this fortified construction and minimal venting forced most of the smoke and heat to stay in the box with the food.

In the end, this grill's competence and versatility, its sturdiness, and its easy cleanup (including the largest, most stable grease tray, which can be lined with a disposable pan) earned it the top spot. The Weber Spirit E-310 ($499) is an updated three-burner version of our former favorite. Weber moved the control knobs to the front, freeing up space on the side table, and added a hook that holds the propane tank and shows the fuel level at a glance. This grill is fairly basic, with no side burner (available on model E-320 for about $50 more), but it does the job. For the same price, you may buy a bigger grill with more frills, but you won't get a better one.

KEY
GOOD ★★★
FAIR ★★
POOR ★

We tested six gas grills priced under $500. Grills appear in order of preference. All were purchased online.

BURNERS: Gas grills heat via perforated tubes called burners that emit flames when ignited. Grills are described by their number of burners, though we found that this did not correlate with performance or capacity.

GRATES: The grill grates are made of either cast iron or stainless steel.

SIZE OF MAIN COOKING GRATE AND HEAT OUTPUT: Manufacturers typically list the combined total square inches, including warming racks and side burners. More usefully, we list the dimensions of the main cooking grate and how many 4-inch burgers each can fit. Similarly, we only list the BTU (British Thermal Units—a measure of heat output per hour) numbers of the main burner.

FEATURES: Some grills offer more extra features than others.

GRILLING: We grilled hamburgers and steaks over direct heat, looking for distinct grill marks, well-browned crusts, and moist interiors. We mapped the heat pattern of each grill by covering its preheated surface with white bread slices and examining the toast.

INDIRECT COOKING: We prepared pulled pork, keeping the grill at 300 degrees for more than 4 hours. Thermocouples confirmed whether lid thermometers were accurate. We rated the pork on smoky flavor and tender, moist texture.

DESIGN: Grills received higher marks if their designs made it easier to set them up and cook.

DURABILITY: Models that were hard to roll; lost wheels, doors, or other parts; or showed greater wear and tear received lower scores.

CLEANUP: We rated whether grates were easy to scrub clean and whether grills had secure, large grease trays and catch pans that were easy to reach.

TESTING GAS GRILLS UNDER $500

WEBER Spirit E-310 Gas Grill

MODEL: 46510001 **PRICE:** $499.00

BURNERS: 3 **GRATES:** Enameled cast iron

SIZE OF MAIN COOKING GRATE: 24" x 17"

HEAT OUTPUT OF MAIN BURNERS: 32,000 BTUs

CAPACITY: 19 burgers

FEATURES: Fuel gauge, six tool hooks, thermometer

GRILLING	★★★
INDIRECT COOKING	★★★
DESIGN	★★★
DURABILITY	★★★
CLEANUP	★★★

COMMENTS: Our winner put a crisp, brown crust on burgers and steaks. It was equally good at barbecue, rendering tender pulled pork with real smoky flavor. Tasters raved: "Perfect smoke, supermoist and tender" and "the texture is spot-on." With a heavy-duty cookbox of thick cast aluminum and enameled steel and just one narrow vent across the back, it was easy to keep heat steady and distribute smoke. The angle of the lid when open kept smoke out of our faces. Its large, secure grease tray made cleanup easier; the sturdy, compact cart rolled without a struggle.

RECOMMENDED

CHAR-BROIL Commercial Series 4-Burner Gas Grill

MODEL: 463242715 **PRICE:** $499.99

BURNERS: 4 **GRATES:** Enameled cast iron

SIZE OF MAIN COOKING GRATE: 29½" x 17"

HEAT OUTPUT OF MAIN BURNERS: 32,000 BTUs

CAPACITY: 24 burgers

FEATURES: Side burner, heat-spreading radiant steel plates under grates, cast-iron griddle, cleaning tool, thermometer

GRILLING	★★★
INDIRECT COOKING	★★
DESIGN	★★
DURABILITY	★★★
CLEANUP	★★

COMMENTS: Unique, heat-spreading zigzagged steel plates beneath cast-iron grates made this grill the best at direct grilling. But its unusual interior layout left us struggling to figure out where to put water pans for indirect cooking, and there was nowhere to prop wood chip packets above the flames. Pulled pork roasted to tenderness but lacked smoke flavor. If you don't care about indirect cooking, this is a great grill. One quibble: While we liked the side burner, its high, domed cover ate up space.

NOT RECOMMENDED

DYNA-GLO
5-Burner Propane Gas Grill with Side Burner and Rotisserie Burner

MODEL: DGA550SSP-D **PRICE:** $483.65

BURNERS: 5 **GRATES:** Stainless steel

SIZE OF MAIN COOKING GRATE: 29" x 17"

HEAT OUTPUT OF MAIN BURNERS: 55,000 BTUs

CAPACITY: 28 burgers

FEATURES: Side burner, rotisserie burner (rotisserie available separately), thermometer

GRILLING	★½
INDIRECT COOKING	★★
DESIGN	★
DURABILITY	★★★
CLEANUP	★½

COMMENTS: This handsome, roomy grill had five burners plus a side burner, but it ran hot and cold in different zones. Burgers got wedged under a protruding rotisserie burner in back, and a low warming rack blocked our spatula. The grease collection tray didn't channel fat, creating a mess. A big 2-inch gap at the back of the lid, open holes in the sides, and an open back panel let too much hot air and smoke escape. While the pulled pork texture was "nice," it lacked smoky flavor: "Not particularly grill-obvious at all," said one taster.

NEXGRILL 4 Burner Liquid Propane Gas Grill

MODEL: 720-0830H **PRICE:** $269.00

BURNERS: 4 **GRATES:** Stainless steel

SIZE OF MAIN COOKING GRATE: 26" by 17"

HEAT OUTPUT OF MAIN BURNERS: 48,000 BTUs

CAPACITY: 15 burgers

FEATURES: Side burner, thermometer

GRILLING	★
INDIRECT COOKING	★★
DESIGN	★
DURABILITY	★★
CLEANUP	★★

COMMENTS: It was the least expensive grill we tested, so we were dubious about its value. Toast was white with black stripes. The back of the grill surface was hotter than the front. We got visible grill marks on some burgers, while all steak came off the grill pale and soft. The open lid's shape sent smoke straight into our faces. The cookbox was thin and flimsy, and nine large vents and a 2-inch gap across the back let smoke and heat escape; no surprise that the pork butt roast was still tough as a rubber ball after 6 hours of cooking. We repeated the test, putting meat just 7 inches from the lit burner; this time it was tender but "smoke was completely absent."

BROIL KING Baron 440

MODEL: 922164 **PRICE:** $499.00

BURNERS: 4 **GRATES:** Cast iron

SIZE OF COOKING GRATE: 25" x 17"

HEAT OUTPUT OF MAIN BURNERS: 40,000 BTUs

CAPACITY: 22 burgers

FEATURES: Side burner, thermometer

GRILLING	★
INDIRECT COOKING	★★
DESIGN	★½
DURABILITY	★
CLEANUP	★★

COMMENTS: Heating was uneven: Toast and burgers were randomly blackened or pale, and we threw about one-quarter of the burgers away, deeming them unfit to serve. Indirect cooking was more successful, with pork rating well for tenderness and lower for smoke flavor, but the grill needed constant tweaking to stay at 300 degrees, due in part to the thin construction of the cookbox. Also, the side holes and wide slit at the back let the smoke escape. Grates scrubbed down easily, but the grease tray was tiny. The deeply curved lid sent smoke into our eyes. The cabinet door fell off every time we rolled the grill.

KITCHENAID 3 Burner Gas Grill & Side Burner

MODEL: 720-0787D **PRICE:** $469.00

BURNERS: 3 **GRATES:** Stainless steel

SIZE OF COOKING GRATE: 24" x 19"

HEAT OUTPUT OF MAIN BURNERS: 36,000 BTUs

CAPACITY: 20 burgers

FEATURES: Grill cover, side burner, tool hooks, thermometer

GRILLING	★½
INDIRECT COOKING	★½
DESIGN	★
DURABILITY	★
CLEANUP	★

COMMENTS: The direct heat over most of this grill's cooking surface was weak: Toast was too light, and burgers cooked unevenly. Meanwhile food on the back row scorched. Steak was "pretty sad," with flabby, pale crust. The weak heat was a boon for barbecue, which came out tender and moist, but there was "no smoke." Abundant vents channeled heat and smoke out of the cookbox, which was thin stainless steel. A very shallow grease tray was a hazard to move, and grease didn't channel effectively, leaving the grill interior a gummy mess. A wheel popped off the cabinet halfway through testing.

Getting to Know Sherry Vinegar

The woodsy yet vibrant taste of sherry vinegar makes it such a standout that it just might become your favorite everyday vinegar.

⇒ BY KATE SHANNON ⇐

In the test kitchen, when we need a wine vinegar, we've generally turned to the red or white varieties. That's because the third big category of wine vinegar—sherry vinegar—has been far less widely available in supermarkets. Given that it's a Spanish condiment, we've mainly restricted ourselves to calling for it in Spanish recipes like gazpacho, romesco sauce, or Catalan beef stew.

But when we noticed that sherry vinegar is now appearing not just in specialty stores but also in many ordinary supermarkets, we were thrilled. We are big fans of its nutty, oaky, savory flavors and decided it was time to find a favorite that we could use not just in Spanish dishes but in applications across the board.

First, a little background on this interesting ingredient: As its name suggests, sherry vinegar (*vinagre de Jerez*) starts with sherry wine, a white wine aged in oak barrels and traditionally fortified with brandy, which has been made in southern Spain for centuries. The transformation of sherry into vinegar begins with the same process as red and white wine vinegars—the sherry is first acetified to convert its alcohol to acetic acid. (These days, and for all types of vinegars, this is generally done quickly and cheaply in an acetator that exposes the wine to oxygen, rather than the traditional way of inoculating the wine with an acetic acid "mother" bacteria from an established vinegar and allowing the vinegar to convert slowly in wooden barrels.) But unlike red and white wine vinegars, which are typically stored in stainless-steel tanks until bottling, sherry vinegar then undergoes a process of aging and blending known as a "solera" system. Here barrels of sherry vinegar of different ages are blended over time to create an end product that is a combination of young vinegar and old vinegar—a process that is also used to make the sherry wine.

Furthermore, sherry vinegars that bear the *Denominación de Origen Protegida* (or DOP) seal must start with drinking-quality sherry made from one of three grape varieties grown in Andalusia and be aged at least 6 months in the solera. Two other DOP classifications exist: *Vinagre de Jerez Reserva* and *Gran Reserva*, which must have been aged at least two years and 10 years, respectively. With this information under our belt, we gathered nine products from different sources. Most we purchased from conventional supermarkets, but we also included a few vinegars from specialty stores and online. The majority were Spanish imports bearing the DOP seal; one was a domestically produced outlier from California. Some were aged for just six months, others for decades—including one 30-year vinegar and another vinegar aged for an astonishing 50 years.

Vying for the Top

We began by tasting the vinegars plain to see if we could detect any nuances that might carry through when the vinegars were combined with food. Not only did most deliver the "bright," "punchy" acidity that we demand from a good vinegar, but most also elicited descriptions more in line with fine wine. Our tasters described them as containing notes of "berries," "wood," "smoke," even "leather." Only one of the bunch exhibited an "acetone" aroma like nail-polish remover—a flaw caused by an excess of ethyl acetate that forms during the vinegar-making process and which we've noticed more extensively in red and white wine vinegars. When we then sampled the brands stirred into gazpacho and in vinaigrette drizzled over salad greens, many of their complex flavors were still evident or helped enhance the fruity tomato flavors of the soup. In the end, we had something positive to say about all of the vinegars and loved six of the nine enough to recommend them.

But the curious thing was that the two vinegars at the very top didn't embody the characteristics we thought would matter most—they didn't have a DOP seal and they weren't the most aged. While we certainly liked the 50-year-old and 30-year-old vinegars, we didn't find their flavors significantly more complex than the younger vinegars in the lineup, and they came in third and fourth, respectively.

Why might this be so? We did some investigating and discovered that the true age of any sherry vinegar is a complicated matter—and the number listed on the label can be misleading. This number does not represent most of the vinegar in the bottle; it instead represents what the industry calls a "fractional average" of all the vintages that are blended together in varying amounts when the vinegar passes through the solera system. Therefore, vinegar from the most mature batches might make up only a small percentage of what's in the bottle.

Our conclusion? It's hard to go wrong with sherry vinegar, since even minimal aging in porous wood encourages evaporation and the concentration of flavor. There's even scientific evidence to support the idea that sherry vinegar is complex stuff: Studies have identified at least 80 distinct aroma compounds that contribute to its flavor.

Finest of the Fine

So what about the two vinegars that edged out the competition—albeit slightly? These vinegars, from Napa Valley Naturals (which, contrary to the name, sources its vinegar from Spain) and O, were aged 15 and three years respectively, but they share a common feature: Both contain a small amount of sugar per serving (1 and 2 grams per tablespoon), while the others have just a fraction of a gram or none at all. We learned that's not because manufacturers add sugar but likely because the wines they used were sweeter to begin with. The sherry used to make the O vinegar is also supplemented with apricot wine vinegar, which may have contributed its own sweetness to the vinegar.

That sweet boost balanced these vinegars' acidity (which was fairly comparable across samples) so that these products brightened both the dressing and the soup with "the right amount of tang." Either one will add both vibrant acidity and nutty, oaky flavors to any application where we call for wine vinegar, from pan sauces and vinaigrette to soups and stews or roasted vegetables. But since the winner from Napa Valley Naturals costs just $0.43 per ounce and is sold widely in supermarkets, it'll be our go-to sherry vinegar.

Age Can Be Deceiving

PRODUCT **OF SPAIN**

GRAN CAPIRETE 50 *Vinagre de Jerez Reserva Sherry Vinegar*

Don't be misled by the age touted on the label of a bottle of sherry vinegar. It doesn't represent the age of all—or even most of—the vinegar in the bottle. Rather, it represents what manufacturers call a "fractional average" determined by calculating the proportion and age of each batch of vinegar that's been blended into the bottle.

TASTING SHERRY VINEGAR

We selected nine sherry vinegars, including supermarket varieties as well as products sold in specialty shops and online. We tasted them plain, in vinaigrette, and in chilled gazpacho. Results were averaged, and products appear in order of preference. Ingredients and nutrition information were obtained from labels and manufacturers.

RECOMMENDED

NAPA VALLEY NATURALS
Reserve Sherry Vinegar

PRICE: $5.49 for 12.7 oz ($0.43 per fl oz)

INGREDIENTS: Sherry vinegar. Contains sulfites.

SUGAR PER 1-TBS SERVING: 2 g ACIDITY: 7%

AGING AND CLASSIFICATION:
Up to 15 years; no certification

SOURCE: Spain

AVAILABILITY: Supermarkets

COMMENTS: Our slightly sweet winner had "just the right amount of tang" and boasted flavors ranging from "lemony" to "smoky." In gazpacho, it added "nice depth" that highlighted the fresh flavors.

O Sherry Vinegar

PRICE: $9.99 for 6.8 oz ($1.47 per fl oz)

INGREDIENTS: Aged California sherry vinegar, aged apricot wine vinegar. Contains naturally occurring sulfites.

SUGAR PER 1-TBS SERVING: 1 g ACIDITY: 6%

AGING AND CLASSIFICATION: 2 years; no certification

SOURCE: California

AVAILABILITY: Upscale supermarkets and online

COMMENTS: With a sweet boost from apricot wine vinegar, this "rich," "smooth" vinegar contributed fruity depth to the vinaigrette and gazpacho, where the tomato flavor was "prominent" and "bright."

GRAN CAPIRETE
50 Years Aged Sherry Vinegar

PRICE: $16.99 for 8.45 oz ($2.01 per fl oz)

INGREDIENTS: Contains sulfites

SUGAR PER 1-TBS SERVING: 0.03 g ACIDITY: 8%

AGING AND CLASSIFICATION: 50 years; DOP Sherry Vinegar Reserva

SOURCE: Spain

AVAILABILITY: Upscale supermarkets and online

COMMENTS: This pricey vinegar's "rich," "dark" flavors made for an "earthy" but "vibrant" dressing and rounded out the soup with a "nice, easy finish."

RECOMMENDED CONTINUED

COLUMELA Sherry Vinegar Solera 30

PRICE: $14.00 for 12.7 oz ($1.10 per fl oz)

INGREDIENTS: Contains sulfites.

SUGAR PER 1-TBS SERVING: 0 g ACIDITY: 8%

AGING AND CLASSIFICATION:
30 years; DOP Sherry Vinegar Reserva

SOURCE: Spain

AVAILABILITY: Upscale supermarkets and online

COMMENTS: In both applications, this vinegar delivered "nice kick" but offered a "smooth" finish and "fruitiness" that kept it from being too sharp or acidic.

COLUMELA Classic Sherry Vinegar

PRICE: $6.99 for 12.7 oz ($0.55 per fl oz)

INGREDIENTS: Sherry vinegar. Contains sulfites.

SUGAR PER 1-TBS SERVING: 0 g ACIDITY: 7%

AGING AND CLASSIFICATION:
6 months to 2 years; DOP Sherry Vinegar

SOURCE: Spain

AVAILABILITY: Supermarkets

COMMENTS: Though "sharper" and more "bracing" than its pricier older sibling, this vinegar's "woody," "spicy, complex" notes were especially nice in vinaigrette.

MAITRE JACQUES Sherry Vinegar

PRICE: $4.13 for 16.9 oz ($0.24 per fl oz)

INGREDIENTS: Sherry vinegar. Contains sulphites.

SUGAR PER 1-TBS SERVING: 0% ACIDITY: 7%

AGING AND CLASSIFICATION:
6 months to 2 years; DOP Sherry Vinegar

SOURCE: Spain

AVAILABILITY: Supermarkets

COMMENTS: With "just enough tartness," this vinegar allowed the soup's tomato flavor to "come through" and made for a "bright" vinaigrette, even if the complexity was lacking a bit.

RECOMMENDED WITH RESERVATIONS

ROMULO Sherry Vinegar
(also sold as Pons Sherry Vinegar)

PRICE: $7.99 for 12.7 oz ($0.63 per fl oz)

INGREDIENTS: Contains sulfites

SUGAR PER 1-TBS SERVING: 0.03 g ACIDITY: 7%

AGING AND CLASSIFICATION: 6 months to 2 years; DOP Sherry Vinegar

SOURCE: Spain

AVAILABILITY: Supermarkets

COMMENTS: Some tasters enjoyed the "punchy vinaigrette" made with this vinegar; others found its "bracing acidity" too strong. It fared best in gazpacho, where it was "tangy and very bright" but not overly so.

DON BRUNO Sherry Vinegar

PRICE: $5.99 for 12.67 oz ($0.47 per fl oz)

INGREDIENTS: Sherry wine vinegar. Contains sulfites.

SUGAR PER 1-TBS SERVING: 0 g ACIDITY: 8%

AGING AND CLASSIFICATION:
6 months to 2 years; DOP Sherry Vinegar

SOURCE: Spain

AVAILABILITY: Supermarkets

COMMENTS: Even tasted plain, this vinegar was surprisingly mellow. It remained steadfastly "in the middle of the pack" in both applications, where tasters expected more vibrancy and complexity.

POMPEIAN Sherry Vinegar

PRICE: $9.99 for 16 oz ($0.62 per fl oz)

INGREDIENTS: Sherry wine vinegar. Contains naturally occurring sulfites.

SUGAR PER 1-TBS SERVING: 0 g ACIDITY: 7%

AGING AND CLASSIFICATION:
3 years; no certification

SOURCE: Spain

AVAILABILITY: Supermarkets

COMMENTS: Though plagued by the aroma of "acetone" and "cheap alcohol" when tasted plain, this vinegar's flaws (likely due to an excess of the compound ethyl acetate) weren't noticeable once it was added to the dressing and soup. Generally, it fared best among those who liked a "punchy" vinegar.

Barrel Before Bottle

Sherry vinegar's complex, nutty flavor is largely the result of its unique blending and maturation system, called a "solera" system. During this process, multiple batches are stored in a series of tiered oak barrels, with the oldest batches on the bottom. Periodically, a portion of vinegar from the row of oldest barrels is extracted and bottled, the empty space is filled with vinegar from the next-oldest batch, and so on throughout the stack, ensuring a continuous and consistent product over time.

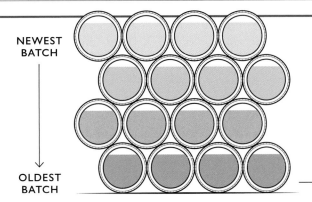

NEWEST BATCH

OLDEST BATCH

Barrels are arranged in tiers called scales. Each scale contains vinegar of the same age. When vinegar is removed from the oldest scale (also called a "solera"), it is replenished by an equal amount from the next-oldest, and so on. Typically, no more than one-third of the vinegar is extracted in any one year.

Tasting Smoked Paprika

Smoked paprika, a specialty of Spain, is traditionally made by slowly drying ripe red chile peppers over a smoldering oak fire for upwards of two weeks and then grinding the peppers into a powder. We use smoked paprika to lend sweet, smoky, raisin-like flavor and deep red color to meats, seafood, sauces, and vegetables.

Spain has two paprika-producing regions. Both have *Denominación de Origen Protegida* (DOP) status, which ensures that paprikas made there and stamped with the DOP seal adhere to traditional production methods. Smoked paprika is a specialty of the La Vera region and is available in three styles: sweet, bittersweet, and hot. For this test, we focused on sweet smoked paprika since it is most commonly called for in recipes.

We tasted seven products in our Smoky Pork and White Bean Stew and in our sauce for Patatas Bravas (page 9). We rated them on flavor, smokiness, and overall appeal. Our tasters strongly preferred smokier paprikas; they gave the lowest score to a paprika that had "almost no perceptible smoke." Our top two, both made in Spain, had an abundance of sweet, intense smoke flavor. One, the DOP offering, is made from peppers smoked for 15 days; the other uses peppers smoked for two to three days. For complete tasting results, go to CooksIllustrated.com/june16.
–Lisa McManus

RECOMMENDED

SIMPLY ORGANIC Smoked Paprika

PRICE: $7.69 for 2.72 oz ($2.83 per oz)

SOURCE: Supermarket ORIGIN: Spain, not DOP certified

PROCESSING: Smoked over oak fire for two to three days, stone-ground in Spain

COMMENTS: This made-in-Spain smoked paprika was redolent with richer, "deeper" smoky flavor than the rest. It was "bright and warm," "sweet and rounded," with smoke that "linger[ed]" "without being overpowering."

LA DALIA Pimentón de La Vera Sweet Smoked Paprika

PRICE: $11.95 for 5 oz ($2.39 per oz, plus shipping)

SOURCE: Online ORIGIN: Spain, DOP certified

PROCESSING: Smoked over oak fire for 15 days, stone-ground in Spain

COMMENTS: This authentic DOP Spanish pimentón de La Vera virtually tied with the top paprika. Our tasters praised its "smoky, warm tones," calling it "nice, strong paprika" that tasted "complex," "sweet, tangy, and earthy."

NOT RECOMMENDED

McCORMICK Smoked Paprika

PRICE: $2.88 for 0.9 oz ($3.20 per oz)

SOURCE: Supermarket ORIGIN: Peppers from Spain and Hungary, ground in USA

PROCESSING: Smoked over oak fire; stone-ground

COMMENTS: Tasters thought that this paprika "taste[d] like plain paprika," with "not much complexity." Some found it "sour and dusty."

Best Way to Revive Wilted Produce

A few years ago we found that soft leafy greens like lettuce, spinach, or arugula can be revived by simply soaking them in a bowl of ice water for 30 minutes. We wondered if a similar technique might be used to revive other types of produce.

Vegetables like broccoli, asparagus, celery, scallions, and parsley won't admit water as quickly along their waxy stalks and stems as they do at their cut base. We found that the best way to revive these kinds of vegetables was to trim their stalks or stems on the bias and stand them up in a container of cold water in the refrigerator for about an hour. This exposes as many of their moisture-wicking capillaries as possible to water. –S.D.

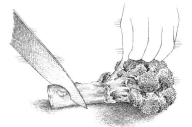

TRIM Cut stalks on bias to expose more water-wicking capillaries.

HYDRATE Stand produce in container filled with cold water for 1 hour.

Swapping Anchovy Paste for Fillets

Our recipes often call for minced anchovy fillets to add savory depth to dishes, but can you save time and avoid fuss by simply substituting anchovy paste from a tube? And, if so, would it be an equal-volume swap?

After determining that one fillet averages ½ teaspoon minced by volume, we ran some tests. In recipes like beef stew, where a modest amount of anchovy is intended to subtly bolster the meaty flavor, 1 teaspoon of anchovy paste made an acceptable substitute for 1 teaspoon of minced anchovy fillets. But in Caesar salad, where anchovies are used in greater concentration and contribute one of the defining flavors, tasters much preferred the fresher and more complex flavor of the salad prepared with actual fillets. They found the dressing made with anchovy paste overpoweringly salty and fishy. So go ahead and substitute anchovy paste for small amounts of minced fillets—but do so only in recipes in which they play a supporting role. –A.G.

Using Active Yeast Instantly

We prefer instant (or "rapid-rise") yeast to active dry yeast in bread recipes because it's easy to use. Active dry yeast package directions call for blooming the yeast in warm water for about 10 minutes before adding it to other ingredients to remove the dead cells that surround the live yeast. Instant yeast granules aren't surrounded by dead cells and can be mixed right into the dry ingredients.

We wondered if there might be enough moisture in a bread dough to allow us to swap active for instant yeast. To find out, we made fast-rising doughs (our Easy Sandwich Bread), slow-rising doughs (No-Knead Brioche), relatively dry doughs (New York Bagels), and wet pizza doughs (Thin-Crust Pizza) with both instant and active dry yeasts. We used 25 percent more active dry yeast than each recipe called for in instant yeast to make up for the volume of the dead yeast cells. In both batches, we mixed the yeasts right into the dry ingredients. In all cases, there was no discernible difference in the rise of the breads. However, the breads made with active yeast had a yeastier (though not offensive) flavor.

The takeaway? We still prefer instant yeast, but you can substitute active dry yeast in all recipes by using 25 percent more of it. –A.J.

Put Leftover Panko to Use

If you've tried store-bought seasoned bread crumbs, you know they are not worth the investment. However, if you happen to have a half-box of panko in your pantry, you can make seasoned bread crumbs that are much better than any store-bought product.

Mix 1 cup panko bread crumbs with 2 tablespoons extra-virgin olive oil, ¼ teaspoon salt, and ¼ teaspoon pepper in 12-inch nonstick skillet to coat evenly. Cook mixture over medium heat, stirring frequently, until golden brown, about 4 minutes. Off heat, stir in 1 of the following: ½ teaspoon grated lemon zest; 1 teaspoon minced fresh thyme, rosemary, or oregano; or 2 tablespoons grated Parmesan cheese. Transfer bread crumbs to rimmed baking sheet and let cool. Transfer to airtight container and store at room temperature for up to 2 days or freeze for up to 1 month. –S.D.

Oil-Cured Olives: A Kalamata Substitute?

Oil-cured black olives aren't really cured in oil. They are cured in salt and then soaked in oil to partially restore their plumpness and to preserve them. The resulting jet-black, wrinkly olives are dense, rich, and meaty, with a very salty and almost smoky flavor. When we swapped them for the kalamatas in our Fougasse (March/April 2016) and in our Spaghetti with Cherry Tomatoes, Olives, Capers, and Pine Nuts (March/April 2005), they made a good, albeit stronger, stand-in. To account for their potency, we recommend using 25 percent fewer olives than the number of kalamatas called for and chopping them finer, as well as seasoning recipes with half the salt called for during cooking and then seasoning to taste at the end, once the olives have been incorporated. –S.D.

Ideal Doneness Temperature for Wild Salmon

We have always preferred salmon cooked to 125 degrees for the ideal balance of firm yet silky flesh. But the majority of the salmon we cook in the test kitchen has been farmed Atlantic salmon. As we've started cooking more wild varieties, we noticed that they seemed dry when cooked to 125 degrees.

To find out why, we cooked multiple samples of four species of wild Pacific salmon—king (Chinook), sockeye (red), coho (silver), and chum—along with farmed Atlantic salmon to both a 120-degree and a 125-degree internal temperature in temperature-controlled water baths. The majority of tasters preferred the wild salmon samples cooked to 120 degrees, while they confirmed our preference for cooking farmed Atlantic salmon to 125 degrees.

Why? Wild salmon has more collagen (and thus connective tissue) and, more important, a significantly greater number of chemical cross-links between collagen molecules. When the wild varieties are cooked to just 120 degrees, the muscle fibers contract less and therefore retain more moisture. The leanest wild salmon also contains less fat, about half as much as farmed salmon, so there is less fat to provide lubrication and the perception of juiciness when cooked.

We'll continue to cook farmed salmon to 125 degrees, but from now on, when we cook wild salmon, we will make sure to cook it to just 120 degrees. –D.S.

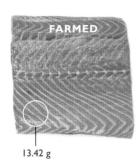

FARMED

13.42 g
Fat

WILD

5.57 g
Fat

THE FAT FACTOR
More fat in farmed salmon is one reason it can be cooked to a higher temperature than the leanest species of wild.

DIY RECIPE Cold-Brew Iced Coffee

Coffee brewed between 195 and 205 degrees will contain more aroma compounds, dissolved solids, and flavor than coffee brewed at 72 degrees, but heat also extracts the bitterness and astringency found in coffee beans. The appeal of cold brew lies in its milder acidity and bitterness, which lets more of the dark chocolate, caramel, ripe black fruit, and vanilla flavors come to the fore.

To make the best cold brew, we tried a number of out-there techniques, including near-continuous agitation and five-day-long extractions in the fridge. But in the end, a simple steep in a French press was the best. Using a high ratio of ground beans to water produces a concentrate that's easy to store and can be diluted as desired. After trying various brew times from 12 to 72 hours, we found that a 24-hour steep delivered the best flavor. Pouring the concentrate through a coffee filter–lined fine-mesh strainer ensures that it's free of sediment. Our finishing touch? A pinch of kosher salt, which rounds out the flavors and further masks cold brew's already minimal bitterness. –D.S.

COLD-BREW COFFEE CONCENTRATE
MAKES ABOUT 1½ CUPS; ENOUGH FOR 3 CUPS ICED COFFEE

This concentrated coffee needs to be diluted before drinking. We recommend a 1:1 ratio of concentrate to water, but you can dilute it more if you like.

- 9 ounces medium-roast coffee beans, ground coarse (3½ cups)
- 3½ cups filtered water, room temperature
- Kosher salt (optional)

1. Stir coffee and water together in large (about 2-quart) glass French press. Allow raft of ground coffee to form, about 10 minutes, then stir again to recombine. Cover with plastic wrap and let sit at room temperature for 24 hours.

2. Line fine-mesh strainer with coffee filter and set over large liquid measuring cup. Place lid on press and slowly and evenly press plunger down on grounds to separate them from coffee concentrate. Pour concentrate into prepared strainer. Line large bowl with triple layer of cheesecloth, with cheesecloth overhanging edge of bowl. Transfer grounds to cheesecloth. Gather edges of cheesecloth together and twist; then, holding pouch over strainer, firmly squeeze grounds until liquid no longer runs freely from pouch; discard grounds.

3. Using back of ladle or rubber spatula, gently stir concentrate to help filter it through strainer. Concentrate can be refrigerated in jar with tight-fitting lid for up to 1 week.

TO MAKE ICED COFFEE: Combine equal parts coffee concentrate and cold water. Add pinch kosher salt, if using, and pour into glass with ice.

Cooking with Shelf-Stable Milk

While popular in Europe, shelf-stable ultra-high-temperature (UHT) milk is rarely used in the United States—if anything, it's stashed away in the back of the pantry for emergency situations. Wondering how it would fare in recipes, we tried it in chocolate pudding and macaroni and cheese.

UHT milk has a "cooked" flavor that many tasters perceived as sweet (the high-heat processing causes the milk's sugars and proteins to undergo the Maillard reaction, both changing the flavor and giving it a slightly tan color), which came through in both recipes, but they were both perfectly acceptable. Some tasters also noticed a slightly muted chocolate flavor in the pudding and a slightly creamier texture in the mac and cheese.

The bottom line? UHT milk is an acceptable substitute for pasteurized milk when cooking but, depending on the dish, you may notice a slight difference in flavor or texture. –A.P.

PANTRY PICK
Shelf-stable UHT milk is an acceptable substitute for pasteurized milk in all types of recipes.

KITCHEN NOTES

BY STEVE DUNN, ANDREA GEARY, ANDREW JANJIGIAN & LAN LAM

WHAT IS IT?

Separating eggs can be time-consuming and messy. Could this egg separator, manufactured around the turn of the 20th century, make the task easier? After setting the tool over a bowl, you crack the egg into its coiled cup. The space between the coils allows the white through, while the yolk should remain suspended, intact, in the coil. When we gave it a try, we found that the separator performed fairly well. Eggs with loose whites passed through each separator in as little as 10 seconds, though very fresh eggs with thicker whites took up to 1½ minutes to separate (even with persistent shaking). Separating eggs with our hands is faster, but the tool did keep our hands clean for other tasks, and at about $10 on auction sites like eBay, it won't break the bank. –S.D.

ANTIQUE EGG SEPARATOR
Gets the job done, if a bit slowly.

For Better-Tasting Beer, Use a Glass

Many restaurants serve bottles or cans of beer with a glass alongside, or they serve draft beers in special glassware. We wondered: Is this just pomp and circumstance, or does pouring a beer into a glass make a noticeable difference in the drinking experience? We sampled three styles of beer—lager, IPA, and stout—straight from the bottle and in a glass, side by side, and evaluated the differences, if any, in bitterness, maltiness, and aroma.

We expected that a glass might make a difference for the aromatic, hoppy IPA, but we were surprised that tasters noticed that all three beers were more aromatic when sipped from a glass, even the lager. In addition, the IPA was perceived as less bitter and more balanced when sipped from a glass, while the stout tasted fuller and maltier. Why? The glass allows more of a beer's aromas to be directed to your nose than does the narrow opening at the tip of a bottle. Our recommendation: No matter the beer, pouring it into a glass will improve the drinking experience. –L.L.

Cake That Holds Up— and Cake That Doesn't

Faced with having to guess which type of cake—a relatively dense yellow butter cake or an airy sponge cake—was the stronger of the two, some might guess butter cake. We did, and we were unhappy with our decision when we tried using one as a base for our Refined Strawberry Shortcake recipe (page 15). It practically dissolved once it soaked up the strawberry juice. Conversely, the sponge cake (we chose a style known as genoise) held up perfectly in our subsequent rounds of testing. Here's why: A combination of gluten proteins and gelatinized starch provides the structure in a butter cake, but the ample amount of butter it contains and the gentle mixing method it undergoes help minimize gluten development to allow for a more-tender texture. When this sparse network encounters the liquid from the strawberries, the starch softens, causing the delicate network to collapse, and the cake crumbles.

The structure of a genoise cake comes from abundant egg proteins that unwind and link with each other when the eggs are whipped and form a strong mesh once baked. When this mesh encounters liquid, it isn't affected—the water just fills in any gaps in the network. The upshot? The cake holds its shape. –L.L.

SUPER SOAKER
Genoise absorbs juice and holds together.

CRUMBLES UNDER PRESSURE
Butter cake doesn't have the structure to hold up.

Lighting a Chimney Starter: More Tinder Isn't Better

A chimney starter makes lighting briquettes quick and easy without the need for lighter fluid. Simply place wadded-up newspaper in the bottom chamber and briquettes in the top chamber, light the newspaper, and when the top coals are ignited, dump the coals into the grill. Though it might be tempting to pack newspaper tightly into the chamber to ensure there's plenty of fire to light the coals, we found that more isn't necessarily better; too much can actually smother fire. When we compared lighting a full chimney (6 quarts of briquettes) with two sheets and four sheets of newspaper, we found that the extra paper blocked airflow, taking 10 minutes longer to light the coals (40 minutes versus 30). Bottom line: Be careful not to pack the chimney too tightly with newspaper; two sheets should be enough for a standard 7½-inch-diameter chimney. –L.L.

STEP BY STEP | FRUIT PIE FOR A CROWD

When baking for a large group, try a slab pie—it's baked in a rimmed baking sheet and serves up to 20 people. Here's how to convert your favorite 9-inch double-crust fruit pies. To make a lattice top, instead of cutting small slits in the top crust in step 5, use a 1¼-inch cookie cutter to cut holes at 3-inch intervals before transferring it to the pie. –A.G.

    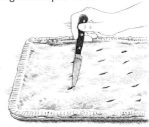

1. Shape 2 batches of your favorite double-crust pie dough into 4 by 6-inch rectangles and refrigerate each until firm.

2. Roll 1 dough piece into large rectangle and fit into large rimmed baking sheet. Refrigerate while making filling.

3. Prepare 1½ batches of your favorite fruit pie filling recipe, shooting for 7 to 8 cups. Spread filling into dough-lined sheet.

4. Roll remaining piece of dough into rectangle and place over filling. Run rolling pin over edges to trim, then crimp edges with fork.

5. Cut slits at 2-inch intervals. Bake at 350 degrees on lower-middle rack until crust is golden brown, 1 to 1¼ hours.

COOK'S ILLUSTRATED

30

THE BEST WAY TO REHEAT A ROAST

We've found the best way to reheat leftover steaks and chicken, but what about a leftover portion of a roast? The key is to fully warm the roast without drying out the exterior or cooking it beyond its original degree of doneness. Wrapping roasts in foil to help retain moisture was a bust: It not only extended the reheating time but also steamed the meat, leaving it wet and gray. The best approach was to reheat the meat in a low oven (which took about 1½ hours for a 2-pound beef roast half and 1 hour for a 1-pound pork roast half) and then finish with a quick sear in an oiled hot skillet. Roasts reheated this way were only slightly less juicy than fresh-cooked roasts. –S.D.

1. Place roast, uncovered, on wire rack set in rimmed baking sheet. Place sheet on middle rack in 250-degree oven.

2. Roast until meat registers 120 degrees (1 to 1½ hours depending on the roast). Pat surface dry with paper towels.

3. Sear roast on all sides in oiled, hot skillet, 1 to 1½ minutes per side. (Do not sear cut ends.)

Leave the Bands on Lobster Claws

For safety reasons, we've always left the rubber bands on lobster claws in place when adding lobsters to a pot of boiling water. But after a recent test kitchen photo of rubber-banded lobsters going into a pot appeared on our website, we received a number of emails and letters from readers stating that the rubber bands would affect the flavor of the cooked lobster. To find out if this is true, we decided to run a test.

We cooked lobsters with and without rubber bands in separate pots of boiling water and then tasted both the lobster meat and the cooking water. While a few tasters claimed they noticed a subtle difference in the cooking water taken from the pot in which we cooked the banded lobsters, no one could detect any flavor differences between the lobster meat samples. Our takeaway? We'll keep our fingers safe and continue to leave the rubber bands in place on the claws until after the lobsters are cooked. –A.J.

A TIDY WAY TO PORTION STICKY BUNS

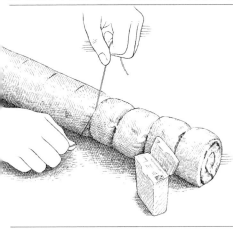

When making our Sticky Buns (page 21), cutting the rolled dough cylinder into buns can be tricky—the soft dough sticks to the knife, or the dough flattens and tears. Here's how we make a tidier, easier job of it. –A.G.

Hold strand of plain dental floss taut and slide under cylinder of dough. Cross floss ends over each other, then pull ends to cut off clean, neat portion of dough.

EXPERIMENT

Whipping Whites and Sugar: Timing Matters

Meringue cookies and all types of sponge cake, including angel food and chiffon, depend on whipped egg whites for both leavening and structure. The sugar that's added to the whites contributes not only sweetness but also stability. But does it matter when you add the sugar?

EXPERIMENT

To find out, we made three batches each of meringue cookies, angel food cake, and chiffon cake, adding the sugar to the whites before whipping, after a minute of whipping, or at the very end, once the foam had reached the "soft peaks" stage. We baked them and compared the results.

RESULTS

In all three recipes, the timing made a difference. Adding the sugar after a minute of whipping was clearly best across the board. In both types of cake, the crumb structure was compromised when the sugar was added at the very end: The chiffon was dense and flat, while the angel food was coarse and almost crumbly. Adding sugar before whipping was also not ideal, leading to cakes that baked up a bit too dry.

In the case of the meringues, adding the sugar at the start of mixing produced a cookie that was dull on the exterior, with a too-fine crumb within. The cookies made when the sugar was added at the very end had an overly airy texture (tasters compared it to Styrofoam) and a grainy consistency. To top it off, they took on an unappealing brown color.

TOO EARLY	ON TIME	TOO LATE
Dull exterior and too-fine crumb	Snow-white color and ideally airy texture	Browned, with grainy, Styrofoam-like texture

EXPLANATION

When egg whites are whipped, the eggs' proteins unfold and then cross-link to form a network that stabilizes the air bubbles. At the same time, the sugar dissolves in the water from the eggs to form a viscous liquid that helps stabilize the structure. If the sugar is added too early, the sugar granules interfere with the proteins' ability to unfold, resulting in a weaker network that can only support small air bubbles (this is why these cakes and meringues had a finer interior texture). If the sugar is added too late, either the sugar, which is hygroscopic, draws water out of the foam and causes the structure to weaken (as in the dense, crumbly cakes), or the sugar doesn't fully dissolve (as in the meringue cookies that were grainy and brown from undissolved sugar caramelizing). Adding the sugar after a brief amount of whipping gives the protein network time to form while leaving enough time for the sugar to dissolve.

TAKEAWAY

For ideal volume and stability, add the sugar to whipped egg whites after the eggs have started to get foamy but well before they have started to form peaks. –A.J.

▶ SCIENCE OF COOKING:
THE MAGIC OF MERINGUE
See exactly how much difference proper timing makes—and why. A step-by-step video is available at CooksIllustrated.com/june16

EQUIPMENT CORNER

⋙ BY MIYE BROMBERG ⋘

RECOMMENDED	**RECOMMENDED**	**RECOMMENDED**	**HIGHLY RECOMMENDED**	**RECOMMENDED WITH RESERVATIONS**
BEE HOUSE Salt Box MODEL: BCB-01 PRICE: $20.80	**PADERNO** World Cuisine Tri-Blade Spiral Slicer MODEL: A4982799 PRICE: $33.24	**OXO** Good Grips Flat Whisk MODEL: 74391 PRICE: $6.95	**ELIZABETH KARMEL** Super Silicone Angled BBQ Brush MODEL: 60500 PRICE: $9.16	**OXO** Good Grips 3-in-1 Avocado Slicer MODEL: 1252180 PRICE: $9.95

Salt Storage Containers

Salt containers placed near the stove put salt at your fingertips, making it easy to season a steak or a pot of boiling water on the fly. They come in two basic styles: Salt pigs are open-mouthed cylindrical vessels, while salt boxes have lids and usually are slightly smaller. We tested two salt pigs and three boxes ranging in price from $8.99 to $37.99, hoping to find a sturdy container that could hold a useful amount of salt; be easy to fill, clean, and access; and defend the salt against humidity and splatters better than an open prep bowl.

While none of the containers kept the salt from clumping in humid conditions, the lidded salt boxes did a better job of this than the open pigs (no great surprise, as the pigs expose the salt to the air). Also not surprising, the boxes better protected the salt from kitchen splatter; plus, they were generally easier to fill and use. Our favorite, the solid and roomy Bee House Salt Box ($20.80), holds 2 cups of salt. It sat sturdily on the counter, required infrequent refilling, and did the best job of accommodating cooks with large hands.

Spiralizers

Spiral vegetable cutters, or spiralizers, cut fruits and vegetables into long noodles and ribbons for "pastas," garnishes, salads, and side dishes. A surge in popularity has led to new models flooding the market since we last tested them several years ago, so we decided to revisit these gadgets. We tested six countertop spiralizers (handheld models tanked in our previous testing) priced from $24.99 to $48.46, plus a spiralizing attachment for KitchenAid stand mixers ($99.95). In the end, our previous winner, the Paderno World Cuisine Tri-Blade Spiral Slicer ($33.24), once again took first place. It's easy to use and made the best noodles with the least waste from a wide range of produce. One gripe: Though many of the models we tested were ambidextrous, this one favors right-handed cooks.

Flat Whisks

Flat (or roux) whisks have a unique shoehorn-like shape that allows them to get into the corners and sides of pans for more efficient stirring when making sauces and gravies. We tested six models priced from about $7 to $22, using them to make a béchamel sauce and a sage-vermouth pan sauce, alongside the tools we'd ordinarily use for these dishes—a wooden spoon and our favorite all-purpose whisk, the OXO Good Grips 11" Balloon Whisk.

All of the flat whisks excelled at scraping the fond off the skillet in the pan sauce recipe. And they really shone when making béchamel. While the fat balloon whisk struggled to reach and scrape the outer edges and sides of the pan, the flat whisk's narrower, more two-dimensional profile made it easy to control, maneuver, and get into corners, thus keeping the béchamel from settling, scorching, or forming lumps. Our favorite, the OXO Good Grips Flat Whisk ($6.95), was also the least expensive model we tested.

Barbecue Basting Brushes

Barbecue basting brushes have extra-long handles so you can paint sauce or oil onto food on the grill without burning your fingers. We've seen lots of new models on the market since our last testing, so we decided to revisit this category, rounding up five new silicone-bristled brushes (we've learned that silicone is much more durable than nylon or boar's hair) to test against our old winner from Elizabeth Karmel. All of the brushes got the job done eventually, but some were easier than others to use, and we found a few keys to the best models: handles around 12 inches long for the best mix of protection and control, bristles that were at least 1½ inches long for optimal coverage, and, in the case of our repeat winner, the Elizabeth Karmel Super Silicone Angled BBQ Brush ($9.16), a slightly angled brush head for extra protection against singed knuckles.

Avocado Gadgets

Over the past decade, Americans' consumption of avocados has doubled to more than one billion per year. And as avocados have become more common in American kitchens, so, too, have specialized gadgets that promise to make it easier, neater, and safer than using a knife to halve, pit, slice, and scoop the flesh from them. We bought 10 models (priced between $5.90 and $11.19) and put them to work prepping smaller, denser Hass and bigger, more watery Florida avocados. We included a chef's knife and a spoon—our usual avocado-prep tools—as a baseline. While a few of the gadgets completed some of the prep tasks more quickly than the knife and spoon, none was capable of performing all of the tasks more neatly or precisely. Some were much messier or even dangerous. The verdict? We'll stick with the knife and spoon. But for those who find it unwieldy or even intimidating to remove an avocado pit with a knife, the two-headed OXO Good Grips 3-in-1 Avocado Slicer ($9.95) might be a worthy investment. Though its slicing end wasn't very precise, it made fast, easy, and safe work of pitting avocados of all sizes.

For complete testing results, go to CooksIllustrated.com/june16.

INDEX
May & June 2016

BONUS ONLINE CONTENT

*More recipes, reviews, and videos are available
at* **CooksIllustrated.com/june16**

RECIPES

Argentinian Chimichurri Sauce
Cilantro-Mint Chutney
Mushroom Farrotto
Pan-Seared Salmon for Two
Roasted Red Pepper Sformati
Spinach Sformati

EXPANDED REVIEWS

Avocado Gadgets
Barbecue Basting Brushes
Dry Storage Containers
Flat Whisks
Salt Storage Containers
Smoked Paprika
Spiralizers

⏵ RECIPE VIDEOS

Want to see how to make any of the
recipes in this issue? There's a video for that.

⏵ MORE VIDEOS

Testing Gas Grills
Science of Cooking: The Magic of Meringue

FOLLOW US ON SOCIAL MEDIA

facebook.com/CooksIllustrated
twitter.com/TestKitchen
pinterest.com/TestKitchen
google.com/+AmericasTestKitchen
instagram.com/TestKitchen
youtube.com/AmericasTestKitchen

Sticky Buns, 21

Patatas Bravas, 9

Refined Strawberry Shortcake, 15

Korean Rice Bowl (Dolsot Bibimbap), 13

Pan-Seared Salmon, 10

Grill-Roasted Beef Tenderloin, 7

Farrotto with Pancetta, Asparagus, and Peas, 18

Skillet-Roasted Chicken in Lemon Sauce, 5

Lemon-Herb Sformati, 11

Sugar Snap Peas with Pine Nuts and Fennel, 19

PHOTOGRAPHY: CARL TREMBLAY; STYLING: MARIE PIRAINO

Doughnut Holes

Jelly

Cinnamon-Sugar Cake

French Cruller

Coffee Roll

Beignet

Boston Cream

Cruller

Chocolate Glazed

Honey Glazed

DOUGHNUTS

NUMBER 141

JULY & AUGUST 2016

COOK'S
ILLUSTRATED

Superjuicy Steak
Freezer-to-Grill Technique

Chicken Tacos
Smoky, Spicy—and Easy

Best Grilled Onions
More Than a Condiment

Is It Done Yet?
Our Complete Guide to
Judging Food Doneness

Paella on the Grill
New Trick for Even Cooking

Tasting Parmesans
Can You Buy the Cheap Stuff?

New Vegetable Slaws
Move Over, Cabbage

Pesto Calabrese
Walkaway Ratatouille
Great Grilled Pizza

CooksIllustrated.com
$6.95 U.S. / $7.95 CANADA

08>

7 25274 62805 6

COOK'S
ILLUSTRATED
JULY & AUGUST 2016

PAGE 12

SEED SPICES

BACK COVER ILLUSTRATED BY JOHN BURGOYNE

Seed Spices

CORIANDER tastes like a cross between roasted nuts and vibrant citrus. CUMIN perfumes Indian, Latin, and Middle Eastern dishes with earthy bitterness and hints of lemon. Crisp YELLOW MUSTARD seeds are often added to pickling brine. Anise-y CARAWAY, also a pickling spice, is used in German cooking. Grating acorn-like NUTMEG adds warm sweetness to baked goods, mulled drinks, and cheese sauces. Tiny CELERY seeds lend a warm, bitter kick to potato salads and Bloody Marys. Sweet, rice-shaped FENNEL seeds are an Italian sausage staple. There's no substitute for the smoky maple flavor of FENUGREEK, particularly in Indian and Ethiopian dishes. The bright pigment of ground ANNATTO tints Latin rice dishes and orange cheeses alike. Crack open GREEN CARDAMOM pods to access their fragrant, piney seeds, essential to Middle Eastern and Indian dishes. The seeds encased in pointy, stellar STAR ANISE pods are more fragrant and distinct than other anise seeds, adding licorice-like fragrance to Chinese and Indian dishes.

AMERICA'S
TEST KITCHEN
RECIPES THAT WORK®

America's Test Kitchen is a real 2,500-square-foot kitchen located just outside Boston. It is the home of more than 60 test cooks, editors, and cookware specialists. Our mission is to test recipes until we understand exactly how and why they work and eventually arrive at the very best version. We also test kitchen equipment and supermarket ingredients in search of products that offer the best value and performance. You can watch us work by tuning in to *America's Test Kitchen* (AmericasTestKitchen.com) and *Cook's Country from America's Test Kitchen* (CooksCountry.com) on public television, or listen to us on our weekly radio program on PRX. You can also follow us on Facebook, Twitter, Pinterest, and Instagram.

EDITORIAL STAFF

Chief Executive Officer David Nussbaum
Chief Creative Officer Jack Bishop
Editorial Director John Willoughby
Executive Editor Amanda Agee
Deputy Editor Rebecca Hays
Executive Managing Editor Todd Meier
Executive Food Editor Keith Dresser
Senior Editors Andrea Geary, Andrew Janjigian, Dan Souza
Senior Editors, Features Elizabeth Bomze, Louise Emerick
Senior Editor, Photo Team Chris O'Connor
Associate Editor Lan Lam
Test Cooks Daniel Cellucci, Steve Dunn, Matthew Fairman,
   Annie Petito
Assistant Test Cook Allison Berkey
Copy Editors Jillian Campbell, Krista Magnuson
Science Editor Guy Crosby, PhD

Executive Tastings & Testings Editor Lisa McManus
Managing Editor Scott Kathan
Deputy Editor Hannah Crowley
Associate Editors Kate Shannon, Lauren Savoie
Assistant Editor Miye Bromberg
Editorial Assistant Carolyn Grillo

Test Kitchen Director Erin McMurrer
Assistant Test Kitchen Director Leah Rovner
Test Kitchen Manager Alexxa Grattan
Lead Senior Test Kitchen Assistant Meridith Lippard
Lead Kitchen Assistant Ena Gudiel
Kitchen Assistants Blanca Castanza, Gladis Campos,
   Heather Ecker, Maria Elena Delgado

Design Director, Print Greg Galvan
Photography Director Julie Cote
Art Director Susan Levin
Deputy Art Director Lindsey Chandler
Art Director, Marketing Melanie Gryboski
Deputy Art Director, Marketing Janet Taylor
Associate Art Director, Marketing Stephanie Cook
Senior Staff Photographer Daniel J. van Ackere
Staff Photographer Steve Klise
Assistant Photography Producer Mary Ball
Styling Catrine Kelty, Marie Piraino

Senior Director, Digital Design John Torres
Executive Editor, Web Christine Liu
Managing Editor, Web Mari Levine
Senior Editor, Web Roger Metcalf
Associate Editors, Web Terrence Doyle, Briana Palma
Senior Video Editor Nick Dakoulas
Test Kitchen Photojournalist Kevin White

BUSINESS STAFF

VP, Print & Direct Marketing David Mack
Circulation Director Doug Wicinski
Circulation & Fulfillment Manager Carrie Fethe
Marketing Assistant Andrea Hampel
Production Director Guy Rochford
Imaging Manager Lauren Robbins
Production & Imaging Specialists Heather Dube,
   Sean MacDonald, Dennis Noble, Jessica Voas

Chief Digital Officer Fran Middleton
Chief Financial Officer Jackie McCauley Ford
Senior Controller Theresa Peterson
Director, Creative Operations Alice Carpenter
Director, Business Partnerships Mehgan Conciatori

VP, Strategic Analytics Deborah Fagone
Partnership Marketing Manager Pamela Putprush
Client Services Manager Kate Zebrowski
Sponsorship Sales Associate Morgan Mannino
Director of Customer Support Amy Bootier
Senior Customer Loyalty & Support Specialist
   Andrew Straaberg Finfrock
Customer Loyalty & Support Specialists Caroline Augliere,
   Rebecca Kowalski, Ramesh Pillay
Senior VP, Human Resources and Organizational
   Development Colleen Zelina
Human Resources Director Adele Shapiro
Director, Retail Book Program Beth Ineson
Retail Sales Manager Derek Meehan
Associate Director, Publicity Susan Hershberg

Cover Illustration (Grapes) Robert Papp

PLAYING WITH FIRE

We are big fans of cooking over live fire. It not only gives food a distinctive flavor that's unattainable in any other way, but its lack of predictability also makes it uniquely engaging.

Given that this cooking method has been around since before the beginning of recorded history, you might think that by now we would have discovered all its secrets. But you would be wrong. Exactly because live fire is unpredictable, every grilled dish presents unique challenges. But by fiddling and investigating and thinking long enough—and by making the dish maybe 60 or 70 times—we discover solutions.

For evidence, just check out the recipes in this issue. When Lan Lam took on grilled paella (page 12), she was faced with the fact that a standard charcoal fire would not last long enough to fully cook the dish. Since she was using a large, heavy pan to make enough for a crowd, moving it off the hot grill to refuel was far from ideal. So Lan came up with an arrangement combining lit and unlit coals in a way that allows the fire to last just long enough at the right temperature.

Andrew Janjigian, too, faced a structural fire problem when creating his new recipe for grilled pizza (page 19). When he was cooking over charcoal, the bottom crusts of his pizzas mysteriously kept burning right in the middle. Reducing the amount of charcoal, and thus the heat of the fire, didn't solve the problem. Eventually Andrew figured out that the curved walls of the kettle grill were acting as a kind of parabolic mirror, creating a hot spot at the center. His solution? A custom arrangement of charcoal in the grill, the first new one we've seen in the test kitchen in a long time.

When Annie Petito took on the task of making grilled onions into a worthy side dish rather than a condiment (page 10), she chose another tack: Rather than rearranging the fire, she changed the way the onions are cut and approached the flame in two different ways. And Andrea Geary perfected a seemingly illogical recipe that calls for taking a steak out of the freezer and putting it directly on the grill—and the resulting steak was just as juicy as if it had never been frozen (page 6).

None of this is magic. In fact, you might have found these solutions yourself if you had unlimited time to play with fire in your backyard. But since that's a luxury we actually do have, we've solved the problems for you; all you have to do is light the fire and start cooking.

The Editors

FOR INQUIRIES, ORDERS, OR MORE INFORMATION

COOK'S ILLUSTRATED MAGAZINE

Cook's Illustrated magazine (ISSN 1068-2821), number 141, is published bimonthly by Boston Common Press Limited Partnership, 17 Station St., Brookline, MA 02445. Copyright 2016 Boston Common Press Limited Partnership. Periodicals postage paid at Boston, MA, and additional mailing offices, USPS #012487. Publications Mail Agreement No. 40020778. Return undeliverable Canadian addresses to P.O. Box 875, Station A, Windsor, ON N9A 6P2. POSTMASTER: Send address changes to *Cook's Illustrated*, P.O. Box 6018, Harlan, IA 51593-1518. For subscription and gift subscription orders, subscription inquiries, or change of address notices, visit AmericasTestKitchen.com/support, call 800-526-8442 in the U.S. or 515-248-7684 from outside the U.S., or write to us at *Cook's Illustrated*, P.O. Box 6018, Harlan, IA 51593-1518.

CooksIllustrated.com

At the all new CooksIllustrated.com, you can order books and subscriptions, sign up for our free e-newsletter, or renew your magazine subscription. Join the website and gain access to 23 years of *Cook's Illustrated* recipes, equipment tests, and ingredient tastings, as well as companion videos for every recipe in this issue.

COOKBOOKS

We sell more than 50 cookbooks by the editors of *Cook's Illustrated*, including *The Cook's Illustrated Cookbook* and *Paleo Perfected*. To order, visit our bookstore at CooksIllustrated.com/bookstore.

EDITORIAL OFFICE 17 Station St., Brookline, MA 02445; 617-232-1000; fax: 617-232-1572. For subscription inquiries, visit AmericasTestKitchen.com/support or call 800-526-8442.

QUICK
TIPS

⤳ COMPILED BY ANNIE PETITO ⤫

Seed-Free Citrus Juicing

Christina Wyman of Virginia Beach, Va., saves the netting from garlic and shallot bulbs for juicing lemons and limes. With the cut side of a citrus half placed inside the netting before squeezing, the fine-mesh weave easily keeps seeds out of her juice and doesn't impart any flavors or odors.

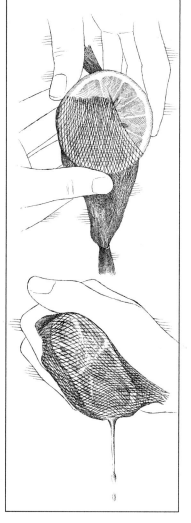

Quick Food Processor Cleaning

When Marilyn Whitlock of Austin, Texas, needs to quickly rinse her food processor between tasks, she adds a couple of drops of dish soap and warm water up to the recommended liquid line, runs the machine for a few minutes, and then rinses the bowl well before moving on to the next task.

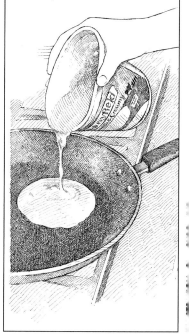

Plastic Bags in Lieu of Plastic Wrap

After seasoning a large roast that needed to rest overnight in the refrigerator, Tom Jury of Ames, Iowa, realized he was out of plastic wrap. His stand-in: a clean plastic bag from the grocery store, which was just as easy to wrap tightly around the meat (and might otherwise have gone to waste).

Easy Way to Core a Jalapeño

Jim Summerour of Atlanta, Ga., discovered a way to remove the seeds and ribs from large fresh jalapeños without having to touch the chile's hot interior. He plunges his apple corer through the top (no need to trim); when he removes it, the ribs and seeds come out, too.

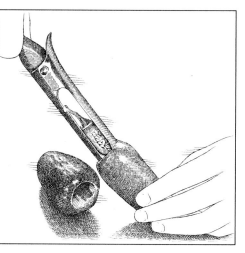

No-Drip Pancake Batter Portioning

Rather than ladling—and dripping—portions of pancake batter onto the griddle, John Audley of Kennebunk, Maine, first pours the batter into a large, clean yogurt container. By bending the vessel's flexible sides, he can pour portions into the pan with no mess.

Who Gets Which Burger?

When making burgers of various degrees of doneness for a crowd, Lacey Matthews of Boise, Idaho, keeps track of which finished patty goes to which guest by writing each person's initials on one cut side of the bun with ketchup or mustard from a squirt bottle. She keeps the initialed side faceup as she hands them out.

SEND US YOUR TIPS We will provide a complimentary one-year subscription for each tip we print. Send your tip, name, address, and daytime telephone number to Quick Tips, *Cook's Illustrated*, P.O. Box 470589, Brookline, MA 02447, or to QuickTips@AmericasTestKitchen.com.

Rinsing Rice with Less Cleanup

After reading our note about rinsing rice in a fine-mesh strainer (May/June 2015), Eugene Prial of Westfield, N.J., offered a suggestion for streamlining the method: Instead of rinsing the rice over a bowl, he holds it over the pot in which the rice will be cooked. Once he can see that the water is running clear, he dumps out the cloudy water and adds fresh water to the pot for cooking.

Muffin Tin "Crate" For Ripe Peaches

To prevent ripe peaches from bruising, Cynthia Craig of Longboat Key, Fla., stores them in the cups of a muffin tin, where they can't touch each other.

Containing Seeds When Slicing Bagels

Slicing seeded bagels often results in a mess of toppings all over the counter. Scott Kleiman of Providence, R.I., avoids this by placing a sheet of newspaper underneath the cutting board to collect the escaped seeds. When he's done, he simply rolls up the paper and pitches it in the trash.

Gently Drying Berries

To gently dry berries after rinsing, Kate Hunter of Allentown, Pa., places a dry dish towel on the counter with the long side facing her. She then encloses the rinsed berries in the center by folding the towel like a business letter. She grasps the towel ends in either hand and holds them loosely apart, tilting the bundle back and forth so that the berries roll until dry.

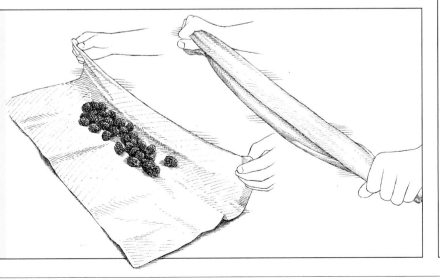

Orange Wedges to Go

To cut citrus wedges for packing in a lunchbox so that the fruit stays juicy, Tommy Ledet of Thibodaux, La., uses the following method.

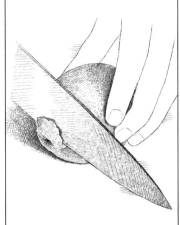

1. Trim the bottom of the fruit to make a flat surface. Place the fruit flat side down on the cutting board.

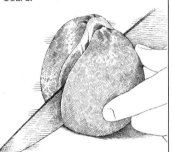

2. Halve the fruit without cutting all the way through it.

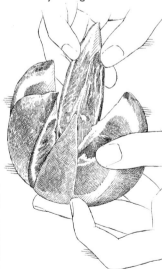

3. Continue to cut the fruit into sixths and then close it back up before wrapping it in plastic. The wedges won't dry out and can be pulled apart at lunchtime.

Shredded Chicken Tacos

Smoky, earthy *tinga de pollo* may share the same flavors as the shredded pork version of this saucy taco filling, but it often lacks the same depth. We set out to change that.

⇒ BY STEVE DUNN ⇐

I've long been a fan of pork *tinga*, a taco filling hailing from the Puebla region of Mexico that features supertender shredded pork (and often chorizo) bathed in a boldly flavored sauce anchored by tomatoes and smoky-spicy chipotle chiles. Fresh toppings like cilantro, salty Cotija cheese, and a squeeze of lime provide a perfect contrast to the rich, meaty filling. But since it's usually made with cuts that take several hours to turn tender, pork tinga isn't practical to make on a weeknight. I'd thought about adapting a recipe to work with chicken, but after a little research I realized there was no need: Lots of authentic recipes for *tinga de pollo* already exist.

I gave the most common—and speedy—approach I found a test run. Similar to the recipe for pork tinga, it called for poaching the chicken (I chose boneless breasts) in water in one pot as you prepare the sauce in another. This was as simple as softening some chopped onions with oil before simmering them with canned diced tomatoes, chicken broth, and—of course—a few tablespoons of minced chipotle chiles in adobo sauce. As soon as the chicken was poached, I shredded it and stirred it into the pot with

For deeper flavor, we use thighs instead of breasts and cook the meat directly in the sauce instead of poaching it separately in water.

Integrating Sauce and Chicken

After cooking the chicken in the sauce, removing it, and shredding it, we return it to the sauce to simmer for a full 10 minutes before serving. This thickens the sauce so it coats the meat better; plus, the simmering action and frequent stirring loosen the chicken's muscle fibers, which in turn allows the sauce to work its way into the meat and take hold. The result is a cohesive taco filling with sauce and meat that are fully integrated.

SAUCE IN EVERY BITE
A 10-minute simmer lets the sauce work its way into every shred of chicken.

the sauce. After cooking the mixture briefly to give the flavors a chance to meld, I gave it a taste. Fast? Yes. But as I had suspected, the time savings just weren't worth it. The chicken was bland, and the sauce was thin in both flavor and texture. Could I deliver the full-flavored smoky, spicy, hearty filling that I craved while keeping the recipe on a weeknight time frame?

A Savory Boost

I began by making three immediate changes. First, I swapped out the breasts for more flavorful boneless thighs. This was such an obvious improvement that I couldn't believe more recipes didn't call for it, particularly since the thighs took only about 15 minutes to cook through, barely longer than the breasts I'd used in my first attempt. Second, I ditched one of my pots. By cooking the chicken and sauce in separate pots, I had missed an opportunity to infuse both components with more flavor. Instead, I simmered them together from the start. And third, to address the sauce's watery consistency, I dialed back on the tomatoes and chicken broth, going from a 28-ounce

can of tomatoes to a 14.5-ounce can and from 1 cup to ½ cup of chicken broth.

These changes helped, but they weren't enough. Most tinga de pollo recipes didn't call for browning the meat, but this would certainly give the chicken more flavor as well as leave behind flavorful bits of fond in the pot that could be stirred into the sauce (and wouldn't add much more time). I also wondered if browning the onions instead of just softening them would make a difference. After browning the chicken on both sides and setting it aside, I added the onions to the pot and let them go several minutes longer before introducing the other ingredients and proceeding with the recipe. I also decided to cook the chicken a little longer, until it reached 195 degrees. Though we typically cook thigh meat to 175 degrees, we've found that longer braising allows even more of its collagen to break down, delivering meat that's more tender. For my purposes, this meant the meat was even easier to shred. Tasters approved of all these changes: The chicken was more tender, and the thicker sauce now boasted savory flavor and depth. But I had higher ambitions: I wanted the dish to have even more complexity.

Fired Up

The diced tomatoes in the sauce were fine, but what if I swapped them for a can of the fire-roasted kind? One test confirmed that their lightly charred flavor noticeably enhanced the smokiness of the chipotles. I also opted to add some of the adobo sauce from the can of chipotles; just 2 teaspoons added a layer of vinegary, smoky complexity. I continued to experiment with other ingredients I'd seen in tinga recipes. Tasters thought that oregano made my recipe taste like an Italian pasta sauce, so it was out. Tomatillos, thyme, and bay leaf didn't offer enough flavor to justify their inclusion. However, garlic and cumin, plus a little sweet warmth from cinnamon, earned a thumbs-up. Authentic recipes seemed to end here, but I found that stirring in just ½ teaspoon of brown sugar had a surprisingly big impact, lending a necessary balancing sweetness. A little acidity and floral flavor from fresh lime juice and zest brightened the dish just enough. With just these simple pantry ingredients, I had the richly smoky, spicy, tomatoey sauce that I'd been hoping for.

MAKE YOUR OWN CORN TORTILLAS

If you have a little extra time, homemade tortillas will take these tacos to the next level. To learn how to make them, see our recipe on page 29.

Perfect Saucy Shreds

There was just one thing I still wasn't happy with: The shreds of chicken and the sauce seemed like separate entities, with much of the sauce dripping from the chicken as I dished it out of the pot. But I had an idea. Thanks to the fact that I was cooking the chicken to 195 degrees, its muscle fibers were looser than they would have been at 175 degrees. So instead of briefly warming the shredded chicken in the pureed sauce before serving, as I'd been doing, I let it simmer for a full 10 minutes. As I'd hoped, the simmering action loosened the muscle fibers even further and gave the sauce a chance to really take hold of the meat. It also allowed the sauce to thicken further. The upshot: a more cohesive taco filling with sauce that clung to the meat.

All I had left to do was iron out the toppings. Minced fresh cilantro and scallions, some avocado pieces, crumbled Cotija cheese, and fresh lime juice added the right amount of contrasting fresh, cool flavors. For some textural interest, I also whipped up a quick *escabèche*, a traditional quick-pickled Mexican condiment, as the chicken cooked. All it took was giving some sliced red onion, jalapeño, and carrots a 30-minute soak in a spiced pickling brine. With that, I had tacos that satisfied all my cravings—plus a simple recipe that also had deep, complex flavor.

SHREDDED CHICKEN TACOS (TINGA DE POLLO)
SERVES 6

In addition to the Mexican-Style Pickled Vegetables (Escabèche) and the toppings included here, Mexican *crema* (or sour cream) and minced onion are also good choices. If you can't find Cotija cheese, you can substitute crumbled feta. The shredded chicken mixture also makes a good topping for tostadas.

Chicken

2 pounds boneless, skinless chicken thighs, trimmed
 Salt and pepper
2 tablespoons vegetable oil
1 onion, halved and sliced thin
3 garlic cloves, minced
1 teaspoon ground cumin
¼ teaspoon ground cinnamon
1 (14.5-ounce) can fire-roasted diced tomatoes
½ cup chicken broth
2 tablespoons minced canned chipotle chile in adobo sauce plus 2 teaspoons adobo sauce
½ teaspoon brown sugar
1 teaspoon grated lime zest plus 2 tablespoons juice

Tacos

12 (6-inch) corn tortillas, warmed
1 avocado, halved, pitted, and cut into ½-inch pieces
2 ounces Cotija cheese, crumbled (½ cup)
6 scallions, minced
 Minced fresh cilantro
 Lime wedges

1. FOR THE CHICKEN: Pat chicken dry with paper towels and season with salt and pepper. Heat 1 tablespoon oil in large Dutch oven over medium-high heat until shimmering. Add half of chicken and brown on both sides, 3 to 4 minutes per side. Transfer to large plate. Repeat with remaining chicken.

2. Reduce heat to medium, add remaining 1 tablespoon oil to now-empty pot, and heat until shimmering. Add onion and cook, stirring frequently, until browned, about 5 minutes. Add garlic, cumin, and cinnamon and cook until fragrant, about 1 minute. Add tomatoes, broth, chipotle and adobo sauce, and sugar and bring to boil, scraping up any browned bits.

3. Return chicken to pot, reduce heat to medium-low, cover, and simmer until meat registers 195 degrees, 15 to 20 minutes, flipping chicken after 5 minutes. Transfer chicken to cutting board.

4. Transfer cooking liquid to blender and process until smooth, 15 to 30 seconds. Return sauce to pot. When cool enough to handle, use two forks to shred chicken into bite-size pieces. Return chicken to pot with sauce. Cook over medium heat, stirring frequently, until sauce is thickened and clings to chicken, about 10 minutes. Stir in lime zest and juice. Season with salt and pepper to taste.

5. FOR THE TACOS: Spoon chicken into center of each warm tortilla and serve, passing avocado, Cotija, scallions, cilantro, and lime wedges separately.

MEXICAN-STYLE PICKLED VEGETABLES (ESCABÈCHE)
MAKES ABOUT 2 CUPS

For less spicy pickled vegetables, remove the seeds from the jalapeño.

½ teaspoon coriander seeds
¼ teaspoon cumin seeds
1 cup cider vinegar
½ cup water
1½ teaspoons sugar
¼ teaspoon salt
1 red onion, halved and sliced thin
2 carrots, peeled and sliced thin
1 jalapeño chile, stemmed and sliced thin into rings

Toast coriander seeds and cumin seeds in medium saucepan over medium heat, stirring frequently, until fragrant, about 2 minutes. Add vinegar, water, sugar, and salt and bring to boil, stirring to dissolve sugar and salt. Remove saucepan from heat and add onion, carrots, and jalapeño, pressing to submerge vegetables. Cover and let cool completely, 30 minutes. (Cooled vegetables can be refrigerated for up to 1 week.)

▶ **Watch Steve Cook It**
A step-by-step video is available at CooksIllustrated.com/aug16

THREE WAYS TO WARM TORTILLAS

Warming tortillas not only makes them more pliable but can also add flavorful toasty char, depending on the method. Wrap the tortillas in foil or clean dish towels to keep them warm until serving.

GAS FLAME Using tongs, place tortilla directly over medium flame of gas burner until lightly charred, about 30 seconds per side.

SKILLET Toast tortilla in dry nonstick skillet over medium-high heat until softened and spotty brown, 20 to 30 seconds per side.

MICROWAVE Wrap up to 6 tortillas in damp, clean dish towel and microwave until warm, 30 to 45 seconds.

Spur-of-the-Moment Grilled Steak

Got a thick-cut steak in the freezer? You're 40 minutes away from a great dinner.

⇒ BY ANDREA GEARY ⇐

I recently watched in disbelief as a fellow test cook took a rock-hard steak from the freezer and clunked it into a screaming-hot skillet. I'm all for questioning conventional wisdom, but really—could this possibly end well?

He seared the steak until it was well browned, about 90 seconds on each side, and then transferred it to the oven for 20 minutes to finish cooking. After letting it rest briefly, he sliced it. It was perfect. The exterior had developed an impressive sear while the superchilled interior was resistant to overcooking, so the meat within was juicy and rosy from edge to edge.

The approach is a clever one, and skipping the thawing step is certainly appealing for those of us who like to keep steaks on hand in the freezer. But the prospect of a perfectly cooked steak, even one that is really convenient to make, isn't quite enough to induce me to fire up both an oven and a stovetop skillet on a hot summer evening. So what about adapting the technique for the grill?

I knew from the outset that I'd use a two-level fire. The hotter side of the grill would stand in for the skillet; I'd cook my steak there until it was deeply browned all over. The cooler side of the grill would play the part of the oven, where the interior of the steak would come up to temperature more slowly. If I could make it work, I'd happily stock my freezer with steaks so I could grill them on the spur of the moment—with no forethought about thawing them—all summer long.

Frozen thick-cut steaks will thaw at just the right pace, resulting in meat with a deep sear on the exterior and a perfect rosy interior when cooked.

Thin Doesn't Win

But before I focused on perfecting my grilling method, I'd have to decide what kind of steak to use. My colleague had done his indoor testing with thick-cut steaks (think rib-eye and strip), so I'd certainly test those. But thin, quick-cooking flank and skirt steaks are favorites on the grill, so I wanted to give them a try, too. I froze my assortment of steaks overnight until they were solid.

I started by grilling the flank and skirt steaks, and I quickly learned an important lesson: Searing in a hot skillet is very different from cooking on a grill. The browning step took three times longer on the grill than it had in my colleague's skillet. That's because the radiant energy of the average grill isn't nearly as focused or efficient as the conductive energy of a heated skillet.

The longer period over high heat on the grill meant that these thinner steaks thawed quickly, and the interiors overcooked by the time the exteriors were properly charred. The flavor was also a bit lackluster. I usually apply a spice rub to a flank steak before grilling, but applying a rub or even just salt and pepper to a frozen steak is like seasoning a brick: Everything bounces right off.

In the Thick of It

Though somewhat discouraging, these initial results actually made me hopeful about my chances with the thicker steaks. Rib-eye and strip steaks taste great with very little embellishment—there's no need for a spice-heavy rub—so a bit of salt and pepper sprinkled on as the steaks thawed on the grill would probably be sufficient. And at about 1½ inches thick, these steaks would be less vulnerable to overcooking.

I put my frozen rib-eye and strip steaks on the grill, first cooking them over the hotter side until they were nicely charred, about 7 minutes per side, and then sliding them over to the cooler side. At that

---

CORE TECHNIQUE | HOW TO FREEZE STEAKS

Frozen steaks at the grocery store are packaged to prevent freezer burn. When freezing fresh steaks at home, the keys are to limit air exposure and to freeze the meat rapidly to create small ice crystals that won't damage the meat's texture. Well-wrapped steaks will stay free from freezer burn for up to two months.

1. WRAP IN PLASTIC WRAP
Wrap each individual steak in plastic wrap to help keep out air and prevent freezer burn.

2. FREEZE ON BAKING SHEET
Place wrapped steaks on a baking sheet to keep them flat for more even cooking. A single layer also ensures faster freezing.

3. PUT IN ZIPPER-LOCK BAG
Freeze until the steaks are solid, about 4 hours. Transfer to a zipper-lock bag, which offers another layer of protection.

DISCOVERY
Frozen Steaks Cook up Just as Juicy as Thawed

Grilling a frozen steak sounds like a bad idea. Given the longer cooking time, it couldn't possibly turn out as juicy as a thawed steak, right? In fact, we found that thick-cut steaks we grilled straight from the freezer were just as juicy as steaks we grilled after thawing, despite needing more than double the time on the grill. The moisture loss averaged about 17 percent in each steak.

point the internal temperature was a reassuring 70 degrees—no overcooking here.

After about 12 minutes over indirect heat, the temperature had risen to 115 degrees, so I took the steaks off the grill and let them rest; then I sliced them. These steaks were perfect: crusty and charred on the outside yet still pink and juicy inside, with a big beefy flavor that needed nothing else. Best of all, they had taken less than 30 minutes to go from freezer to serving platter.

To make the most of my summery grilled steak, I re-created a simple dinner salad I had eaten once in Italy. I sliced the steaks, shingled the slices on a platter, and topped them with a big tangle of arugula dressed with lemony vinaigrette and studded with small shards of salty Parmesan. I sprinkled a bit more Parmesan on top, and I was done: a company-worthy dinner salad, made with straight-from-the-freezer steaks and only four other ingredients, in less than 40 minutes. From now on, I'll definitely be stocking my freezer so I can grill a steak whenever the urge strikes.

GRILLED FROZEN STEAKS
SERVES 4

Do not substitute thinner steaks for the thick-cut steaks called for in this recipe. Thinner steaks cannot be grilled successfully when taken directly from the freezer.

2 (1-pound) frozen boneless strip or rib-eye steaks, 1½ inches thick, trimmed
Kosher salt and pepper

1A. FOR A CHARCOAL GRILL: Open bottom vent completely. Light large chimney starter mounded with charcoal briquettes (7 quarts). When top coals are partially covered with ash, pour evenly over half of grill. Set cooking grate in place, cover, and open lid vent completely. Heat grill until hot, about 5 minutes.

1B. FOR A GAS GRILL: Turn all burners to high, cover, and heat grill until hot, about 15 minutes. Leave primary burner on high and turn off other burner(s).

2. Clean and oil cooking grate. Place steaks on hotter side of grill and cook (covered if using gas) until browned and charred on first side, 5 to 7 minutes. Flip steaks, season with salt and pepper, and cook until browned and charred on second side, 5 to 7 minutes. Flip steaks, season with salt and pepper, and move to cooler side of grill, arranging so steaks are about 6 inches from heat source. Continue to cook until meat registers 115 to 120 degrees for rare or 120 to 125 degrees for medium-rare, 10 to 15 minutes longer. Transfer steaks to wire rack set in rimmed baking sheet and let rest for 5 minutes before serving.

A Perfect Summer Meal

For a complete meal that requires minimal planning and only seven ingredients, we took inspiration from a recipe for grilled Roman steak with olive oil and lemon. In our version, we top the steak slices with bitter baby arugula dressed in a simple lemon vinaigrette and salty shredded Parmesan cheese. We serve the dish with extra wedges of lemon.

GRILLED FROZEN STEAKS WITH ARUGULA AND PARMESAN
SERVES 4 TO 6

Use the large holes of a box grater to shred the Parmesan.

1 recipe Grilled Frozen Steaks
6 tablespoons extra-virgin olive oil
2 tablespoons lemon juice, plus lemon wedges for serving
   Salt and pepper
8 ounces (8 cups) baby arugula
2 ounces Parmesan cheese, shredded (⅔ cup)

Slice steaks thin against grain. Fan slices on either side of large platter. Whisk oil, lemon juice, ¾ teaspoon salt, and ¼ teaspoon pepper together in large bowl. Add arugula and three-quarters of Parmesan and toss to combine. Arrange arugula down center of platter, allowing it to overlap steak. Sprinkle remaining Parmesan over steak and arugula. Serve with lemon wedges.

How Far From the Heat Is "Indirect"?

The heat-generating burner tubes of our former winning gas grill and of other older grills run horizontally beneath the cooking grate, but the burners on newer gas grills—including our winning Weber Spirit E-310—are positioned vertically. When cooking with indirect heat on a grill with horizontal burners, there isn't much variation in the distance food can be placed from the primary (lit) burner, meaning that food will cook pretty consistently from recipe to recipe and from grill to grill. But there's more real estate beside a primary vertical burner (especially if your grill has a large cooking surface), so where, exactly, the food should be placed is open to much greater interpretation. Placed far from the primary (lit) burner, the food will cook at a temperature that's too low.

Our solution? Specify in our recipes how far the food should be from the primary burner. The size of the food being grilled and the temperature determine the spacing. We found that 6 inches was the sweet spot for our grilled steaks.

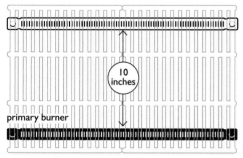

HORIZONTAL BURNERS
On older grills like our former winner, food can be no more than 10 inches from the primary burner, so it will still cook efficiently even when placed at the farthest point.

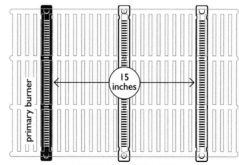

VERTICAL BURNERS
On newer grills like our current winner, the burners run vertically, so food can be placed more than 15 inches from the primary burner—too far away for it to cook efficiently.

▶ **Seeing Is Believing**
A step-by-step video is available at CooksIllustrated.com/aug16

Walkaway Ratatouille

The secret to great yet easy ratatouille? Overcook some of the vegetables, barely cook the others—and let the oven do the work.

⇛ BY ANNIE PETITO ⇚

Ratatouille is a rustic Provençal specialty that transforms late-summer produce—tomatoes, eggplant, zucchini, and bell peppers—by simmering the vegetables, scented with garlic, onion, and herbs, until they have softened into a rich stew. It's a satisfying dish that can be served as an accompaniment or even turned into a light main course by topping it with an egg, sandwiching it between slices of bread, or spooning it over pasta or rice.

The problem with ratatouille boils down to one thing: water. More specifically, each of the primary ingredients contains more than 90 percent water. If all that liquid isn't dealt with somehow, you end up with a wet, pulpy mess of ingredients that are indistinguishable in taste, color, and texture.

To remedy this, many cooks complicate what is already a prep-heavy dish (cutting multiple pounds of vegetables into ¼- or ½-inch pieces is the norm). Techniques like salting, microwaving, and pressing are often used to extract excess moisture. The individual vegetables are then typically sautéed in batches to create some flavorful browning before being simmered to cook off more water.

Recipes that skip these steps and call for simply throwing everything into a pot on the stove fared exactly as I anticipated: They were soggy, mushy, and bland. Surely I could come up with a more hands-off approach that would hold ratatouille to its rustic roots but still deliver complex flavor and tender-yet-toothsome texture.

Oven Me Tender

I definitely wanted to skip any type of pretreatment, and that meant finding a method that could efficiently draw out moisture during cooking. On the stovetop, the heat must be kept low in order to avoid burning the food on the bottom of the pot, but this also means that liquid does not readily

▶ Watch Annie in Action
A step-by-step video is available at CooksIllustrated.com/aug16

Eggplant, tomatoes, and onions melt down into a thick, silky sauce that envelops tender, intact chunks of zucchini and bell peppers.

evaporate. How about using the oven, where the ambient dry heat would evaporate moisture with less risk of burning?

Roasting the vegetables in batches on baking sheets would be almost as bothersome as sautéing each vegetable individually, so I limited myself to using only a Dutch oven and started with the least amount of chopping that I thought I could get away with. I cut onions, plum tomatoes (meatier than round types, with less watery gel), bell peppers, and zucchini into quarters and an eggplant into eighths, figuring that large pieces would retain their shape and texture better than small ones. I tossed the vegetables with olive oil, salt, and pepper (I'd fiddle with other seasonings later) and slid the Dutch oven, uncovered, into a 400-degree oven. Sure enough, after about 2 hours, the moisture had mostly evaporated and the top layer of vegetables was deeply caramelized. But I wasn't done yet.

Season As You Go

To give salt time to migrate into food for even seasoning and fully developed flavor, don't wait until the end of cooking to season. Here, we add salt each time we put vegetables in the pot.

It had taken so long for any significant amount of moisture to evaporate from the vegetables that some of them (like the zucchini) were blown out and overcooked. What's more, any intact pieces were unwieldy to eat. I reduced the vegetable size to more manageable 1-inch chunks, which would cook more quickly but still wouldn't require too much time at the cutting board. I also decided to jump-start the cooking of the onions on the stovetop, which would cut down the oven time and would give me the opportunity to sauté some smashed garlic cloves before I stirred in the remaining vegetables. These procedural tweaks cut the oven time in half, but even after I stirred partway through, the more delicate vegetables were overdone by the time any browning happened.

The eggplant had even begun to disintegrate, leaving its soft pulp and slivers of peel behind. That was unacceptable. Or was it? If eggplant cooks long enough, its flesh becomes downright silky. Perhaps, I thought, I should embrace eggplant's texture and allow it to break down completely. It just might make for a creamy sauce to unify the stew.

Cooking in Stages

I decided to peel the eggplant to create a smooth sauce with no distractions, and since tomatoes supply so much juice, I added them (also peeled) to the pot with the sautéed onions, garlic, and herbs and seasonings, knowing that their moisture would evaporate for even more concentrated flavor. I would hold the quicker-cooking zucchini and bell peppers back until near the end of the cooking time.

I put my plan into action. After 40 minutes in the oven, the eggplant, onions, and tomatoes were so meltingly soft that they yielded to gentle smashing with a potato masher, turning them into the velvety sauce that I had envisioned. What's more, most of the onions and eggplant had become so deeply browned and full of concentrated flavor that I wouldn't need to worry about getting color on the zucchini and bell peppers. Giving these later additions just a short time in the pot would

Secrets to Faster, More Flavorful Ratatouille

Classic ratatouille recipes call for cutting vegetables into small pieces, pretreating them to remove moisture, and then cooking them in batches on the stovetop. Our streamlined oven method eliminates the need for batch cooking and pretreatments—plus, it tastes better.

➤ STREAMLINE THE PREP
Chop the onions into chunks and smash the garlic cloves instead of mincing them. A brief stovetop sauté cuts down on oven time.

➤ GIVE SOME VEGETABLES A HEAD START
Add the eggplant and tomatoes and then transfer the pot to the oven where moisture evaporates, flavors concentrate, and browning occurs.

➤ MAKE AN EGGPLANT MUSH
Cook eggplant long enough and it becomes soft and creamy. We exploit this trait by mashing the eggplant (along with tomatoes and onions) into a velvety sauce.

➤ FINISH WITH FRESHNESS
Added to the pot toward the end of cooking, zucchini and bell peppers maintain freshness and bite.

SCIENCE Better Browning in the Oven

In a liquid-y dish like ratatouille, the vegetables can brown only when most of the moisture has evaporated. That's because the exteriors of the vegetables must rise beyond the boiling point of water (212 degrees) to about 300 degrees, the temperature at which browning occurs. On the stovetop, this can take a long time if the heat must be kept low to avoid scorching. However, in the dry, ambient heat of the oven, evaporation and subsequent browning happen quickly, especially since we sauté the onions and garlic in the pot on the stovetop first, preheating the pot before it goes into the oven. Another benefit of oven cookery is that as moisture evaporates, a dark, flavorful fond develops around the inside edge of the pot. Such a fond would take much longer to develop over the low flame of the stovetop.

ON THE STOVE
Heat below the pot: less browning and less fond

IN THE OVEN
Heat around the pot: more browning and more fond

maintain some pleasing bite to contrast with the smooth sauce.

I stirred in the zucchini and bell peppers and returned the pot to the oven for 20 minutes. When I checked, a few pieces of zucchini were still on the cusp of being done, but rather than return the pot to the oven, I simply covered it and let it rest for 10 minutes. Now a paring knife just slipped in and out of the pieces.

I noticed that the pot had a dark ring of fond around the inside edge. When left to sit with the lid on, the steam moistened the fond, so I could easily scrape the browned bits back into the ratatouille, making for a simple but robust flavor boost. For

spice and heady fragrance, I also added red pepper flakes, a bay leaf, and herbes de Provence (a French blend usually consisting of dried basil, fennel, lavender, marjoram, rosemary, savory, and thyme). In fact, the dish now tasted so rich that I felt that some freshening up was in order.

The intensely caramelized, almost jammy quality of the ratatouille needed a touch of acid. Although entirely untraditional, a splash of sherry vinegar helped wake up the flavors of the sweet vegetables. Finally, just before serving, I stirred in chopped fresh basil and parsley and gave the stew a glossy drizzle of extra-virgin olive oil. And there it was, a ratatouille that was simultaneously flavorful and easy to make.

This dish is best prepared using ripe, in-season tomatoes. If good tomatoes are not available, substitute one 28-ounce can of whole peeled tomatoes that have been drained and chopped coarse. Ratatouille can be served as an accompaniment to meat or fish. It can also be served on its own with crusty bread, topped with an egg, or over pasta or rice. This dish can be served warm, at room temperature, or chilled.

- ⅓ cup plus 1 tablespoon extra-virgin olive oil
- 2 large onions, cut into 1-inch pieces
- 8 large garlic cloves, peeled and smashed
  Salt and pepper
- 1½ teaspoons herbes de Provence
- ¼ teaspoon red pepper flakes
- 1 bay leaf
- 1½ pounds eggplant, peeled and cut into 1-inch pieces
- 2 pounds plum tomatoes, peeled, cored, and chopped coarse
- 2 small zucchini, halved lengthwise and cut into 1-inch pieces
- 1 red bell pepper, stemmed, seeded, and cut into 1-inch pieces
- 1 yellow bell pepper, stemmed, seeded, and cut into 1-inch pieces
- 2 tablespoons chopped fresh basil
- 1 tablespoon minced fresh parsley
- 1 tablespoon sherry vinegar

1. Adjust oven rack to middle position and heat oven to 400 degrees. Heat ⅓ cup oil in Dutch oven over medium-high heat until shimmering. Add onions, garlic, 1 teaspoon salt, and ¼ teaspoon pepper and cook, stirring occasionally, until onions are translucent and starting to soften, about 10 minutes. Add herbes de Provence, pepper flakes, and bay leaf and cook, stirring frequently, for 1 minute. Stir in eggplant and tomatoes. Sprinkle with ½ teaspoon salt and ¼ teaspoon pepper and stir to combine. Transfer pot to oven and cook, uncovered, until vegetables are very tender and spotty brown, 40 to 45 minutes.

2. Remove pot from oven and, using potato masher or heavy wooden spoon, smash and stir eggplant mixture until broken down to sauce-like consistency. Stir in zucchini, bell peppers, ¼ teaspoon salt, and ¼ teaspoon pepper and return to oven. Cook, uncovered, until zucchini and bell peppers are just tender, 20 to 25 minutes.

3. Remove pot from oven, cover, and let stand until zucchini is translucent and easily pierced with tip of paring knife, 10 to 15 minutes. Using wooden spoon, scrape any browned bits from sides of pot and stir back into ratatouille. Discard bay leaf. Stir in 1 tablespoon basil, parsley, and vinegar. Season with salt and pepper to taste. Transfer to large platter, drizzle with remaining 1 tablespoon oil, sprinkle with remaining 1 tablespoon basil, and serve.

Dressing Up Grilled Onions

We wanted grilled onions that were worthy of being a stand-alone side dish.

⇾ BY ANNIE PETITO ⇽

While grilled onions are typically used as part of a grilled vegetable mix, their sharp, sweet bite; caramelized edges; and crisp-tender texture are so good that I wondered if I could create a version worthy of being a side dish all on its own. I'd opt for the common yellow variety and would serve onion halves, rather than separating them into rings or cutting them into wedges, since I wanted a substantial side dish that presented well. The trick would be figuring out how to cook them evenly. To serve the onions as a stand-alone dish, I wanted to cook them longer in order to mellow their sharp bite and soften their texture. I would have to figure out how to achieve this without burning their exteriors.

To that end, medium heat was my best bet for giving the halves enough time to cook through without burning. But simply putting the onion halves on the grill and cooking them until charred and tender left a lot to be desired. The onions had dried out too much and required frequent turning to make sure they didn't burn. And with all the handling, they came apart by the time they were done.

My first change was to modify the way I prepped them. Following the lead of other recipes I'd found, I had been cutting the onions crosswise through the middle. But cut this way, they had no chance of holding together—the rings toward the center popped right out. Cutting them from pole to pole (in other words, from root end to stem end) gave each half a better chance of staying in one piece.

To prevent them from drying out too much, I tried wrapping each half in foil before grilling; I hoped that the onions would cook through gently in the moist heat while developing some browning through the foil. Indeed, these onions were very tender, but the flat side, which had been facing the grate, bordered on burnt. And even worse, they lacked any charred flavor from the grill since they hadn't been directly exposed to the flames.

I needed a hybrid approach. I scrapped the fussy

For onions that are both charred and tender, we start them over the coals and finish them in a disposable pan.

FAILED TEST:
Cooking whole onions in the coals makes them taste steamed versus grilled.

individual packets and instead arranged the halves cut side down in an aluminum roasting pan. And to keep the exteriors from charring, I left the skins on. I covered the pan and let the onions cook until they were softened before transferring them to the grill grate to finish cooking. Unfortunately, there was so much residual moisture from the steaming that the onions didn't pick up much char, and they were difficult to handle since they were so soft.

So I reversed the order. I began grilling the halves cut side down on the grate until charred. Then I transferred them cut side up to pan, covered the pan, and let them steam until a paring knife slipped easily in and out of each half. These onions held together and had a buttery-rich texture, with great caramelization on the bottom side that had been against the pan. But the char, though impressive going into the pan, had washed out a bit in the steamy environment. The fix was twofold: I left the onions cut side down on the grate for several minutes to bolster the char, and I briefly grilled the rounded side over direct heat, too.

My tender, caramelized, smoky onions just needed a quick, flavorful finish. An herb-flecked butter seemed promising, but the richness overwhelmed the onions. Instead, I whisked together a simple balsamic vinaigrette to drizzle over the onions before serving. The dressing complemented their sweetness and provided some necessary contrasting acidity. With a final sprinkling of minced chives, I had grilled onions well worthy of side-dish status.

GRILLED ONIONS WITH BALSAMIC VINAIGRETTE
SERVES 4

The size of the onions will affect the cooking time, so it's important to choose onions that weigh between 7 and 8 ounces each and measure about 3 inches in diameter. In step 3, be sure to err on the side of achieving darker charring, as the steaming step will soften the char's appearance and flavor. The onions can be served hot, warm, or at room temperature.

½ cup extra-virgin olive oil
3 tablespoons balsamic vinegar
　Kosher salt and pepper
4 onions
1 (13 by 9-inch) disposable aluminum roasting pan
1 tablespoon minced fresh chives

1. Whisk 6 tablespoons oil, vinegar, 1 teaspoon salt, and ¼ teaspoon pepper together in bowl; set aside.

2. Trim stem end of onions and halve onions from root end to stem end, leaving skin intact. (Root end can be trimmed, but don't remove it.) Brush cut sides of onions with remaining 2 tablespoons oil and sprinkle each half with ⅛ teaspoon salt.

3. Arrange onions cut side down on grill over medium heat and cook (covered if using gas) until well charred, 10 to 15 minutes, moving onions as needed to ensure even cooking. Flip onions and cook cut side up until light charring develops on skin side, about 5 minutes.

4. Transfer onions cut side up to disposable pan and cover tightly with aluminum foil. Return disposable pan to grill and cook over medium heat (covered if using gas) until onions are tender and easily pierced with paring knife, 10 to 15 minutes.

5. When onions are cool enough to handle, remove and discard charred outer skin; arrange onions cut side up on large platter. Rewhisk vinaigrette and drizzle evenly over onions. Sprinkle with chives, season with salt and pepper to taste, and serve.

▶ **Annie Shows You How**
A step-by-step video is available at CooksIllustrated.com/aug16

Red Pepper–Ricotta Pesto

Basil and pine nuts get the boot in this creamy-spicy pesto from southern Italy.

⇒ BY STEVE DUNN ⇐

I make pesto often, and for all the usual reasons: It's simple and easy to prepare, it's rich but fresh-tasting, and it can function not just as a pasta sauce but also as a vibrant dip, dressing for meat or vegetables, or sandwich spread. Like most cooks, I default to the familiar Genovese puree of basil, pine nuts, Parmesan, garlic, and olive oil. But almost every region of Italy lays claim to its own version, and I'm often tempted to branch out and try other styles—most recently, *pesto alla calabrese*. Calabria's namesake sauce looks and tastes nothing like the raw Genovese puree for two key reasons: First, it trades the base of basil and nuts for the red bell peppers, creamy ricotta and tangy Parmesan cheeses, and hot chiles native to that part of southern Italy. Some versions also include tomato, onion or shallot, garlic, or basil. Second, at least some of the components are cooked, either before or after the mixture is pureed. The coral-colored sauce is lush and creamy, nicely balanced by a pepper flavor that's at once sweet, fresh, and slightly spicy.

At least, it should be. But the consistencies and the flavors of the recipes I tried ranged dramatically—from dense and cloying (one taster compared it to pimento cheese) to sharp and vegetal. Surely a little kitchen work could lead me to a superior version.

Most recipes call for cooking the bell peppers, either by roasting or sautéing them (with the onion and tomato, if using) in strips so that they brown and sweeten or by steaming or blanching them so that the pieces soften somewhat but don't brown. From there, it's just a matter of blitzing the peppers with the cheeses and any other ingredients in the food processor and tossing the puree with hot pasta.

Usually I consider the rich browning and sweetness produced by roasting or sautéing a plus for peppers, but here their deeply cooked flavor was one-dimensional. Steaming or blanching them simply washed away their flavor; plus, they didn't soften sufficiently, which made the pesto grainy. My best attempt was a hybrid method: starting the peppers in a covered skillet to soften them before finishing them with the lid off so that they developed some flavorful browning. I built in some complexity by adding onion, garlic, tomato, and basil during the uncovered cooking phase before pureeing the vegetables

▶ **Look: Pesto Diverso**
A step-by-step video is available at CooksIllustrated.com/aug16

Just enough cheese lends the pesto rich, creamy body.

with the ricotta and Parmesan. The pesto still tasted a bit flat, but I hoped that the hot pepper component would add some fresh bite as well as heat.

And herein was the big problem: Calabrian chiles—variously sold fresh, packed in oil or brine, or as a paste—are the traditional heat source in this dish, but they aren't readily available in domestic supermarkets. There wasn't an obvious substitute. In their absence, most recipes call for hot pepper flakes—and while I found that ½ teaspoon or so gave the sauce just enough kick, they of course added none of the fruity bite of a fresh chile. For that, I had to circle back to the bell peppers: Adding one additional raw pepper to the food processor along with the cooked mixture and pepper flakes delivered the complex flavor I was after, and it did so without turning the sauce grainy.

Now to enrich the pepper puree with just enough cheese to make it creamy but not stodgy. Making a few more batches with varying amounts of cheese proved that it was easy to go overboard, and I eventually settled on just ¾ cup total, a 2:1 ratio of ricotta to Parmesan. Processing a couple of tablespoons of oil with the pesto made it a touch smoother, and I balanced the extra richness with a splash of white wine vinegar. Tossed with penne (the short tubes captured the sauce nicely), this pesto was rich, bright, and just a touch spicy—a nice change from better-known versions and just as satisfying.

PENNE WITH RED PEPPER PESTO (PESTO CALABRESE)
SERVES 4

Other short, tubular pastas can be used. A rasp-style grater makes quick work of turning the garlic into a paste. Adjust the amount of red pepper flakes depending on how spicy you want the dish. For our recipe for Penne with Red Pepper Pesto (Pesto Calabrese) for Two, go to CooksIllustrated.com/aug16.

- 3 red bell peppers, stemmed, seeded, and cut into ¼-inch-wide strips (5 cups)
- 3 tablespoons extra-virgin olive oil
- Salt and pepper
- 1 small onion, chopped
- 1 plum tomato, cored, seeded, and chopped
- ⅓ cup chopped fresh basil
- ½–¾ teaspoon red pepper flakes
- 1 teaspoon garlic, minced to paste
- ½ cup whole-milk ricotta cheese
- ¼ cup grated Parmesan cheese, plus extra for serving
- 1 teaspoon white wine vinegar
- 1 pound penne

1. Toss two-thirds of bell peppers with 1 tablespoon oil and ¼ teaspoon salt in 12-inch nonstick skillet. Cover and place over medium-low heat. Cook, stirring occasionally, until bell peppers are softened and just starting to brown, about 15 minutes.

2. Add onion, tomato, basil, pepper flakes, and ½ teaspoon garlic and continue to cook, uncovered, stirring occasionally, until onion is softened and bell peppers are browned in spots, 6 to 7 minutes longer. Remove skillet from heat and let cool for 5 minutes.

3. Place ricotta, Parmesan, remaining one-third of bell peppers, remaining ½ teaspoon garlic, ¾ teaspoon salt, and ¼ teaspoon pepper in bowl of food processor. Add cooked bell pepper mixture and process for 20 seconds. Scrape down sides of bowl. With processor running, add vinegar and remaining 2 tablespoons oil; process for about 20 seconds. Scrape down sides of bowl, then continue to process until smooth, about 20 seconds longer.

4. Meanwhile, bring 4 quarts water to boil in large pot. Add pasta and 1 tablespoon salt and cook, stirring often, until al dente. Reserve ½ cup cooking water, then drain pasta and return it to pot. Add pesto and toss to combine, adjusting consistency with reserved cooking water as needed. Season with salt and pepper to taste. Serve, passing extra Parmesan separately.

Paella on the Grill

A live fire lends Spain's beloved rice dish subtle smoke and a beautifully caramelized crust, but it can make evenly cooking the other elements a challenge.

≥ BY LAN LAM ≤

If you've ever made paella, you probably know that no two versions of this famous Spanish rice dish are prepared the same way. The basic template consists of medium-grain rice cooked in a wide, shallow vessel (traditionally, a *paellera*) with a flavor base called *sofrito*, broth and maybe wine, and a jumble of meat and/or seafood. Within this framework, the proteins can be anything from poultry to pork to any species of shellfish; the seasonings may include garlic, saffron, smoked paprika—or all of the above; and the embellishments might be peas, bell peppers, or lemon. As the rice absorbs the liquid, the grains in contact with the pan form a caramelized crust known as *socarrat*—the most prized part of the dish. The final product is colorful and flavor-packed: a one-pot showpiece that's perfect for entertaining.

What you might not know is that while most modern recipes are cooked on the stove or in the oven, paella was originally made on the grill, and many Spanish cooks still make it that way today. The live fire gives the dish a subtle smokiness and provides an extra-large cooking surface that encourages even socarrat development—a distinct advantage over a stove's burners or the indirect heat of an oven, which often yield a spotty or pale crust.

But in my experience, grilling comes with challenges of its own. Besides the usual problem—the quicker-cooking proteins overcook while they wait for heartier items to cook through—keeping a charcoal fire alive can be tricky. Plus, most recipes call for a paella pan, which only enthusiasts keep on hand (see our latest reviews of paella pans on page 32).

The grilled paella I had in mind would feature tender-chewy rice strewn with moist chicken, sausage, and shellfish; a uniformly golden, crisp crust; and an efficient, reliable cooking method.

Getting Set Up

A paella pan alternative had to be grill-safe, deep enough to accommodate the food (I wanted a recipe that serves eight), and broad to maximize the amount of socarrat. A disposable aluminum pan was large enough, but its flimsy walls made it a nonstarter given the hefty amount of food I was cooking. But a sturdy stainless-steel roasting pan was easy to maneuver, and

Placed hinge side down, the clams in our paella are able to open wide and release their flavorful juices over the rice, chicken, shrimp, and sausage.

its surface area was generous—three times as spacious as a large Dutch oven. I worried that the pan's underside would darken on the grill, but during testing I quickly discovered that the exterior stayed remarkably clean on both charcoal and gas grills.

As for the fire setup, I needed a single layer of coals to expose the pan's base to even heat, but I also needed long-lasting heat output that wouldn't require refueling. So I lit 7 (rather than our usual 6) quarts of charcoal and poured them evenly across the kettle's surface, hoping that would be enough. (On a gas grill, I'd simply crank the burners to high.)

Staggering Along

Knowing I'd have to stagger the additions of the proteins to get them to finish cooking at the same time, I first set the roasting pan over the fire and browned boneless, skinless chicken thighs (richer in flavor than breasts) that I'd halved for easier portioning. From there, I pushed the meat to the side, sautéed the sofrito (finely chopped onion, bell pepper, and tomato) until it softened, and followed with minced garlic, smoked

paprika, and saffron. Then came the rice. Traditional Bomba and Valencia have more bite than other medium-grain rices, but Arborio is easier to find and made a good substitute. I stirred it in with a mixture of chicken broth, clam juice, and dry sherry that I hoped would highlight the proteins. Once the rice had absorbed most of the liquid, I scattered chunks of slightly spicy, smoky, cured Spanish chorizo; shrimp (seasoned first with oil, garlic, smoked paprika, and salt); and littleneck clams over the top and let the paella cook until the grains were plump and the underside sizzled—the audible cue that a flavorful crust was forming.

My staggering strategy wasn't quite right. The chicken was a tad dry, while the sausage wasn't warmed through and the shellfish were just shy of done. Maybe part of the problem was not only when I was adding the proteins but also where I was placing them in the pan. Thinking that the thighs would stay moist if they cooked more gently, I arranged them around the cooler perimeter of the pan. As for the chorizo, shrimp, and clams, they merely sat on top of the rice and received relatively little heat when I added them after most of the liquid had been absorbed. Instead, I partially submerged the shrimp and clams (hinge side down so that their juices could be absorbed by the rice) in the center of the rice after the liquid came to a simmer and then scattered the chorizo over top. As the liquid reduced, all three components would stay warm without overcooking.

Divide and Conquer

Back to the heat output: The larger fire *almost* held out until the rice was cooked. But to completely close the gap between the cooking time and the fuel output, I made adjustments to both.

First, I covered the lit coals with 20 fresh briquettes that would gradually ignite during cooking. Next, I seared the chicken thighs directly on the grates rather than in the roasting pan (they'd still finish cooking at the edges of the pan). They browned in half the time and picked up valuable grill flavor.

Then, I retooled the sofrito to make it quicker. Instead of waterlogged fresh peppers and tomato, I used roasted red peppers and tomato paste—shortcuts to the caramelized sweetness achieved in a long-cooked sofrito. I also divided the sofrito into two parts, sautéing the peppers with the onions in the roasting pan but adding the tomato paste and aromatics (toasted first to deepen their flavor) to the cooking liquids. Finally, I brought the seasoned broth to a boil in a saucepan so that it would quickly simmer when I poured it into the roasting pan.

Finally, the proteins were spot-on, but I took a couple of extra steps to ensure that the rice cooked evenly from top to bottom, periodically shuffling the pan around over the fire to avoid any hot spots and scraping a corner of the rice with a spoon to track the socarrat development. When the grains were almost cooked through, I scattered thawed frozen peas over the surface (they would add sweet pop and color) and covered the grill so that the trapped steam would heat them through and finish cooking any underdone grains at the surface.

The finished paella was a stunner—as impressive to eat as it was to behold. And now that I had the blueprint for making it successfully on the grill, I wasn't sure I'd ever go back to the indoor version.

PAELLA ON THE GRILL
SERVES 8

This recipe was developed using a light-colored 16 by 13.5-inch tri-ply roasting pan; however, it can be made in any heavy roasting pan that measures at least 14 by 11 inches. If your roasting pan is dark in color, the cooking times will be on the lower end of the ranges given. The recipe can also be made in a 15- to 17-inch paella pan. If littlenecks are unavailable, use 1½ pounds shrimp in step 1 and season them with ½ teaspoon salt.

1½	pounds boneless, skinless chicken thighs, trimmed and halved crosswise
	Salt and pepper
12	ounces jumbo shrimp (16 to 20 per pound), peeled and deveined
6	tablespoons extra-virgin olive oil
6	garlic cloves, minced
1¾	teaspoons hot smoked paprika
3	tablespoons tomato paste
4	cups chicken broth
1	(8-ounce) bottle clam juice
⅔	cup dry sherry
	Pinch saffron threads (optional)
1	onion, chopped fine
½	cup jarred roasted red peppers, chopped fine
3	cups Arborio rice
1	pound littleneck clams, scrubbed
1	pound Spanish-style chorizo, cut into ½-inch pieces
1	cup frozen peas, thawed
	Lemon wedges

1. Place chicken on large plate and sprinkle both sides with 1 teaspoon salt and 1 teaspoon pepper. Toss shrimp with 1 tablespoon oil, ½ teaspoon garlic, ¼ teaspoon paprika, and ¼ teaspoon salt in bowl until evenly coated. Set aside.

A Blueprint for Paella on the Grill

Producing perfectly cooked paella on the grill isn't hard; it just takes some planning as to exactly where and when to add each element.

PEAS
Scattered across the surface at the end of cooking, the peas stay plump.

CHORIZO
Added before the liquid is absorbed, the precooked cured sausage warms through without drying out.

SHRIMP & CLAMS
Partially submerging the shellfish in the simmering liquid in the center of the pan ensures that they stay warm without overcooking.

CHICKEN
After being seared on the grill, the thighs are arranged around the pan's cooler perimeter, where they cook through slowly and gently.

LARGE ROASTING PAN
Thanks to the roasting pan's generous surface area—nearly triple that of a Dutch oven—the rice develops lots of the prized crust called *socarrat*. (Don't worry; the pan won't burn.)

2. Heat 1 tablespoon oil in medium saucepan over medium heat until shimmering. Add remaining garlic and cook, stirring constantly, until garlic sticks to bottom of saucepan and begins to brown, about 1 minute. Add tomato paste and remaining 1½ teaspoons paprika and continue to cook, stirring constantly, until dark brown bits form on bottom of saucepan, about 1 minute. Add broth, clam juice, sherry, and saffron, if using. Increase heat to high and bring to boil. Remove saucepan from heat and set aside.

3A. FOR A CHARCOAL GRILL: Open bottom vent completely. Light large chimney starter mounded with charcoal briquettes (7 quarts). When top coals are partially covered with ash, pour evenly over grill. Using tongs, arrange 20 unlit briquettes evenly over coals. Set cooking grate in place, cover, and open lid vent completely. Heat grill until hot, about 5 minutes.

3B. FOR A GAS GRILL: Turn all burners to high, cover, and heat grill until hot, about 15 minutes. Leave all burners on high.

4. Clean and oil cooking grate. Place chicken on grill and cook until both sides are lightly browned, 5 to 7 minutes total. Return chicken to plate. Clean cooking grate.

5. Place roasting pan on grill (turning burners to medium-high if using gas) and add remaining ¼ cup oil. When oil begins to shimmer, add onion, red peppers, and ½ teaspoon salt. Cook, stirring frequently, until onion begins to brown, 4 to 7 minutes. Add rice (turning burners to medium if using gas) and stir until grains are well coated with oil.

6. Arrange chicken around perimeter of pan. Pour broth mixture and any accumulated juices from chicken over rice. Smooth rice into even layer, making sure nothing sticks to sides of pan and no rice rests atop chicken. When liquid reaches gentle simmer, place shrimp in center of pan in single layer. Arrange clams in center of pan, evenly distributing with shrimp and pushing hinge sides of clams into rice slightly so they stand up. Distribute chorizo evenly over surface of rice. Cook (covered if using gas), moving and rotating pan to maintain gentle simmer across entire surface of pan, until rice is almost cooked through, 12 to 18 minutes. (If using gas, heat can also be adjusted to maintain simmer.)

7. Sprinkle peas evenly over paella, cover grill, and cook until liquid is fully absorbed and rice on bottom of pan sizzles, 5 to 8 minutes. Continue to cook, uncovered, checking bottom of pan frequently with metal spoon, until uniform golden-brown crust forms, 8 to 15 minutes longer. (Rotate and slide pan around grill as necessary to ensure even crust formation.) Remove pan from grill, cover with aluminum foil, and let stand for 10 minutes. Serve with lemon wedges.

▶ **See the Setup**
A step-by-step video is available at CooksIllustrated.com/aug16

Korean Fried Chicken Wings

One bite of this exceptionally crunchy, sweet-spicy style
of fried chicken and you'll understand its cult-like popularity.

⋟ BY ANDREA GEARY ⋞

I crave fried chicken as much as the next person, but I have never been partial to fried wings. To me, they're bar snacks—fine for occasionally sharing with friends but not substantial or satisfying enough to make a meal out of—and certainly not worth the trouble to make at home.

At least, that's how I felt until I tasted the fried wings at a Korean restaurant in my neighborhood. The biggest selling point of this style is its thin, crackly exterior that gives way to juicy meat with an audible crunch—an especially impressive trait considering that the surface of the chicken is doused with a wet sauce. And unlike many styles of wings that are just sweet, salty, or fiery, these delivered a perfect balance of all those flavors.

That profile has made this style of fried chicken wildly popular as an accompaniment to beer and the pickled side dishes known as *banchan* in South Korean bars and restaurants. In fact, the fried chicken–beer combination is now a multibillion-dollar industry that has spawned the term *chimaek* (*chi* for "chicken" and *maek* for "maekju," the Korean word for beer), a South Korean festival, and (in the past decade or so) worldwide restaurant chains like Bon Chon that are centered on this particular dish.

Needless to say, I was hooked and was determined to make Korean fried chicken for myself. Once I started to research the recipe, I also learned a practical explanation for using wings: In Korea, where chickens are smaller, restaurants often cut up and fry the whole bird, but because the larger breasts and thighs on American birds are harder to cook evenly, wings are the easier choice. The more I thought about it, I didn't see why I couldn't make a meal out of Korean fried chicken wings; their bold flavors would surely pair well with a bowl of rice and (in place of the banchan) a bright, fresh slaw.

The Crust of the Matter

Replicating the sauce would be easy enough once I figured out the ingredients. So I first focused on nailing the wings' delicate but substantial crunch, reviewing the coatings and frying methods I found in a handful of recipes. The coatings varied considerably—from a simple cornstarch dredge to a thick

A brief rest after frying allows the wings' crispy crust to cool slightly and set before the sauce is applied.

batter made with eggs, flour, and cornstarch—and I found methods for both single frying and double frying. Figuring I'd start with a minimalist approach, I tossed 3 pounds of wings (which would feed at least four people) in cornstarch before frying them once, for about 10 minutes, in a Dutch oven filled with 2 quarts of 350-degree oil.

The meat on these wings was a tad dry, but their worst flaw was the coating—or lack thereof. Most of the cornstarch fell off as soon as the wings hit the oil, so the crust was wimpy—nothing that could stand up to a sauce—and only lightly browned.

Thinking that the starch needed some moisture to help it cling to the chicken, I next tried a series of batter coatings. Not surprisingly, the shaggy mixture of flour, cornstarch, and egg fried up thick and craggy, more like the coating on American

Double Frying Isn't Double the Work

Double frying is crucial for the crunchy texture of our wings because it drives more moisture from the skin—but it's not as onerous as you might think. Each batch of wings takes just 7 minutes, and the second fry can be done in one large batch.

fried chicken. I also tried a combination of just cornstarch and water, but it was another bust: Adding enough liquid to make the mixture loose enough to coat the chicken also made it too runny to cling, but without enough water the mixture thickened up like liquid cement. Coating the wings with a creamy, loose slurry of flour and water yielded a nicely thin crust, though it was a bit tough and lacked the elusive shattery texture I was after. From there, I tried various ratios of flour and cornstarch and found that supplementing a flour-based batter with just 3 tablespoons of cornstarch helped the coating crisp up nicely. I understood why once I learned that flour and cornstarch play different but complementary roles in frying: The proteins in wheat flour help the batter bond to the meat and also brown deeply; cornstarch (a pure starch) doesn't cling or brown as well as flour, but it crisps up nicely. Why? Because pure starch releases more amylose, a starch molecule that fries up supercrispy. Cornstarch also can't form gluten, so it doesn't turn tough.

I dunked the wings in the batter and let the excess drip back into the bowl before adding them to the hot oil. When they emerged, I thought I'd finally nailed the crust, which was gorgeously crispy and brown. But when I slathered the wings with my placeholder sauce (a mixture of the spicy-sweet Korean chile-soybean paste *gochujang*, sugar, garlic, ginger, sesame oil, soy sauce, and a little water) and took a bite, I paused. They'd gone from supercrispy to soggy in minutes.

On the Double

It was a setback that made me wonder if double frying might be worth a try, so I ran the obvious head-to-head test: one batch of wings fried continuously until done versus another fried partway, removed from the oil and allowed to rest briefly, and then fried again until cooked through. After draining them, I would toss both batches in the same amount of sauce to see which one stayed crispier.

It wasn't even a contest: Whereas the wings that

Winging It, Korean-Style

Korean fried chicken wings boast a big crunch and a complex sauce that make them appealing to eat, but they also employ a relatively quick and easy cooking method that makes them more appealing to prepare than many other styles of fried chicken.

Supercrispy
Double frying ensures that the skin stays crispy long after being sauced.

Cook Quickly
Because they're small, wings will be fully cooked by the time they're brown and crispy, 28 minutes in total for both rounds.

Lots of Skin
A high ratio of skin to meat protects the meat and keeps it moist and also means crunch in every bite.

Complex Sauce
Gochujang chile paste, soy sauce, sesame oil, sugar, and aromatics make a savory, spicy, sweet sauce.

A rasp-style grater makes quick work of turning the garlic into a paste. Our favorite rasp-style grater is the Microplane Classic Zester Grater. *Gochujang*, a Korean chile-soybean paste, can be found in Asian markets and in some supermarkets. Tailor the heat level of your wings by adjusting its amount. If you can't find gochujang, substitute an equal amount of Sriracha sauce and add only 2 tablespoons of water to the sauce. See page 30 for tips on cutting wings. For a complete meal, serve with steamed white rice and a slaw.

- 1 tablespoon toasted sesame oil
- 1 teaspoon garlic, minced to paste
- 1 teaspoon grated fresh ginger
- 1¾ cups water
- 3 tablespoons sugar
- 2–3 tablespoons gochujang
- 1 tablespoon soy sauce
- 2 quarts vegetable oil
- 1 cup all-purpose flour
- 3 tablespoons cornstarch
- 3 pounds chicken wings, cut at joints, wingtips discarded

1. Combine sesame oil, garlic, and ginger in large bowl and microwave until mixture is bubbly and garlic and ginger are fragrant but not browned, 40 to 60 seconds. Whisk in ¼ cup water, sugar, gochujang, and soy sauce until smooth; set aside.

2. Heat vegetable oil in Dutch oven over medium-high heat to 350 degrees. While oil heats, whisk flour, cornstarch, and remaining 1½ cups water in second large bowl until smooth. Set wire rack in rimmed baking sheet and set aside.

3. Place half of wings in batter and stir to coat. Using tongs, remove wings from batter one at a time, allowing any excess batter to drip back into bowl, and add to hot oil. Increase heat to high and cook, stirring occasionally to prevent wings from sticking, until coating is light golden and beginning to crisp, about 7 minutes. (Oil temperature will drop sharply after adding wings.) Transfer wings to prepared rack. Return oil to 350 degrees and repeat with remaining wings. Reduce heat to medium and let second batch of wings rest for 5 minutes.

4. Heat oil to 375 degrees. Carefully return all wings to oil and cook, stirring occasionally, until deep golden brown and very crispy, about 7 minutes. Return wings to rack and let stand for 2 minutes. Transfer wings to reserved sauce and toss until coated. Return wings to rack and let stand for 2 minutes to allow coating to set. Transfer to platter and serve.

had been fried once and then sauced started to soften up almost instantly, the double-fried batch still delivered real crunch after being doused with the sauce. What's more, the double-fried wings were juicier than any batch I'd made before. Why? Chicken skin contains a lot of moisture, so producing crispy wings (which have a higher ratio of skin to meat than any other part of the chicken) means removing as much moisture as possible from the chicken skin before the meat overcooks. When you fry just once, the meat finishes cooking before all of the moisture is driven out of the chicken skin, and the remaining moisture migrates to the crust and turns it soggy. Covering the wings with sauce makes the sogginess even worse. But when you fry twice, the interruption of the cooking and the brief cooldown period slow the cooking of the meat; as a result, you can extend the overall cooking time and expel all the moisture from the skin without overcooking the chicken.

There was my proof that double frying was worth the time—and, frankly, it wasn't the tediously long cooking process I thought it would be. Yes, I had to do the first fry in two batches, for two reasons: The oil temperature would drop too much if I put all the chicken in at once because there would be so much moisture from the skin to cook off; plus, the wet coating would cause the wings to stick together if they were crowded in the pot. But the frying took only about 7 minutes per

Temp Drops? Don't Worry

The oil temperature will drop when the chicken is added, but as long as it stays above 250 degrees (where there is enough energy to evaporate water and brown the exterior), the results will be fine.

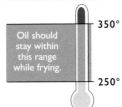

Oil should stay within this range while frying.

350°
250°

batch. As the parcooked wings rested on a wire rack, I brought the oil temperature up to 375 degrees. Then, following the lead of one of the more prominent Korean fried chicken recipes I'd found, I dumped all the wings back into the pot at once for the second stage. After another 7 minutes, they were deeply golden and shatteringly crispy. All told, I'd produced 3 pounds of perfectly crispy wings in roughly half an hour. Not bad.

Savory, Spicy, Sweet

Back to my placeholder sauce, which was close but a tad sharp from the raw minced garlic and ginger. Instead, I placed the ginger and garlic in a large bowl with a tablespoon of sesame oil and microwaved the mixture for 1 minute, just long enough to take the edge off. Then I whisked in the remaining sauce ingredients. The sweet-savory-spicy balance was pitch-perfect.

Before tossing them in the sauce, I let the wings rest for 2 minutes so the coating could cool and set. When I did add them to the sauce, they were still so crispy that they clunked encouragingly against the sides of the bowl. In fact, the crust's apparent staying power made me curious to see how long the crunch would last, so I set some wings aside and found that they stayed truly crispy for 2 hours. Impressive—even though I knew they'd be gobbled up long before that.

▶ **Watch: How to Wing It**
A step-by-step video is available at CooksIllustrated.com/aug16

How to Know When Food Is Done

Don't flub a beautifully rosy steak or a perfectly chewy batch of cookies because you couldn't pinpoint the moment to stop cooking. BY ELIZABETH BOMZE

For the Best Results, Get Out Your Thermometer

The axiom "knowledge is power" holds especially true in the kitchen—the more you know about what's going on inside your food as it cooks, the more you can control the result. That's why we're so gung ho about using an instant-read thermometer in the kitchen, as more control means less stress and better results.

➤ Our Favorite Instant-Read Thermometers

The **ThermoWorks Thermapen Mk4** (left, $99) and our Best Buy, the **ThermoWorks ThermoPop** (right, $29), are accurate, fast, and easy to use.

➤ Take Multiple Readings

Especially with large roasts and turkeys, it's important to take the temperature in multiple places since it can vary in thicker and thinner areas, as well as near bones. Food is only done once all parts reach the target temperature.

MEAT AND POULTRY

Don't Forget Carryover Cooking

The temperature of many proteins will continue to rise once they're taken off heat and allowed to rest before serving, a phenomenon known as carryover cooking. This is particularly true for thick roasts cooked at high temperatures, which must be removed from the heat as much as 10 to 15 degrees below the desired doneness. We've also learned that carryover cooking is negligible in burgers, whole chickens, and whole fish; the loose grain of the burgers and the hollow cavities of the chicken and fish allow heat to escape, so these items should be cooked to the desired degree of doneness.

	COOK TO	SERVE AT
BEEF/LAMB		
Rare	115°F–120°F	125°F
Medium-Rare	120°F–125°F	130°F
Medium	130°F–135°F	140°F
Medium-Well	140°F–145°F	150°F
Well-Done	150°F–155°F	160°F
GROUND BEEF		
Medium-Rare*	125°F	125°F
Medium*	130°F	130°F
Medium-Well*	140°F	140°F
Well-Done	160°+	160°+
PORK		
Medium	140°F–145°F	150°F
Well-Done	150°F–155°F	160°F
CHICKEN		
White Meat	160°F	160°F
Dark Meat	175°F	175°F

Cook Some Cuts Longer

Whereas most proteins are best cooked just to an internal temperature at which they're safe to eat, items like braised or slow-roasted dark-meat chicken, pork butt, and beef chuck often taste better when they're cooked longer. That's because these tough cuts are loaded with collagen, which breaks down into gelatin between 140 and 195 degrees and lubricates the muscle fibers, making them seem more moist and tender. It's also important to cook these cuts slowly; the longer they spend in that collagen breakdown window, the more tender the meat will be.

Pink Poultry and Pork Can Be Safe

Pink-tinted turkey and pork aren't necessarily undercooked. Often, the color is an indication that the pH of the meat is relatively high, which stabilizes the meat's pink pigment so that it doesn't break down when exposed to heat. As long as the meat registers the prescribed temperature, it's safe to eat.

*The USDA recommends cooking all ground beef to 160 degrees.

Tips for Taking Meat's Temperature

Steaks and chops: Hold the steak or chop with tongs and insert the thermometer through the side of the meat. This method also works for chicken parts.

Burgers: Leaving the burger in the pan (or on the grill), slide the tip of the thermometer into the top edge and push it toward the center, making sure to avoid hitting the pan (or grate).

Roasts: Insert the thermometer at an angle, pushing the probe deep into the roast and then slowly drawing it out. Look for the lowest temperature to find the center of the meat.

Whole poultry, breast: Insert the thermometer from the neck end, holding it parallel to the bird. (Avoid hitting the bone, which can give an inaccurate reading.)

Whole poultry, thigh: Insert the thermometer at an angle away from the bone into the area between the drumstick and breast.

Whole stuffed poultry: In addition to taking the temperature of the white and dark meat, insert the thermometer directly into the center of the cavity. The stuffing is food-safe at 165 degrees.

FISH AND SHELLFISH

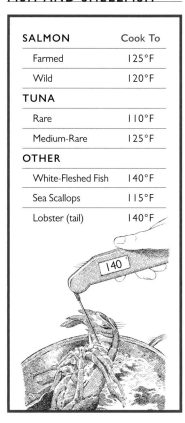

SALMON	Cook To
Farmed	125°F
Wild	120°F
TUNA	
Rare	110°F
Medium-Rare	125°F
OTHER	
White-Fleshed Fish	140°F
Sea Scallops	115°F
Lobster (tail)	140°F

Salmon: With less fat than farmed salmon, wild salmon is more prone to drying out and overcooking, so we cook it to a lower temperature.

Swordfish: The exterior of cooked swordfish should feel firm while the inside is just opaque but still moist.

Shrimp: Cooked shrimp should look pink, feel just firm to the touch, and be slightly translucent at the center.

Mussels: An opened mussel is cooked, but one that remains closed might just need more cooking. Microwave it for 30 seconds; if it still doesn't open, discard it.

Clams: Open clams are done—and overcook quickly. Remove clams as they open and keep them warm in a covered bowl while the rest finish cooking.

DISCOVERY
Temp Baked Potatoes
Baking a potato to between 205 and 212 degrees ensures that the interior will be uniformly fluffy. To learn why, go to CooksIllustrated.com/bakedpotato.

BAKED GOODS AND SWEETS

We use a thermometer to gauge the doneness of not just proteins but also many baked goods and desserts. And when a food doesn't lend itself to temperature-taking, our visual guidelines can be just as helpful.

WHEN TO USE A THERMOMETER

Yeast Breads
We have found that yeast bread can reach its recommended temperature for doneness well before the loaf is actually baked through. You should take the temperature of your bread as a backup, but stick to the recommended baking time and make sure the crust is well browned before removing the loaf from the oven and checking its temperature.

Lean (e.g., sandwich bread)	205–210°F
Enriched (e.g., brioche)	190–195°F

Loaf-pan loaves: Insert the thermometer from the side, just above the pan edge, and direct it at a downward angle into the center of the loaf.

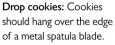
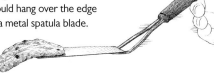

Free-form loaves: Tip the loaf (cover your hand with a dish towel) and insert the probe through the bottom crust into the center.

Cheesecake
New York cheesecake: The velvety consistency of this style is achieved when the center registers 165 degrees.

Other baked cheesecakes: For an all-over creamy consistency, we bake them to between 145 and 150 degrees.

Custards and Puddings
Stovetop custards: We cook custards like crème anglaise to a relatively low 175 degrees to prevent the egg proteins from curdling.

Ice cream bases: Custard bases for ice cream should be thicker than conventional stovetop custards, so we cook them to 180 degrees.

Baked custards: Applications such as flan and crème brûlée should jiggle but not slosh when gently shaken and should register between 170 and 180 degrees (depending on the ratio of eggs to other ingredients).

Custard Pie Fillings
Because baked custard fillings like pumpkin pie filling continue to set up as they cool, it's important to remove custard pies from the oven when they're slightly underdone. The edges of the filling should be set, while the center should jiggle slightly (but not slosh) when the pie is shaken and should register between 170 and 175 degrees.

WHEN TO USE VISUAL CUES

Cakes, Muffins, and Quick Breads
➤ For thin (less than ¾-inch) items: Test for springback. Gently press the center of the food; it should feel springy and resilient. If your finger leaves an impression or the center jiggles, it's not done.

➤ For thick (at least ¾-inch) items: Use a skewer. Poke a wooden skewer or toothpick into the center; it should emerge with no more than a few crumbs attached. If you see moist batter or lots of crumbs, bake it longer.

Cookies, Bar Cookies, and Brownies
➤ For chewy centers, underbaking is key—but tricky to gauge. Look for these visual cues.

Drop cookies: Cookies should hang over the edge of a metal spatula blade.

Crackly cookies: Cracks should appear shiny.
Stamped and sliced cookies: Edges should be light brown and centers slightly moist.

➤ For uniformly crisp cookies, remove the cookies when the edges are deep golden brown and crisp, and the centers yield to slight pressure.

➤ For perfect brownies, poke a wooden toothpick into the center and look for a few moist crumbs; moist batter means they're not ready. Overbaking will yield dry, chalky results with diminished chocolate flavor.

Pie Crust
The pastry should be well browned (deep color equals deep flavor). We bake in glass pie plates, which allow us to monitor browning on the sides and bottom of the crust.

Fruit Pies
Filling should bubble at the edges and in the vents.

Vegetable Slaws

Root vegetables can add a lively twist to coleslaw. You just need to treat them right.

⇒ BY ANDREW JANJIGIAN ⇐

Just because cabbage is the traditional choice for coleslaw doesn't mean it's the only option. I suspected that root vegetables like beets, carrots, celery root, and kohlrabi would stay just as crisp once dressed, and their distinctive flavors would enliven a slaw. And while mayonnaise-based dressings are a common choice, I liked the idea of pairing my shredded root vegetables with a tangy vinaigrette.

With their deep, rich color and earthy-sweet flavor, beets seemed like a great starting place for my testing. But unlike cabbage, which succumbs to a sharp knife with little effort, dense beets would take more elbow grease to turn them into shreds thin enough to be palatable raw. A mandoline could do the job, but I ruled it out since it's not a tool that everyone owns. Fortunately, I found that both the shredding disk of a food processor and the large holes of a box grater made relatively quick work of the task.

We typically pretreat cabbage to remove much of its abundant water; otherwise, you'd wind up with a slaw that's a waterlogged mess. I had hoped I could skip this step for beets, but one test confirmed that they contain enough water to cause problems. Plus, while the shreds were thin, they were still too woody for tasters. Some sort of pretreatment was a must.

Tossing a vegetable with salt and letting it sit is a common way to pull out water. I worked my way up to using 1 teaspoon of salt with the beets before I had to put on the brakes—any more and the slaw was too salty. It also took an hour, which was too long to wait. Luckily, salt wasn't my only pretreatment option. Just as it does with fruit, sugar can extract liquid from vegetables. It isn't as effective as salt at the task—how quickly water gets pulled to the surface is determined by how many dissolved particles are in the solution, and sugar remains one molecule when dissolved whereas salt breaks down into two ions—but the combination of the two would speed up the process. And I liked the idea of the contrast that the sweetness would provide against the tangy vinaigrette.

I tossed a new batch of shredded beets with 1 teaspoon of salt plus ¼ cup of sugar and let the mixture sit. By the time I'd finished prepping my other ingredients (which took about 15 minutes),

▶ **See the Slaw Come Together**
A step-by-step video is available at CooksIllustrated.com/aug16

they were sufficiently wilted; I gave them a quick spin in a salad spinner, and they were ready to go.

Now I just needed a few complementary ingredients and a dressing. I settled on endive since its bitterness would make a nice foil to the sweet beets. For another layer of texture and some floral sweetness, I added some pears. And finally, for contrasting color and another layer of flavor, I tossed in some cilantro.

As for the vinaigrette, sherry vinegar offered an oaky complexity that complemented the beets, and adding plenty of Dijon mustard punched up the flavor and lent the dressing body.

From here, it was easy to create a few variations based on the formula. I paired celery root with celery, earthy carrots with peppery radishes, and sweet kohlrabi with bitter radicchio. Changing out the pear for apple and swapping in different vinegars—rice, white wine, or cider—and alternate herbs helped give each slaw a unique profile. And with so much texture, flavor, and alluring color, these slaws were sure to appear on my dinner table throughout the year.

BEET, ENDIVE, AND PEAR SLAW
SERVES 4 TO 6

To save time, we recommend shredding and treating the beets before prepping the remaining ingredients. Shred the beets on the large holes of a box grater or with the shredding disk of a food processor. For our free recipe for Celery Root, Celery, and Apple Slaw, go to CooksIllustrated.com/aug16.

1½	pounds beets, trimmed, peeled, and shredded
¼	cup sugar, plus extra for seasoning
	Salt and pepper
½	cup extra-virgin olive oil
3	tablespoons sherry vinegar, plus extra for seasoning
2	tablespoons Dijon mustard
2	heads Belgian endive (4 ounces each), cored and sliced thin on bias
2	pears, peeled, halved, cored, and cut into ⅛-inch matchsticks
1	cup fresh cilantro leaves

1. Toss beets with sugar and 1 teaspoon salt in large bowl and let sit until partially wilted and reduced in volume by one-third, about 15 minutes.
2. Meanwhile, whisk oil, vinegar, mustard, ½ teaspoon salt, and ½ teaspoon pepper in large bowl until combined.
3. Transfer beets to salad spinner and spin until

In this carrot slaw, as well as our other root vegetable slaws, salt and sugar draw out excess water.

excess water is removed, 10 to 20 seconds. Transfer beets to bowl with dressing. Add endive, pears, and cilantro to bowl with beets and toss to combine. Season with salt, pepper, extra sugar, and/or extra vinegar to taste. Serve immediately.

CARROT, RADISH, AND ASIAN PEAR SLAW

Shred the carrots on the large holes of a box grater or with the shredding disk of a food processor.

Substitute carrots for beets and rice vinegar for sherry vinegar. Add 1 tablespoon toasted sesame oil to dressing in step 2. Substitute 12 ounces radishes, trimmed, halved, and sliced thin, for endive; Asian pears for pears; and 10 scallions, green parts only, sliced thin on bias, for cilantro.

KOHLRABI, RADICCHIO, AND APPLE SLAW

Shred the kohlrabi on the large holes of a box grater or with the shredding disk of a food processor.

Substitute kohlrabi for beets and white wine vinegar for sherry vinegar. Substitute 1 small head radicchio, halved, cored, and sliced ½ inch thick, for endive; Granny Smith apples for pears; and ½ cup coarsely chopped fresh mint for cilantro.

Great Grilled Pizza

After weeks of making burnt, puffy pies, we learned that the keys to crisp-tender, lightly charred pizza from the grill are quite simple: a strategic setup and a glug of oil.

> BY ANDREW JANJIGIAN <

I like to host pizza parties year-round, but come summertime the last thing I want to do is crank up the oven and cook in a hot kitchen. That's when I opt to grill pizza. Not only does this approach allow me to move both the kitchen and the party outdoors, but when made well, the pie is a lighter and fresher style of pizza, perfect for summer appetites: a thin, audibly crisp, lightly charred crust that's tender within and topped judiciously (so as not to saturate the crust) with a simple tomato sauce, pockets of cheese, and fresh herbs.

My standards for grilled pizza are admittedly high, since I was introduced to this style at Al Forno in Providence, Rhode Island, the restaurant where the dish is said to have been invented more than three decades ago. There, the pies are cooked on a custom-made wood-fired grill, which produces a gorgeously charred, crisp-tender oblong crust that the kitchen tops with alternating islands of bright, well-rounded tomato sauce and gooey melted cheese, a few shallow pools of rich olive oil, and zippy raw scallion curls.

But as proficient as I am at baking pizzas, I've found it much trickier to grill one. That's because unlike an oven, which browns pizza from both the bottom and the top, a grill cooks pizza entirely from the bottom, which leaves the top soft and blond and the toppings undercooked, even when the grill is covered. To brown the second side, many recipes call for flipping the dough before applying any toppings, but I've found that this also causes the dough to puff up from edge to edge—more like a flatbread than pizza.

The grill at Al Forno solves this problem because it features a brick enclosure that absorbs heat and then reflects it back onto the top of the pie, much like an oven would. Without that setup, I'd need to test other ways to achieve the results I was after.

Slick Move

Grilling the dough on both sides was a must if I wanted flavorful browning on the top and bottom, so I focused my first tests on keeping the dough flat. I used our Thin-Crust Pizza dough (January/February 2011) as a jumping-off point; it's a mixture of bread flour, instant yeast, water, vegetable oil, salt, and sugar

Instead of blanketing the pie with sauce and cheese, we dollop these toppings over the crust so that they don't saturate it and make it soggy.

that comes together in minutes in the food processor and stretches beautifully without tearing or springing back. It also boasts a tight crumb with complex flavor thanks to a prolonged fermentation in the fridge, where the dough's yeast produces sugars, alcohol, and acids. As for the grill setup, for now I'd cook the pies on a gas grill with all the burners set to high and revisit the method later if necessary.

Back to the puffiness issue: I wondered if the solution might be as simple as pressing the dough as thin as possible, which I tried with both my hands and a rolling pin. But neither of the mechanical methods worked: No matter how thin I stretched it, the dough inevitably puffed back up once it hit the grill. My only recourse was to try tweaking the dough formula itself. First I halved the amount of yeast, which did minimize the air bubbles but didn't make the dough easier to stretch. What I really needed was a looser dough that would naturally spread more, so I gradually upped the amount of water until the dough was soft enough to stretch into a thin sheet but not so wet that it was

soupy. The difference—an extra ½ ounce of water—made for a dough that not only stretched thinner and puffed less but also boasted a moister, more tender crumb.

But adding more water presented a catch-22: The wetter dough was stickier and required a liberal dusting of flour to keep it from clinging to my fingers and the grill grates (which I'd already oiled generously), but more flour made the exterior of the crust leathery and tough.

Stumped, I arranged a visit with Al Forno's executive chef, David Reynoso, hoping there was more to the restaurant's great results than the custom grill. And as it turned out, there was a subtle but significant difference to his method. Rather than stretching the dough in flour, he did so in a generous amount of olive oil. It made sense, as the fat not only kept the dough from sticking but essentially fried the exterior a bit and helped it crisp: As water in the dough's exterior is driven away by the high temperatures, the starch molecules lock into place, forming a rigid, brittle network with a porous, open structure.

Back at work, I whipped up another batch of dough. This time I poured ¼ cup of olive oil onto a rimmed baking sheet, dipped both sides of the dough ball into it, and then used my palms to stretch and spread the dough into a thin oval sheet that measured roughly 16 by 12 inches, just about filling the pan. It was a little messy, but the dough stretched easily beneath my hands and peeled cleanly from my fingers and the grates: So far

At Al Forno in Providence, R.I., the brick enclosure that surrounds the grill reflects heat downward onto the pie, cooking the top of it, as heat from beneath the grate cooks the bottom.

Conventional Dough Won't Do

When we tried grilling our conventional pizza dough, we were met with a number of problems. Instead of the thin, even crust we were after, we ended up with a thick, bubbly flatbread.

➤ DOESN'T SPREAD
Too little water in our conventional dough makes it impossible to roll it as flat as we wanted.

➤ PUFFS UP
Too much yeast causes large air pockets to form and the crust to bubble as it cooks on the first side.

➤ BROWNS UNEVENLY
The bubbling gives the top side an uneven surface that, when flipped, doesn't lie flat on the cooking grate.

---

so good. The finished product was proof that using lots of oil was well worth it: This pie was thin, tender, and richly flavorful, with a crisp shell—and it wasn't the least bit greasy.

Playing with Fire
I should clarify that these pies had cooked nicely on a gas grill with the lid closed, but when I tried mimicking the results over a single-level charcoal fire, things got trickier. Simply put, it was much harder to maintain even heat over the entire surface, and the bottom of the crust tended to burn in the center before the outer edges had browned and the cheese had melted.

It wasn't that the fire was too strong; I proved that to myself when I reduced the amount of charcoal and the same bull's-eye effect happened, only more slowly. The problem was the shape of the kettle grill; even though the coals were spread in an even layer, the curved walls reflected heat and created a hot spot at the very center. The solution was to make the shape of the grill work in my favor by arranging the coals in a ring around the exterior of the grill with a void at the center; that way, the concentrated heat on the outside edge would reflect in. With that setup, I was able to achieve a more-even spread of heat from edge to edge.

However, this setup meant that I could cook just one pie at a time. But this was just as well: I'd also realized during testing that grilled pizza is more ephemeral than other styles and goes from perfectly crisp to limp in minutes, so serving one at a time was better. Going forward, I made sure to have everything I needed—all three sheets of stretched dough, sauce, cheese, and tools—at the ready so that I could cook and serve the pies as quickly as possible. In fact, it was best to pargrill all three pies before topping, grilling, and serving them one by one.

In Top Form
With my dough and my cooking method locked down, it was time to turn my attention to finessing the toppings, which, up to this point, had been just a coarse puree of whole tomatoes and seasonings along with some shredded mozzarella. The sauce needed nothing more than a little olive oil and sugar to balance the tomatoes' bright acidity, but the cheese, which was a tad bland and had never fully melted in previous tests, needed rethinking. After a few tests, I switched from the block mozzarella we typically use on pizza to the softer, faster-melting fresh kind and supplemented it with salty-sharp finely grated Parmesan.

I was also strategic about how and when I added the toppings: First, I applied a thin but even layer of Parmesan (plus a little more olive oil), which created a flavorful barrier against the other toppings' moisture, ensuring that the crust would stay crisp. Since slathering the thin dough with sauce and cheese would surely thwart crispness, I instead dolloped spoonfuls of sauce (warmed on the stove first to ensure it would be piping hot by the time the pizza was done) over the pargrilled dough surface, along with bite-size pieces of the mozzarella. I slid the pie back over the heat for 3 to 5 minutes to crisp up the crust and cook the toppings, checking the underside and rotating the pizza as necessary to make sure that it browned evenly. When it came off the grill, I finished it with chopped fresh basil, one more drizzle of oil, and a bit of coarse salt for crunch.

This was the closest replica of the Al Forno pie that I'd ever had: a crisp-tender crust that boasted richness from that oil bath and just a touch of smoke and char, simply and judiciously covered with pockets of bright, balanced sauce and just enough gooey cheese. It didn't need any other toppings (though applying certain fresh items that don't weigh down the pie after cooking is fine; see "Toppings with a Light Touch" for suggestions) and was as addictive to eat as it was fun to make.

GRILLED PIZZA
SERVES 4 TO 6

The dough must sit for at least 24 hours before shaping. We prefer the high protein content of King Arthur bread flour for this recipe, though other bread flours are acceptable. For best results, weigh your ingredients. It's important to use ice water in the dough to prevent it from overheating in the food processor. Grilled pizza cooks quickly, so it's critical to have all of your ingredients and tools ready ahead of time. We recommend pargrilling, topping, and grilling in quick succession and serving the pizzas one at a time, rather than all at once.

Dough
- 3 cups (16½ ounces) King Arthur bread flour
- 1 tablespoon sugar
- ¼ teaspoon instant or rapid-rise yeast
- 1¼ cups plus 2 tablespoons ice water (11 ounces)
- 1 tablespoon vegetable oil, plus extra for counter
- 1½ teaspoons salt

Sauce
- 1 (14-ounce) can whole peeled tomatoes, drained with juice reserved
- 2 tablespoons extra-virgin olive oil
- 2 teaspoons minced fresh oregano
- ½ teaspoon sugar, plus extra for seasoning Salt
- ¼ teaspoon red pepper flakes

Pizza
- ½ cup plus 1 tablespoon extra-virgin olive oil, plus extra for drizzling
- 3 ounces Parmesan cheese, grated (1½ cups)
- 8 ounces fresh whole-milk mozzarella cheese, torn into bite-size pieces (2 cups)
- 3 tablespoons shredded fresh basil Coarse sea salt

To Avoid a Hot Spot, Make a Ring

Though it sounds counterintuitive, a conventional single-level fire with the coals spread across the grill causes the crust to burn at the center. This is because the pizza is not just subjected to heat from below; the curved kettle walls also reflect the heat inward, creating a hot spot at the center of the grill. For more even heat, we arrange the coals in a ring, which cooks the center of the pizza through reflected heat only.

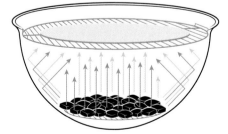

HOTTER AT THE CENTER
A single-level fire concentrates both direct and indirect heat in the center of the grill, burning the pizza.

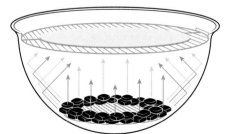

EVEN ALL OVER
A ring of coals heats the grill center through reflected heat, avoiding the creation of a hot spot.

Because grilled pizza cooks exclusively from the bottom up and browns only on the side in contact with the grate, we pargrill the dough on both sides before applying toppings.

1. FOR THE DOUGH: Process flour, sugar, and yeast in food processor until combined, about 2 seconds. With processor running, slowly add ice water; process until dough is just combined and no dry flour remains, about 10 seconds. Let dough stand for 10 minutes.

2. Add oil and salt to dough and process until dough forms satiny, sticky ball that clears sides of bowl, 30 to 60 seconds. Transfer dough to lightly oiled counter and knead until smooth, about 1 minute. Divide dough into 3 equal pieces (about 9⅓ ounces each). Shape each piece into tight ball, transfer to well-oiled baking sheet (alternatively, place dough balls in individual well-oiled bowls), and coat top of each ball lightly with oil. Cover tightly with plastic wrap (taking care not to compress dough) and refrigerate for at least 24 hours or up to 3 days.

3. FOR THE SAUCE: Pulse tomatoes in food processor until finely chopped, 12 to 15 pulses. Transfer to medium bowl and stir in reserved juice, oil, oregano, sugar, ½ teaspoon salt, and pepper flakes. Season with extra sugar and salt to taste, cover, and refrigerate until ready to use.

4. One hour before cooking pizza, remove dough from refrigerator and let stand at room temperature.

5A. FOR A CHARCOAL GRILL: Open bottom vent halfway. Light large chimney starter three-quarters filled with charcoal briquettes (4½ quarts). When top coals are partially covered with ash, pour into ring around perimeter of grill, leaving 8-inch clearing in center. Set cooking grate in place, cover, and open lid vent halfway. Heat grill

until hot, about 5 minutes.

5B. FOR A GAS GRILL: Turn all burners to high, cover, and heat grill until hot, about 15 minutes. Leave all burners on high.

6. While grill is heating, transfer sauce to small saucepan and bring to simmer over medium heat. Cover and keep warm.

7. FOR THE PIZZA: Clean and oil cooking grate. Pour ¼ cup oil onto center of rimmed baking sheet. Transfer 1 dough round to sheet and coat both sides of dough with oil. Using your fingertips and palms, gently press and stretch dough toward edges of sheet to form rough 16 by 12-inch oval of even thickness. Using both your hands, lift dough and carefully transfer to grill. (When transferring dough from sheet to grill, it will droop slightly to form half-moon or snowshoe shape.) Cook (over clearing if using charcoal; covered if using gas) until grill marks form, 2 to 3 minutes. Using tongs and spatula, carefully peel dough from grate, then rotate dough 90 degrees and continue to cook (covered if using gas) until second set of grill marks appears, 2 to 3 minutes longer. Flip dough and cook (covered if using gas) until second side of dough is lightly charred in spots, 2 to 3 minutes. Using tongs or pizza peel, transfer crust to cutting board, inverting so side that was grilled first is facing down. Repeat with remaining 2 dough rounds, adding 1 tablespoon oil to sheet for each round and keeping grill cover closed when not in use to retain heat.

8. Drizzle top of 1 crust with 1 tablespoon oil. Sprinkle one-third of Parmesan evenly over surface. Arrange one-third of mozzarella pieces, evenly spaced, on surface of pizza. Dollop one-third of sauce in evenly spaced 1-tablespoon mounds over surface of pizza. Using pizza peel or overturned rimmed baking sheet, transfer pizza to grill; cover and cook until bottom is well browned and mozzarella is melted, 3 to 5 minutes, checking bottom and turning frequently to prevent burning. Transfer pizza to cutting board, sprinkle with 1 tablespoon basil, drizzle lightly with extra oil, and season with salt to taste. Cut into wedges and serve. Repeat with remaining 2 crusts.

Toppings with a Light Touch

Because grills don't heat the top of a pizza, and because the ultrathin crust can't support much weight beyond sauce and cheese, it's important to choose lightweight toppings that require little to no cooking—and to not go overboard. The following can be scattered over the pies once they come off the grill.

- baby arugula or spinach (lightly dressed with lemon juice, olive oil, salt, and cracked pepper)
- paper-thin slices of prosciutto
- pickled hot pepper rings
- roasted red peppers, sliced into strips
- thin-sliced scallion or onion
- chopped or torn fresh herbs
- red pepper flakes

Be Prepared!

Grilled pizza cooks quickly and is best eaten right away, so be sure to have everything you'll need at the ready:

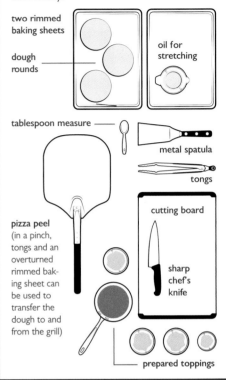

two rimmed baking sheets

dough rounds

oil for stretching

tablespoon measure

metal spatula

tongs

pizza peel (in a pinch, tongs and an overturned rimmed baking sheet can be used to transfer the dough to and from the grill)

cutting board

sharp chef's knife

prepared toppings

DON'T SKIMP ON THE OIL

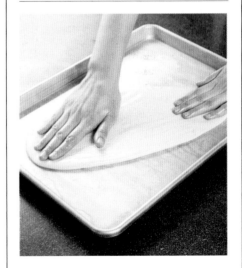

Stretching the dough in a generous amount of olive oil not only prevents it from sticking to your hands and to the cooking grate but also crisps the exterior without rendering it greasy.

▶ **Watch Dough Become Pizza**
A step-by-step video is available at CooksIllustrated.com/aug16

The Best Homemade Frozen Yogurt

In most homemade fro yo, tangy taste and a creamy, smooth texture are mutually exclusive. We wanted both qualities in the same scoop.

> BY DAN SOUZA <

When I set out to make frozen yogurt for the first time, I thought the task would be simple. Unlike ice cream recipes, which typically call for cooking (and then cooling) a finicky custard for a base, most of the fro yo recipes I came across required nothing more than throwing yogurt, sugar, and maybe a few flavorings into an ice cream maker and churning. But these recipes were hugely disappointing: The fro yo turned out icy and rock-hard. I realized that this was partly because frozen yogurt doesn't have the advantage of yolks or cream, both of which give ice cream proportionally more fat and less water. Fat makes ice cream taste creamier and smoother, while less water in the base means there's less of it to form ice crystals, leading to a more velvety, scoopable texture. I found a few frozen yogurt recipes that tried to improve texture by adding cream to the mix. But while these versions did turn out less icy, their tangy yogurt flavor had been muted.

For me, this was a nonstarter. I wanted my frozen yogurt to put the fresh-tasting tartness of yogurt front and center. The challenge was to figure out how to do that and achieve a dense, creamy-smooth texture at the same time.

For tangy flavor that's front and center, we keep the sweetness in check, and we use only yogurt (no cream, like some recipes call for).

Strain and Drain

The obvious thing was to try to eliminate some water from the yogurt. In my initial tests, I had been using regular whole-milk yogurt (plain was a must, since I wanted to be able to control flavorings and sweetness myself). What if I switched to Greek yogurt, which has had much of the liquid whey strained out? When my first test produced an oddly crumbly texture, I switched to another brand and then another—but they all produced unappealing results. (To learn why, see "For Creamier Fro Yo, Forgo Greek Yogurt").

So I considered another option: straining regular yogurt. I spooned a quart of yogurt into a fine-mesh

▶ **See the Science At Work**
A step-by-step video is available at CooksIllustrated.com/aug16

strainer lined with cheesecloth and set over a bowl and left it overnight. By the following morning, a generous amount of whey had drained into the bowl. The fro yo I made with this yogurt was much smoother; I knew this step was a must.

Inverting the Problem

The next ingredient to go under my microscope was sugar. Just as in ice cream (and sorbet for that matter), sugar doesn't serve as a mere sweetener in frozen yogurt. It also affects the texture. Once dissolved, sugar depresses the freezing point of water, which means the more you use, the more water in the mix will stay in liquid form after churning. That translates not only to fewer ice crystals but also to a softer, more scoopable product straight from the freezer. But balance would be key—I didn't want to make it so sweet that the yogurt's flavor was overshadowed. I found that I could go up to a full cup of sugar per quart before the yogurt turned too sweet.

I also knew from my ice cream testing that there were other sweeteners worth considering beyond the granulated stuff. One secret to the velvety texture of an ice cream recipe I'd developed a few years back was swapping out some of the granulated sugar for corn syrup. This sweetener contains starch chains that keep water molecules from joining up and forming large ice crystals. When I tried it in my frozen yogurt, it worked pretty well at minimizing iciness, but the yogurt's flavor seemed muted. A little research informed me why: Those starch chains trap flavor molecules. This wasn't a problem in tame vanilla ice cream, but in tart frozen yogurt, the dulling effect was clear.

My next thought was to try incorporating a source of invert sugar, which is better than granulated sugar at depressing the freezing point of water. Why? Unlike granulated sugar, which is made up of larger sucrose molecules, invert sugar is made up of two smaller molecules, glucose and fructose. Freezing-point depression is directly related to the number of molecules dissolved in the water. So a tablespoon of invert sugar provides twice as many sugar molecules and roughly twice as much freezing-point depression as a tablespoon of granulated sugar. Supermarket options for invert sugar include honey and agave syrup, but each has a distinct flavor that I didn't want in my frozen yogurt. Luckily, I knew of another option: Lyle's Golden Syrup. While only half invert sugar (the other half is sucrose), Lyle's was good enough

A Soft Touch

One key to the creamy texture of our frozen yogurt is Lyle's Golden Syrup, a British pantry staple that is also readily available in American markets. Its lightly caramelized flavor distinguishes it from honey, maple syrup, and even corn syrup. The Brits use it to sweeten baked goods or drizzle it over pancakes or porridge. So what's it doing in our fro yo? As a partial invert sugar, Lyle's contains small fructose and glucose molecules that can interfere with ice crystal formation more readily than the larger sucrose molecules in table sugar can. With Lyle's in the mix, more water stays in liquid form, and that translates to a less icy, more scoopable frozen yogurt.

LYLE'S GOLDEN SYRUP

For Creamier Fro Yo, Forgo Greek Yogurt

Making creamy, smooth frozen yogurt is largely about limiting water, since less water translates to fewer large ice crystals. Thus we were surprised when frozen yogurt made with Greek-style yogurt, which has been strained of excess liquid, churned up crumbly and chalky. The reason for these results is twofold: First, Greek-style yogurt has a particularly high protein content (in lab tests, we found that it had almost twice as much protein as regular yogurt we strained ourselves). Second, it's often strained by centrifuge, which can damage these proteins and increase the likelihood of a chalky texture. So while it may seem like a timesaver to reach for Greek when making frozen yogurt, you'll pay for that convenience in texture. That's why we take the time to strain regular yogurt for the creamiest, smoothest results.

FASTER BUT FLAWED
Greek yogurt gave us chalky, crumbly frozen yogurt.

to work magic. Just 3 tablespoons (along with ¾ cup of granulated sugar) noticeably reduced the iciness. This was impressively creamy frozen yogurt. But I suspected I could do better.

Getting Trapped
Many manufacturers add pectin, gums, or modified starches to get smoother, less icy results. These ingredients essentially trap water, which will minimize large water droplets—and thus large ice crystal formation. Pectin and gelatin seemed most promising, but the citric acid in pectin made the frozen yogurt taste almost fruity. Gelatin, however, was perfect. I needed a liquid to bloom it in, so I reserved ½ cup of whey when I drained the yogurt and microwaved the whey with the gelatin to quickly dissolve the gelatin before incorporating the mixture into my base. Just 1 teaspoon of gelatin gave me the smoothest, creamiest frozen yogurt yet.

There were just a few more details to attend to. Quickly freezing the base was key, since faster freezing, along with agitation, promotes the formation of smaller ice crystals. I refrigerated my base until it registered 40 degrees or less before churning. And as with my ice cream recipe, in addition to churning until it looked like "thick soft-serve," I also made sure it registered 21 degrees (the temperature at which roughly 50 percent of the water has frozen) for the most consistent results.

My frozen yogurt took some time, but it was mostly hands-off. And best of all, it boasted a wonderfully creamy, smooth texture as well as the distinctively tangy, fresh flavor of its namesake ingredient.

FROZEN YOGURT
MAKES ABOUT 1 QUART

This recipe requires draining the yogurt for 8 to 12 hours. We prefer the flavor and texture that Lyle's Golden Syrup lends this frozen yogurt, but if you can't find it, you can substitute light corn syrup. Any brand of whole-milk yogurt will work in this recipe. You can substitute low-fat yogurt for whole-milk yogurt, but the results will be less creamy and flavorful.

1	quart plain whole-milk yogurt
1	teaspoon unflavored gelatin
¾	cup sugar
3	tablespoons Lyle's Golden Syrup
⅛	teaspoon salt

1. Line colander or fine-mesh strainer with triple layer of cheesecloth and place over large bowl or measuring cup. Place yogurt in colander, cover with plastic wrap (plastic should not touch yogurt), and refrigerate until 1¼ cups whey have drained from yogurt, at least 8 hours or up to 12 hours. (If more than 1¼ cups whey drains from yogurt, simply stir extra back into yogurt.)

2. Discard ¾ cup drained whey. Sprinkle gelatin over remaining ½ cup whey in bowl and let sit until gelatin softens, about 5 minutes. Microwave until mixture is bubbling around edges and gelatin dissolves, about 30 seconds. Let cool for 5 minutes. In large bowl, whisk sugar, syrup, salt, drained yogurt, and cooled whey-gelatin mixture until sugar is completely dissolved. Cover and refrigerate (or place bowl over ice bath) until yogurt mixture registers 40 degrees or less.

3. Churn yogurt mixture in ice cream maker until mixture resembles thick soft-serve frozen yogurt and registers about 21 degrees, 25 to 35 minutes. Transfer frozen yogurt to airtight container and freeze until firm, at least 2 hours. Serve. (Frozen yogurt can be stored for up to 5 days.)

GINGER FROZEN YOGURT

Stir 1 tablespoon grated fresh ginger and 1 teaspoon ground ginger into whey-gelatin mixture as soon as it is removed from microwave. After mixture has cooled for 5 minutes, strain through fine-mesh strainer, pressing on solids to extract all liquid. Proceed with recipe as directed.

ORANGE FROZEN YOGURT

Substitute ½ cup orange juice for ½ cup whey in step 2. Stir ½ teaspoon grated orange zest into orange juice–gelatin mixture as soon as it is removed from microwave.

STRAWBERRY FROZEN YOGURT

Substitute ¾ cup strawberry puree for ½ cup whey in step 2.

What's the Best Digital Scale?

No matter what you're cooking or baking, weighing the ingredients helps guarantee perfect results. But only if your scale is accurate and easy to use.

⇒ BY KATE SHANNON ⇐

A digital scale is a game changer in the kitchen. A scale is critical for baking recipes, where measuring dry ingredients by weight is the only way to guarantee accuracy. We've proven this in tests where we've repeatedly measured a cup of flour by volume, using a "dip and sweep" method, and found that there can be up to a 20 percent difference in the weight—a variance that can mean the difference between a cake that's squat and dense and one that's fluffy and tender.

Scales have many applications in cooking, too. Using one to portion burgers, for example, means no more guessing if the patties are the same size and will thus cook at the same rate. They can even make cooking and cleanup more efficient, thanks to the help of the "tare" function; with the push of this button, you can reset the displayed weight on the scale to zero, allowing you to skip the fussy "dip and sweep" method (for more information, see "On a Tare").

For years, we've relied on the OXO Good Grips 11 lb Food Scale with Pull Out Display ($49.95), but many new (and some cheaper) models have since hit the market, so we decided to take another look. We bought 10 scales, priced from $11.79 to $67.27, with maximum capacities between 9 and 15 pounds. We tested them for accuracy and also assessed their design, countertop stability, and how easy they were to clean and store.

Measuring Pros and Cons

The good news: All of the scales were acceptably accurate. When we weighed calibrated lab weights on multiple copies of each model, most gave the exact same reading every time. Only two of them consistently displayed fluctuating readings, and even those were just a few grams off the mark. (Note that

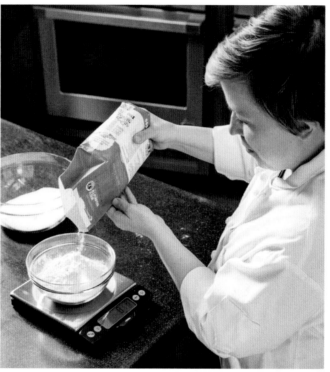
One important feature of a digital scale? A large digital display window.

◐ See Why It Won
We work through all the details at CooksIllustrated.com/aug16.

Bonus Web-Only Exclusive: To read about our testing of scales that communicate with smartphones, go to CooksIllustrated.com/aug16.

we tested only consumer-grade scales, which are not certified by the National Conference on Weights and Measures, as more-expensive commercial-grade scales are too pricey for the home cook.)

The bad news was that half the scales were either so unintuitive to operate or so hard to read that we can't recommend them. The first flaw became obvious when we timed testers as they weighed 5 ounces of flour on each model and watched them fumble around for a switch or button to change the unit of measurement from grams to ounces. On one of the losing models, this was a tiny toggle on the underside of the scale underneath the battery cover, which we only found once we referred to the owner's manual. On another, you must gently press the "on/off" button as the scale powers up—and if you miss that brief window, you have to turn it off and start all over. Start to finish, it took roughly twice as long to complete the task on these models as it did on our top-rated scales.

Legibility was problematic on models with tiny, hard-to-read, or obscurely labeled buttons but was even more of an issue on scales where the control panel was flush with the platform rather than set into a separate part of the scale body. No matter

how big and crisp the display was on these scales, larger bowls cast a shadow over, or completely blocked, the screen, forcing us to bend down to peer underneath or nudge the bowl backward until it threatened to fall off the back end of the platform. Only the OXO truly excelled in this test: Its display bar can be pulled out 4 inches from the platform, ensuring that the screen is visible under even the biggest, bulkiest items.

When it came to countertop stability, lighter-weight (under 1 pound) scales with feet frequently teetered back and forth or slid around on the counter. In general, squat scales with smooth bottoms stayed put more reliably; plus, they were easier to store.

Cleanup was a finicky job for a few models, which trapped flour—or, worse, water that could seep in and damage the internal hardware—in their crevices. In this evaluation, we preferred two models that featured removable platforms, which allowed us to scrub them without risking water damage.

Worth Their Weight

By the end of testing, we'd found three scales that impressed us with accuracy; intuitive design; responsive, clearly labeled buttons positioned on an easily visible control panel; and slim frames that were easy to slip into a drawer or cabinet. The best of these, our previous champ from OXO, also boasted great stability, a bright backlight, and a removable platform that made cleanup a snap. But if its nearly $50 price tag is too steep, consider our Best Buy from Ozeri ($11.79). Though it feels a bit lightweight and lacks the winner's removable platform, its performance was otherwise stellar.

On a Tare

When measuring multiple ingredients that will be combined, such as the dry mix for baked goods, using a digital scale's tare button is more accurate than the "dip and sweep" method and reduces the number of dirty dishes. Set one bowl on the scale for measuring each ingredient and a larger one next to the scale for compiling the measured ingredients, and then press the tare button to reset the scale to zero. Add the ingredient to the bowl on the scale until it registers the correct amount, and then transfer the measured item to the larger bowl. Repeat with the now-empty bowl and another item.

TESTING DIGITAL KITCHEN SCALES

ACCURACY

We tested three units of each model, weighing 30-, 200-, and 500-gram lab-calibrated weights 10 times on each unit, at the beginning and end of testing. We preferred scales that gave consistently accurate readings; models that routinely varied by more than 2 grams lost points.

EASE OF USE

We timed how long it took to turn on the scales, switch from grams to ounces, and measure 5 ounces of flour. Several test cooks also subjected top-performing models to a week of daily use. The best models had intuitive controls that were easy to access.

LEGIBILITY

We preferred digital displays with sharp color contrast or a backlight option, big digits, and large screens. Scales lost points if a 5-quart mixing bowl blocked or obscured the screen.

DURABILITY

We dropped each model onto the counter from a height of 2 inches, checking to see if any pieces fell off or if the scales became damaged.

CLEANUP

We stained the platforms with a measured amount of yellow mustard, tomato paste, and canola oil; after 36 hours, we washed them by hand. The best models had removable platforms that we could wipe off or scrub. Scales that trapped water and food residue lost points.

We tested 10 digital kitchen scales, priced from $11.79 to $67.27, with maximum capacities between 9 and 15 pounds. All models display weights in at least two units of measurement, which we've listed below. "Ounces" indicates a display that can show a total weight in ounces, while "pounds/ounces" indicates a display that will show pounds and ounces for items heavier than 16 ounces. "Grams" indicates a display that can show a total weight in grams, while "kilograms/grams" indicates a display that will show kilograms and grams for items heavier than 1,000 grams. Prices shown were paid online. Models appear below in order of preference.

HIGHLY RECOMMENDED

	CRITERIA		TESTERS' COMMENTS

OXO Good Grips 11 lb Food Scale with Pull Out Display
MODEL: 1130800 PRICE: $49.95
MAXIMUM WEIGHT: 11 lb
UNITS DISPLAYED: Pounds/ounces, kilograms/grams

ACCURACY	★★★
EASE OF USE	★★★
LEGIBILITY	★★★
DURABILITY	★★★
CLEANUP	★★★

Our longtime favorite scale has it all: consistent accuracy; a clear digital display (which pulls out from the frame and includes a backlight); responsive, clearly labeled, accessible buttons; a removable platform that makes cleanup a breeze; and a sturdy, slim body that stores easily. It's a pricier package but worth the investment.

POLDER Easy Read Digital Kitchen Scale
MODEL: KSC-310-28 PRICE: $27.98
MAXIMUM WEIGHT: 11 lb
UNITS DISPLAYED: Pounds/ounces, kilograms/grams

ACCURACY	★★★
EASE OF USE	★★★
LEGIBILITY	★★★
DURABILITY	★★★
CLEANUP	★★½

Like the OXO, this model is accurate, intuitive, and easy to read, thanks to its offset digital screen. Our only complaint is that the platform isn't removable, so we had to wash it slowly and carefully to avoid getting the interior mechanism wet.

OZERI Pronto Digital Multifunction Kitchen and Food Scale
MODEL: ZK14 PRICE: $11.79
MAXIMUM WEIGHT: 11 lb
UNITS DISPLAYED: Ounces, pounds/ounces, grams

BEST BUY

ACCURACY	★★★
EASE OF USE	★★½
LEGIBILITY	★★★
DURABILITY	★★★
CLEANUP	★★½

Though its relatively lightweight frame feels flimsier than those of our top performers and it lacks a removable platform, this simple scale is impressive for the money. It's accurate and easy to use, with a digital screen that's bright and visible even when weighing large items.

RECOMMENDED

SALTER Aquatronic Glass Electronic Kitchen Scale
MODEL: 3003BDSS PRICE: $36.23
MAXIMUM WEIGHT: 11 lb
UNITS DISPLAYED: Pounds/ounces, kilograms/grams

ACCURACY	★★½
EASE OF USE	★★★
LEGIBILITY	★★★
DURABILITY	★★
CLEANUP	★★½

Its accuracy consistently fluctuated a few grams—not a deal breaker, but it was enough to set this sleek scale apart from the top performers. Clearly marked buttons were easily accessible, and the digital display was crisp. Small drops of water became trapped under the glass platform during cleaning.

RECOMMENDED WITH RESERVATIONS

ESCALI Alimento Digital Scale
MODEL: 136DK PRICE: $67.27
MAXIMUM WEIGHT: 13 lb
UNITS DISPLAYED: Ounces, pounds/ounces, grams

ACCURACY	★★★
EASE OF USE	★½
LEGIBILITY	★★
DURABILITY	★★★
CLEANUP	★★★

The perks of this scale include spot-on accuracy, clearly marked buttons, a bright backlight, and a removable platform for easy cleanup. But a few design flaws detract from its appeal: It's bulky but lightweight, making it a challenge to store and hold steady, and taller testers found the sharp angle of its screen difficult to read from above.

NOT RECOMMENDED

ESCALI Arti Glass Kitchen Scale	AMERICAN WEIGH EDGE-5K Digital Kitchen Scale	AMERICAN WEIGH CITRON-5K Digital Kitchen Scale	SOEHNLE Page Evolution	POLDER Slimmer Stainless Digital Kitchen Scale
MODEL: 157	MODEL: EDGE-5K	MODEL: CITRON-5K	MODEL: 66189	MODEL: KSC-345-95
PRICE $32.38	PRICE: $18.34	PRICE: $14.99	PRICE: $35.06	PRICE: $35.76
MAXIMUM WEIGHT: 15 lb	MAXIMUM WEIGHT: 11 lb	MAXIMUM WEIGHT: 11 lb	MAXIMUM WEIGHT: 9 lb	MAXIMUM WEIGHT: 11 lb
UNITS DISPLAYED: Ounces, pounds/ounces, grams	UNITS DISPLAYED: Pounds/ounces, grams	UNITS DISPLAYED: Pounds/ounces, grams	UNITS DISPLAYED: Pounds/ounces, grams	UNITS DISPLAYED: Pounds/ounces, grams
ACCURACY ★★★	ACCURACY ★★★	ACCURACY ★★★	ACCURACY ★★½	ACCURACY ★★★
EASE OF USE ★	EASE OF USE ★	EASE OF USE ★	EASE OF USE 0	EASE OF USE 0
LEGIBILITY ★★	LEGIBILITY ★★	LEGIBILITY ★	LEGIBILITY ★★½	LEGIBILITY ★★★
DURABILITY ★★★	DURABILITY ★★★	DURABILITY ★★★	DURABILITY ★★★	DURABILITY ★★★
CLEANUP ★★★	CLEANUP ★★★	CLEANUP ★★★	CLEANUP ★★★	CLEANUP ★½

The Great Parm Debate

For a cheese with all the nutty, savory flavor and crumbly, crystalline texture of the original, do the cows really have to eat Italian grass?

⇒ BY HANNAH CROWLEY ⇐

There's a heated debate raging in the cheese world. On one side, Parmigiano-Reggiano, the so-called king of cheese. Complex, with fruity, nutty, savory notes; a dry, crumbly texture; and a crystalline crunch, this cheese has been made in precisely the same way in northern Italy for the past 800 years. Its adversary? Imitators like Parmesan, Parmezan, Regginito—takes on the classic made under varying regulations in the United States and around the world. (We'll refer to this group of cheeses simply as "Parmesan" from here on out.) Parmigiano-Reggiano producers want clearer labeling to call out these imitators. The European Union and the United States are currently debating how to label cheese as part of a massive trade agreement.

But nomenclature aside, how's the cheese? Do the imitators actually rival the real thing, or are their knockoff names where the similarity ends? To find out, we chose the top seven nationally available supermarket products—five domestic Parmesans and two certified Parmigiano-Reggianos from Italy—priced from $5.38 to $19.99 per pound. We asked 21 tasters to evaluate them plain at room temperature and cooked in polenta. We sent samples of each cheese to an independent laboratory for evaluation.

Even before tasters took a bite, differences among the cheeses were noticeable. On the whole, domestic products were smoother, almost waxy in appearance; the two Parmigiano-Reggianos appeared drier and had visible white flecks of crystallization. In the plain tasting, tasters in general panned the domestics, criticizing them for being rubbery and bland. The two Parmigiano-Reggianos, on the other hand, earned praise for being dry and crumbly, with flavor that was "robust," "nutty," and "clear and bright." While the textural differences didn't come out as clearly in the polenta tasting, the preference for the imports held up. But when we took a closer look at the results, we noticed that one domestic cheese fared impressively well, earning praise for both its flavor and texture. It even had those crystalline flecks.

So what are these producers doing differently? For an explanation, we looked into how the cheeses are made, starting with the cows and what they eat.

From Cow to Wheel

In the highly sanctioned world of Parmigiano-Reggiano, cows graze in pastures; their diet must consist of at least 75 percent local grass. Here in the United States, the U.S. Food and Drug Administration (FDA) doesn't mandate diet, and cows typically aren't pastured; manufacturers reported using various feeds, including hay, corn, soybeans, and grains.

According to Dean Sommer, cheese and food technologist at the University of Wisconsin's Center for Dairy Research, diet has a major effect on the flavor of the cheese. Pastured cows that feed mostly on fresh grass and various other naturally growing plants tend to have more complexly flavored milk than those with grain-based diets.

Another factor: raw versus pasteurized milk. In Italy, Parmigiano-Reggiano is always made from raw milk. In the States, the milk is typically pasteurized first. This step kills off potentially dangerous organisms and yields a more consistent product. The downside? The heating process also kills off flavorful microorganisms.

Fat content plays a role as well. Before the milk is made into cheese, some of the milk fat is skimmed off, but that amount can vary. Our lab reports showed that the Italian cheeses contain more fat than the domestics. Fat equals flavor, and our tasters enthusiastically approved of cheeses that had more of it.

To make the cheese, milk is warmed and combined with a starter culture to kick off the curdling process. Then rennet (enzymes that further facilitate curd formation) goes in. The mixture is stirred to evaporate some moisture, the curds are formed into wheels, and the wheels go into salt baths for preservation and flavor. There's one key difference in this stage: Domestic wheels range in size from 20 to 24 pounds, while wheels of Parmigiano-Reggiano weigh at least 66 pounds. Domestic producers make smaller wheels for various reasons, including that

they're easier to work with, age faster, and result in a smoother cheese that's easier to slice into uniform wedges. Smaller wheels also pull in salt faster than larger ones because they have more exposed surface area. Our lab results confirmed this: The domestic cheeses had an average of 40 percent more sodium than the Italian cheeses. We typically prefer saltier products, but in this case manufacturers seem to be using the salt to flavor otherwise very bland cheeses—which would explain why tasters found that the domestic cheeses on the whole had simple savory notes at best.

See the Difference

Lengthy aging—two years on average—helps give Italian Parmigiano-Reggiano its complex flavor and dry, crumbly texture. When we put domestic Parms, which are typically aged for less than half that time, alongside two imports for our tasting, it wasn't hard for our panel to pick out the impostors on sight.

WAXY WANNABE
A telltale smooth, waxy texture identified last-place Belgioioso as a domestic Parm.

CRUMBLY CHAMP
Our imported winner, from Boar's Head, boasts Italian Parm's trademark crystalline flecks and dry texture.

Aged to Perfection

The aging step affects both flavor and texture. Once the wheels come out of the salt bath, they're set on racks in climate-controlled rooms to age. As the cheese sits, lactic acid forms, and the acid causes proteins in the cheese to squeeze together, which in turn forces out moisture. Parmigiano-Reggianos are required to age for at least 12 months, though most are left for 24. Meanwhile, the FDA mandates a minimum of just 10 months for Parmesan. Thus, the domestic cheeses tended to be rubbery, while the imports were dry and crumbly. Lab results backed this up, showing that the domestic cheeses had an average of 34.61 percent moisture, while the imports averaged 30.11 percent. Interestingly, according to the FDA, domestic Parmesans must contain no more than 32 percent moisture, yet our lab results showed three products above that limit, at 35.62, 36.49, and 37.99 percent—a significant difference, according to industry experts. These higher levels could be attributed to natural variation among batches, attempts to eke out a bit more product, a bid to boost flavor since more moisture can make flavor develop faster early in the process, or a goal of making a cheese that melts and grates better.

To that point, we discovered that the cheese with the highest moisture content in the lineup—Sargento Hard Grating Parmesan—is a different type of cheese altogether under FDA regulations. Cheeses categorized as "hard-grating" require less aging and allow for more moisture. It's no surprise that this product fell near the bottom of our rankings.

As the cheese ages, enzymes from the starter culture and rennet continue to break down the cheese at the molecular level. Complex fats are broken down into individual free fatty acids, which give the cheese a sharp flavor. They also convert into aromatic compounds called esters when they combine with naturally present alcohols, contributing a layer of fruitiness. The enzymes break down proteins in the cheese into shorter peptides and individual amino acids, both of which give the cheese its appealing nuttiness. Sommer called this process "a giant Scrabble game in reverse." The more time allowed for these reactions to occur, the more flavor there will be, so not surprisingly, tasters liked older cheeses. At 24 months, our winner was the oldest in the lineup.

These enzymatic reactions are also responsible for those crunchy, appealing crystals. Over time, some of the peptides continue to break down into individual amino acids. Two amino acids, tyrosine and leucine, become visible as white crystals and larger white pearls, respectively. The younger domestic cheeses had few, if any, noticeable crystals or pearls, while the two older Parmigiano-Reggianos had constellations of them.

Could It Be a Contender?

Considering the whole picture, all the way from feed to aging, it's clear why so many domestics don't measure up. But what about that one that came close? Our third-place cheese, Sarvecchio, is made in Wisconsin and aged for at least 20 months, twice as long as its domestic counterparts. Its manufacturer also reported the most varied feed. It didn't quite have the depth the Parmigiano-Reggianos had—it's aged four months less than our winner, doesn't have the same diet regulations, and is made with pasteurized milk—but we think it deserves a nod as a good domestic option. If domestic producers—or producers anywhere—were to follow more of the Parmigiano-Reggiano specifications, we think they could make a comparable cheese.

But for now, for that classic, craggy, crystalline cheese with elegant depth, you still have to look to a roughly 8,500-square-mile patch of land in northern Italy. You'll pay a higher price for the quality exacted by Parmigiano-Reggiano regulations—our winner costs $19.99 a pound, while most domestic Parms were half that. But because of its fuller flavor, you can use it more sparingly. Our winner is sold by Boar's Head, an American company that purchases Parmigiano-Reggiano and sells it under its name. Tasters were unanimous, voting Boar's Head Parmigiano-Reggiano the best supermarket Parmesan of all the products we sampled.

TASTING SUPERMARKET PARMESAN

Twenty-one editors and cooks at America's Test Kitchen sampled each cheese plain (at room temperature) and stirred into our recipe for Creamy Parmesan Polenta; scores were averaged, and the cheeses are listed below in order of preference. Details on age, origin, pasteurization, and cow diet were obtained from manufacturers and the *Journal of the European Union's Council Regulation on "Parmigiano-Reggiano."* Nutritional data was analyzed by an independent laboratory and is reported per 100 grams of cheese. Prices were paid in Boston-area supermarkets.

RECOMMENDED | COMMENTS

BOAR'S HEAD Parmigiano-Reggiano

PRICE: $19.99 per lb ($1.25 per oz)
COW DIET: Local grass
MOISTURE: 31.48%
ORIGIN: Italy
MILK: Raw
AGE: 24 months
SODIUM: 674.8 mg
FAT: 31.06 g

This "robust" Parmigiano-Reggiano was the most aged in our lineup. It earned raves from tasters, who pronounced it "intensely flavorful," "strong," and "nutty." "Piquant," with notes of fruit and umami, it was "very dry" with a delightfully crystalline texture. In a word: "Delicious!"

IL VILLAGGIO Parmigiano-Reggiano 18 Month

PRICE: $19.99 per lb ($1.25 per oz)
COW DIET: Local grass
MOISTURE: 28.74%
ORIGIN: Italy
MILK: Raw
AGE: 18 months
SODIUM: 544.4 mg
FAT: 30.88 g

Tasters found this Parmigiano-Reggiano to be "more assertive" than its domestic counterparts, with an "authentic tang and nuttiness." It was "robust" and "pungent," with "a little funk" that spoke of both "tropical fruits" and "savory mushrooms." It was "dry and crumbly," with a "nice crystal structure."

SARVECCHIO Parmesan

PRICE: $17.99 per lb ($1.12 per oz)
COW DIET: Alfalfa hay, grass hay, corn silage, soybeans
ORIGIN: Wisconsin
AGE: At least 20 months
MOISTURE: 31.68%
FAT: 28.85 g
MILK: Pasteurized
SODIUM: 948.6 mg

This was the best domestic Parmesan we sampled, likely because it's aged twice as long as the four other American cheeses in our lineup. Tasters called it "nutty" and "pleasant," with a "sweet start" and hints of "caramel" and "butterscotch." The structure was "crumbly," though "slightly waxy," with "a little crystal crunch."

RECOMMENDED WITH RESERVATIONS

DIGIORNO Natural Cheese Wedge Parmesan

PRICE: $11.49 per lb ($0.72 per oz)
COW DIET: Corn, alfalfa, soybeans
ORIGIN: Wisconsin
AGE: 10 months
MOISTURE: 35.62%
MILK: Pasteurized
FAT: 26.39 g
SODIUM: 929.7 mg

Tasters picked up on savory, umami notes in this cheese, "like chicken stock." But it was muted, and in polenta it provided no "clear central cheesy note." Others compared it to gouda, cheddar, or Swiss cheese. Its "creamy," "gummy" texture was "too soft."

STELLA Parmesan Cheese

PRICE: $10.99 per lb ($0.69 per oz)
COW DIET: Proprietary
MOISTURE: 36.49%
ORIGIN: USA
MILK: Proprietary
AGE: At least 10 months
SODIUM: 920.2 mg
FAT: 26.65 g

This cheese was "slightly nutty," "briny," "milky," and "meaty" but "overall bland." In polenta, where it melted readily, it didn't foster any complaints about texture, but tasters noted that it was "soft" and "waxy" when eaten plain. "No crystalline crunch! Disappointing!"

SARGENTO Hard Grating Parmesan

PRICE: $5.38 per lb ($0.34 per oz)
COW DIET: Unknown
MOISTURE: 37.66%
ORIGIN: USA
MILK: Pasteurized
AGE: At least 6 months
SODIUM: 1,173.4 mg
FAT: 25.78 g

This little wedge had a hint of Gruyère-like nuttiness but was otherwise "quite mild," so much so that tasters "hardly knew there was cheese" in the polenta made with 2 cups of it. It was inoffensive but more cheddar-like, "moist" and "creamy," without the "crystalline snap."

BELGIOIOSO Parmesan

PRICE: $9.99 per lb ($0.62 per oz)
COW DIET: Grass and grains
ORIGIN: Wisconsin
AGE: At least 10 months
MOISTURE: 31.60%
MILK: Raw
FAT: 28.21 g
SODIUM: 1,041.0 mg

"Impostor!" declared one taster sampling this younger cheese. It didn't taste bad, but it was denser and softer than a Parmesan should be. Tasters compared it to gouda, cheddar, and mozzarella. It was "mild" with no real tang."

Tasting Almond Butter

In recent years, almond butter has emerged as a popular alternative to peanut butter. To find the best, we rounded up the four top-selling national products (as reported by IRI, a Chicago-based market research firm) and tasted them plain and in cherry-almond smoothies.

Note that while you can buy almond butters that are made solely from almonds that have been roasted and ground, none in that unadulterated style sell well enough to have made our lineup. The top-selling almond butters all add a solid fat (palm oil or hydrogenated vegetable oil) to create the homogeneous, spreadable consistency many consumers like. Three of the four products were labeled "creamy," but only the two winners were totally smooth. According to their ingredient lists, the smooth almond butters were made with blanched and skinned almonds, while at least one of the coarse-textured products was made with skin-on almonds. Our tasters also preferred products with a bit of salt and sugar added to the mix.

Our favorite, Jif Creamy Almond Butter, had a "mild," "clean" almond flavor and a perfectly even, creamy consistency. It included plenty of salt and sugar and was made with blanched almonds. Go to CooksIllustrated.com/aug16 for the complete tasting results. –Miye Bromberg

RECOMMENDED

JIF Creamy Almond Butter

PRICE: $7.99 for 12 oz ($0.67 per oz)

SALT: 110 mg (per 2-tbs serving) SUGAR: 3 g

COMMENTS: Tasters loved its "supercreamy," "velvety" texture. Made with blanched, skinned almonds; sugar; and the largest amount of salt of any product we tasted, this "crowd-pleaser" had a "mild," "fairly sweet," "clean nutty flavor."

KEEP 'EM SEPARATED
Even though it doesn't prolong their life, storing greens separately makes cleaning them easier.

Keeping Root Vegetable Greens Fresh

Although the leafy green tops of beets, turnips, and radishes are sometimes removed at the store, we like to buy these vegetables with their greens still attached since they're great for cooking. (Beet and turnip tops can be cooked like Swiss chard, while peppery radish tops can be cooked like mustard greens.) Some sources recommend removing the greens and storing them separately to extend their life. To test this, we stored samples of each of these vegetables. We left the tops attached to the roots on some, wrapping the bunches in paper towels and sealing them in zipper-lock bags. We refrigerated these alongside batches of greens and roots wrapped and bagged separately. In the end, both sets lasted about the same amount of time. That said, while separating the greens won't extend their life, we'll still do it simply because once they are removed from the root bulbs, it is much easier to sort through the greens to rid them of any beginning-to-rot leaves. –A.J.

Honey That Won't Recrystallize

We've found we can clear up a jar of crystallized honey by putting the opened jar in a saucepan with 1 inch of water, heating the water (and honey) gently over low heat, and then transferring the now-smooth honey to a clean jar—but it's never a lasting fix. Rather than repeatedly perform this trick, we wanted a more permanent solution.

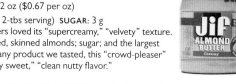

Over time, honey crystallizes when moisture evaporates, causing the individual sugar molecules to interlock and form a lattice. But this can happen only when the sugars are all of the same structure. Corn syrup never crystallizes because it contains fragments of glucose chains.

With that in mind, we heated jars of crystallized honey until the honey was smooth and then evenly divided it between two containers. We stirred a small amount of light corn syrup (2 teaspoons per cup of honey) into one half and left the other untreated. And then we waited. And waited. It took some time to get an answer, but the corn syrup did the trick in the end. The untreated honey started to recrystallize after three months, while the honey mixed with corn syrup stayed fluid and clear even after six months of storage. So the next time your honey crystallizes, heat it with 2 teaspoons of light corn syrup per cup for a long-term fix. –A.J.

SYRUPY FIX
Corn syrup keeps honey from recrystallizing.

Wings: Dark Meat or White?

We recently polled our test cooks, asking whether they thought chicken wings were white or dark meat. The majority said dark meat. A small but vocal minority claimed they are white meat. When asked to compare samples of breast, wing, and thigh meat cooked to 170 degrees (a temperature at which dark meat is still juicy but white meat is dried out), the dark meat camp changed its tune: Tasters unanimously said the wings were closer to the dried-out white meat. Lab analysis backed this up: With an average fat content of 1.1 percent, wings are more similar to breast meat, which registered 0.7 percent fat compared with the 2.5 percent fat of thigh meat. This makes sense since fat lends richness and helps retain juices. The wings' dry texture also indicated a lack of collagen, which breaks down into gelatin and helps lubricate the protein fibers in dark meat. –D.S.

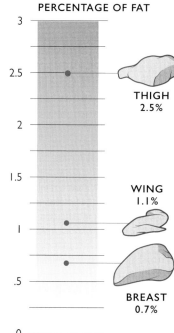

PERCENTAGE OF FAT

THIGH 2.5%

WING 1.1%

BREAST 0.7%

Baking with Rainier Cherries

These spectacular yellow cherries with their distinctive red-pink blush are the stars of the late spring/early summer produce section. But how do they taste, and can they be used as a substitute for Bing cherries in recipes?

Eaten out of hand, tasters found that large, meaty Rainiers were noticeably sweeter, more floral, and less acidic than Bing cherries. Baked into a pie, however, the Rainier cherries made a filling that tasted a bit flat, and their golden color, unexpected in a cherry pie, was off-putting to some. In our recipe for Cherry Clafouti (July/August 2015), where a contrast between creamy custard and bright-tasting fruit is vital, the pale, sweet Rainier cherries also failed to measure up.

Seeing that Rainier cherries can cost 20 to 50 percent more than common sweet cherry varieties like Bing, we recommend reserving them for eating raw, not cooking. –A.G.

Better Fried Tofu

When preparing tofu for frying, we've always blotted it dry and tossed it in cornstarch, which absorbs exuded moisture and ensures a crispy exterior and better browning. Recently we came across another method: Soaking the tofu in a hot-water brine and then letting it drain for 15 minutes before frying. In the end, we got the best results by marrying old and new. We found that using a brine that was four times stronger than what we'd seen published delivered the best seasoning and crust, and tossing the hot-brined tofu in cornstarch after the draining period improved the crust even more. Why does the brine work? Both the heat and the salinity of the water draw moisture out of the surface of the tofu, helping it crisp and brown. The hot water also gradually tightens the proteins at the surface of the tofu, helping keep any remaining moisture inside. Here's how to do it. –S.D.

1. SOAK Dissolve ¼ cup salt in 4 cups boiling water. Slice 14 ounces firm tofu crosswise into 1-inch-thick planks and soak in brine for 15 minutes.

2. DRAIN Transfer planks to quadruple layer of paper towels and top with another 4-ply layer. Press gently, then let sit for 15 minutes.

3. TOSS Cut tofu planks into cubes and toss with cornstarch to lightly coat. Shallow-fry cubes in hot oil for 4 to 5 minutes until golden brown and crispy.

Cooking Broccolini

Broccolini is a hybrid of broccoli and Chinese broccoli that typically costs a bit more than broccoli. Tasters described plain steamed broccolini as having a tender-crisp texture and a sweet, slightly mineral flavor, like a cross between spinach and asparagus. When we substituted broccolini for broccoli in a stir-fry, some tasters felt that its mild flavor was masked by the soy sauce and chili-garlic sauce, but despite this, they preferred it to the same recipe made with broccoli. Tasters also preferred broccolini when we swapped it into a creamy broccoli salad recipe. In both cases, tasters pointed to the comparatively delicate texture and slim, easier-to-eat pieces of stalk along with buds that held together better than the fragile buds of broccoli florets.

To prep broccolini, simply discard the bottom ¼ inch of stalks and cut any stems thicker than ½ inch in half lengthwise. Broccolini, and its slender stalks in particular, will cook more quickly than broccoli; you'll typically need to reduce the cooking time by 1 to 2 minutes. –A.P.

BROCCOLINI
This hybrid has slim stems, delicate flavor, and buds that hold up when cooked.

DIY Corn Tortillas

While supermarket tortillas are convenient, they pale in comparison to home-made versions. Luckily, making them is easier than you might think. The ingredient list is short, the dough is forgiving, and you don't need a tortilla press. –The Editors at America's Test Kitchen

CORN TORTILLAS
MAKES ABOUT TWENTY-TWO 5-INCH TORTILLAS

Pressing the dough between a zipper-lock bag that has been cut open at the sides prevents it from sticking to the pie plate. Distribute your weight evenly over the dough when pressing. Using a clear pie plate makes it easy to see the tortilla. A tortilla press, of course, can also be used. You can find masa harina in the international aisle or near the flour.

- 2 cups (8 ounces) masa harina
- 2 teaspoons vegetable oil
- ¼ teaspoon salt
- 1¼ cups warm water, plus extra as needed

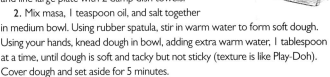
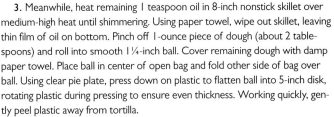

1. Cut sides of sandwich-size zipper-lock bag but leave bottom seam intact so that bag unfolds completely. Place open bag on counter and line large plate with 2 damp dish towels.

2. Mix masa, 1 teaspoon oil, and salt together in medium bowl. Using rubber spatula, stir in warm water to form soft dough. Using your hands, knead dough in bowl, adding extra warm water, 1 tablespoon at a time, until dough is soft and tacky but not sticky (texture is like Play-Doh). Cover dough and set aside for 5 minutes.

3. Meanwhile, heat remaining 1 teaspoon oil in 8-inch nonstick skillet over medium-high heat until shimmering. Using paper towel, wipe out skillet, leaving thin film of oil on bottom. Pinch off 1-ounce piece of dough (about 2 tablespoons) and roll into smooth 1¼-inch ball. Cover remaining dough with damp paper towel. Place ball in center of open bag and fold other side of bag over ball. Using clear pie plate, press down on plastic to flatten ball into 5-inch disk, rotating plastic during pressing to ensure even thickness. Working quickly, gently peel plastic away from tortilla.

4. Carefully place tortilla in skillet and cook, without moving it, until tortilla moves freely when pan is shaken, about 30 seconds. Flip tortilla and cook until edges curl and bottom surface is spotty brown, about 1 minute. Flip tortilla again and continue to cook until bottom surface is spotty brown and puffs up in center, 30 to 60 seconds. Place toasted tortilla between 2 damp dish towels; repeat shaping and cooking with remaining dough. (Cooled tortillas can be transferred to zipper-lock bag and refrigerated for up to 5 days. Reheat before serving.)

Tomato Leaves in the Sauce?

We've read that adding tomato leaves to recipes can boost a dish's fresh tomato flavor. Those of us with tomatoes in our home gardens thought this trick was worth looking into, so we sampled two batches of tomato sauce, one cooked with leaves and one without. Compared with the sweet-savory flavor of a classic tomato sauce, the batch with leaves tasted less sweet but more complex, according to tasters. The leaves added an aroma that one taster described as the "earthy and slightly waxy smell of a tomato plant."

Was this a positive addition? Our tasters' opinions were divided. If you grow tomatoes, we think it's worth a try to decide for yourself. We recommend using ¼ cup of chopped leaves per 8 cups of tomato sauce and tying the leaves in a cheesecloth bag so that they can be easily removed. Because the compound responsible for the aroma is unstable, add the leaves only during the last 10 minutes of cooking. Freezing the sauce will also diminish the leaves' contribution. –L.L.

KITCHEN NOTES

⇒ BY STEVE DUNN, ANDREA GEARY, LAN LAM & DAN SOUZA ⇐

WHAT IS IT?

SPONG MARMALADE SLICER

This kitchen tool dating from around 1900 was made by one of the Victorian era's greatest inventors, James Osborne Spong. The industrial-era Spong Marmalade Slicer was, and continues to be, famous in Britain for slicing citrus wedges for marmalade, and it can also be used for slicing firm vegetables like cucumber and squash. To use it, you push produce through the feed tube with a plunger while simultaneously cranking the handle to spin the five-bladed rotary cutter.

We purchased one online and found that despite its age, the tool worked quite well. Putting too much pressure on the plunger jammed up the works, making the handle tough to crank and mashing rather than slicing produce, but once we lightened up a little, the cutting barrel moved smoothly and produced uniform slices of lemon, orange, and cucumber. The only real flaw was that the countertop clamp tended to loosen, causing the tool to slide off the counter. –S.D.

Quick Clarified Butter

Clarified butter is often served alongside lobster and used for making hollandaise and baklava. Because of its high smoke point, it's also ideal for pan frying. Our typical clarifying method calls for melting the butter; letting it sit to let the milk solids, butterfat, and water separate; skimming off the milk solids; refrigerating the remaining mixture until it solidifies; and then finally popping the solidified fat out of the container (where the water and trace amounts of other dissolved ingredients will remain).

We recently discovered a faster method that calls for bringing melted butter and cornstarch—½ tablespoon per ½ cup butter—to a simmer in a pot with high sides (the mixture will foam). After just 30 seconds, the cornstarch will trap the butter's water as well as any water-soluble proteins in the milk solids; any non-water-soluble proteins will separate out of the liquid. Strain the mixture through a coffee filter–lined fine-mesh strainer to remove the cornstarch and milk solids, and you're left with clarified butter. –L.L.

FROM DINNER ROLLS TO TOP-LOADING BUNS

Moving en Papillote Recipes Outside

Our recipe for Cod Baked in Foil with Leeks and Carrots (March/April 2009) calls for cooking the fish and vegetables in a foil packet, or *en papillote*, for 15 minutes in a 450-degree oven. But during the summer, turning on the oven is often a nonstarter. Could we get the same results on a gas grill?

After preheating the grill for 15 minutes, we left on only the primary burner, adjusting it to maintain the temperature at 450 degrees. We then placed our packets on a baking sheet and placed the sheet on the cooler side of the grill. Just as we'd hoped, the packets' contents cooked through perfectly in the same amount of time called for in the oven version. Further testing confirmed that we could apply this method to any en papillote recipe. Simply heat the grill to the same temperature called for in the oven-based recipe, place the packets on a baking sheet on the cooler side of the grill, and grill for the same amount of time. Note that keeping the packets on the sheet is important: It tempers the direct heat from the cooking grate and minimizes handling. –S.D.

HOW TO CUT UP CHICKEN WINGS

Our recipe for Korean Fried Chicken Wings (page 15) calls for cutting the wings into three parts: drumettes, midsections, and wingtips. Here's how to do it. –A.G.

1. Using your fingertip, locate joint between wingtip and midsection. Place blade of chef's knife on joint, between bones, and using palm of your nonknife hand, press down on blade to cut through skin and tendon, as shown.

2. Find joint between midsection and drumette and repeat process to cut through skin and joint. Discard wingtip.

Top-loading buns, which are good for lobster rolls and hot dogs, are likable because their sides can be toasted. Since they can be hard to find outside New England, we figured out how to make them using our Fluffy Dinner Rolls recipe (January/February 2016). For our dinner roll recipe, go to CooksIllustrated.com/dinnerrolls. –A.G.

    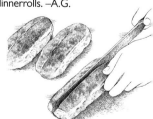

1. Prepare dough as directed in recipe through step 4. Pat and stretch dough into rectangle, then divide rectangle into eight 3-ounce portions.

2. Press each portion into 5-inch square, roll into cylinder, and pinch seam.

3. Arrange cylinders seam side down in 2 rows of four in greased 13 by 9-inch baking pan. Cover pan with plastic wrap and let rise until doubled in size, 45 minutes to 1 hour.

4. Bake on middle rack of 375-degree oven until rolls are golden brown, about 20 minutes. Let rolls cool for 3 minutes in pan, then transfer to wire rack and let cool completely.

5. Once rolls have cooled, gently pull them apart at seams. Using serrated knife, slice each roll lengthwise, stopping three-quarters of way from bottom.

CHOP (AND MINCE) LEAFY HERBS LIKE A PRO

To chop cilantro or parsley, some home cooks make thin, loose piles of herbs on their cutting boards and then run their knives back and forth over the piles. But this isn't the most efficient approach, and often the leaves are chopped inconsistently. Here's how to chop (and mince) large amounts of leafy herbs quickly. –A.G.

TO CHOP
Gather washed, dried leaves into a tight pile and hold them with your nonknife hand. Using your chef's knife in a rocking motion, slice thinly, working your way through the pile. Turn the sliced leaves 90 degrees, gather them, and repeat.

TO MINCE
For a smaller mince, chop as before and then go over the pile once more, placing the fingertips of your nonknife hand flat on the top of the knife's tip and moving the blade up and down with your other hand while using the knife's tip as a pivot.

Cloudy Tea Made Clear
In the past, we've found that cold-brewing iced tea is an effective way to avoid cloudiness, which is caused by caffeine and tannins bonding with each other and precipitating out of the solution when the hot tea is then chilled. We recently came across a different approach for producing clear tea: Brew the tea the traditional way with hot water and then chill it. Before serving, add boiling water to the chilled tea to break the bonds between the tannins and caffeine. The key, we found, is to add enough water: Most online sources call for only a splash, but we found that we needed a full ¼ cup of boiling water per cup of cloudy tea to make it clear again. To allow for the dilution, we simply brewed extra-strong tea, upping the standard 5 tea bags called for per quart of water to 8.

Here's how: Steep 8 tea bags in 4 cups hot water for 5 minutes. Refrigerate tea until thoroughly chilled. Add 1 cup boiling water to chilled tea and stir, then pour over ice and serve. (Note that rechilling the tea will cause cloudiness.) –S.D.

No Newspaper? Other Options for Lighting Coals

In our May/June 2016 issue, we included a note about how to properly pack the bottom of a charcoal chimney starter with newspaper, but some readers reported a problem: They no longer get a paper. One option: buy starters (see page 32). We also wondered if there wasn't a suitable alternative in the recycling bin.

In lieu of the paper, we first tried 10 crumpled pages from a glossy magazine (enough to provide fuel without overpacking), but they smoldered slowly—a half-full chimney took a full 30 minutes before the coals were ready. Half a cardboard six-pack carrier, crumpled into the lower chamber, did the job in 20 minutes but generated a lot of smoke and flyaway embers. Corrugated cardboard torn into strips behaved the same way.

The best bet? A cardboard egg carton torn into rough 4-inch chunks and lightly packed into the lower chamber. It produced minimal smoke and ash as it burned, and our coals were grill-ready in 20 minutes, about the same amount of time it takes with newspaper. –A.G.

GLOSSY MAGAZINES? NO

CARDBOARD SIX-PACK CARRIER? NO

EGG CARTON? YES

EXPERIMENT
Mushrooms: Impossible to Overcook?
Cooks often lump mushrooms into the category of vegetables (they're actually a fungus). While mushrooms display characteristics of vegetables (high water content) as well as meat (savory flavor), they are unique in their ability to maintain a pleasant texture over a wide range of cooking times. We set up the following experiment to illustrate how a mushroom's texture changes with cooking as compared with that of a green vegetable and a cut of beef.

EXPERIMENT
We cut ½-inch-thick planks of portobello mushroom, zucchini, and beef tenderloin and steamed them in a basket in a large Dutch oven for 40 minutes. At 5-minute intervals we used a piece of equipment called a CT3 Texture Analyzer to determine how much force was required to "bite" into each piece of food.

RESULTS
After 5 minutes of steaming, the tenderloin, portobello, and zucchini required 186, 199, and 239 grams of force, respectively, to be compressed (or "bite") 3 millimeters into the food. Tasters noted that all of these samples were tender. This picture changed rapidly after 5 more minutes of steaming. At the 10-minute mark, the tenderloin, portobello, and zucchini samples required 524, 195, and 109 grams of force, respectively. Tasters found the tenderloin tough and leathery and the zucchini overly soft. The portobello, on the other hand, remained largely unchanged. Over the course of the next 30 minutes, the tenderloin continued to toughen, eventually turning a whopping 293 percent tougher, while the zucchini decreased in firmness 83 percent and turned mushy and structureless. The portobello, meanwhile, increased in firmness just 57 percent over the same period of time; after a full 40 minutes of cooking, tasters found the mushroom to still be properly tender.

TAKEAWAY
While many foods we cook require precise attention to internal temperature and cooking time, mushrooms are remarkably forgiving. The key to their resiliency lies in their cell walls, which are made of a polymer called chitin. Unlike the proteins in meat or the pectin in vegetables, chitin is very heat-stable. This unique structure allows us to quickly sauté mushrooms for a few minutes or roast them for the better part of an hour, all the while achieving well-browned, perfectly tender specimens. –D.S.

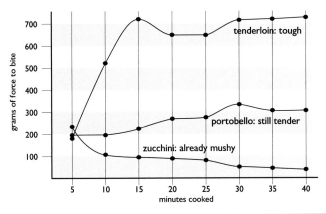

Graph: grams of force to bite vs. minutes cooked
- tenderloin: tough
- portobello: still tender
- zucchini: already mushy

⊙ SCIENCE OF COOKING:
The Key To Tender Mushrooms
We show why mushrooms simply can't be overcooked in a video available at CooksIllustrated.com/aug16.

EQUIPMENT CORNER

⇒ BY MIYE BROMBERG AND HANNAH CROWLEY ⇐

RECOMMENDED

KNAPP MADE Small Ring CM Scrubber
MODEL: SM6X6
PRICE: $19.98

HIGHLY RECOMMENDED

WEBER Lighter Cubes
MODEL: 7417
PRICE: $3.29 for 24 cubes ($0.14 per cube)

RECOMMENDED

KUHN RIKON Spider Skimmer, Small
MODEL: 22315
PRICE: $19.69

HIGHLY RECOMMENDED

BALL Secure-Grip Jar Lifter
MODEL: 382779
PRICE: $10.99

HIGHLY RECOMMENDED

MATFER BOURGEAT Black Steel Paella Pan
MODEL: 062052
PRICE: $49.98

UPDATE Knapp Made Small Ring CM Scrubber

The Knapp Made Classic CM Scrubber (the "CM" stands for "chain mail"), a 4 by 4-inch square of interlinked stainless-steel rings that sells for $14.99, makes easy work of cleaning nasty messes out of cast-iron pans. Recently, Knapp Made released a new model, the Small Ring CM Scrubber ($19.98), that's about an inch larger and has smaller, thinner rings. The manufacturer claims that both scrubbers can be used not just on cast iron but also on dark-finish enameled cast iron, stainless steel, and Pyrex. To see which scrubber we liked better, we tested both using all of these types of pans.

After making lots of messes and washing lots of pans, we crowned the larger scrubber the new king—its smaller rings make it more agile and adept at removing crusty, burnt-on residue. However, we found that both scrubbers scratched and damaged enameled cast-iron and stainless-steel pans, so we don't recommend them for those surfaces. No matter what you're cleaning with these scrubbers, use a light hand and let the metal do the work for you. –M.B.

Charcoal Fire Starters

How do you light charcoal in a chimney starter if you don't have newspaper? One answer: Use an egg carton (see page 31). Another option is to use charcoal fire starter cubes, tiles, or nuggets, which manufacturers claim ignite easily—even when wet. To see if these starters worked as advertised, we bought five varieties, priced from $0.13 to $1.25 per unit, and started playing with fire. We used the lowest number of starters recommended for each product (between one and three) to light full chimneys of briquettes, and then we grilled zucchini planks and flank steak over the coals to see if the starters imparted any off-flavors. They all ignited relatively easily, and all of the food tasted fine.

To see if these starters did work when wet, we submerged them in water for 2 hours and then tried to light them with a match. While none ignited when dripping wet, all lit relatively easily after a quick blot dry with paper towels. Our favorite, the Weber Lighter Cubes, were the most water-resistant of the bunch. –M.B.

Spider Skimmers

Sure, you could use a slotted spoon to remove boiled, blanched, or fried foods from a pot, but a spider skimmer—a long-handled stainless-steel wire basket—has a larger capacity and more open area for more efficient scooping and draining. To find the best spider, we tested six models, priced from $11.99 to $41.68, while cooking ravioli, fried chicken, and French fries.

Every spider worked fine, but some were clearly better than others. Models with long handles and large grips provided better protection and stability. Some spiders had baskets that were too small to hold much or so big that they felt clumsy and awkward; we liked the efficiency and agility of models with moderately deep baskets. Our favorite spider, the lightweight Kuhn Rikon Spider Skimmer, Small, has a long handle; a large, comfortable rubberized grip; and a perfectly sized webbed basket that made it quick and easy to extract food of all sizes and shapes. –M.B.

Canning Jar Lifters

Canning jar lifters are essential for home canning: Their curved grabbing arms are specifically designed to securely grasp hot jars. To find the very best one—a lifter that was comfortable, safe, and strong—we tested four nationally available models, priced from $6.32 to $10.99, moving filled cup, pint, and quart jars into and out of a boiling water bath. To simulate extended use, we also repeatedly opened and closed the lifters, washed them 10 times, and left them damp overnight to check for rusting.

In the end, one lifter—the Ball Secure-Grip Jar Lifter—stood head and shoulders above the others. It had a comfortable handle (other handles dug into our hands when lifting heavier jars), well-designed grabbers that felt secure on jars of all sizes, and one game-changing innovation: a spring-loaded hinge that pops the grabbers open when the handles are released. This feature means the user has to use only one hand to release each jar and grab the next one—other models often require two hands for this task—making the process easier, safer, and more efficient. –H.C.

Paella Pans

You can cook paella in a Dutch oven or roasting pan (see our recipe for Paella on the Grill on page 13), but a carbon-steel *paellera*, or paella pan, is the traditional vessel. This pan's shallow, wide shape maximizes the surface area of the paella, allowing for rapid evaporation of the cooking liquid and optimal *socarrat* (golden rice crust) development. To find the best paella pan for the home cook, we rounded up five models, priced from $24.95 to $79.00, and used each pan to prepare paella on both gas and charcoal grills.

All five pans held up to the heat of the grill and made good paella, but our winning pan, a carbon-steel beauty from Matfer Bourgeat, stood out from the rest. It was the thickest and heaviest of the lot, so it held and distributed the heat most evenly, resulting in fantastic socarrat. Much like a cast-iron skillet, this pan did require initial seasoning and light maintenance between uses, but in the end its superior performance and nearly nonstick surface made the extra effort well worth it. –M.B.

For complete testing results, go to CooksIllustrated.com/aug16.

INDEX

July & August 2016

BONUS ONLINE CONTENT

More recipes, reviews, and videos are available at **CooksIllustrated.com/aug16.**

RECIPES AND REVIEWS

Celery Root, Celery, and Apple Slaw
Penne with Red Pepper Pesto
   (Pesto Calabrese) for Two
Tasting Almond Butter
Testing Canning Jar Lifters
Testing Cast Iron Scrubbers
Testing Charcoal Fire Starters
Testing Digital Scales
Testing Ice Cream Makers
Testing Paella Pans
Testing Smart Scales
Testing Spider Skimmers

▶ RECIPE VIDEOS

Want to see how to make any of the recipes in this issue? There's a video for that.

▶ MORE VIDEOS

Science of Cooking: The Key to
   Tender Mushrooms

FOLLOW US ON SOCIAL MEDIA

facebook.com/CooksIllustrated
twitter.com/TestKitchen
pinterest.com/TestKitchen
google.com/+AmericasTestKitchen
instagram.com/TestKitchen
youtube.com/AmericasTestKitchen

Shredded Chicken Tacos (Tinga de Pollo), 5

Beet, Endive, and Pear Slaw, 18

Paella on the Grill, 13

Grilled Pizza, 20

Frozen Yogurt, 23

Korean Fried Chicken Wings, 15

Walkaway Ratatouille, 9

Grilled Steaks with Arugula and Parmesan, 7

Grilled Onions with Balsamic Vinaigrette, 10

Penne with Red Pepper Pesto, 11

PHOTOGRAPHY: CARL TREMBLAY; STYLING: MARIE PIRAINO

Caraway

Star Anise

Fennel

Green Cardamom

Fenugreek

Annatto

Yellow
Mustard

Celery

Cumin

Nutmeg

Coriander

SEED SPICES

COOK'S
ILLUSTRATED

Perfect Boiled Corn
The Secret? Don't Boil It

Easy Cheese Lasagna
New Noodle Technique

Smoked Pork Roast
Barbecue Flavor in 2 Hours

The Best Small
Kitchen Appliances

Shrimp Kebabs
Ingenious Kebab Design

Oatmeal Cookies
Crispy Edges, Chewy Centers

Turkey Meatballs
Deep Flavor Plus Tenderness

Rating Serrated Knives
Easier Chicken Mole
No-Knead Sourdough Bread
What's the Best Soy Sauce?

CooksIllustrated.com
$6.95 U.S. & $7.95 CANADA

10>

7 25274 62805 6

COOK'S
ILLUSTRATED

SEPTEMBER & OCTOBER 2016

PAGE 10

PRESERVED FISH

BACK COVER ILLUSTRATED BY JOHN BURGOYNE

Preserved Fish

Salt and smoke (alone or in combination) have been used to preserve many kinds of fish for thousands of years. SALT COD, made by heavily salting and drying cod fillets, is the simplest example of salt preservation. ANCHOVIES are layered in barrels with salt and cured for several months, which gives them their pungent flavor, before being packed in jars or tins with oil or more salt. Similarly, PICKLED HERRING are cured and then immersed in a flavored vinegar solution. COLD-SMOKED SALMON is not heated, resulting in a lush, delicate texture. Nordic GRAVLAX is cured with a combination of salt, sugar, and dill. SABLEFISH, also called butterfish, has a rich, buttery texture and a mild flavor when cured and cold-smoked. HOT-SMOKED SALMON (sometimes sold encrusted in crushed black pepper), meaty SMOKED TROUT, and whole smoked MACKEREL all have a mild smoke flavor and a moist, flaky texture. SARDINES are small, oily fish that are cooked, dried, packed into tins, and covered with oil.

AMERICA'S
TEST KITCHEN
RECIPES THAT WORK®

America's Test Kitchen is a real 2,500-square-foot kitchen located just outside Boston. It is the home of more than 60 test cooks, editors, and cookware specialists. Our mission is to test recipes until we understand exactly how and why they work and eventually arrive at the very best version. We also test kitchen equipment and supermarket ingredients in search of products that offer the best value and performance. You can watch us work by tuning in to *America's Test Kitchen* (AmericasTestKitchen.com) and *Cook's Country from America's Test Kitchen* (CooksCountry.com) on public television and listen to us on our weekly radio program on PRX. You can also follow us on Facebook, Twitter, Pinterest, and Instagram.

QUEST FOR THE BEST

It's not uncommon, as you walk through our offices, to pass a table of 25 or so staffers silently concentrating on tasting a dozen varieties of olive oil, peanut butter, or soy sauce. If you continue to the main test kitchen, you might see a lineup of eight slow cookers, each outfitted with a thermometer that is connected to a computer so we can gauge how evenly they maintain a given temperature over time. Walk out the back door and you could find someone dropping one portable grill after another onto the pavement from a specified height to see how well the grills stand up to abuse.

It's all in a day's work for our tastings and testings team. And if you think the test cooks here at America's Test Kitchen are obsessive in their quest for the best—and you're quite right, they are—you should spend some time with this team. The lengths they go to in order to be sure that their tests are accurate, comprehensive, and conducted on a level playing field are enough to make the rest of us look relaxed.

There are strict written protocols for selecting the items to be tested, for running the tests themselves, and for evaluating them. There are detailed instructions for tasters. And if there is ever a question, our team will go back and run the tests again, just to be sure.

But even when that rigorous (and sometimes seemingly endless) process is over, their work is really just beginning. Because it's not enough to say which product or piece of equipment came out on top—we need to know why. Sometimes it seems random to the rest of us, but these folks don't believe in that word, so they keep digging and analyzing, consulting experts all over the world and sending samples to labs for analysis, until they find the keys to the particular

puzzle. It might be the number of bevels on a serrated knife (spoiler: fewer are actually better) or the processing method used in making a particular soy sauce, but there will be a reason. Once they find it, we can appreciate even more clearly how solid a foundation our tastings and testings rest on.

This all holds true even for the smallest tools, like the slotted spoons and gourd seeding tools evaluated in this issue's Equipment Corner. You may see only a few sentences on the page, but the testing process has been just as disciplined, extensive, and intensive as ever, because this group has never heard of cutting corners. (The details can always be found at CooksIllustrated.com.)

The result of all this obsessiveness? You can truly trust our recommendations. In a kind of celebration of that, this issue includes a guide to the best countertop appliances—though we don't recommend tossing any of them onto the pavement.

—The Editors

FOR INQUIRIES, ORDERS, OR MORE INFORMATION

COOK'S ILLUSTRATED MAGAZINE

Cook's Illustrated magazine (ISSN 1068-2821), number 142, is published bimonthly by America's Test Kitchen Limited Partnership, 17 Station St., Brookline, MA 02445. Copyright 2016 America's Test Kitchen Limited Partnership. Periodicals postage paid at Boston, MA, and additional mailing offices, USPS #012487. Publications Mail Agreement No. 40020778. Return undeliverable Canadian addresses to P.O. Box 875, Station A, Windsor, ON N9A 6P2. POSTMASTER: Send address changes to *Cook's Illustrated*, P.O. Box 6018, Harlan, IA 51593-1518. For subscription and gift subscription orders, subscription inquiries, or change of address notices, visit AmericasTestKitchen.com/support, call 800-526-8442 in the U.S. or 515-248-7684 from outside the U.S., or write to us at *Cook's Illustrated*, P.O. Box 6018, Harlan, IA 51593-1518.

CooksIllustrated.com

At the all-new CooksIllustrated.com, you can order books and subscriptions, sign up for our free e-newsletter, or renew your magazine subscription. Join the website and gain access to 23 years of *Cook's Illustrated* recipes, equipment tests, and ingredient tastings, as well as companion videos for every recipe in this issue.

COOKBOOKS

We sell more than 50 cookbooks by the editors of *Cook's Illustrated*, including *Master of the Grill* and *Foolproof Preserving*. To order, visit our bookstore at CooksIllustrated.com/bookstore.

EDITORIAL OFFICE 17 Station St., Brookline, MA 02445; 617-232-1000; fax: 617-232-1572. For subscription inquiries, visit AmericasTestKitchen.com/support or call 800-526-8442.

Baste Away Excess Water from a Coffee Maker

Anne Marie Draganowski of Saint Paul, Minn., occasionally adds too much water to her drip coffee maker's reservoir. Rather than precariously tip the entire machine over to empty just the right amount into the sink, she uses a turkey baster to remove the water, checking against the machine's water gauge until there is just the right amount of water left.

A New Way to Crush Garlic and Ginger

Smashing garlic or ginger with the flat side of a knife blade can feel unsteady, so Doug Schifter of Thornhurst, Pa., uses a meat pounder to quickly and safely do the job instead.

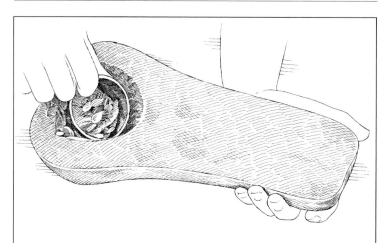

A Simple Squash Cleaning Tool

To clean out the seeds and fibers from a squash, you can use a seeding tool (see page 32), or you can follow the lead of Kris Widican of Needham, Mass., and use a stainless-steel biscuit cutter. Its sharp edge cuts through the squash's flesh, allowing her to grab all the fibers and seeds within.

Fish Spatula as a Flat Whisk

The narrow profile of a flat whisk makes it easy to maneuver around the edges of a saucepan. Since Gladys Heaton of Richardson, Texas, didn't have one, she searched for a worthy stand-in and found it in her slotted fish spatula. Its curved corners proved very effective at clearing sauces and puddings from the edges of the saucepan, preventing scorches or lumps.

A Compartmentalized Lunch Bag

Megan Mazzocco of Wauconda, Ill., recommends saving bread bags and fasteners to use as multicompartment lunch bags. She puts the first item in a bag, twists and secures it, and then repeats the process a few more times. This keeps potentially leaky containers of yogurt or applesauce separate from her other food.

Submerge Food with a Steamer Basket

When Edmund Gallizzi of St. Petersburg, Fla., wants to keep artichokes or other foods submerged in a cooking liquid, he pulls out his folding steamer basket. He removes the basket's handle, inverts the basket, and places it on top of the food. The leaves cover the surface of the food and keep it from bobbing above the liquid, ensuring even cooking.

SEND US YOUR TIPS We will provide a complimentary one-year subscription for each tip we print. Send your tip, name, address, and daytime telephone number to Quick Tips, *Cook's Illustrated*, P.O. Box 470589, Brookline, MA 02447, or to QuickTips@AmericasTestKitchen.com.

Homemade Skimming Spoon

Rather than purchase a specially made offset spoon, Adrian Bartoli of San Francisco, Calif., made his own by simply putting a 90-degree bend in one of the soupspoons he already owns. The angle lets him dip the spoon into deep pots or pans without tipping the vessel, and the bend makes it less awkward to scoop pan juices or skim a simmering stock.

A Better Way to Chop Through Bone-In Cuts

Some chopping jobs require both a full-powered swing and considerable precision, like cutting up bone-in chicken parts. For the cleanest cuts, Marvin Swartz of Durham, N.C., places the blade of his chef's knife or meat cleaver directly on the target and then sharply strikes the back of the knife with a rubber mallet.

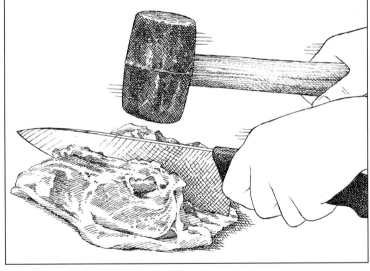

Cocktails in a Fat Separator

Whenever Maddy Reed of Kamuela, Hawaii, makes a batch of cocktails for a party, she uses her fat separator for mixing and serving the drinks—it strains the ice out with no mess.

How to Use up Expired Baking Soda

When her baking soda reaches its expiration date, Ann O'Rourke of West Covina, Calif., doesn't throw it away. Instead, she keeps it in a jar under her sink for all kinds of kitchen cleaning tasks—whether it's smothering a spill in the oven or removing stains from glassware.

Save Your Crumbs for Tasty Toppings

After letting cookies or cakes cool, there are always crumbs left beneath the cooling rack. Rather than throw them away, Denise Gardberg of Aurora, Colo., places parchment paper beneath the rack so that she can transfer the crumbs to a container or bag to store them in the freezer. They make a quick, tasty topping for ice cream, fruit, or even yogurt.

Easy Pie Shield

Miriam Clubok of Athens, Ohio, was inspired by our recent idea for a homemade pie shield (November/December 2015) and wanted to share her own method: She cuts out the center of a disposable pie plate and uses the rim as the shield. If the crust's edges are looking too brown, she can easily place the ring on top to protect the edge while the pie continues to bake. Plus, the pie shield can be washed and reused.

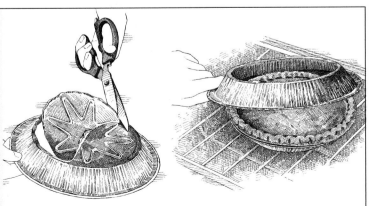

Two-Hour Smoked Pork Roast

Classic barbecue recipes take most of a day. We wanted a smoky, company-worthy pork roast that cooked in just a couple of hours.

≥ BY STEVE DUNN ≤

I haven't met many people who can resist a plateful of smoky, tender barbecue like pork butt or ribs, but I also haven't met many who can regularly commit to the half-day required to make them. So what can you do to create a meaty, smoky pork roast fit for a crowd in less time? After some thinking, I settled on using a pork loin. Because it isn't loaded with collagen, a pork loin doesn't require nearly as much cooking time as ribs or a pork butt—maybe a couple of hours, tops. It has a drawback, though—namely, a very mild flavor. But smoking seemed like a great way to give this mild cut a big flavor boost. The challenge? I'd need to be careful with the smoke. I'd want enough to amplify the roast's meaty taste but not overwhelm it. And because pork loin doesn't have much fat and has a tendency to dry out, I'd also need to take steps to ensure that my roast came off the grill tender and juicy.

A Slow Start

My first step was to pick the best cut from the loin. Here's the thing: All pork loin roasts are not created equal. You've actually got two options: blade-end or center-cut. The blade roast comes from the end of the loin closest to the shoulder, so it has relatively more fat (and flavor) than roasts cut from the center of the loin. That made the blade-end roast my clear choice.

I also knew I'd either salt or brine my roast since both of these pretreatments season the meat and help it retain juices during cooking. In both cases, the salt works its way into the meat and alters the meat's muscle proteins, making them better at holding on to water. Though brining tends to be quicker, it also impedes browning and would require making room for a large container in the fridge, so I settled on salting. Covering a roast with ¼ cup kosher salt, which is easier to distribute than table salt, and refrigerating it for 6 hours before grilling (I used a stripped-down grilling method for now) worked well enough. But

An overnight rub of salt and brown sugar is a triple win, seasoning our roast, keeping it juicy, and giving it a caramelized exterior.

letting it sit overnight worked much better, giving the salt time to penetrate deeper into the meat.

Following the lead of a few of the roast pork recipes the test kitchen has done in the past, I decided to add a good amount of brown sugar to the salt rub. This would have several benefits. First, like salt, sugar would help the meat retain moisture and stay juicy (it's less effective at the job but still makes

a difference). Second, sugar dissolved on the surface of the meat would encourage caramelization, delivering both more flavor and improved color. Finally, opting for brown sugar over granulated would add a hint of molasses flavor that would nicely complement the pork.

With my pork roast ready to go, I headed outside. First up: the grill setup. A lean roast like pork loin benefits from low-and-slow indirect cooking since this allows the interior to cook through evenly and gently, helping it retain as much moisture as possible. We've had a lot of experience with indirect cooking on the grill, so I arranged our standard setup: I banked the coals on one side of the grill and placed the roast opposite them, on the cooler side, with a pan filled with water beneath it to help keep the meat moist. The water pan also kept the temperature in the grill stable by absorbing heat.

So how low, exactly, did I need to go? I began with a grill temperature of 375 degrees (7 quarts of charcoal), but the roast came out dry. So I worked my way down in temperature. While lower temperatures led to better results, too low was too hard to maintain and took too long to cook the pork through. I found that 300 degrees was my best bet for a juicy roast in a reasonable time frame. Cooked at this temperature, the roast needed 1½ to 2 hours to hit the ideal internal temperature of 140 degrees.

The problem was, I had to refuel my fire partway through. Luckily, we had already devised a solution for this when developing our recipe for Memphis-Style Barbecued Spareribs (July/August 2010): We

▶ **Steve Shows You How**
A free video is available at
CooksIllustrated.com/oct16

SCIENCE **The Magic of Wood Smoke**

Leave unassuming wood chips to smolder in your grill and they produce smoke that adds incredible complexity to food. What exactly is behind the transformation?

When wood burns, one of its primary components, lignin, breaks down into the smoky aroma compounds that we readily associate with barbecue, as well as clove and vanilla aromas. The sugars in cellulose and hemicellulose, wood's other major components, break apart into many of the same molecules found in caramel. These aromas and many others drift up in the form of smoky vapors that dissolve in the surface moisture of the food, imbuing it with flavor. Hickory and fruit-tree woods produce the most pleasing, balanced-tasting smoke. We don't typically use mesquite because it contains much more lignin than other woods; its pungent flavor can overpower food.

Smoke also makes food look better. Some of the compounds produced by the breakdown of cellulose and hemicellulose react with the proteins on the meat's surface, and this gives the meat a lacquered appearance.

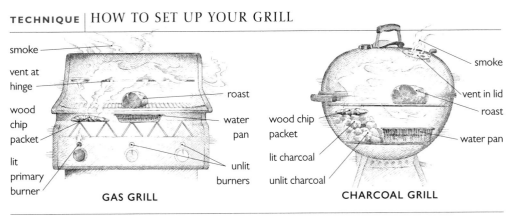

GAS GRILL

CHARCOAL GRILL

arranged a layer of unlit coals in the grill and then topped those with a layer of lit coals. This stretched out the life of the flame, so there was no need to refuel. To achieve the steady 300 degrees that I wanted, I just needed to bump up the coal count from the rib recipe since that recipe calls for a grill temperature of 275 degrees. Some simple math and a few roasts later, I found that a combination of 25 unlit and 40 lit coals (or 4 quarts) was just the ticket for a 300-degree fire that would burn for 2 hours.

And what about a browning step? We often brown the exterior of a roast for deeper flavor and improved color. Happily, the salt–brown sugar rub contributed enough on both fronts that I could skip it.

Smoking Out the Solution

The final detail was the smoke. As wood smolders, it breaks down into numerous flavorful compounds that vaporize, waft up, and settle on the food, infusing it with smoky, spicy pungency but also a complex sweetness. (For more detail, see "The Magic of Wood Smoke.") Combined with the flavor that grilling adds—which would mainly be Maillard browning along with some flavor from the coals since pork loin has little to offer in the way of fatty drippings—smoking meat delivers a lot of bang for the buck. But how much smoke did my recipe need?

I started with 4 cups of wood chips, the same amount we used for Smoky Pulled Pork on a Gas Grill (July/August 2014), but that much smoke was overkill for mild pork loin. Two cups produced just the right amount of smoke to add flavor but not overwhelm, and setting the lid vents over the meat ensured that the smoke drifted by the meat before exiting the grill. The smoking process also gave my roast a beautifully lacquered appearance.

Translating my charcoal-grill recipe to gas was easy enough: I placed the wood chip packet on the primary burner and placed the roast beside it so that the smoke would drift over the meat on its way out of the vents at the back.

As a finishing touch, I put together a quick dried-fruit chutney to serve alongside the roast. Brightened with vinegar, ginger, and mustard, it was the perfect complement to the deeply smoky meat. This recipe certainly satisfied my barbecue cravings, and I didn't have to put in half a day's work to enjoy it.

SMOKED PORK LOIN WITH DRIED-FRUIT CHUTNEY
SERVES 6

Note that the roast needs to be refrigerated for at least 6 hours or up to 24 hours after the salt rub is applied. A blade-end roast is our preferred cut, but a center-cut boneless loin roast can also be used. Any variety of wood chip except mesquite will work; we prefer hickory. If you'd like to use wood chunks instead of wood chips when using a charcoal grill, substitute two medium wood chunks, soaked in water for 1 hour, for the wood chip packet.

Pork

½	cup packed light brown sugar
¼	cup kosher salt
1	(3½- to 4-pound) blade-end boneless pork loin roast, trimmed
2	cups wood chips
1	(13 by 9-inch) disposable aluminum roasting pan (if using charcoal) or 1 (9-inch) disposable aluminum pie plate (if using gas)

Chutney

¾	cup dry white wine
½	cup dried apricots, diced
½	cup dried cherries
¼	cup white wine vinegar
3	tablespoons water
3	tablespoons packed light brown sugar
1	shallot, minced
2	tablespoons grated fresh ginger
1	tablespoon unsalted butter
1	tablespoon Dijon mustard
1½	teaspoons dry mustard
	Kosher salt

1. FOR THE PORK: Combine sugar and salt in small bowl. Tie roast with twine at 1-inch intervals. Rub sugar-salt mixture over entire surface of roast, making sure roast is evenly coated. Wrap roast tightly in plastic wrap, set roast in rimmed baking sheet, and refrigerate for at least 6 hours or up to 24 hours.

2. Just before grilling, soak wood chips in water for 15 minutes, then drain. Using large piece of heavy-duty aluminum foil, wrap soaked chips in 8 by

4½-inch foil packet. (Make sure chips do not poke holes in sides or bottom of packet.) Cut 2 evenly spaced 2-inch slits in top of packet.

3A. FOR A CHARCOAL GRILL: Open bottom vent halfway. Arrange 25 unlit charcoal briquettes over half of grill and place disposable pan filled with 3 cups water on other side of grill. Light large chimney starter two-thirds filled with charcoal briquettes (4 quarts). When top coals are partially covered with ash, pour evenly over unlit briquettes. Place wood chip packet on coals. Set cooking grate in place, cover, and open lid vent halfway. Heat grill until hot and wood chips are smoking, about 5 minutes.

3B. FOR A GAS GRILL: Remove cooking grate and place wood chip packet directly on primary burner. Place disposable pie plate filled with 1 inch water directly on other burner(s). Set grate in place, turn all burners to high, cover, and heat grill until hot and wood chips are smoking, about 15 minutes. Turn primary burner to medium and turn off other burner(s). (Adjust primary burner as needed to maintain grill temperature of 300 degrees.)

4. Clean and oil cooking grate. Unwrap roast and pat dry with paper towels. Place roast on grill directly over water pan about 7 inches from heat source. Cover (position lid vent over roast if using charcoal) and cook until meat registers 140 degrees, 1½ to 2 hours, rotating roast 180 degrees after 45 minutes.

5. FOR THE CHUTNEY: Combine wine, apricots, cherries, vinegar, water, sugar, shallot, and ginger in medium saucepan. Bring to simmer over medium heat. Cover and cook until fruit is softened, 10 minutes. Remove lid and reduce heat to medium-low. Add butter, Dijon, and dry mustard and continue to cook until slightly thickened, 4 to 6 minutes. Remove from heat and season with salt. Transfer to bowl and let stand at room temperature.

6. Transfer roast to cutting board, tent with foil, and let stand for 30 minutes. Remove and discard twine. Slice roast ¼ inch thick and serve with chutney.

Best Leftovers Sandwich Ever

We were so happy with this recipe that we wanted to make it even when there were only two or three people at dinner. But what about the leftovers?

Turning a problem into a plus, we came up with a shortcut version of the classic pressed Cubano sandwich, a perfect use for our juicy, flavorful pork. Slices of Smoked Pork Loin make a great stand-in for the roast pork and ham in this sandwich, which also features Swiss cheese, pickles, and mustard on a pressed and toasted roll. Our free recipe is available for four months at CooksIllustrated.com/oct16.

Perfecting Cheese Lasagna

Without meat or vegetables, cheese lasagna can be dull to eat. For a great version, the cheese and the tomato sauce—and even the noodles—needed an upgrade.

≳ BY STEVE DUNN ≲

When I make lasagna, I usually turn to the Bolognese kind, layered with plenty of ground meats, or perhaps a vegetarian version bulked up with things like eggplant, zucchini, or mushrooms. But I recently decided to try my hand at a simpler classic enjoyed in southern Italy. Called *lasagne di magro* ("lasagna without meat"), it strips the dish down to its most basic elements: noodles, cheese (usually a trio of ricotta, mozzarella, and Parmesan), and tomato sauce.

I was excited when I found this dish, and trying a few recipes confirmed that it was considerably faster to make than the more familiar kind. But these tests also revealed a shortcoming—namely, that a lasagna with only cheese and tomato can be plain old boring. Without meat and vegetables to add complex flavor, the tomato sauce came across as thin and acidic. The mozzarella and ricotta were bland, and the latter cooked up grainy rather than creamy. These lasagnas also lacked the stature and distinct layering of meat or vegetable versions; the noodles seemed to be swallowed up by the sauce and cheese.

To make this simpler lasagna work, I'd need to amp up the basic elements so that they offered bold, balanced flavor and substance of their own.

Between the Sheets

There was plenty of room to enhance the flavor and body of the tomato sauce, since the recipes I'd tried called for nothing more than canned tomatoes (usually crushed), garlic, onion, red pepper flakes, and basil. My first additions were tomato paste (a generous ¼ cup) and minced anchovies—both contribute glutamates that would give the sauce a savory boost in the absence of meat (the anchovies leave no trace of fishiness). The tomato paste also added body, but the sauce still came across as thin and one-dimensional. A small can of diced tomatoes in addition to

To give our lasagna more bite, we use traditional wavy noodles. But instead of cooking them in a pot, we soak them in a small amount of boiling water.

● See It Step-by-Step
A free video is available at
CooksIllustrated.com/oct16

the larger can of crushed ones broke up the uniform texture (they're treated with calcium chloride and thus don't break down much during cooking), while some grated Pecorino Romano tightened up the sauce and further enhanced its savory depth. A touch of sugar tempered the tomatoes' acidity. Those additions, along with a low 20-minute simmer, produced a sauce that was altogether different from the starting point: complex and balanced, with distinct body and substance.

Ricotta and mozzarella are naturally mild, so my next move was to replace them with stronger, more assertive cheeses. I briefly considered bolstering the ricotta with creamy, tangy additions like mascarpone or cream cheese, but I held off when I remembered that we'd come up with an effective ricotta substitute in other pasta casserole recipes: cottage cheese, which is both creamier and tangier than ricotta. I whisked the cottage cheese together with heavy cream, grated Parmesan, a touch of cornstarch (to prevent the dairy proteins from curdling when cooked), garlic, salt, and pepper to make a quick

no-cook sauce. When I swapped in this mixture for the ricotta, it was not only more flavorful but also smoother and more lush. In later versions, I took the flavor boost one step further and traded the Parmesan for saltier, stronger Pecorino Romano.

As for replacing the mozzarella, I needed another good melting cheese that also had enough flavor to stand up to my now-robust tomato sauce. Thankfully, I didn't need to look beyond the Italian border for the perfect candidate: fontina. A great melter prized for its nuttiness, it delivered just as much gooeyness as mozzarella but with a more distinctive flavor.

No Boil, No Problem

On to the noodles, which needed to not only separate the lasagna into distinct layers but also provide resiliency and bite. No-boil noodles, which I'd been using for convenience and because they have a delicacy reminiscent of fresh pasta, were the wrong choice here, as demonstrated by the squat, uniformly soft lasagna I'd produced thus far. Switching to thicker, ruffly traditional lasagna noodles would be a convenience trade-off but would hopefully yield a taller, more substantial slice.

I boiled the sheets until they were al dente and then layered them in the baking dish with the tomato sauce, cottage cheese sauce, and shredded fontina, topping the layers with a mixture of fontina (tossed with a bit of cornstarch to prevent the shreds from clumping) and Pecorino. I covered the casserole with aluminum foil and baked it for 35 minutes in a moderate oven; I then removed the foil and cranked the heat for the last 15 minutes of cooking so that the top layer of cheese bubbled and browned.

The finished product certainly looked more substantial than my past attempts, but by the time the fully boiled noodles had baked and soaked up more moisture from the sauces, they, too, were softer than I wanted, which defeated the purpose of using them in the first place. I could parboil them, but bringing a whole pot of water to a boil just for a quick dip seemed like a lot of fuss. But how about simply soaking them in hot water before baking? I laid the noodles in the dish I would use to bake the lasagna (to keep the dirty dishes to a minimum) and soaked them in boiling water for 15 minutes until they were

Our novel way of soaking—not fully cooking—traditional noodles means they don't expand as much in the oven, leaving gaps at the short sides of the baking dish. Our fix: We arrange the soaked noodles so only one short side of the baking dish is left uncovered and then lay a half noodle across it. For a level lasagna, we alternate which short side gets the half noodle with every layer.

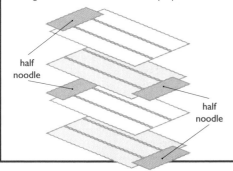

pliable but not fully hydrated. I drained them and then built another lasagna, which turned out to be the best one yet—substantial, with a good balance of noodles, sauce, and cheese.

I made just two more tweaks: rinsing the soaked noodles before baking to wash off some residual starch that had made the lasagna a tad gummy and reworking the assembly of the noodles. Now that I was simply soaking them before they went into the casserole, they weren't expanding as much, leaving empty spaces at the short sides of the baking dish. The simple fix? I arranged the soaked noodles so only one short side was left uncovered and then laid a half noodle across that open area. To keep the lasagna level, I alternated which short end got the half noodle with every layer. (See "Mind the Gap(s).")

A lasagna that wasn't a project yet still delivered the satisfying flavor and texture of the meat and vegetable versions? If you ask me, this lasagna should become a classic, too.

INGREDIENT
Cornstarch Does Double Duty

Though not traditional, cornstarch plays two small but important roles in our lasagna. In the cheese sauce, it coats the dairy proteins, preventing them from linking tightly and curdling. Tossed with the shredded fontina, the cornstarch absorbs moisture that would make the shreds clump so they'd be hard to sprinkle.

CLUMPY FONTINA   FLUFFY FONTINA

CHEESE AND TOMATO LASAGNA
SERVES 8

Do not substitute no-boil noodles for regular noodles, as they are too thin. Alternating the noodle arrangement in step 4 keeps the lasagna level. For a vegetarian version, omit the anchovies.

Cheese Sauce

- 4 ounces Pecorino Romano cheese, grated (2 cups)
- 8 ounces (1 cup) cottage cheese
- ½ cup heavy cream
- 2 garlic cloves, minced
- 1 teaspoon cornstarch
- ¼ teaspoon salt
- ¼ teaspoon pepper

Tomato Sauce

- ¼ cup extra-virgin olive oil
- 1 onion, chopped fine
- 1½ teaspoons sugar
- ½ teaspoon red pepper flakes
- ½ teaspoon dried oregano
- ½ teaspoon salt
- 4 garlic cloves, minced
- 8 anchovy fillets, rinsed, patted dry, and minced
- 1 (28-ounce) can crushed tomatoes
- 1 (14.5-ounce) can diced tomatoes, drained
- 1 ounce Pecorino Romano cheese, grated (½ cup)
- ¼ cup tomato paste

Lasagna

- 14 curly-edged lasagna noodles
- 8 ounces fontina cheese, shredded (2 cups)
- ⅛ teaspoon cornstarch
- ¼ cup grated Pecorino Romano cheese
- 3 tablespoons chopped fresh basil

1. FOR THE CHEESE SAUCE: Whisk all ingredients in bowl until homogeneous. Set aside.

2. FOR THE TOMATO SAUCE: Heat oil in large saucepan over medium heat. Add onion, sugar, pepper flakes, oregano, and salt and cook, stirring frequently, until onions are softened, about 10 minutes. Add garlic and anchovies and cook until fragrant, about 2 minutes. Stir in crushed tomatoes, diced tomatoes, Pecorino, and tomato paste and bring to simmer. Reduce heat to medium-low and simmer until slightly thickened, about 20 minutes.

3. FOR THE LASAGNA: While sauce simmers, lay noodles in 9 by 13-inch baking dish and cover with boiling water. Let noodles soak until pliable, about 15 minutes, separating noodles with tip of paring knife to prevent sticking. Place dish in sink, pour off water, and run cold water over noodles. Pat noodles dry with clean dish towel; dry dish. Cut two noodles in half crosswise.

4. Adjust oven rack to middle position and heat oven to 375 degrees. Spread 1½ cups tomato sauce in bottom of dish. Lay 3 noodles lengthwise in dish with ends touching 1 short side, leaving space on opposite short side. Lay 1 half noodle crosswise in empty space to create even layer of noodles. Spread half of cheese sauce over noodles, followed by ½ cup fontina. Repeat layering of noodles, alternating which short side gets half noodle (alternating sides will prevent lasagna from buckling). Spread 1½ cups tomato sauce over second layer of noodles, followed by ½ cup fontina. Create third layer using 3½ noodles (reversing arrangement again), remaining cheese sauce, and ½ cup fontina.

5. Lay remaining 3½ noodles over cheese sauce. Spread remaining tomato sauce over noodles. Toss remaining ½ cup fontina with cornstarch, then sprinkle over tomato sauce, followed by Pecorino.

6. Spray sheet of aluminum foil with vegetable oil spray and cover lasagna. Bake for 35 minutes. Remove lasagna from oven and increase oven temperature to 500 degrees.

7. Remove foil from lasagna, return to oven, and continue to bake until top is lightly browned, 10 to 15 minutes longer. Let lasagna cool for 20 minutes. Sprinkle with basil, cut into pieces, and serve.

A Triple Threat to Dull Cheese Lasagna

Without meat or vegetables, plain old cheese lasagna can taste flat. Or it can be an opportunity to bring the three classic components—tomato sauce, cheese, and noodles—into the spotlight.

➤ ROBUST TOMATO SAUCE
Tomato paste, minced anchovies, and grated Pecorino Romano ramp up savory depth.

➤ CREAMY, TANGY CHEESE
We forgo the usual ricotta, mozzarella, and Parmesan for tangy cottage cheese (whisked into a creamy sauce); nutty, smooth fontina; and richer, saltier Pecorino Romano.

➤ NOODLES WITH BITE
Ruffly lasagna noodles make for a more substantial dish than do thinner no-boil noodles.

Chicken Mole Poblano

Mexico's iconic sauce is rich and complex—and requires dozens of ingredients and days in the kitchen. Could a simpler method deliver equally good results?

≥ BY ANDREW JANJIGIAN ≤

Even if you've never tasted mole poblano, you might know of its prominent place in Mexican cuisine. The legends associated with its origin all seem to agree on one thing: This rich, velvety, deeply complex sauce, the hallmark of the Puebla region and widely considered the country's national dish, was conceived centuries ago to serve to dignitaries. To make it, cooks spent days gathering, frying or roasting, and then grinding nuts and seeds, dried chiles, herbs and warm spices, dried fruit, aromatics such as garlic and onion, and tomatoes into a paste thickened with stale bread or tortillas. The earthy, faintly bitter, fruity-sweet, smoky, and subtly spicy mixture (the term *mole* stems from the Nahuatl word *molli*, which means "sauce" or "concoction") was then fried to deepen its flavor; enriched with a little dark chocolate; thinned with liquid left over from poaching a chicken or turkey to yield a smooth, dark sauce; and poured over the poached poultry. Sopping it up with corn tortillas or rice meant not a drop was wasted.

To this day, preparing mole is a ritual in Mexican households, one that's often tackled over multiple days and reserved for special occasions. But stateside, it's also become a familiar dish in traditional Mexican restaurants and one that home cooks are often tempted to try. There are plenty of published recipes to choose from, many of which, I've found, are quite good—and, not surprisingly, incredibly labor-intensive. Then there are approaches that reduce the ingredients and the work to convenience products like commercial chili powder and no more than an hour or so of prepping and cooking, but they result in a rather lackluster sauce.

What I wanted was a mole recipe that struck a compromise between the depth and complexity of authentic versions and the more reasonable workload of modern approaches. My strategy: Start with a classic formula, and then, testing carefully, evaluate

Traditional recipes call for pouring mole over poached chicken. We cook the chicken pieces in the rich sauce, which makes them more flavorful.

▶ Watch the Mole Happen
A free video is available at
CooksIllustrated.com/oct16

which components and steps could be simplified or cut altogether without sacrificing the end result.

Cuts and Adds

I would begin with the chiles. Some recipes call for as many as six varieties, the most common being rich, raisiny sweet anchos; fruity and slightly spicy pasillas; and smoky chipotles (or mulatos). I tried a blend of all three, toasting them in the oven before letting them cool; removing their stems, seeds, and ribs; tearing them into pieces; and then soaking them so that they softened. To prepare the rest of the paste, I fried sesame seeds, peanuts, almonds, walnuts, and pecans in oil (rather than the traditional lard), followed by coriander and cumin and a couple of corn tortillas; pureed the nut-seed mixture with raisins (plumped beforehand in warm water), onion, garlic, tomato, dried oregano and thyme,

Much More Than a Chocolate Sauce

Mole famously contains chocolate, which adds depth and luxurious texture to the sauce. But mole's complex flavors also encompass spicy, smoky, and earthy-sweet notes contributed by chiles, nuts, warm spices, raisins, and tomato.

ground cinnamon, and the drained chiles; and finally fried the paste to deepen and meld the flavors. In went a few ounces of bittersweet Mexican chocolate, which had been hard to track down but made the paste richer, darker, and a touch more bitter. I thinned it with chicken broth and then ladled it over a whole poached chicken—my placeholder poultry for the moment.

The sauce certainly was complex, but with so many components in the mix, the flavors of the individual chiles were subtle, and I guessed that only a very attuned palate would notice if I further downsized the list. Anchos made a good base chile, especially since I could enhance their earthy-sweet profile with the nuts, spices, raisins, and dark chocolate I was already using. Chipotles were a must for their smokiness and heat, but instead of fussing with another dried chile, I minced a tablespoon of the easier-to-find canned kind, which also came with the benefit of punchy adobo sauce. The others could go.

I spent my next few tests weeding out some of the nuts. Ultimately, almonds were the only essential variety; they provided a baseline of richness and body, and the sesame seeds offered their distinctively earthy flavor, making walnuts, pecans, and peanuts superfluous. I also switched from corn tortillas to a slice of white sandwich bread—an ingredient I am more likely to have on hand—and no one was the wiser.

Those changes took care of the earthy, smoky, and spicy flavors I'd wanted to hit, but I also needed to tweak the tomato component. Tomato paste was better than the fresh tomatoes I'd been using: A couple of tablespoons rounded out the sauce with acidity as well as depth, and it was more convenient to use.

Finally, I circled back to the Mexican chocolate: The two biggest differences between this kind and European and American chocolate are that the former boasts a relatively coarse, rustic texture and is scented with cinnamon and sometimes other warm spices. You can really taste the difference between the two types if you try them in bar form, but once melted into the mole, the Mexican chocolate's distinctiveness was almost imperceptible. A few ounces of unsweetened chocolate made a fine stand-in.

A Method Without Madness

I'd cut the ingredient list down considerably, and I was anxious to do the same with the method—particularly the frying part, since frying each component once before grinding and then for a second time as a paste was a laborious process.

Instead, I tried toasting the chiles, nuts, seeds, spices, and bread together on a rimmed baking sheet in the oven and happily found that this delivered comparably rich-tasting results. And as long as I added the same amount of oil to the food processor as I had been using to fry, the consistency and richness of the paste weren't any different. But as it turned out, I didn't even need to go that far. Just to see how streamlined I could make the recipe, I skipped the toasting and simply fried the paste, and my tasters still didn't pick up on the change. I did need to toast the anchos to make them pliable enough to stem and seed, but otherwise I'd eliminated about an hour of work with no loss in flavor.

I also made a few tweaks to the soaking and frying steps. I sped up the soaking process by zapping the anchos and raisins together in the microwave. After processing all the ingredients for the paste, instead of frying it on the stove, where it required constant stirring to prevent scorching, I moved the pot to a low oven, where it required just a few stirs.

Back to my placeholder poached chicken: The broth it produced worked nicely for thinning the paste, but simply pouring the sauce over the cooked bird didn't yield a very cohesive dish. Switching to chicken parts allowed me to stew the meat directly in the sauce, where it soaked up much more flavor; plus, it enabled me to increase the amount of meat to serve at least six guests (mole is a for-company dish, after all). For the sauce base, I simply switched to using store-bought chicken broth, and that was fine.

When I tallied up all my changes, I'd cut the ingredient list by 30 percent (and limited it to supermarket staples only) and the marathon-like process by several hours—taking this from a dish I'd like to make to one that I actually would. But the most convincing part was the flavors, which were deeply complex and balanced.

CHICKEN MOLE POBLANO
SERVES 6 TO 8

Our preference is to cook the chicken with the skin on, but it can be removed before cooking, if desired. Serve with white rice and/or corn tortillas. Vary the amount of cayenne (or omit it altogether) depending on how spicy you like your food.

3	ounces (6 to 8) dried ancho chiles
3½	cups chicken broth
½	cup raisins
1	onion, cut into 1-inch pieces
¼	cup vegetable oil
2	tablespoons tomato paste
4	garlic cloves, peeled
1	tablespoon minced canned chipotle in adobo sauce
¾	cup sliced almonds
1	slice hearty white sandwich bread, torn into 1-inch pieces
3	tablespoons sesame seeds
2	teaspoons salt
1–2	teaspoons cayenne pepper (optional)
1	teaspoon dried oregano
½	teaspoon dried thyme
½	teaspoon ground cinnamon
½	teaspoon ground cumin
½	teaspoon ground coriander
½	teaspoon pepper
2	ounces unsweetened chocolate, chopped coarse
4	pounds bone-in chicken pieces (split breasts cut in half, drumsticks, and/or thighs), trimmed

1. Adjust oven rack to middle position and heat oven to 325 degrees. Place anchos on rimmed baking sheet and toast until fragrant and pliable, about

Sauce for Special Occasions

Because traditional mole is so labor-intensive and requires so many ingredients—some cooks add as many as six varieties of chiles alone—it is often made over several days and reserved for special occasions like weddings, baptisms, and holidays. It can be made in such big batches that cooks may take their roasted and fried ingredients to a neighborhood *molino*, or mill, to grind them into a sauce that is then thinned with stock at home.

5 minutes. Transfer to medium bowl and let cool for 5 minutes. Remove seeds, stems, and ribs from anchos and discard; tear flesh into ½-inch pieces and return pieces to bowl.

2. Add 2 cups broth and raisins to bowl with anchos, cover, and microwave until steaming, about 2 minutes. Let stand until softened, about 5 minutes. Drain mixture in fine-mesh strainer set over bowl, reserving liquid.

3. Process onion, 2 tablespoons oil, tomato paste, garlic, chipotle, and ancho-raisin mixture in food processor until smooth, about 5 minutes, scraping down sides of bowl as needed. Add almonds; bread; 2 tablespoons sesame seeds; salt; cayenne, if using; oregano; thyme; cinnamon; cumin; coriander; pepper; and ¼ cup reserved ancho soaking liquid and continue to process until smooth paste forms, about 3 minutes, scraping down sides of bowl as needed and adding additional soaking liquid if necessary.

4. Heat remaining 2 tablespoons oil in Dutch oven over medium-high heat until shimmering. Add mole paste and cook, stirring frequently, until steaming, about 3 minutes. Stir in chocolate until incorporated. Transfer pot to oven and cook, uncovered, for 30 minutes, stirring twice. (Paste will darken during cooking.) (Paste can be refrigerated for up to 1 week or frozen for up to 1 month.)

5. Place pot over medium-high heat and whisk remaining reserved soaking liquid and remaining 1½ cups broth into mole paste until smooth. Place chicken in even layer in pot, reduce heat to low, cover, and cook until breasts register 160 degrees and drumsticks/thighs register 175 degrees, 25 to 30 minutes, stirring halfway through cooking. Transfer chicken pieces to serving dish as they come up to temperature. Pour sauce over chicken, garnish with remaining 1 tablespoon sesame seeds, and serve.

RECIPE SHORTHAND ## Simpler Chicken Mole

Fewer (and more accessible) ingredients and an efficient method help streamline what's traditionally a very complicated recipe into one that's eminently doable.

PREPARE CHILE BASE
Toast anchos in oven; microwave them with broth and raisins.

PROCESS INTO PASTE
Process all remaining mole ingredients except chocolate.

HEAT; ADD CHOCOLATE
Cook paste in oil on stove; stir in chocolate.

TRANSFER TO OVEN
Continue to cook 30 minutes longer. Paste will darken.

ADD CHICKEN
Thin paste with liquid, add chicken, and continue to cook until chicken is done.

Shrimp and Vegetable Kebabs

Can shrimp and vegetables ever achieve perfection on a single skewer?

> BY STEVE DUNN

Shrimp and vegetable kebabs have a sad but well-earned reputation. When the shrimp are perfectly cooked, the vegetables come off the skewer almost raw; when the vegetables are properly done, the shrimp are so overcooked that they're rubbery and tough. One obvious solution is to cook the shrimp on one skewer and the vegetables on another. But the ability to deliver a variety of flavors, colors, and textures to the plate in one attractive package seemed like a goal worth achieving.

My first decision was to use jumbo shrimp, since their larger size would translate into a longer cooking time. I also found that submerging the peeled shrimp in a quick pregrill brine plumped and seasoned them and allowed them to stay on the grill a touch longer without drying out. Most important, after trying a few ways of organizing the components, I discovered that nestling mushrooms tightly into the curve of the shrimp extended the shrimp's cooking time by providing them with additional insulation.

As for the remaining vegetables, I found that using quick-cooking varieties such as scallions and bell peppers was essential. Cutting them into plank-like pieces about the same width as the shrimp created a uniform profile for everything on the skewer; this way, the kebabs laid flat on the cooking grate, maximizing contact with the grill and promoting even cooking and caramelization along the entire skewer.

I was making good progress, but the vegetables, while nicely charred, still tasted a bit raw when the shrimp were properly cooked. At this point I decided a little precooking was in order. The scallions didn't need it, but lightly salting and microwaving both the peppers and the mushrooms for a few minutes before loading them onto the skewers made a big difference. Prepared this way, the kebabs came off the grill beautifully charred, sporting crisp-tender vegetables and rosy-pink shrimp that were just cooked through.

Now, I wanted to explore ways to bring more flavor to my kebabs. Marinating the kebabs caused them to steam and prevented them from picking up sufficient char, while rubbing them with spice mixes before grilling masked the delicate sweetness of the shrimp. In the end I found that drizzling a bright lemon-thyme vinaigrette over the kebabs just after they came off the grill worked best.

▶ **See the Skewer Action**
A free video is available at
CooksIllustrated.com/oct16

GRILLED SHRIMP AND VEGETABLE KEBABS
SERVES 4 TO 6

Small mushrooms measuring about 1¼ to 1½ inches in diameter work best in this recipe. If using larger mushrooms, halve them before microwaving in step 3. You will need eight 12-inch metal skewers for this recipe. Our free recipe for Grilled Shrimp and Vegetable Kebabs for Two is available for four months at CooksIllustrated.com/oct16.

Shrimp

> Salt and pepper
> 2 tablespoons sugar
> 1½ pounds jumbo shrimp (16 to 20 per pound), peeled and deveined
> 3 large red or yellow bell peppers, stemmed, seeded, and cut into ¾-inch-wide by 3-inch-long strips
> 24 cremini mushrooms, trimmed
> 12 scallions, cut into 3-inch lengths
> 2 tablespoons vegetable oil

Vinaigrette

> ¼ cup lemon juice (2 lemons)
> ¼ cup extra-virgin olive oil
> 2 teaspoons minced fresh thyme
> 1 garlic clove, minced
> ½ teaspoon salt
> ¼ teaspoon Dijon mustard
> ⅛ teaspoon pepper

1. FOR THE SHRIMP: Dissolve 2 tablespoons salt and sugar in 1 quart cold water in large container. Submerge shrimp in brine, cover, and refrigerate for 15 minutes. Remove shrimp from brine and pat dry with paper towels.

2. Line large microwave-safe plate with double layer of paper towels. Spread half of bell peppers skin side down in even layer on plate and sprinkle with ⅛ teaspoon salt. Microwave for 2 minutes. Transfer bell peppers, still on towels, to cutting board and let cool. Repeat with fresh paper towels and remaining bell peppers.

3. Line second plate with double layer of paper towels. Spread mushrooms in even layer on plate and sprinkle with ⅛ teaspoon salt. Microwave for 3 minutes. Transfer mushrooms, still on towels, to cutting board and let cool.

4. Lay 1 shrimp on cutting board and run 12-inch metal skewer through center. Thread mushroom onto skewer through sides of cap, pushing so it nestles tightly into curve of shrimp. Follow mushroom with

Cutting the vegetables into planks the width of the shrimp allows the kebabs to lay flat for even cooking.

2 pieces scallion and 2 pieces bell pepper, skewering so vegetables and shrimp form even layer. Repeat shrimp and vegetable sequence 2 more times. When skewer is full, gently press ingredients so they fit snugly together in center of skewer. Thread remaining shrimp and vegetables on 7 more skewers for total of 8 kebabs. Brush each side of kebabs with oil and season with pepper.

5A. FOR A CHARCOAL GRILL: Open bottom vent completely. Light large chimney starter mounded with charcoal briquettes (7 quarts). When top coals are partially covered with ash, pour evenly over grill. Set cooking grate in place, cover, and open lid vent completely. Heat grill until hot, about 5 minutes.

5B. FOR A GAS GRILL: Turn all burners to high, cover, and heat grill until hot, about 15 minutes. Leave all burners on high.

6. FOR THE VINAIGRETTE: While grill heats, whisk all ingredients together in bowl.

7. Clean and oil cooking grate. Place kebabs on grill and cook (covered if using gas) until charred, about 2½ minutes. Flip kebabs and cook until second side is charred and shrimp are cooked through, 2 to 3 minutes, moving kebabs as needed to ensure even cooking. Transfer kebabs to serving platter. Rewhisk vinaigrette and drizzle over kebabs. Serve.

A New Way to Cook Broccoli Rabe

The tricks to taming this notoriously bitter green? How you cut it and how you cook it.

⇒ BY STEVE DUNN ⇐

In the past I rarely, if ever, cooked broccoli rabe. (Rabe, or *rapini*, as it's known in Italy where the vegetable is a mainstay in the cuisine, is actually more closely related to spicy turnips than to regular, more-mellow broccoli.) While I'm a fan of this green's bitter, mustardy bite, I seem to be in the minority on this. As a result, the majority of recipes you find jump through hoops to subdue its characteristic flavor. One of the most popular approaches calls for chopping, blanching, shocking, draining, and sautéing the pieces with strong-flavored aromatics—a lengthy ordeal that wipes out just about any trace of the green's pungency and leaves you with a sink full of dirty dishes. At that point, why bother?

I've always thought that if you could temper rabe's bitterness but not eliminate it entirely, this green would offer much more character than most vegetables. As a bonus, it would need little or no dressing before it hit the plate. The trick would be figuring out the most efficient way to do this.

I made some headway by researching where broccoli rabe gets it bitter flavor. The technical explanation is that when the plant is cut or chewed and its cells thus damaged, two components stored mainly in its florets—the enzyme myrosinase and a bitter-tasting substrate of the enzyme called glucosinolate—combine, and some of the glucosinolates are converted into even harsher-tasting isothiocyanates. In other words, the pungency we taste is the plant's defense mechanism when under attack.

The upshot was that the way in which I cut the rabe seemed likely to be at least as important as how I cooked it. I proved this to myself with a quick side-by-side test: I divided a bunch of rabe in half and fully chopped one portion, florets and all. Then, I cut the remaining stalks roughly where the leaves and florets start to branch off from the stems, leaving the leafy parts intact, and cut the stem segments (where less of the enzyme resides) into bite-size pieces. For the sake of ease, I simply sautéed both batches and took a taste. Sure enough, the intact pieces were considerably more mellow. It also turns out that there was another factor at play: The high heat of cooking deactivates the myrosinase enzyme in the vegetable and thus stops the reaction that contributes most of the bitter flavor in the first place.

I could have stopped right there and created a recipe for sautéing chopped stems and whole leaves

Broiling broccoli rabe browns the vegetable, creating sweetness that complements its bitterness.

Nipping Bitterness in the Bud

Cutting and chewing broccoli rabe releases compounds that are bitter. Since more of these compounds are in the florets, we leave the leafy part whole. Broiling the rabe also reduces bitterness, as heat exposure deactivates the enzyme (myrosinase) that causes the bitterness.

and florets, but I'd found a few recipes that called for roasting the rabe, which was an interesting alternative. Plus, I hoped that the rabe would brown deeply and take on a rich caramelized flavor that would balance out the remaining bitterness. I prepared another batch, giving the stalks a quick rinse before cutting them using my new technique; tossing them with extra-virgin olive oil, garlic, red pepper flakes, and salt; spreading them on a rimmed baking sheet (which was big enough to arrange them in an even layer); and sliding the sheet into a 400-degree oven.

After 10 minutes, the rabe had caramelized nicely, and the leaves now also offered a delicate crunch—that part was good. But texturally, the stems had suffered, turning soft and stringy by the time they had browned.

Part of the problem, I realized, was that the water droplets left over from washing the rabe were taking a long time to burn off and therefore delaying browning. Going forward, I got serious about drying the greens by rolling them in clean dish towels to blot away as much moisture as possible. I also cranked the heat to 450, but even then the stems were limp by the time they were browned.

It was time to take it up a notch to the broiler. I adjusted the oven rack 4 inches from the heating element, popped in another oiled and salted batch, and kept a close watch. In less than 3 minutes, half the rabe's leaves and florets were lightly charred and crisp at the edges, and the stems were also browned yet still bright green and crisp—so far so good. I gave them a quick toss with tongs and slid the sheet back into the oven. Two minutes later, the results were perfect: lightly charred, crisp leaves and florets and perfectly crisp-tender stalks.

BROILED BROCCOLI RABE
SERVES 4

Because the amount of heat generated by a broiler varies from oven to oven, we recommend keeping an eye on the broccoli rabe as it cooks. If the leaves are getting too dark or not browning in the time specified in the recipe, adjust the distance of the oven rack from the broiler element.

- 3 tablespoons extra-virgin olive oil
- 1 pound broccoli rabe
- 1 garlic clove, minced
- ¾ teaspoon kosher salt
- ¼ teaspoon red pepper flakes
- Lemon wedges

1. Adjust oven rack 4 inches from broiler element and heat broiler. Brush rimmed baking sheet with 1 tablespoon oil.

2. Trim and discard bottom 1 inch of broccoli rabe stems. Wash broccoli rabe with cold water, then dry with clean dish towel. Cut tops (leaves and florets) from stems, then cut stems into 1-inch pieces (keep tops whole). Transfer broccoli rabe to prepared sheet.

3. Combine remaining 2 tablespoons oil, garlic, salt, and pepper flakes in small bowl. Pour oil mixture over broccoli rabe and toss to combine.

4. Broil until half of leaves are well browned, 2 to 2½ minutes. Using tongs, toss to expose unbrowned leaves. Return sheet to oven and continue to broil until most leaves are lightly charred and stems are crisp-tender, 2 to 2½ minutes longer. Transfer to serving platter and serve immediately, passing lemon wedges.

▶ **Behold the Broil**
A free video is available at
CooksIllustrated.com/oct16

Bringing Home Scallion Pancakes

We made batch after gummy batch of this Chinese restaurant staple until we discovered a method that produced crispy, gorgeously layered results.

⇒ BY ANDREA GEARY ⇐

Forget casinos and racetracks: I do my gambling at Chinese restaurants when I order scallion pancakes. Hitting the jackpot means digging into deep golden-brown flatbread wedges with crispy exteriors that break away in flaky shards to reveal paper-thin, scallion-studded layers within. But as luck more often has it, I usually end up with floppy, pallid triangles with doughy inner leaves that fuse to form a single dense, gummy layer.

I decided it was time to stop leaving good scallion pancakes to chance and develop my own recipe. A quick look at a few recipes was encouraging. Their ingredient lists included just flour, water, oil, scallions, and salt. And the way the layers were formed seemed clever and interesting: You coat the rolled-out dough with oil and sliced scallions and then fold it up and roll it out again in such a way that you produce multiple sheets of dough separated by fat. When you fry the pancakes, the water in the dough turns to steam, which is trapped between the layers and so forces them apart.

However, opinions about the proper temperature of the water in the dough, the perfect size for the pancake, and the amount of oil used for frying differed. If I wanted a scallion pancake that was a sure bet every time, I'd have to explore all the options.

Hot and Cold

Here's the procedure: Make a dough with just flour and water, separate it into pieces, let them rest for a bit to allow the gluten (the stretchy network of proteins that gives dough its structure) to relax and the starches to hydrate, and then roll each piece into a very thin round. Brush each round with oil, sprinkle it with sliced scallions, and then roll it into a cylinder. Coil the cylinder into a spiral and roll the spiral out again into a pancake. Fry the pancakes until crispy and brown and cut them into wedges to serve with a dipping sauce.

Scallion pancake dough is usually 2 parts flour

We fry the pancakes in an oiled cast-iron skillet for its steady, even heat. If you use a stainless-steel skillet, you may need to increase the heat slightly.

to 1 part water by volume, but some recipes called for boiling water and others for cool. I tried it both ways, keeping all other variables the same. The cool-water dough proved noticeably stickier and forced me to use a lot of flour on the counter, which I knew would stick to the pancakes and burn in the pan during cooking. The cool-water dough also kept springing back when I tried to roll it out. The dough made with boiling water was not only firmer and less

sticky but also more relaxed. Our science editor explained that hot water dissolves the flour's tightly packed starch molecules to a greater extent than cold water does, allowing the starch to absorb the free water that would otherwise make the dough overly sticky. It also decreases the elasticity of the gluten network, so the dough is less prone to snapping back.

Since the finished pancakes in each batch were comparable and the hot-water dough was much easier to work with, the choice was clear. I made another batch, mixing 1½ cups of flour and ¾ cup of boiling water with a wooden spoon and then kneading the dough by hand for a few minutes. I separated it into four pieces and let them rest for 30 minutes before rolling them out into thin rounds. Next I brushed each round with a mixture of vegetable oil and toasted sesame oil added for flavor, sprinkled on the scallions, and proceeded with the rolling into a cylinder, coiling, and second rolling steps, which sounds time-consuming but was actually quickly accomplished. Lastly, I heated 2 teaspoons of vegetable oil in a nonstick skillet and fried my four pancakes, replenishing the oil as needed.

These pancakes definitely had some issues. Steam built up under some of them as they fried, lifting large parts away from the skillet, so they didn't brown evenly. The exteriors were tough and chewy rather than crispy, and the inside was undercooked, verging on raw. Maybe that's why the layers were not as separate as I would have liked. And I wasn't wild about repeating the rolling, coiling, and frying steps four times.

Two Tweaks to Ensure the Best Texture

▶ **See Every Step**
A free video is available at
CooksIllustrated.com/oct16

PIERCE YOUR PANCAKES
Cutting a ½-inch slit in the center of each pancake before cooking allows for the release of steam that would otherwise cause the pancake to puff. By staying flat, the pancakes brown and crisp evenly.

TAKE COVER
During the first few minutes of cooking, we cover the pan to trap steam, which helps the dough cook through from edge to edge. Then we uncover the pan for the final moments of cooking to thoroughly brown and crisp the exterior.

HOW TO GET THE LAYERED LOOK

A great scallion pancake boasts multiple paper-thin layers studded with scallions. Here's how we achieve it.

ROLL OUT dough into 12-inch round.

BRUSH with oil and flour; sprinkle with salt and scallions.

ROLL UP round into cylinder.

COIL cylinder, tucking end underneath, then flatten.

ROLL OUT flattened spiral into 9-inch round; cut slit.

Full Steam Ahead

Reducing the repetition was easy: I simply rolled out two larger pancakes instead of four smaller ones. I also realized that I might be able to increase the inner flakiness if I created a more distinct barrier between the folds to keep them separated, so I added a bit of flour to the oil that I brushed on the rounds. As for the exterior toughness, I suspected it might be because I had skimped on the oil in the frying step, so I tried the other extreme: deep frying, as many restaurants do. But while the interiors were a bit more cooked through (and the oil-flour mixture did make the pancakes more layered), deep frying turned out to be more trouble than it was worth. The pancakes wouldn't stay submerged, so I had to hold them under the surface of the oil, which splashed when I tried to flip them. I went back to a skillet, but this time I added 2 tablespoons of oil per pancake—enough that I no longer needed to use a nonstick pan. Instead, I switched to a cast-iron skillet, which offered steadier, more even heat that encouraged better browning.

The other tweak I made was to cut a slit in the center of each pancake before cooking, hoping that it would allow steam to escape from underneath so the pancake would lie flush against the skillet rather than ballooning in the center. Then, after placing the pancake in the skillet, I covered it, thinking that doing so might trap some heat and cook the interior more thoroughly while the exterior browned and crisped.

After about 1½ minutes, I brushed the top of the pancake with a bit more oil, flipped it (it had indeed remained flat) and covered it again to brown the second side. After another minute or so, both sides were nicely browned but not very crispy. Covering the skillet had trapped not only heat but also steam, which made the pancakes soggy.

Another 40 seconds on each side with the skillet uncovered took care of that.

These pancakes were as crispy, as flaky, as layered, and as well cooked as the best I'd ever eaten, and they had been so easy to make that I had time to stir together a quick sauce for dipping. Now that I'm assured of hitting the jackpot every time, I know exactly where to place my bet.

SCALLION PANCAKES WITH DIPPING SAUCE
SERVES 4 TO 6

For this recipe, we prefer the steady, even heat of a cast-iron skillet. A heavy stainless-steel skillet may be used, but you may have to increase the heat slightly.

Dipping Sauce

- 2 tablespoons soy sauce
- 1 scallion, sliced thin
- 1 tablespoon water
- 2 teaspoons rice vinegar
- 1 teaspoon honey
- 1 teaspoon toasted sesame oil
  Pinch red pepper flakes

Pancakes

- 1½ cups (7½ ounces) plus 1 tablespoon all-purpose flour
- ¾ cup boiling water
- 7 tablespoons vegetable oil
- 1 tablespoon toasted sesame oil
- 1 teaspoon kosher salt
- 4 scallions, sliced thin

1. FOR THE DIPPING SAUCE: Whisk all ingredients together in small bowl; set aside.

2. FOR THE PANCAKES: Using wooden spoon, mix 1½ cups flour and boiling water in bowl to form rough dough. When cool enough to handle, transfer dough to lightly floured counter and knead until tacky (but not sticky) ball forms, about 4 minutes (dough will not be perfectly smooth). Cover loosely with plastic wrap and let rest for 30 minutes.

3. While dough is resting, stir together 1 tablespoon vegetable oil, sesame oil, and remaining 1 tablespoon flour. Set aside.

4. Place 10-inch cast-iron skillet over low heat to preheat. Divide dough in half. Cover 1 half of dough with plastic wrap and set aside. Roll remaining dough into 12-inch round on lightly floured counter. Drizzle with 1 tablespoon oil-flour mixture and use pastry brush to spread evenly over entire surface. Sprinkle with ½ teaspoon salt and half of scallions. Roll dough into cylinder. Coil cylinder into spiral, tuck end underneath, and flatten spiral with your palm. Cover with plastic and repeat with remaining dough, oil-flour mixture, salt, and scallions.

5. Roll first spiral into 9-inch round. Cut ½-inch slit in center of pancake. Cover with plastic. Roll and cut slit in second pancake. Place 2 tablespoons vegetable oil in skillet and increase heat to medium-low. Place 1 pancake in skillet (oil should sizzle). Cover and cook, shaking skillet occasionally, until pancake is slightly puffy and golden brown on underside, 1 to 1½ minutes. (If underside is not browned after 1 minute, turn heat up slightly. If it is browning too quickly, turn heat down slightly.) Drizzle 1 tablespoon vegetable oil over pancake. Use pastry brush to distribute over entire surface. Carefully flip pancake. Cover and cook, shaking skillet occasionally, until second side is golden brown, 1 to 1½ minutes. Uncover skillet and continue to cook until bottom is deep golden brown and crispy, 30 to 60 seconds longer. Flip and cook until deep golden brown and crispy, 30 to 60 seconds. Transfer to wire rack. Repeat with remaining 3 tablespoons vegetable oil and remaining pancake. Cut each pancake into 8 wedges and serve, passing dipping sauce separately.

TO MAKE AHEAD: Stack uncooked pancakes between layers of parchment paper, wrap tightly in plastic wrap, and refrigerate for up to 24 hours or freeze for up to 1 month. If frozen, thaw pancakes in single layer for 15 minutes before cooking.

Scallions: Whites versus Greens

Scallion flavor depends on which part of the stalk you're using and how you're treating it. Used raw, the white (which includes the light green part) is mildly sweet, while the green is grassy and peppery. We've found that these differences become less apparent when the two parts are cooked. However, the reverse is true of scallion texture: Whereas both parts are crisp when raw, cooked whites soften and turn tender, while the greens can become unappealingly limp and even chewy if cooked too long.

dividing line

Rescuing Turkey Meatballs

Turkey meatballs have a justifiably bad reputation. But if you boost the flavors and treat ground turkey like, well, turkey, you get great results.

⋝ BY ANDREW JANJIGIAN ⋜

I can see the appeal of using ground turkey in place of beef or pork in a meatball, since many folks these days want to eat less red meat. But when I swapped ground turkey into my usual meatball recipe (an Italian red-sauce version), I got something that was altogether disappointing. The meat mixture was so wet that it was difficult to shape, and the meatballs slumped during the frying step, leaving them more pyramid-shaped than spherical. Once cooked, they were mushy overall yet grainy inside. And their flavor was entirely uninspiring. I wanted an easy-to-form turkey meatball with the same traits as a knockout beef or pork version: a moist, tender, slightly springy texture and rich, savory flavor.

My standard meatball recipe (like most) goes like this: Combine ground meat and seasonings with egg and a panade—a moistened bread-crumb mixture that helps the meat hold on to liquid as it cooks and keeps its texture open and tender. With beef or pork, you want to handle the mixture as gently as possible, since overworking can cause the meat proteins to tighten up, creating a too-springy, sausage-like consistency. But as I had already discovered, turkey is another beast altogether: Although it contains the same sticky proteins as beef and pork, it also has a higher moisture content (ground turkey contains about 71 percent moisture versus 66 and 61 percent for pork and beef, respectively). This means that even after a good amount of mixing, ground turkey remains wet and hard to work with. Commercially ground turkey also has a finer texture than beef or pork, which is why it cooks up mushy. The fine consistency also means the meat has a harder time holding on to moisture.

There are three options when buying commercially ground turkey: 85 percent lean, 93 percent lean, and 99 percent lean. I tried all three, and I wasn't surprised when the 99 percent lean type produced ultradry, nearly inedible results. I would go with the fattier options, both of which produced moister meatballs.

▶ **Andrew Makes the Meatballs**
A free video is available at
CooksIllustrated.com/oct16

Once the meatballs are browned, we braise them in a well-seasoned sauce, which gives them time to soak up extra flavor.

My recipe called for panko (Japanese dried bread crumbs, which we like for their consistently dry texture) soaked in milk. Since the turkey was so wet to begin with, I figured that the milk was unnecessary and probably partly why the meatballs were so difficult to roll. Indeed, when I left out the milk and just stirred the meat, egg, and panko together, the mixture was stiffer and easier to work with—but the cooked meatballs were somewhat dense.

A better solution was switching to sandwich bread, which I ground to fine crumbs in a food processor. In terms of moisture content, the crumbs were midway between milk-soaked panko and dry panko—dry enough to soak up some of the water in the turkey yet still moist enough to keep meatballs from becoming dense.

But the meatballs were still too mushy, and they continued to be grainy. In an attempt to repair the

Don't Skip Chilling

A stint in the fridge makes the meat mixture easier to shape and also gives the meatballs a springy texture once they are cooked. The quick chill gives the gelatin time to stiffen, helps solidify the fat, and gives the myosin (a sticky, soluble protein in ground turkey) time to bind the meat together.

mushiness, I added another egg, hoping it would firm up the meatballs once cooked, but the extra liquid once again made the mixture too hard to work with. Ultimately, I found that a 15-minute postshaping refrigeration period was the key to creating a springy, not mushy, texture in the cooked meatballs. That's because it gave the myosin, a sticky, soluble protein in meat, time to bind the meat together. (It also firmed up the mixture, making it the easiest yet to shape.)

Finally, it occurred to me that adding some powdered gelatin might help mitigate the graininess of the meat by trapping some of its moisture, and indeed it did. The slick gelatin also created a juicy mouthfeel.

I'd solved the textural problems; now I needed to work on flavor. Italy isn't the only country with a vibrant meatball culture, so I knew I'd want to come up with some variations once I'd perfected my Italian version. I considered Parmesan cheese, which is rich in glutamates, compounds that enhance the meaty umami flavor of foods; it added a savory boost but was subtle enough to work with any flavor profile. Glutamate-rich anchovies worked similarly, amplifying meatiness without announcing their presence.

The last umami-enhancing ingredient I used was a seemingly unusual one: dried shiitake mushrooms. Shiitakes are naturally high in glutamates, and though they are most commonly used in Asian cooking, their flavor is relatively neutral, so I knew they'd work no matter how I flavored the meatballs. I reconstituted them in hot water (making sure to add the soaking liquid to the sauce to retain all of the mushrooms' flavor) and then chopped them fine in the food processor.

Lastly, I tackled the cooking method. For ease, I'd been browning the meatballs in oil in a skillet before removing them, making a quick tomato sauce, and returning them to the skillet to cook through. As they simmered in the sauce, the meatballs picked up that rich flavor.

Move over, pork and beef. I'll still use you to make meatballs—but maybe not quite as often.

ITALIAN-STYLE TURKEY MEATBALLS
SERVES 4 TO 6

Serve with spaghetti. Our free recipes for Asian-Style and Moroccan-Style Turkey Meatballs are available for four months at CooksIllustrated.com/oct16.

I	cup chicken broth
½	ounce dried shiitake mushrooms
2	slices hearty white sandwich bread, torn into 1-inch pieces
I	ounce Parmesan cheese, grated (½ cup), plus extra for serving
I	tablespoon chopped fresh parsley
1½	teaspoons unflavored gelatin
	Salt and pepper
4	anchovy fillets, rinsed, patted dry, and minced
1½	pounds 85 or 93 percent lean ground turkey
I	large egg, lightly beaten
4	garlic cloves, minced
I	(14.5-ounce) can whole peeled tomatoes
½	teaspoon dried oregano
⅛	teaspoon red pepper flakes
3	tablespoons extra-virgin olive oil
2	tablespoons tomato paste
¼	cup chopped fresh basil
	Sugar

1. Microwave broth and mushrooms in covered bowl until steaming, about 1 minute. Let sit until softened, about 5 minutes. Drain mushrooms in fine-mesh strainer and reserve liquid.

2. Pulse bread in food processor until finely ground, 10 to 15 pulses; transfer bread crumbs to large bowl (do not wash processor bowl). Add Parmesan, parsley, gelatin, 1 teaspoon salt, and ¼ teaspoon pepper to bowl with bread crumbs and mix until thoroughly combined. Pulse mushrooms and half of anchovies in food processor until chopped fine, 10 to 15 pulses. Add mushroom mixture, turkey, egg, and half of garlic to bowl with bread-crumb mixture and mix with your hands until thoroughly combined. Divide mixture into 16 portions (about ¼ cup each). Using your hands, roll each portion into ball; transfer meatballs to plate and refrigerate for 15 minutes.

3. Pulse tomatoes and their juice in food processor to coarse puree, 10 to 15 pulses. Combine oregano, pepper flakes, remaining anchovies, remaining garlic, and ¼ teaspoon pepper in small bowl; set aside.

4. Heat oil in 12-inch nonstick skillet over medium-high heat until shimmering. Add meatballs and cook until well browned all over, 5 to 7 minutes. Transfer meatballs to paper towel–lined plate, leaving fat in skillet.

5. Add reserved anchovy mixture to skillet and cook, stirring constantly, until fragrant, about 30 seconds. Increase heat to high; stir in tomato paste, reserved mushroom liquid, and pureed tomatoes; and bring to simmer. Return meatballs to skillet, reduce heat to medium-low, cover, and cook until meatballs register 160 degrees, 12 to 15 minutes, turning meatballs once. Transfer meatballs to platter, increase heat to high, and simmer sauce until slightly thickened, 3 to 5 minutes. Stir in basil and season with sugar, salt, and pepper to taste. Pour sauce over meatballs and serve, passing extra Parmesan separately.

Ground Turkey Tips

➤ DON'T SKIMP TOO MUCH ON FAT
We found that 99 percent lean commercial ground turkey yielded meatballs that were irreparably dry and grainy, so we recommend avoiding it. However, our meatball recipe works well with both 93 and 85 percent lean ground turkey, so use whichever of these you can find. (Packages usually state the fat percentage, though it is not always displayed prominently; another tip-off is that, typically, the darker the meat, the higher the fat content.)

➤ BUY STORE-GROUND IF YOU CAN
We developed our turkey meatball recipes using commercial ground turkey, which tends to have a very fine texture. If your supermarket or butcher grinds turkey in house, buy that instead. Store-ground turkey is typically more coarsely ground than commercial ground turkey and will produce meatballs with a slightly less compacted texture.

➤ CONSIDER GRINDING YOUR OWN
If you have the time and inclination, we recommend grinding your own turkey thighs for the very best results: Start with one 2-pound turkey thigh, skinned, boned, trimmed, and cut into ½-inch pieces. Place pieces on large plate in single layer. Freeze until pieces are very firm and hardened around edges, 35 to 45 minutes. Pulse one-third of turkey in food processor until chopped into ⅛-inch pieces, 18 to 22 pulses, stopping and redistributing turkey around bowl as needed to ensure even grinding. Transfer turkey to large bowl and repeat 2 times with remaining turkey. Yields 1½ pounds.

Turkey Meatball Variations

Ground turkey's mild taste makes it ideal for adding flavors. We kept the key umami boosters but switched up ingredients to produce recipes for Asian- and Moroccan-Style Meatballs. The free recipes are available for four months at CooksIllustrated.com/oct16.

ASIAN-STYLE MEATBALLS
We mix scallions and plenty of ground white pepper into the turkey mixture before simmering the meatballs in a brothy sauce augmented with soy sauce, garlic, and sesame oil.

MOROCCAN-STYLE MEATBALLS
We season the turkey mixture with warm spices, add chopped carrots, and simmer the meatballs in a tomatoey broth infused with saffron, ginger, and cilantro.

Which Ingredients Add Up to Great Meatballs?
Settling on 85 or 93 percent lean ground turkey was only half the battle. We tried multiple additions to our meatballs until we landed on the perfect recipe.

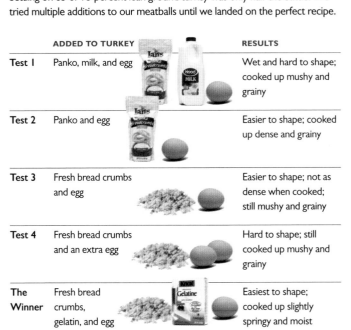

	ADDED TO TURKEY	RESULTS
Test 1	Panko, milk, and egg	Wet and hard to shape; cooked up mushy and grainy
Test 2	Panko and egg	Easier to shape; cooked up dense and grainy
Test 3	Fresh bread crumbs and egg	Easier to shape; not as dense when cooked; still mushy and grainy
Test 4	Fresh bread crumbs and an extra egg	Hard to shape; still cooked up mushy and grainy
The Winner	Fresh bread crumbs, gelatin, and egg	Easiest to shape; cooked up slightly springy and moist

The Best Countertop Appliances

The right appliances not only make cooking easier and more enjoyable but can also help your recipes turn out better. BY KEITH DRESSER

Too often, appliances promising convenience wind up as clutter. Decades of testing have taught us which pieces of equipment are the most useful and which models are the highest quality and most durable. Here's our guide to the best options for key appliances that can improve how you bake and cook.

FOOD PROCESSOR

CUISINART Custom 14 Food Processor ($199.99)
A food processor is essential for kneading dough, cutting butter into pastry, and grinding meat. With a powerful motor, responsive pulsing action, and sharp blades, this model effortlessly handles these tasks. It also chops, slices, and shreds neatly and with ease.

SMALL FOOD PROCESSOR

CUISINART Elite Collection 4-Cup Chopper/Grinder ($59.95)
Smaller processors can't handle doughs or large-quantity prep, but the powerful motor on this model makes it superconvenient for zipping through smaller-quantity jobs like chopping nuts, grinding bread crumbs, or dicing an onion or two.

BLENDER

VITAMIX 5200 ($449.00)
This impressive, powerful (1,380-watt) commercial-style blender crushes ice with ease and makes lump-free smoothies, hummus, and more. Its performance commands a steep price, but it is exceptionally durable and comes with a seven-year warranty.

➤ **Best Buy: Breville The Hemisphere Control ($199.99)**
If you subject your blender to heavy-duty use, we recommending saving up for a Vitamix. However, at less than half the price, the relatively powerful (750-watt) Breville is an excellent choice for routine use.

The best cooks invest in the right tools—and we'll tell you exactly which ones to look for. Browse up-to-date reviews, buying guides, and expert tips on CooksIllustrated.com.

IMMERSION BLENDER

KITCHENAID 3-Speed Hand Blender ($59.99)
An immersion blender is a great backup to a traditional blender, saving time, effort, and cleanup. Soups can be pureed right in the pot, and small jobs like blending vinaigrette or even whipping cream take mere seconds. This model is comfortable and simple to use as well as tough and durable.

➤ **Quick Vinaigrette:** Using an immersion blender allows you to add all the oil to a vinaigrette at once. Add the solids and vinegar to a tall, narrow container and pour in the oil. Place the blender at the bottom of the container and blend at the lowest speed. Gradually increase the speed to medium and slowly pull the blender to the top. For more tips on using an immersion blender, see page 31.

SLOW COOKER

KITCHENAID 6-Quart Slow Cooker with Solid Glass Lid ($99.99)
This digital cooker simmers food gently and evenly. Testers liked its cool-to-the-touch handles and intuitive-to-use control panel.

ELECTRIC CITRUS JUICER

BREVILLE Stainless Steel Juicer ($199.99)
The Breville extracts every last drop of juice with minimal effort. This attractive stainless-steel machine is easy to clean (all nonmotorized parts are dishwasher-safe) and quiet enough to use in the early morning.

➤ **Best Buy: Dash Go Dual Citrus Juicer ($19.99)**
Don't think twice about buying this inexpensive juicer over the Breville. While it lacks the Breville's motorized lever, it still performed every bit as well.

Stand or Handheld?

If you are a regular baker, a stand mixer is imperative for mixing pizza and bread doughs, whipping cream and egg whites, and creaming butter and sugar. However, if you seldom bake, you can get by with a handheld mixer for occasional mixing, whipping, and creaming.

STAND MIXER
KITCHENAID Pro Line Series 7-Qt Bowl Lift Stand Mixer ($549.95)
Its robust motor, durability, and smart design make this mixer truly worth the investment if you do a lot of heavy-duty baking. It effortlessly handles a range of volumes of food, from small amounts of whipped cream to heavy batches of bread or pizza dough to stiff cookie dough.

➤ **Best Buy: KitchenAid Classic Plus Series 4.5-Quart Tilt-Head Stand Mixer ($229.99)**
This basic, compact machine is an excellent choice for budget-conscious bakers. We wish that its bowl had a handle and that the machine had a bowl lift, but these are small concessions given its affordable price.

HANDHELD MIXER
KITCHENAID 5-Speed Ultra Power Hand Mixer ($69.99)
A handheld mixer lacks the power of a stand mixer but works just fine for occasional light tasks. (It's also just nice to have on hand, even if you own a stand mixer. It's far easier to pull out when all you need to do is whip ½ cup of cream.) This model is light, maneuverable, and efficient.

➤ **Best Buy: Cuisinart PowerSelect 3-Speed Hand Mixer ($26.77)**
Though it has just three speeds compared with our winner's five, this comfortable-to-hold mixer is plenty powerful for simple tasks.

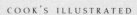

Forget Toasters. Buy a Toaster Oven.

Our advice on buying toasters and toaster ovens has changed: In 2009, we halfheartedly recommended our winning toaster oven because of the expense and said that you'd be better off buying a toaster and using your oven (unless you do a lot of small cooking projects). Today, the best two-slot toaster we can find (the MagiMix by Robot-Coupe Vision Toaster) costs a staggering $249.00, and our Best Buy, the KitchenAid 2 Slice Manual High-Lift Lever with LCD Display, can't be counted on to consistently produce evenly browned toast—and still costs $99.99. Our new recommendation? Consider skipping a toaster altogether. Instead, choose a regular or "compact" toaster oven that can perform as both a toaster and a small oven—our winners are exceptional and serve both functions well.

TOASTER OVEN
BREVILLE The Smart Oven by Breville ($249.95)
A small second oven is handy for preparing side dishes, toasting nuts and bread crumbs, or even roasting a chicken, and it helps keeps the kitchen cool in hot weather. Five quartz heating elements consistently cool and reheat, producing uniform browning and cooking.

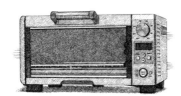

COMPACT CHOICE
BREVILLE Mini Smart Oven with Element IQ ($149.95)
This toaster oven, which is roughly 25 percent smaller than the full-size model, aced every test we threw at it, from roasting chicken breasts to baking cookies and toasting bread. It's a great choice—even if you just use it for toast.

DRIP COFFEE MAKER
TECHNIVORM Moccamaster 10-Cup Coffee Maker with Thermal Carafe ($299.00)
This hand-built, intuitive Dutch machine is utterly consistent, producing pot after pot of a "smooth," "velvety" brew by hitting the ideal temperature zone for the optimal length of time.

➤ **Best Buy: Bonavita 8-Cup Coffee Maker with Thermal Carafe ($189.99)** This brewer is also an excellent choice, producing "rich," "full-flavored" coffee. Its thermal carafe kept coffee very hot for up to 3 hours.

SPICE/COFFEE GRINDER
KRUPS Fast-Touch Coffee Mill ($19.99)
This model produces an exceptionally fine, uniform grind and easily pulverizes spices of varying hardness, density, and shape. What's more, it is easy to fill and use. If you grind coffee beans regularly, we advise buying two mills and using one exclusively for coffee and one for spices.

➤ **"Dry Clean" Your Grinder:** The oils in coffee beans, spices, and chiles can cling to the insides of grinders. Since the appliances can't be washed, here's how to clean them: Pulverize a few tablespoons of raw rice in the grinder to a fine powder. The powder will absorb any residues and oils. Discard the powder, and the tool will be clean.

ICE CREAM MAKER
CUISINART Automatic Frozen Yogurt, Ice Cream & Sorbet Maker ($53.99)
This exceptionally affordable model churns out frozen desserts that are "even-textured" and "velvety." We appreciate its lightweight, compact design and its one-button operation. If you like to make batches of ice cream in succession, buy a second canister to store in your freezer.

Angling for a Sharper Edge?
We've long appreciated the thinner blade of our winning chef's knife, the Victorinox 8" Swiss Army Fibrox Pro, which boasts the finer 15-degree angle more typically found on Japanese knives. Many other European bladesmiths are now making knives with a similar ultrathin edge. But if you have a traditional Western knife with a 20-degree blade angle, our winning Trizor electric sharpener offers a great perk: It can hone a wider cutting edge to 15 degrees.

ELECTRIC KNIFE SHARPENER
CHEF'SCHOICE Trizor XV Knife Sharpener ($149.99)
Its diamond abrasives consistently produced 15-degree edges that were sharper than those on new knives. After 10 minutes of sharpening, a severely nicked knife looked and cut like a brand-new blade.

➤ **Best Buy: Chef'sChoice Diamond Sharpener For Asian Knives ($79.99)**
Also fitted with diamond abrasives, this model wasn't quite as effective at sharpening to 15 degrees as its winning sibling. It removed nicks in the blade, though it took 30 minutes and a tiring 223 swipes.

RICE COOKER
AROMA 8-Cup Digital Rice Cooker and Food Steamer ($29.92)

This inexpensive appliance makes cooking white, brown, and sushi rice convenient and entirely foolproof. Useful features include a digital timer that lets the cook know when the rice is nearly ready, a clear audio alert, and a delayed-start function.

➤ **Faster Rice:** Brown rice can take up to an hour to cook. To reduce the cooking time to just 30 minutes, soak the rice (1½ cups of water per cup of rice) directly in the rice cooker pot for 6 to 24 hours in the refrigerator. When you're ready to cook, add salt, put the pot in the cooker, and turn on the heat.

HOME SELTZER MAKER
SODASTREAM Source Starter Kit ($99.95)
This countertop machine transforms tap water into sparkling water by applying light pressure to a carbonating block that allows you to choose between gentle carbonation or intense effervescence. Long-lasting CO_2 canisters are convenient to exchange (at 50 percent of the price of new) in dozens of retail stores.

➤ **For the Most Fizz, Use Ice-Cold Water:** When we carbonated 32-degree water, 68-degree water, and 140-degree water, the 32-degree sample was by far the most effervescent, with small, long-lasting bubbles. That's because cold water can hold five times more carbon dioxide than warmer water can.

Perfect Boiled Corn

The best way to guarantee perfectly crisp, juicy kernels? Not boiling the corn at all.

⇒ BY LAN LAM ⇐

I almost didn't pursue a boiled corn recipe. I'd never consulted one, and as one of my colleagues asked dubiously, what was wrong with the usual method? Bring a pot of water to a boil, drop in the ears, and wait. When the kernels turn bright yellow, they're done.

I was inclined to agree with her, until I thought about how rarely I've produced perfectly crisp, juicy corn. Usually, I pull the ears out too early and the kernels are underdone and starchy, or I let them sit in the cooling water while I get the rest of dinner on the table—and find that they've shriveled and turned to mush. Given how fleeting corn season is, I decided it was worth figuring out a method that delivers perfect results every time.

First, I took a close look at exactly what happens to corn as it goes from raw to cooked. There are two key variables at play: the starches and the pectin. Anyone who's bitten into an ear of raw corn knows that the liquid inside the kernels (referred to as the "milk") is chalky, thanks to the presence of raw starches. As corn heats, those starches absorb water, swell, and gelatinize, and the starchy liquid becomes seemingly smoother, silkier, and more translucent.

Tracking How Corn Cooks

It's easy to overcook boiled corn, since the corn's temperature soon approaches that of the boiling water (212 degrees) and its pectin rapidly dissolves. But if the heat is shut off right before the corn is added to the water, the temperatures of both will equalize somewhere between 150 and 170 degrees, the sweet spot where the corn's starches have gelatinized but little of its pectin has broken down and the kernels still remain snappy.

When water continues to boil after corn is added:	When water is turned off right before corn is added:
water 212°	water
170°	170°
150°	150°
corn	corn
Corn temperature overshoots its ideal doneness range, and corn turns mushy.	Corn and water meet at about 160°, ensuring perfect texture every time.

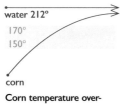

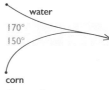

▶ **Look: No-Boil Corn**
A free video is available at
CooksIllustrated.com/oct16

Simultaneously, the pectin (which is essentially glue holding together the cell walls inside each kernel) dissolves, and the cell walls no longer stick together, so the corn softens. The more pectin that dissolves, the mushier the corn becomes.

All of this meant that the key to perfectly cooked corn would be pinpointing when the starches had gelatinized but the pectin hadn't dissolved so much that the kernels lost their crisp bite. Fortunately, I was able to attach temperatures to these phases: Corn starch begins to gelatinize at 144 degrees, while pectin starts dissolving at 176 degrees and does so rapidly at 194 degrees. Using those temperatures as parameters, I would aim for a doneness zone of 150 to 170 degrees—hot enough to cook the starches quickly but cool enough to keep the majority of the pectin intact.

On to the cooking method: Figuring that the only way to guarantee consistent results would be to cook a certain number of ears in a measured amount of water for a certain amount of time, I settled on six ears and began experimenting with various amounts of boiling water and cooking times. But it wasn't that simple; sometimes the corn would cook perfectly, and other times it would emerge under- or overdone. Eventually I realized that the problem was the varying sizes of the ears. They weighed anywhere between 6 and 9 ounces, so depending on the total weight of corn in the pot, the water temperature dropped accordingly, and the cooking time varied.

I wasn't about to settle for a recipe that worked only with a specific size ear, but it occurred to me that I could ensure that the water never got hot enough to overcook the corn in the first place. The idea is based on the popular restaurant method of *sous vide*, where food cooks in a water bath set at a specific temperature and can get only as hot as that temperature. We've hacked that technique in the past by bringing water to a boil, adding the item(s), and shutting off the heat. The food increases in temperature as the water

temperature decreases, until an equilibrium is reached; the final temperature depends on the relative amounts of water and food.

So I experimented: I dropped six ears of various sizes into 3, 4, and 5 quarts of boiling water; shut off the heat; and let them sit between 10 and 30 minutes. About a dozen batches later, I'd nailed the formula: six ears of any size in 4 quarts of cooling water ensured that the water didn't stay hot long enough for much pectin to dissolve, yielding snappy, not starchy, kernels every time.

My method had another perk: I could achieve these results whether I left the corn in the water for as little as 10 minutes or as long as 30 minutes, since the water temperature continued to drop and the corn would never overcook—an advantage for those who eat a couple of ears but don't want to pull both from the water at the same time. When all was said and done, my method was not only more reliable but also more forgiving than not using a recipe at all.

FOOLPROOF BOILED CORN
SERVES 4 TO 6

Success depends on using the proper ratio of hot water to corn. Eight ears of corn can be prepared using this recipe, but let the corn sit for at least 15 minutes before serving. Use a Dutch oven with a capacity of at least 7 quarts. Serve with Chili-Lime Salt (recipe follows), if desired. Our free recipes for Cumin-Sesame Salt and Pepper-Cinnamon Salt are available for four months at CooksIllustrated.com/oct16.

6   ears corn, husks and silk removed
    Unsalted butter, softened
    Salt and pepper

1. Bring 4 quarts water to boil in large Dutch oven. Turn off heat, add corn to water, cover, and let stand for at least 10 minutes or up to 30 minutes.
2. Transfer corn to large platter and serve immediately, passing butter, salt, and pepper separately.

CHILI-LIME SALT
MAKES 3 TABLESPOONS

This spice mix can be refrigerated for up to one week.

2   tablespoons kosher salt
4   teaspoons chili powder
¾   teaspoon grated lime zest

Combine all ingredients in small bowl.

Sourdough Start-Up

Making a starter requires time but very little effort. And once it's established, it opens up a whole new universe of homemade breads with sourdough's trademark tang.

⇒ BY ANDREW JANJIGIAN ⇐

My foray into sourdough baking wasn't as romantic as some. I wasn't bequeathed an heirloom starter from my grandmother. Nor did I acquire one that's ripe with exotic flora while traveling abroad. I was a hobbyist baker when I made my first homegrown batch, and I was tempted to do so not only because I love the tang, complexity, and chew of a good sourdough loaf but also because I was intrigued by the idea of making bread entirely from scratch.

Making a sourdough starter is actually dead simple: All you have to do is stir together some flour and water and let it ferment for a couple of days at room temperature. As the mixture sits, yeast and bacteria already present in the flour wake up and start to multiply, and the mixture evolves into a damp, bubbly, boozy-scented blob. This is your starter—a culture of yeast and bacteria. From here, you help it grow strong by "feeding" it regularly, which might sound intimidating but really isn't once you get the hang of it. You simply combine a small amount of the starter with more flour and water until, after a few weeks, it becomes chock-full of enough bacteria and yeast that a portion can flavor and leaven bread. You can save what's left, and as long

A sourdough starter begins with stirring together just flour and water. Given care and time, this mixture can leaven and flavor bread.

as you keep it healthy and alive, you can continue to use it for months and even years. The process is a commitment but one that's rewarding—even addictive. Just ask some of my colleagues, who've confessed to extreme measures like taking their starters on airplanes so as not to miss a feeding.

So why don't more home bakers try making their own starter? My guess is that the process seems mysterious and complicated. That's why I decided to come up with a straightforward, reliable recipe for creating and maintaining a sourdough starter—so even the most inexperienced baker would feel confident trying it. Then I wanted to develop two sourdough bread recipes: one that would be the easiest, quickest way to use the starter in a baked loaf and another more involved recipe that would produce the most classic form of sourdough, the rustic loaf known as *pain au levain*.

Culture Club

Mixing together flour and water is a pretty straightforward business, but I did make a few discoveries about even these two simple ingredients. After making a few slow-to-grow starters that took a week or longer to establish themselves, I learned that starting with a 50/50 mix (by weight) of whole-wheat and all-purpose flours worked much faster than using just all-purpose flour because the whole-wheat flour provided some extra nutrition for the budding organisms. Using filtered or bottled water was also important; when I used tap water, the chlorine it contains weakened the starter, causing it to die.

After mixing the flours and water together, I waited. After two or three days at room temperature, the loose, batter-like mixture was bubbly and fragrant, a sign that microorganisms were alive and consuming the nutrients in the flour. It wasn't a pleasant aroma at this point (it was like sour milk or dirty socks), but it was a positive sign that the starter was established.

Time to Hit Refresh

The goal of the next stage is to get those microorganisms thriving by regularly refreshing their food supply. The method—mixing a small amount of the starter with fresh flour and water and leaving it to sit at room temperature—is pretty standard across recipes; it's just the frequency that varies. Many recipes call for feeding every 12 hours, but this was overkill. I found that every 24 hours was totally sufficient.

It took about two weeks of daily feedings using my mix of all-purpose and whole-wheat flours before my starter was ready, or mature. At this point it had a pleasant aroma (no more funky smell), was bubbly, and nearly doubled in size 8 to 12 hours after the last feeding. From here, I could use some of my starter to bake a loaf, or I could shift it into maintenance mode. I'd get to the bread baking soon enough, so I moved on to figuring out the easiest, least-involved method for keeping my starter healthy between bakes.

▶ **See How It's Done**
A free video is available at
CooksIllustrated.com/oct16

PROOF IN THE OVEN
Sourdoughs can take much longer to rise than doughs leavened with commercial yeast. That's because the bacteria and yeast in a sourdough metabolize starch much more slowly than baker's yeast does, and they also prefer slightly higher temperatures for proofing. You can't do much about the metabolism of the sourdough's bacteria and yeast, but you can accommodate their temperature needs. That's why we set the shaped loaf, in the pot, in the oven and place a pan of hot water beneath it. This creates a warm, steamy environment—a "proofing box"—that encourages the dough to rise and keeps it from drying out.

Making a Sourdough Loaf: Starter to Finish

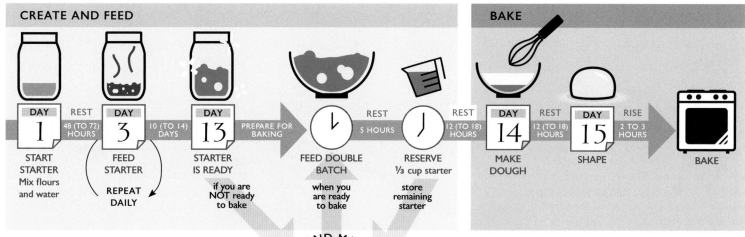

CREATE AND FEED

DAY 1 — START STARTER — Mix flours and water

REST 48 (TO 72) HOURS

DAY 3 — FEED STARTER — REPEAT DAILY

REST 10 (TO 14) DAYS

DAY 13 — STARTER IS READY — if you are NOT ready to bake

PREPARE FOR BAKING

FEED DOUBLE BATCH — when you are ready to bake

REST 5 HOURS

RESERVE ⅓ cup starter — store remaining starter

REST 12 (TO 18) HOURS

BAKE

DAY 14 — MAKE DOUGH

REST 12 (TO 18) HOURS

DAY 15 — SHAPE

RISE 2 TO 3 HOURS

BAKE

STORE AND MAINTAIN
FEED REPEAT WEEKLY

WHY DISCARD STARTER?
Each time you feed your starter, you measure out a portion of existing starter, add flour and water to that, and throw out the rest. Why? As the microorganisms consume nutrients, they also produce waste, so disposing of some starter helps refresh their living environment. Also, if you kept all the starter, you'd have enough to fill a bathtub after a few weeks.

IS YOUR STARTER READY FOR BAKING?
A starter that is ready for baking will double in size 8 to 12 hours after feeding. Want to double-check that it is ready? Here's a quick test you can do to find out. Drop a spoonful of starter into a bowl of water. If it floats, the culture is sufficiently active. If it sinks, let your starter sit for another hour or so.

Low Maintenance

During the maintenance stage, you aren't trying to multiply the number of microorganisms but rather simply to maintain what you have and keep the starter healthy through regular feedings (ideally, it will live indefinitely). My goal would be to keep the feedings down to as few as possible—which would mean storing the starter in the fridge. (At room temperature, the bacteria and yeast would be more active, consuming food more quickly and requiring more feedings.) From then on, I'd just have to take the starter out every so often, refresh the food supply, and give the culture some time at room temperature to wake up and start feeding and reviving before putting it back in the fridge. What I needed to determine was just how often I would have to feed the starter and how long I would need to leave it out when I did.

First I tried feeding my starter once a week and leaving it out for 12 hours before putting it back in the fridge. But it began looking gray and smelling sour, as if all those millions of microorganisms were feeling sick. After talking to Ciril Hitz, a friend who is also an award-winning master baker, I learned that 12 hours was too long—the yeast and bacteria consumed the food so fast that they starved over the course of the next week in the fridge. Hitz suggested leaving the starter out for just 5 hours, which would be long enough for the culture to get a foothold but not consume all of the food. In the fridge, the starter would continue to feed and grow at a very slow pace, staying healthy all the while.

This worked beautifully. I also learned that during this stage it was best to use just all-purpose flour. The whole-wheat flour proved a bit too nutritious, causing the starter to grow too fast and get too sour.

When I wanted to bake with my starter, I fed it a double portion so that I would have plenty to use for baking, plus leftovers to continue to store. I left the starter out at room temperature for 5 hours as before. It then needed an additional 12 to 18 hours in the refrigerator to rest—and it was ready to go.

In the end, my starter recipe was pretty simple: Mix the flours and water together, let it sit for a few days, feed it daily for 10 to 14 days, and then feed it just once a week. Whenever I wanted to bake, I just gave it one last big feeding, let it go for a day, and that was it.

Culture in Action

Now I just needed to iron out the bread recipes. Our Almost No-Knead Bread (January/February 2008) makes a great artisanal loaf with minimal work; it seemed like a good framework to start with. It's called "almost" no-knead because while it relies mainly on gluten's ability to develop structure in a dough on its own given enough time (and plenty of water), kneading the dough for a few seconds before shaping it evens out the texture and ensures a well-risen loaf. Baking the loaf in a Dutch oven also helps it rise well and creates a crackly-crisp crust.

What Happens When You "Feed" a Starter

A sourdough starter begins with mixing together just flour and water. As the mixture sits, wild yeast and lactic acid–producing bacteria that are already present in the flour wake up and start to multiply. This is the beginning of your culture of microorganisms that, once healthy and plentiful, will be able to leaven bread and also imbue it with that trademark sour flavor.

So how do you help those microorganisms multiply and grow? By "feeding" the culture daily for a few weeks with fresh flour and water, you provide a new supply of nutrients. (Leaving the culture at room temperature after each feeding is also key—it does best in warmer environments.) At each feeding, you use only a portion of your existing starter and throw away the rest. This encourages faster growth by getting rid of waste the microorganisms have produced. The microorganisms consume the food and multiply and grow until there is no more food left; you then repeat the cycle with another feeding. After a couple of weeks of this, you'll know the microorganisms are plentiful and healthy because the mixture doubles in size 8 to 12 hours after a feeding—a sign the culture is really active. Your starter is ready for bread baking.

To make a no-knead sourdough version, all I needed was flour, salt, and water, along with my starter. The only question was, how much starter did I need to swap in for the commercial yeast? After a few trials, I settled on ⅓ cup of starter; this gave me a dough that proofed and baked in the same time frame as in the original recipe. The loaf had the bold tang, open crumb, and perfectly crisp, burnished crust I was after. My pain au levain recipe required more work, but it delivered complex flavor and a classic appearance.

With that, I had the straightforward, reliable starter recipe I'd hoped for, as well as two bread recipes to use it in. If you just give it a try, I'll bet you'll be surprised at how easy the world of sourdough is. What could be more satisfying than being part of the act of creating bread from the very first step?

SOURDOUGH STARTER

It's okay to occasionally miss a daily feeding in step 2, but don't let it go for more than 48 hours. For the best results, weigh your ingredients and use organic flour and bottled or filtered water to create the starter. Once the starter is mature, all-purpose flour should be used to maintain it. Placing the starter in a glass bowl will allow for easier observation of activity beneath the surface. Discarding some starter before each feeding gets rid of waste and keeps the amount of starter manageable.

4½	cups (24¾ ounces) whole-wheat flour
5	cups (25 ounces) all-purpose flour, plus extra for maintaining starter
	Water, room temperature

1. Combine whole-wheat flour and all-purpose flour in large container. Using wooden spoon, mix 1 cup (5 ounces) flour mixture and ⅔ cup (5⅓ ounces) room-temperature water in glass bowl until no dry flour remains (reserve remaining flour mixture). Cover with plastic wrap and let sit at room temperature until bubbly and fragrant, 48 to 72 hours.

2. **FEED STARTER:** Measure out ¼ cup (2 ounces) starter and transfer to clean bowl or jar; discard remaining starter. Stir ½ cup (2½ ounces) flour mixture and ¼ cup (2 ounces) room-temperature water into starter until no dry flour remains. Cover with plastic wrap and let sit at room temperature for 24 hours.

3. Repeat step 2 every 24 hours until starter is pleasantly aromatic and doubles in size 8 to 12 hours after being fed, 10 to 14 days. At this point starter is mature and ready to be baked with, or it can be moved to storage. (If baking, use starter once it has doubled in size during 8-to-12-hour window. Use starter within 1 hour after it starts to deflate once reaching its peak.)

4A. TO STORE AND MAINTAIN MATURE STARTER: Measure out ¼ cup (2 ounces) starter and transfer to clean bowl; discard remaining starter.

Our Almost No-Knead Sourdough Bread recipe is an easy approach to making an artisanal sourdough loaf.

Stir ½ cup (2½ ounces) all-purpose flour and ¼ cup (2 ounces) room-temperature water into starter until no dry flour remains. Transfer to clean container that can be loosely covered (plastic container or mason jar with its lid inverted) and let sit at room temperature for 5 hours. Cover and transfer to refrigerator. If not baking regularly, repeat process weekly.

4B. TO PREPARE FOR BAKING: Eighteen to 24 hours before baking, measure out ½ cup (4 ounces) starter and transfer to clean bowl; discard remaining starter. Stir 1 cup (5 ounces) all-purpose flour and ½ cup (4 ounces) room-temperature water into starter until no dry flour remains. Cover and let sit at room temperature for 5 hours. Measure out amount of starter called for in bread recipe and transfer to second bowl. Cover and refrigerate for at least 12 hours or up to 18 hours. Remaining starter should be refrigerated and maintained as directed.

ALMOST NO-KNEAD SOURDOUGH BREAD
MAKES 1 LARGE ROUND LOAF

We prefer King Arthur all-purpose flour in this recipe; if you can't find it, you can substitute any brand of bread flour. For the best results, weigh your ingredients. The dough can rise at room temperature in step 3 (instead of in the oven), but it will take 3 to 4 hours. Do not wait until the oven has preheated in step 4 to start timing 30 minutes or the bread will burn.

3⅔	cups (18⅓ ounces) King Arthur all-purpose flour
1¾	teaspoons salt
1½	cups plus 4 teaspoons (12⅔ ounces) water, room temperature
⅓	cup (3 ounces) mature sourdough starter

1. Whisk flour and salt together in medium bowl. Whisk room-temperature water and starter in large bowl until smooth. Add flour mixture to water mixture and stir using wooden spoon, scraping up dry flour from bottom of bowl until dough comes together, then knead by hand in bowl until shaggy ball forms and no dry flour remains. Cover bowl with plastic wrap and let sit at room temperature for at least 12 hours or up to 18 hours.

2. Lay 12 by 12-inch sheet of parchment paper on counter and spray generously with vegetable oil spray. Transfer dough to lightly floured counter and knead 10 to 15 times. Shape dough into ball by pulling edges into middle. Transfer dough, seam side down, to center of parchment. Pick up dough by lifting parchment edges and lower into heavy-bottomed Dutch oven. Cover with plastic wrap.

3. Adjust oven rack to middle position and place loaf or cake pan in bottom of oven. Place pot on middle rack and pour 3 cups of boiling water into pan below. Close oven door and let dough rise until doubled in size and does not readily spring back when poked with your floured finger, 2 to 3 hours.

4. Remove pot and water pan from oven; discard plastic from pot. Lightly flour top of dough and, using razor blade or sharp knife, make one 7-inch-long, ½-inch-deep slit along top of dough. Cover pot and place on middle rack in oven. Heat oven to 425 degrees. Bake bread for 30 minutes (starting timing as soon as you turn on oven).

5. Remove lid and continue to bake until loaf is deep brown and registers 210 degrees, 20 to 30 minutes longer. Carefully remove bread from pot; transfer to wire rack and let cool completely before serving.

Take It to the Next Level

Our recipe for the classic sourdough loaf known as *pain au levain* takes more time and effort than our Almost No-Knead Sourdough Bread, but the result is a bread with more complex flavor, a more open crumb, and the classic rustic loaf appearance. Our free recipe is available for four months at CooksIllustrated.com/oct16.

Classic Chewy Oatmeal Cookies

Knowingly or not, most folks use the cookie recipe from the Quaker canister. We wanted a cookie that was chewier, moister, and easier to make.

⇒ BY ANDREA GEARY ⇐

Why does the man on the Quaker oatmeal package look so smug? Maybe it's because he's the cunning perpetrator of a wildly successful cookie con. The evidence is anecdotal but persuasive: When I asked several friends to share their favorite family recipe for oatmeal cookies, many produced (often unbeknownst to them) the recipe from the Quaker Oatmeal website, Quaker's Best Oatmeal Cookies. The guy on the canister has apparently cornered the market, but do his cookies really deserve all the love?

The recipe goes like this: Use a mixer to cream the butter and sugar and then add an egg and some vanilla. Stir in some flour, leavening, salt (oddly optional in this recipe), spices (a generous amount), and old-fashioned rolled oats, and then spoon the mixture onto baking sheets. As they bake, the cookies fill the house with the heady scents of butter and cinnamon.

One bite of a cooled cookie, though, and the problems were apparent: The Quaker standby was crumbly at the edges and dry and cakey in the middle. Plus, the abundant spices overpowered the subtle flavor of the oats. I wanted a cookie with a crispy edge; a dense, chewy middle; and true oaty flavor. I was confident I could attain these goals and, in doing so, topple the oatmeal cookie kingpin. But I wasn't above using his recipe as a starting point.

Mixed Up

I planned to make the salt mandatory instead of optional and to tone down the spices, but other than that I saw no reason to change the key ingredients in the Quaker recipe at this point—they each played a role—so I turned my attention to the ingredient proportions.

Most of those seemed OK, too. Only one, the 2½ sticks of butter, stood out as scandalously extravagant. The only cookie I know that has such a high

The right ratio of unsaturated to saturated fats creates the perfect texture.

▶ Watch the Cookies Happen
A free video is available at
CooksIllustrated.com/oct16

proportion of butter to flour is shortbread, and that was definitely not the texture I was after. Instead, I placed a more reasonable 1½ sticks of softened butter in the mixer bowl. The brown sugar, granulated sugar, egg, vanilla, flour, and baking soda amounts all remained the same. But because I wanted just a hint of spice, I cut the cinnamon back to a mere ¼ teaspoon and eliminated the nutmeg altogether.

All was going well until it was time to add the oats. The mixture was simply too dry to accommodate all of them; I ended up with something that resembled crumble topping more than it did cookie dough.

I abandoned that batch and started over, keeping the butter to 1½ sticks but reducing the flour to 1 cup. This worked better: The cookies weren't as dry, and with less flour in the mix, the flavor of the oats stood out more.

Unfortunately, these cookies tasted a bit tinny. They also seemed rather lean, and the cakey texture remained. The metallic flavor, I knew, was coming from the baking soda—a full teaspoon was too much for the reduced amount of flour, especially now

that there wasn't as much spice to hide behind. The excess soda might have been contributing to the cakey texture, too, but I suspected something else was at play.

The whole point of creaming butter and sugar when baking is to seed the softened butter with millions of tiny air bubbles. When the alkaline leavener reacts with acidic ingredients in the dough to produce carbon dioxide, the gas inflates the air bubbles, producing a light texture. If I wanted flatter, less cakey cookies, I probably didn't need—or want—the mixer.

But combining the butter and sugar by hand sounded like a chore. Then it occurred to me: If I wasn't whipping air into it, there was no need for the butter to be solid. Instead, I melted it. Eliminating the creaming step made the recipe easier and, along with cutting the baking soda amount in half, produced cookies that were flatter and denser in a good way. They were still a bit lean, but I didn't want to increase the butter because of the textural issues, so I'd need to enrich them in another way. And they still weren't as chewy as I wanted.

Fat Factor

Luckily, I had some experience with making baked goods chewy, having developed our recipe for Chewy Brownies (March/April 2010). The key lies in the chemistry of fats. Both saturated fats (such as butter) and unsaturated fats (such as vegetable oil) consist of long chains of carbon atoms strung together with hydrogen atoms attached to them. The carbon chains in saturated fats have the maximum number of hydrogen atoms attached, so they can pack together more closely into a solid like butter. Unsaturated fats have fewer hydrogen atoms attached, so the chains pack more loosely and thus remain fluid, like vegetable oil. The right combination of loosely and tightly packed chains will produce the ideal chewy texture. When developing my brownie recipe, I learned that 3 parts unsaturated fat to 1 part saturated fat was the magic ratio.

Would the same hold true for my oatmeal cookies? With 12 tablespoons of butter (which is mostly saturated fat) and 1 egg, the fat in my recipe was currently 35 percent unsaturated and 65 percent saturated. For my next batch of cookies, I switched out 8 tablespoons of butter for ½ cup of vegetable oil.

Save the Thick Oats for Breakfast

Bob's Red Mill Organic Extra Thick Rolled Oats are the test kitchen's favorite for breakfast cereal because they cook up plump and chewy, but they're not so great for baking because they come across as tough. For cookies and other baked goods, we prefer the relative delicacy of Quaker Old-Fashioned Rolled Oats.

I also added an extra egg yolk for richness. Now the cookies had 71 percent unsaturated fat and 29 percent saturated, which was much closer to that 3:1 ideal.

So how were they? Crispy on the edges and chewy in the middle, the texture was at last spot-on. But with so much of the butter replaced by neutral-tasting vegetable oil, they were a bit bland and boring. The recipe would need a few more tweaks.

If I had only 4 tablespoons of butter to work with, I was determined to get as much flavor out of it as I could, so I cooked it in a skillet until it was fragrant and the milk solids had turned a dark golden brown before transferring it to the mixing bowl. And rather than increasing the amount of cinnamon, I added the ¼ teaspoon to the warm browned butter to let it bloom, making its flavor rounder and more complex. Correct seasoning is every bit as important in sweets as it is in savory dishes; for my last adjustment, I bumped up the salt to ¾ teaspoon.

The three tweaks were, in combination, surprisingly effective. My cookies now had not only the right texture but also a rich, toasty flavor: buttery, sweet oats with a subtle spice background. A small handful of raisins stirred into the last batch of dough added pops of bright flavor and reinforced the cookies' chew. Knowing that they're a controversial addition, I kept them optional in the recipe.

The Quaker guy no longer has the best recipe, so I guess I'll have to come up with another reason for his smug expression now. Maybe it's the hat.

For a Chewy Cookie, Cut the (Saturated) Fat

When our cookies were coming out cakey and tender rather than dense and chewy, we knew to look at the fat—specifically, the types of fat we were using and their proportion to each other. More saturated fat (e.g., butter) will produce baked goods with a tender texture, while more unsaturated fat (e.g., vegetable oil) leads to a chewier baked good. We were using all butter up to this point, so swapping in vegetable oil for some of that butter (and adding another egg yolk) gave us a ratio of about 3 parts unsaturated fat to 1 part saturated—and cookies that met our chewy, dense ideal.

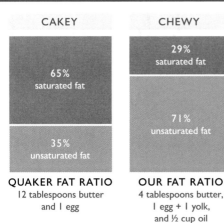

CAKEY	CHEWY
65% saturated fat	29% saturated fat
35% unsaturated fat	71% unsaturated fat
QUAKER FAT RATIO 12 tablespoons butter and 1 egg	**OUR FAT RATIO** 4 tablespoons butter, 1 egg + 1 yolk, and ½ cup oil

CLASSIC CHEWY OATMEAL COOKIES
MAKES 20 COOKIES

Regular old-fashioned rolled oats work best in this recipe. Do not use extra-thick rolled oats, as they will bake up tough in the cookie. For cookies with just the right amount of spread and chew, we strongly recommend that you weigh your ingredients. If you omit the optional raisins, the recipe will yield 18 cookies.

1	cup (5 ounces) all-purpose flour
¾	teaspoon salt
½	teaspoon baking soda
4	tablespoons unsalted butter
¼	teaspoon ground cinnamon
¾	cup (5¼ ounces) dark brown sugar
½	cup (3½ ounces) granulated sugar
½	cup vegetable oil
1	large egg plus 1 large yolk
1	teaspoon vanilla extract
3	cups (9 ounces) old-fashioned rolled oats
½	cup raisins (optional)

1. Adjust oven rack to middle position and heat oven to 375 degrees. Line 2 rimmed baking sheets with parchment paper. Whisk flour, salt, and baking soda together in medium bowl; set aside.

2. Melt butter in 8-inch skillet over medium-high heat, swirling pan occasionally, until foaming subsides. Continue to cook, stirring and scraping bottom of pan with heat-resistant spatula, until milk solids are dark golden brown and butter has nutty aroma, 1 to 2 minutes. Immediately transfer browned butter to large heatproof bowl, scraping skillet with spatula. Stir in cinnamon.

3. Add brown sugar, granulated sugar, and oil to bowl with butter and whisk until combined. Add egg and yolk and vanilla and whisk until mixture is smooth. Using wooden spoon or spatula, stir in flour mixture until fully combined, about 1 minute. Add oats and raisins, if using, and stir until evenly distributed (mixture will be stiff).

4. Divide dough into 20 portions, each about 3 tablespoons (or use #24 cookie scoop). Arrange dough balls 2 inches apart on prepared sheets, 10 dough balls per sheet. Using your damp hand, press each ball into 2½-inch disk.

5. Bake, 1 sheet at a time, until cookie edges are set and lightly browned and centers are still soft but not wet, 8 to 10 minutes, rotating sheet halfway through baking. Let cookies cool on sheet on wire rack for 5 minutes; using wide metal spatula, transfer cookies to wire rack and let cool completely.

No Mixer? No Need

A lot of oatmeal cookie recipes, including Quaker's Best Oatmeal Cookies, call for using a mixer, but we realized that hauling one out was not only unnecessary but even counterproductive. Mixers are great for incorporating air into cake batters, but that's exactly what you *don't* want for a dense, chewy oatmeal cookie. So we skipped the mixer and simply stirred our dough together in a bowl. And since we didn't need to whip air into the butter, there was no reason for it to stay in solid form. Melting it made for easier mixing and also gave us the chance to brown it for a flavor boost that enhanced the oaty flavor.

How Oats Work in Cookies

Because oats are a starch like flour, you might think they would behave the same way in cookie dough. In some ways, they do. Just as with flour, the more oats in the dough, the thicker the resulting cookie. However, flour limits a cookie's spread by soaking up moisture. Oats, on the other hand, don't have time to absorb much free water and instead limit the spread of the dough by acting as physical barriers. In effect, oats behave more like solid mix-ins such as nuts, remaining suspended and discrete in dough rather than being an integral part of it.

RAW COOKIE DOUGH . . .

. . . SPREADS IN THE OVEN.

FEW OATS
Fewer oats means fewer impediments to the flow of liquid, so the cookies spread more.

MORE OATS
More oats means that the liquid's flow is more restricted, resulting in a thicker cookie.

The Secrets of Serrated Knives

Why are some knives a pain and others a pleasure? Everything counts, from the number and shape of the serrations to the width of the blade.

∋ BY HANNAH CROWLEY ∈

Some people call them bread knives, but we think serrated knives are more versatile than that. We use them to cut everything from crusty baguettes and buttery brioche to tender cakes and squishy tomatoes. We last tested serrated knives in 2008; with new options on the market, we decided it was time to revisit the category. We selected nine serrated knives, priced from $19.99 to $199.99, and ran them through a series of tests to find one capable of handling all our usual tasks. We focused on knives with blades around 10 inches long—in past tests, shorter blades couldn't cut through wide loaves or split cake layers horizontally, while longer blades simply got in the way. We included the all-around winner and the Best Buy from our 2008 testing in our new lineup and started slicing.

To find the best, we worked our way through 50 pounds of tomatoes, 18 yellow cakes, nine loaves of challah, 30 crusty rustic loaves, and nine towering BLT sandwiches loaded with extra fillings. Multiple testers, with varying dominant hands, hand sizes, and skill levels, assessed the knives and rated them on their cutting ability and comfort. We also evaluated how well the knives retained their edges throughout testing.

Here's the news: If you hate slicing bread because it makes you think of sawing or struggling, it's probably your knife's fault—we were shocked by how bad some of the knives were. Brand-new blades turned glossy loaves of challah into shaggy piles that looked as if they'd been run through a blender. Others were so uncomfortable to use or so terrible at slicing that testers begged to quit halfway through their loaves. But others were a pleasure to use. The best glided through the crustiest of loaves with minimal effort, leaving behind even, tidy slices. Why were some great while others failed so spectacularly?

▶ **Slice Along with Us**
A free video is available at
CooksIllustrated.com/oct16

What's the Point?

The point (pun intended) of using a serrated blade instead of a straight-edge blade (like that of a standard chef's knife) is the serrated blade's ability to bite into foods that are too hard or squishy for straight knives to get a purchase on. The points sink into the food while the scooped-out gullies between them reduce the blade's friction as it moves through the food. Less friction makes it easier for the user to saw back and forth and cut through the food cleanly.

We examined the serration patterns of our nine knives and found two distinct styles. The first, which we noticed on two of the knives, didn't have any points. Instead, the serrations were scalloped or rounded. This style is purportedly designed to dull more slowly and to create more cutting angles for more effective slicing, the theory being that by rounding the serration, more of it will hit the food at the point of contact. But we found just the opposite: Knives with rounded serrations struggled.

Those with the classic serration style of pointed tips were, in general, much more successful. But there were some exceptions. What made the difference? After counting and measuring the serrations along all nine blades, we landed on a surprising discovery. The best knives had broad, deep, pointed serrations and, most interestingly, fewer of them. Our top-ranked knife had 29 serrations compared with the 55 on our bottom-ranked blade. The idea seemed counterintuitive, so we turned to Sarah Hainsworth, knife expert and professor of materials and forensic engineering at the University of Leicester, to help us understand why the number and shape of serrations matter.

Hainsworth explained that when a user pushes down on a serrated knife, the force exerted is divided among the serrations. The more serrations there are, the less power each one gets. Conversely, the fewer the serrations, the more power each serration gets. This is why we observed blades with fewer serrations biting into food much more readily than those with more serrations.

Next, we zoomed in and looked at the shape of

Making the Cut

Some serrated blades breeze through food, while others make slicing a chore. Here's what to look for.

LOTS OF BITE

deep, wide gullies — few serrations — pointed tips

NO BITE

shallow gullies — lots of serrations — rounded tips

each individual serration. Deeper serrations with pointier tips are better at biting into food than rounded or shallow serrations because the force is also spread over the surface area of each tip. So the same force distribution theory applies: A narrower tip will have more force concentrated behind it and will thus have more power to bite into food.

Angling for the Win

Since we last tested serrated knives, we noticed that manufacturers are now following the same trend we've seen in chef's knives: They're making the blades narrower. Narrower blades, sharpened to 16 degrees or fewer (from the very tip of the serrations to the top of the bevel running along the entire edge of the blade) excelled, while those sharpened to 20 degrees or more felt dull. When cutting, you're essentially pushing one object through another object. The narrower the object that you're pushing (i.e., the cutting implement), the less force is required. For a knife, less required force means the knife feels sharper to the user. The notable exceptions to this trend were the two knives with rounded serrations; they had narrow edges, but their serrations were so dull that it didn't matter. And while some blades were curved and others straight and some blade tips were rounded while others were pointed, we found that neither aspect had an impact on the knives' performance.

The knives' handles also affected their rankings. Testers preferred handles made of grippy, rather than smooth, material because they felt more secure. Good handles also had what ergonomists call "affordance," meaning they allowed multiple comfortable grip options. Cutting is a complex task: Usually we hold the knife vertically, but sometimes we want to hold it horizontally (such as when dividing cake layers); sometimes we want to pinch the spine of the blade to maximize our control, but other times we want to use a "power grip" (much like the grip you use when shaking hands), which requires grasping farther back on the handle.

In addition to a grippy handle with several comfortable holding options, our winning knife also had an exceptional blade that was sharp out of the box and, unlike some knives in our lineup, stayed sharp, cutting wafer-thin slices throughout our testing. The best part? The knife costs just $22. A mainstay of culinary schools, the Mercer Culinary Millennia 10" Wide Bread Knife aced every test we threw its way, earning its spot as our new top-rated serrated blade.

TESTING SERRATED KNIVES

HIGHLY RECOMMENDED

	CRITERIA	

MERCER Culinary Millennia 10" Wide Bread Knife

MODEL: M23210
PRICE: $22.10 LENGTH: 10 in
WEIGHT: 5.93 oz BLADE ANGLE: 16°
HANDLE MATERIALS: Polypropylene and Santoprene
NUMBER OF SERRATIONS: 29
AVERAGE SERRATION WIDTH: 7.73 mm
AVERAGE SERRATION DEPTH: 1.81 mm

CUTTING ★★★
COMFORT ★★★
EDGE RETENTION ★★★

COMMENTS

With the fewest, widest, and deepest serrations, this knife was a "standout." Its sharp points bit into everything from the crustiest bread to the squishiest tomato, producing crisp, clean slices. "Perfect, no crumbs, really easy," said one tester. A stellar blade coupled with a grippy, comfortable handle earned this knife the top spot.

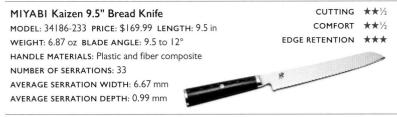

We tested nine knives ranging from 9.5 to 10.25 inches in length and from $19.99 to $199.99 in price. Multiple testers, with varying dominant hands, hand sizes, and skill levels, assessed each knife. We weighed and measured the knives and counted and measured their serrations; blade angle and handle material were reported by manufacturers.

CUTTING: We rated each knife on how well it halved cake layers widthwise and sliced through tomatoes, bread (soft and crusty), and loaded BLT sandwiches. Points were awarded for crisp, tidy cuts that required minimal effort.

COMFORT: We evaluated the ergonomics, grippiness, length, and weight of each knife; those that were comfortable and secure rated highest.

EDGE RETENTION: We used each knife to slice squishy, tactile tomatoes at the beginning and end of testing; those that started and stayed sharp rated highest.

AVERAGE SERRATION WIDTH AND DEPTH: We pressed each knife's nonbeveled side into Silly Putty, measured three serrations on each knife with calipers, and calculated an average for each knife.

RECOMMENDED

MIYABI Kaizen 9.5" Bread Knife

MODEL: 34186-233 PRICE: $169.99 LENGTH: 9.5 in
WEIGHT: 6.87 oz BLADE ANGLE: 9.5 to 12°
HANDLE MATERIALS: Plastic and fiber composite
NUMBER OF SERRATIONS: 33
AVERAGE SERRATION WIDTH: 6.67 mm
AVERAGE SERRATION DEPTH: 0.99 mm

CUTTING ★★½
COMFORT ★★½
EDGE RETENTION ★★★

This blade was supersharp, with broad serrations that showed only the slightest bit of hesitation on crusty loaves. It was perfectly balanced, and testers liked that the handle allowed for multiple comfortable grip options, though a few complained that its straight, smooth design didn't feel as secure.

WÜSTHOF Classic 10-Inch Serrated Bread Knife

MODEL: 4151-7 PRICE: $123.00 LENGTH: 10 in
WEIGHT: 7.08 oz BLADE ANGLE: 14°
HANDLE MATERIAL: Polyoxymethylene
NUMBER OF SERRATIONS: 36
AVERAGE SERRATION WIDTH: 6.15 mm
AVERAGE SERRATION DEPTH: 1.24 mm

CUTTING ★★½
COMFORT ★★½
EDGE RETENTION ★★½

Our previous winner turned in an admirable performance. It was a shade less sharp than our top knives, but it still did well. A minority of testers complained about its handle's smooth, square sides, but most approved. Its edge showed minor damage after testing.

VICTORINOX Swiss Army Fibrox Pro 10¼" Curved Bread Knife with Serrated Edge

MODEL: 40547 PRICE: $39.48 LENGTH: 10.25 in
WEIGHT: 5.00 oz BLADE ANGLE: 18°
HANDLE MATERIAL: Polyamide
NUMBER OF SERRATIONS: 41
AVERAGE SERRATION WIDTH: 5.86 mm
AVERAGE SERRATION DEPTH: 1.15 mm

CUTTING ★★
COMFORT ★★★
EDGE RETENTION ★★

This knife, our former Best Buy, was reasonably sharp but had some trouble biting into crusty loaves. "It takes a little more elbow grease," said one tester. Others noted less bite and more bread "squish" over time. It had a great grippy, ergonomic handle.

DEXTER-RUSSELL 10" Sofgrip Scalloped Bread Slicer

MODEL: SG147-10SC PRICE: $25.34 LENGTH: 10 in
WEIGHT: 4.13 oz BLADE ANGLE: 20°
HANDLE MATERIALS: TPE coating with polypropylene core
NUMBER OF SERRATIONS: 56
AVERAGE SERRATION WIDTH: 4.05 mm
AVERAGE SERRATION DEPTH: 1.22 mm

CUTTING ★★
COMFORT ★★
EDGE RETENTION ★★★

This lightweight knife did the trick but required "a bit more work" to get through crustier loaves. Some found its handle comfortable, but others felt that a protruding knob at the bottom blocked them from being able to choke up for more control. "I'm either too far back or too far forward," said one tester.

NOT RECOMMENDED

MESSERMEISTER Four Season 10 Inch Scalloped Baker's Bread Knife

MODEL: 5033-10
PRICE: $34.40
COMMENTS: This blade felt excessively dull, and its handle was "really uncomfortable." Overall the knife was "quite taxing."

CUTTING ★½
COMFORT ★½
EDGE RETENTION ★★

ZWILLING Pro 10" Ultimate Bread Knife

MODEL: 38406-263
PRICE: $139.99
COMMENTS: This heavy knife felt like "overkill." Its scalloped serrations squished bread or skidded over it. The handle was smooth, large, and uncomfortable for some.

CUTTING ★
COMFORT ★★
EDGE RETENTION ★★

KRAMER BY ZWILLING Essential 10" Bread Knife

MODEL: 34986-263
PRICE: $199.99
COMMENTS: This knife did a terrible job, squashing tomatoes, making ragged slices of challah, and struggling to get into crusty loaves.

CUTTING ★
COMFORT ★★
EDGE RETENTION ★★

CHICAGO CUTLERY Walnut Tradition 10" Serrated Bread/Slicing Knife

MODEL: BT10P
PRICE: $19.99
COMMENTS: With too many narrow serrations, this knife turned challah into a "horror show." In sum, "You're better off tearing your bread."

CUTTING ★
COMFORT ★★
EDGE RETENTION ★

Brewing a Better Soy Sauce

Savory, fragrant, umami-rich soy sauce is a staple in American kitchens. But choose the wrong product and all you get is a salt bomb.

⋟ BY LISA McMANUS ⋞

Packed with flavor-enhancing umami, soy sauce is one of the oldest food products in the world. It originated in China about 2,500 years ago and made the leap to Japan around the seventh century. Over time, it's been produced in a variety of styles and become a pantry staple worldwide; in fact, it's the third best-selling condiment in this country after ketchup and mayonnaise. We feature it in all kinds of Asian dishes, but we also harness its savory flavor in recipes as diverse as barbecue, burgers, fried chicken, corn on the cob, vegetable soup, and lamb chops.

That said, we've learned over the years that not every bottle delivers the kind of nuance and balance that good soy sauce should, so we rounded up 10 top-selling nationally available products made in the United States, Japan, and China to zero in on a soy sauce worthy of being both a condiment and a staple cooking ingredient. Three were tamari, a close relative that's made just like soy sauce but contains little to no wheat. We tasted them plain (with rice to cleanse the palate between samples) and cooked in a teriyaki sauce brushed over broiled chicken thighs.

Due Process

Tasters reported that they could not only taste but also smell distinct differences among the samples. Some boasted sweet-savory aroma and nuances like "caramel," "vanilla," "molasses," and "honeysuckle," while others not only lacked complexity but actually deterred us because they tasted "metallic," "musty," and "fishy." Cooking them with strong aromatics like garlic and ginger muted those off-flavors enough that the sauces were passable, though ultimately they fell near the bottom of the rankings. As for the tamaris, two of the three were true failures; they tasted so harshly salty that we couldn't recommend them. The third was an outlier that balanced salt and sweet better than many of the other soy sauces.

We needed to look only as far as the processing methods for soy sauce to understand where those variations in flavor and complexity came from. Our results show a clear divide between those that were made according to a slower, more traditional method and those produced by a shortcut approach.

The six top-ranking sauces we tasted are made the old-fashioned way: fermented, or "brewed." The process starts by culturing boiled soybeans and roasted wheat with a mold that creates a mixture called *koji*, which functions like a sourdough starter: It begins to break down the carbohydrates and proteins and

Deep Flavor, Naturally

Here's how traditionally fermented (or "brewed") soy sauces get their more balanced, complex flavor.

CREATE KOJI
Soybeans and wheat are cultured with mold to create *koji*.

MAKE MOROMI
Salt and water are added to create liquid-y *moromi*.

FERMENT
Months to years of fermentation intensify moromi's flavor.

PRESS
Moromi is pressed to extract soy sauce.

PASTEURIZE
Heat kills bacteria, starts Maillard reaction to deepen flavor.

provides a sauce's unique flavor profile. (Some manufacturers have used the same koji for decades or even centuries; Kikkoman, for example, claims that its koji dates back 300 years). From there, salt and water are added, and the mash, now called *moromi*, is left to ferment for anywhere from a few months to years. During that time, lactic acid bacteria work with yeasts to further break down proteins and carbohydrates into a mix of flavorful compounds (alcohols, esters, peptides, and acids), including glutamic acid (a major source of umami), and the clear-colored mash darkens to a deep reddish brown. Finally, when the manufacturer decides it's ready—in our lineup, this period ranged from four months to two years—the mash is pressed to extract soy sauce, which is then pasteurized. The heat kills bacteria, stops fermentation, and launches the Maillard reaction, breaking down the proteins into hundreds of new compounds that give soy sauce rich caramelized flavor and aroma.

The two lower-ranking soy sauces are made by hydrolysis, a process that takes just two to three days and involves no wheat or even soybeans, per se. Instead, defatted soy flour (or other flours, such as corn) is boiled with hydrochloric acid to separate the amino acids, which are then neutralized with sodium carbonate. The resulting hydrolyzed vegetable protein is doctored with caramel color, corn syrup, and salt to make it look and taste more like fermented soy sauce.

We found these two hydrolyzed sauces, from La Choy and Crystal, passable—or at least pleasantly familiar—in the teriyaki sauce, where their "intense," "deep and dark" flavors were not out of place and were balanced by the other ingredients. But when we tasted them plain, we picked up on "odd" flavors "like powdered beef soup"—not surprising, since hydrolyzed vegetable protein is used to create the savory, brothy flavor of bouillon cubes—that gave us

reservations about recommending them as all-purpose sauces that might also be used as condiments.

Against the Grain

But what about hydrolysis makes it yield a less balanced and complex product than fermentation does? For one thing, the rapid and thorough protein breakdown. Research has shown that fermentation slowly breaks down proteins and thus allows them to develop multiple types of flavor compounds, whereas hydrolysis quickly converts all of the protein to amino acids, so the end result is relatively one-dimensional.

The other major difference is the absence of wheat, which contributes sweetness and favorable aromas that balance the salt in fermented soy sauces. Without it, the hydrolyzed products tasted "harsh" and "salty" and reminded tasters of "Gravy Master."

The absence of wheat is also likely what accounted for the overly salty flavors we detected in the tamaris, all three of which are fermented products. We noticed that two of the tamaris contain an added sweetener to help balance the salt, though the evaporated cane juice in the losing sample couldn't compensate for a saltiness so harsh that tasters' mouths were "burning." Fortunately, the sugar in the better tamari, from Kikkoman, made for a much more balanced product.

Kikkoman is also the maker of our favorite soy sauce, which achieves good salty-sweet balance and plenty of complexity from its six to eight months of fermentation, one of the longer spans of our lineup. What's more, it does so with just four ingredients—wheat, soybeans, water, and salt—whereas other recommended sauces add flavor enhancers and sugar to achieve a similar effect. Bottom line: You can't go wrong as long as you buy a soy sauce that's labeled "fermented" or "brewed," but we'll stick with Kikkoman's simpler approach.

TASTING SOY SAUCE

We sampled 10 top-selling nationally available supermarket varieties of soy and tamari sauce, selected from sales data gathered by Chicago-based market research firm IRI, in two blind tastings: plain and in our recipe for Chicken Teriyaki, where the sauces were combined with ginger, garlic, sugar, and mirin and reduced on the stove to concentrate flavors. We rated them on aroma, flavor, saltiness, and overall appeal. All products were purchased at Boston-area supermarkets or online. Sodium levels (per 1-tablespoon serving) and ingredients were taken from product labels. We averaged tasting results; products appear below in order of preference.

RECOMMENDED

KIKKOMAN Soy Sauce

PRICE: $2.79 for 10 oz ($0.28 per oz)
STYLE: Fermented
TIME TO PRODUCE: 6 to 8 months
MADE IN: Walworth, Wis.
INGREDIENTS: Water, wheat, soybeans, salt, sodium benzoate: less than 1/10 of 1% as a preservative.
SODIUM: 920 mg

COMMENTS: Thanks to its relatively long fermentation time, our favorite soy sauce came across as "rich," "well-balanced," and "complex," with notes of "caramel," a level of saltiness that was "just right," and a "pleasant," "sherry-like" aroma.

LEE KUM KEE Table Top Premium Soy Sauce

PRICE: $3.49 for 5.1 oz ($0.68 per oz)
STYLE: Fermented
TIME TO PRODUCE: Manufacturer did not respond
MADE IN: China
INGREDIENTS: Water, salt, soybeans, sugar, wheat flour, sodium benzoate added as a preservative, disodium 5'-inosinate and disodium 5'-guanylate as flavor enhancers
SODIUM: 1,030 mg

COMMENTS: The "dark and earthy" flavor of this Chinese product may have been bolstered by its added sugar as well as disodium 5'-inosinate and disodium 5'-guanylate, nucleotides that work with glutamates in soy sauce to magnify the umami impact. It was especially nice in teriyaki, where tasters found it "sweet, rich," "buttery, complex, and tasty."

KIKKOMAN Gluten-Free Tamari Soy Sauce

PRICE: $3.99 for 10 oz ($0.40 per oz)
STYLE: Fermented
TIME TO PRODUCE: 6 to 8 months
MADE IN: Walworth, Wis.
INGREDIENTS: Water, soybeans, salt, sugar
SODIUM: 980 mg

COMMENTS: The only tamari we liked, this sibling of our winning soy sauce contains sugar that adds sweetness in wheat's absence. It makes a good, "classic"-tasting soy substitute in cooked applications, though tasters still found it too salty when sampled straight.

OHSAWA Organic Nama Shoyu

PRICE: $9.99 for 10 oz ($1.00 per oz)
STYLE: Fermented, unpasteurized
TIME TO PRODUCE: 2 years
MADE IN: Japan
INGREDIENTS: Organically grown soybeans, mountain spring water, organically grown whole wheat, sea salt
SODIUM: 720 mg

COMMENTS: Despite this soy sauce's exceptionally long fermentation time, its flavor came across as relatively subtle in the plain tasting, perhaps because it's unpasteurized and thus didn't develop the deep-tasting Maillard compounds that other products had. But once cooked in teriyaki sauce, it won high praise for its complexity that boasted "buttery, savory, nutty, sweet" flavors.

LEE KUM KEE Panda Brand Premium Soy Sauce

PRICE: $7.50 for 16.9 oz ($0.44 per oz)
STYLE: Fermented
TIME TO PRODUCE: Manufacturer did not respond
MADE IN: China
INGREDIENTS: Water, salt, soybeans, sugar, wheat flour
SODIUM: 1,080 mg

COMMENTS: With more salt than soy or wheat, it's no surprise that this Chinese product tasted "aggressively salty" straight from the bottle. Perhaps that's why the manufacturer also adds sugar. But once cooked with the teriyaki ingredients, it took on a "savory caramel" flavor that tasters enjoyed.

RECOMMENDED WITH RESERVATIONS

YAMASA Soy Sauce

PRICE: $2.49 for 10 oz ($0.25 per oz)
STYLE: Fermented
TIME TO PRODUCE: 6 months
MADE IN: Salem, Ore.
INGREDIENTS: Water, wheat, soybeans, salt, alcohol (to retain freshness)
SODIUM: 920 mg

COMMENTS: This soy sauce boasted a "big umami aroma" but actually tasted "mild" and "not terribly complex." Even cooked in chicken teriyaki, tasters found its flavor "shallow" and slightly out of balance, noting that "more sweet than salty comes through."

LA CHOY Soy Sauce

PRICE: $2.59 for 10 oz ($0.26 per oz)
STYLE: Hydrolyzed
TIME TO PRODUCE: "A few days"
MADE IN: United States
INGREDIENTS: Water, hydrolyzed soy protein, corn syrup, salt, caramel color
SODIUM: 1,250 mg

COMMENTS: America's iconic hydrolyzed soy sauce was familiar—and polarizing: Some appreciated its "deep, dark" flavor, while others rejected its recognizably "supersalty," "cheap takeout soy" profile. (It was, in fact, the saltiest sauce in the lineup.) It fared better in the cooked sauce, though even there it met criticism for tasting "fake," like "canned beef broth."

CRYSTAL Soy Sauce

PRICE: $2.53 for 12 oz ($0.21 per oz)
STYLE: Hydrolyzed
TIME TO PRODUCE: Manufacturer did not respond
MADE IN: Metairie, La.
INGREDIENTS: Hydrolyzed soybean and corn protein, water, corn syrup, salt, caramel color
SODIUM: 950 mg

COMMENTS: Made by the popular hot sauce manufacturer, this hydrolyzed soy sauce tasted unacceptably "harsh" and "salty" straight from the bottle, though it was passable as a cooking ingredient. Corn syrup lent it plenty of sweetness, which tasters noticed—but didn't dislike—in the teriyaki sauce.

NOT RECOMMENDED

SAN-J Tamari Gluten Free Soy Sauce

PRICE: $2.99 for 10 oz ($0.30 per oz)
STYLE: Fermented
TIME TO PRODUCE: 4 to 6 months
MADE IN: Henrico, Va.
INGREDIENTS: Water, soybeans, salt, alcohol (to preserve freshness)
SODIUM: 980 mg

COMMENTS: Without wheat or any added sweeteners, this tamari tasted "quite salty" and even "fishy" to some in both the plain and teriyaki tastings. In general, tasters found it "overpowering" and plagued by off-flavors.

WAN JA SHAN Organic Tamari Gluten-Free

PRICE: $3.99 for 10 oz ($0.40 per oz)
STYLE: Fermented
TIME TO PRODUCE: 4 to 6 months
MADE IN: Middletown, N.Y.
INGREDIENTS: Water, organic whole soybeans, salt, and organic evaporated cane juice
SODIUM: 910 mg

COMMENTS: "Sodium afterburn" and "salt bomb" were common complaints about this tamari, which clearly lacked balance despite the addition of cane juice to compensate for the lack of wheat. One taster even called it "misery."

INGREDIENT NOTES

⇒ BY ANDREA GEARY, ANDREW JANJIGIAN & ANNIE PETITO ⇐

Tasting Anchovies

These little fish deserve a spot in your pantry. When minced and stirred into pasta sauce, stew, or dressing, they amplify savory flavor without making the dish taste fishy. At more than $6.00 per ounce, our old winner is expensive. Could we find great anchovies that wouldn't break the bank?

We limited our lineup to whole fillets found in grocery stores (priced from $0.68 to $1.40 per ounce). In all, we had five products to pit against our old favorite. Although most supermarket anchovies have been cured in salt for several months and then packed in oil, we included one widely available product that's not cured. We evaluated the anchovies plain and in Caesar dressing.

In the plain tasting, most samples received high marks; the one exception was the uncured product, which was downgraded for lacking potency. The Caesar dressing tasting followed the same pattern, with tasters liking all the anchovies save the uncured ones, which dissolved into the dressing, giving it a murky appearance and "canned tuna" flavor. What made some anchovies better than others? Curing time. We found that the sweet spot for curing was between three and six months—just long enough for the fillets to develop rich flavor but not so long that they got funky and shrunken. We fully recommend five of the six products we tasted, with the top two scoring especially well for their balanced potency and clean finish. Our new winner, King Oscar Anchovies, even edged out our pricey old favorite from Ortiz. To read the complete tasting results, go to CooksIllustrated.com/oct16. –Kate Shannon

RECOMMENDED

KING OSCAR Anchovies – Flat Fillets in Olive Oil

PRICE: $2.79 for a 2-oz can ($1.40 per oz)

CURING TIME: 4 to 6 months

COMMENTS: Sampled plain, these rosy-red anchovies were "meaty with intense flavor" but not too salty or pungent. They were also "firm" and uniform. In Caesar dressing, tasters praised the "great balance of briny and savory notes."

ORTIZ Anchovies in Olive Oil

PRICE: $12.59 for a 1.9-oz jar ($6.63 per oz)

CURING TIME: 6 months

COMMENTS: Our old winner still impressed, thanks in large part to a texture that tasters described as "tender" and pleasantly "dense." In both tastings, they were "richly flavored" and had a clean finish. These anchovies are far more expensive than any of the others in our lineup.

How to Handle Monster Squash

Breaking down a massive, rock-hard squash like a Blue Hubbard with a knife can seem downright dangerous. We prefer using two alternative tools: gravity and asphalt. Place the squash in a large, clean plastic bag and drop it from chest height onto a hard surface. Remove the pieces from the bag, scrape out the pulp and seeds, and prepare as desired. –A.G.

Introducing Teff

Supermarkets are increasingly stocking teff, a gluten-free whole grain that's been a staple of Ethiopian cooking for thousands of years. Teff has a mildly nutty, earthy flavor and can range in color from dark brown to red to white, with the lighter grains correspondingly lighter in flavor. Despite being the smallest grain in the world (it is the size of a poppy seed), teff is a nutritional powerhouse. In Ethiopia, teff is typically ground into flour to make the flatbread known as *injera*, but we wanted to explore using the whole grain in two untraditional applications: hot breakfast cereal and savory polenta.

TINY GRAIN

After experimenting with different ratios of liquid to grain for both dishes, we found we agreed with some package directions advising a 4:1 ratio, which created a thick but pourable consistency. We also preferred the teff polenta when we cooked it in broth and the teff porridge when it was sweetened with maple syrup. To serve two to four people, add ½ cup teff to 2 cups boiling water (or stock for polenta). Cover, reduce heat to low, and simmer, stirring occasionally, until liquid is absorbed, 15 to 20 minutes. Stir in 2 tablespoons maple syrup and chopped nuts for porridge and 2 tablespoons grated Parmesan for polenta, adding additional syrup and cream or milk to porridge and extra Parmesan to polenta as desired. The teff will continue to thicken as it cools and can be thinned with extra milk or broth. –A.P.

TECHNIQUE 24-Hour Preserved Lemons

Preserving lemons in salt softens their rinds and imbues the fruit with a floral, pungent flavor through fermentation. A staple of North African cuisines, preserved lemons are preserved whole or in wedges and then sliced or chopped and added to recipes, pith and all. They often appear in tagines but can bring depth to seafood, dressings, and even roasted vegetables. Because the process takes a month or longer, we were excited when we found a "quick" version from Jeff Cerciello, chef at Los Angeles's Farmshop. While these lemons lack the intensity of the real deal, they still boast complexity. The trick is to slice them thin, add sugar to help offset the acidity and bitterness, and add oil to help soften the pith. Here's our adaptation of the method. The lemons will keep, refrigerated, for two weeks. –A.J.

SLICE THIN Slice 3 lemons thin crosswise.

MIX Toss with 3 tablespoons each sugar and salt. Stir in ¾ cup extra-virgin olive oil.

STORE Pack into bowl or jar, cover, and refrigerate for at least 24 hours or up to 2 weeks.

How Slicing Impacts Onions

Because the layers of plant cells in an onion run from the root to the stem end of the bulb, the direction in which you slice onions can make a big difference in their cooked appearance and texture. When you slice across these layers, you separate them into small pieces that soften when cooked—ideal for pureeing into a smooth soup or sauce. However, when you slice with the direction of the fibers, you preserve their structure. That means the onions will maintain their shape even when cooked for a long time until deeply browned and flavorful, which makes them perfect for French onion soup or caramelized onions. –A.G.

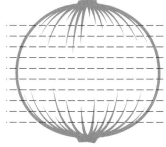 

CROSSWISE TO SOFTEN   **LENGTHWISE TO RETAIN SHAPE**

Using Sprouted Wheat Flour

We've been spotting sprouted-wheat flour in the supermarket. Made from wheat berries that have been soaked and allowed to sprout before being dried and ground into flour, it is often sought out for nutritional reasons: Sprouting grain is said to make vitamins, minerals, and protein easier to absorb. But how does it behave in recipes? To find out, we substituted it for regular whole-wheat flour in whole-wheat pancakes, whole-wheat sandwich bread, and whole-wheat pizza. In all cases, the swap worked fine. Sprouted-wheat flour has fewer gluten-forming proteins than whole-wheat flour, so the doughs and batters were slightly wetter than the original versions, but ultimately only the pizza's structure was noticeably affected. The sprouted-wheat version came out less airy and crisp, but not unacceptably so. As for flavor, tasters found the sprouted versions sweeter and less bitter, even preferring the sprouted-wheat sandwich bread to the whole-wheat original.

Bottom line? For a flavor that's sweeter and less bitter (and a nutritional boost), substitute sprouted-wheat flour for whole-wheat flour, though in recipes like pizza that are heavily dependent on gluten, you might also notice a slight structural difference. –A.J.

Does Freezing Take the Crispness out of Toasted Nuts?

Toasting nuts brings out their flavor through browning reactions and gives them an appealingly crisp texture. We typically toast only the amount a recipe calls for, but toasting a whole bag would mean we'd always have them at the ready. The only issue? Storage. Nuts go stale quickly at room temperature, so we like to keep them in the freezer. Would freezing and thawing harm the toasted nuts' crisp texture? To find out, we toasted separate batches of walnuts, almonds, and pecans following our skillet method: toasting them in a dry skillet over medium heat, stirring frequently, until they were fragrant and slightly darkened, 3 to 5 minutes. We let the nuts cool, placed them in zipper-lock freezer bags, and stored them in the freezer for a month. When brought back to room temperature, these nuts were indistinguishable from batches of freshly toasted nuts. So as long as you seal them tightly to prevent freezer burn and softening, feel free to store toasted nuts in the freezer for up to one month. –A.J.

Almond Butter

Almond butter makes a great alternative to everyday peanut butter, and making your own is dead simple. A surprising number of recipes call for vegetable oil, but the nuts don't need any help turning into a smooth paste—in the food processor, the nuts' oils are released, and that's all you need. Roasting the nuts before grinding them gives the almond butter a more complex flavor while seasoning with kosher salt delivers distinct salty bites. Add almond butter to smoothies for a touch of floral, sweet nutty flavor; use it in our recipe for Chicken Mole Poblano (page 9); or simply spread it on a slice of Almost No-Knead Sourdough Bread (page 21) with a little honey. –Amy Graves

ALMOND BUTTER
MAKES 2 CUPS

4	cups (1¼ pounds) whole almonds
1	teaspoon kosher salt

1. Adjust oven rack to middle position and heat oven to 375 degrees. Spread almonds in single layer on rimmed baking sheet and roast until fragrant, 8 to 10 minutes, rotating sheet halfway through roasting. Transfer sheet to wire rack and let cool until almonds are just warm, about 20 minutes.

2. Process almonds in food processor until oil is released and loose paste begins to form, 5 to 7 minutes, scraping down bowl often. Add salt and pulse to incorporate, about 3 pulses. Transfer to jar with tight-fitting lid. (While best when served at room temperature, almond butter can be refrigerated for up to 2 months.)

How to Cut an Apple Without Coring

If you're cutting just a few apples for a salad or a garnish, it can be easier to skip coring and simply cut the flesh off the core. There's a little more waste, but the time savings can be worth it. Try these techniques. –A.G.

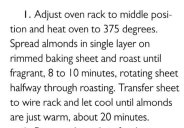

WEDGES: Placing knife just to side of core, slice down to remove 1 side of apple. Turn apple 180 degrees and repeat. Slice off remaining sides. Lay chunks core side down on cutting board and cut lengthwise into wedges.

MATCHSTICKS: Slice off 1 side of apple in ¼-inch-thick planks, stopping just before core. Gather slices into stack. Turn apple 180 degrees and repeat. Slice and stack remaining sides in same manner. Slice stacks lengthwise into ¼-inch-thick matchsticks.

DICE: Follow directions for matchsticks, but slice into ½-inch-thick planks, then ½-inch-thick matchsticks. Turn sticks 180 degrees and slice into cubes.

KITCHEN NOTES

⇛ BY STEVE DUNN, ANDREA GEARY, ANDREW JANJIGIAN, LAN LAM & DAN SOUZA ⇚

WHAT IS IT?

This clever little object is a Wesson Oil Mayonnaise Maker, first produced in the 1930s when it sold for about $0.98. We picked up ours on eBay for considerably more than that: $40.00. The tool consists of a tall glass jar; a "dasher," or plunger, with a mesh screen attached to its bottom; and a screw-top lid. The lid has a hole in the center where the dasher runs through and can be pumped up and down. To try it out, we followed Wesson's recipe for mayonnaise, which is embossed on the outside of the jar: We placed an egg, vinegar, mustard, and salt and pepper in the jar; screwed on the lid; and then slowly poured 2 cups of oil through the lid's center hole while constantly pumping the dasher to churn the ingredients. After about 4 minutes of churning, the ingredients emulsified into a creamy mayonnaise. Though the Wesson Oil Mayonnaise Maker is no match for the speed of a food processor (our preferred appliance for making this creamy sauce), it worked well and with little fuss. –S.D.

WESSON OIL MAYONNAISE MAKER

ULTIMATE ODOR FIGHTERS
Finely grated apple or potato eliminated the pungent smell of garlic.

Wipe out Garlic Odor on Cutting Boards

In the past we've advocated rubbing cutting boards with a water–baking soda paste to remove potent garlic smells, but some of the smell has always lingered. When we read about a study in the online magazine *Science World Report* that found that garlic breath can be eliminated by eating foods that brown, like apples and potatoes, we wondered if we could apply the concept to removing the odor from our boards. The principle is this: Browning is a sign that a certain enzyme (polyphenol oxidase) has been released by bruising or cutting and is reacting with oxygen. This enzyme can oxidize sulfurous compounds, including the thiols and thiocyanates that give garlic its pungent odor, turning them into odorless compounds.

We knew that a prepared product like applesauce wouldn't work since the pasteurization process inactivates the enzyme, so we grabbed a fresh potato and apple and got to work. We took three cutting boards, each of which we'd rubbed with garlic paste over a small area for long enough to leave a noticeable odor even after washing. On one board we applied our old baking soda paste. For the other two, we grated a few tablespoons of either potato or apple over the offending area; grating finely ensured that the maximum amount of enzyme was released. We let the treatments sit for 10 minutes and then washed them off.

The results? The two boards treated with apple or potato had no trace of garlicky smell, winning the contest hands down. From now on, for boards free from garlic odors, we'll keep an apple or potato at the ready. –L.L.

LET COME TO ROOM TEMP

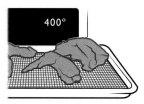
BAKE ON RACK

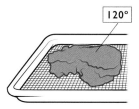
REHEAT TO INTERNAL TEMP OF 120 DEGREES

Best Way to Reheat Fried Chicken

Reheated fried chicken is often a disappointment, featuring dried-out or unevenly heated meat and/or a coating that never adequately recrisps. We tried several approaches recommended by sources online, including wrapping the chicken in foil and baking it (this steamed the coating and sogged it out) and baking it after placing it in a paper bag (this wicked oil from the coating and toughened it). Microwaving was also a bust because the skin didn't recrisp and the heating was uneven.

We had the most success when we allowed the chicken to come up to room temperature for 30 minutes to 1 hour before rewarming it in the oven, which helped it heat more quickly and ensured that the odd-shaped pieces would heat more evenly. We placed it on a wire rack set in a baking sheet to keep the bottom from steaming and then baked it in a 400-degree oven, which quickly recrisped the crust before the meat had time to dry out. Heating the chicken to an internal temperature of 120 degrees, which took 14 to 18 minutes for breasts and 8 to 12 minutes for legs and thighs, gave us chicken at the perfect serving temperature. –S.D.

Flavoring Corn's Cooking Water: Is It Worth It?

When developing our recipe for Foolproof Boiled Corn (page 18), we couldn't tell the difference between corn cooked in water seasoned with sugar or salt and corn cooked in plain water. To find out why that might be, we ran a test. We cooked three ears of corn for various amounts of time. To represent the seasoning, we dissolved a blue compound known as copper sulfate in the water. We chose copper sulfate because its penetration rate would be comparable to that of the sodium ions in salt.

Interestingly, the blue dye made its way into the kernels by traveling through the cob and then into the kernels. Given this long route, it wasn't too surprising that it took a very long time to "season" a whole ear. Even after 3 minutes, the first ear showed hints of blue only in the kernels at the tip and base of the cob. After 30 minutes, the blue had progressed a mere ½ inch from each end toward the middle. It took a full 2 hours for all of the kernels in the last ear to take on any color, and even then the color was very faint toward the center of the cob.

The takeaway? Salt will eventually season an ear of corn if added to the cooking water, but it will take so long that it's just not worth it. Sugar molecules are larger than salt, so they would take even longer to penetrate—if they could at all. Season corn on the cob at the table instead. –L.L.

SALT MOVES TOO SLOWLY TO SEASON
Blue dye added to corn cooking water mimics salt's slow progression through the cob to penetrate all the kernels. It takes 2 hours for the dye to penetrate the whole ear.

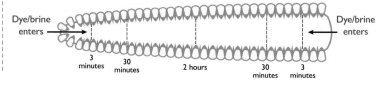

Dye/brine enters →   ← Dye/brine enters

3 minutes   30 minutes   2 hours   30 minutes   3 minutes

Fermentation Explained

When we realized how many ingredients highlighted in this issue—soy sauce, sourdough starter, anchovies, preserved lemons—are fermented, we decided that a closer look at fermentation was in order.

Fermentation is a process in which bacteria and/or yeasts consume carbohydrates and proteins often naturally present in food, producing alcohols, lactic acid, acetic acid, and/or carbon dioxide as byproducts. Water and salt are often added to the mix because both create a fermentation-friendly environment. (Salt can also keep bad bacteria at bay.) Fermentation helps preserve food and alters its texture, scent, and flavor. When we compared fresh lemon to store-bought preserved lemons (our quick-preserved lemons on page 28 do not actually ferment), the fresh lemons were bright, sharp, and citrusy, while the preserved lemons were floral, briny, and pungent, with a slight chemical-like flavor.

Fermented foods are also easy to digest, and their bacteria are thought to offer health benefits (which helps explain their recent uptick in popularity). –A.J.

FERMENTED FOODS ARE EVERYWHERE

Foods like pickles, vinegar, and yogurt have the tang that we often associate with fermentation. And of course beer and wine are fermented. But all these everyday foods also get deep flavor from fermentation.
• Chocolate
• Coffee
• Olives
• Bread
• Vanilla
• Hot sauce
• Cheese

Make Your Immersion Blender More Effective

An immersion blender is less fussy than a countertop blender since you don't have to blend in batches or clean a blender jar or lid. Immersion blenders can't produce the same silkiness as countertop models, but here's how to get the best results. –A.G.

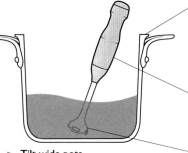

Use a deep, narrow pot when possible. A smaller surface area enables an immersion blender to draw food toward and through its blades, which decreases the likelihood of unblended chunks.

Angle the blender. To blend chunks that won't fit through the holes in the blender head, hold the blender at a slight angle.

Submerge the blender head. To prevent splatter, make sure that the blender head is always fully submerged when the blender is on.

➤ **Tilt wide pots.**
If your recipe requires a broad pot, tilt it slightly while blending so the food concentrates in one area.

Better Brown Butter

Brown butter—butter cooked until the solid milk proteins color—adds a deep, nutty flavor to everything from savory sauces to our Classic Chewy Oatmeal Cookies (page 23). We've always browned butter by melting it in a skillet (a traditional one to easily monitor browning), swirling it until the solids brown, and then pouring it into a heatproof bowl, using a spatula to attempt to scrape out the milk protein solids that cling to the skillet. But this was an imperfect method, as a lot of the solids were inevitably left behind. Though the milk proteins make up only 2 percent of butter's mass, they are mainly responsible for browned butter's nutty flavor, and we wondered if there was a better way. We melted butter in a skillet until the sputtering subsided and then stirred and scraped constantly until the solids browned so that none stuck to the pan. When we compared pasta dressed with stirred-and-scraped brown butter with non-stirred, tasters unanimously preferred the pasta tossed with the stirred batch, calling it "nuttier" and "toastier." From now on, we'll be stirring butter as it browns to ensure that every last bit of the flavorful solids leaves the pan. –A.G.

EXPERIMENT   Parm's Most Flavorful Part

When buying wedges of Parmigiano-Reggiano at the supermarket, we've typically avoided corner pieces that have rind on two sides, aiming for pieces with more usable interior cheese. But anecdotally, we've also noticed that cheese closer to the rind seems to be crumblier, with more of the pleasant crunchy crystals (aggregates of the amino acid tyrosine) that help give this cheese its nutty flavor. We decided to put this observation to the test.

EXPERIMENT

We first set up a tasting of samples of cheese we excised from three locations on one wheel of 18-month-old Parmigiano-Reggiano: the first from the very center of the wheel, the second from a location 1 inch in from the side and bottom rind, and the third from a location between these two points. We asked tasters to describe the texture and flavor of each sample and rank them based on overall preference. Next, we took additional core samples from the center and edge locations, shaved them into thin strips, and manually counted the number of tyrosine crystals in each.

RESULTS

Tasters were clear about their preferences. The sample taken from closest to the rind earned near-unanimous support for its "nutty," "complex," "sharp" flavor and "pleasantly crumbly" texture—it ranked first. The sample taken from the center of the wheel ranked third and was often described as "clean-tasting," with a "smoother," "plasticky" texture. The core sample taken between these two points landed in second place and was described, fittingly, as "middle-of-the-road" in terms of both flavor and texture. The crystal counts also painted a clear picture. Cheese right next to the rind averaged 20 crystals per 10 grams of cheese, while the center cheese averaged fewer than 9 crystals per 10 grams.

TAKEAWAY

When cheese ages, it undergoes a complex process called proteolysis that affects its texture, melting qualities, and flavor. Proteolysis works from the outside in, so the outer portions of the Parmigiano-Reggiano show more of the telltale signs of advanced aging—a dry, crumbly texture; a high proportion of tyrosine crystals; and a deep, complex flavor. Moving forward, we'll be seeking out corner pieces of Parmigiano-Reggiano at the supermarket. While we'll get a little less cheese for shaving or grating, we'll also be buying the best part of the wheel. –D.S.

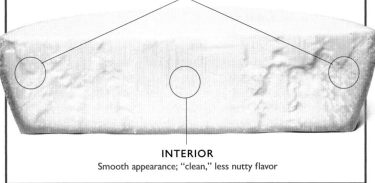

EXTERIOR
Visible tyrosine crystals; cheese tastes very complex

INTERIOR
Smooth appearance; "clean," less nutty flavor

▶ SCIENCE OF COOKING: The Secret to Porterhouse Steaks

Beware: The steak that looks the most luscious might end up wasting your money. Watch our free video at CooksIllustrated.com/oct16 to find out why.

EQUIPMENT CORNER

⇒ BY MIYE BROMBERG AND KATE SHANNON ⇐

HIGHLY RECOMMENDED

OXO
On Clarity Cordless Glass
Electric Kettle
MODEL: 8710300
PRICE: $89.95

RECOMMENDED

CUISINART
Stainless Steel
Slotted Spoon
MODEL: CTG-08-SLS
PRICE: $9.12

**RECOMMENDED
WITH RESERVATIONS**

CHEF'N
ScoopSaw Squash
and Melon Tool
MODEL: 102-804-062
PRICE: $9.99

HIGHLY RECOMMENDED

EXCALIBUR
Food Dehydrator
MODEL: 3926T
PRICE: $241.50

RECOMMENDED

RSVP
Classic Rotary Food Mill
MODEL: VEG-3
PRICE: $24.95

Electric Kettles

Electric kettles are handy for making coffee and tea but are also great for any cooking task that requires boiling water: rehydrating dried mushrooms, softening lasagna noodles, or reconstituting stock base. To find out if our 2008 winner from Capresso ($55.69) was still the best kettle on the market, we rounded up five stainless-steel and four glass models, priced from $32.89 to $99.95, to pit against it. After days of testing—including a taste test of the water boiled in each kettle—we found that we preferred kettles that sat securely on their bases and had glass pitchers, clearly visible power indicators, comfortable grips, and spouts that poured neatly. Boiling speed, of course, was also important. Our new winner, a tall, sleek model from OXO, met all of our criteria and narrowly edged out our old winner, which is now our Best Buy. –K.S.

Slotted Spoons

Slotted spoons are kitchen workhorses, useful for removing all manner of small foods from boiling water, hot oil, or sauce. To find the best model, we rounded up eight dishwasher-safe nylon, silicone, and stainless-steel spoons, priced from $6.99 to $34.00, and tested them by using each to remove green peas, poached eggs, meatballs, and jumbo shrimp from liquids in different pots and pans.

Despite different perforation sizes and configurations, all the spoons filtered out water, oil, and sauce equally well. But we did have a preference for shallow, broad spoon bowls that easily slid under food and held it securely. And while nylon and silicone spoons were lighter than their metal counterparts, their bowls tended to be thicker, making it harder to get them up and under food in skillets and saucepans. Our new favorite, the Cuisinart Stainless Steel Slotted Spoon, $9.12, has a wide, shallow, thin bowl that slides under food effortlessly, and because its comfortable, rounded handle is hollow, it's almost as light as a nonmetal spoon. –M.B.

Gourd Seeding Tools

Two specialized tools—the Messermeister Pro-Touch Plus Culinary Spoon ($12.95) and the Chef'n ScoopSaw Squash and Melon Tool ($9.99)—promise to remove the seeds and strings from gourds more easily than our tool of choice, a soupspoon. To test their claims, we pitted both tools against our trusty spoon, using each to scoop halved honeydew melons, butternut squash, and pumpkins. We also tried a taxidermy fleshing tool, a $6.99 serrated metal loop that has found favor with serious pumpkin carvers. In the end, none of the tools bested the spoon at removing seeds and strings from gourds. The ScoopSaw also features a narrow, flexible saw nested inside its hollow scoop to use for cubing squash and slicing melon—a task it didn't perform well. However, it did a nice job of carving a pumpkin. If you carve a lot of pumpkins, the ScoopSaw might be a worthwhile investment. –M.B.

Food Dehydrators

Like kale chips? How about beef jerky? Food dehydrators are better than ovens or microwaves for making dried foods like these because they continually circulate warm air over the food for even, controlled moisture removal. In addition, some models include timers that automatically shut off the machine at the end of the dehydrating cycle. But which model should you buy? To find out, we purchased five dehydrators priced from $64.94 to $241.50 and put them through their paces making beef jerky, dried tomatoes, dried thyme, kale chips, apple chips, and fruit leather.

Dehydrators come in two styles—large boxes with sliding trays and round, stackable trays that seal together and are capped by a lid. While one style isn't necessarily better than the other, all the stackable models have donut-shaped trays with holes in the middle for air flow; these holes made it difficult to fit lots of food at once. In general, it was also easier to check on the doneness of food in sliding-shelf models. And while dehydrating is an inherently slow process, we preferred models that got the job done more quickly. At the end of testing, one model came out on top for its flawlessly dehydrated food, speed, and ease of use. The most expensive machine we tested at $241.50, the Excalibur Food Dehydrator (a sliding-shelf-style dehydrator) isn't cheap, but if you dry a lot of food, it's worth every penny. We also found a Best Buy. At $74.47, the Presto Dehydro Electric Food Dehydrator produced great results. –K.S.

Food Mills

Food mills are hand-cranked tools that simultaneously grind and strain fruits and vegetables. Since you typically don't need to peel or seed produce before milling, these gadgets can save a lot of time and effort. To find the best one, we tested five models, priced from $24.95 to $106.05, using them to make mashed potatoes, applesauce, raspberry coulis, and tomato sauce.

Every mill we tested comes with at least three interchangeable disks with different-size perforations for fine, medium, and coarse purees. All five models produced smooth purees and handled each type of produce equally well—the tomato sauce, coulis, and applesauce made with each mill were great, although all mills ground some potato skin into the mash. Some, however, were easier and more efficient to use. The best models had comfortable handles, sat stably on all manner of bowls and pots, were easy to set up and break down, and were calibrated (via spring tension) to produce just enough force to push food through the disk quickly and without also pushing through seeds and skins. Our new favorite mill, the RSVP Classic Rotary Food Mill, hit all the marks and, as a bonus, was the least expensive model we tested. –M.B.

Complete results are free for four months at CooksIllustrated.com/oct16.

INDEX

September & October 2016

BONUS ONLINE CONTENT

More recipes, reviews, and videos are available
at **CooksIllustrated.com/oct16**

RECIPES

Asian-Style Turkey Meatballs
Classic Sourdough Bread (Pain au Levain)
Cuban-Style Sandwiches with Smoked
    Pork Loin
Cumin-Sesame Salt
Grilled Shrimp and Vegetable Kebabs
    for Two
Moroccan-Style Turkey Meatballs
Pepper-Cinnamon Salt

EXPANDED REVIEWS

Tasting Anchovies
Testing Electric Kettles
Testing Food Dehydrators
Testing Food Mills
Testing Gourd Seeding Tools
Testing Slotted Spoons

▶ RECIPE VIDEOS

Want to see how to make any of the recipes
in this issue? There's a video for that.

▶ MORE VIDEOS

Science of Cooking: The Secrets
to Porterhouse Steaks

FOLLOW US ON SOCIAL MEDIA

facebook.com/CooksIllustrated
twitter.com/TestKitchen
pinterest.com/TestKitchen
google.com/+AmericasTestKitchen
instagram.com/CooksIllustrated
youtube.com/AmericasTestKitchen

Almost No-Knead Sourdough Bread, 21

Foolproof Boiled Corn with Chile-Lime Salt, 18

Grilled Shrimp and Vegetable Kebabs, 10

Chicken Mole Poblano, 9

Classic Chewy Oatmeal Cookies, 23

Broiled Broccoli Rabe, 11

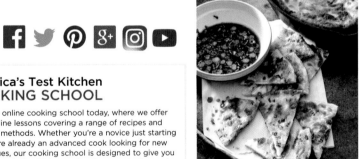
Scallion Pancakes with Dipping Sauce, 13

Smoked Pork Loin with Dried-Fruit Chutney, 5

Cheese and Tomato Lasagna, 7

Italian-Style Turkey Meatballs, 15

PHOTOGRAPHY: CARL TREMBLAY; STYLING: MARIE PIRAINO

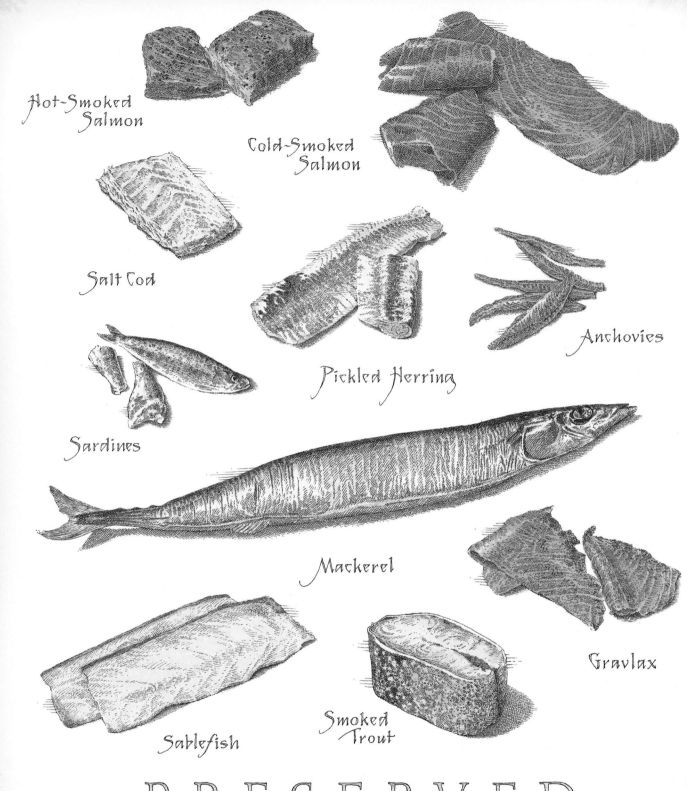

Hot-Smoked Salmon

Cold-Smoked Salmon

Salt Cod

Pickled Herring

Anchovies

Sardines

Mackerel

Gravlax

Sablefish

Smoked Trout

PRESERVED FISH

COOK'S
ILLUSTRATED

French-Style
Mashed Potatoes

Fuss-Free Turkey
with Quick Pan Gravy

Best Stovetop Steak
The Secret's in the Pan

All About Chocolate
Tips for Buying, Storing, Cooking

Dinner Frittatas
Fast, Easy Weeknight Meal

Apple Strudel
Best-Tasting Filling Ever

Rating Cinnamons
Is It Worth Spending More?

Millionaire's Shortbread
Testing Baking Sheets
Braised Root Vegetables
Pad Thai at Home

CooksIllustrated.com
$6.95 U.S. & $7.95 CANADA

COOK'S
ILLUSTRATED

NOVEMBER & DECEMBER 2016

PAGE 14

TEAS

BACK COVER ILLUSTRATED BY JOHN BURGOYNE

Teas

Made from the cured leaves of the *Camellia sinensis* shrub, teas are categorized based on how they are processed. Oxidation determines the color of tea; in general, the more processing, the stronger the flavor. White teas like SILVER NEEDLE are made from young leaves that are minimally processed, giving them delicate character. SENCHA and JASMINE PEARLS are grassy green teas that are heated before they are dried and rolled. MATCHA, a green tea powder, is whisked when brewed to make a frothy beverage. GENMAICHA is green tea blended with toasted and popped rice, giving it roasted notes. JADE OOLONG is lightly bruised to produce partial oxidation, giving it a balanced flavor. ENGLISH BREAKFAST and EARL GREY are full-bodied black teas; the latter is blended with bergamot orange oil. Made from fermented leaves, PU-ERH yields a strong, smoky brew. MASALA CHAI, a blend of black teas and whole spices, is often served with plenty of milk and sugar.

AMERICA'S TEST KITCHEN
RECIPES THAT WORK

America's Test Kitchen is a real 2,500-square-foot kitchen located just outside Boston. It is the home of more than 60 test cooks, editors, and cookware specialists. Our mission is to test recipes until we understand exactly how and why they work and eventually arrive at the very best version. We also test kitchen equipment and supermarket ingredients in search of products that offer the best value and performance. You can watch us work by tuning in to *America's Test Kitchen* (AmericasTestKitchen.com) and *Cook's Country from America's Test Kitchen* (CooksCountry.com) on public television and listen to us on our weekly radio program on PRX. You can also follow us on Facebook, Twitter, Pinterest, and Instagram.

IS IT TOO MUCH?

One question we're always asking around here is, "How much is too much for this recipe?" That can apply to cooking time, to butter or pork fat, or just to hassle. In the photo at right, you see Lan Lam making apple strudel the classic way. This involves rolling out the dough until it's more than 4 feet long and so thin you can read a newspaper through it. Lan knew that would be too much work for most of us, but she had to find out what she would be striving to duplicate when she simplified the recipe. The lower photo shows Andrew Janjigian halfway through the process of developing his recipe for *porchetta*, the classic (and incredibly delicious) Italian street food. The traditional approach involves boning a whole pig, letting it sit overnight, and then spit-roasting it all day on a wood fire. Out of the question for the home cook. But was pork belly too fatty to make a decent substitute? That's what Andrew was testing. Similarly, when Steve Dunn developed his version of *pommes purée*, he started with a recipe that called for a full pound of butter for every 2 pounds of potatoes, plus 10 minutes of arm-numbing whisking. Way too much—but could Steve keep the rich, silky appeal of the dish while cutting down on fat and work? For each of our recipes, the cook's task is to arrive at the precise point where the investment of time, effort, and calories is perfectly balanced with the flavor, texture, and all-around appeal that attracted us to the dish in the first place. It's a balancing act worthy of the Flying Wallendas (remember them?), but it's what we strive to achieve here every day.

The Editors

FOR INQUIRIES, ORDERS, OR MORE INFORMATION

COOK'S ILLUSTRATED MAGAZINE

Cook's Illustrated magazine (ISSN 1068-2821), number 143, is published bimonthly by America's Test Kitchen Limited Partnership, 17 Station St., Brookline, MA 02445. Copyright 2016 America's Test Kitchen Limited Partnership. Periodicals postage paid at Boston, MA, and additional mailing offices, USPS #012487. Publications Mail Agreement No. 40020778. Return undeliverable Canadian addresses to P.O. Box 875, Station A, Windsor, ON N9A 6P2. POSTMASTER: Send address changes to *Cook's Illustrated*, P.O. Box 6018, Harlan, IA 51593-1518. For subscription and gift subscription orders, subscription inquiries, or change of address notices, visit AmericasTestKitchen.com/support, call 800-526-8442 in the U.S. or 515-248-7684 from outside the U.S., or write to us at *Cook's Illustrated*, P.O. Box 6018, Harlan, IA 51593-1518.

CooksIllustrated.com

At the all-new CooksIllustrated.com, you can order books and subscriptions, sign up for our free e-newsletter, or renew your magazine subscription. Join the website and gain access to 23 years of *Cook's Illustrated* recipes, equipment tests, and ingredient tastings, as well as companion videos for every recipe in this issue.

COOKBOOKS

We sell more than 50 cookbooks by the editors of *Cook's Illustrated*, including *Cook's Science* and *Bread Illustrated*. To order, visit our bookstore at CooksIllustrated.com/bookstore.

EDITORIAL OFFICE 17 Station St., Brookline, MA 02445; 617-232-1000; fax: 617-232-1572. For subscription inquiries, visit AmericasTestKitchen.com/support or call 800-526-8442.

QUICK TIPS

COMPILED BY ANNIE PETITO

A Stand-In for Pie Weights

When prebaking 9-inch tart shells, instead of covering the dough with foil and weighing it down with pie weights after trimming the dough, Jaime Pedraza of Minneapolis, Minn., puts an 8- to 8½-inch-diameter pot lid on top of the foil. It's effective at preventing the pastry from puffing up as it bakes, and it is even easier to put in place and remove than weights are.

Homemade Makeshift Apron

Not having an apron handy, Lynda Crowley of Kill Devil Hills, N.C., fashioned one with a few items in her kitchen: a large dish towel, two clothespins, and two long pieces of kitchen twine—one for around her neck and one to fasten at her waist.

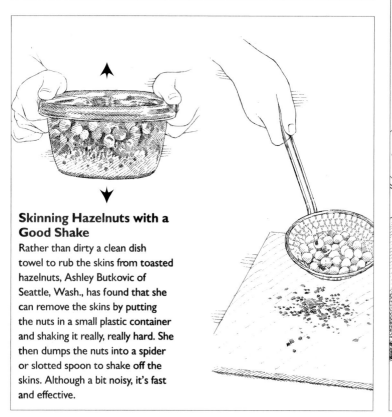

Skinning Hazelnuts with a Good Shake

Rather than dirty a clean dish towel to rub the skins from toasted hazelnuts, Ashley Butkovic of Seattle, Wash., has found that she can remove the skins by putting the nuts in a small plastic container and shaking it really, really hard. She then dumps the nuts into a spider or slotted spoon to shake off the skins. Although a bit noisy, it's fast and effective.

Sandwich Bread Swaps in Panades

We often call for hearty white bread when making a panade, a paste of starch and dairy that helps keep meatballs, meatloaf, and burgers tender and moist. But when Jessica Pantzer of Brooklyn, N.Y., is out of sandwich bread, she swaps in hamburger or hot dog buns. After determining that one slice of sandwich bread weighs 1½ ounces and yields ½ cup of crumbs when coarsely ground in a food processor, it's easy to make the swap by using a volume or weight equivalent of her available alternative.

A Better Way to Transport Roll-Out Cookies

Using a spatula to transfer cut-out cookies from the counter to the baking sheet inevitably means some shapes bend or break in transport. Lily Giordano of Arlington, Va., has devised a less frustrating approach. She rolls out the dough to the desired thickness on parchment cut to fit her baking sheets and then cuts the cookies right on the parchment, spaced according to the recipe. She peels away the scraps and transfers the parchment with the cookies to the baking sheet.

SEND US YOUR TIPS We will provide a complimentary one-year subscription for each tip we print. Send your tip, name, address, and daytime telephone number to Quick Tips, *Cook's Illustrated*, P.O. Box 470589, Brookline, MA 02447, or to QuickTips@AmericasTestKitchen.com.

COOK'S ILLUSTRATED

2

Securing Jars and Bottles in Your Cabinet

Tina Nelissen of Anaheim, Calif., has found that securing bungee cords across the fronts of her kitchen shelves prevents bottles and jars at the front from falling when she's searching behind them for an ingredient. She first screws circular eye hooks into both sides of the cabinet and then loops the bungee cord through the hooks to hold it in place.

Seasonings Test for Meatloaf and Burgers

Marcia Schjavland of Mystic, Conn., always taste-tests her meatloaf or burger meat before cooking to check for seasoning. But rather than heating up a frying pan to test a small amount, she just puts a tablespoon of the meat mixture in the microwave on high for about 30 seconds until cooked through.

A Better Way to Stir Peanut Butter

A new jar of natural peanut butter has a layer of oil sitting on top of the peanut butter. Rather than making a mess by trying to swirl them together in the jar, Brian King of Sonoma, Calif., pours the jar's contents into a stand mixer and beats them for a few minutes on low speed. Then, using a rubber spatula, he scrapes the perfectly mixed peanut butter back into the jar and stores it in the refrigerator so it won't separate again.

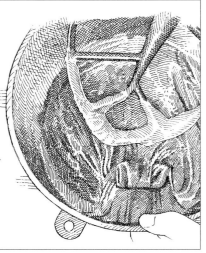

A Clever Strainer for Frozen Shrimp

Our standard method for thawing frozen shrimp is to place them in a colander under cool running water. Jeff Levine of Maplewood, N.J., has come up with a method that doesn't require a colander. Instead, he turns the shrimp's bag into a strainer by snipping a few small holes in the bottom; he then runs water through the opening in the top.

A Slick Way to Chop Sticky Foods

When Joyce Siegel of North Bethesda, Md., chops dried fruit or minces garlic, some always sticks to the knife. One day she tried oiling the knife, using a paper towel to distribute a thin coat evenly along the blade before chopping dried fruit—it worked perfectly. The pieces slid right off the blade.

Dry Baking Sheets on a Roasting Rack

When she runs out of space for drying baking sheets, Jennifer Clayton of Cheektowaga, N.Y., pulls out her V-shaped roasting rack. She turns it upside down, and— *voilà*—she can place the sheets in the slots created while the handles keep the rack from tipping over.

Dry Chicken Skin in a Flash

Letting salted skin-on chicken sit overnight helps dry the skin so it crisps up when cooked, but sometimes Ben Dahlberg of Houston, Texas, forgets to plan ahead, so he came up with a fast alternative: a hair dryer. He pats the chicken dry with paper towels and then waves a hair dryer set on high heat back and forth over the chicken pieces for about 2 minutes per piece, until the skin looks dry. It roasts beautifully, with very crispy skin.

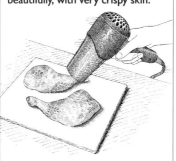

Cleaning Nonstick Pans

Bill McDonald of Vancouver, Wash., finds that food or grease sometimes stays stuck in the nooks and crannies of his nonstick pans, especially around the handle. A clean electric toothbrush, he's discovered, is perfect for this cleaning task. The stiff bristles' circular motion acts like a buffer, removing stuck-on grime, but the bristles are still soft enough for a nonstick surface.

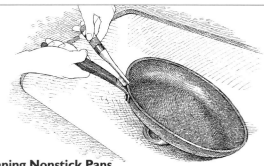

Easier Roast Turkey and Gravy

No flipping. No long-simmered gravy. For fuss-free turkey and a fast, richly flavored gravy, we borrow a tool from pizza making.

⋗ BY LAN LAM ⋖

An idyllic roast turkey isn't hard to envision: Picture crispy, well-browned skin and moist, juicy, well-seasoned meat. And don't forget a lightly thickened, full-flavored gravy. But alas, the perfect bird is not easy to come by. Crispy skin is elusive, and an ever-present hurdle when roasting whole poultry is that while the dark meat needs to reach 175 degrees, the delicate breast meat will dry out if it's cooked beyond 160 degrees. The gravy is easier to get right, but it takes about an hour of simmering to produce rich, well-rounded flavor.

Over the years, we've jumped through all kinds of hoops to try to get both the dark and white meat properly cooked: separating the breast from the leg quarters and roasting them individually, butterflying the turkey so it lies flat, flipping the hot turkey over partway through roasting (using wadded-up paper towels as hand protection), and even icing down the breasts before putting the turkey in the oven. But this year, I wanted to find a simpler way: In other words, I wanted all the advantages of a great roasted turkey with none of the disadvantages.

First on my agenda: salt, which alters the proteins in meat and helps it retain moisture as it cooks. There are two ways to introduce salt into a turkey: brining and salting. A brine penetrates the flesh rather quickly, in 6 to 12 hours, but there are drawbacks. For one, brining adds water to the skin, which hinders browning. Another is that the process requires a container large enough to hold 2 gallons of brine along with a 14-pound turkey—that takes up a lot of refrigerator space.

Salting a turkey (underneath the skin, for proper penetration) works a little differently. Salt draws out moisture from the meat, and this moisture mixes with the salt to form a concentrated brine. Over time, the salt migrates back into the meat, seasoning it and helping keep it juicy. Salt also dries out the

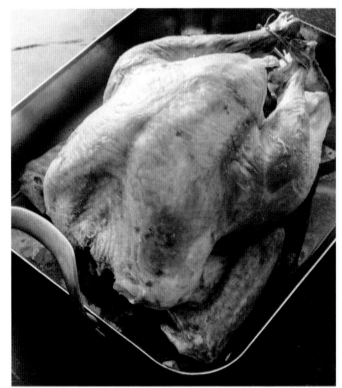

Roasting the bird directly in a preheated roasting pan (with no V-rack) helps the dark meat finish cooking at the same time as the white meat.

skin, so it browns more readily. And although salting requires more time—24 to 48 hours—it eventually results in fully seasoned meat. Another bonus of salting is that it occupies less fridge space since no large container is required.

Salting, it seemed, was the way to go, and while I was at it, I also wanted to incorporate sugar, which helps accentuate turkey's mild flavor. I found that 4 teaspoons of sugar and 4 tablespoons of salt were the right amounts for a 12- to 14-pound bird. Using my fingers, I loosened the skin of the turkey and then rubbed my salt-sugar blend on the flesh and in the cavity of the bird. I then arranged the bird on a wire rack set in a rimmed baking sheet, transferred it to the fridge, and waited 24 hours for the salt to do its work.

The Keystone

Because the dark meat needs to cook to a higher temperature than the white meat, some of our turkey recipes call for starting the bird breast side down on a V-rack set inside a roasting pan, an

arrangement that shields the breast from some of the heat. The bird is then flipped breast side up partway through cooking. But handling a heavy, steaming-hot bird in the middle of the roasting period is never an easy task. In the spirit of producing a supersimple recipe, I looked at our recipe for Weeknight Roast Chicken (September/October 2011). There, we skip the awkward flip by placing the bird breast side up directly in a preheated skillet. The pan transfers heat into the portion of the bird that needs it most—the thighs and legs. At the same time, the convection currents act more slowly on the breasts. The result? A perfectly cooked chicken.

A skillet was too small for a turkey, but a roasting pan would work. I placed one on the bottom rack of the oven and turned the dial to 500 degrees. When the oven was up to temperature, I swirled 2 tablespoons of oil into the hot pan before setting my salted turkey in place. To avoid overheating the oil and smoking out the kitchen, I dropped the oven temperature to 425 degrees immediately after putting in the turkey. Then, after about 45 minutes, I reduced the temperature to 325 degrees for a gentle finish. An hour and a half later, the breast hit 160 degrees. However, the dark meat was well short of the 175 degrees I was shooting for. I needed a better way to slow down the breast and speed up the leg quarters.

Turning the oven above 500 degrees wasn't possible. If I couldn't get the oven any hotter, I needed to find a way to store some of the heat it produced and then direct that heat at the turkey. How about using a baking stone? Baking stones are designed to absorb heat and then deliver that heat to whatever is placed on top of them (usually, a pizza). For my next go-round, I slipped a baking stone under my roasting pan in the oven. While they preheated, I

Speed the Way Even More

Want to streamline your turkey prep even more? Buy a kosher bird and you can skip salting altogether, since the koshering process involves bathing the bird in salt. Our favorite supermarket turkey is Empire Kosher Turkey. It boasts a dense, moist texture and buttery white meat with nice poultry flavor.

▶ Watch: It's Easy
A step-by-step video is available at CooksIllustrated.com/dec16

Salting Under the Skin

In order to apply salt to turkey flesh, the skin must first be loosened. Here are a couple of tips:

➤ Don't detach the membrane along the breastbone—it's hard to loosen without ripping the skin. Plus, the membrane helps you divide the salt evenly.

➤ The skin around the curve at the neck end can be difficult to loosen. To make the job easier, first loosen the skin on the bottom two-thirds of the breast and the legs, and then turn the turkey 180 degrees and come in through the neck end to loosen the skin on the top third of the breast.

Note: Don't forget to salt the cavity of the bird as well; when we skipped this step, the turkey didn't taste as deeply seasoned.

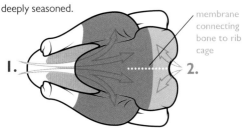

membrane connecting bone to rib cage

1. Working from tail end, rub salt under loosened skin on bottom two-thirds of breast and legs.

2. Working from neck end, rub salt on remaining breast meat.

covered the breast of a salted turkey with a double layer of aluminum foil, which would shield it from some heat. I would pull off the foil when I turned the oven down to 325 so that the breast could brown. Sure enough, this approach produced exactly the results I wanted. This was no small victory: With no extra effort—just a strategically placed piece of kitchenware—the turkey legs and thighs registered 175 degrees just as the breasts reached 160.

My only critique was that the skin wasn't quite brown or crispy enough, so I employed a test kitchen trick that makes all the difference: rubbing baking powder onto the skin. Baking powder has alkaline properties that speed up browning. It also causes proteins in the skin to break down more readily and produce crispier results.

I prepared one last bird, salting it overnight and then rubbing 1 teaspoon of baking powder (combined with 1½ teaspoons of oil for easy distribution) on top before following my new roasting protocol. When I pulled this bird out of the oven, I knew instantly that the baking powder had done its job. The skin was deeply bronzed and beautifully crispy. I transferred the turkey to a carving board to rest while I contemplated the drippings in the pan.

The Rest Is Gravy

When I tasted the drippings, one thing jumped out at me: They were salty and intensely flavorful. The supplementary heat from the baking stone had caused the juices to reduce far more than usual, making them superconcentrated. I transferred the drippings to a fat separator, making sure to scrape the flavorful fond from the bottom of the pan. I pro-

ceeded with a classic gravy-making routine, starting with browning the neck and giblets from the turkey along with onion, carrot, and herbs in some of the reserved fat and then stirring in flour to make a roux. Finally, I whisked in chicken broth and white wine and let the gravy simmer to thicken.

After about 10 minutes (the drippings were so intense that no real reduction was necessary), I dipped a spoon in for a taste and found that the superconcentrated jus had produced a gravy that was far too salty, even though I hadn't added any additional seasonings. The solution was simple: Instead of using chicken broth, I swapped in water (unsalted broth was an option, but it seemed unnecessary since I already had flavor in spades). Now I had a deeply flavorful gravy—in record time.

Roasting a turkey was now less of a hassle, and I could produce the gravy while the bird rested. From now on, the first thing I'll be reaching for when roasting a turkey is a baking stone.

EASIER ROAST TURKEY AND GRAVY
SERVES 10 TO 12

Note that this recipe requires refrigerating the seasoned bird for 24 to 48 hours. This recipe was developed and tested using Diamond Crystal Kosher Salt. If you have Morton Kosher Salt, which is denser than Diamond Crystal, reduce the salt in step 1 to 3 tablespoons and rub 1 tablespoon of the salt mixture into each breast, 1½ teaspoons into each leg, and the remainder into the cavity. If using a self-basting turkey (such as a frozen Butterball) or a kosher turkey, do not apply the salt-mixture to the bird. The

success of this recipe is dependent on saturating the baking stone and roasting pan with heat.

	Kosher salt and pepper
4	teaspoons sugar
1	(12- to 14-pound) turkey, neck and giblets removed and reserved for gravy
2½	tablespoons vegetable oil
1	teaspoon baking powder
1	small onion, chopped fine
1	carrot, sliced thin
5	sprigs fresh parsley
2	bay leaves
5	tablespoons all-purpose flour
3¼	cups water
¼	cup dry white wine

1. Combine 4 tablespoons salt and sugar in bowl. Place turkey, breast side up, on counter. Using your fingers, carefully loosen skin covering breast and legs. Rub 4 teaspoons salt-sugar mixture under skin of each breast, 2 teaspoons under skin of each leg, and remaining salt-sugar mixture inside cavity. Tuck wings behind back and tie legs together with kitchen twine. Place turkey on wire rack set in rimmed baking sheet and refrigerate, uncovered, for 24 to 48 hours.

2. At least 30 minutes before roasting turkey, adjust oven rack to lowest position, set baking stone on rack, set roasting pan on baking stone, and heat oven to 500 degrees. Combine 1½ teaspoons oil and baking powder in small bowl. Pat turkey dry with paper towels. Rub oil mixture evenly over turkey. Cover turkey breast with double layer of aluminum foil.

The Setup for Easier Turkey and Gravy

We place the turkey in the preheated roasting pan, cover the breast with aluminum foil to protect it from overcooking, and place the pan on a preheated baking stone. The benefits of this arrangement are twofold:

WHITE AND DARK MEAT FINISH CONCURRENTLY
The baking stone's heat is transferred through the roasting pan to the leg quarters, so they finish cooking at the same time as the more delicate breast meat.

FASTER GRAVY
The extra heat provided by the baking stone also causes the juices that accumulate in the bottom of the roasting pan to reduce very quickly, so the drippings left in the pan at the end of roasting are superconcentrated. Starting with intensely flavored drippings means that the gravy can be made with water, not broth, and it needs only 10 minutes of simmering time to reach its full flavor potential.

3. Remove roasting pan from oven. Drizzle remaining 2 tablespoons oil into roasting pan. Place turkey, breast side up, in pan and return pan to oven. Reduce oven temperature to 425 degrees and roast for 45 minutes.

4. Remove foil, reduce oven temperature to 325 degrees, and continue to roast until breast registers 160 degrees and drumsticks/thighs register 175 degrees, 1 to 1½ hours longer.

5. Using spatula, loosen turkey from roasting pan; transfer to carving board and let rest, uncovered, for 45 minutes. While turkey rests, using wooden spoon, scrape up any browned bits from bottom of roasting pan. Strain mixture through fine-mesh strainer set over bowl. Transfer drippings to fat separator and let rest for 10 minutes. Reserve 3 tablespoons fat and defatted liquid (you should have 1 cup; add water if necessary). Discard remaining fat.

6. Heat reserved fat in large saucepan over medium-high heat until shimmering. Add reserved neck and giblets and cook until well browned, 10 to 12 minutes. Transfer neck and giblets to large plate. Reduce heat to medium; add onion, carrot, parsley sprigs, and bay leaves; and cook, stirring frequently, until vegetables are softened, 5 to 7 minutes. Add flour and cook, stirring constantly, until flour is well coated with fat, about 1 minute. Slowly whisk in reserved defatted liquid and cook until thickened, about 1 minute. Whisk in water and wine, return neck and giblets to pan, and bring to simmer. Simmer for 10 minutes, then season with salt and pepper to taste. Discard neck. Strain gravy through fine-mesh strainer, discarding solids, and transfer to serving bowl. Carve turkey and arrange on serving platter. Serve with gravy.

No Neck? Just Wing It.

As we were developing our gravy recipe, we found that not all turkeys come with a neck—a flavor booster. Luckily, a portion of the wings makes a great substitute. In fact, some tasters preferred gravy made from the wings (which have more meat and collagen) to gravy made from the neck.

Use kitchen shears to cut between the midsection and drumette of each wing, leaving the drumette in place both for appearance and to keep the bird stable during roasting and carving. Use a chef's knife to separate the wingtip and midsection.

EQUIPMENT TESTING Baking Stones

A good baking stone or steel takes your oven to the next level, absorbing and radiating heat to create flavorful crisping on pizza and bread—or even helping you roast a better turkey. But the consumer looking to buy one faces a lot of questions regarding material, shape, and size. To find the best option, we rounded up five nationally available stones (made of a durable ceramic called cordierite) and steels (made of low-carbon steel); we used our prior findings to limit our lineup to those that are rectangular, which is a more versatile and forgiving shape than round (see "Why a Square Baking Stone Beats a Round One" on page 31). We also eliminated models that couldn't be used at 500 degrees (or higher); high temperatures are essential for great pizza crust.

We put each stone or steel through the wringer, using it to bake thin-crust pizza, rustic bread, and our Easier Roast Turkey and Gravy. To test for toughness, we dropped each onto the floor from a height of 2 to 3 inches and examined it for cracks or chips; we also had users of various heights move each stone in and out of different ovens.

When all was said and done, we could fully recommend all the stones and steels in our lineup—there were a few minor blips with the food tests, but everything came out acceptably well. The stones scored slightly higher than the steels, whose minor fault was that they can throw off too much heat (you've got to watch what's cooking closely); one of them was also so big that it was hard to maneuver. Our old favorite, the 16 by 14-inch Old Stone Oven Pizza Baking Stone ($59.95), took top honors once again. It put a great crust on pizza and bread, its moderate size makes it versatile without being too bulky, and we especially liked its raised feet, which make moving it a breeze. Our Best Buy—the Pizzacraft All-Purpose Baking Stone ($28.99)—is harder to handle with its lack of feet and larger size, but it performs well in all other respects. For complete testing results, go to CooksIllustrated.com/dec16. –Lisa McManus

HIGHLY RECOMMENDED	RECOMMENDED	
OLD STONE OVEN Pizza Baking Stone	**PIZZACRAFT All-Purpose** Baking Stone	**PIZZACRAFT Rectangular Steel** Baking Plate
Model: 4467	Model: PC0102 *BEST BUY*	Model: PC0313
Price: $59.95	Price: $28.99	Price: $43.99
Material: Cordierite	Material: Cordierite	Material: Low-carbon steel
Weight: 9.5 lb	Weight: 10.9 lb	Weight: 11.8 lb
Dimensions: 16 in x 14 in	Dimensions: 20 in x 13.5 in	Dimensions: 22 in x 14 in
Comments: Our durable former favorite stone wins again. Pizza and bread came out deeply golden brown and crisp, and light and dark turkey meat cooked evenly. The raised feet built into the underside of this stone make it easy to grab and maneuver.	Comments: Four inches longer than our winner, this inexpensive stone was plenty roomy, but it was also somewhat cumbersome to pick up, maneuver, and store, since it is very large and has no feet. Pizza and breads came out nicely browned and crisp.	Comments: This fourth-place huge steel slab browned bread and pizza crust beautifully but was cumbersome for some testers to maneuver. It filled our oven rack from wall to wall, so be sure to measure your oven if you are tempted to buy it.

How a Baking Stone Gets a Roasting Pan Hotter Faster

A baking stone was so helpful in jump-starting the cooking of the dark meat that we decided to quantify the heat gains it produced. First, we measured what happened without a stone by placing a cool turkey in a preheated roasting pan and monitoring the temperature of the pan with a thermocouple. The temperature of the pan dropped from 201 degrees to 165 degrees over a period of 45 minutes before it stabilized. Conversely, a pan sitting on a baking stone actually increased in temperature after the turkey was added, rising from 210 degrees to 246 degrees over the same period of time. The upshot? Heat is quickly transferred to the leg quarters, so they finish cooking concurrently with the delicate breast meat.

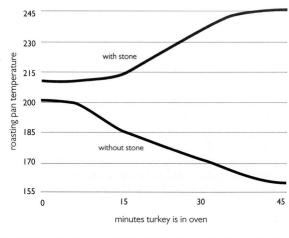

roasting pan temperature

with stone

without stone

245 / 230 / 215 / 200 / 185 / 170 / 155

0 — 15 — 30 — 45

minutes turkey is in oven

Ultimate French Mashed Potatoes

The luxuriously rich and silky puree served in Paris is the result of tedious mixing by hand and a sinful amount of butter. But does it have to be?

⮞ BY STEVE DUNN ⮜

In the early 1980s, Parisian chef Joël Robuchon turned mashed potatoes into an utterly sublime experience by employing two hallmarks of French cooking: tireless attention to detail and a whole lot of butter.

His method: Boil 2 pounds of whole unpeeled potatoes and then peel them while hot before passing them through a food mill. Next, incorporate a full pound of cold butter, 1 tablespoon at a time, by beating vigorously with a wooden spoon—a 10-minute, arm-numbing process. Finally, thin the puree with warm milk and pass it repeatedly through a *tamis* (a flat, drum-shaped ultrafine sieve). Robuchon's painstaking efforts produced the ultimate example of *pommes purée*, ethereally smooth and laden with butter.

While I love Robuchon's recipe, the scandalous fat content and the drudgery of sieving make it unrealistic for a home cook. But if I could streamline the process and cut back somewhat on the fat, it would be a dish I'd love to make for special occasions.

In France, the puree is made with ratte potatoes, medium-starch fingerlings. I used Yukon Golds, a close substitute. For my first go-round, I cut the amount of butter in half and poured in extra milk to compensate; I used a food mill, but I skipped the tamis.

Was the resulting puree as gloriously smooth as Robuchon's? Perhaps not, but tasters still called it "pillow-soft," so I happily gave up any thoughts of trying to jury-rig a tamis. That said, the potatoes did lack the richness of Robuchon's version. Adding butter back a little at a time, I found that 2½ sticks elevated these spuds to pommes purée status: a rich, silky step above regular mashed potatoes.

Now that I had experienced beating cold butter into potatoes, I was eager to find a way around it. How about melting the butter? Sadly, with so much of it in the mix, the butter and potatoes didn't fully integrate, so the puree was separated and greasy.

Setting that problem temporarily aside, I turned my attention to the literal pain of peeling hot potatoes. I compared a puree made with peeled and diced potatoes (rinsed to remove surface starch) to one made with whole, skin-on spuds. The latter required more than a cup of milk to achieve the proper silken consistency. However, the peeled, diced potatoes

Passing the potatoes through a food mill gives the buttery puree a silky, almost pourable consistency.

absorbed so much cooking water that they could accommodate only ½ cup of milk. The result? A weaker-tasting mash. This got me thinking: Since potatoes are so absorbent, why not peel them and cook them in liquid I'd actually want them to soak up (the milk and butter)? I gave it a try, reserving the buttery cooking milk and whisking it into the milled potatoes. The puree was velvety-smooth and tasted rich and buttery. What's more, it was not at all separated or greasy. This was a double victory: no more beating in cold butter or peeling hot potatoes.

Why did simmering the potatoes directly in milk and butter result in a more cohesive puree than adding melted butter and milk to boiled potatoes? It all comes down to the potato starch, which is critical for helping fat emulsify with potatoes. When peeled potatoes are boiled in water, much of their starch is released and eventually poured down the drain. With too little gluey starch in the mix, the melted butter struggles to form a smooth emulsion with the wet spuds, resulting in a slick, greasy puree. When the potatoes are cooked directly in the milk and butter, none of the released

starch gets lost, and it is thus available to help the butter emulsify with the water in the potatoes. (In Robuchon's recipe, the whole, skin-on potatoes retain their starch during cooking; vigorous beating liberates the starch and helps stabilize the emulsion, while the generous amount of butter prevents the released starch from turning the puree gluey.)

In the end, my simplified recipe delivered a rich, silky-smooth mash while allowing me to wave *au revoir* to an exhausted arm.

FRENCH-STYLE MASHED POTATOES (POMMES PURÉE)
SERVES 8

When serving, keep the richness in mind. A small dollop on each plate should suffice.

- 2 pounds Yukon Gold potatoes, peeled and cut into 1-inch pieces
- 20 tablespoons (2½ sticks) unsalted butter
- 1⅓ cups whole milk
  Salt and white pepper

1. Place potatoes in fine-mesh strainer and rinse under cold running water until water runs clear. Set aside to drain.

2. Heat butter, milk, and 1 teaspoon salt in large saucepan over low heat until butter has melted. Add potatoes, increase heat to medium-low, and cook until liquid just starts to boil. Reduce heat to low, partially cover, and gently simmer until paring knife can be slipped into and out of centers of potatoes with no resistance, 30 to 40 minutes, stirring every 10 minutes.

3. Drain potatoes in fine-mesh strainer set over large bowl, reserving cooking liquid. Wipe out saucepan. Return cooking liquid to saucepan and place saucepan over low heat.

4. Set food mill fitted with finest disk over saucepan. Working in batches, transfer potatoes to hopper and process. Using whisk, recombine potatoes and cooking liquid until smooth, 10 to 15 seconds (potatoes should almost be pourable). Season with salt and pepper to taste, and serve immediately.

⊙ **See Silkiness Happen**
A step-by-step video is available at CooksIllustrated.com/dec16

Porchetta for the Holidays

Italy's rich herb-and-garlic-infused slow-cooked pork is one of the world's best street foods. We wanted to transform it into a roast for company.

⇒ BY ANDREW JANJIGIAN ⇐

Italy's *porchetta*—fall-apart tender, rich pieces of slow-cooked pork, aromatic with garlic, fennel seeds, rosemary, and thyme and served with pieces of crisp skin on a crusty roll—is one of the world's greatest street foods. Traditionally a whole pig is boned and the meat is rubbed with an herb-spice paste. The pig is then tied around a spit and allowed to sit overnight. The next day, it's slow-roasted over a wood fire until the meat is ultratender and the skin is burnished and crackling-crisp.

Recently, porchetta came to mind as I pondered my holiday roast options. It may sound strange, given that a sandwich doesn't offer much in the way of presentation, but it's such a knockout for flavor that I had to wonder: Could I make a few tweaks to transform porchetta from street-fare sandwich to holiday centerpiece?

Going whole hog wasn't an option, so my first task was picking the right substitute. Some recipes call for wrapping a pork belly around a pork loin. I ruled out that scenario from the get-go for being too fussy; plus, pork loin takes more work to keep juicy. Pork belly alone is also a popular choice since it comes with skin attached and it's very fatty (it's what you make bacon from, after all). I found that it was easy to tie into a compact roll that sliced neatly, its skin cooked up crisp and crackly, and the meat was tender and moist. But I ultimately decided against it, too, since it's often composed of more fat than meat—fine for bacon but a bit much for porchetta.

Pork butt, cut from the upper portion of the shoulder, was my best bet. It generally cooks up flavorful and moist, and it's fatty without being over the top. Its lack of skin was a drawback, but I decided I could live with it since I suspected I could brown and crisp the fat cap as a stand-in.

That said, the recipes I tried featuring pork butt left something to be desired. Even though the meat was tender and juicy at the center, it got progressively drier and tougher toward the exterior. The herb paste

A sharp, boldly flavored paste made with fennel seeds, plenty of herbs, a dozen cloves of garlic, and ground black pepper complements the rich meat.

was poorly distributed, and the irregular, loose shape of the roast meant it was hard to slice into neat pieces elegant enough for a holiday dinner.

The Skin I'm In

When cooking a pork butt, low-and-slow is best since it allows the ample collagen time to melt, creating an ultratender roast; it also helps mitigate the difference in cooking between the interior and exterior. I found that 6 hours produced the best results, but that was just too long. Cutting the roast in half lengthwise decreased the cooking time by almost half, and it gave me two cylindrical roasts that sliced nicely, especially when I tied them with twine.

Now the meat was cooking through more evenly and more quickly, but the exterior was still a bit dry. I had noticed when testing the pork belly version that all of the meat was juicy and tender despite having been cooked at a much higher temperature than my pork butts were. Was it the greater amount of fat? Or was it the fact that when tied into a roll, the meat in

the pork belly was entirely encased within a layer of skin?

Increasing the amount of fat in my pork butt wasn't on the table, but I had a notion for how to fake a layer of skin around it: aluminum foil. For my next test, I covered the roasting pan tightly with foil, roasted the pork until its interior registered 180 degrees, and then removed the foil. A billow of steam wafted up, and I noticed that the meat had shed about a cup of brothy liquid into the pan—good signs. While the roasts were pale and wan on the exterior, the meat was tender and juicy throughout, with little discernible difference between the exterior and the core. Here's why: The steam kept the surface temperature of the roast from exceeding the boiling point of water (212 degrees), preventing the exterior from overcooking as the interior came up to temperature. Cooking with steam also sped up the cooking, since steam is a better conductor of heat than air is. The cooking time was down to about 2 hours.

I drained the juices from the pan, untied the roasts, and returned them to a 500-degree oven for a short stint to brown.

A Cut Above

Next, I shifted my focus to the paste. Some recipes called for rubbing the paste onto the roast, with the hope that the flavor would penetrate. Others called for poking holes in the roast with a knife and stuffing the paste into them. The latter approach worked better than the former, but it was slow work and impossible to tell whether I'd done a good job until serving time. There had to be a better way.

I tried pulling each roast apart along the seams while still keeping the pieces attached to each other—basically unfolding each roast—and then rubbing the

Why Some Fat Melts and Some Crisps

For fat to render, or melt, the fat has to be released from the bounds of its cells—that's why cutting shallow slits in the fat cap helps. But when exterior fat that's still trapped within cells is exposed to the heat of the oven and reaches a high enough temperature (well beyond 300 degrees), it oxidizes, leading to a series of reactions that produces flavorful molecules and brown pigments and leads to cross-linking of those pigments, which delivers that familiar crisp texture.

▶ **Watch Every Step**
A step-by-step video is available at CooksIllustrated.com/dec16

CROSSHATCH FAT CAP
Crosshatching the fat cap allows heat to penetrate, which helps the fat render just below the surface.

HALVE ROAST Two smaller roasts are evenly shaped and cook more quickly.

CUT SLITS INTO ROASTS These openings allow for even, thorough seasoning and also ensure that the roast holds its shape when sliced.

TIE ROASTS Tying the roasts along their length before cooking gives them an even shape that allows for neat slicing.

TREAT FAT CAP A rub of baking soda (which accelerates browning) and salt and an overnight stint in the fridge dry out the fat cap to help it cook up crisp.

paste all over before tying each piece back together. That worked in terms of distribution, but the roasts fell apart at the seams during slicing. A similar thing happened when I butterflied the roasts along their length. The problem in both cases was that I had created seams that ran perpendicular to the direction in which the roast would be sliced. So what if the cuts ran in the *same* direction as the slices?

For my next test, I cut a series of parallel slits through each roast along its length, stopping 1 inch from each end. Getting the paste into the roast was easy since the slits were big enough to let me use my hands to push the paste in from both sides. I rubbed each roast with salt, applied the paste, and let the roasts sit overnight in the fridge, which gave the salt time to penetrate the meat. This worked perfectly and guaranteed that every serving was deeply flavored and that the meat would slice neatly.

All that remained was to improve the appearance and texture of the fat cap "skin." I had avoided putting the herb paste on the fat cap to give it a better chance of crisping up, but it was still a bit pale, and the fat just below the surface wasn't particularly well rendered. To improve things, I used a sharp knife to create 1-inch-wide crosshatches through the cap, which would let heat penetrate and the fat render out. To help it dry out and thus crisp up, I rubbed the fat cap with salt and left the roasts uncovered for their overnight rest. Finally, to boost browning, I added a bit of baking soda to the salt rub. Baking soda creates a more alkaline environment, which makes browning

reactions more likely to occur. Crisp, rich, and deeply browned, the fat cap was the perfect complement to the tender, moist, boldly flavored meat beneath. This porchetta might have simple street-food roots, but it's worthy of taking center stage on any holiday table.

PORCHETTA
SERVES 8 TO 10

Pork butt roast is often labeled Boston butt in the supermarket. Look for a roast with a substantial fat cap. If fennel seeds are unavailable, substitute ¼ cup of ground fennel. The *porchetta* needs to be refrigerated for 6 to 24 hours once it is rubbed with the paste, but it is best when it sits for a full 24 hours.

- 3 tablespoons fennel seeds
- ½ cup fresh rosemary leaves (2 bunches)
- ¼ cup fresh thyme leaves (2 bunches)
- 12 garlic cloves, peeled
    Kosher salt and pepper
- ½ cup extra-virgin olive oil
- 1 (5- to 6-pound) boneless pork butt roast, trimmed
- ¼ teaspoon baking soda

1. Grind fennel seeds in spice grinder or mortar and pestle until finely ground. Transfer ground fennel to food processor and add rosemary, thyme, garlic, 1 tablespoon pepper, and 2 teaspoons salt. Pulse mixture until finely chopped, 10 to 15 pulses. Add oil and

process until smooth paste forms, 20 to 30 seconds.

2. Using sharp knife, cut slits in surface fat of roast, spaced 1 inch apart, in crosshatch pattern, being careful not to cut into meat. Cut roast in half with grain into 2 equal pieces.

3. Turn each roast on its side so fat cap is facing away from you, bottom of roast is facing toward you, and newly cut side is facing up. Starting 1 inch from short end of each roast, use boning or paring knife to make slit that starts 1 inch from top of roast and ends 1 inch from bottom, pushing knife completely through roast. Repeat making slits, spaced 1 to 1½ inches apart, along length of each roast, stopping 1 inch from opposite end (you should have 6 to 8 slits, depending on size of roast).

4. Turn roast so fat cap is facing down. Rub sides and bottom of each roast with 2 teaspoons salt, taking care to work salt into slits from both sides. Rub herb paste onto sides and bottom of each roast, taking care to work paste into slits from both sides. Flip roast so that fat cap is facing up. Using 3 pieces of kitchen twine per roast, tie each roast into compact cylinder.

5. Combine 1 tablespoon salt, 1 teaspoon pepper, and baking soda in small bowl. Rub fat cap of each roast with salt–baking soda mixture, taking care to work mixture into crosshatches. Transfer roasts to wire rack set in rimmed baking sheet and refrigerate, uncovered, for at least 6 hours or up to 24 hours.

6. Adjust oven rack to middle position and heat oven to 325 degrees. Transfer roasts, fat side up, to large roasting pan, leaving at least 2 inches between roasts. Cover tightly with aluminum foil. Cook until pork registers 180 degrees, 2 to 2½ hours.

7. Remove pan from oven and increase oven temperature to 500 degrees. Carefully remove and discard foil and transfer roasts to large plate. Discard liquid in pan. Line pan with foil. Remove twine from roasts; return roasts to pan, directly on foil; and return pan to oven. Cook until exteriors of roasts are well browned and interiors register 190 degrees, 20 to 30 minutes.

8. Transfer roasts to carving board and let rest for 20 minutes. Slice roasts ½ inch thick, transfer to serving platter, and serve.

TECHNIQUE **Roasting Under Wraps**

Italian *porchetta* made with a whole pig stays moist over a long cooking time because the pig's skin acts as a protective layer. Since pork butt lacks skin, we use aluminum foil to trap the steam created from the roasts' drippings and keep the meat moist. Covering the pan with foil has two other benefits. First, because the temperature of water (here in the form of steam) cannot go above 212 degrees, the temperature gradient between the outer portion of the roast and the interior is minimized, and the roast cooks more evenly. Second, because water conducts heat better than air, the foil cover helps speed up the cooking time.

Perfect Cast Iron Steak

This pan's unbeatable heat retention should create the deepest, richest sear on a steak. But you first need to know your cast iron.

⇒ BY RUSSELL SELANDER ⇐

I have long been a fan of cooking in cast iron. So when I set out to develop a recipe for a great steak—one with a perfectly seared exterior and an interior that was evenly cooked from edge to edge—of course I turned to my great-grandmother's well-worn Wagner cast-iron skillet.

After an initial round of testing, though, I had found out a little secret: Despite cast iron's many virtues, you can't just plunk a steak into the pan and expect success. The recipes that I tried produced varied results, but none of them were encouraging. There were steaks with burnt exteriors and raw interiors and steaks with pale exteriors and overcooked interiors, and the browning was uneven across the board.

I decided to take a step back and investigate the cast-iron skillet a little more. It's said to produce a great seared steak because it retains heat well, but I suspected there was more to it than that. I knew from previous test kitchen testing that cast iron does not heat up evenly, and that seemed likely to be the root of the problem with the recipes I tried. I wanted to know just how unevenly cast iron heats and whether there was a way I could fix that.

Going Toe to Toe

I started by pitting cast-iron skillets against stainless steel–clad skillets to see how the heat was distributed in each. I lightly dusted both types of skillet with flour—since I wanted to be sure that the evenness of heating was not due to any inherent quality of the heat source—and, without any preheating, set the skillets over gas, electric, and induction burners at both medium and medium-high heat. The results were consistent for all three types of heat: evenly toasted, nicely golden-brown flour in the steel-clad skillets, and in the cast-iron skillets, pale flour with black splotches marking the places where the heat source actually came into contact with the pan (see "How Cast Iron Heats").

▶ See Them Sizzle
A step-by-step video is available at CooksIllustrated.com/dec16

For the ultimate sear in cast iron, how you preheat the pan matters at least as much as how you cook the steaks. We preheat it in the oven.

But, I thought, since the dark spots were more well defined over medium-high heat than medium heat, maybe the heat level was the problem. To find out,

I heated a cast-iron skillet over small and large gas flames, as well as over electric and induction burners. I took the temperature at the center, 3 inches off center, and at the inside edge of the skillet every 30 seconds for about 10 minutes during each test. The results confirmed what I was seeing with the flour test: No matter the level of heat or its source, the skillet had hot and cool spots.

Our science editor explained that most stainless steel–clad cookware is made up of layers of stainless steel around a core of aluminum, which conducts heat about $2\frac{1}{2}$ times better than cast iron. Therefore, the heat moves across the skillet very easily. Since heat doesn't move as easily across cast iron, the skillet initially develops hot spots where it is directly touching the heat source.

Oven to the Rescue

But I realized there was a change that could provide a solution: heating the pan in the oven. It would take a little longer, but because the oven's heat is not concentrated on a single part of the pan but rather comes at the pan more or less evenly from all directions, it guaranteed an evenly heated pan. An added advantage was that the oven could be set to a specific temperature, no matter what the heat source, whereas when using the stovetop I had found it difficult to accurately specify a single burner setting that worked across all types of heat sources.

PERFECT STEAK, INSIDE AND OUT

Searing steak in cast iron can produce the ultimate crust—but often at the expense of a rosy, tender interior. Here's how to get both.

USE LOTS OF OIL A generous 2 tablespoons of oil keeps the steak (which contracts during cooking) in contact with the heat, for more even browning.

TURN THE HEAT DOWN After the initial sear, reduce the flame to medium-low; the pan will stay hot enough to sear the meat.

FLIP REPEATEDLY Turning the steak every 2 minutes prevents a gray, overcooked band from forming under the surface.

But what was the best oven temperature? My goal was to get the skillet hot enough so that vegetable oil, which has a smoke point of between 400 and 450 degrees, would start to smoke as soon as I added it to the skillet. I put the skillet in the cold oven, as there was no sense in waiting for the oven to heat before adding the skillet, and set the oven temperature to 400 degrees. However, when I added the oil after heating the skillet, it took some time to start smoking. I continued to test temperatures at 25-degree intervals, pulling the skillet out and searing steaks, and eventually worked my way up to 500 degrees, which I found to be the ideal setting.

Now for the steak itself. I chose thick boneless strip steaks because they have big, beefy flavor and are easy to find. Salting the steaks and letting them sit while my pan heated in the oven would not only season the meat throughout but also help keep it moist and juicy. Patting them dry before searing helped them brown even more.

My next question was how much oil to use—and it turned out that I needed more than I thought I would. As meat cooks, it contracts; any ridges or divots get bigger, and without oil, they don't touch a heat source, resulting in a spotty brown steak rather than a gorgeously browned one. I settled on 2 tablespoons of oil, a hefty but necessary amount.

Flipping Out

Two problems remained: I was still getting a rather large gray band, the area between the crust and interior that dries out and turns chalky. And my beautifully preheated pan was so hot that the crust it produced was actually too good—it was too thick and almost unpleasantly crunchy. To eliminate the gray band, one of my coworkers suggested that I try flipping the steak more often (I had been flipping it only once). The idea made sense, since each time a steak is flipped, the side not touching the skillet cooks with residual heat, which penetrates the meat more slowly, resulting in a smaller gray band. I wondered if flipping might also help prevent an overly thick crust. I found that flipping once every 2 minutes was just the right amount to ensure a perfectly rosy interior, but the crust was still thicker than I liked.

Then I did something I never thought I would do when searing: I turned down the heat. Because the cast iron retained the heat so well once it got up to the proper temperature, turning down the heat actually maintained the temperature I wanted, whereas keeping the heat high increased the skillet's temperature as time went on. So I got a great initial sear over medium-high heat and then reduced the heat until I found a sweet spot: about 8 minutes over medium-low heat. Combined with flipping every 2 minutes, this produced a perfect, gorgeously browned crust and a rosy interior from edge to edge.

The steak was now fantastic on its own, but a simple accompaniment would make it that much more special. Mixing up a compound butter to melt over the resting steaks was easier than making a pan sauce and was just as flavorful.

SCIENCE | HOW CAST IRON HEATS

Cast iron doesn't heat as quickly as stainless steel–clad cookware because its thermal conductivity—the ability to transfer heat from one part of the metal to another—is lower. But it holds heat much more effectively; even when a relatively cool steak is added, the pan's temperature drop is minimal and the steak browns better. The trick is to make sure that the pan preheats thoroughly and evenly, which we do in a very hot oven (not on the stovetop) because the convective heat minimizes hot spots. Once the pan is hot, we set it over a moderate flame to maintain the heat and to avoid creating an overly thick crust.

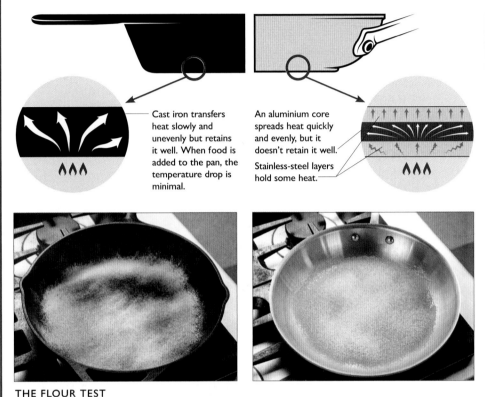

Cast iron transfers heat slowly and unevenly but retains it well. When food is added to the pan, the temperature drop is minimal.

An aluminium core spreads heat quickly and evenly, but it doesn't retain it well. Stainless-steel layers hold some heat.

THE FLOUR TEST
Heating flour in cast-iron and stainless-steel skillets illustrates the difference between the two: In the cast-iron skillet, the flour burns in spots while remaining raw in others; in the stainless-steel skillet, it browns more evenly.

CAST IRON STEAKS WITH HERB BUTTER
SERVES 4

Don't forget to take the butter out to soften at least 30 minutes before you start to cook.

- 2 (1-pound) boneless strip steaks, 1½ inches thick, trimmed
  Salt and pepper
- 4 tablespoons unsalted butter, softened
- 2 tablespoons minced shallot
- 1 tablespoon minced fresh parsley
- 1 tablespoon minced fresh chives
- 1 garlic clove, minced
- 2 tablespoons vegetable oil

1. Adjust oven rack to middle position, place 12-inch cast-iron skillet on rack, and heat oven to 500 degrees. Meanwhile, season steaks with salt and let sit at room temperature. Combine butter, shallot, parsley, chives, garlic, and ¼ teaspoon pepper in bowl; set aside.

2. When oven reaches 500 degrees, pat steaks dry with paper towels and season with pepper. Using potholders, remove skillet from oven and place over medium-high heat; turn off oven. Being careful of hot skillet handle, add oil and heat until just smoking. Cook steaks, without moving them, until lightly browned on first side, about 2 minutes. Flip steaks and cook until lightly browned on second side, about 2 minutes.

3. Flip steaks, reduce heat to medium-low, and cook, flipping every 2 minutes, until steaks are well browned and meat registers 120 to 125 degrees (for medium-rare), 7 to 9 minutes. Transfer steaks to carving board, dollop 2 tablespoons herb butter on each steak, tent with aluminum foil, and let rest for 5 to 10 minutes. Slice steaks ½ inch thick and serve.

CAST IRON STEAKS WITH BLUE CHEESE–CHIVE BUTTER

Omit shallot and parsley. Increase chives to 2 tablespoons and add ⅓ cup crumbled mild blue cheese to butter with chives.

Hearty Frittata

Loading up a frittata with meat, vegetables, and cheese can yield a simple, satisfying meal—or a rubbery egg disk with a wet, runny core.

⋺ BY LAN LAM ⋶

The frittata is sometimes called a lazy cook's omelet. After all, it contains the same ingredients but doesn't require folding the eggs around the filling, a skill that takes practice to master. But it's not just the fold that distinguishes the two. Frittatas sport a golden-brown exterior, whereas any browning on a French-style omelet is a sign of poor technique. Also, an omelet should be custardy and just set, whereas a frittata must be firm enough to hold a filling in place.

But even the practical frittata requires a little know-how, lest the bottom turn rubbery or the center end up loose and wet. I wanted to uncover the keys to a tender, evenly cooked, cohesive frittata. I also wanted it to be big and hearty enough to serve at least four for dinner.

Stir and Scrape

With plenty of filling ingredients and a 12-inch nonstick skillet at the ready, I evaluated common cooking methods. I immediately dismissed what I call "the inversion method," since it can be even harder to pull off than folding an omelet. It calls for cooking the frittata in an oiled skillet on the stove until the bottom sets, sliding it onto a plate, placing the overturned skillet on top of the frittata, inverting it back into the skillet, and returning the skillet to the stove to finish cooking. Yes, it's as tricky as it sounds. No thanks.

Instead, I tried a method that skips the difficult flipping step and calls for covering the skillet to trap the steam and cook the eggs through. I poured a dozen beaten eggs (enough to serve four to six people) on top of 3 cups of a hot placeholder filling (the right amount for a substantial frittata) and gave it a try. Unfortunately, this was a miss: While I waited for the eggs to set, the bottom of the frittata overcooked.

Another popular approach, cooking the frittata entirely in the oven, didn't fare much better. Recipes

Thanks to a hybrid stove-oven approach, our frittata turns out nicely browned on the exterior and tender inside.

▶ Look: It's So Easy
A step-by-step video is available at CooksIllustrated.com/dec16

were either too time-consuming, requiring a low temperature and at least 40 minutes to cook the eggs, or they called for the use of a broiler, which produced a spotty brown top that hid runny pockets.

In the end, I got the best results using a hybrid stove-oven approach. But it wasn't as straightforward as pouring the eggs over a filling on the stovetop, letting it cook for a couple of minutes, and then popping the pan into the oven. When made this way, the frittata overcooked on the bottom.

Stirring the eggs as they began to set on the stovetop was crucial. After pouring the eggs over the filling, I scraped the bottom of the pan as curds formed. This action prevented overcooking by pushing the partially cooked egg away from the pan bottom and allowing raw egg to flow in. After just 30 seconds, my spatula left a wide trail through the curds, at which point I smoothed the eggs into an even layer and transferred the skillet to a 350-degree oven, where the frittata finished cooking in less than 10 minutes. Progress, indeed: This frittata was evenly cooked from top to bottom and edge to edge. However, the eggs were rather rubbery. Here was my next challenge.

The Proteins That Bind

Many frittata recipes call for the addition of dairy, claiming that it tenderizes eggs. So I whipped up frittatas using milk, heavy cream, sour cream, and crème fraîche, happily finding that they all produced roughly the same tender texture—any variation in richness wasn't noticeable because of the substantial

Two Great Egg Tenderizers: Liquid and Salt

The combination of milk and salt gives our frittata its tender texture. The addition of any type of liquid makes it more difficult for egg proteins to bond, and when they do bond, they hold more moisture that contributes to increased tenderness. Salt weakens the protein networks, further tenderizing the eggs. The upshot is softer, more tender curds, even at relatively high temperatures. To demonstrate this concept, we cooked batches of eggs *sous vide* in plastic containers and then placed weights on top to gauge their tenderness.

| EGG
FIRMEST | EGG + SALT
SLIGHTLY TENDER | EGG + MILK
TENDER | EGG + SALT + MILK
MOST TENDER |

THE TRAIL TO SUCCESS

Stirring the eggs with a rubber spatula as they cook on the stovetop helps all the eggs set up evenly. When the spatula leaves a trail in the skillet, it's time to transfer the pan to the oven. Look for a trail that fills in slowly; if it fills in quickly, not enough egg has coagulated and the finished frittata will contain pockets of undercooked egg.

filling. And because any subtle flavor differences in the dairy were also obscured by the filling, I settled on milk. One-third cup of milk per dozen eggs was just the right amount. Any more made the eggs too delicate.

It was at this point that a colleague made an interesting observation. The frittata was emerging piping hot from the oven; when I took its temperature, it registered between 185 and 195 degrees. Scrambled eggs cooked to that temperature would be tough and bouncy—and yet the frittata was still tender. Exactly what was the milk doing to keep the eggs tender?

Here's what I learned: First, when it comes to tenderizing eggs, there's nothing special about dairy; any liquid will do the job. That said, after experimenting with water (too bland), chicken broth (too chicken-y), and even wine (too acidic), I decided to stick with understated milk.

To understand how liquid makes eggs tender, you first need to understand the composition of an egg: It is mainly water, fat, and proteins. At room temperature, the proteins are isolated and coiled up. But when heat is added, the proteins begin to unwind and move more. As they move, they bump into each other, and because they are unwound, they tangle and form a mesh that holds the water and fat in place. This reaction starts when the eggs hit 160 degrees, the temperature at which curds first take shape. As the temperature increases, the number of bonds increases and the mesh gets stronger. As this happens, the eggs move from just set to firm to rubbery.

That's where the extra liquid comes in: Liquid dilutes the proteins, making it harder for them to coagulate and turn rubbery even as the temperature rises. What's more, even when they do bond, there is a lot of extra water in the mesh, which further contributes to tenderness. The result is eggs that remain tender even when heated to nearly 200 degrees.

As I read about egg cookery, I was reminded that the salt I was using for seasoning also played a role in protein coagulation. Salt weakens the protein network, a disruption that further tenderizes the eggs.

Filled to Capacity

To finish, I drew up some guidelines for the fillings. First, I chose bold ingredients to complement the mild eggs, cooking them in the skillet before building the frittata. Second, I chopped the ingredients into ½-inch pieces (or smaller) because large chunks broke up the frittata's structure, making it prone to falling apart. Third, I seasoned not just with salt but also with a touch of acid, which provided a flavor boost without affecting the texture of the eggs.

My first creation was a broccoli and feta frittata seasoned with lemon and red pepper flakes. As I worked my way through other combinations, three favorites emerged: asparagus with tangy goat cheese, Yukon Gold potatoes paired with garlicky chorizo, and earthy shiitake mushrooms with nutty Pecorino Romano cheese. Move over, omelets—when eggs are for dinner, a simple frittata will be my new go-to dish.

BROCCOLI AND FETA FRITTATA
SERVES 4 TO 6

This frittata can also be served warm or at room temperature. When paired with a salad, it can serve as a meal. Variations scaled to serve two people for all of the frittatas are available for free for four months at CooksIllustrated.com/dec16.

    12 large eggs
    ⅓   cup whole milk
        Salt
    1   tablespoon extra-virgin olive oil
    12 ounces broccoli florets, cut into ½-inch
        pieces (4 cups)
        Pinch red pepper flakes
    3   tablespoons water
    ½   teaspoon grated lemon zest plus ½ teaspoon
        juice
    4   ounces feta cheese, crumbled into ½-inch
        pieces (1 cup)

1. Adjust oven rack to middle position and heat oven to 350 degrees. Whisk eggs, milk, and ½ teaspoon salt in bowl until well combined.

2. Heat oil in 12-inch ovensafe nonstick skillet over medium-high heat until shimmering. Add broccoli, pepper flakes, and ¼ teaspoon salt; cook, stirring frequently, until broccoli is crisp-tender and spotty brown, 7 to 9 minutes. Add water and lemon zest and juice; continue to cook, stirring constantly, until broccoli is just tender and no water remains in skillet, about 1 minute longer.

3. Add feta and egg mixture and cook, using rubber spatula to stir and scrape bottom of skillet until large curds form and spatula leaves trail through eggs but eggs are still very wet, about 30 seconds. Smooth curds into even layer and cook, without stirring, for 30 seconds. Transfer skillet to oven and bake until frittata is slightly puffy and surface bounces back when lightly pressed, 6 to 9 minutes. Using rubber spatula, loosen frittata from skillet and transfer to cutting board. Let stand for 5 minutes before slicing and serving.

ASPARAGUS AND GOAT CHEESE FRITTATA

This recipe works best with thin and medium-size asparagus.

Substitute 1 pound asparagus, trimmed and cut into ¼-inch lengths, for broccoli and ¼ teaspoon pepper for pepper flakes. Reduce cooking time in step 2 to 3 to 4 minutes. Omit water. Substitute goat cheese for feta and add 2 tablespoons chopped fresh mint to eggs with cheese.

CHORIZO AND POTATO FRITTATA

Be sure to use Spanish-style chorizo, which is dry-cured and needs only to be heated through.

Substitute 1 pound Yukon Gold potatoes, peeled and cut into ½-inch pieces, for broccoli and ¼ teaspoon ground cumin for pepper flakes. In step 2, cook potatoes until half are lightly browned, 8 to 10 minutes. Substitute 6 ounces Spanish-style chorizo sausage, cut into ¼-inch pieces, and 1 teaspoon sherry vinegar for lemon zest and juice. Substitute ½ cup chopped fresh cilantro for feta.

SHIITAKE MUSHROOM FRITTATA WITH PECORINO ROMANO

While the shiitake mushrooms needn't be cut into exact ½-inch pieces, for a cohesive frittata, make sure that no pieces are much larger than ¾ inch.

Substitute 1 pound shiitake mushrooms, stemmed and cut into ½-inch pieces, for broccoli and ¼ teaspoon pepper for pepper flakes. Reduce water to 2 tablespoons and substitute 2 minced scallion whites, 1 tablespoon sherry vinegar, and 1½ teaspoons minced fresh thyme for lemon zest and juice. Substitute ¾ cup shredded Pecorino Romano for feta and add 2 thinly sliced scallion greens to eggs with cheese.

Fill 'er up with Small Pieces
Taking the time to cut the filling ingredients into small pieces improves the frittata's cohesiveness. The eggs can easily surround small pieces of filling and hold them in place, whereas larger pieces can lead to gaps in the frittata, making it prone to breaking.

Millionaire's Shortbread

Britain's triple-decker combo of buttery cookie, sweet caramel, and dark chocolate makes a perfect holiday gift. But only if every layer is flawless.

⇒ BY ANDREA GEARY ⇐

I'll concede that millionaire's short-bread is a corny name, but it fits this impressively rich British cookie/confectionery hybrid: a crunchy, buttery shortbread base topped with a chewy, caramel-like layer, which is in turn topped with a thin layer of shiny, snappy chocolate. It's an indulgent combination of textures and flavors, all stacked in a sleek package.

I ate a lot of it when I lived in the United Kingdom, and since it has a good shelf life (more than a week), I figured it would make an ideal holiday gift. But after giving a few recipes a try, I realized that a gift-worthy recipe wasn't going to just come to me wrapped neatly with a bow.

The shortbread base in most recipes was easy enough in terms of composition—just flour, butter, sugar, and salt—but they differed in terms of procedure, calling for softened butter and a stand mixer, cold butter and a food processor, or getting in there and rubbing everything together with your fingers as you would for pie dough. The caramel portion of this cookie is unique: It's based on sweetened condensed milk, which gives it a luxurious creaminess. Instructions were all simple—cook sweetened condensed milk, butter, sugar, and corn syrup in a saucepan until thickened—yet unpredictable. In some batches the butter separated out, but in other batches it didn't, and I wasn't entirely sure why. As for the chocolate, you can't just melt it any which way and expect it to reset with its original sheen and snap. With each batch, I was left with dull, soft chocolate that was a mess as soon as I touched it. I was determined to devise strategies that delivered three perfect layers every time, and I would streamline as much as possible along the way.

Beta Testing

Knowing that the other two layers were going to be challenging, I gave myself a break with the shortbread and turned to an approach I've used before that skips the solid butter. I whisked together 2½ cups of flour,

▶ **Andrea Shows You How**
A step-by-step video is available at CooksIllustrated.com/dec16

These bars make a great gift since they keep so well. For the cleanest cuts, use a serrated knife and a gentle sawing motion to portion the bars.

½ cup of sugar, and ¾ teaspoon of salt and stirred in 2 sticks of melted butter. I patted the dough into a foil-lined baking pan, pricked it all over with a fork to prevent pockets of steam from building up underneath, and then baked it until it was golden brown and firm. My melted butter shortcut produced a level, crunchy shortbread layer in no time flat. On to the chocolate.

It would be so handy if chocolate were like wax: You could melt it and cool it, and it would always have that same texture and appearance when it resolidified. Sadly, it's not that forgiving. Good chocolate right out of the package has a nice snap and sheen. But when you heat it past 94 degrees and leave it to resolidify, it takes on a dull, dusty appearance and soft texture. This is because the crystal structure of the cocoa butter fats in the chocolate has changed. Cocoa butter can solidify into any of six different crystal formations, but only one—beta crystals—sets up dense and shiny. For the layer of chocolate for my millionaire's shortbread,

Tidy Transfer

To easily and neatly transfer the grated chocolate to a bowl, grate the chocolate over parchment paper, rapping the grater to collect all of the shavings.

there was no settling for anything but beta.

Since heating chocolate beyond 94 degrees destroys the beta crystal structure, a chocolatier would temper the chocolate to reestablish that beta structure. It's an elaborate process of melting chocolate, cooling it, warming it, holding it at that temperature for a while, and then warming it a bit more (but not too much!). Luckily, I came up with an alternative that's much easier and more foolproof: Melt a portion of the chocolate very gently, being careful not to let it get too warm, and then stir in the remaining chocolate, which has been finely grated. These small flakes disperse throughout the melted chocolate, and their temperature remains so low that most of their beta crystals remain intact, triggering the formation of new crystals as the chocolate cools so it sets up perfectly shiny and snappy.

I melted 6 ounces of finely chopped chocolate in the microwave at 50 percent power (small pieces would melt more quickly and help minimize the chance of overheating). I stirred the chocolate every 15 seconds, holding the bowl in the palm of my hand so I could monitor the temperature: If it felt warmer than my hand, I stirred until it cooled down before returning it to the microwave. Once it was all melted and still a bit warm, I deployed my secret weapon: 2 ounces of finely grated chocolate. Finely grating the chocolate would ensure even dispersal and mean it needed minimal, if any, additional heating to fully melt; plus, it seeded the melted chocolate with beta crystals. I stirred the grated chocolate into the bowl, heating for only 5 seconds at a time if necessary. I poured it onto the caramel (a placeholder recipe for now) and spread it into an even layer. It started to set right away—a hallmark of beta chocolate. With top and bottom squared away, I moved on to the middle: the caramel.

Breaking Bad

Recipes for the caramel layer were all about the same: Dump one can of sweetened condensed milk, some butter, brown sugar, and corn syrup (my substitute for Britain's golden syrup) into a saucepan and cook the mixture over medium heat while stirring until it

Millionaire's Shortbread, Perfected

Most versions of millionaire's shortbread rely on a labor-intensive shortbread layer, and they produce a caramel filling that separates during cooking and a chocolate layer that's dull and soft. Here's how we make a cookie that's easier and a step above.

CHOCOLATE WITH SHINE AND SNAP Grated chocolate and gentle heating in the microwave are the keys to an easy faux-tempered chocolate layer.

FILLING THAT DOESN'T BREAK Supplementing the usual filling ingredients with a little heavy cream prevents the butter from separating out.

QUICK, PAT-IN-THE-PAN SHORTBREAD Opting for melted butter means we need just a bowl and spoon, no food processor or stand mixer.

---

turns thick and brown. Pour it over the baked shortbread, and that's it.

Except that it wasn't. My results were inconsistent. Sometimes the sauce broke; sometimes it didn't—and I couldn't figure out why. I also noticed that when I added ½ teaspoon of salt to help offset the sweetness, breaking was pretty much a given. I was baffled.

It must have been fate that just at this point in my testing, Dr. Janice Johnson, a food scientist from Cargill who specializes in salt, paid the test kitchen a visit. I told her all about my breaking filling. She was not surprised. She explained that whey proteins in the sweetened condensed milk were one of the major classes of proteins responsible for keeping the caramel mixture emulsified but that those proteins had two enemies: salt and heat. As the mixture cooked, moisture evaporated, which increased the concentration of salt. At high concentrations of salt, proteins can fall out of solution and the caramel can take on a grainy appearance. At the same time, the heat was also damaging the proteins, which had already been compromised during the processing that transforms fresh milk into sweetened condensed milk.

If too much heat was a problem, maybe all my recipe needed was more precision. After several tests, I determined that I should cook the mixture to 236 degrees—hot enough to give it the proper texture but, most of the time, not so hot that it broke. But maddeningly, I found that I got different results when I used different brands of sweetened condensed milk, with some more prone to breaking than others (see "The Problem with Sweetened Condensed Milk").

And then it occurred to me: If the compromised whey proteins in sweetened condensed milk were the problem, why not use fresh dairy since its proteins haven't been damaged by processing? But subbing it in for the canned stuff would change the flavor profile of the filling, so I decided to try using it as a supplement. I knew from experience that milk didn't have enough fat to prevent curdling at high temperatures, so it would have to be cream. Indeed, the whey in just ½ cup of cream proved to be enough to keep my caramel intact without compromising the flavor. Finally, I knew it would work to my satisfaction every time.

From top to bottom, my version of this British classic was as perfect—and as gift-worthy—as I could have hoped.

MILLIONAIRE'S SHORTBREAD
MAKES 40 COOKIES

For a caramel filling with the right texture, monitor the temperature with an instant-read thermometer. We prefer Ghirardelli 60% Cacao Bittersweet Chocolate Premium Baking Bar for this recipe. Grating a portion of the chocolate is important for getting the chocolate to set properly; the small holes on a box grater work well for this task. Stir often while melting the chocolate and don't overheat it.

Crust

2½	cups (12½ ounces) all-purpose flour
½	cup (3½ ounces) granulated sugar
¾	teaspoon salt
16	tablespoons unsalted butter, melted

Filling

1	(14-ounce) can sweetened condensed milk
1	cup packed (7 ounces) brown sugar
½	cup heavy cream
½	cup corn syrup
8	tablespoons unsalted butter
½	teaspoon salt

Chocolate

8	ounces bittersweet chocolate (6 ounces chopped fine, 2 ounces grated)

---

1. FOR THE CRUST: Adjust oven rack to lower-middle position and heat oven to 350 degrees. Make foil sling for 13 by 9-inch baking pan by folding 2 long sheets of aluminum foil; first sheet should be 13 inches wide and second sheet should be 9 inches wide. Lay sheets of foil in pan perpendicular to each other, with extra foil hanging over edges of pan. Push foil into corners and up sides of pan, smoothing foil flush to pan. Combine flour, sugar, and salt in medium bowl. Add melted butter and stir with rubber spatula until flour is evenly moistened. Crumble dough evenly over bottom of prepared pan. Using your fingertips and palm of your hand, press and smooth dough into even thickness. Using fork, pierce dough at 1-inch intervals. Bake until light golden brown and firm to touch, 25 to 30 minutes. Transfer pan to wire rack. Using sturdy metal spatula, press on entire surface of warm crust to compress (this will make finished bars easier to cut). Let crust cool until it is just warm, at least 20 minutes.

2. FOR THE FILLING: Stir all ingredients together in large, heavy-bottomed saucepan. Cook over medium heat, stirring frequently, until mixture registers between 236 and 239 degrees (temperature will fluctuate), 16 to 20 minutes. Pour over crust and spread to even thickness (mixture will be very hot). Let cool completely, about 1½ hours.

3. FOR THE CHOCOLATE: Microwave chopped chocolate in bowl at 50 percent power, stirring every 15 seconds, until melted but not much warmer than body temperature (check by holding in palm of your hand), 1 to 2 minutes. Add grated chocolate and stir until smooth, returning to microwave for no more than 5 seconds at a time to finish melting if necessary. Spread chocolate evenly over surface of filling. Refrigerate shortbread until chocolate is just set, about 10 minutes.

4. Using foil overhang, lift shortbread out of pan and transfer to cutting board; discard foil. Using serrated knife and gentle sawing motion, cut shortbread in half crosswise to create two 6½ by 9-inch rectangles. Cut each rectangle in half to make four 3½ by 9-inch strips. Cut each strip crosswise into 10 equal pieces. (Shortbread can be stored at room temperature, between layers of parchment, for up to 1 week.)

RECIPE TESTING The Problem with Sweetened Condensed Milk

While developing the caramel filling for our Millionaire's Shortbread, we found that fillings made with some brands of sweetened condensed milk were more prone to breaking—meaning that the butter separated out and pooled on the surface instead of staying emulsified—than others. When we took a closer look at the milks, we noticed that the ones that broke more often were darker in color than the ones that tended to stay emulsified. What was the connection? The temperature used in processing.

Some manufacturers process their milks at high temperatures, speeding up the Maillard reaction, which leads to more browned sugars and proteins, and damaging more whey proteins in the milk, which are key to keeping the fat emulsified. For a foolproof filling that won't break, no matter the brand of sweetened condensed milk, we add fresh dairy. Just ½ cup of cream bolsters the mixture with enough undamaged whey proteins to prevent the butter from separating out.

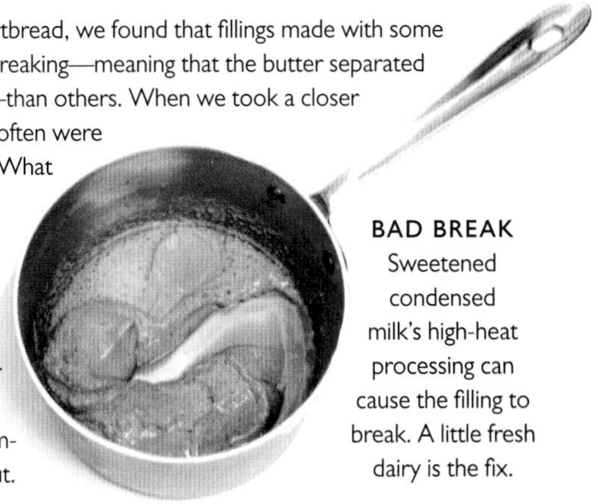

BAD BREAK Sweetened condensed milk's high-heat processing can cause the filling to break. A little fresh dairy is the fix.

Our Guide to Chocolate

Chocolate is notoriously fussy—even choosing the wrong brand can ruin dessert. Here's what you need to know for foolproof baking and cooking. BY KEITH DRESSER

WHAT IS CHOCOLATE, ANYWAY?

The base of all processed chocolate is chocolate liquor, a dark paste produced from grinding the nibs extracted from dried, fermented, roasted cacao beans. In its natural state, chocolate liquor is about 55 percent cocoa butter, which gives chocolate its unique texture. The remaining 45 percent is the cocoa solids responsible for chocolate's flavor. The cocoa butter and cocoa solids in chocolate liquor may be separated and recombined in different ratios; together, they make up the cacao percentage in a processed chocolate.

SHOPPING

Brand really matters with chocolate. In tastings we found that nearly half (or even more) of the products in our lineup weren't up to par, no matter the type of chocolate. So for best results, stick with our winners.

BITTERSWEET/SEMISWEET CHOCOLATE

WHAT IT IS: Also known as dark chocolate, bittersweet and semisweet chocolates (there is no official distinction) must contain at least 35 percent cacao; the remainder is mainly sugar with a small amount of emulsifiers and flavorings.

HOW WE USE IT: With its strong chocolate flavor and smooth texture, bittersweet is our go-to chocolate. We use it for most baked goods and desserts and for dipping and coating.

GOOD TO KNOW: Cacao percentage matters. It affects the flavor as well as the texture of creamy desserts. For cooking and baking, we prefer 60 percent cacao. In tests, some chocolates with cacao percentages even a few points less than 60 percent (and thus a lower percentage of cacao solids) produced loose custards. Chocolates with cacao percentages higher than this (and thus with more cacao solids) turned out chalky custards.

FAVORITE: Ghirardelli 60% Cacao Bittersweet Chocolate Premium Baking Bar ($2.99 for 4 oz)

SUBBING WITH UNSWEETENED: In a pinch, replace 1 ounce of bittersweet chocolate with ⅔ ounce of unsweetened chocolate and 2 teaspoons of sugar, but note that texture may be affected.

MILK CHOCOLATE

WHAT IT IS: With only 10 percent cacao required, milk chocolate tastes more milky than chocolaty. Milk fat, along with cocoa butter, gives it its ultracreamy texture.

HOW WE USE IT: We generally like milk chocolate more for snacking than baking.

FAVORITE: Dove Silky Smooth Milk Chocolate ($2.79 for 3.53 oz)

COCOA POWDER

WHAT IT IS: Cocoa powder is chocolate liquor that has been pressed to remove most of the cocoa butter, leaving behind cocoa solids that are then finely ground. Dutch-processed cocoa is less acidic than natural cocoa, but their flavors are similar.

HOW WE USE IT: Ounce for ounce, cocoa powder packs more chocolate flavor than any other form of chocolate. Because it is relatively low in fat, we like to use cocoa powder in applications that already contain a lot of fat, like cakes and cookies.

FAVORITE: Hershey's Natural Cocoa Unsweetened ($3.49 for 8 oz)

UNSWEETENED CHOCOLATE

WHAT IT IS: Typically, unsweetened chocolate is pure chocolate liquor formed into bars.

HOW WE USE IT: In recipes like brownies or chocolate cake, unsweetened chocolate's lack of sugar allows us to control more variables to achieve a desired texture.

WHY IT HAS NO SUBSTITUTE: Some sources recommend subbing cocoa powder and butter or oil for unsweetened chocolate, but these fats don't have the subtle cocoa flavor or contribute the same texture as cocoa butter.

GOOD TO KNOW: Because unsweetened chocolate isn't for snacking, some manufacturers don't use the best beans. But since it's also not typically refined or conched (a process that mellows harsh flavors), there's no hiding the flavor of mediocre beans. In taste tests, we had reservations about or disliked four out of nine products.

FAVORITE: Hershey's Unsweetened Baking Bar ($1.99 for 4 oz)

DARK CHOCOLATE CHIPS

WHAT THEY ARE: Dark chocolate chips are bittersweet chocolate with at least 35 percent cacao—the same as for dark bar chocolate—but they typically have less cocoa butter, so they're cheaper to make and will hold their shape on the production line.

HOW WE USE THEM: Chocolate chips get the most use as mix-ins for cookies and brownies.

GOOD TO KNOW: Most companies don't cite cacao percentages for chips. And in lab tests, we found that chips produced by such companies had far less cacao than in bar chocolate—and correspondingly weaker flavor and grainier texture.

FAVORITE: Ghirardelli 60% Cacao Bittersweet Chocolate Chips ($3.50 for 11.5 oz)

With the same cacao percentage as our winning bittersweet bar (their sibling), these morsels have complex chocolate flavor. They also have comparable cocoa butter, for morsels that melt appealingly in cookies.

SUB CHIPS FOR CHOPPED? Unless you use our winner, forget it. Chips have less flavor than most bar chocolates, and because they usually have less cocoa butter, most chips left behind graininess in sauces, mousses, and custard.

WHITE CHOCOLATE

WHAT IT IS: Technically not chocolate since it's made with cocoa butter, milk, sugar, emulsifiers, and flavorings but no cocoa solids, white chocolate has a milky taste and satiny texture. Some products substitute other fats for all or some of the cocoa butter; these can only be labeled "white" and not "chocolate."

HOW WE USE IT: In mousses, frostings, and soufflés, it adds creaminess and subtle milky flavor.

GOOD TO KNOW: Products with "fake" flavor and "chalky" texture abound. We had reservations about four out of 10 in our tasting lineup.

FAVORITE: Guittard Choc-Au-Lait White Chips ($3.29 for 12 oz)

Though they're not real white chocolate since they contain palm kernel oil, we found that the refined fat helped these chips melt and solidify at higher temperatures, preventing crystals in mousse.

Seized Chocolate

Seizing—the nearly instantaneous transformation of melted chocolate from a fluid state to a stiff, grainy one—is usually the result of a tiny amount of moisture being introduced.

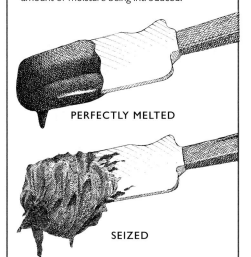

PERFECTLY MELTED

SEIZED

Preventing Seizing

In recipes that contain no liquid, don't let moisture get into the melted chocolate. Even a tiny amount will form a syrup with the sugar in the chocolate to which the cocoa particles will cling, creating grainy clumps. In recipes containing liquids like melted butter, liqueur, or water, always melt the chocolate along with these ingredients.

Fixing Seizing

Surprisingly, adding liquid will return seized chocolate to a fluid state, as the liquid dissolves seized sugar and cocoa particles. Add boiling water to the chocolate, 1 teaspoon at a time, stirring vigorously after each addition until smooth. But don't use the diluted chocolate for baking; use it for chocolate sauce or hot chocolate.

STORING

Wrap open bars of chocolate tightly in plastic wrap and store them in a cool pantry. Avoid the refrigerator or freezer, as cocoa butter easily absorbs off-flavors from other foods and temperature changes can alter its crystal structure so it behaves differently in recipes. Note: The milk solids in white and milk chocolate give them a shorter shelf life.

SHELF LIFE

2 YEARS
UNSWEETENED AND DARK CHOCOLATE

6 MONTHS
WHITE AND MILK CHOCOLATE

WORKING WITH CHOCOLATE

Finely Chopping Chocolate

Finely chopping chocolate helps it melt more evenly and quickly. Place the tip of a serrated knife on a cutting board and the blade on a corner of the chocolate and bear down with both hands. The serrations will break the chocolate into fine shards.

How to Make Chocolate Curls

Chocolate curls add a professional touch to cakes, pies, and mugs of hot cocoa. Use block (not bar) chocolate—bittersweet/semisweet and white chocolate work well—that's at least 1 inch thick. Soften the chocolate slightly by microwaving it on the lowest power setting for 1 minute. (It shouldn't melt, but it should soften a little.) Run the blade of a vegetable peeler along the width of the softened chocolate, creating a curl. The longer the block, the bigger the curl.

An Easier Way to Temper Chocolate

Good chocolate has a sheen and a satisfying snap. But if you simply melt chocolate to use as a coating or for drizzling, it will cool into a soft, dull-looking mess. That's because the cocoa butter's crystal structure has changed. Of cocoa butter's six different crystal types, only beta crystals set up dense and shiny and stay that way, even well above room temperature. Chocolate with a uniform beta crystal structure is said to be "in temper." The traditional way to ensure that melted chocolate returns to temper requires a painstaking process of heating, cooling, and reheating. In our easier method, we

1. Microwave 3 ounces finely chopped chocolate (decrease or increase amount here and below as needed) at 50 percent power, stirring every 15 seconds, until fully melted but not much warmer than body temperature, 1 to 2 minutes. (Stir often while melting and monitor temperature by holding bowl in palm of your hand.)

2. Add 1 ounce finely grated chocolate (use small holes of box grater; see tip on page 14) and stir until smooth, returning to microwave for no more than 5 seconds at a time if necessary.

melt three-quarters of the chocolate very gently and then stir in the remaining portion, which has been very finely grated. These small flakes appear to melt, but their temperature is so low that most of the beta crystals remain intact, triggering the formation of new beta crystals as the chocolate cools.

Don't Overbake

The volatile compounds in cocoa solids that give chocolate much of its flavor are also driven away by heat. The longer chocolate is heated, the more compounds are driven off, so don't bake chocolate desserts a minute longer than you need to. In tests, chocolate crinkle cookies baked for 2 minutes longer than the recipe calls for had a less intense flavor than cookies baked according to the recipe.

BLOOMED CHOCOLATE: CAN I USE IT?

Storing chocolate at temperatures that are either too warm or too cool will cause a white film, or bloom, to develop on the surface. One type of bloom occurs when cocoa butter crystals melt and migrate to the surface. Another type happens in humid conditions when water condenses on bittersweet and milk chocolate, dissolving some of its sugar before evaporating and leaving behind a fine layer of sugar crystals.

In tests, we found that bloomed chocolate of either type was fine for baking. But when we dipped cookies in melted chocolate with cocoa butter bloom, the chocolate took longer to set up and the bloom reappeared. This is because the chocolate's fat structure had changed. Also, the sugar crystals in the melted sugar–bloomed chocolate never dissolved, resulting in a grainy coating. Bottom line: Bloomed chocolate is fine for baking—just don't use it for dipping.

USING CACAO NIBS

We like crunchy, bitter cacao nibs best in baked goods where there aren't many other competing flavors or textures; they're also great in granola. Use ½ to ⅔ cup per loaf of quick bread, dozen muffins, or 9-cup batch of granola.

Hearty Butternut Squash Soup

For a satisfying main-dish soup, we treat the squash like two different vegetables.

⇒ BY STEVE DUNN ⇐

A cup of pureed butternut squash soup is fine as a dinner starter or as a side to a sandwich. But this winter I wanted a heartier soup that I could enjoy as a stand-alone meal. I've seen a few versions that pair chunks of squash with creamy cannellini beans, which sounded like just what I was after.

I sautéed sliced leeks, added diced squash and chicken broth, simmered it all for 10 minutes, added the beans, and simmered a little longer to warm them through. I wanted simple, but this was too simple, as the soup was thin in taste and texture. Furthermore, the squash had cooked unevenly.

There was one clear reason for the uneven cooking: It's easy to evenly dice the neck of a butternut squash but not the bulb end: I ended up with oddly shaped bits. I could cut the bulb into equal pieces if I made them larger, but tasters found these unwieldy to eat.

The flesh from the squash neck is also much more dense, and thus slower to cook, than that of the bulb, which tended to blow out and turn stringy. I tried cutting the neck into smaller pieces than the bulb to equalize their cooking times, but the oddly shaped bits of bulb nagged at me. Then a fellow test cook made a suggestion: Why not cut the bulb into wedges, cook these in the broth until they were completely soft, and then mash them to create a "squash stock" for the soup's base? Then I'd cook the diced neck pieces in the stock. Good idea—this gave my soup body and flavor and avoided the issue of uneven cooking.

But the soup had a one-note sweetness from the squash. Two of our favorite umami boosters, soy sauce and tomato paste (along with some minced garlic), lent needed depth. Sautéing tomato paste with the leeks deepened its flavor further.

My soup still tasted lean, though, so I tried drizzling it with olive oil. Unfortunately, the oil didn't provide the infusion of richness I was after. Cream was a poor fit in this brothy soup and muted the flavors. Then my mind drifted to the technique of enriching sauces by whisking in butter toward the end. Adding butter at the end would be difficult given everything in the pot, so I added it to the stock at the start of its

An earthy sage and walnut pesto finishes the soup.

cooking. The lengthy agitation of the simmer fully emulsified the butter, no fussy whisking required.

For a final touch I prepared a sage and walnut pesto to swirl into the soup at the table. This was just the satisfying, hearty main dish I'd set out to make.

BUTTERNUT SQUASH AND WHITE BEAN SOUP WITH SAGE PESTO
SERVES 6 TO 8

For the best texture, it's important to remove the fibrous white flesh just below the squash's skin.

Pesto
- ½ cup walnuts, toasted
- 2 garlic cloves, minced
- 1 cup fresh parsley leaves
- ½ cup fresh sage leaves
- ¾ cup extra-virgin olive oil
- 1 ounce Parmesan cheese, grated (½ cup), plus extra for serving
- Salt and pepper

Soup
- 1 (2- to 2½-pound) butternut squash
- 4 cups chicken broth
- 3 cups water
- 4 tablespoons unsalted butter
- 1 tablespoon soy sauce
- 1 tablespoon vegetable oil
- 1 pound leeks, white and light green parts only, halved lengthwise, sliced thin, and washed thoroughly
- 1 tablespoon tomato paste
- 2 garlic cloves, minced
- Salt and pepper
- 3 (15-ounce) cans cannellini beans
- 1 teaspoon white wine vinegar

1. FOR THE PESTO: Pulse walnuts and garlic in food processor until coarsely chopped, about 5 pulses. Add parsley and sage; with processor running, slowly add oil and process until smooth, about 1 minute. Transfer to bowl, stir in Parmesan, and season with salt and pepper to taste. Set aside.

2. FOR THE SOUP: Using sharp vegetable peeler or chef's knife, remove skin and fibrous threads just below skin from squash (peel until squash is completely orange with no white flesh remaining, roughly ⅛ inch deep). Cut round bulb section off squash and cut in half lengthwise. Scoop out and discard seeds; cut each half into 4 wedges.

3. Bring squash wedges, broth, water, butter, and soy sauce to boil in medium saucepan over high heat. Reduce heat to medium, partially cover, and simmer vigorously until squash is very tender and starting to fall apart, about 20 minutes. Using potato masher, mash squash, still in broth, until completely broken down. Cover to keep warm; set aside.

4. While broth cooks, cut neck of squash into ⅓-inch pieces. Heat oil in large Dutch oven over medium heat until shimmering. Add leeks and tomato paste and cook, stirring occasionally, until leeks have softened and tomato paste has darkened, about 5 minutes. Add garlic and cook until fragrant, about 30 seconds. Add squash pieces, ¾ teaspoon salt, and ¼ teaspoon pepper and cook, stirring occasionally, for 5 minutes. Add squash broth and bring to simmer. Partially cover and cook for 10 minutes.

5. Add beans and their liquid, partially cover, and cook, stirring occasionally, until squash is just tender, 15 to 20 minutes. Stir in vinegar and season with salt and pepper to taste. Serve, passing pesto and extra Parmesan separately.

Squash Two Ways
Since the bulb of the squash is awkwardly shaped and cooks more quickly than the neck, we use it to make a "squash stock." We cut the neck into tidy cubes and cook them in our flavorful base.

▶ **Watch the Squash**
A step-by-step video is available at CooksIllustrated.com/dec16

Braised Root Vegetables

Braising root vegetables leaves the oven free for the roast—plus, you get a sauce.

⪴ BY ANDREW JANJIGIAN ⪵

My go-to cooking method for root vegetables has always been to roast them in a hot oven until they are caramelized and tender. This year, though, I wanted to come up with something more elegant and interesting that would leave the oven free to cook the holiday roast. Braising—cooking food in a small amount of flavorful liquid that then serves as a sauce—seemed promising. But I wanted to avoid recipes that left the vegetables swimming in bland, soupy liquid or, alternatively, cooked down the sauce to the point that it was a glaze. I wanted my braised vegetables to be napped in a generous amount of rich, flavorful sauce with appealing body.

Carrots possess a sweetness that plays well with a range of flavors—plus, they offer an appealing bright color—so I decided I would pair them with another vegetable in a few different recipes. I started with the classic combination of carrots and parsnips. I began by sautéing a minced shallot in butter. I then added the carrots and parsnips, which I'd cut crosswise into ¼-inch-thick coins to encourage even cooking. I added enough chicken broth to cover the vegetables, brought the mixture to a simmer, covered the pot, and lowered the heat. After 15 minutes, the vegetables were tender, but the sauce was thin in both consistency and flavor.

The quantity of sauce was where I wanted it, so I didn't want to reduce the amount of liquid I started with. As it turned out, the best approach was actually to do the opposite. When I increased the amount of liquid I started with, I was able to reduce it for 5 minutes before adding the vegetables, which gave the sauce better body and a more concentrated flavor. To lend it a bit more silkiness, I also whisked in a couple of tablespoons of butter at the end.

But could I give the sauce even more character? I tried replacing half the broth with white wine, but it made the sauce too tart. I wanted something that would underscore the flavor of the root vegetables yet remain in the background. The answer turned out to be apple cider, which enhanced the earthy sweetness of the vegetables. And its natural sugars, once cooked down, gave the reduced sauce even more body. Bay leaves and thyme sprigs added savoriness, and a tablespoon of mustard gave it a punch. Dried cranberries lent texture, color, and bright, tart flavor while parsley provided a colorful finish.

From here, it was easy to come up with variations on the theme: carrots and celery root with apples and marjoram, carrots and turnips with golden raisins and chives, and carrots and sweet potatoes with candied

Sweet, bright carrots anchor each of our recipes.

ginger and cilantro. I'd welcome any one of these side dishes to my holiday table.

BRAISED CARROTS AND PARSNIPS WITH DRIED CRANBERRIES
SERVES 4 TO 6

For a vegetarian version, you can substitute vegetable stock or water for the chicken broth. Our recipe for Braised Carrots and Sweet Potatoes with Candied Ginger is available for free for four months at CooksIllustrated.com/dec16.

 3 tablespoons unsalted butter, cut into ½-inch pieces
 1 shallot, minced
 1 cup chicken broth
 1 cup apple cider
 6 sprigs fresh thyme
 2 bay leaves
    Salt and pepper
 1 pound carrots, peeled and sliced on bias ¼ inch thick
 1 pound parsnips, peeled and sliced on bias ¼ inch thick
 ½ cup dried cranberries
 1 tablespoon Dijon mustard
 2 tablespoons minced fresh parsley

1. Melt 1 tablespoon butter in large Dutch oven over high heat. Add shallot and cook, stirring frequently, until softened and just beginning to brown, about 3 minutes. Add broth, cider, thyme sprigs, bay leaves, 1½ teaspoons salt, and ½ teaspoon pepper; bring to simmer and cook for 5 minutes. Add carrots and parsnips, stir to combine, and return to simmer. Reduce heat to medium-low, cover, and cook, stirring occasionally, until vegetables are tender, 10 to 14 minutes.

2. Remove pot from heat. Discard thyme sprigs and bay leaves and stir in cranberries. Push vegetable mixture to sides of pot. Add mustard and remaining 2 tablespoons butter to center and whisk into cooking liquid. Stir to coat vegetable mixture with sauce, transfer to serving dish, sprinkle with parsley, and serve.

BRAISED CARROTS AND CELERY ROOT WITH APPLE

Substitute 1½ pounds celery root, peeled, halved if medium or quartered if large, and sliced ¼ inch thick, for parsnips; 1 Fuji or Honeycrisp apple, cored and cut into ¼-inch dice, for dried cranberries; and 1 teaspoon minced fresh marjoram or thyme for parsley. In step 1, cook celery root in braising liquid by itself for 15 minutes before adding carrots and proceeding with recipe.

BRAISED CARROTS AND TURNIPS WITH GOLDEN RAISINS

Reduce chicken broth and apple cider to ¾ cup each. Substitute turnips, peeled, halved if medium (2- to 3-inch diameter) or quartered if large (3- to 4-inch diameter), and sliced ¼ inch thick, for parsnips; golden raisins for dried cranberries; and 10 chives, cut into 1-inch lengths, for parsley.

The Secret Sauce
We discovered that a trio of chicken broth, apple cider, and mustard created a braising liquid with a savory, sweet flavor; a little punch; and good body that pairs well with most any root vegetable.

▶ **Watch Andrew Braise**
A step-by-step video is available at CooksIllustrated.com/dec16

Pad Thai at Home

In Thailand, pad thai is built on pantry staples. Could we create a satisfying, authentic-tasting version using mostly ingredients from the American pantry?

⋟ BY ANNIE PETITO ⋞

I once pulled out all the stops to make an entirely authentic version of pad thai, and the result was a real stunner: tender rice noodles entwined in a sweet, sour, salty sauce and stir-fried with garlic, shallot, sweet shrimp, soft curds of scrambled egg, and nuggets of tofu. Chopped dried shrimp and pungent preserved daikon radish contributed intense flavor and chewy, crunchy textures that made me think I'd been transported to Bangkok. Chopped roasted peanuts, crisp bean sprouts, and garlic chives scattered over the top ensured that every bite was as exciting as the next.

My only quibbles? After all that work, the recipe yielded only two servings. Also, although it was incredibly satisfying to eat, my homemade pad thai had required a lot of forethought. Sourcing ingredients like dried shrimp and preserved radish demanded an excursion to an Asian market. Instead, could I create a satisfying version of pad thai using mostly everyday ingredients?

The Basics

Thankfully, the dried rice noodles that form the base of pad thai are available at most supermarkets. Having dealt with rice noodles before, I knew exactly how to treat them. I put 8 ounces in a bowl with boiling water and let them sit until they were pliant, about 8 minutes. After draining and rinsing the noodles with cold water, I tossed them with oil for antistick insurance.

With the noodles sorted out, I moved on to the sauce. The interplay of salty, sweet, and sour tastes is the primary characteristic of pad thai. These flavors typically come from pungent, saline fish sauce; caramel-like palm sugar; and sour, fruity tamarind. Fish sauce is now available in most supermarkets, so it would need no substitute. Next up: thick palm sugar disks. Rather than hunt them down, I made test batches with brown and white sugar. Finding no

▶ See How Annie Does It
A step-by-step video is available at CooksIllustrated.com/dec16

Lime wedges, chile vinegar, and chopped peanuts are the garnishes for our authentic-tasting—but easy to make—pad thai.

discernible flavor difference, I opted to use white.

Tamarind, a fruit that grows as a round, brown pod, is also available as pure tamarind concentrate. I was committed to using everyday ingredients in my recipe, but after some testing I concluded that tamarind is essential to pad thai and is worth seeking out. Happily, tamarind is increasingly available in the Asian or Latin section of supermarkets. I chose the juice concentrate, since it is easier to work with (see "All About Tamarind").

On to the protein. Pad thai typically includes three types: firm tofu, shrimp, and eggs. To keep the ingredient list manageable, I omitted tofu and added more of the latter two. One pound of large shrimp and four beaten eggs were adequate.

Most recipes call for adding the many ingredients in pad thai to the skillet sequentially. But to avoid overcrowding the pan, the volume of food must be kept low, so only one or two servings can be produced. By cooking in batches rather than gradually adding ingredients to the skillet, I could make enough to serve four. I started with minced garlic

and scallion whites (instead of the usual shallot since I planned on using the scallion greens in place of relatively obscure garlic chives) and then mixed in the shrimp and eggs. Once they were cooked, I transferred them to a bowl and stir-fried the noodles and sauce. I tossed in a handful of bean sprouts and the green parts of the scallions, and the dish was ready to be garnished with lime and chopped peanuts.

Fake It 'til You Make It

My pad thai was now in very good shape, but I pined for those salty bits of chewy dried shrimp and crunchy preserved daikon that help make it unique.

Hoping to replicate the daikon, which has a crunchy texture akin to pickled cabbage, I thought of similar salty, pickled options. Everything from sauerkraut (too vinegary) to pickles (too briny) to dried apricots that I brined (too sweet and sticky) took a turn in the dish. In the end, the most successful option was, not too surprisingly, fresh radishes. Simply soaking matchsticks of red radish in a warm solution of salt, sugar, and water created a fresh, crunchy, salty mix-in that added its own dimension.

Next, I considered the dried shrimp. In Thailand, the tiny shellfish are peeled, salted, and dried in the sun, giving them a meaty flavor and a firm, chewy texture. In Thai cooking, they are typically fried and used as a garnish or seasoning. My thought was to use a portion of the shrimp I was

---

TECHNIQUE DIY Dried Shrimp

Small dried shrimp, which are firm and chewy when reconstituted, add savory depth to many Asian dishes. Since they're not readily available in most supermarkets, we created a faux version using fresh shrimp. This is how we did it:

Cut shrimp in half lengthwise, then cut each half into ½-inch pieces. Toss with salt and sugar, then microwave until shrimp are dried and have reduced in size by half. Cook shrimp pieces in oil until they turn golden brown and crispy.

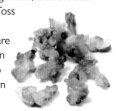

already calling for—just treated in a different manner. I cut a handful of shrimp into small bits and gently cooked them with the scallions and garlic, hoping to create a kind of shrimp paste. However, the shrimp pieces just plumped as they cooked, making them indistinguishable from the rest.

To produce a better facsimile, I would have to overcook the shrimp. Doing so in a skillet set over low heat took 20 minutes, so I turned to the microwave. I nuked shrimp pieces until they were shriveled and then fried the nuggets in the skillet until they were golden. I continued with the recipe as before, tossing in my makeshift pickled radishes and dried shrimp. Both were huge hits, giving my pad thai authentic character.

Thai'ing It All Together

Typically pad thai is served with condiments such as fish sauce, sugar, Thai chile powder, and vinegar. Instead, I stirred thinly sliced serrano chiles into white vinegar. Drizzling this concoction onto the noodles brightened all the other flavors.

My pad thai boasted all the right flavors and textures, and I could have it almost any time I wanted.

EVERYDAY PAD THAI
SERVES 4

Since pad thai cooks very quickly, prepare everything before you begin to cook. Use the time during which the radishes and noodles soak to prepare the other ingredients. We recommend using a tamarind juice concentrate made in Thailand in this recipe. If you cannot find tamarind, substitute 1½ tablespoons lime juice and 1½ tablespoons water and omit the lime wedges. Our recipe for Everyday Pad Thai for Two is available for free for four months at CooksIllustrated.com/dec16.

Chile Vinegar
- ⅓ cup distilled white vinegar
- 1 serrano chile, stemmed and sliced into thin rings

Stir-Fry
- Salt
- Sugar
- 2 radishes, trimmed and cut into 1½-inch by ¼-inch matchsticks
- 8 ounces (¼-inch-wide) rice noodles
- 3 tablespoons plus 2 teaspoons vegetable oil
- ¼ cup fish sauce
- 3 tablespoons tamarind juice concentrate
- 1 pound large shrimp (26 to 30 per pound), peeled and deveined
- 4 scallions, white and light green parts minced, dark green parts cut into 1-inch lengths
- 1 garlic clove, minced
- 4 large eggs, beaten
- 4 ounces (2 cups) bean sprouts
- ¼ cup roasted unsalted peanuts, chopped coarse
- Lime wedges

Noodle Is Your Lunch

Despite pad thai being widely regarded as a quintessential Thai dish, its history is a bit murky. Many sources point to China. The technique of stir-frying and many of the ingredients are Chinese, and even the dish's full name, *kway teow pad thai*, refers to the origin of one of its ingredients (*kway teow* is Chinese for "rice noodles"). No matter where it came from, pad thai's salty, sour, and sweet flavors make it distinctly Thai.

The popularization of pad thai was part of a campaign led by Thai prime minister Plaek Phibunsongkhram in the late 1930s and early 1940s. He wanted to introduce Thai cuisine to the rest of the world as part of a bigger plan to transform the country's identity into a strong, nationalistic, and modern one. To popularize the dish, the Public Welfare Department distributed a basic recipe for pad thai, launched an advertising campaign with the slogan "Noodle is your lunch," and prompted Bangkok vendors to sell pad thai from mobile carts. Meanwhile, other foreign food vendors were banned from the streets as part of a "Buy Thai" campaign.

---

1. FOR THE CHILE VINEGAR: Combine vinegar and chile in bowl and let stand at room temperature for at least 15 minutes.

2. FOR THE STIR-FRY: Combine ¼ cup water, ½ teaspoon salt, and ¼ teaspoon sugar in small bowl. Microwave until steaming, about 30 seconds. Add radishes and let stand for 15 minutes. Drain and pat dry with paper towels.

3. Bring 6 cups water to boil. Place noodles in large bowl. Pour boiling water over noodles. Stir, then let soak until noodles are almost tender, about 8 minutes, stirring once halfway through soaking. Drain noodles and rinse with cold water. Drain noodles well, then toss with 2 teaspoons oil.

4. Combine fish sauce, tamarind concentrate, and 3 tablespoons sugar in bowl and whisk until sugar is dissolved. Set sauce aside.

5. Remove tails from 4 shrimp. Cut shrimp in half lengthwise, then cut each half into ½-inch pieces. Toss shrimp pieces with ⅛ teaspoon salt and ⅛ teaspoon sugar. Arrange pieces in single layer on large plate and microwave at 50 percent power until shrimp are dried and have reduced in size by half, 4 to 5 minutes. (Check halfway through microwaving and separate any pieces that may have stuck together.)

6. Heat 2 teaspoons oil in 12-inch nonstick skillet over medium heat until shimmering. Add dried shrimp and cook, stirring frequently, until golden brown and crispy, 3 to 5 minutes. Transfer to large bowl.

7. Heat 1 teaspoon oil in now-empty skillet over medium heat until shimmering. Add minced scallions and garlic and cook, stirring constantly, until garlic is golden brown, about 1 minute. Transfer to bowl with dried shrimp.

8. Heat 2 teaspoons oil in now-empty skillet over high heat until just smoking. Add remaining whole shrimp and spread into even layer. Cook, without stirring, until shrimp turn opaque and brown around edges, 2 to 3 minutes, flipping halfway through cooking. Push shrimp to sides of skillet. Add 2 teaspoons oil to center, then add eggs to center. Using rubber spatula, stir eggs gently and cook until set but still wet. Stir eggs into shrimp and continue to cook, breaking up large pieces of egg, until eggs are fully cooked, 30 to 60 seconds longer. Transfer shrimp-egg mixture to bowl with scallion-garlic mixture and dried shrimp.

9. Heat remaining 2 teaspoons oil in now-empty skillet over high heat until just smoking. Add noodles and sauce and toss with tongs to coat. Cook, stirring and tossing often, until noodles are tender and have absorbed sauce, 2 to 4 minutes. Transfer noodles to bowl with shrimp mixture. Add 2 teaspoons chile vinegar, drained radishes, scallion greens, and bean sprouts and toss to combine.

10. Transfer to platter and sprinkle with peanuts. Serve immediately, passing lime wedges and remaining chile vinegar separately.

All About Tamarind

The tart, fruity flavor of tamarind is essential for authentic-tasting pad thai. The fruit is sold in a variety of forms, from fresh pods to bricks of pulp to pure concentrate and powder. The pods must be opened to remove the seedy pulp; the bricks require soaking and straining. Concentrate is used straight from the container, as is tamarind powder.

When we tasted the options while developing our recipe, we liked the fresh flavor of pods or pulp, but they required the most preparation. Tamarind powder was easy to use but had a faint flavor. Tamarind juice concentrate offered the best of both worlds: tangy, fresh flavor and ease of use. Look for tamarind juice concentrate manufactured in Thailand, which is thinner and tastes brighter than the paste concentrate produced in other countries. (If all you can find is a paste concentrate, mix 1½ tablespoons with 1½ tablespoons hot water to use it in our Everyday Pad Thai recipe.)

FRESH PODS
Too much prep

JUICE CONCENTRATE
Easy to use

Easier Apple Strudel

Unless you're a skilled pastry chef, wrapping ultrathin, delicate dough around a wet filling is usually a recipe for disaster. We wanted a strudel recipe for the rest of us.

⋟ BY LAN LAM ⋞

In the world of pastries, apple strudel seems unassuming. It's not over-the-top buttery or sweet. It's not loaded with a rich filling. Yet its marriage of flaky pastry and just-sweet-enough raisin-studded apples is perfect: ideal for dessert, with afternoon coffee, or even for breakfast. No wonder it's an everyday favorite all over central Europe.

And yet making strudel, at least the traditional way, is not at all simple. To create the swirl of delicate pastry that defines it (*strudel* means "whirlpool" or "eddy" in German), you start by stretching a piece of dough the size of a brick until it measures well over 4 feet long and 4 feet wide and is so thin you can read a newspaper through it. You brush it with butter and then pile a mixture of chopped apples, sugar, spice, raisins, and toasted bread crumbs (to absorb exuded juice) along one edge. The sides are folded over, and then it's ever-so-carefully rolled up, transferred to a baking sheet, and baked.

The dough is such an ordeal (and requires so much counter space) that rarely does anyone other than a professional baker make strudel this way anymore. The modern approach is to swap in a stack of store-bought phyllo sheets. Yet after making a few of these "simpler" recipes, I discovered that these versions are still rife with problems. Brushing each sheet with butter (for both flavor and to make the sheets more pliable) and rolling up the strudel without ripping the pastry was tricky. Plus, the bottom crusts all came out dense and tough, while the top was a mess of flyaway sheets that flaked off as soon as I started slicing (if not before). The fillings weren't so great either. Many

To prevent the confectioners' sugar from dissolving too quickly, dust the strudel just before serving.

had collapsed, leaving a gaping void between the filling and the top of the pastry, and they all had a gummy, pasty texture and muted apple flavor. And despite the bread crumbs, sweet juice still leaked out, gluing the pastry to the pan. I wanted to come up with a phyllo-based strudel recipe that was easy to make, had a flavorful and tender apple filling that stayed put, and featured a crust that held together but was still flaky.

Liquid Fix

First, I needed a filling. I quickly settled on Golden Delicious apples since they are easy to find and hold their shape when cooked. After cutting the apples into ½-inch pieces (1¾ pounds of apples seemed about right for six servings), I tossed them with sugar, cinnamon, ground ginger, and some lemon zest and juice. Since I suspected that the bread crumbs were responsible for dulling the flavor and creating the pasty texture, I decided to leave them out. I had a par-cooking technique in mind that I hoped would not only eliminate excess liquid (and thus the need for bread crumbs) but also keep the filling from collapsing.

We've found that parcooking apples briefly can set off an enzymatic reaction that causes the pectin in the fruit to set, meaning the fruit will hold its shape when it continues cooking at higher temperatures. A couple of minutes in the microwave warmed the apples just enough. They also exuded about ⅓ cup of liquid, which I drained off and reserved before stirring in the raisins. I wrapped this simple filling up in a stack of phyllo, placed it seam side down on a baking sheet, and baked it in a 375-degree oven until it was golden.

On the upside, the apples were now tender yet still held their shape—no collapsed filling. But clearly I hadn't drained off enough of the apples' juice, which had seeped through, caramelized in the hot oven, and glued the strudel to the pan.

Instead of turning to the usual freshly toasted bread crumbs to soak up the juice, I decided to reach for panko. Commercially dried panko bread crumbs are drier than homemade, which meant I could use

Fixing a Sad Strudel

GUMMY, PASTY FILLING
SOLUTION: We drain off some of the liquid before wrapping the filling in phyllo. We also use panko instead of toasted fresh bread crumbs; because they are drier, we can use less of them for the same effect.

THICK, TOUGH BOTTOM
SOLUTION: We use fewer sheets of phyllo overall and arrange the seam on top, where it won't compress and toughen from the filling's weight.

FLYAWAY PHYLLO
SOLUTION: Sprinkling confectioners' sugar between the layers helps fuse them together. We slice the strudel while it's warm, before the sheets have crisped up.

GAPPING
SOLUTION: We parcook the apples briefly, which causes an enzymatic reaction that "sets" the pectin in the fruit, allowing the slices to hold their shape even after further cooking.

less of them and soak up a comparable amount of liquid (we avoid regular commercial bread crumbs in the test kitchen since they are too fine and dusty). After a few tests, I found that just 1½ tablespoons of panko stirred into the parcooked apples was all my filling needed to effectively contain the juice. And best of all, the filling tasted bright and appley—no dull flavor or pasty texture. It was time to deal with the pastry.

In the Fold

Phyllo can be intimidating to work with, but a few tips that we've come up with in the past helped make it easier out of the gate (see "Phyllo Without Fear" on page 29). I also made an immediate change to the strudel's assembly. Rolling the phyllo around all that filling and getting it onto the baking sheet was cumbersome and tricky. Instead, I'd divide it up and make two smaller strudels.

First, I decided to tackle the layers of tough, dense phyllo on the bottom of the strudel. Some recipes use as many as 11 sheets of phyllo, and while flakiness is a goal, I had to wonder if more was necessarily better. The weight of the filling seemed to be compressing the layers on the strudel's bottom, making them tough. Maybe using fewer sheets would give me a more delicate, tender base? Indeed, going down to seven sheets made a noticeable difference. But it wasn't perfect.

By rolling the strudels like logs and placing them seam side down, I'd created areas with overlapping layers of phyllo on the undersides of the strudels—there were 14 sheets where the edges overlapped rather than just seven. What if I put the seam on the top, where toughness wasn't an issue? For the next strudel, I placed the filling on the phyllo stack, folded the sides up over the filling, and then folded the top and bottom up and over, much like folding a letter. To seal the seam, I brushed the dough with some of the sticky apple liquid that had been released in the microwave (and while I was at it, I also brushed the liquid over the entire surface to help the strudels brown). I transferred the strudels to a baking sheet and popped them into the oven. Finally, the undersides were perfect: crisp on the exterior yet tender and easy to get a fork through. Plus, this method was much easier, with less risk of tearing since I didn't have to manipulate the strudels so much.

On to the messy top layers. To keep them from shattering everywhere, I came up with a two-pronged solution. First, I lightly "glued" the sheets together by sprinkling each one with confectioners' sugar after brushing it with butter. In the heat of the oven, the sugar melted and sealed the sheets together just enough to keep them from flying apart. And second, as soon as the strudel was out of the oven, I transferred it to a cutting board and sliced it after just a few minutes. When hot, the pastry was softer and thus less prone to shattering; once cooled, it crisped up beautifully.

At last, I had a simpler strudel that was so good, I could see myself enjoying it on a regular basis.

APPLE STRUDEL
SERVES 6

Gala apples can be substituted for Golden Delicious. Phyllo dough is also available in larger 18 by 14-inch sheets; if using, cut them in half to make 14 by 9-inch sheets. Thaw phyllo in the refrigerator overnight or on the counter for 4 to 5 hours; don't thaw it in the microwave. Our recipe for Apple Strudel for Two is available free for 4 months at CooksIllustrated.com/dec16.

1¾	pounds Golden Delicious apples, peeled, cored, and cut into ½-inch pieces
3	tablespoons granulated sugar
½	teaspoon grated lemon zest plus 1½ teaspoons juice
¼	teaspoon ground cinnamon
¼	teaspoon ground ginger
	Salt
3	tablespoons golden raisins
1½	tablespoons panko bread crumbs
7	tablespoons unsalted butter, melted
1	tablespoon confectioners' sugar, plus extra for serving
14	(14 by 9-inch) phyllo sheets, thawed

1. Toss apples, granulated sugar, lemon zest and juice, cinnamon, ginger, and ⅛ teaspoon salt together in large bowl. Cover and microwave until apples are warm to touch, about 2 minutes, stirring once halfway through microwaving. Let apples stand, covered, for 5 minutes. Transfer apples to colander set in second large bowl and let drain, reserving liquid. Return apples to bowl; stir in raisins and panko.

2. Adjust oven rack to upper-middle position and heat oven to 375 degrees. Spray rimmed baking sheet with vegetable oil spray. Stir ⅛ teaspoon salt into melted butter.

3. Place 16½ by 12-inch sheet of parchment paper on counter with long side parallel to edge of counter. Place 1 phyllo sheet on parchment with long side parallel to edge of counter. Place 1½ teaspoons confectioners' sugar in fine-mesh strainer (rest strainer in bowl to prevent making mess). Lightly brush sheet with melted butter and dust sparingly with confectioners' sugar. Repeat with 6 more phyllo sheets, melted butter, and confectioners' sugar, stacking sheets one on top of other as you go.

4. Arrange half of apple mixture in 2½ by 10-inch rectangle 2 inches from bottom of phyllo and about 2 inches from each side. Using parchment, fold sides of phyllo over filling, then fold bottom edge of phyllo over filling. Brush folded portions of phyllo with reserved apple liquid. Fold top edge over filling, making sure top and bottom edges overlap by about 1 inch. (If they do not overlap, unfold, rearrange filling into slightly narrower strip, and refold.) Press firmly to seal. Using thin metal spatula, transfer strudel to 1 side of prepared baking sheet, facing seam toward center of sheet. Lightly brush top and sides of strudel with half of remaining apple liquid. Repeat process

STEP BY STEP | THAT'S A WRAP

Most strudel recipes call for rolling the strudel up like a log and placing it seam side down on a baking sheet. This risks tearing the phyllo and creates too many layers on the underside where the seam overlaps, which we found leads to toughness. Here's our better, easier way.

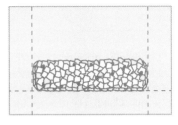

1. Mound half of filling along bottom third of 7 layered phyllo sheets on parchment paper, leaving 2-inch border at bottom edge and sides of phyllo.

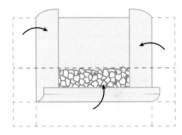

2. Using parchment, fold sides of phyllo over filling, then fold over bottom edge of phyllo. Brush folded portions with apple liquid.

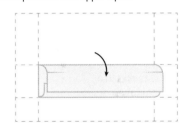

3. Fold top edge of phyllo over mounded filling, which should overlap the bottom edge by about 1 inch. Press to seal. Repeat with second strudel.

with remaining phyllo, melted butter, confectioners' sugar, filling, and apple liquid. Place second strudel on other side of prepared sheet, with seam facing center of sheet.

5. Bake strudels until golden brown, 27 to 35 minutes, rotating sheet halfway through baking. Using thin metal spatula, immediately transfer strudels to cutting board. Let cool for 3 minutes. Slice each strudel into thirds and let cool for at least 20 minutes. Serve warm or at room temperature, dusting with extra confectioners' sugar before serving.

▶ **See the Assembly Process** A step-by-step video is available at CooksIllustrated.com/dec16

The Busiest Pan in Our Kitchen

A rimmed baking sheet is essential for sheet cakes and handy for cookies. But if yours is flimsy or you use it only for baking, you're not getting your money's worth.

> BY KATE SHANNON

Rimmed baking sheets, also called half-sheet pans, are true workhorses in the test kitchen. We have stacks of them that we use every day for obvious tasks like baking cookies or roasting oven fries or root vegetables. But we also use them for baking chicken or fish, toasting nuts and seeds, roasting vegetables such as green beans and asparagus, and baking jelly roll cakes. More unusually, we use baking sheets for sorting dried beans or spreading out cooked rice or pasta to cool before making salads. In a pinch, an inverted baking sheet can even stand in for a pizza peel or baking stone. And that's just the start. Slipping a wire cooling rack inside (to elevate food for increased air circulation and also to contain mess) makes these pans even more versatile—it's our go-to setup for roasting and broiling meats, holding breaded foods before and after frying, and drizzling chocolate over desserts.

To find the best rimmed baking sheet on the market, we selected eight standard-size models (priced from $7.43 to $23.69) to put through their paces in the test kitchen. We baked our way through jelly roll cakes and dozens of sugar cookies and then roasted 30 pounds of chicken thighs and more parsnips than anyone should ever have to look at. For each recipe, we examined how evenly foods browned across the surface of the pan, as well as how cleanly they released. Throughout testing, we kept a close eye on warping and evaluated how comfortable each pan felt when loaded with heavy foods.

Sizing up the Competition

First, some good news: It's possible to bake, roast, and broil using all of the pans we tested. Most cookies and cakes baked to an appropriate pale golden brown. Meanwhile, chicken thighs and parsnips browned and cooked evenly in most of the pans and didn't stick to any of the pans. But some pans made it harder to achieve good results.

We selected pans that either listed their dimensions as approximately 18 by 13 inches or that called themselves "standard" size; the dimensions refer to the lip-to-lip measurements, and the actual usable cooking surface on most of these pans was about 16½ inches by 11½ inches. There was one noticeable outlier. Its cooking surface was 18 inches by 12 inches, so a jelly roll cake made in this pan was too thin, which threw off the ratios of the filled and rolled cakes. Even more damning was that this irregularly sized pan wasn't compatible with our favorite wire cooling rack (see our testing of cooling racks on page 32). The rack slid around precariously and left swirls of scratches. Racks sat snugly and securely in most other models.

The style of the pans' edges also mattered. One had low, sloped sides; when we walked around the kitchen with it, liquid threatened to spill over the edges, which were just ⅞ inch tall. Another pan had unique ridged edges. The cakes that emerged from these pans tasted fine, but they looked odd. We much preferred models with straighter, smooth sides that were 1 inch or taller. They not only contained liquid and produced straight-sided cakes but also gave us something sizable to grip—especially important when carrying a hot pan using a bulky potholder.

The Heat Is On

Over the years, we've learned some tricks to get the most out of our baking sheets. When roasting meats and vegetables, more browning generally means more flavor. Much as you preheat a skillet before searing, say, a pork chop, we like to preheat baking sheets in a hot oven to create increased browning on roasted beef, chicken, root vegetables, cauliflower, and so on. That said, this preheating puts stress on the pan and can lead to warping. In fact, every pan we tested warped at least a little.

Happily, only one sheet in our lineup permanently warped enough to have an actual impact on cooking. In this model, the oil ran away from the center of the pan and pooled in the lower corners. As a result, some parsnips sizzled in a deep layer of oil, while others never made contact with the fat and emerged from the oven dry and leathery. (For more information, see "Truly Warped.")

Superior Sheets

In the end, we were able to recommend nearly all of the baking sheets we tested. Most were good for both baking and roasting and cooked food uniformly. Cooling racks fit snugly, and jelly roll cakes came out perfectly. Still, two jumped ahead of the pack. Their cooking surfaces were the right size for a wire rack to fit snugly, and both boasted straighter, taller sides that contained food and offered us a good grip. They were also hard to scratch and turned out to be the most warp-resistant pans in the lineup. Even if warping doesn't have much of an effect on cooking, given the choice we'd still rather have a pan that lies flat than one that doesn't. The inexpensive Nordic Ware Baker's Half Sheet ($14.97) was slightly sturdier, which gave it the edge over our old favorite from Vollrath ($20.99). This is a workhorse baking sheet we'll be happy to use for years to come.

Dynamic Duo

Setting a wire rack inside a baking sheet promotes air circulation, encouraging crisping and preventing sogginess when roasting or broiling meats. This setup can also hold breaded foods before and after frying and desserts while drizzling with chocolate or icing.

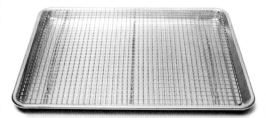

PERFECT FIT
Our favorite rack—the Libertyware Half Size Sheet Pan Cooling Rack—fits snugly in our winning baking sheet from Nordic Ware.

Truly Warped

All of the pans we tested warped at least a little bit during testing—the result of metal expanding as it heats. When relatively cool food (like chicken thighs or parsnips) is placed in a hot pan, the metal directly below the food cools and starts to contract. The combination of expanding and contracting areas on a single pan creates a sort of twisting effect. Though most pans spring back into place when the hot and cool spots across the pan equalize, the pan will remain warped if the thermal stress is too great and the pan twists too much—what people in the metal industry refer to as exceeding its "elastic limit." If you ever see a pan that won't sit flat on the counter but instead rocks back and forth when you tap on it, that's why. That's what happened to the Fat Daddio's ProSeries Jelly Roll Pan: It became dramatically warped and stayed that way, which contributed to its last-place ranking.

TESTING RIMMED BAKING SHEETS

We tested eight rimmed baking sheets, all measuring roughly 18 by 13 inches from rim to rim, using each to bake a jelly roll cake and lemon sugar cookies, roast parsnips, and roast and broil chicken thighs. We evaluated how evenly the food cooked and how cleanly it released from the sheets. We also rated their handling, strength, and resistance to warping and measured the dimensions of their cooking surfaces. All models were purchased online and appear below in order of preference.

BAKING

We baked a jelly roll cake and cookies in each sheet, giving higher scores for appropriately light golden-brown baked goods that baked evenly across the entirety of the cooking surface.

ROASTING

We preheated the sheets and roasted parsnips and chicken thighs on them, observing how evenly foods cooked across the entirety of the cooking surface. Those that browned and cooked foods evenly scored the highest.

WARPING

We preferred sheets that withstood high-heat ovens and rapid temperature changes with minimal warping.

HANDLING

To test comfort and ease of use, we fitted each sheet with a wire rack, prepared a mock roast (placing a 5-pound bag of flour atop the rack and ½ cup of water underneath it), and did a lap around the test kitchen. The best sheets felt comfortable and secure in hand, with tall, straight sides that were easy to grip and helped contain liquid.

RACK COMPATIBILITY

We often use wire cooling racks inside baking sheets. We deducted points if standard-size racks moved around inside the sheets or didn't fit inside them completely.

▶ **See Why It Won**
We work through all the details at CooksIllustrated.com/dec16

HIGHLY RECOMMENDED

NORDIC WARE Baker's Half Sheet

MODEL: 43100 **PRICE:** $14.97

COOKING SURFACE: 16½ x 11½ in

MATERIAL: Aluminum

CRITERIA		TESTERS' COMMENTS
BAKING	★★★	Everything prepared in this sturdy, warp-resistant sheet cooked appropriately and evenly. Best of all, our new favorite is a few bucks cheaper than our old winner.
ROASTING	★★★	
WARPING	★★½	
HANDLING	★★★	
RACK COMPATIBILITY	★★★	

VOLLRATH Wear-Ever Heavy Duty Sheet Pan (13 gauge)

MODEL: 5314 **PRICE:** $20.99

COOKING SURFACE: 16½ x 11½ in

MATERIAL: Aluminum alloy

CRITERIA		TESTERS' COMMENTS
BAKING	★★★	Our old favorite performed flawlessly when baking cookies and cakes. It did warp slightly when roasting, but the food still came out well. It resisted scratching and snugly fit wire racks.
ROASTING	★★★	
WARPING	★★½	
HANDLING	★★★	
RACK COMPATIBILITY	★★★	

RECOMMENDED

CHICAGO METALLIC Traditional Large Jelly Roll Pan

MODEL: 49813

PRICE: $15.51

COOKING SURFACE: 16½ x 11½ in

MATERIAL: Aluminized steel

CRITERIA	
BAKING	★★★
ROASTING	★★★
WARPING	★★
HANDLING	★★★
RACK COMPATIBILITY	★★★

COMMENTS: The sole aluminum-coated steel sheet in our lineup, it matched the performance of the all-aluminum models. Although it didn't warp noticeably more than most other sheets, it rested unevenly at the end of testing and made a disconcerting rumbling, popping noise when we pressed against it.

NORDIC WARE Prism Half Sheet Baking Pan

MODEL: 43170

PRICE: $17.95

COOKING SURFACE: 16½ x 11½ in

MATERIAL: Aluminum

CRITERIA	
BAKING	★★★
ROASTING	★★★
WARPING	★★
HANDLING	★★★
RACK COMPATIBILITY	★★★

COMMENTS: This sheet has a ridged pattern on the cooking surface (ostensibly for increased strength and easy release) that left a houndstooth pattern on the undersides of the cake and parsnips. It held a wire cooling rack as snugly as our top models did.

NORPRO Heavy Gauge Aluminum Jelly Roll Pan

MODEL: 3271

PRICE: $17.36

COOKING SURFACE: 16½ x 11½ in

MATERIAL: Aluminum

CRITERIA	
BAKING	★★★
ROASTING	★★★
WARPING	★★
HANDLING	★★★
RACK COMPATIBILITY	★★½

COMMENTS: This sheet cooked and browned foods evenly in both baking and roasting tests. It was less warp-resistant than our favorites, especially when we roasted chicken thighs. A wire cooling rack fit fairly well and left behind minimal marks.

RECOMMENDED

CHICAGO METALLIC StayFlat NSF Half-Size Sheet Pan

MODEL: 30850

PRICE: $7.43

COOKING SURFACE: 16¾ x 11¾ in

MATERIAL: Aluminum

CRITERIA	
BAKING	★★★
ROASTING	★★★
WARPING	★★
HANDLING	★★★
RACK COMPATIBILITY	★★

COMMENTS: This bargain-priced sheet felt exceptionally strong and sturdy. It did twist slightly in our chicken thigh test. The sides have a unique ridged shape that imprinted on the edges of the cake, but most testers didn't mind.

ISLAND WARE Baker's Half Sheet Pan

MODEL: Half Sheet Pan

PRICE: $20.99

COOKING SURFACE: 15¾ x 11½ in

MATERIAL: Aluminum

CRITERIA	
BAKING	★★★
ROASTING	★★½
WARPING	★½
HANDLING	★½
RACK COMPATIBILITY	★★★

COMMENTS: Although this sheet cooked parsnips, chicken, and cookies well, it warped awkwardly, and its low, flared sides gave us pause. Chicken fat almost spilled out of it, and our cake had odd beveled edges.

NOT RECOMMENDED

FAT DADDIO'S ProSeries Jelly Roll Pan

MODEL: JRP-12181

PRICE: $23.69

COOKING SURFACE: 18 x 12 in

MATERIAL: Aluminum

CRITERIA	
BAKING	★★
ROASTING	★½
WARPING	★
HANDLING	★★
RACK COMPATIBILITY	★

COMMENTS: This sheet was the longest in our lineup; it made a jelly roll cake that was too thin, and a wire rack slid around. It browned foods almost too well, and we had to watch them carefully so they didn't burn. It warped dramatically.

Shopping for Cinnamon

Labels touting origin imply there's more to this standby spice than there once was. How much does source influence flavor?

⇉ BY LAUREN SAVOIE ⇇

Few spices feel as familiar as ground cinnamon: We swirl it into oatmeal; sprinkle it on top of lattes; bake it into pies, cakes, and cookies; and even add it to savory dishes. But when it comes to shopping for cinnamon, the choices sound exotic. Instead of picking up simple "ground cinnamon," you can choose from among bottles specifying "Vietnamese" or even "Saigon" on the label. Such cinnamons also command a higher price—up to about $4.00 per ounce, compared with as little as $0.90 per ounce for those with generic labeling. Does origin really matter, or is it just a clever marketing tool?

To find out, we rounded up eight cinnamons, most nationally available in supermarkets and one purchased online from the spice purveyor Penzeys. Half the products were Vietnamese cinnamon. The other half didn't specify origin on their labels, but we confirmed with manufacturers that they all hailed from Indonesia, the source for most generic cinnamon sold in this country. Tasters sampled the products stirred into chilled rice pudding, baked into cinnamon rolls, and sprinkled and baked on cinnamon-sugar pita chips.

It took one test—the rice pudding tasting—to determine that cinnamons are noticeably different, mainly when it comes to heat. Some were markedly spicy (a few even bordered on too intense), while the others had more-tempered heat that allowed hints of sweetness and clove to come through. When we compared comments to products, we discovered that origin does matter: The Vietnamese cinnamons all fell on the spicier end of the spectrum, while the Indonesian cinnamons were milder. And there were tasters who championed each style.

We looked deeper into cinnamon production and learned that "cinnamon" is actually an umbrella term for several different species of evergreen trees in the genus *Cinnamomum*. Moreover, the species grown in Vietnam is different from the species grown in Indonesia. Vietnamese growers cultivate *Cinnamomum loureiroi*, which is naturally higher in the volatile oils that provide heat and carry cinnamon's trademark flavors than the *Cinnamomum burmannii* grown in Indonesia. A less common third type, *Cinnamomum verum*, is grown in Sri Lanka (see "Three Cinnamons, Oceans Apart"). Another species (*Cinnamomum cassia*) grown in China is mainly imported to the United States in the form of oils for flavoring in food manufacturing.

The age of the bark at harvesting also affects the amount of volatile oils. Harvesting entails stripping the exterior bark from the tree and then scraping its interior into strips, or quills, that are then sun-dried and ground. Older trees contain the most oils. Indonesian cinnamon typically comes from the bark of trees that are less than 10 years old, while

Three Cinnamons, Oceans Apart

Most of the cinnamon sold in supermarkets is harvested from the bark of trees grown in Indonesia and Vietnam. But in many parts of the world, Ceylon cinnamon, or "true" cinnamon, which is grown primarily in Sri Lanka, is more common. When we pitted three Ceylon cinnamons against our favorite Indonesian cinnamon, tasters easily singled out the Ceylon products, finding them milder and more subtle. Lab tests backed this up, confirming that all of the Ceylon cinnamons had lower percentages of key volatile oils than did our favorite Indonesian product. In general, our tasters preferred the bolder, spicier flavor profile of Indonesian- and Vietnamese-grown cinnamons, but if you like a floral, more delicate flavor, Ceylon (our favorite is by Frontier) could be a good choice.

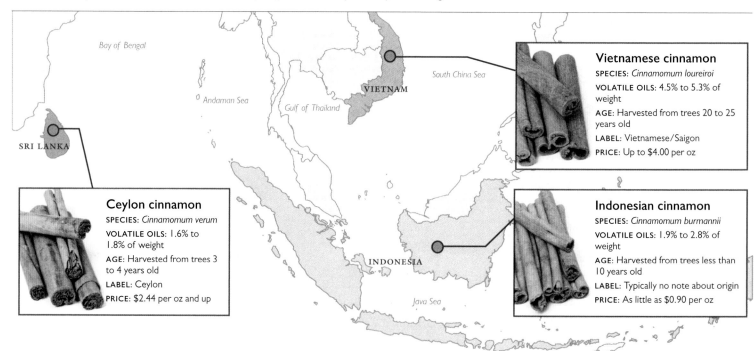

Vietnamese cinnamon
SPECIES: *Cinnamomum loureiroi*
VOLATILE OILS: 4.5% to 5.3% of weight
AGE: Harvested from trees 20 to 25 years old
LABEL: Vietnamese/Saigon
PRICE: Up to $4.00 per oz

Indonesian cinnamon
SPECIES: *Cinnamomum burmannii*
VOLATILE OILS: 1.9% to 2.8% of weight
AGE: Harvested from trees less than 10 years old
LABEL: Typically no note about origin
PRICE: As little as $0.90 per oz

Ceylon cinnamon
SPECIES: *Cinnamomum verum*
VOLATILE OILS: 1.6% to 1.8% of weight
AGE: Harvested from trees 3 to 4 years old
LABEL: Ceylon
PRICE: $2.44 per oz and up

Vietnamese cinnamon is often harvested from trees between 20 and 25 years old. Lab analysis confirmed these differences: The Vietnamese cinnamons in our tasting contained between 4.5 and 5.3 percent volatile oils, while the Indonesian cinnamons contained 1.9 to 2.8 percent.

The Great Equalizer

Tasters felt the burn of many of the Vietnamese cinnamons when tasting them sprinkled on rice pudding, but that heat all but disappeared when we sampled the cinnamons baked into cinnamon rolls and on pita chips. In fact, tasters struggled to detect differences of any kind in these baked items, deeming every product acceptable except for one outlier (more on that in a minute). What had happened to the heat?

Three main chemical compounds comprise the bulk of volatile oils in cinnamon. The compound responsible for spiciness, cinnamaldehyde, is by far the most abundant of the three, but it's also the least stable in the presence of heat. The other two compounds—eugenol and linalool—provide cinnamon's floral, woodsy, and clove aromas, but they are present in very tiny amounts, hence the subtlety of these flavors. Some of the cinnamaldehyde and virtually all of the eugenol and linalool will be carried off by steam once the moisture in a baked good (or any cooked, moist foodstuff) starts to evaporate. Eugenol helps stabilize cinnamaldehyde, and without its protection, cinnamaldehyde will start to break down once the temperature of the food reaches 140 degrees—a temperature easily exceeded during baking. No wonder the cinnamons all tasted virtually the same in the baked applications.

And what about that outlier cinnamon that nobody really liked? Tasters singled it out for its dull flavor and musty aftertaste in all three applications. This product turned out to be an Indonesian-sourced cinnamon from Badia. The manufacturer told us that it adds 2 percent soybean oil to its cinnamon as a processing aid, which had to help explain its lingering "musty" flavor.

Split Decision

With the exception of this one product, we found that it's hard to go wrong with cinnamon. If you like a big, spicy flavor and use cinnamon frequently in unheated applications, we recommend springing for Penzeys Vietnamese Cinnamon Ground. At $4.09 per ounce, it was the most expensive product in our lineup, but it also had the highest percentage of volatile oils: 5.3 percent. And while a few of the other Vietnamese cinnamons seemed to be all punch and no nuance, this product offered an array of floral, earthy notes in addition to heat. But if you use cinnamon just for baking, or if you prefer a milder, sweeter cinnamon in unheated applications, stick with cheaper cinnamons that make no claim to origin. Our favorite among these cinnamons was Morton & Bassett Spices Ground Cinnamon ($2.72 per ounce), which had tempered heat and a complex bouquet of floral, woodsy, and earthy aromas.

TASTING CINNAMON

We sampled eight nationally available varieties of cinnamon in three blind tastings: swirled into rice pudding, baked into cinnamon rolls, and baked on homemade pita chips. We found that, depending on their origins, the cinnamons were either spicy or mild and sweet. All products were purchased at Boston-area supermarkets or online, and prices shown are what we paid. An independent lab analyzed each cinnamon for its percentage of volatile oils. Information about origin, additives, and processing was obtained from manufacturers. For complete testing results and results of our Ceylon cinnamon tasting, go to CooksIllustrated.com/dec16.

RECOMMENDED

MORTON & BASSETT SPICES Ground Cinnamon
PRICE: $5.99 for 2.2 oz ($2.72 per oz)
ORIGIN: Indonesia
STYLE: Mild and sweet
ADDITIVES: None
VOLATILE OILS: 1.9%
COMMENTS: In the rice pudding tasting, this Indonesian cinnamon struck "the perfect balance of sweet and spicy." Its flavor dramatically mellowed when baked into cinnamon rolls and on pita chips.

MOST VERSATILE

PENZEYS Vietnamese Cinnamon Ground
PRICE: $6.95 for 1.7 oz ($4.09 per oz)
ORIGIN: Vietnam
STYLE: Spicy
ADDITIVES: None
VOLATILE OILS: 5.3%
COMMENTS: With the highest percentage of volatile oils in the bunch, this Vietnamese cinnamon boasted a "bold" heat that didn't overpower its "woodsier" flavors in rice pudding. But it lost heat in baked applications.

SPICY FAVORITE

McCORMICK Ground Cinnamon
PRICE: $2.99 for 2.37 oz ($1.26 per oz)
ORIGIN: Indonesia
STYLE: Mild and sweet
ADDITIVES: None
VOLATILE OILS: 2.2%

SIMPLY ORGANIC Ground Cinnamon
PRICE: $4.49 for 2.45 oz ($1.83 per oz)
ORIGIN: Vietnam
STYLE: Spicy
ADDITIVES: None
VOLATILE OILS: 4.8%

FRONTIER CO-OP Organic Ground Cinnamon
PRICE: $3.69 for 1.92 oz ($1.92 per oz)
ORIGIN: Indonesia
STYLE: Mild and sweet
ADDITIVES: None
VOLATILE OILS: 2.8%

McCORMICK GOURMET Organic Saigon Cinnamon
PRICE: $4.19 for 1.25 oz ($3.35 per oz)
ORIGIN: Vietnam
STYLE: Spicy
ADDITIVES: None
VOLATILE OILS: 4.5%

SPICE ISLANDS Saigon Cinnamon
PRICE: $6.49 for 1.9 oz ($3.42 per oz)
ORIGIN: Vietnam
STYLE: Spicy
ADDITIVES: None
VOLATILE OILS: 5.0%

RECOMMENDED WITH RESERVATIONS

BADIA Cinnamon Powder
PRICE: $1.79 for 2 oz ($0.90 per oz)
ORIGIN: Indonesia
STYLE: Mild and sweet
ADDITIVES: Less than 2% soybean oil added as processing aid
VOLATILE OILS: 2.6%

COMMENTS: The only product with soybean oil added during processing, this cinnamon received low marks for its "sour," "musty" aftertaste. However, these off-notes mostly disappeared when we baked with it.

Baking With Cinnamon? Any Will Do

We found differences among cinnamons, mainly in terms of heat, when we sampled them stirred into chilled rice pudding. But those distinctions faded when we baked the spices in cinnamon buns and on pita chips. That's because, of the three main volatile oils responsible for cinnamon's flavor, the most abundant oil is spicy-tasting cinnamaldehyde, which is also the least stable in the presence of heat. So if you're buying the spice primarily for baking, any of our recommended products will do.

⇒ BY ANDREA GEARY, ANDREW JANJIGIAN, LAN LAM & ANNIE PETITO ⇐

Tasting Whole-Milk Ricotta

A good ricotta should be both creamy and dense, with a fresh dairy flavor that adds richness to dishes like lasagna, cannoli, and cheesecake. To find the best supermarket whole-milk ricotta, we scooped up four contenders and had our tasting panel sample them plain and in baked manicotti.

In the plain tasting, tasters lauded the three creamy, smooth cheeses and panned the lone "granular" product. Our two top scorers were cheeses with a mild sweetness, which we preferred to those with tang. In manicotti, the grainy ricotta that stood out in the plain tasting once again received low marks.

In Italy, ricotta is made with whey (a byproduct of cheese making), which is heated with a small amount of acid to form curds and then drained. Ideally, the delicate curds are then hand-scooped into packaging to preserve their texture. Many American ricottas replace some or all of the whey with milk (our two lowest-scoring ricottas contain no whey) and are mechanically packaged. Our winner uses more whey than milk (resulting in a sweeter cheese) and is packaged using a special pump designed to maintain the cheese's texture. BelGioioso Ricotta con Latte Whole Milk is our new favorite. For complete tasting results, go to CooksIllustrated.com/dec16. –Kate Shannon

RECOMMENDED

BELGIOIOSO Ricotta con Latte Whole Milk

PRICE: $3.99 for 16 oz ($0.25 per oz)

INGREDIENTS: Pasteurized whey and milk, vinegar, salt

COMMENTS: This cheese was slightly sweet, with a dense, "luscious" consistency. In manicotti, it was rich without being overwhelming.

GALBANI Whole Milk Ricotta Cheese

PRICE: $6.29 for 32 oz ($0.20 per oz)

INGREDIENTS: Whey, milk, vinegar, and xanthan gum, locust bean gum, guar gum (stabilizers)

COMMENTS: A mildly sweet flavor and "dense," "velvety" texture made for exceptional manicotti.

CALABRO Whole Milk Ricotta Cheese

PRICE: $4.49 for 16 oz ($0.28 per oz)

INGREDIENTS: Whole milk, starter, salt

COMMENTS: This product was slightly tangy, with a "fresh, clean ricotta flavor" in manicotti. Some tasters found it a bit "dry."

NOT RECOMMENDED

ORGANIC VALLEY Whole Milk Ricotta Cheese

PRICE: $6.99 for 15 oz ($0.47 per oz)

INGREDIENTS: Organic whole milk, organic skim milk, organic vinegar, salt

COMMENTS: Most tasters objected to the "pebbly," "cottage cheese"–like texture. Plain, it was weepy. In manicotti, it was "grainy" and "lumpy."

All About Celery Root

WHAT IT IS: A variety of celery cultivated not for its stalks but for its knobby root bulb, celery root (also known as celeriac) boasts a crisp, firm, parsnip-like texture under its tough peel and a mild, celery-like flavor that sweetens with cooking.

HOW WE USE IT: A classic application is celery root rémoulade, where the raw root is grated or cut into matchsticks and tossed with a tangy mustard dressing. This versatile bulb can also be braised, baked, roasted, or made into a mash on its own or in combination with other vegetables.

DOES SIZE MATTER? We found that smaller bulbs (less than 1¼ pounds) had more flavor than larger bulbs both when sampled raw and when cooked simply in butter and water. The difference was more subtle when we compared smaller and larger bulbs in root vegetable gratin. We'll seek out smaller bulbs when we're using celery root on its own or in simple applications without a lot of competing flavors, but when adding it to a more complex recipe like a stew or gratin, we'll use whatever is available.

TO PREVENT BROWNING: To avoid discoloration, place the prepped vegetable in acidulated water (1 teaspoon lemon juice or vinegar per 1 cup water).

HOW TO PREP: The tough exteriors of smaller bulbs can simply be cut away using a chef's knife. Here's a safe way to prepare bulbs larger than 1¼ pounds. –L.L.

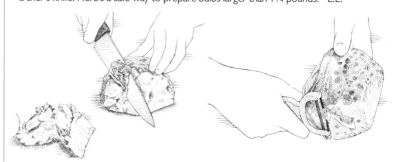

1. Trim stem end to create flat surface, then halve vertically. Lay flat on side and use knife to trim away knotty roots.

2. Using vegetable peeler, remove remaining skin.

Getting Nondairy Milks to Froth

Recently we had some colleagues report that they couldn't always get alternative milks to froth properly for homemade coffee drinks. To see for ourselves, we purchased several almond, soy, rice, and coconut milks and tried to froth them using our French press method (May/June 2012). Indeed, some frothed up just fine. But others couldn't hold a foam no matter how hard we tried. We found the reason for this on the ingredient label.

Only nondairy milks that contain gellan, a fermented food additive that's added to help thicken these thinner liquids, could hold a foam. Here's why: The proteins and water in cow's milk form the walls of air bubbles in foam. The proteins, which unwind during agitation, buttress and stabilize the walls, slowing the process in which the water drains out and causes the foam to collapse. The proteins in nondairy milks are weaker (and there are fewer of them) and can't support air bubbles as well. But when gellan is in the mix, it bonds with the calcium in nondairy milks to create a strong matrix that makes up for the lack of strong proteins and results in a more stable foam. So when buying alternative milks that you want to froth, make sure gellan is on the ingredient list. –L.L.

FOR FROTH, GELLAN IS THE KEY

**3 OUNCES OF PARMESAN =
2 OUNCES OF PECORINO ROMANO**

Substituting Pecorino Romano for Parmesan

Pecorino Romano and Parmigiano-Reggiano are very similar: They're both aged, salty hard cheeses, and they're both high in glutamates, compounds that boost umami flavors. Parmesan (we're referring to both Parmigiano-Reggiano and domestic Parmesan here), made from cow's milk, has a more neutral flavor than sheep's milk–based Pecorino, which is more pungent and assertive. But if you already have Pecorino Romano on hand, will it work as a Parmesan substitute?

In polenta, a direct swap proved too salty. Reducing the amount by one-third made the salt level acceptable, but the cheese flavor was less distinctive. In our Turkey Meatballs (September/October 2016), where the Parmesan is used as a background savory flavor booster, the Pecorino didn't come across as too salty, but its flavor was more noticeable. Using one-third less cheese was a good workaround.

The bottom line? You can substitute Pecorino Romano for Parmesan, but use one-third less than the recipe calls for to keep the salt level and flavor in line. –A.J.

Phyllo Without Fear

Delicate phyllo can be difficult to work with. When developing our Apple Strudel recipe (page 23), we came up with some tricks.

➤ **WARM UP SLOWLY** For even thawing, let the phyllo defrost overnight in the refrigerator, and then let it rest on the counter for 30 minutes before opening the package and unrolling the leaves.

➤ **KEEP COVERED** To keep phyllo from drying out, most recipes recommend covering the stack with a damp towel, but the dough can easily turn sticky. We prefer to cover the stack with plastic wrap and then a damp towel to weigh it down and keep the plastic flush against the phyllo.

➤ **STAGGER CRACKS** Because phyllo is so fragile, some sheets inevitably crack or even tear while still in the box. Don't worry—just make sure to adjust the orientation of the sheets as you stack them so that cracks in different sheets don't line up.

➤ **TRIM STUCK EDGES** When phyllo sheets emerge from the box fused at their edges, don't try to separate the sheets. Instead, trim the fused portions and discard them. –L.L.

Piquillos: More Than a Pricey Roasted Red Pepper?

On the shelf near jarred roasted red peppers in some supermarkets, you'll see bright red, comparatively expensive (about 20 percent more) piquillos, a pepper common in Spanish cuisine. Are they worth the extra money?

Piquillos have thinner flesh, with a complex, slightly bitter flavor underlying their sweetness; roasted red peppers tasted fruitier in comparison. We didn't find the piquillos spicy at all, as some sources claim. They are also smaller, making them perfect for a stuffed tapas-style appetizer. But when we used both peppers in a filling for grilled meat and in a pureed sauce for chicken, they were indistinguishable.

Our advice? For recipes that call for chopped piquillos, go ahead and swap in the more-affordable, easier-to-find roasted red peppers. Save the pricey piquillos for making authentic tapas. –A.G.

**GOOD FOR
APPS**

A Different Way to Chop Onions

The most widely known method for chopping an onion involves making a series of vertical and then horizontal cuts, the latter requiring cutting toward the hand holding the onion. Here's a different method that's just as fast but doesn't require the horizontal cuts, which some cooks don't like to make. To watch a free video of this technique, go to CooksIllustrated.com/dec16. –A.P.

1. Halve onion through root end and peel. Make several vertical cuts, starting 1 inch from root end.

2. Extend middle cut to divide onion half into 2 even quarters.

3. Flip quarters onto newly cut sides, then align quarters so that vertical cuts are horizontal.

4. Make vertical cuts as in step 1, starting 1 inch from root end.

5. Cut across onion quarters to dice. Repeat with remaining onion half.

KITCHEN NOTES

≫ BY KEITH DRESSER, STEVE DUNN, ANDREA GEARY, ANDREW JANJIGIAN, LAN LAM & ANNIE PETITO ≪

WHAT IS IT?

SUNBEAM PARTY GRILL
Good for retro party snacks

A cross between a waffle maker and a panini press, this electric gadget known as the Sunbeam Party Grill was popular in the 1960s and was used to make hot snacks for cocktail parties or treats for the kids. Lift the lid and spoon batter into the 12 small nonstick cups to make mini muffin–type treats, or make filled snacks by laying down one square of bread, topping it with a dollop of filling, and then topping that with another piece of bread and closing the lid to cook. We put the grill through its paces using recipes from the original manual. All three items we made—muffin-like Chocolate Chippers, Stuffed Quick Pizzas, and Peanut Butter and Chocolate Bites—were big hits with tasters (especially the peanut butter bites, with their molten centers). In each case the grill worked as promised, delivering golden snacks that cooked perfectly in 3 minutes and released easily from the grill. The only issue we encountered was cheese oozing out of the pizza bites and down the sides of the grill, which left a baked-on mess. With a little tinkering, we could probably avoid that issue in future batches. –S.D.

The Proper Way to Use a Probe

A probe thermometer allows you to track the temperature of large roasts, turkeys, and chickens as they cook so that you don't have to repeatedly open the oven door and test with an instant-read thermometer. Proper placement is particularly important when cooking at higher heat as opposed to low and slow, because there will be a large differential within just an inch of space in the food. Follow these tips for proper usage. –L.L.

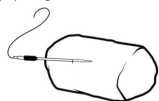   

FOR UNIFORMLY SHAPED ROASTS
Place tip of probe in center of meat, which will hit target temperature last.

FOR POULTRY
Place in thickest part of breast since this area is easiest to overcook, while dark meat can handle being slightly overdone.

AVOID BONE	**ENSURE PROBE IS SECURE**	**SPOT-CHECK**	**HANDLE WITH CARE**
Touching bone will give incorrect reading. Insert probe until you hit bone, then pull back about ¼ inch.	Check probe after closing oven door to ensure that it hasn't been displaced.	When thermometer nears target temperature, spot-check other areas to see if they are also close.	Remember that probe and its wire are hot.

How to Hack a Tart Pan

A round tart pan's removable bottom allows you to turn out beautiful crusts without marring the sides. But what if you don't own a tart pan? We tried various options, including cutting out the bottom of a disposable aluminum pan, but our favorite hack for both press-in and roll-out crusts was a 9-inch springform pan. Its removable collar helped release both types of crusts without damaging them. With the roll-out crust, we found it simplest to leave the collar closed but unfastened when fitting the dough and then fasten it once the dough was in place. Here's what to do:

➤ **PRESS-IN CRUST:** Pat dough into pan (with collar fastened), pressing dough 1 inch up sides to approximate height of sides of tart pan, and bake as directed.

➤ **ROLL-OUT CRUST:** Follow tart recipe directions, rolling dough into circle approximately 2 inches larger than size of pan and about ¼ inch thick. Gently ease dough into springform pan with collar closed but unfastened. Once dough is fitted into pan, snap collar shut and trim edge to 1-inch height using paring knife. –A.P.

Thawing Frozen Meat and Poultry

We always thaw large cuts (entire roasts and whole birds) in the refrigerator, but we also use the quick-thaw method for cuts that are 1 inch thick or less. Simply seal the meat in zipper-lock bags and submerge the bags in very hot (140-degree) water. This way, the meat defrosts quickly and bacterial growth remains in the "safe" range. We've found that quick-thawed meat is indistinguishable from meat defrosted in the refrigerator (including chicken breasts, which may turn slightly opaque once thawed).

Follow the chart of thawing times below to help you plan ahead; separating items such as steaks will help them thaw faster.

REFRIGERATOR THAWING	TIME
Thin steaks, chops, boneless chicken breasts	8 to 12 hours
Thick steaks, chops, bone-in chicken parts	24 hours
Whole chickens, turkeys, roasts	5 hours per pound
HOT-WATER THAWING	
Boneless chicken breasts	8 minutes
Thin steaks and chops	12 minutes

Note: Unless you are following our quick-thaw method, always defrost frozen meat and poultry in the refrigerator; frozen meat left on the counter can begin to grow microorganisms in as little as 2 hours. –K.D.

Sourdough Starter Rescue Remedy

Experienced sourdough bakers know that even a healthy sourdough starter can occasionally lose vigor—either because it hasn't been fed regularly or simply for reasons unknown (which can, and does, happen)—leaving it unable to leaven a loaf of bread. Fortunately, a little love is all it usually takes to revive an ailing starter.

Here's what to do: Feed ¼ cup (2 ounces) starter with ½ cup (2½ ounces) all-purpose flour and ¼ cup (2 ounces) water twice daily (approximately every 12 hours) and let it sit, covered with plastic wrap, at room temperature. It will be ready to use again when it smells pleasantly yeasty and sweet (rather than sour) and doubles in volume 8 to 12 hours after a feeding.

Sadly, this doesn't always work. If the starter doesn't revive at all after a day or two of feedings—it doesn't double in volume even more than 12 hours after a feeding—it is probably beyond saving, and it's time to start a new one from scratch. –A.J.

Keeping Cookies Ship-Shape

To find out how to ship cookies and bars so that they arrive in perfect condition, we made nine varieties and boxed them up in various combinations using different packing materials. We stored the boxes for six days to simulate shipping time, occasionally tossing them around to mimic the indignities that happen along the way. Then we unpacked them. Lessons learned:

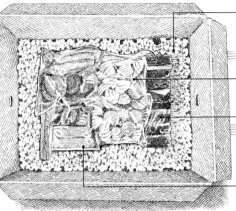

LIGHT PACKING MATERIAL
3 to 4 inches on all sides and top and bottom

MOST-DELICATE ITEMS
in the center

BAR COOKIES
stacked with parchment between each, then wrapped entirely in plastic wrap

STURDY COOKIES
in zipper-lock bags

➤ **SELECT WISELY** Gingersnaps, biscotti, meringues, and spritz cookies—varieties that are baked until dry throughout—remained intact, crunchy, and fresh-tasting. Moist, dense brownies and pecan bars also fared well. But chewy cookies that started out just slightly moist (including our Perfect Chocolate Chip Cookies) ended up stale, while delicate lace cookies were reduced to shards.

➤ **COMBINE LIKE WITH LIKE** Moist items like brownies turned crisp meringues to mush, and gingersnaps transferred their spicy flavors to mild spritz cookies.

➤ **STACK BARS IN SMALL SETS** Place parchment between each piece and wrap the stack tightly with plastic wrap. Enclose cookies in zipper-lock bags; how many cookies we packed into each bag didn't matter as long as we packed the box properly.

➤ **PACK WITH PADDING** For maximum shock absorption, surround your wrapped cookies with plenty of lightweight bulk; recycled packing peanuts, bubble wrap, and (our favorite) air-popped popcorn work well. Place the most delicate items in the very center of the box. –A.G.

Why a Square Baking Stone Beats a Round One

During our testing of baking stones (page 6), we eliminated circular models early on. While a round stone might seem practical since one of a baking stone's most popular uses is baking pizzas, there are good reasons to opt for a rectangular model instead.

BIGGER TARGET: While round and rectangular stones usually have roughly the same depth, rectangular stones are wider, giving you more wiggle room for mistakes when loading a pizza into the oven.

GREATER VERSATILITY: We commonly use baking stones to lend intense, sustained heat to foods beyond pizza, many of which get baked in rectangular pans (such as our Easier Roast Turkey and Gravy on page 6 and baking-sheet pizzas) that would overhang a circular stone. Similarly, many breads (such as baguettes and long *bâtardes*) are not circular.

BETTER BROWNING: Since round stones offer less surface area than even similar-size rectangular stones and are thus lighter than rectangular ones, they are less able to retain heat (and release it to the food being baked on it), which translates to inferior browning and slower cooking. –A.J.

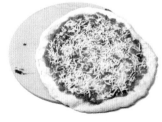

LESS WIGGLE ROOM
Round stones are narrower than rectangular stones, so even though they're the same shape as pizzas, they make it harder to hit the target.

SCIENCE **Is Basting Really Worth It?**

Basting is a time-honored method for keeping a turkey or chicken moist and helping brown the skin to improve both appearance and flavor. We wondered, though, if tradition has it right, so we ran a few tests.

EXPERIMENT

We roasted three turkey breasts (which we chose over whole turkeys to minimize variables) in 350-degree ovens until they reached 160 degrees. One breast we left in the oven undisturbed to act as a control. The second we roasted in another oven and basted every 20 minutes. The third we didn't baste, but we opened and closed the oven door every time we basted the second breast to evaluate the effect of simply opening the door. We weighed all three turkey breasts before and after cooking to determine the percentage of moisture lost and recorded the total cooking time. We also roasted three whole chickens (again, easier to manage than whole turkeys) under the same circumstances and compared the level of browning.

RESULTS

The total cooking time was 59 minutes for the control, 66 minutes for the unbasted breast exposed to the opening and closing oven door, and 69 minutes for the basted breast. Most important, the moisture loss of all three was comparable, ranging from 22.4 to 24.0 percent—a statistically insignificant difference—and tasters found all the birds comparably moist. In terms of browning, the basted chicken was evenly bronzed, while the other two exhibited slightly lighter, less glossy browning that was also a bit patchy.

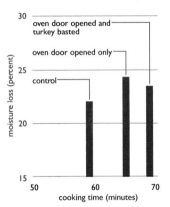

ADDS TIME AND EFFORT BUT NOT MUCH MOISTURE
The small increase in juiciness isn't worth the effort or time.

EXPLANATION

Basting purportedly keeps meat more moist by cooling the surface and thus slowing down the rate at which the meat cooks. And the more gently the meat cooks, the juicier it will remain. Basting did slow the cooking down more than just opening and closing the oven door but not enough to make a difference in moisture loss. In terms of browning, the drippings used for basting contain a lot of fat and protein, which encourage browning because they provide some of the starting materials (amino acids) for the Maillard reaction.

TAKEAWAY

Basting not only makes a negligible difference in moisture loss but also prolongs the cooking time and requires more hands-on work. For a really juicy turkey, we prefer a more hands-off approach such as brining or salting, which not only helps turkey retain moisture but also seasons the bird. And while basting did improve appearance, we don't think the difference is significant enough to make it worth it. –L.L.

▶ **SCIENCE OF COOKING: Making the Best-Tasting Quinoa**
Quick-cooking quinoa has a lot going for it, but does it really need to be washed before cooking? We answer that question in a video available at CooksIllustrated.com/dec16.

EQUIPMENT CORNER

⋗ BY MIYE BROMBERG AND KATE SHANNON ⋖

 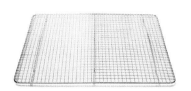  

HIGHLY RECOMMENDED	RECOMMENDED	HIGHLY RECOMMENDED	RECOMMENDED	RECOMMENDED
PYREX Easy Grab 3-Quart Oblong Baking Dish	**CUISIPRO Fat Separator**	**LIBERTYWARE Half Size Sheet Pan Cooling Rack**	**TOVOLO Stainless Steel 4-in-1 Cocktail Shaker**	**DESIGN TRIFECTA 360 Knife Block**
MODEL: 1085782	MODEL: 747301	MODEL: GRA4	MODEL: n/a	MODEL: HB360 002
PRICE: $7.29	PRICE: $33.95	PRICE: $15.99 for set of two	PRICE: $8.99	PRICE: $248.64

Glass Baking Dishes

Three-quart, or 13 by 9-inch, glass baking dishes are ideal for bringing lasagnas, casseroles, cobblers, and crumbles straight from the oven to the table. And because they're transparent, it's easy to monitor browning. You can't broil in them, but these inexpensive pans are dishwasher-, microwave-, oven-, and freezer-safe.

So does it matter which dish you buy? To find out, we tested five baking dishes priced from $7.29 to $18.77 (including the favorite from our previous testing, the Pyrex 3-Quart Oblong Baking Dish), using them to make sheet cake and lasagna. The good news: All the dishes did an excellent job of cooking the food, and there were only minor differences in how easy they were to use. We still like our old Pyrex favorite, but we like its newer sibling, the Pyrex Easy Grab 3-Quart Oblong Baking Dish ($7.29) even better. It's a bit heavier, but its larger handles are more comfortable to grip, and it's the cheapest pan in our lineup. –M.B.

Fat Separators

Fat separators help you say goodbye to greasy gravy and slick soups by removing settled fat from stocks and other liquids. To find the best, we tested six 4-cup models priced from $11.99 to $34.95, using them to strain aromatics and separate fat from both large and small volumes of stock. There are two types of separators: pitchers (where the fat is poured off from a spout set into the base) and bottom-drainers (where the liquid drains from a trigger-released plug in the bottom of the vessel). We tested four of the former and two of the latter. Our winner, the bottom-draining Cuisipro Fat Separator ($33.95), consistently did the best job of defatting stock. It had a big, comfortable handle and a wide, tall-sided strainer that contained splashes and was easy to pour into. And with a detachable canister, it was the easiest separator to clean by hand. The only knock against this model is that its measurement lines are hard to read, but that's a minor quibble for a tool that performs its primary function very well. –M.B.

Cooling Racks

The combination of a cooling rack set in a rimmed baking sheet gets a lot of action in the test kitchen; it is our top choice for roasting or broiling meats and holding breaded foods before and after frying. The rack elevates food so air can circulate underneath for even cooking and cooling, while the baking sheet below contains any mess. Our winning rack has been discontinued, so we set out to find a new favorite. We considered only racks that measured roughly 16½ by 12 inches (and thus fit inside most rimmed baking sheets, whose flared sides allow a rack to drop in and fit securely).

We also looked for racks whose bars were arranged in a grid (parallel bars can let food drop through), and that were broiler-safe. These qualifiers left us with just three contenders. Our winner, from Libertyware, did everything we asked of it and, at just $15.99 for two racks, was the least expensive rack we tested. –K.S.

Cocktail Shakers

A good cocktail shaker should allow a home bartender to shake drinks with the same efficiency as the professionals. There are two basic types of shaker: Boston shakers (favored by professional bartenders), which consist of two cups that you seal together, and cobbler shakers, which typically have a bottom cup and a top half with a built-in strainer and cap. To find the best cocktail shaker in each style, we bought three Boston and eight cobbler shakers priced from $8.99 to $41.95 and used them to make shaken, stirred, and muddled drinks. Because we wanted to be able to make one or two cocktails at a time, we focused on models with a capacity of at least 18 ounces. Our top cobbler shaker was from Tovolo ($8.99): It was easy to load and grip, it strained drinks well, and it fit together easily to make a great seal that never leaked. If you're up for the slight learning curve required by a Boston shaker, try our favorite in that category: The Boston Shaker Professional Boston Shaker, Weighted ($14.50). –M.B.

Universal Knife Blocks

Universal knife blocks, which use magnets, bristles, folds, or a grid to hold knives, are better than traditional knife blocks because they allow the cook to store knives of all sizes in any configuration. To find the best model, we purchased 10 universal blocks priced from $24.99 to $248.64 and got to work inserting our winning and our Best Buy 6-piece à la carte knife sets, which include our winning and Best Buy kitchen shears. We preferred magnetic blocks to other styles. While typically more expensive, magnetic blocks generally exposed less of the blades and held the knives more securely. Durability came into play, as cheaper plastic models showed significant nicks and wear. Finally, we found the best blocks to be heavy, with a tacky bottom—no one wants a collection of sharp knives sliding around the counter. Our winner, the handsome bamboo 360 Knife Block by Design Trifecta ($248.64), isn't cheap, but it passed all of our tests with flying colors and should take care of your knives for a lifetime. For a lower-priced alternative, we also recommend the Schmidt Brothers Midtown Block ($67.99) –M.B.

For complete testing results, go to CooksIllustrated.com/dec16.

INDEX
November & December 2016

BONUS ONLINE CONTENT
*More recipes, reviews, and videos are available
at **CooksIllustrated.com/dec16***

RECIPES
Apple Strudel for Two
Asparagus and Goat Cheese
    Frittata for Two
Braised Carrots and Sweet Potatoes
    with Candied Ginger
Broccoli and Feta Frittata for Two
Chorizo and Potato Frittata for Two
Everyday Pad Thai for Two
Shiitake Mushroom Frittata with Pecorino
    Romano for Two

EXPANDED REVIEWS
Tasting Ceylon Cinnamon
Tasting Cinnamon
Tasting Whole-Milk Ricotta
Testing Baking Stones
Testing Cocktail Shakers
Testing Cooling Racks
Testing Fat Separators
Testing Glass Baking Dishes
Testing Universal Knife Blocks

▶ RECIPE VIDEOS
Want to see how to make any of the recipes
in this issue? There's a free video for that.

▶ MORE VIDEOS
Science of Cooking: Making the
    Best-Tasting Quinoa
A Different Way to Chop Onions

FOLLOW US ON SOCIAL MEDIA
facebook.com/CooksIllustrated
twitter.com/TestKitchen
pinterest.com/TestKitchen
google.com/+AmericasTestKitchen
instagram.com/CooksIllustrated
youtube.com/AmericasTestKitchen

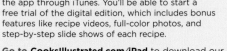

Apple Strudel, 23

Braised Carrots and Parsnips, 19

French-Style Mashed Potatoes, 7

Easier Roast Turkey and Gravy, 5

Broccoli and Feta Frittata, 13

Porchetta, 9

Millionaire's Shortbread, 15

Butternut Squash and White Bean Soup, 18

Cast Iron Steaks with Herb Butter, 11

Everyday Pad Thai, 21

PHOTOGRAPHY: KELLER + KELLER, CARL TREMBLAY, DANIEL J. VAN ACKERE; STYLING: MARIE PIRAINO, SALLY STAUB

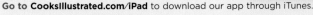

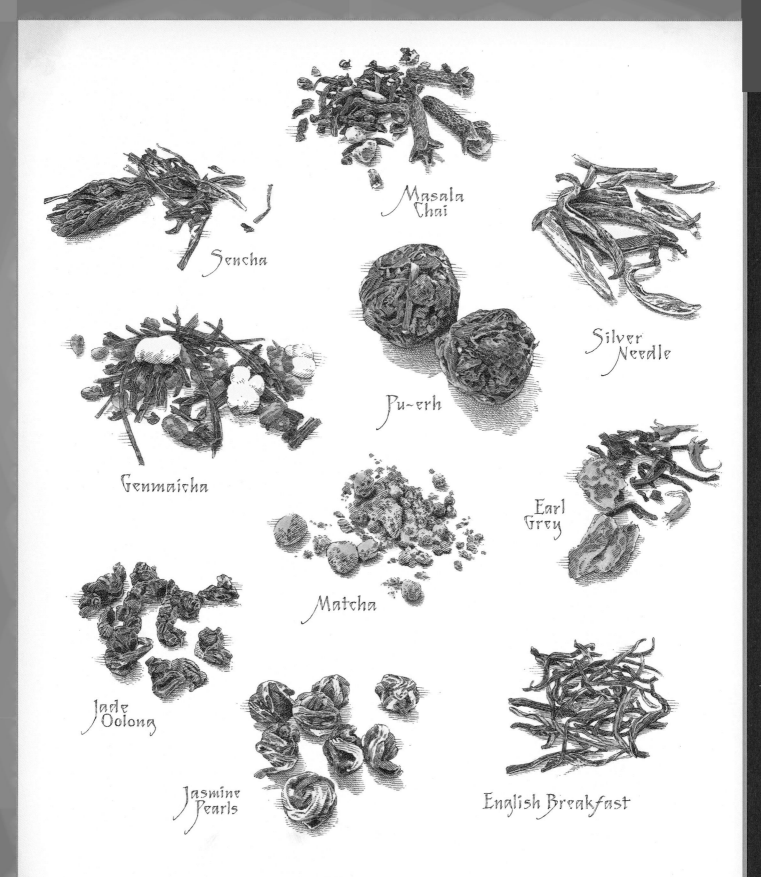

Masala Chai

Sencha

Silver Needle

Genmaicha

Pu~erh

Earl Grey

Matcha

Jade Oolong

Jasmine Pearls

English Breakfast

T E A S